The Jews In Canada

Robert J. Brym

William Shaffir

Morton Weinfeld

Toronto
OXFORD UNIVERSITY PRESS
1993

Oxford University Press, 70 Wynford Drive, Don Mills, Ontario M3C 1J9

Toronto   Oxford   New York
Delhi   Bombay   Calcutta   Madras   Karachi   Kuala Lumpur
Singapore   Hong Kong   Tokyo   Nairobi   Dar es Salaam
Cape Town   Melbourne   Auckland   Madrid

and associated companies in
Berlin   Ibadan

This book is printed on permanent (acid-free) paper ∞.

Canadian Cataloguing in Publication Data

Main entry under title:

The Jews in Canada

Includes bibliographical references and index.
ISBN 0-19-540829-2

1. Jews — Canada.   I. Brym, Robert J., 1951-   .
II. Shaffir, William, 1945-   .   III. Weinfeld, Morton.

FC106.J5J5   1993   971'.004924   C92-095578-9
F1035.J5J5   1993

Design by Marie Bartholomew

1   2   3   4   —   96   95   94   93

Printed in Canada

For Rhonda, Shira, and Talia — R.J.B.

For Rivka, Yael, Elichai, and Ariel — W.S.

For Phyllis, Rebecca, David, and Joanna — M.W.

Acknowledgements

Robert Brym 'A Socio-Demographic Profile of Canadian Jews' appeared originally as 'The Rise and Decline of Canadian Jewry? A Socio-demographic Profile' in E. Lipsitz, ed. *Canadian Jewry Today: Who's Who in Canadian Jewry* (Downsview, Ont.: JESL Educational Products, 1989). Reprinted by permission.

Robert Brym and Rhonda Lenton 'The Distribution of Anti-Semitism in Canada in 1984', *Canadian Journal of Sociology* (1981). Reprinted by permission.

Robert Brym, Michael Gillespie, and Ron Gillis 'Anomie, Opportunity, and the Density of Ethnic Ties: Another View of Jewish Outmarriage in Canada', *Canadian Review of Sociology and Anthropology*, vol. 22 (1985). Reprinted by permission.

Leo Davids 'Yiddish in Canada: Picture and Prospects', *Canadian Ethnic Studies*, vol. 16, no. 2 (1984). 'Marital Status and Fertility Among Sub-Groups of Canadian Jews', *Jewish Population Studies/Papers in Jewish Demography, 1985* (Jerusalem, 1989). Both reprinted by permission.

Jean Laponce 'Left or Centre? The Canadian Jewish Electorate, 1953-1983', *The Canadian Journal of Political Science* XXI, no. 4 (December 1988). Reprinted by permission.

Jean-Claude Lasry 'Sephardim and Ashkenazim in Montreal', *Contemporary Jewry* 6, 2 (Fall 1983). Reprinted by permission.

Cyril Levitt and William Shaffir 'The Swastika as Dramatic Symbol: A Case-Study of Ethnic Violence in Canada' from *The Jewish Journal of Sociology* vol. 31, no. 1 (June 1989). 'Aliyah and Return Migration of Canadian Jews: Personal Accounts of Incentives and of Disappointed Hopes' from *The Jewish Journal of Sociology* vol. 32, no. 2 (December 1990). Both reprinted by permission.

Roberta L. Markus and Donald V. Schwartz 'Soviet Jewish Emigrés in Toronto: Ethnic Self-Identity and Issues of Integration' from *Canadian Ethnic Studies* vol. 16, no. 2 (1984). Reprinted by permission.

Sheva Medjuck 'Jewish Survival in Small Communities in Canada' in E. Lipsitz, ed. *Canadian Jewry Today: Who's Who in Canadian Jewry* (Downsview, Ont.: JESL Educational Products, 1989). Reprinted by permission.

William Shaffir 'Separation from the Mainstream in Canada: The Hassidic Community of Tash' from *The Jewish Journal of Sociology* vol. 29, no. 1 (June 1987). Reprinted by permission.

David Taras and Morton Weinfeld 'Continuity and Criticism: North American Jews and Israel', *International Journal* (Summer 1990). Reprinted by permission of the Canadian Institute of International Affairs.

Harold Troper and Morton Weinfeld 'Jewish-Ukrainian Relations in Canada Since World War II and the Emergence of the Nazi War Criminal Issue', *American Jewish History* 77, 1 (Sept. 1987). Reprinted by permission.

Gerald Tulchinsky 'The Contours of Canadian Jewish History', *Journal of Canadian Studies*, vol. 17, no. 4 (1982-3). Reprinted by permission.

Morton Weinfeld 'The Jews of Quebec: An Overview' from R. Aigen and G. Hundert, eds. *Community and the Individual Jew: Essays in Honor of Lavy M. Becker* (Philadelphia: reconstructionist Rabbinical College Press, 1986). Reprinted by permission.

Morton Weinfeld 'The Ethnic Sub-economy: Explication and Analysis of a Case Study of the Jews of Montreal', *Contemporary Jewry* 6, 2 (Fall 1983). Reprinted by permission.

Morton Weinfeld and Phyllis Zelkowitz 'Reflections on the Jewish Polity and Jewish Education' in Daniel Elazar ed. *Authority, Power, and Leadership in the Jewish Polity* (University Press of America and the Jerusalem Center for Public Affairs, 1991). Reprinted by permission.

Gabriel Weinmann and Conrad Winn, from *Hate on Trial: The Zundel Affair, The Media and Public Opinion in Canada* (Mosaic Press, 1986). Reprinted by permission of the publisher.

Contents

Preface

Robert J. Brym

In 1939, Arthur Ruppin, the first demographer of world Jewry, wrote that 'the veil of darkness hitherto hanging over the position of Canadian Jewry has now been lifted' (Ruppin, 1939). The event that led Ruppin to compose such florid prose was the publication of Louis Rosenberg's *Canada's Jews*. Rosenberg headed—more accurately, alone constituted—the Bureau of Social and Economic Research of the Canadian Jewish Congress. He had indeed performed a monumental task by scrupulously analysing census data and vital statistics pertaining to Jews. Single-handedly, Rosenberg ensured that the social and economic data available on Canadian Jews were in many ways comparable, and in some respects superior, to similar data on Jewish communities in the United States, Great Britain, the Soviet Union, Palestine, and elsewhere.

That rough parity did not last long. Over the next 40 years, particularly in the United States and Israel, there accumulated a large body of research on the sociology of the Jews, much of it based on sample surveys and ethnographic fieldwork. Meanwhile, as the Canadian Jewish community matured, prospered, and doubled in size to 300,000 members, Rosenberg's book remained virtually the sole sociological study of Canadian Jewry. By 1980 the historians had at least published some respectable, if generally somewhat pietistic and unanalytical, works that sketched the broad outlines of Canadian Jewish life since its origins. But apart from Rosenberg's volume, about all the sociological material one could find on the subject of the Jews in Canada was a dozen or so published articles on specialized themes, several MA and PhD theses focusing on specific locales, some commissioned reports on various communities, and William Shaffir's ethnography of the Lubavitcher Chassidim in Montreal (Shaffir, 1974).[1] In one week of not overly strenuous work one could consume the entire literature, emerging from the exercise with a far from extensive understanding of the social structure and behaviour of Canadian Jewry. Not surprisingly, when Morton Weinfeld, William Shaffir, and Irwin Cotler edited the first sociological anthology on Canadian Jewry in 1981, only eight of the 21 articles were written by sociologists (Weinfeld, Shaffir, and Cotler, 1981).

It would be embellishing the truth to claim that the sociological study of Canadian Jewry has since become a growth industry. Several areas in the sociology of Canadian Jewry still require basic research. In reviewing the published literature and work in progress, we were especially disappointed to see how little sociological material is available on the Canadian-Jewish

family, the changing roles of Canadian-Jewish women, problems bound up
with the integration of immigrants (especially Soviet Jews and Israelis) in the
community, the place of religion and, more generally, culture in Canadian-
Jewish life, and the Jews in Western Canada.[2] That said, the quantity and
quality of research *has* increased since 1980—so much so that it is now
possible to offer a detailed and fairly comprehensive sociological portrait of
the Canadian Jewish community for the first time. That is the aim of this
book.

The articles in this volume represent some of the most recent sociological
or near-sociological research on Canadian Jewry. How recent? Four of the
articles were prepared especially for this volume; the mean first publication
date of all 24 articles is 1988. How sociological? Of the 38 authors who
contributed to this volume, 70 per cent are sociologists and most of the rest
are political scientists.[3]

We have divided the book into seven substantive topics that reflect the major
research interests of students of Canadian Jewry: comparative perspectives,
anti-Semitism, culture, intercommunal relations, politics, women and the family, and minorities. Broadly speaking, however, most of the authors are concerned with only two analytical themes. First, how does Canadian Jewry today
compare—in terms of organization, attitudes, and behaviour—to the Jewish
community of the United States and to Canadian Jewry in the past, and what
accounts for the similarities and differences? Second, what are the sources and
dimensions of the challenges faced by the Canadian Jewish community in its
attempt to survive the exigencies of modern life?

Neither question is surprising. Both are solidly Canadian in origin; both
are solidly Jewish. Canadians stand in the shadow of the world's most
powerful country, and out of a slightly neurotic mixture of admiration and
insecurity they are always comparing themselves to Americans, sometimes
inventing differences when none spring immediately to mind. The enduring
myth that the United States is an ethnic melting pot while Canada is an
ethnic mosaic is one of those inventions. Without the benefit of systematically collected and uniform data on ethnic groups in the two countries, and
without the benefit of controlled comparisons—in short, largely on the
basis of anecdotes and casual impressions—the view has become widespread that ethnic differences are encouraged in Canada and effaced in the
US. Only recently has this view been critically scrutinized and found inadequate (Brym with Fox, 1989). One of the chief virtues of this volume is that it
adds to the ongoing critique by examining one case in depth: Canadian Jews.
Differences between Canadian and American Jewry are highlighted in many
of the following essays, but they are typically explained less in terms of
national differences in 'tolerance' or 'culture' than in terms of different immigration patterns, concrete historical experiences, organizational foundations,
and other structural conditions.

The second analytical theme of this book—the possibility of survival in
the face of modernity—may at first seem an especially Jewish concern.

Rising intermarriage rates, low fertility rates, changing gender roles, an aging population, the abandonment of ethnic languages, the decline of small communities, and the problematic role of parochial education are all facets of the Canadian-Jewish response to the challenge of modernity, and all these issues figure prominently in this volume. The authors seek to uncover their causes and occasionally offer policy recommendations. But reflecting on these issues for a moment shows that they are by no means exclusively Jewish concerns; *la survivance* is, after all, no stranger to these parts. As in the case of the first broad theme noted above, the Jewish question is only one variant of a more universal one. Ultimately, then, the two issues that form the real spine of this book reflect the everyday hopes and anxieties not just of Canadian Jewish academics, not just of educated Canadian Jews, but of educated Canadians in general.

★   ★   ★

Editing this book was so much fun I am still not sure how it got finished at all, let alone on schedule. Our editorial meetings were utterly anarchic and our frequent e-mail messages more or less beside the point. As a result, errors doubtless remain in the manuscript. The public should know, however, that that is completely the fault of the other two editors.

Notes

[1]Ten reports on the governance of Jewish communities were only recently revised and published (Elazar and Waller, 1990). For a comprehensive bibliography of sources *circa* 1980, see Weinfeld, Shaffir, and Cotler (1981).

[2]Unfortunately, we were unable to secure permission to reprint Stuart Schoenfeld's (1978) still-useful account of Canadian-American differences in the Jewish religion, and due to space limitations we were unable to include Michael Greenstein's (1992) analysis of themes in Canadian-Jewish literature. On the Jews in Western Canada, Leo Driedger's (1980) analysis of the Winnipeg Jewish community is somewhat dated but still interesting.

Researchers interested in up-to-date references should consult the bibliographies of the articles in this volume, as well as Schoenfeld and Daigneault (1992). They can also search the key words 'Canadian Jews' in machine-readable bibliographies of social science articles, such as *Sociofile*. The editors wish to thank Ms Marilyn Fransiszyn of McGill University's Humanities and Social Sciences Library for assisting in a preliminary computer search of the recent periodical literature.

[3]Authors were counted more than once if they contributed to more than one article.

References

Brym, Robert J. with Bonnie J. Fox
1989 *From Culture to Power: The Sociology of English Canada* (Toronto: Oxford University Press).

Driedger, Leo
  1980 'Jewish identity: the maintenance of urban religious and ethnic boundaries', *Ethnic and Racial Studies* 3, 1: 67–88.

Elazar, Daniel J. and Harold M. Waller
  1990 *Maintaining Consensus: The Canadian Jewish Polity in the Postwar World* (Lanham, MD: University Press of America).

Greenstein, Michael
  1992 'Nobody chasing everyman: dominant themes in Canadian-Jewish literature', unpublished paper.

Ruppin, Arthur
  1939 'Foreword', in Louis Rosenberg, *Canada's Jews: A Social and Economic Study of the Jews in Canada* (Montreal: Canadian Jewish Congress): xxvii.

Schoenfeld, Stuart
  1978 'The Jewish religion in North America: The Canadian experience', *Canadian Journal of Sociology* 3: 209–33.

Schoenfeld, Stuart and Dwight Daigneault
  1992 *Contemporary Jewish Life in Canada: A Bibliography* (Toronto: Centre for Jewish Studies, York University).

Shaffir, William
  1974 *Life in a Religious Community: The Lubavitcher Chassidim in Montreal* (Toronto: Holt, Rinehart and Winston of Canada).

Weinfeld, Morton, William Shaffir and Irwin Cotler, eds
  1981 *The Canadian Jewish Mosaic* (Toronto: John Wiley and Sons).

part one

Canadian

Jews in

Comparative

Perspective

Introduction

Morton Weinfeld

Canadian Jews, like any ethnic and/or religious group, are best studied in a comparative framework (Lipset, 1963). To understand Canadian Jewry we must understand the similarities and differences with other diaspora Jewish communties, and indeed with non-Jewish communities in Canada.

Just as Canada's environment for ethnic minorities is often termed 'a "mosaic" in contrast to the American "melting pot", so are Canadian Jews considered to be more "Jewish" than are American Jews' (Weinfeld *et al.*, 1981: 13). Two questions must be asked. First, is this conventional wisdom still correct? And if it is, do these differences reflect differences in the generational composition of the two Jewish communities, or more fundamental differences in the historic foundations and broader socio-historical contexts of Canada and the United States? In this latter view, the longer Canada persists as a 'distinct society' compared to the United States, the longer may Canadian Jews remain distinct from their American cousins.

In fact, the images of the mosaic and the melting pot are both overdone. In the United States, the substantial evidence of assimilation among white European groups (Alba, 1990; Waters, 1990) has not led to the complete irrelevance of ethnicity in other areas, such as politics, and the racial divisions remain acute. In Canada, the high immigrant proportion of the population (16 per cent in 1986 compared to 6.2 per cent in the United States in 1980) and the government policies of multiculturalism have masked steady generational acculturation, notably in areas such as language loss or observance of cultural rituals (Breton *et al.*, 1990).

While we can indeed identify broad patterns of assimilation, acculturation, or in some perspectives, transformation (Cohen, 1988), one thing stands out. Canadian Jews are the most survivalist of any comparable ethnic or ethno-religious group in Canada. While Jews attend synagogue rather infrequently, comparable here to Christians, they do regularly practise religious rituals of all kinds. And when compared even to fairly survivalist ethnic groups such as Ukrainian Canadians, Jews are noteworthy for their high levels of Jewish identification and communal involvement (Troper and Weinfeld, 1988: ch.2; Breton *et al.*, 1990).

Gerald Tulchinsky's article, 'The Contours of Canadian Jewish History' begins the section with a review of the historical differences in the early experience of Canadian and American Jews. Tulchinsky explains how the specific socio-political Canadian environment, coupled with the specificity of Canadian Jewry's immigration sequence in the early decades of the cen-

2

tury (and indeed in the post-war period as well), created a distinctive Canadian Jewish community. It remains to be seen whether this pattern of historical distinctiveness will continue.

To answer the latter question requires extensive social scientific data. The student of Canadian Jewry is particularly well served. The Canadian census has contained data on Jews since the turn of the century, and has usually provided separate counts of Jews as a religion and as an ethnic group. As a result, reasonably reliable data on demographic variables such as linguistic ability, birthplace, intermarriage, fertility, education, occupation, and income have been available for some time. The American census has never collected data on religion, and Jews have never been treated as a distinct ancestry category. Thus 'Russian Americans' have often been surrogates for Jews.

Surveys of representative samples of Jews provide the best alternate quantitative data source. Sample surveys permit the researcher to probe more deeply than the census into questions of ethno-religious identity. Recently — in 1990 — two important sample surveys of Canadian Jews have been undertaken. The first, a survey sponsored by the CRB Foundation, directed by Goldfarb Consultants and Steven M. Cohen, covered a representative sample of close to 1000 Jewish households in Canada. The Montreal responses have been analysed separately by Charles Shahar of Montreal's Allied Jewish Community Services. The second is a survey of the Jewish community of Toronto undertaken for the Toronto Jewish Congress and the Jewish Federation of Greater Toronto, and analysed by Jay Brodbar-Nemzer with Gary Tobin and Allan Reitzes.

These Canadian surveys may be compared with a nationwide survey of American Jewry completed in 1990 for the Council of Jewish Federations. Thus for the first time we can make, with some minimal confidence, comparative evaluations of Canadian and American Jewish attitudes and behaviours.

Robert Brym, in his 'A Socio-Demographic Profile of Canadian Jews' uses the Canadian census data for 1986 to develop an analysis of future socio-demographic prospects for Canadian Jewry. These he sees as dim, and links his demographic analysis to a provocative sociological perspective, stressing the need for a transformative community to appeal to the increasing number of alienated or marginal Canadian Jews. In his use of census data, Brym is continuing in a tradition pioneered by Louis Rosenberg, researcher for the Canadian Jewish Congress from the 1930s to the 1970s. Rosenberg's volume *Canada's Jews*, published in 1939, was an exhaustive analysis of the 1931 census, as well as other statistical data available at the time. (For example, it includes a detailed analysis of Jewish involvement in criminal activity based on official government statistics — no longer collected in Canada — which refuted the stereotype of Jewish over-representation among arsonists!)

The final selection is a synthesis of the three surveys described above. These provide data which include comparisons between Canada and the United States, as well as among the major Canadian Jewish communities.

The findings confirm the prevailing notions of a more rooted, more committed, Canadian Jewish comunity.

Within Canadian Jewry, we can also note distinctions. Montreal seems most religiously traditional, and also enjoys a greater internal diversity provided by the large francophone/Sephardic Jewish community. Winnipeg and Vancouver are communities with identities in flux. Yet as a whole, the Canadian survey data reveal the complex, indeed contradictory, nature of contemporary Jewish identification. Some of the data, such as decreasing rates of in-marriage in Toronto in the 1980s, may point to decline; others, such as comparable or increasing religiosity among younger compared to older respondents in Canada, point to renewal. As Yiddish language and culture decline, Hebrew and Israel increase their salience. A more detailed analysis of these data may help resolve these ambiguities.

References

Alba, Richard
  1990 *Ethnic Identity: The Transformation of White America* (New Haven: Yale University Press)

Breton, Raymond, Wsevolod W. Isajiw, Warren E. Kalbach, and Jeffrey G. Reitz
  1990 *Ethnic Identity and Equality: Varieties of Experience in a Canadian City* (Toronto: University of Toronto Press)

Cohen, Steven M.
  1988 *American Assimilation or Jewish Revival* (Bloomington: University of Indiana Press)

Lipset, Seymour Martin
  1963 'The Study of Jewish Communities in a Comparative Context', *Jewish Journal of Sociology* 5: 157–66

Troper, Harold and Morton Weinfeld
  1988 *Old Wounds: Jews, Ukrainians, and the Hunt for Nazi War Criminals in Canada* (Toronto: Penguin)

Waters, Mary
  1990 *Ethnic Options: Choosing Identities in America* (Berkeley: University of California Press)

Weinfeld, Morton, William Shaffir, Irwin Cotler, eds
  1981 *The Canadian Jewish Mosaic* (Rexdale, Ont.: John Wiley of Canada)

The Contours of Canadian Jewish History

Gerald Tulchinsky

To describe adequately the contours of Canadian Jewish history requires a discussion of the character of the past experience of the Jewish people in Canada. How they got here, where they went, how they earned their living, and what they thought, wrote, sang, and hoped all form part of the story. Some features of Canadian Jewish history suggest that certain of the assumptions about the Jewish-Canadian past are open to serious doubt and are badly in need of revision. One of these major assumptions is that Canadian Jewry was a sort of colony of the American Jewish communities.[1] From this viewpoint, most of what happened to the Canadian Jewish community can be seen as a reflection of occurrences and trends taking place first in the American mainstream and then, years later, happening also to the northern cousins. Thus, the Americanization of the Jews, i.e. their gradual or rapid (depending on the circumstances) adaptation to and acceptance in the mainstream of American culture, and the development of what might be called the American-Jewish symbiosis are mirrored in the same kind of process taking place in Canada. In this analysis a Canadian Jew who becomes Chief Justice of the Supreme Court of Canada, or Governor of the Bank of Canada, or a member of a federal cabinet, or a senior officer in the Royal Canadian Air Force, or a leading literary figure is the northern equivalent of American Jews like Justice Brandeis, Henry Morgenthau, Bernard Baruch, Admiral Rickover, or Philip Roth.

To be sure, there are many significant — almost overpowering — similarities between American and Canadian Jewish historical experiences and in certain respects the communities in both countries are so similar as to be indistinguishable. Without doubt, the more numerous and more highly developed American Jewish communities exercised strong and continuing influences on Canadian Jewry. After all, most of their people came from the Russian empire in sudden and vast waves of immigration before 1914. And, of course, the cultural baggage they brought with them was identical in both countries: a hybrid mixture of deeply pious, rigid orthodoxy in many, and a complex mélange of philosophies such as Marxism, socialism, anarchism, Zionism, bundism and other ideals, especially among the young who had been exposed to the intellectual world outside of the Pale of Settlement, the vast Jewish ghetto. And the historical developments of both American and Canadian Jewries were also, in important respects, highly similar. This was particularly the case in such things as post-1900 settlement patterns, aspects of cultural life including the use of the Yiddish language in newspapers, theatre, and schools, and the economic struggle, especially in the arena of the clothing industry. These and other similarities, interchanges, and influences must be acknowledged.

What should not be conceded, however, is that all of the major forces that shaped the Jewish historical experience in Canada were the same or even similar to those in the United States. This paper is an attempt to examine some of these differences in an effort to explain the contours of Canadian Jewish history. Some of these issues were broached by Jonathan Sarna who, in a brief paper a few years ago in the *Canadian Jewish Historical Journal*, suggested some important differences.[2] The case presented here is that, notwithstanding the many strong similarities, Canadian Jewry evolved in a significantly different fashion from its American counterparts as a result of the Canadian national context in which it was situated. It is, of course, not enough to say that Canada before 1945 was a different country than the United States. Canada's proximity to the American giant and the similarity of peoples and outlook inevitably resulted in very strong American influences affecting all aspects of Canadian life throughout its history, including the evolution of the Jewish community. At the same time, it is important to understand that there were different co-ordinates to the Canadian constitutional structure, political life, national composition, urban pattern and economic development which all directly affected the evolution of Jewish life in Canada and determined that in certain important respects it would be different from the American. The point is that some of the most significant factors influencing the Jewish community in this country had no counterparts in the United States. Consequently, if Canadian and American Jewry have now in certain respects become indistinguishable from one another, they reached this commonality by different routes.

The duality of Canada's national personality posed particularly acute problems for Canadian Jewry or for that very large part of it—until recently it was nearly half—that lived in the province of Quebec. There the confessional school system established at Confederation put the Jewish community at a serious disadvantage because there was no legal provision for them in either the Catholic or Protestant systems of schooling. The winning of the right to send their children to schools was a testy legal and political question which was resolved in stages over nearly thirty years of struggle between 1903 and 1930.[3] Periodically, between 1850 and the end of the first world war, Canada was riven with several lengthy and bitter disputes over religious instruction and the languages used in its schools. The Jewish school question in the province of Quebec did not, of course, assume the proportions of a national issue and certainly pales to insignificance when compared to some of the other schools questions in Canada. (The Manitoba and Ontario battles come to mind.) But one can understand the seriousness of the issue at least among Jews in that province. It was, first of all, a battle for fundamental civil rights that were being denied to them by the Protestant School Commissioners of Montreal and the Quebec provincial government. Minor victories in the courts and in the legislative assembly after 1903 were the outcome of a galvanization of the Jewish community on a massive scale and resulted in the emergence of a collective Montreal Jewish consciousness noteworthy for its major political leadership, newspaper development, intense intra-communal discussion, and greatly heightened awareness of their place in the legal, political, and social context of the province of Quebec.[4] Nothing like this kind of Jewish civil rights occurred in the United States because nowhere in the Republic did the same kind of co-ordinates exist to bar the Jewish advance to social equality.

Paradoxically, however, the schools issue did not completely unify all Montreal Jews. In fact, for many years the debate had the reverse effect of fostering increasingly divisive and bitter discussion over the most desirable solution to the problem. In this conflict, which was especially acute during 1920s, one side favoured a strictly civil rights solution and integration of Jews on a basis of complete equality into existing Protestant schools, while others were interested in a communal or confessional solution by which the Jews would be on an equal footing with Protestants and Catholics enjoying their own separate school systems. The fact that most of those participating in the dispute came from conflicting economic and social groups tended to exacerbate the already sensitive relations between working-class 'down-town' Montreal Jewry and the patricians and clothing-factory owners of the west end. Seeking social acceptance by the Anglophone élite, the latter segment of Montreal Jewry wanted their children to attend the Protestant schools, while the downtowners—who were usually more recent immigrants—tended to favour the protection which a completely separate system would provide.[5]

The great importance of this contest and its ramifications through all sectors of life in a community that included half of all Jews in the Dominion was, of course, only one feature of Canadian Jewish history in Quebec that was so strongly affected by the French-English duality of Canada's nationality. In fact, while living in Montreal, the rapidly expanding Jewish community ran directly afoul of French-Canadian nationalism at the very height of its late nineteenth and early twentieth-century efflorescence. This nationalism with its blend of what the French-Canadian historian, Michel Brunet, calls agriculturalism, anti-statism, and messianism combined a militant ultramontane Catholic faith with the national rebirth of an agricultural French-speaking republic on the St Lawrence.[6] In this visionary frame of reference, in this French-Canadian Catholic utopia, the Jew was a standing affront, an insidious poison representing all that was dangerous to its establishment and survival.[7] Among other things, the Jew was the infidel, the Christ-killer whose continuing rejection of Christianity constituted a standing insult to the faith and whose rapidly increasing presence in Montreal posed a dire threat to the purity of the French-Canadian ideal. He was also viewed by certain segments of French-Canadian society as the arch traitor, the perfidious vendor of France's honour as was proven beyond a shadow of doubt in the conviction in 1894 of Captain Alfred Dreyfus for treason.[8] The Jew was an economic threat as well, both as unscrupulous exploiter in the clothing industry where Jewish contractors worked the piecing-out system on the basis of Jewish and French-Canadian sweated labour in home or attic shops with eighty-hour weeks not uncommon, and as a competitor in the market for unskilled or semiskilled jobs.[9] Besides being clothing workers, considerable numbers of Jews worked as skilled tradesmen in local shoe factories, in the CPR and Grand Trunk repair shops, abattoirs, bakeries, tanneries, and various metal, electrical, printing, and woodworking shops as well as on construction sites around the city.[10] The Jew was also perceived as the political and social radical and trade-union activist, the purveyor of insidious socialist and anarchist ideas which French-Canadian clerical and lay leaders saw as infectious and corrosive poisons in the pure springs of their people's religious and social life.[11] Thus, paradoxically, in the tumultuous and volatile clothing industry the Jew was seen at one and the same time as exploiter and radical. In all, then, the Jew was a significant threat to the destiny of the French-Canadian people to survive and thrive as a distinctive Catholic and French agrarian polity on the banks of the St Lawrence.

That the Jews should have attracted the French-Canadian hatred which welled up repeatedly in newspapers, pamphlets, and church sermons should not surprise us. Jews were, first of all, the largest minority in the province outside of the old stock English-speaking groups which — though separated by certain class and religious issues — nevertheless maintained a certain transcendent coherence and unity, and were headed by a tight, tough, wealthy, and influential élite. Montreal's Jewish quarter, which stretched north from the docks along St Lawrence Street to Dorchester by about 1900, had mushroomed in size with the pre-1914 infusions of immigrants.[12] By the 1920s, virtually the entire city section from the waterfront north in a belt along St Lawrence-Main to the lower reaches of Outremont constituted a huge, predominantly Jewish enclave of factories, shops, synagogues, and tightly-packed housing. Although it was not the only sector of Montreal in which Jews lived, the fact that this 'Jewish quarter' was at the geographical centre of the city and divided the French from the English sections of Montreal was also symbolic of the precarious marginality of the Jewish presence to both communities. Insofar as most Anglophones were concerned, the Jews were not particularly welcome, as indicated by the treatment which Jewish pupils and teachers received from the Protestant School Commissioners.[13] The Francophones, however, because of their closer physical proximity, far greater numbers, and local political prowess, were able to manifest their anti-Semitism much more effectively and do much more visible damage to the vast majority of Jews than the Anglo Protestants who made Jews uncomfortable in their schools (by means of a variety of indignities as well as an exclusion of Jewish teachers) and kept the upstart Westmount Jews out of their golf clubs. French-Canadian anti-Semitism was very serious business and it must be understood that although it was obviously far less dangerous than the uniquely venomous and murderous Polish or Ukrainian varieties, it was nevertheless extremely disquieting. More important, it had a long-lasting effect on the political and social well-being of the large Jewish population of Quebec.

In the spring of 1910 the whole of Canadian Jewry was deeply shocked by the virulently anti-Semitic speeches and publications of one Plamondon, a Quebec City notary who accused the Jews of numerous sins including the charge that the Talmud permitted Jewish men to violate the purity of Christian women, and taught Jews that Jesus Christ was conceived in vice and sin and that Christians were animals.[14] Hints of arson, well-poisoning and, worst of all, allegations that Jews practised ritual murder completed Mr Plamondon's Jewish demonology. This Quebec blood libel which was so reminiscent of the worst East European anti-Semitism — and an excuse for many a pogrom — foreshadowed by two years the famous Beilis case in Kiev, Russia. Plamondon was taken to court two years later in a civil suit for slander and, under cross-examination, he and the six Roman Catholic priests who appeared to substantiate his allegations admitted that they had never read the Talmud or any other Jewish works, and that their information was derived from anti-Semitic publications which came to them from France. This case, which so deeply distressed Canadian Jewry, was only one of a whole series of anti-Jewish occurrences in the province of Quebec during those years. In 1901 and 1909, the old Jewish cemeteries in Trois Rivières had been seized by the municipality, the graves dug up and the remains reinterred elsewhere.[15] During the 1905 debates in the House of Commons over the Lord's Day Act, prominent nationalist Henri Bourassa had attacked the proposal to exclude Jews from its provisions because 'they are the most undesirable class that can be brought into this country'.[16] Montreal's tough Sunday-closing municipal by-laws worked a hardship on sabbath-observing Orthodox Jews, and tactics occasionally employed to disenfranchise Jews and to weaken their electoral muscle in other ways kept reminding them that they were *persona non grata* in the province of Quebec.

Although these incidents — with the exception of the Plamondon case — were by themselves relatively harmless, they did underscore the fact that anti-Semitism in Quebec seemed to possess a special force, a greater depth and virulence than anywhere else in North America. So violent did physical attacks on Jews and their property become that in the summer of 1909 a Jewish defence league was formed in the Montreal ghetto.[17] A force of 500 vigilantes was set up to patrol the streets against hooligans — perhaps using some of the tactics employed to deter similar attacks during the bloody 1903 pogroms in parts of the Ukraine. Though disbanded under the combined pressures of the Montreal police and the west-end Jewish patricians, the experience in organized self-defence and the reasons for it constituted an important historical occurrence in Jewish self-awareness in Montreal. During the 20s, 30s and 40s, this kind of French-Canadian anti-Semitism welled up time and again, not only to remind Jews of their inferior position in the eyes of Canadians, but also to reduce their presence in sectors where they had achieved some prominence. The 1920s 'Achats Chez Nous' movement aimed at Jewish storekeepers; the pro-Fascist or anti-Semitic utterances of major Quebec provincial and municipal politicians; the rise of Adrien Arcand and his Blue-shirts; the attempts by the Catholic syndicates to engender anti-Semitism among French-Canadian clothing workers; and the widespread campaign mounted by the Société Saint-Jean Baptiste and other organizations against the immigration of Jewish refugees during the 1930s all combined to let Jews know that in its special brand of anti-Semitism, as in most other respects, 'La province de Québec n'est pas un province comme les autres.'

Thus, what is unique about this experience is not that Jews felt anti-Semitism in Canada. This phenomenon was North America-wide and, as Michael Dobkowski has recently explained in an important new work on anti-Semitism in the United States, it was—and, no doubt, still is—deeply rooted in western Christian culture, stemming largely from religious sources.[18] He points out that anti-Semitism since colonial times found frequent expression in various forms reflecting these religious origins. Although there are no similar studies of anti-Semitism in Canada, evidence suggests that the same could be said of English Canada where this phenomenon also received widespread expression. But if Jews were targets for various kinds of discrimination outside Quebec as well, it appears that anti-Semitism was not nearly as strong as the anti-Oriental feelings on the Canadian west coast or the anti-Slavic attitudes manifested on the Prairies.[19] What is evident, however, is that the special character, dimensions, and perseverance of the French-Canadian variety shaped a community-consciousness in approximately one half of Canada's Jews and, indirectly through national organizations dominated by Montreal, of a significant portion of the remainder. If the Canadian Jewish community has always been much more effectively governed in national organizations than American Jewry, this was largely attributable to the fact that Canadian Jewry has felt more threatened from the aforementioned forces. A leading reason for the reactivation of the Canadian Jewish Congress after 1933 was the need to counter the increasingly virulent anti-Semitism in Quebec.

Governance through national organizations like the Congress, which was originally established in 1919, was also facilitated by another peculiar feature of Canadian Jewry: its overwhelming concentration in a few metropolitan centres after the 1880s. In contrast to the state of American Jewish demography where, by the 1840s, significant Jewish communities existed in all major cities up and down the eastern seaboard, in the mid-West, and on the Gulf coast, Canada's Jews before 1900 overwhelmingly chose Montreal or Toronto; later Winnipeg became a third centre. The Three Rivers community declined; Quebec City withered, and Maritimes centres barely began in the nineteenth century.[20] In the United States, however, even before the Civil War, there were nearly 210 congregations in existence across the country, including major southern cities.[21] In the 1870s Cincinnati emerged as a leading centre of Jewish religious life and Philadelphia as a major educational and cultural hub, while Chicago attracted a huge Jewish population after the 1880s. All of these communities were independent of New York, the Jerusalem of America (or really Warsaw, Minsk, Pinsk, and Odessa all rolled into one), a city one quarter Jewish by 1914 and the residence of about half of all America's Jews. In the establishment of Jewish community life in Canada there were no counterparts to Cincinnati, Philadelphia, Chicago, Boston, or other Jewish centres which so diffused power and influence among American Jewry that national organizations have always been relatively weak. As a result of a high concentration of Canadian Jews in two or three cities and of about half in one particular metropolis, countervailing influences did not develop here on anything like the scale that they did in the United States. Hence, Jewish national organizations in Canada apparently were able to establish themselves more effectively than their American counterparts.

After 1898 the Zionist Federation of Canada, for example, was greatly envied by the Americans because of its impressive national structure, active branches, and tight organization controlled from Montreal by the Spanish-Portuguese patrician, Clarence de Sola.[22] With its reestablishment in 1933, the Canadian Jewish Congress, which was also based in Montreal, served as a forum for all shades of political, religious, and cultural expression. As a spokesman for Canadian Jewry on major issues it was far more effective than the American Jewish Congress which suffered from the rivalry of a number of competing national organizations.[23] This is not to say that the Canadian Jewish community was more politically or intellectually homogeneous than the American or necessarily always unified, or that, notwithstanding Montreal's obvious importance, there were fewer regional and other conflicts of interest. The leadership of Toronto's Jewish community strongly resented the control of national organizations by the Montreal patricians, while in Winnipeg and elsewhere on the Prairies an independent spirit emerged early and persisted for many years.[24] Yet virtually all elements agreed on the need — most of the time — for strong national Jewish organizations. Winnipeg Zionists, for example, were always more active in cultural and fundraising activities than those of any other centre in Canada; their youth groups were more strongly politicized than any others, and they strove to radicalize the Zionist movement in Canada.[25]

Certain factors help to explain the broad commonality of purpose upon which these national Canadian Jewish organizations were based and for many years embodied. The most important one, I think, is the comparatively strong religious homogeneity of Canadian Jewry. This is the third major point of difference between the two North American communities and it constitutes an essential ingredient in any understanding of the contours of Canadian Jewish history. American Jewry was shaped and, until at least 1900, was dominated by the German immigrants who arrived in the United States during the 1840s and 1850s.[26] The cultural baggage of many early nineteenth-century German Jews included fragments of the enlightenment philosophy of Moses Mendelssohn and some of the influences of the new scientific study of Jewish culture, *Wissenschaft des Judentums*, begun by Leopold Zunz.[27] From this early nineteenth century German-Jewish Reformation, a new synagogue, theology and liturgy had emerged in which virtually all elements of Jewish particularism were expunged and Jewish universalism celebrated; thus many Jews were transformed into Germans of the Mosaic persuasion. Jewish religious beliefs were reinterpreted and reformulated root and branch by the rabbis of the new Judaism. In the transposition to America these Germans erected their Reform synagogues, established Cincinnati as their centre, and so dominated American Jewish religious life that, by 1880, of 270 synagogues in the United States most were Reform.[28] Furthermore, they now became Americans of the Mosaic persuasion. Acquiring wealth, influence, power, and social prestige, the Loebs, Kuhns, Gimbels, Guggenheims and other of 'Our Crowd' began to merge into the American mainstream, while still others made significant contributions to American progressivism.[29] Thus, not only did they imprint upon American Jewish life a strong Reform synagogue, they also implanted a dominant philosophy or mystique of American-ness, as in Germany they had come to believe in their German-ness (this was sometimes expressed as the German-Jewish symbiosis). The fact that this mystique of American-Jewish identity fitted neatly into the prevailing ethos of American nationality served only to accentuate this identity. Is it sheer coincidence that Jews wrote some of the most patriotic American popular songs, including 'God Bless America' and 'White Christmas'? Likely not, in that American-Jewish song-writers like Lorenz Hart, Oscar Hammerstein, Richard Rodgers, Irving Berlin, Jerome Kern and the Gershwin brothers are among the most rhapsodic celebrants of American life. The fact that there were no parallels in Canada is a reflection of the differences in Canadian self-consciousness.

North of the 49th parallel the Jewish community developed in a much different way. Its historical evolution, demography, and culture through most of the nineteenth century were very much at variance with those in the Great Republic. In the first place, it must be emphasized that Canada did not receive sufficient numbers of German-Jewish immigrants to overwhelm existing religious institutions in that era and thus escaped being heavily influenced by their Reformation movement and their accompanying philosophy of emancipation. Not that Canadian Jews, small in numbers and concentrated in very few centres, refrained from trying to adjust economically, politically, and in every other way. But the important point here is that they were not Germans, and they were not exposed either to the German-Jewish Reform synthesis or to the enlightenment-influenced Orthodoxy of Germany's Samson Raphael Hirsch. Indeed, the most influential elements culturally in Montreal until the 1880s were the Spanish and Portuguese, while in Toronto British and Lithuanians outnumbered all other elements including a few Germans.[30] While there is evidence of some enlightenment influences among a few of Montreal's Spanish and Portuguese, both of these groups were essentially conservative and observantly Orthodox in religious practice. The historian of Toronto Jewry, Stephen Speisman, points out that until the early twentieth century 'the division between the traditional and liberal wings of the [Holy Blossom] congregation appears to have been minor. . . . There were no major departures from orthodoxy while the congregation remained [without its own premises].'[31] And while certain German Reform influences began to affect the main group in Toronto in the 1880s, the Montrealers remained adamantly, almost pugnaciously, Orthodox. Rabbis Abraham de Sola and his son, Meldola, who held the pulpit of the Spanish and Portuguese synagogue in succession for about seventy years, acted as stout defenders of the old faith in Montreal and successfully kept the tiny Reform group out of the mainstream of religious life in the community.[32]

The absence of a German migration to Canada large enough to overwhelm or replace the old Spanish and Portuguese communities, as occurred in the United States, is thus highly significant. For while American Jewry was highly influenced by the Reform philosophy, Canadian Jews were affected to a much lesser degree. Indeed, in Montreal, a certain counter-reformation spirit prevailed. Canadian Jewry overwhelmingly remained, therefore, nominally tied to the old faith even though some assimilation was already underway. This outlook may also have reflected the comparatively conservative ethos of nineteenth-century Canada where traditional monarchical values, established churches (official in all but name), and certain quasi-aristocratic trappings related to Canada's British connection held sway. Canadian Jews like the influential de Sola family saw themselves as defenders of the British tradition as well as of Jewish Orthodoxy. Although this outlook never had the philosophical respectability of the ideal German or American-Jewish symbiosis, it did lend a certain tone or shading to the Canadian Jewish community. In Canada, especially in Quebec, Jews knew that they were different and would remain so, equal in law perhaps but distinct, whereas in the United States there was a belief—especially among the second generation—in a larger degree of integration into a culture which, because it was by definition republican, democratic, and libertarian, would allow the Jewish admixture.[33]

With Orthodoxy and tradition still firmly in place and centred in a very much smaller, more concentrated group of communities by the 1880s and 1890s, Canadian Jewry faced the hordes of arrivals who continued to come until World War I. Indeed, this is the point at which many of the dissimilarities between the two North American communities begin to diminish. In both Canada and the United States the East European Jews, both traditional and radical, came increasingly into communal prominence. They thronged into the clothing factories and concentrated themselves in urban ghettos, while in Canada a significant percentage moved out to settle on the Prairies. But previously developed national differences in the two Jewries nevertheless continued to influence the ways in which certain institutions and organizations evolved, while the timing of national economic development somewhat affected the subsequent demographic distribution of Jews.[34] Thus the differences, some subtle and some blatant, continued. For example, Zionism became from the 1890s until the present a continuous and dominant part of the Canadian Jewish identity. This is not to say that even a majority of Canadian Jews became identified officially as Zionists. But significant segments of the old patrician and *nouveaux riches* élites did so.[35] American Jewry, or at least its leadership and moneyed élite, on the other hand, either held back from Zionism or actively opposed it.[36] For many American Jews, especially those who shared the ideal of the symbiosis — that goal implanted by the mid-nineteenth-century German immigrants — Zionism was a threat because it raised the problem of dual loyalty. The nagging question of how one could become a Zionist — that is, one who believed in the return of Jews to the ancient homeland — while still being loyal American dedicated to the achievement of cultural integration in the United States, could not be easily answered. Even after Louis D. Brandeis, the famous Justice of the US Supreme Court, developed a partially satisfying answer to this dilemma, most of the old German community — now America's Jewish élite — continued a sustained and militant anti-Zionist stance.[37] And it is interesting to note that the Reform synagogue — the quintessential expression of the German-American-Jewish quest for symbiosis — was a major vehicle of opposition to Zionism although there were inevitably a few significant Reform leaders who actively espoused Zionism. At the Cincinnati seminary, rabbinical students were taught by outspoken opponents of the idea of a Jewish homeland in Palestine; consequently, this message was heard from many American Reform pulpits.[38] When one American rabbi, Maurice Eisendrath, tried to bring this anti-Zionism into his Toronto Reform congregation in the late 1920s, the community was outraged and a sizeable secession from the synagogue took place, although the rabbi — unrevised and unrepentant — continued to attack this form of Jewish nationalism.[39] But Rabbi Eisendrath was the one exceptional case of a major Canadian Jewish figure publicly opposing Zionism. And, let it be noted, he ceased his opposition during the 1930s as did most of the rest of Reform Jewry for one principal, terrible reason.

What explains the more favourable attitude towards Zionism among Canadians brings me to my penultimate point, which has already been to some extent anticipated. Jews in Canada did not understand that there were any tests of Canadian nationalism they had to meet. The situation of Jews in Montreal was such that, insofar as both French and English were concerned, they were pariahs barely tolerated by both camps. But the predominant strain of pre-1914 Canadian nationalist thought, that of the Imperial Federationists, though expressing a narrowly British view of history, national character, and mission for Canada, also implied indirectly an integration into British imperialism, a toleration, an openness, a liberality towards racial and cultural diversity, and a grudging acceptance in this polity in which freedom is said to wear a Crown.[40] From the standpoint of J.S. Woodsworth's Social Gospel outlook Jews were, like Galicians and Chinese in Canada, one of the communities which could be absorbed.[41] It may be that the origins of the idea of the Canadian mosaic lie somewhere in these attitudes and in the fact that there appears to have been no public ethos in English Canada which necessarily overrode all other loyalties. In any event, Canada was without the intellectual influences of the German Jews who might have been inclined to make an issue out of this and think their way into a loyalty conundrum for which there could only be one logical answer.

In the circumstances of no competing nationalism and no opposing Reformation ideology, the Zionist movement in Canada thrived. Under the leadership of Clarence de Sola, a member of the Spanish-Portuguese aristocracy of Montreal Jewry who headed the Canadian Zionist Federation from 1898 to 1920, the movement grew. It spread quickly through the metropolitan centres, into small communities across the country and even into the few scattered farming colonies on the Prairies.[42] So successful was this organization to which de Sola — a wealthy timber exporter — devoted so much of his time and money, that he proudly held it up as a model for Zionists in other countries to follow, especially for the Americans who were grappling with a multitude of problems, the most serious being the need for an intellectual justification of the movement's first principles. No such problem bothered de Sola. His followers were the Russian and Romanian Jews who were pouring into the country in the early 1900s, completely outnumbering all previous waves of Jewish immigration. By 1911, the Jewish population of Canada reached 75,681, a figure which represents an increase of almost 370 per cent over just one decade.[43] After 1901, when the nation's Jewish population stood at about 16,000, an average of 6,000 Jews arrived every year and in 1913-14 alone over 18,000 reached Canada.[44] Even during World War I an annual average of 4,000 Jews arrived. The resurgence of Jewish immigration in the 1920s brought waves from the Ukraine, Poland, and Lithuania (and in the 1930s a tiny trickle from Germany, Austria, and Czechoslovakia). To most of these Eastern European Jews, modern political Zionism came as one major vehicle of redemption from a hateful and oppressive Czarist regime which was also semi-officially anti-Semitic. Very few Russian-Ukrainian Jews saw themselves as Russians or, much less, as Ukrainians. Consequently, they arrived in Canada with no predispositions toward symbiosis. (I should say parenthetically that this is not to deny that a form of enlightenment [the *Haskalah*] had penetrated into the Polish-Ukrainian Jewish towns and villages in the great Pale of Settlement.) Indeed Zionism thrived perhaps also because some Canadian Jewish leaders like Clarence de Sola and Rabbi Ashinsky saw the movement as potentially an integral part of British imperialism.[45] De Sola waxed eloquent on this theory and claimed later to have broached the idea of a British pro-Zionist declaration several months before the famous Balfour Declaration of November 1917.

But the Canadian Zionist Federation, which because of its universal —

though even among both religious and secular Russian immigrants, not unanimous — support became a kind of national Jewish congress, was only the first of such organizations to be followed by the Congress after World War I. Zionism thus went deeper into the Canadian Jewish context than into the American because of the conjunction of separate and distinctive cultural, demographic, and political factors and the unique constitutional and racial structures of Canada. Perhaps Canadian Jews may also have absorbed some nationalistic influences from the French Canadians in Montreal. At any event Zionism's greater strength and support from Canadian Jewry was noted by the world leaders of the movement and was expressed by larger *per capita* financial contributions and emigration to Palestine before and after 1948.

A further determining factor in Canadian Jewish history is its pace of development around the turn of the century. This country began to 'hit its stride' somewhat later than the United States. In terms of economic growth, historians are successfully demonstrating that the 1880s and 1890s were not nearly as stagnant a period as had previously been thought.[46] Nevertheless, there is a point in dating the Canadian takeoff as occurring between 1900 and 1914 if only because that was when the East-West integration, massive development projects, and large-scale investment began to take place. What effect does this generation gap in Canadian economic development (as compared to the American) have upon the Jews? It is that massive Jewish immigration to Canada began and continued a good decade later than it did to the United States. Canada continued to receive relatively substantial Jewish immigration flows through the 1920s while the tide to the US, though numerically larger, was relatively far less significant as a proportion of the total Jewish population.[47] The point is a double one. Historians George Rawlyk and Gordon Stewart identify a 'missing decade' as having been crucial in Nova Scotia's lack of revolutionary politicization just prior to the American Revolution.[48] I have already borrowed the idea by identifying Canadian Jewry's 'missing Germans'. Turning that interesting concept on its head we can say that in respect to its Jewish immigration Canada enjoyed a 'bonus decade': that is, almost ten additional years of people flowing from the cultural centres of Jewish tradition in Eastern Europe. We must not overstress or romanticize the importance of this group. The philosopher A.J. Heschel — a Holocaust survivor writing after 1945 on the inner European Jewish world, the life of the mind of Eastern European Jewry — calls this epoch the 'golden period in the history of the Jewish soul'.[49] But the intellectual baggage that accompanied these Jews to Canada was a complex mixture and consisted not just of an adherence to tradition, however rich and culturally edifying that might be. The typical immigrant of 1924 was considerably different from his counterpart of 1914 or earlier. He had experienced firsthand the European turmoil of 1914-18, the massive upheaval of the Russian Revolution, the ensuing devastating civil war, and the terrible Ukrainian pogroms. Recent East European history as well as the modernization of Russia before 1914, and the cultural resonances of the old world (through the arrival of nearly 50,000 Jewish immigrants during the 1920s) probably had a deeper, more pervasive, and more lasting effect on the Canadian community than on the American.[50] Moreover, this wave of immigration in the 1920s, which included a small number of young intellectuals, likely had a strong enriching influence on Jewish cultural life in Canada from that point forward.

Thus, in conclusion, the contours of Canadian Jewish history were determined by the intermixing of forces which were unique to the northern half of this continent and which resulted in the evolution of a community with a personality different from that of American Jewry. Canadian Jews were immersed in a country with a different history, polity, and culture, and with varying immigration, economic, and urban growth patterns. Not surprisingly, there evolved from it a community that was more traditional, more organizationally unified, and more culturally homogeneous than that of American Jewry. While American Jews yearned for integration into the mainstream of the Great Republic, Canadians stove to express their Jewishness in a country that had no coherent self-definition — except perhaps the solitudes of duality, isolation, northernness, and borrowed glory. In America, Irving Berlin wrote 'God Bless America'; in Canada the quintessential Jewish literary figure, who is probably this country's greatest twentieth-century poet — Abraham Moses Klein — wrote poems of anguish expressing longing for redemption of the Jewish soul lost in a sea of modernity. 'Go catch the echoes to the ticks of time; Spy the interstices between its sands,' he tells us in 'Of Remembrance'.[51] And while he was able in his collection of poems, *The Rocking Chair*, to capture brilliantly the culture of French Canada better than any Anglophone has done in recent times, he continuously reiterated throughout his career his Jewish frame of reference. And towards the end his thoughts returned to 'the ghetto streets where a Jewboy dreamed pavement into pleasant Bible-land':

> It is a fabled city that I seek;
> It stands in Space's vapours and Time's haze;
> Thence comes my sadness in remembered joy
> Constrictive of the throat;
> Thence do I hear, as heard by a Jewboy,
> The Hebrew violins,
> Delighting in the sobbed Oriental note.[52]

We have thus returned to the beginning and to the features that make Canadian Jewish history a separate study. To be sure, they are not unique, *sui generis*, or entirely distinct from the American Jewish experience. Many similarities exist. But the differences remain, and as Canadian history is in certain respects both different from and similar to the American, the historical experience of at least one ethnic group in this country is a reflection of that reality. Can one perhaps generalize from this Jewish history to the history of other ethnic groups in Canada? It is not for me to answer this question. But if the Jewish experience is in any way representative, the peculiarities of this country's history, culture, and pace of evolution must be considered in understanding the development of Ukrainian, Polish, or Hungarian communities in Canada. In this way we can begin to explain not only ethnic history but also some of the only partially explored dimensions of Canada's past and present personality that affect us all and help us understand how we got to where we are now. The rewriting of post-1900 Canadian history from an ethnic perspective will add immeasurably to an understanding of the fascinating complexity of our national experience.

Notes

[1]Michael Brown, 'The American Connection of Canadian Jews: 1959-1919', *Association for Jewish Studies Review* 3 (1978): 21-77.

[2]Jonathan Sarna, 'The Value of Canadian Jewish History to the American Jewish Historian and vice-versa', *Canadian Jewish Historical Society Journal* 5, 1 (Spring 1981): 17-22.

[3]See Bram de Sola, 'The Jewish School Question', *The University Magazine* December (1909): 533-60; D. Rome, 'On the Jewish School Question in Montreal: 1903-1931' (Montreal: National Archives, Canadian Jewish Congress, Canadian Jewish Archives, New Series, no. 3, 1975).

[4]Maxwell Goldstein, 'The Status of the Jew in the Schools of Canada' in Arthur D. Hart, ed., *The Jews in Canada* (Montreal, 1926): 497-8; Public Archives of Canada, M.G. III, C23, Peter Bercovitch Collection; William Nadler, 'The Jewish-Protestant School Problem', typescript, 1925; Rome, *op. cit.*

[5]See Bernard Figler, *Louis Fitch Q.C.* (Montreal, 1969).

[6]M. Brunet, 'Trois Dominantes de la Pensée Canadienne-Française', *La Présence Anglaise et les Canadiennes* (Montreal, 1964): 113-66.

[7]Susan Mann Trofimenkoff, *Action Française: French Canadian Nationalism in the Twenties* (Toronto: University of Toronto Press, 1975): 76-7, 78.

[8]*La Patrie*, 14, 23 Nov., 14, 27 Dec. 1894. See A.I. Silver, *The French Canadian Idea of Confederation, 1864-1900* (Toronto, 1981): 232.

[9]*Report of the Royal Commission Upon The Sweating System in Canada*, Canada, *Sessional papers* (1896), no. 61: 10-11.

[10]Louis Rosenberg, *Canada's Jews: A Social and Economic Study of the Jews in Canada* (Montreal: Bureau of Social and Economic Research, Canadian Jewish Congress, 1939): 377.

[11]Trofimenkoff, *op. cit.*: 78-9; *Labour Gazette* (1933): 1183; *Les Midinettes*: 18, 80; *Canadian Jewish Chronicle*, 6 July 1934.

[12]See Louis Rosenberg, 'A Study of the Growth and Changes in the Distribution of the Jewish Population of Montreal', Canadian Jewish Population Studies, Canadian

Jewish Community Series, no. 4 (Montreal: Bureau of Social and Economic Research, Canadian Jewish Congress, 1955): 8-14.

[13]See Elson I. Rexford, *Our Educational Problem: The Jewish Population and the Protestant Schools* (Montreal: Renouf, n.d.).

[14]See *Canadian Jewish Times*, 8 April, 4 November 1910; 17 March 1911; 9, 30 May 6, 13, 20, 27 June, 1 July 1913.

[15]'Desecration of the Jewish Cemeteries at Three Rivers', in Hart (ed.), *op. cit.*: 499-500.

[16]Quoted in J.M. Bumsted, *Documentary Problems in Canadian History: Post Confederation* (Georgetown, Ont.: Irwin Dorsey, 1969) II: 37. See also *Canadian Jewish Times*, 20 September 1911.

[17]*Canadian Jewish Times*, 17 August 1909.

[18]Michael N. Dobkowski, *The Tarnished Dream: The Basis of American Anti-Semitism*, Contributions to American History, no. 81 (Westport, Conn.: Greenwood Press, 1979): Chapter 1.

[19]See H. Palmer (ed.), *Immigration and the Rise of Multiculturalism* (Toronto: Copp Clark, 1975): 44-53; W. Peter Ward, *White Canada Forever: Popular Attitudes and Public Policy Toward Orientals in British Columbia* (Montreal: McGill-Queen's University Press, 1978).

[20]Rosenberg, *op. cit.*: 9-16.

[21]Bertram W. Korn, *American Jewry and the Civil War* (New York: Atheneum, 1970): 1.

[22]See Leon Goldman, 'Zionist Organization of Canada', in Hart, ed., *op. cit.*: 291-320; Central Zionist Archives, Jerusalem, Z1/244, Jacob de Haas to Dr Theodore Herzl, 14 April 1903.

[23]See Daniel J. Elazar, *Community and Policy: The Organizational Dynamics of American Jewry* (Philadelphia: The Jewish Publication Society of America, 1980): chapter 5.

[24]Harry Gutkin, *Journey Into Our Heritage* (Toronto: Lester & Orpen Dennys, 1980): 195-96.

[25]NAC, Samuel J. Zacks Papers, M.G. 30, C144, Vol. IX, file 1946-7, 'Midwestern Region'.

[26]Nathan Glazer, *American Judaism* (Chicago: University of Chicago Press, 1972, second edition): Chapter 3.

[27]Bertram W. Korn, *German-Jewish Intellectual Influences on American Jewish Life*, B.G. Rudolph Lectures in Judaic Studies (Syracuse, 1972): 1, 6.

[28]Glazer, *op. cit.*: 44, 60.

[29]See Stephen Birmingham, *'Our Crowd': The Great Jewish Families of New York* (New York: Dell, 1967): Part 4; Arthur Mann, *Yankee Reformers in the Urban Age: Social Reform in Boston, 1880-1900* (New York: Harper & Row, 1966): Chapter 3.

[30]Benjamin G. Sack, *History of the Jews in Canada* (Montreal: Harvest House, 1965): Chapter 14.

[31]Stephen A. Speisman, *Jews of Toronto: A History to 1937* (Toronto: McClelland & Stewart, 1979): 32.

[32]Michael Brown, 'The Beginnings of Reform Judaism in Canada', *Jewish Social Studies* 34, 4 (October 1972): 322-42, 323, 330-1.

[33]Will Herberg, *Protestant-Catholic-Jew: An Essay in American Religious Sociology* (New York: Doubleday, Anchor Books, 1960); ch. 7.

[34]See Jonathan D. Sarna's article 'Jewish Immigration to North America: The Canadian Experience (1870-1900)', *Jewish Journal of Sociology* 17, 1 (June 1976): 31-42. He argues that Canadian Jews were more receptive to East European Jewish immigrants than contemporary US Jews (p. 35).

[35]Goldman, *op. cit.*: 291-313. See Bernard Figler, *Lillian and Archie Freiman* (Montreal, 1959).

[36]Melvin I. Urofsky, *American Zionism From Herzl to the Holocaust* (New York: Doubleday, Anchor Books, 1976): 85-91.

[37]See Allon Gal, *Brandeis of Boston* (Cambridge: Harvard University Press, 1980).

[38]Kenneth I. Cleator and Harry J. Stern, *A Rabbi's Journey* (New York: Bloch, 1981): 9.

[39]See Speisman, *op. cit.*: p. 242; see (Rabbi) Maurice Eisendrath, *The Never Failing Stream* (Toronto: Macmillan, 1939): 224-42, for his sermon, 'Nation, Race or Religion', in which he attacked the Zionist cause as 'ridiculous and . . . . symptomatic of the blind conceit which afflicts every nationalist!' (p. 236).

[40]Carl Berger, *The Sense of Power: Studies in the Ideas of Canadian Imperialism, 1867-1914* (Toronto: University of Toronto Press, 1970): 9; John Farthing, *Freedom Wears a Crown* (Toronto: Kingswood House, 1957).

[41]J.S. Woodsworth, *Strangers Within Our Gates* (Toronto, 1911): 150-9, 279-89.

[42]Goldman, *op. cit.*, passim.

[43]Rosenberg, *op. cit.*, 4.

[44]*Ibid.*: 134.

[45]*Canadian Jewish Times*, 17 August 1900. See also *The Maccabean* Dec. 1903: 363-5; Goldman, *op. cit.*: 302.

[46]G.W. Bertram, 'Economic Growth in Canadian Industry, 1870-1915: The Staple Model', in W.T. Easterbrook and H.G.J. Aitken, *Approaches To Canadian Economic History* (Toronto: McClelland and Stewart, 1967): 74-98.

[47]Rosenberg, *op. cit.*, 134.

[48]Gordon Stewart and George Rawlyk, *A People Highly Favoured of God: The Nova Scotia Yankees and the American Revolution* (Toronto: Macmillan, 1972): chapter 1.

[49]Abraham J. Heschel, *The Earth Is the Lord's* (New York: Harper Torchbook, 1962): 10.

[50]Simon Belkin, *Through Narrow Gates: A Review of Jewish Immigration Colonization and Immigrant Aid Work in Canada (1840-1940)* (Montreal: Canadian Jewish Congress and The Jewish Colonization Assn., 1966): Chapters 9-13; Joseph Kage, *With Faith and Thanksgiving: The Story of Two Hundred Years of Jewish Immigration and Immigrant Aid Work in Canada (1760-1960)* (Montreal: Eagle, 1962): 87.

[51]Abraham M. Klein, *The Second Scroll*, New Canadian Library, no. 22 (Toronto: McClelland & Stewart, 1961): 138.

[52]*Ibid.*, 95, 97.

I wish to thank my Queen's colleagues, Rabbi Herbert Basser, Donald Schurman, Roger Graham, Klaus Hansen, and George Rawlyk for their helpful comments on this paper.

The Rise and Decline of Canadian Jewry?

A Socio-Demographic Profile

Robert J. Brym

The Paradox of Success

Starting for the most part as workers and small business owners one, two, or three generations ago, Jews have moved quickly up Canada's socioeconomic hierarchy, contributing significantly to the worlds of business, the professions, academic life, and public service along the way. It has not, however, been an easy climb. As our historians have ably shown, anti-Semitism, both popular and official, has made it difficult for Jews to get into the country and, once here, to gain acceptance. Justifiably, therefore, the chroniclers of Canadian Jewry have tended to focus on a single, compelling theme: tragedy and triumph.

But the story of success in the face of adversity is by no means the only possible account of Canadian Jewish history. Indeed, devotion to that theme obscures an important paradox of Canadian Jewish life, a paradox that forms the subject of this essay. From a sociological viewpoint, 'success' means that Jews have moved into social and economic positions from which they were previously excluded. In these new positions, Jews have established increasingly numerous and intimate ties with non-Jews. The result: widespread acculturation and, for some, considerable assimilation. The conditions in which Jews earn a livelihood today also compel Jewish women to have fewer children than are needed to replace the current parental generation. The result: population decline. Canada has, on the whole, been relatively good to the Jews, especially in the last 30 years. But the largely agreeable circumstances of Canadian Jewish life are weakening the community. The main exception to this pattern is Orthodox Jewry, whose survival chances are significantly above average.

This essay documents some dimensions of the dilemma of Canadian Jewry's success. I will first try to answer the apparently simple, but actually quite complex, questions of how many Canadian Jews there are, and how the size of the community has fluctuated over time. I will next document some aspects of the Jew's impressive economic successes. Indicators of assimilation and population decline will then be examined in the light of these accomplishments. Finally, I will outline some policy implications of my analysis.

Throughout the essay I will rely mainly on census data collected by Statistics Canada. These data are not without flaws. But they permit one to move beyond impressionistic statements and describe with some precision the paradox of Canadian Jewry's success.

Who is a Jew?

The 1981 Canadian census asked people to specify their ethnic origin(s) and religious identification (if any). This allows one to divide the Canadian Jewish population into four groups (see Table 1). The first and by far the largest group, amounting to 84 per cent of the total, is composed of 246,130 'high identifiers' — those who indicated that both their religion and their ethnic origin was Jewish. The smallest group (2.9 per cent of the total), is composed of apostates, who considered themselves ethnic Jews but had converted to a non-Jewish religion. Not much more numerous are the secularists (3.2 per cent of the total), who considered themselves ethnic Jews but stated they have no religion. Altogether, these three groups — Canada's 'ethnic Jews' — represent over 90 per cent of the Canadian Jewish population. The fourth group of Canadian Jews, comprising people who specified multiple ethnic origins (e.g., Jewish and British), I have labelled 'assimilated'. The term seems entirely appropriate. Researchers widely acknowledge that people who specify multiple ethnic origins tend to identify comparatively weakly with any one ethnic group (Reitz, 1980); and Jews with multiple ethnic origins are proportionately more numerous in provinces that rank high on other indicators of assimilation, such as the rate of mixed marriage.[1]

The 1986 'mini-census' asked no questions about respondents' religion, so for that year one can divide Canada's Jews into only two groups — ethnic and assimilated Jews. This is where the numbers start to get interesting. In 1986, the most recent year for which we have figures, the total number of Jews in Canada, both ethnic and assimilated, stood at 343,505, up an impressive 17 per cent over 1981. However, that increase is attributable to a tripling in the number of *assimilated* Jews in the five years between censuses. Thus, in 1986 there were only 245,855 *ethnic* Jews in Canada, *down* nearly 7 per cent from five years earlier. Meanwhile, the number of assimilated Jews increased by 236 per cent to 97,650.[2]

I will discuss the significance of these changes below. But for the moment, in concluding this brief survey of the size of the Canadian Jewish community, I want to note that the number of ethnic Jews in Canada may have been declining since about 1971.[3] By 1986 ethnic Jews comprised just under 1 per cent of Canada's population. Between 1981 and 1986 Canada's ethnic Jewish population shrank at a brisk 1.4 per cent annual rate (see Table 3). If that trend continues — and, I emphasize, this is an extrapolation, not a forecast — Canada's total Jewish population will be about 150,000 and Canada's ethnic Jewish population will be under 100,000 in the year 2050, just 57 years from now (cf. Davids, 1989: 53).

Table 1 Number of Jews in Canada, 1981 and 1986

	1981	1986
HIGH IDENTIFIERS		
(ethnic Jewish and Jewish religious identification)	246,130 (84.0%)	n.a.
SECULARISTS		
(ethnic Jewish and no religious identification)	9,265 (3.2%)	n.a.
APOSTATES		
(ethnic Jewish and non-Jewish religious identification)	8,625 (2.9%)	n.a.
ETHNIC JEWS		
(subtotal)	264,020 (90.1%)	245,855 (71.6%)
ASSIMILATED		
(ethnic Jewish and other ethnic origin)	29,055 (9.9%)	97,650 (28.4%)
TOTAL	293,075 (100.0%)	343,505 (100.0%)

Sources: Calculated from Statistics Canada (1984: 1-7 to 1-8, 5-15 to 5-16; n.d. [1988?]).

Socioeconomic Attainment

The good news about Canadian Jews concerns their socioeconomic achieve-ments, which are impressive by any standard, even allowing for the fact that they started out with some clear advantages over other immigrant groups. In 1931, 56 per cent of Canada's Jews were immigrants and another 39 per cent were first generation born in Canada. While most Canadian immigrants in that era had been peasants or unskilled workers in their countries or origin, most Jewish newcomers arrived urbanized and skilled. As a result, in 1931 about 30 per cent of Jews in the labour force were employed as skilled workers in manufacturing (mainly textiles and clothing) and 36 per cent were engaged in trade. Some 10 per cent of Jews were clerks, another 5 per cent professionals, and the remaining 19 per cent were scattered among the various service, primary, and blue-collar occupations where non-Jews pre-dominated (Rosenberg, 1939: 72, 172, 176).

The following half century witnessed enormous changes in the Canadian, and Canadian-Jewish, occupational structures. The growth of giant enter-prises and the mechanization and automation of production reduced the proportion of blue-collar workers and small-business people and increased

Table 2 Jews in Canada by Province and Territory, 1931, 1981, 1986 (per cent of total in brackets)

	1931 JEWISH BY "RACE"		1981 ETHNIC JEWISH		1981 ETHNIC JEWISH AND OTHER ETHNIC ORIGIN		1986 ETHNIC JEWISH		1986 ETHNIC JEWISH AND OTHER ETHNIC ORIGIN	
NFLD	—	(—)	285	(0.1)	185	(0.6)	150	(0.1)	390	(0.4)
PEI	20	(0.0)	80	(0.0)	50	(0.2)	40	(0.0)	125	(0.1)
NS	2,046	(1.3)	2,085	(0.8)	725	(2.5)	1,760	(0.7)	2,650	(2.7)
NB	1,262	(0.8)	720	(0.3)	370	(1.3)	610	(0.3)	910	(0.9)
PQ	60,087	(38.4)	90,360	(34.2)	4,755	(16.4)	81,195	(33.0)	17,030	(17.4)
ONT	52,383	(39.8)	131,320	(49.7)	14,525	(50.0)	127,030	(51.7)	49,510	(50.7)
MAN	19,341	(12.4)	14,950	(5.7)	1,235	(4.3)	13,875	(5.6)	4,400	(4.5)
SASK	5,116	(3.3)	1,515	(0.6)	465	(1.6)	990	(0.4)	1,620	(1.7)
ALTA	3,722	(2.4)	9,460	(3.6)	2,340	(8.1)	7,950	(3.2)	7,160	(7.3)
BC	2,743	(1.8)	13,170	(5.0)	4,345	(15.0)	12,230	(5.0)	13,635	(14.0)
NWT & YKN	6	(0.0)	80	(0.0)	50	(0.2)	40	(0.0)	225	(0.2)
TOTAL	156,726	(100.2)	264,020	(100.0)	29,055	(100.2)	245,855	(100.0)	97,550	(100.0)

Sources: Calculated from Rosenberg (1939: 19–20); Statistics Canada (1984: 1–7 to 1–8, 10–17 to 1–18; n.d. [1988?]).

Table 3 *Average Annual Growth Rate of Ethnic Jewish and Total Population of Canada, 1931–86 (in per cent) and Ethnic Jews as per cent of Total Population, 1941–86*

	ETHNIC JEWISH GROWTH RATE	ALL ETHNIC ORIGINS GROWTH RATE	ETHNIC JEWS AS PER CENT OF ALL ETHNIC ORIGINS AT END OF PERIOD
1931–41	0.8	1.0	1.5
1941–51	0.7	1.7	1.3
1951–61	−0.5	2.6	0.9
1961–71	5.6	1.7	1.4
1971–81	−1.2	1.2	1.1
1981–86	−1.4	1.0	1.0
1931–86	0.8	1.6	

Sources: Calculated from Beaujot and McQuillan (1982: 112); Kalbach and McVey (1979 [1971]: 195, 198–9); Statistics Canada (1984: 1-7 to 1-8; n.d. [1988?]).

Note: Since the 1981 census was the first to allow respondents to acknowledge multiple ethnic origins, responses to the ethnic origin question in 1981 and thereafter are not strictly comparable to pre-1981 responses: some of the people listed as Jews in 1971, for example, would have acknowledged multiple ethnic origins if that had been permissible. On the other hand, less distortion results from comparing 1981 and later censuses with, say, the 1931 census because the 1931 Canadian Jewish population consisted largely of immigrants; it is unlikely that many of them would have been inclined to indicate multiple ethnic (or 'racial') origins if that had been allowed.

the proportion of white-collar employees and professionals in the labour force. The Jews' 'entrance status' was relatively high among immigrants, and that advantage enabled them to rise quickly in the new occupational structure. Indeed, they soon achieved high socioeconomic status among the native-born population as well.

The socioeconomic position of Jews in Canada is well illustrated by Tables 4, 5 and 6, all based on the 1981 census.[4] Table 4 shows how Jews and people of all ethnic origins are distributed among the sixteen main census occupational groupings. The chief lesson to be learned from the table is that both Jewish men and Jewish women tend to be concentrated at the top of the occupational hierarchy. Thus, Jewish men are about 4.5 times more likely than all men in Canada to be in a medical profession; 4.1 times more likely to have a social science job; 2.4 times more likely to be a salesperson; and 2.3 times more likely to occupy a managerial or administrative position. On the other hand, all men in Canada are 14.5 times more likely than Jewish men to be engaged in primary production other than farming; 7.7 times more likely to be farmers; 4.7 times more likely to be construction workers; and 3.6 times more likely to process materials.

The picture for Jewish women differs only in detail. Jewish women are 2.8 times more likely than all women to be employed in artistic, literary, and

Table 4 Occupational Distribution of Jews and all Ethnic Groups, Canada, 1981, by Sex (in per cent)

	ETHNIC JEWISH		ALL ETHNIC ORIGINS	
	MALE	FEMALE	MALE	FEMALE
Managerial, administrative	25.1	10.5	10.9	5.1
Natural science	5.0	1.9	4.8	1.1
Social science	5.3	5.1	1.3	2.0
Teaching	4.5	9.8	2.8	6.1
Medical	7.6	5.7	1.7	8.2
Artistic, literary, recreational	3.1	4.2	1.6	1.5
Clerical	8.0	34.5	7.2	35.4
Sales	20.5	18.5	8.6	9.8
Service	5.7	4.6	9.9	16.8
Farming	0.7	0.4	5.4	2.4
Other primary	0.2	0.1	2.9	0.2
Processing	1.5	0.5	5.4	2.3
Machining and repairing	5.7	2.7	14.0	5.3
Construction	2.3	0.1	10.8	0.3
Equipment operating	2.3	0.1	6.0	0.7
Other	2.4	1.3	6.7	2.6
Total	100.0	100.0	100.0	100.0

Source: 1981 Census of Canada, Public Use Sample Tape, Individual File.

recreational work; 2.6 times more likely to be employed in social science professions; and 2.1 times more likely to work as managers and administrators. But all Canadian women are 7 times more likely than Jewish women to have jobs operating equipment; 6 times more likely to be farmers; 4.6 times more likely to do processing work; and 3.7 times more likely to be engaged in service jobs.

Table 5 presents additional indicators of the Jew's socioeconomic attainment. In 1981 Jews were 5.3 times more likely than all Canadians to earn

Table 5 Some Indicators of the Socioeconomic Status of Selected Ethnic Groups, Canada, 1981 (in per cent)

	JEWISH	BRITISH	ITALIAN	CHINESE	ALL
Income $50,000 +	6.4	1.5	0.8	1.3	1.2
Completed university	32.1	10.4	6.1	20.7	10.2
Employers, managers, administrators and professionals	46.5	25.7	16.9	32.2	25.0

Sources: Li (1988: 76, 90); 1981 Census of Canada, Public Use Sample Tape, Individual File.

Table 6   *Annual Income of Jews and Selected Other Ethnic Groups in Canada, 1981 (in dollars)*

INCOME	JEWISH	BRITISH	ITALIAN	CHINESE
Above or below mean	6,262	356	−2158	−2209
Adjusted for age, gender, nativity	4,975	306	−1138	−1035
Adjusted for age, gender, nativity and years of schooling	2,794	−128	1224	−1020

Source: Li (1988: 116-17).

very high incomes ($50,000 + per year), 3.1 times more likely to have a university degree, and 1.9 times more likely to have high status jobs (employer, manager, administrator, professional).

In 1981 Jews had the highest average income of any ethnic group in Canada—$6,232 above the mean (see Table 6). Part of the reason for the Jews' high average income was demographic: compared to many other ethnic groups in Canada, Jews are on average older and there are proportionately more native-born people among them. Taking these factors into account statistically—that is, calculating income on the assumption that Jews had the same demographic characteristics as all Canadians—Jews' mean income was only $4,975 higher than the average in 1981. Another source of the Jews' high income is that they are the most highly educated ethnic group in Canada. Taking years of schooling into account in addition to demographic factors, we see that the Jews' average income drops to only $2,794 above the mean. Although relevant quantitative data are not available, my sense is that a large part of the remaining Jewish income advantage can probably be explained by the Jews' relatively high entrance status. In sum, it seems that Jews earn more than other Canadians because of their demographic characteristics, their devotion to education, and the relatively advantaged positions from which they began their climb up Canada's socioeconomic hierarchy.

Assimilation

The development of Canada's occupation structure has affected Jewish life in profound and complex ways, but it is generally acknowledged that one of the most consequential changes derives from the partial breakdown of social boundaries between Jews and non-Jews. The erosion of group boundaries is most evident in public educational institutions and bureaucratic work settings. For most Canadian Jews, these are arenas in which one can meet, learn about, befriend, date, and court people of all ethnic origins. Jews are still among the most socially cohesive ethnic groups in Canada, but their educa-

Table 7 Opposition to Intermarriage in Canada, 1968-83

	1968	1973	1978	1983
Per cent opposed to marriage between . . .				
Catholics and Protestants	28	16	10	9
Jews and non-Jews	28	16	11	10
Whites and Blacks	53	35	23	21

Source: Lambert and Curtis (1984: 44, n. 9).

tional and occupational aspirations have led most of them to enter a new and basically accepting world.

There are many indicators of growing ethnic tolerance in Canada, but the overall picture is well summarized in Table 7 on Canadian attitudes towards intermarriage.[5] Surveys conducted by the Canadian branch of the Gallup organization show that the period 1968-82 witnessed a dramatic decline in opposition to all forms of intermarriage. By 1983 only 10 per cent of Canadians opposed marriage between Jews and non-Jews—practically the same as the proportion opposing marriage between Catholics and Protestants (and, incidentally, exactly the same proportion as in the United States). Moreover, older people tend to oppose intermarriage more than younger people, so it is not unreasonable to expect that acceptance of intermarriage will grow over time.

Table 8 illustrates the Jewish response to this liberal climate of opinion. The mixed marriage rate has risen steadily since the 1930s, substantially since the 1960s, and it reached 25 per cent in 1984. That is, by 1984 about a quarter of Jewish brides and grooms were marrying non-Jews.

These figures refer to marriages in which Jews' spouses identified with a non-Jewish religion at the time of marriage. They do not provide a full picture of intermarriage because some non-Jews who marry Jews convert—and converts add more than just numbers to the community. As American studies have shown, converts tend to be somewhat more religiously involved with the Jewish community than the average Jew. However, surveys also reveal that only about a third of American-Jewish intermarriages involve conversion of the non-Jewish spouse (Mayer, 1985: 282), and the Canadian figure is nearly identical (Broadbar-Nemzer, Cohen, and Shahar, this volume). Since non-conversionary intermarriages involve a weakening of Jewish identity, especially for the offspring, there can be little doubt that intermarriage is not only increasing but that, on the whole, it promotes assimilation.

The rising marriage rate is, then, one factor underlying the growth in the number of assimilated Jews between the 1981 and 1986 censuses, reported above: it seems likely that children of non-conversionary intermarriages are especially prone to be reported as having multiple ethnic origins. Additional

Table 8 Jewish Mixed Marriages in Canada by Sex, 1931-1984 (in per cent)

	MALE[a]	FEMALE[b]	TOTAL[c]
1931	3	2	2
1941	7	3	5
1951	7	3	5
1961	10	4	7
1971	18	12	15
1981[d]	24	20	22
1984	26	22	25

Sources: Calculated from Cohn (1976: 92-3); Statistics Canada (1974-86).
Notes:
[a]Per cent of Jewish grooms who married non-Jews.
[b]Per cent of Jewish brides who married non-Jews.
[c]Jews who married non-Jews as a per cent of all Jewish brides and grooms.
[d]Quebec data are not available after 1973 and Alberta data are not available after 1982. The figures for these years were estimated as follows. In the period 1951-71 Jewish marriages in Quebec were 39 per cent of all Jewish marriages in Canada, while in 1971 the total Quebec Jewish mixed marriage rate was 45 per cent of the rest-of-Canada rate. Assuming that these proportions remained constant until 1976, they were used to estimate the contribution of Quebec to the Canadian rate for 1974-76. For 1977-84 the estimate was based on the assumption that Jewish marriages in Quebec fell to 34 per cent of all Jewish marriages in Canada (since Quebec Jews were 34 per cent of Canadian Jews according to the 1981 census). A similar estimation procedure was followed for Alberta in 1983-84.

sources of new assimilated Jews include some immigrants; natural increase among Jews in the 1981 assimilated population; conversions to Judaism; and the secular drift of Jews in the 1981 Jewish population out of the 'ethnic' category. This drift is caused by some second- and third-generation Canadian Jews beginning to think of themselves as people not just of Jewish origin, but of Canadian origin too.[6]

But that is very far from the whole story. Recall that the number of assimilated Jews rose by nearly 69,000 in the intercensal period. The sources of new, assimilated Jews enumerated above can account for perhaps a third of the increase.[7] One is obliged to conclude that the remainder came from inside Canada but outside the 1981 Canadian Jewish population. That is, most of the 69,000 additional assimilated Jews recorded in the 1986 census are people who had lived in Canada in 1981 but who had not specified Jewish as one of their ethnic origins in 1981.

For the most part these people appear to have recently 'discovered' their Jewish roots. For large numbers of North Americans, being a member of a minority group is no longer stigmatizing, and ethnicity in general has even become fashionable. As a result, it is not uncommon for people with comparatively remote ethnic ancestry, who formerly considered themselves to be majority group members, to now acknowledge some minority group attachment (Lieberson, 1989; Silberman, 1985). The rapid increase in the number of assimilated Jews in Canada between 1981 and 1986 is, I suggest, more an outcome of the rediscovery of suppressed Jewish ethnicity than an indication of assimilation among former ethnic Jews.

Although some analysts might be inclined to think of this rediscovery as an ethnic 'revival', it is unclear whether we are dealing here with anything more than a symbolic phenomenon that amounts to little in real terms (Gans, 1979). Any conclusive statement on the subject must await the collection of relevant survey data, but my impression is that, with some well-publicized exceptions, people who rediscover their Jewish identity rarely join Jewish organizations, give money to Jewish causes, learn Jewish languages, study Jewish history, or otherwise participate actively in the life of the community. Certainly the organized Jewish community does not actively seek to attract and involve new, assimilated Jews in Jewish life. The rise of the new, assimilated Jew thus does little to alter the basic picture sketched above: the core of the Canadian Jewish community — Canada's ethnic Jews — is shrinking in size, partly due to assimilation.

Declining Fertility

A low and declining fertility rate is a second important source of population decline among Canada's ethnic Jews: Jewish women are having too few babies to sustain the size of the community.

Table 9 corroborates this point. Look first at the right-hand column, which pertains to women past the age of procreation who have ever been married. Among these women, Jews gave birth to substantially fewer children than did members of any other religious group — an average of about 2.2 children. Given current mortality rates, each woman, whether married or not, must give birth to 2.1 children on average in order for the population to maintain its current size. Thus, if one assumes that 5 per cent of Jewish women fail to marry and have children,[8] the completed fertility rate for Jewish women in 1981 was 2.1. In other words, as of 1981, Jewish women who had passed childbearing age — women born before 1936 — had given birth to just enough children to maintain the size of the Jewish population.

What is crucial for the future of the Canadian Jewish community, however, is the childbearing practice of women still in their procreative years. The left-hand column of Table 9 pertains to women aged 15 to 44. As of 1981 the Jews among them had by far the lowest fertility rate — less than 1.6 children per ever-married woman (or about 1.5 children per woman). Note that this figure refers to Jews by religion. The figure for all Jewish women is lower still. Can we know how many more children will be born to these women before they all reach their mid-40s? All that can be said with certainty on the basis of available data is that (1) the predicted completed fertility rate for *all* Canadian women in their childbearing years has been declining steadily

Table 9   Children Ever Born per 1,000 Ever-Married Women, by Religion, 1981

	WOMEN 15-44	WOMEN 45 AND OVER
Catholic	1,781	3,848
Mainline Protestant	1,797	2,806
Eastern Orthodox	1,798	2,793
Jewish	1,596	2,236
All	1,781	3,304

Source: Statistics Canada (1983: 11-1 to 11-2).

since 1959, falling to 1.7 in 1981 (Romaniuc, 1984: 124);[9] and (2) we may safely assume that Jewish women have a below-average rate. On this basis it seems safe to conclude that Canadian-Jewish women born after 1936 are likely to have fewer children than are needed to replace the current generation (cf. Davids, 1989: 53).

Low fertility is a response to the social and economic demands of modern life. The fertility rate declines among women who are more urbanized, more highly educated, more involved in the paid labour force, and more highly paid (Romaniuc, 1984: 59-75). Jewish women rank high on all these dimensions. To the degree that careers demand more years of schooling and add to total work time, Jewish women often make choices that reduce fertility, delaying childbirth, waiting longer between births, even foregoing childbirth altogether.

Fertility rates below the replacement level result in an aging population, unless, of course, young immigrants make up for natural population loss. In Canada, however, there are too few Jewish immigrants to offset the losses caused by natural decrease (see Table 10). As a result, Canada's Jewish population is aging quickly. The aging process is illustrated by the population pyramids in Figure 1, which graph the age-sex distribution of the Canadian-Jewish population and the Canadian population as a whole

Table 10   Post-War Jewish Immigrants in Canada, 1946-1986

PERIOD OF IMMIGRATION	ETHNIC JEWISH PER YEAR	ETHNIC JEWISH AND OTHER ETHNIC ORIGIN PER YEAR	TOTAL JEWISH PER YEAR
1946-55	1,731	472	2,203
1956-66	1,234	519	1,753
1967-77	1,869	876	2,745
1978-82	2,196	687	2,883
1983 to 31 May 1986	1,013	390	1,403

Source: Calculated from Statistics Canada (1989: 2-36).

Figure 1 Jewish and All Origins by Age and Sex, 1931 and 1981

1931 Jews   male   female
           65 + | | |
approximate   55–64 | | | | | |
mean age: 45–54 | | | | | | | | | | | |
27.4   35–44 | | | | | | | | | | | | | | | | |
                25–34 | | | | | | | | | | | | | | | | | | |
                15–24 | | | | | | | | | | | | | | | | | | | | | | | | | | | |
                ⟨15 | | | | | | | | | | | | | | | | | | | | | | | | | | | | | |
                      30   15   0   15   30
                                         per cent

1931 all origins   male   female
           65 + | | | | | | |
approximate   55–64 | | | | | | |
mean age: 45–54 | | | | | | | | | | |
28.5   35–44 | | | | | | | | | | | |
                25–34 | | | | | | | | | | | | |
                15–24 | | | | | | | | | | | | | | |
                ⟨15 | | | | | | | | | | | | | | | | | | | | | | | | | | | | | | | |
                      30   15   0   15   30
                                         per cent

1981 Jews   male   female
           65 + | | | | | | | | | | | | | | | | | | |
approximate   55–64 | | | | | | | | | | | | | |
mean age: 45–54 | | | | | | | | | | |
38.1   35–44 | | | | | | | | | | | |
                25–34 | | | | | | | | | | | | | | | | | | |
                15–24 | | | | | | | | | | | | | | |
                ⟨15 | | | | | | | | | | | | | | | | |
                      30   15   0   15   30
                                         per cent

1981 all origins   male   female
           65 + | | | | | | | | | |
approximate   55–64 | | | | | | | | | |
mean age: 45–54 | | | | | | | | | | |
32.6   35–44 | | | | | | | | | | | | |
                25–34 | | | | | | | | | | | | | | | | |
                15–24 | | | | | | | | | | | | | | | | | | |
                ⟨15 | | | | | | | | | | | | | | | | | | | | | | | | | |
                      30   15   0   15   30
                                         per cent

Sources: Calculated from Dominion Bureau of Statistics (1936: 736-7); Rosenberg (1939: 46); Statistics Canada (1984: 1-1 to 1-2, 1-7 to 1-8, 3-1 to 3-4).

in 1931 and 1981. The top two graphs—of Jews and all Canadians in 1931—show that for both groups the number of people increases as the age of the cohort declines. Young, dynamic, growing groups have population pyramids like these. Turning to 1981, one notes significant bulging at the top of the 'all origins' pyramid—evidence of an aging Canadian population at or near the point of zero population growth. Alarmingly, however, the 1981 Jewish population 'pyramid' looks more like an hourglass: in 1981 there were nearly as many Canadian Jews over the age of 65 as there were under the age of 15. In 32 years, when the members of the large baby-boom generation (roughly the 25-34 cohort in 1981) will have reached retirement age, the Jewish age-sex distribution may again resemble a pyramid—but this time an inverted one, with the largest age group at the top and the smallest at the bottom.

Policy Implications

To recapitulate: In this essay I have posed a central paradox of Canadian Jewish life. Starkly stated, the socioeconomic accomplishments of Canadian Jews may also be their undoing. The development of Canada's social and economic institutions has set in motion forces that heighten assimilation and depress fertility. As a result, the number of Jews who strongly identify with and participate in the community is declining.

Do countervailing forces change this outlook? Few Jews have immigrated to Canada in recent years and in any case many of the immigrants are highly assimilated and/or want little to do with organized Jewish life. The Jewish community's panacea will not be found among the Russian, Israeli, and American Jews who come to Canada.

Nor can one seriously expect an outbreak of virulent anti-Semitism to 'rescue' Canada's Jews. True, the organizational and intellectual leaders of Canadian Jewry tend to argue that anti-Semitism is growing and taking on more subtle and invidious forms (Arnold, 1989; Wilson, 1989). But these arguments are politically tendentious and based on fragmentary and misleading data.[10] Since the Second World War, the main thrust of Canadian social development has been towards greater acceptance of all ethnic minorities, including Jews. This is reflected in more liberal immigration regulations and the results of attitudinal surveys and behavioural studies. In such an atmosphere it is unlikely that Jews will feel more threatened and therefore inclined to establish a more cohesive community. The plain fact is that anti-Semitism is no longer the major threat to the Canadian Jewish community. Dissipation is.

The only segments of Canadian Jewry that appear to be more or less immune to the tendencies just described are the Orthodox and ultra-Orthodox. Orthodox families in Canada average 3-4 children and ultra-Orthodox families average 6-8 children. Their commitment to Jewish religion and education in particular ensures a degree of community cohe-

siveness unmatched by other subgroups of Canadian Jewry. Now constituting about 25 per cent of the community, the Orthodox and ultra-Orthodox
will comprise more than half of Canadian Jewry by the middle of the next
century (Broadbar-Nemzer, Cohen, and Shahar, this volume; Davids, this
volume; Davids, 1989).

We may infer that it is the non-Orthodox who must worry most about their
group survival. I conclude by noting that a key to changing their prospects
may lie in their liberalism. The more assimilated members of the Jewish
community—especially the third of Canadian Jews who are Reform or
unaffiliated—are the most liberal in their attitudes concerning a wide range of
Jewish and general social and political issues (cf. Cohen, 1983: 133-53).[11] It
follows that if Canadian Jewish leaders espouse hard-line, right-wing views on
Israel; if they fail to encourage the growth of religious forms that can appeal to
highly educated and cosmopolitan young people; if they keep broad issues of
universal concern off the Jewish agenda (issues such as poverty, publicly
funded daycare, the environment, and so forth); if, in short, they continue on
their present course, then assimilating Jews will be permanently lost to the
community and the assimilated Jews who are beginning to show some interest
in their roots will find nothing appealing in what the community has to offer.
In that event the Canadian Jewish community is likely to age, shrink in size and
influence, and leave itself open to the charge of having had a too-narrow vision
of how to fulfil the first commandment of Jews: survive.

Notes

[1]For example, in 1986, British Columbia, a province with one of the highest rates of
mixed marriage in the country, contained proportionately nearly three times as many
assimilated Jews as ethnic Jews (14.0 versus 5.0 per cent). In contrast, Quebec, which
has the lowest provincial rate of mixed marriage, contained proportionately nearly
twice as many ethnic Jews as assimilated Jews (33.0 versus 17.4 per cent). See Table 2
and, for provincial mixed marriage rates, Cohn (1976). (Note that in Table 2 and
elsewhere, columns may not total 100.0 per cent due to rounding error. Note also that
Statistics Canada now randomly rounds figures up or down to multiples of five.)

[2]This runs parallel to tendencies in other Canadian ethnic groups.

[3]There is, however, some difficulty involved in comparing pre-1981 census data on
ethnicity with census date on ethnicity collected in 1981 and after (see the note to
Table 3).

[4]The tables are based on data from Statistics Canada's Public Use Sample Tape,
Individual File, for the 1981 Census. The PUST is a two per cent probability sample
of the total population. The tabulations exclude people under 15 years of age,
people who have not worked since 1 January 1980, and inmates. I am grateful to
Kim Hall of the Population Research Laboratory, Erindale College, University of
Toronto, for conducting computer runs to supplement Li's (1988) data.

[5]It makes sense to pay special attention to intermarriage because, as at least one

survey has shown, marrying a Jew is the single most important 'cultural identity factor' for Canadian Jews (Driedger 1975).

[6]The 1981 census was the first to allow 'Canadian' as an ethnic origin.

[7]My *very* rough calculation is based on the following considerations: (1) At most, mixed marriages account for about 10 per cent of Canadian families in which at least one adult is ethnically Jewish (estimated from Schoenfeld, 1987: 26). Generously assuming a 3 per cent annual rate of growth on the grounds that mixed marriages tend to occur among people in their procreative years, these families added 4,200 children to the assimilated category in the five-year period. (2) Some converts to Judaism are likely to define themselves as being of mixed ethnic origin. There were perhaps 1,250 conversions to Judaism in Canada between 1981 and 1986 (estimated from Schoenfeld, 1987: 42). (3) Extrapolating from available figures (see Table 7), only about 2,250 assimilated Jews moved to Canada between 1981 and 1986 while a small but unknown number of assimilated Jews must have left the country. (4) Again assuming a 3 per cent annual rate of growth, natural increase accounts for another 4,600 new people in the assimilated category over the five-year period. (5) Drift from the ethnic to the assimilated category is difficult to quantify. However, given the ethnic Jewish women are apparently having children below the replacement level (see below), and that there were only 18,000 fewer ethnic Jews in 1986 than in 1981, it seems unlikely that all the new, 1986 assimilated Jews were recruited from the ranks of the 1981 ethnic Jews: the low fertility rate of Jewish women could easily account for most of the decline in the number of ethnic Jews. If one nonetheless arbitrarily allows that 9,000 Jews drifted between categories in the intercensal period, the maximum number of people accounted for by the sources just enumerated is only 21,300 (4,200 + 1,250 + 2,250 + 4,600 + 9,000), i.e., just under a third of the increase in the number of assimilated Jews.

[8]In the US in the early 1980s, 92 to 95 per cent of Jewish women had been married by the time they reached the 35-44 age bracket (Silberman, 1985: 279). On this basis it seems safe to assume that 5 per cent of Canadian Jewish women will (a) never marry and (b) have no children.

[9]The most recent figure available, for 1987, is 1.67 and is based on still-unpublished Statistics Canada data. I am grateful to Drs Madhera and Ram of Statistics Canada in Ottawa for the 1987 rate and for investigating the possibility of obtaining data that would allow the calculation of a total fertility rate for Jews.

[10]Thus, the B'nai B'rith annual reports on anti-Semitic incidents neglect to mention that the number of swastikas etched on synagogue doors by Ku Klux Klan members can go up in a context of increasing ethnic tolerance: there is a big difference between the behaviour of a lunatic fringe group and the attitudes and actions of the mass of the population. And those who argue that criticism of Israel represents a new form of anti-Semitism deny legitimate political debate. The most recent public opinion polls show that 65 per cent of Israeli Jews would give up some of the occupied lands and 53 per cent would talk to the PLO if they could be persuaded that Arafat will renounce terrorism; and Israel's top strategic analysts are now urging such a conciliatory course of action (Barthos, 1989a; 1989b). To argue in this context that criticism of Israeli policy is anti-Semitic is to suggest that most Israeli Jews and the country's top military strategists are anti-Semites.

[11]The most conservative are the most observant *and* the most assimilated.

References

Arnold, Janice
1989 'New kind of anti–Semitism gaining acceptability', *Canadian Jewish News* (2 March): 22.

Barthos, Gordon
1989a 'Israeli analysts urge talks with PLO', *Toronto Star* (8 March): A1, A5.

———

1989b 'Israelis willing to give up land for peace: poll', *Toronto Star* (11 February): A3.

Beaujot, Roderic and Kevin McQuillan
1982 *Growth and Dualism: The Demographic Development of Canadian Society* (Toronto: Gage).

Brym, Robert J., Michael W. Gillespie and A. Ronald Gillis
1985 'Anomie, opportunity and the density of ethnic ties: another view of Jewish outmarriage in Canada', *Canadian Review of Sociology and Anthropology* 22, 1: 102-12.

Cohen, Steven M.
1983 *American Modernity and Jewish Identity* (New York and London: Tavistock).

Cohn, Werner
1976 'Jewish outmarriage and anomie: a study in the Canadian syndrome of polarities', *Canadian Review of Sociology and Anthropology* 13, 1: 90-105.

Davids, Leo
1989 'The Canadian Jewish population picture: today and tomorrow', in E. Lipsitz, ed., *Canadian Jewry Today: Who's Who in Canadian Jewry* (Downsview, Ont.: JESL Educational Publications, 1989): 52-9.

Dominion Bureau of Statistics
1936 *Seventh Census of Canada: 1931: Volume 1: Summary* (Ottawa).

Driedger, Leo
1975 'In search of cultural identity factors: a comparison of ethnic students', *Canadian Review of Sociology and Anthropology* 12: 150-62.

Gans, Herbert J.
1979 'Symbolic ethnicity: the future of ethnic groups and cultures in America', in Herbert J. Gans *et al.*, eds, *On the Making of Americans: Essays in Honor of David Reisman* (Philadelphia: University of Pennsylvania Press): 193-220.

Kalbach, Warren E. and Wayne W. McVey
1979
[1971] *The Demographic Bases of Canadian Society*, 2nd edn (Toronto: McGraw-Hill Ryerson).

Lambert, Ronald D. and James E. Curtis
1984 'Quebecois and English Canadian opposition to racial and religious intermarriage, 1968-1983', *Canadian Ethnic Studies* 16, 2: 30-46.

Li, Peter
1988 *Ethnic Inequality in a Class Society* (Toronto: Wall and Thompson).

Lieberson, Stanley
  1989 'Ethnic groups in the United States: some odd census results', paper presented in the Department of Sociology, University of Toronto (Toronto).

Mayer, Egon
  1985 *Love and Tradition: Marriage between Jews and Christians* (New York: Plenum).

Reitz, Jeffrey
  1980 *The Survival of Ethnic Groups* (Toronto: McGraw–Hill Ryerson).

Romaniuc, A.
  1984 'Fertility in Canada: from baby-boom to baby-bust', *Current Demographic Analysis* (Ottawa: Statistics Canada).

Rosenberg, Louis
  1939 *Canada's Jews: A Social and Economic Study of the Jews in Canada* (Montreal: Bureau of Social and Economic Research, Canadian Jewish Congress).

Schoenfeld, Stuart
  1987 'An invitation to a discussion: a perspective on assimilation, intermarriage and Jewish identity in Ontario', report submitted to the Sub-committee on Assimilation and Intermarriage of the Planning and Priorities Committee of the Ontario Region, Canadian Jewish Congress (Toronto).

Silberman, Charles E.

  1985 *A Certain People: American Jews and Their Lives Today* (New York: Summit).

Statistics Canada
  1976-86 *Vital Statistics, Vol. II: Marriages and Divorces* (Ottawa).

————

  1983 *1981 Census of Canada: Population: Nuptiality and Fertility: Canada, Provinces, Urban Size Groups, Rural Non-Farm and Rural Farm* (Ottawa).

————

  1984 *1981 Census of Canada: Population: Ethnic Origin: Canada Provinces, Urban Size Groups, Rural Non-Farm and Rural Farm* (Ottawa).

————

N.D.
  [1988?] *Population by Ethnic Origin, 1986 Census: Canada, Provinces and Territories and Census Metropolitan Areas* (Ottawa).

————

  1989 *Dimensions: Profile of Ethnic Groups: Census Canada 1986* (Ottawa).

Wilson, Deborah
  1989 'Anti-Semitism on the rise in Canada, B'nai B'rith says', *Globe and Mail* (14 March): A15.

An Overview of the Canadian Jewish Community

Jay Brodbar-Nemzer, Steven M. Cohen,

Allan Reitzes, Charles Shahar, Gary Tobin

This chapter presents recent data on the social, demographic, and cultural characteristics of Canadian Jewry. The data are taken from two 1990 surveys. The first is a Canada-wide survey sponsored by the CRB Foundation, which included subsamples from Toronto, Montreal, and other areas. The second is a survey of the Toronto Jewish community sponsored by the Toronto Jewish Congress.

The first part of the chapter is drawn from a report prepared by the sociologist Steven M. Cohen, and focuses primarily on Canadian national patterns revealed by the CRB survey, as compared to those of the United States. This review also includes a section comparing patterns found in the major Canadian cities. The second section is drawn from a report prepared for the TJC by Dr Jay Brodbar-Nemzer, focusing on Toronto Jewry. The third section contains highlights of a report on Montreal Jewry prepared by Charles Shahar for the Allied Jewish Community Services of Montreal, based on the Montreal unweighted sub-sample of the CRB survey. The reports of both local cases are brief, to try to minimize duplication of data with the national report.

Both these data sets represent valuable research assets, particularly when used in conjunction with the data from the 1991 census. Scholars of Canadian Jewry are now equipped to conduct the first detailed, quantitative assessments of Canadian Jewish life.

The Canadian Picture

What is the nature and quality of Jewish commitment and involvement among Canadian Jews today? To what extent are the characterizations of Canadian Jewish identity advanced by most knowledgeable observers in Canada truly valid and accurate?

Probably the most fundamental and widely held assumption is that the identity of Canadian Jews is quite distinctive from that found among their Jewish counterparts in the United States. In the view of many leaders, Canadian Jewry is 'one generation behind' the United States in the 'assimilation' process.

A second critical assumption entails regional diversity. Canadian Jewish communal leaders often speak of significant regional variations across their vast country.

The third key assumption entails the younger generation. Notwithstanding what they regard as a well-founded pride in current high levels of Jewish involvement and participation, many Canadian Jewish leaders also express fears for the persistence of intensive Jewish commitment in the next generation.

Drawing upon these three elements in the self-image of Canadian Jewish communal leadership, this report revolves around these questions:

1. To what extent are Canadian Jews qualitatively different from American Jewry? Specifically, are Canadian Jews really 'more Jewish' than US Jews?

2. To what extent do Canadian Jews in the major population centres exhibit significant regional variations in the distributions of key measures of Jewish involvement and participation? Are the Jews in some cities generally 'more Jewish' than those elsewhere?

3. How do younger adults differ from their older counterparts in their Jewish behaviour and attitudes? More critically, is Canadian Jewry becoming less Jewishly active with the passing of earlier generations? Are older Jews 'more Jewish' than younger Jews?

Data, Methods, and Measures

This analysis relies primarily upon data collected in a survey of a national sample of 972 Canadian Jewish households conducted in late 1990. Goldfarb Consultants of Toronto untertook the study on behalf of the CRB Foundation of Montreal. On the provincial level, the regional breakdown of the sample closely approximates the geographic distribution of Canadian Jews reported in the 1986 Canadian census.

The principal aim of the original research was to learn how to stimulate travel to Israel by teen-agers and young adults. Consistent with this aim, interviewers intentionally over-sampled areas with higher concentrations of married couples. Owing to this over-sampling, comparisons of the survey's unweighted results with other studies of Canadian Jews reveal some predictable discrepancies that conceivably could affect our analysis of Jewish identity characteristics. Most significantly, with respect to what we believe are the accurate distributions in the Canadian Jewish population, this sample contains too many married couples (i.e., too few single, widowed, or divorced) and too few mixed married respondents. That is, of the married, too many are married to other Jews. (The relatively small number of mixed married respondents in the survey precludes a useful and reliable analysis of the implications of mixed marriage for Canadian Jewish identity.) Flowing from these biases, and consistent with the explicit design of the survey, the sample also seems to under-represent the elderly, independent adults under thirty years of age, and lower income households.

The analysis below weights the sample so as to correct for these biases. It down-weights both the married and the in-married. The application of these weights, in turn, results in collateral changes in the distributions of age and income that bring the distribution of these variables closer to those found in other studies of Canadian Jews.

As a check on these procedures, after the weights for marriage and inter-marriage were applied, the Toronto portion of this sample was compared with the Jewish identity measures found in the recently conducted Toronto Jewish community study, sponsored by the Toronto Jewish Congress and the Jewish Federation of Greater Toronto. It was reassuring to note that the proportion of households in the Toronto sub-sample of the Goldfarb sample who undertake various sorts of ritual practices and acts of communal affilia-tion came to closely approximate results reported in the Toronto community study.

The survey's sampling unit is the Jewish household. Aside from the inten-tional over-sampling of married households in Jewish neighbourhoods, every Canadian household with at least one Jew had a theoretically equal chance of entering the sample. The complications for the analysis derive from the indisputable fact that some households have more (or fewer) Jews than others. Thus, those individual Jews in households with many Jewish family members had a far smaller chance of having their views and behavi-ours represented in the sample than those Jews who are the only Jew in their home, as is the case for most unmarried Jewish adults and for many Jews married to non-Jews. To address this problem, additional weighting proce-dures took into account the number of Jewish adults, or, where appropriate, the number of Jewish individuals in the household (the tables are so labelled). That is, for certain items reported below, homes with two Jewish adults were, in effect, counted twice as heavily as those with one Jewish adult. For other items (such as ritual observance), homes with larger numbers of Jews were weighted more heavily than those with smaller numbers of Jews. In effect, and to simplify, these procedures assure that households with more Jews get more 'votes' in the analysis.

For these and other reasons, the results presented in this report differ in small ways from those presented in a full and comprehensive earlier report on these data by Goldfarb Consultants ('The Canadian Jewish Community: A Research Report for the CRB Foundation', April 1991). The Goldfarb report also provides additional details on sampling and methodology.

For comparative purposes, this research draws upon data on American Jews. The data set used most extensively is the recently conducted National Jewish Population Study (NJPS), sponsored by the Council of Jewish Federa-tions. The NJPS data are presented below in the comparative analysis of religious life, communal affiliation, and Israel travel. The other extensively utilized data set is the 1989 National Survey of American Jews sponsored by the American Jewish Committee, as well as, in few instances, earlier parallel surveys conducted in 1986 and 1988. We turned to these surveys to present comparative data on American Jews' attitudes toward Israel.

(For further details on these studies see the following reports by Steven M. Cohen, published by the American Jewish Committee: 'Ties and Tensions: The 1986 Survey of American Jewish Attitudes Toward Israel and Israelis'; 'Ties and Tensions: An Update — The 1989 Survey of American Jewish Attitudes Toward Israel and Israelis'; and 'Content or Continuity? Alternative Bases for Commitment — The 1989 National Survey of American Jews'.)

The NJPS results reported below differ slightly from those reported earlier by other researchers. To achieve maximal comparability of the NJPS data with the Goldfarb sample, the analysis of the NJPS was restricted to those households where at least one adult head of household identifies as a Jew in answer to a question on religious preference. This restriction excludes the NJPS respondents who are of Jewish ancestry but do not currently identify as Jews. In addition, the NJPS results below were weighted as were the Canadian data for number of Jews in the household or, where appropriate, for number of Jewish adult heads of household. As a result of these procedures, the levels of Jewish involvement for US Jews reported below tend to exceed those reported in other published analyses of NJPS data.

The comparisons below between Canadian and US Jews obscure significant internal variations within US Jewry. Level of ritual observance and communal participation vary dramatically by region and community throughout the United States. In particular, Jews living in the major metropolitan areas of the American Northeast, Midwest, and southern Florida report higher rates of involvement than those living elsewhere.

The implication is that gaps reported below between Canadian and US levels of Jewish involvement ought to be understood as comparing a large and diverse collection of US Jewish communities with a smaller collection of more compact Canadian Jewish communities, heavily concentrated in just two places (Toronto and Montreal). While the gaps in Jewish identity measures between Canadian and American may appear, at times, rather sizeable, we need to recognize that many of these gaps would be much smaller were we to compare Canadian Jews with only those American Jews living in certain American communities. That is, differences in Jewish activity levels between Canada and specific US communities (such as New York, Detroit, Cleveland, and Baltimore, to name just a few with higher than average rates of involvement) are much smaller than the differences between all of Canadian Jewry and all of US Jewry.

Religion

As in all other countries, in Canada certain Jewish ritual practices are far more popular than others (see Table 1). The results suggest that ritual practices fall into three tiers, based upon frequency of observance. First, the vast majority of Canadian Jews live in homes that in some way commemorate

Table 1 Measures of Religious Involvement in Canada and the US (Entries are percentages; data weighted by number of Jews in the household)

	CANADA	UNITED STATES*
Attends Passover seder	92	76
Lights Hanukkah candles	87	78
Fasts Yom Kippur	77	64
Lights Sabbath candles	54	26
Has meat and dairy dishes	46	18
Handles no money on the Sabbath	15	14
Observes Fast of Esther	11	6
DENOMINATION		
Orthodox	19	9
Conservative	37	38
Reconstructionist	1	1
Reform	11	43
Other Jewish	32	9
Synagogue member	67	50
SYNAGOGUE MEMBERS' DENOMINATION		
Orthodox	25	12
Conservative	43	45
Reconstructionist	1	1
Reform	14	38
Other Jewish	19	5

*Source of US data: The 1990 National Jewish Population Study.

Passover, Hanukkah, and the High Holidays. Second, about half of Canadian Jews also maintain such practices as lighting Sabbath candles or maintaining two sets of dishes at home for meat and dairy products as required by traditional Jewish dietary laws. Third, only a small number of Canadian Jews — one sixth or less — practise rituals associated with more strict adherence to Jewish religious law such as refraining from handling money on the Sabbath, or observing the Fast of Esther.

(A methodological note: Respondents reported on their households' religious practices and not necessarily their own personal observance. As noted earlier, the entries in the table are weighted for the number of Jews in the household. Thus, they refer to the percentage of the total Jewish population who live in households where a certain practice is observed. To take an example, the entry on Sabbath candle lighting should be understood as saying that an estimated 54 per cent of Canadian Jews live in homes where somebody lights Sabbath candles. In point of fact, fewer than 54 per cent of the respondents said that candles are lit in their homes. But those who so reported tend to reside in homes with larger numbers of Jews and, as noted earlier, their answers count for more than those with fewer Jews in the household.

Why is higher observance associated with larger Jewish households? One reason is that many households with just one Jewish member are those where the only Jew in the household is single or married to a non-Jew. Both singlehood and mixed marriages are linked to lower levels of ritual observance and Jewish communal participation.)

In the United States, we find a similar rank ordering of religious practices by frequency of observance. The major difference is that Canadian Jews observe every practice more frequently than do American Jews. The gaps are especially large with respect to lighting Sabbath candles and to maintaining meat and dairy dishes. Here, the Canadian frequencies are more than double those in the United States.

These patterns suggest that, on a proportional basis, slightly more Canadian Jews are among the most highly observant in Jewish life, as reflected in the number who handled no money on the Sabbath. More significantly, a far greater proportion of Canadian can be regarded as somewhat observant than American Jews, as the answers to the questions on lighting Sabbath candles and owning kosher dishes.

These results offer a slightly different image of Canadian Jewry than that frequently presented by those leaders who speak only of the large Orthodox (or *dati*) segment of Canadian Jewry. Rather, these figures suggest that the real distinction between Canadian and American Jewry lies in the very large number of what we could call *masorati* Jews in Canada, those who are observant of some traditional practices but do not necessarily identify as Orthodox.

Examining the distributions of denominational preferences can augment our understanding of these differences in observance. The questionnaire asked respondents, 'Which of the following describes you and your spouse?' and then presented a list including such choices as 'Orthodox Jew', 'Conservative Jew', etc. We find that only half as many American Jews (9 per cent) live in Orthodox households as in Canada (19 per cent). Among the remainder we find two striking contrasts: far more Americans are Reform, while far more Canadians are 'other Jewish'. These patterns reflect well-known differences in the populations of the two countries. Historically, the Reform movement has been stronger in the United States than in Canada. In contrast, Canada has been home to a visible and institutionalized Jewish secularist population.

To Jewish leaders, the denominational labels have a more concrete organizational and ideological meaning than they might have to many respondents. Orthodox leaders, for example, are often shocked to learn of the significant minority of Jews who call themselves Orthodox on social surveys, yet also readily admit to violating the Sabbath or failing to observe Jewish dietary laws. Large segments of Conservative and Reform Jews do not even belong to a temple or synagogue, let alone one affiliated with the movement with which they identify on a survey. These meaning of these denominational labels should not be exaggerated. To better understand denominational distributions, we would do well to focus just on those Jews who belong to a synagogue.

In Canada, about two-thirds of Jews live in households where the head claims synagogue affiliation. In the United States, about half are affiliated by the same criterion. The last panel of the table reports the denominational distributions only for those households who belong to congregations. Owing to the differential rates of congregational affiliation, we find some marked departures from the distributions reported earlier for all respondents, synagogue-affiliated or not.

In Canada, among synagogue members, about a quarter of the Jews are identified as Orthodox, and almost twice as many (43 per cent) identify with the Conservative movement. The number of Reform Jews is quite small (14 per cent), and just under a fifth of Canadian synagogue members (19 per cent) select other categories of Jewish identity, far fewer than among all Jews regardless of synagogue affiliation.

These results point up some striking contrasts between the two countries. In Canada, two-thirds of synagogue Jews are Conservative or Orthodox. In the United States, over four-fifths of synagogue members are Conservative or Reform. As in Canada, among American synagogue members, Conservatism is the most popular movement (45 per cent). However, almost as many American members are Reform (38 per cent). Just a small number (12 per cent) of American synagogue members are Orthodox and hardly any (5 per cent) fail to identify with the major denominations.

Relative to American Jewry, then, Canadian Jewry is characterized by more sizeable Orthodox and more sizeable secular Jewish population segments. In contrast with the United States, the appeal of Canadian Reform Judaism is, at this date, rather limited.

The Organized Community

Just as frequencies of ritual observance in Canada exceed those in the United States, so too do various measures of communal participation (see Table 2).

About three-fifths of Canadian Jewish adults read a Jewish newspaper regularly, compared with just a third of American Jewish adults. Almost two-fifths (38 per cent) of Canadian Jewish adults are Jewish Community Center or YMHA members, substantially greater than the comparable US average (23 per cent).

The gaps between American and Canadian Jews with respect to other forms of organizational participation are smaller than those for newspaper reading or JCC/YMHA membership.

The fact that as many as a quarter of the adult Jewish population in both societies serve on Jewish agency boards and committees testifies to a high

Table 2 Measures of Jewish Communal Involvement in Canada and the US
         (Entries are percentages; data weighted by number of Jewish adults in the
         household)

	CANADA	UNITED STATES*
Reads a Jewish newspaper	60	33
YMHA or JCC member	38	23
Jewish organization member	47	37
Volunteers for Jewish organization	31	24
Serves on a board or committee	25	24
Donates $100 or more to UJA	41	21
Mean UJA/Federation gift		
All households	$ 700	$ 300
Donors of $100+ only	$1700	$1300
Most close friends are Jewish	78	51
Can converse in Yiddish	37	—
Can converse in Hebrew	25	—

*Source of US data: The 1990 National Jewish Population Study.

level of formal voluntary activity. In these respects, levels of organizational activity in Canada exceed those in the United States from a small to moderate extent. However, much larger differences characterize the arena of Jewish fund-raising. However measured, Canadian Jews make far larger and more frequent contributions to Jewish philanthropic causes than their American counterparts. Here we focus upon giving to the central Jewish philanthropic campaign.

Much of the observed gap between Canadian and American philanthropic giving is attributable to the difference in the number contributing at least $100. Once we restrict the analysis to those who donate at least $100, we find that the Canadian-American gift-gap reduces substantially. Of those contributing $100 or more, Canadian Jews give about $1700 per household as compared with almost as much, $1300, among American Jewish households.

These patterns suggest that much of the strength of Jewish fund-raising in Canada relative to that in the United States lies in the much larger base of support among more donors rather than in the unusual generosity among a small number of big donors. The broad participation in the Canadian philanthropic campaigns is itself a sign of a well-knit and cohesive community.

Further evidence of Canadian Jewish cohesiveness is found in the large majority (78 per cent) who report that at least 'most' of their closest friends are Jewish. In contrast, only about half (51 per cent) of adult American Jews make the same claim. That over three-quarters of Canadian Jewish adults can report that most of their closest friends are Jewish speaks of a very closely knit minority community. Some may call it 'cohesive', others may call it 'insular', but whatever the connotation, Canadian Jews are highly connected to one another, and, by implication, their most intimate social lives are conducted relatively separate and apart from close contact with non-Jewish Canadians.

Two other indicators of communal involvement entail knowledge of Jewish languages, which in this century and continent means Yiddish and Hebrew. Language familiarity, of course, has special meaning for multilingual Canadian society generally and for the Jewish community particular. Owing to the relatively recent influx of East European Jewish immigrants before and after both World Wars, Canadian Jewry established a significant number of Yiddish-speaking schools and cultural institutions. Significantly, as many as 37 per cent of Canadian Jewish adults claim that they are either totally fluent in Yiddish or can at least converse in the language somewhat short of total fluency. No comparable figures exist for the United States, but it is impossible to believe that the number of American Jews who can converse in Yiddish even approaches 37 per cent.

Not only is a significant minority of Canadian Jews reasonably fluent in Yiddish, but a quarter (not necessarily the same people) are also competent in spoken Hebrew. As many as 25 per cent say that they can at least converse in Hebrew, albeit not always with total fluency. In the United States, according to the 1986 National Survey of American Jews, not more than 10 per cent of Jewish adults claim a comparable level of competence in spoken Hebrew. In any event, fluency in both major contemporary Jewish languages — Yiddish and Hebrew — is certainly far more widespread among Canadian Jews than among their American counterparts.

In sum, Canadian Jews are far more close-knit, substantially more Jewishly philanthropic, and somewhat better organized than American Jews. The Canadian-American gaps are especially pronounced with respect to philanthropic giving, in-group friendship, and fluency in Yiddish and Hebrew.

Ties to Israel

Canadian Jewish leaders regularly claim that their community is unusually involved with and supportive of Israel.

As we learn in Table 3, about two-thirds of Canadian Jewish adults (66 per cent) have been to Israel and, of those who have visited Israel, most (39 per cent of the total) have been to Israel more than once. In contrast, according to the NJPS, only half as many adult American Jews (35 per cent) have been to Israel, and just 17 per cent have been there two or more times. Not only do Canadian Jews visit Israel more than American Jews, the Canadians also are in more frequent mail or telephone contact with Israelis.

For Canadian Jews, their connection with Israel is not merely with some

Table 3   *Measures of Israel Involvement in Canada and the US (Entries are percentages; data weighted by number of Jewish adults in the household)*

	CANADA	UNITED STATES[a]
VISITED ISRAEL		
Twice or more	39	17
Just once	27	18
Never	34	65
Corresponded with Israeli	44	23
Spoken by telephone to Israeli	37	10
Israel important to being a Jew	87	73
If Israel destroyed, personal tragedy	85	66
Often talk about Israel	70	62
Feel very close to Israel	42	22
Will visit in three years	44	24
Consider self Zionist	42	25
Fuller Jewish life in Israel	35	10
Considered *aliyah*	21	13
Know year of Independence	79	66
Know year of Six-Day War	72	40
Israel should recognize only Orthodox conversions	14	6
Very upset if Israel recognizes only Orthodox conversions	47	57
FAVOURABLE IMPRESSIONS		
Ultra-Orthodox Israelis	14	8
Modern Orthodox Israelis	53	41
Secular Jewish Israelis	53	49
Israeli doves	35	36
Israeli hawks	23	28

[a]Source of US data: For visiting Israel, the 1990 National Jewish Population Study; for corresponded with Israelis and spoken by telephone with Israelis, the 1988 National Survey of American Jews; for all other variables, the 1989 National Survey of American Jews.

vague and remote symbol in the inner recesses of their Jewish consciousness. Rather, as frequent visitors and as people who maintain family or friendship ties with Israelis, many Canadian Jews maintain some very vivid images of and intimate ties with Israeli loved ones and the Israeli landscape.

The depth of their attachment to Israel is demonstrated in answers to a variety of questions about their feelings and beliefs. Almost nine in ten Canadian Jews (87 per cent) agree that 'Caring about Israel is a very important part of my being a Jew', as compared with 73 per cent of American Jews. In a telling expression of attachment, the vast majority (85 per cent) agree with the statement, 'If Israel were destroyed, I would feel as if I had suffered one of the greatest personal tragedies in my life.' In contrast, a smaller majority (66 per cent) of American Jews say they agree with the same statement. Over two-thirds (70 per cent) of Canadian Jews 'often talk about Israel with friends and relatives', as compared with slightly fewer (62 per cent) American Jews.

The gaps between Canadian and American Jews are even more striking when we turn to more demanding questions, those that signify higher levels of commitment than those reviewed just above. When asked how close they feel to Israel, 42 per cent of Canadian Jews answer in the strongest possible terms ('very close'), roughly double the number of American Jews (22 per cent) who answer in like fashion. Consistent with their higher rates of previous travel to Israel, almost twice as many Canadian as American Jews say they intend to visit Israel within the next three years (44 per cent versus 24 per cent). A large gap also separates the rates at which Canadian and American Jews regard themselves as Zionists (42 per cent versus 25 per cent). Consistent with Zionist ideology, almost as many (35 per cent) feel they can 'live a fuller Jewish life in Israel than in Canada'. (Only 10 per cent of American Jews have similar views about life in Israel and the United States.)

What may be most indicative of the deep and widespread commitment to Israel among Canadian Jews is that over a fifth (21 per cent) say they 'have seriously considered living in Israel', as compared with 13 per cent of American Jews.

Not only are Canadian Jews more attached to Israel than are American Jews, they also seem to know more about Israel, if the answers to two simple questions on recent Israeli history offer any firm indication. Almost four-fifths (79 per cent) of Canadian Jews and just 66 per cent of American Jews could correctly identify the year of Israel's independence as 1948. The gap is even wider with respect to identifying 1967 as the year of the Six-Day War: 72 per cent for the Canadians as against only 40 per cent for the Americans.

American Jews enjoy a reputation for avid and passionate support for Israel. If so, then the attachment and concern of Canadian Jews must be seen as even more avid and more passionate. When compared with American Jews, Canadian Jews are more in touch with Israel and Israelis, more knowledgeable, more involved, more pro-Israel, and more Zionist in many senses of the term. Yet despite these differences, Canadian and American Jews seem to share many of the same instincts toward the major social divisions within Israel.

In late 1988, religious parties in Israel unsuccessfully sought to amend Israeli legislation so as to recognize conversions to Judaism conducted abroad that were supervised only by Orthodox rabbis. The 'Who is a Jew?' crisis precipitated a powerful adverse reaction among North American Jewry. Among Jews in the United States in 1988, hardly anybody (6 per cent) supported the view that Israel should 'change its laws so as to recognize only those conversions performed by Orthodox rabbis'. In Canada, in late 1990, just 14 per cent supported this position. In 1988, in the United States, 57 per cent said they would feel 'very upset' if 'Israel changed its "Who is a Jew" law to recognize *only* Orthodox conversions'; an additional 20 per cent would be 'somewhat upset'. In Canada, in 1990, with the issue somewhat removed in time, as many as 47 per cent still would be 'very upset' with the proposed change and another 19 per cent would be 'somewhat upset'.

These results suggest that with respect to this one hot issue, Canadian and American Jews have basically similar reactions, although the Canadians are slightly more sympathetic to the religious parties' stance, owing in large part to the larger segment of Canadian Jews who are Orthodox.

Other parallel reactions can be seen in answers to questions on impressions of various sorts of Israelis. Among both American and Canadian Jews, very few have positive impressions of so-called Ultra-Orthodox Jews. About half in both countries (slightly more in Canada, slightly less in the United States) have positive impressions of Modern Orthodox and of secular Israelis. (Those lacking positive impressions have either negative impressions or no impression either way regarding these groups.)

The parallels between American Jewish and Canadian Jewish orientations extend to the political sphere as well. Among both Canadian and American Jews, somewhat more individuals express positive views of Israeli doves than who think well of Israeli hawks. In Canada, the doves are endorsed, in effect, by 35 per cent of the respondents in contrast with just 23 per cent for the hawks. The results in the United States are fairly similar.

In sum, Canadian Jews are highly attached to Israel, even more so than their Jewish counterparts to the south. Moreover, like their American counterparts, Canadian Jews are not particularly sympathetic to the ultra-Orthodox or their political agenda, and are more inclined to think well of Israeli doves as opposed to Israeli hawks.

Urban Variations

How do the measures of Jewish involvement differ in the major Canadian Jewish population centres? Toronto, Montreal, Winnipeg, Vancouver, and the several smaller Jewish communities throughout Canada differ in numerous respects. Different sorts of Jewish immigrants came to these destinations from different locations at different times. Certain ideological streams have preferred some places over others. For example, Montreal seems to have been a favoured location for Orthodoxy, while Winnipeg Jews attracted an unusual concentration of secularist-socialist-Yiddishists.

The communities also differ dramatically in size. Toronto and Montreal are, by far, the largest Jewish population centres in Canada. Winnipeg and Vancouver, though much smaller, are still considerably larger than any other communities in Canada. Historically, larger Jewish communities are in a better position to support more complex and more diverse Jewish institutions.

Another key consideration has been the stream of migration of Jews from Montreal to Toronto and other destinations over the last several years. That

Table 4 Religious, Communal, and Israel Involvement by Region in Canada

	TORONTO	MONTREAL	WINNIPEG	BRITISH COLUMBIA	OTHER
Attends Passover seder	90	95	92	83	91
Lights Hanukkah candles	84	90	90	77	88
Fasts Yom Kippur	69	88	77	58	75
Lights Sabbath candles	54	59	46	42	42
Has meat and dairy dishes	42	54	39	34	36
Handles no money on the Sabbath	13	22	2	5	2
Observes Fast of Esther	9	17	1	5	1
DENOMINATION					
Orthodox	14	28	7	10	14
Conservative	39	31	59	32	47
Reconstructionist	1	2	–	2	–
Reform	15	3	11	16	16
Other Jewish	31	37	21	40	22
Synagogue member	61	69	79	54	82
SYNAGOGUE MEMBERS' DENOMINATION					
Orthodox	22	36	8	5	18
Conservative	45	33	62	49	54
Reconstructionist	–	–	–	–	–
Reform	20	5	17	21	18
Other Jewish	14	26	13	25	10
Reads a Jewish newspaper	62	72	41	20	44
YMHA or JCC member	28	48	44	38	40
Jewish organization member	41	47	60	49	60
Donates $100 or more to UJA	42	35	43	36	56
Most close friends are Jewish	81	83	77	48	64
Can converse in Yiddish	38	40	48	28	25
Can converse in Hebrew	24	31	14	16	21
Visited Israel	65	73	47	59	60
Feel very close to Israel	39	51	35	40	31
Often talk about Israel	67	75	72	63	66
Will visit Israel in three years	40	56	20	37	33
Considered *aliyah*	21	26	8	15	18
Considered self Zionist	40	43	45	49	41
Israel important to being a Jew	86	90	90	85	83

migration may well have helped change the character of Montreal to a great extent and the other cities to a lesser extent.

We certainly have many compelling reasons to anticipate significant differences in the Jewish character of the major Jewish population centres. To address this issue, the sample has been divided into four discrete regions and a fifth residual category. The four regions with sufficient numbers of respondents for reliable analysis are: Toronto (409 interviews), Montreal (353), Winnipeg (54), and British Columbia (47 respondents in Vancouver, 3 in Victoria). The remaining interviews are gathered under Table 4's 'other' column. This column combines Ottawa (32), Calgary (21), Hamilton (16), Edmonton (15), Halifax (4), St Catharines (4), Regina, Kitchener, and Moncton (3 each), and Saskatoon and Sydney (2 each). The 'other' category, then, is very diverse with respect to region but is relatively homogeneous with respect to the small size of these eleven Jewish population centres, no one of which is large enough to sustain separate analysis.

On measures of ritual involvement, Montreal emerges as the most observant, and British Columbia is in most respects the least observant.

Consistent with this observation, we see that among the synagogue-affiliated population, Montreal is the only community where the Orthodox exceed the Conservative population (36 per cent versus 33 per cent). In contrast, in Toronto, among the congregationally affiliated, Conservative Jews outnumber the Orthodox by more than two to one (45 per cent to 24 per cent). Among the synagogue members, the Reform population is almost negligible in Montreal, as is the Orthodox population in Winnipeg and British Columbia.

Although the regional variations in ritual observance of denomination are rather pronounced and clear-cut, the variations in communal participation are less uniform. Each region is distinguished in its own way. Toronto and Montreal are notable for their rather high rates of Jewish newspaper readership. Toronto Jews are also noteworthy for their low rates of JCC/YMHA membership. Montreal and Toronto report substantially higher rates of familiarity with Hebrew than the smaller communities. Winnipeg is unusual in the large extent to which people belong to Jewish organizations, belong to synagogues, identify as Conservative Jews, and are familiar with Yiddish. These figures are consistent with the image of Winnipeg as a Conservative town replete with a large number of small Jewish organizations and one where a strong Yiddishist movement has managed to support a Yiddish language day school for decades. British Columbia (largely Vancouver) is distinguished by rather low rates of synagogue membership, of Jewish newspaper readership, and of fluency in Yiddish and in Hebrew.

With respect to Israel attachment and pro-Israel involvement, the several indicators point to a nearly consistent rank order: Montreal leads, followed by Toronto, with British Columbia third, and Winnipeg last.

These results are a thin reed upon which to build an argument about the distinctive Jewish character of the major Canadian Jewish population centres. Nevertheless, the statistical results are consistent with the qualitative impression of many informed Jewish communal leaders. The results serve to fortify, clarify, and amplify several key generalizations. Among them:

1. Montreal Jewry is more observant and more Orthodox than other Canadian Jewry.

2. Montreal Jews are also generally more communally active than Jews elsewhere.

3. Winnipeg Jewry is noted for its Yiddishism, organizational life, Conservative synagogue affiliation, and, for Canada, a lower than average level of attachment to Israel.

4. British Columbian Jewry falls below the national average in several measures of ritual observance and institutional affiliation.

5. Toronto Jewry is distinguished by its typicality. With over 40 per cent of Canada's Jews, Toronto generally scores neither very high nor very low on measures of Jewish involvement. On the whole, Toronto area Jews are somewhat less involved in many aspects of Jewish life than those in Montreal, but more involved than most Jews elsewhere.

6. Last, the major distinguishing feature of Jews subsumed under the 'other' rubric is their high levels of institutional belonging. More than Jews in any of the larger communities, these Jews are synagogue members. They also score relatively high with respect to JCC/YMHA membership as well as affiliating with other Jewish organizations. The acutely felt minority status of Jews in these small communities undoubtedly heightens their interest in formally associating with fellow Jews in one or another sort of Jewish institution.

Age Differences

Are younger Canadian Jews indeed less Jewishly involved than their elders? To address these questions, Table 5 compares those under 35 years of age with those 35-49, 50-64, and 65 and over. Since some expressions of Jewish commitment emerge for many people only when they marry and have children, lower scores among those under 35 may not accurately indicate their eventual levels when most of this group moves into parenthood. Hence, it is also useful to closely examine those 35-49 and compare them with those 50-64. If there is indeed a decline in Jewish commitment among younger Jews, then we should also be able to observe gaps in Jewish involvement scores between those in early middle age and those in later middle age (i.e., between those 35-49 and 50-64).

Whichever younger age group one examines, youth is clearly associated with no decline whatever in ritual observance. More pointedly, with respect to the two most traditional rituals (not handling money on the Sabbath and fasting on the Fast of Esther), the two younger groups are significantly more observant than those 50-64. If the younger groups are a portent of the future, Orthodoxy has been gaining ground at the expense of Conservatism.

Of Jews in families where the respondent is under 35, just 54 per cent are congregationally affiliated, as compared with 66 per cent or more in the

Table 5 Religious, Communal, and Israel Involvement by Age in Canada

	UNDER 34	35–49	50–64	65+
Attends Passover seder	96	91	92	87
Lights Hanukkah candles	86	89	88	80
Fasts Yom Kippur	82	76	76	70
Lights Sabbath candles	50	54	52	58
Has meat and dairy dishes	49	43	44	49
Handles no money on the Sabbath	21	15	8	13
Observes Fast of Esther	15	12	5	9
DENOMINATION				
Orthodox	22	19	13	16
Conservative	35	35	47	36
Reconstructionist	–	2	–	–
Reform	10	13	9	9
Other Jewish	34	31	31	36
Synagogue member	54	70	66	75
SYNAGOGUE MEMBERS' DENOMINATION				
Orthodox	37	25	18	22
Conservative	34	42	54	40
Reconstructionist	–	2	–	–
Reform	13	16	13	10
Other Jewish	18	16	15	28
Reads a Jewish newspaper	52	56	67	70
YMHA or JCC member	41	36	40	37
Jewish organization member	43	39	49	64
Donates $100 or more to UJA	32	42	46	42
Most close friends are Jewish	76	74	84	79
Can converse in Yiddish	14	27	51	64
Can converse in Hebrew	35	25	21	20
Visited Israel	70	64	66	65
Feel very close to Israel	33	37	47	56
Often talk about Israel	58	66	75	81
Will visit Israel in three years	42	43	50	39
Considered *aliyah*	29	22	22	10
Considered self Zionist	40	35	48	51
Israel important to being a Jew	87	85	90	88

older groups. But in families where the respondent is 35–49, fully 70 per cent belong to synagogues or temples, a figure about the same as among the two groups 50 years old and over. These patterns suggest that many adults simply put off joining a synagogue until their thirties, when many marry and have children. These results, then, do not portend any shrinkage in the synagogue membership base.

The stability in most forms of ritual observance, the apparent growth in traditional observance and in Orthodoxy among the young, and the signs of stability in synagogue membership all suggest persistence in the intensity of religious life among younger Jews. Clearly, with respect to religious activity, fears for the commitment of younger Jews are unfounded.

What about indicators of communal involvement? Here we find youngsters matching their elders in most areas, but clearly surpassing them in none. As one might expect, with the advance of generations, fluency in Yiddish is declining; but, at the same time, fluency in Hebrew is increasing, not quite offsetting the implicit losses in Yiddish fluency.

Previous American studies have established that attachment to Israel is declining among younger Jews. Although Canadian Jewry can boast an overall stronger attachment to Israel than American Jewry, declines similar to those seen in the United States can be observed in Canada as well.

For example, the proportion who say they feel 'very close' to Israel declines from 56 per cent among those 65 and over to just 33 per cent among those under 35. Similar gaps between old and young can be seen with respect to the items on talking about Israel with friends and relatives and considering oneself a Zionist. At the same time, younger adults are no less likely than older adults to see Israel as important to their being a Jew, to have travelled to Israel, or to plan to visit in the next three years; in fact younger people are more likely to have at one time considered living in Israel.

Yet despite these areas where younger adults match or exceed their older counterparts in Israel involvement, the key items that measure feelings of closeness to Israel do demonstrate an unmistakable gap between older and younger Canadian Jews.

Taken in their entirety, the diverse findings on differences in Jewish identity between older and younger Jews in Canada present a mixed picture. In some ways, such as traditional ritual observance, younger Jews are actually more involved than older Jews. In other ways, such as many forms of communal affiliation and most forms of ritual practice, younger Jews are hardly different from their elders. In still other ways, such as emotional attachment to Israel or fluency in Yiddish, younger Jews score lower than older Jews. These patterns certainly point to ongoing and anticipated change in the nature of Jewish commitment in Canada. But they do not point to any clear shift in one direction or the other. If these data do tell us something about the future directions of Jewish involvement in Canada, they suggest neither massive erosion of Jewish identity nor wholesale intensification.

Anti-Semitism

Despite their enormous economic, political, and cultural achievements in the United States, from one-half to four-fifths of American Jews express considerable anxiety about their acceptance by the larger society and the phenomenon of American anti-Semitism. For many reasons, we would expect

Canadian Jews to be at least as anxious, if not more so, than American Jews. One consideration is that Canadian Jews are, in absolute and relative terms, a far smaller population than American Jews. Canadian Jews number about 300,000 and comprise just over 1 per cent of their country's population; American Jews amount to almost six million and make up over 2 per cent of their country's population. Another important distinction is that Canadian Jewry is chronologically and generationally closer to Europe and to the Nazi Holocaust. In addition, the political turmoil surrounding the future of Quebec has undoubtedly generated increased anxieties among the Jews of Montreal, in particular, if not all of Canada in general.

In light of these considerations, it is not surprising that nearly four-fifths (79 per cent) of Canadian Jewish adults believe that there is 'a great deal of anti-Semitism in Canada', the most potent answer category available. When offered four choices relating to how well accepted they feel, a clear majority (59 per cent) rejected the opportunity to say that they feel 'completely accepted in Canada'. Not only do Canadian Jews perceive a great deal of anti-Semitism; most (51 per cent) believe that anti-Semitism in Canada has increased in recent years. Certainly these are signs of a group fairly insecure with its position in the larger society.

To what extent are these anxieties buttressed by personal experiences? Despite widespread fears of anti-Semitism, relatively few respondents could report direct encounters with anti-Semitic injury of one sort or another. Just under a quarter (22 per cent) report that they have been the target of any anti-Semitic ethnic slurs in the last five years. While verbal abuse has afflicted only a minority, outright discrimination is even more rare. In the last five years, rather small numbers of Canadian Jewish adults have suffered from what they perceive as anti-Semitic discrimination in finding a job or being promoted (3 per cent), in 'your work, business, or profession, other than in finding a job or being promoted' (7 per cent), in housing (1 per cent), or in education (3 per cent). Taken together, just one in ten claim to have suffered any form of discrimination in any of these concrete ways.

To what extent do discrimination and the accompanying anxieties differ by region? Variations are small and inconsistent, but the Jews of Montreal seem the most anxious and also among the most likely to report actual incidents of discrimination. Jews in the smaller communities (outside Montreal and Toronto) are more likely to report being the brunt of anti-Semitic verbal abuse.

Younger and older respondents are equally likely to express concerns about Canadian anti-Semitism and their acceptance by the larger society. The experiences of outright discrimination are fairly evenly distributed over the age spectrum, but encounters with anti-Semitic slurs are more frequent among younger than among older Canadian Jews. Perhaps the increased exposure of younger Jews to less ethnically insulated (or more ethnically integrated) work and educational environments increase their chances of encountering anti-Semitic remarks.

One theme that runs through these findings on perceived anti-Semitism is that the actual experience with anti-Semitic behaviour is not a prerequisite to the perception of anti-Semitic threat. Vast numbers of Canadian Jews express anxieties about anti-Semitism even though very few have suffered verbal or more serious abuse because they are Jews.

Conclusion

In so many respects, Canadian Jewry constitutes a strong and vital Jewish community. Throughout this report, we have seen relatively high rates of ritual observance, communal affiliation, pro-Israel attachment, and in-group friendship patterns. Moreover, for the most part, these high levels of Jewish involvement persist among younger adults who, in most respects, are as Jewishly involved as middle-aged and older Jews. Moreover, the distinctive character of the major Canadian Jewish population centres is quite apparent in the analysis. Just as living a Jewish life in Canada is quite different from doing so in the United States, so too is Jewish living in Montreal quite different from that found in Winnipeg (or Toronto, or Vancouver, or numerous other cities as well).

There are certainly some disquieting signs. The possible fall-off in attachment to Israel among younger adults (which this report documents) and the impact of rising intermarriage (which we could not satisfactorily investigate owing to sampling limitations) do raise some concerns. These areas merit close attention and further investigation.

However, notwithstanding the impact of a rising intermarriage rate over the last two decades, Canadian Jews generally and younger Canadian Jews in particular (those with the higher rates of mixed marriage) continue to display extraordinary levels of involvement in Jewish life both in the home and in the community. Certainly Canadian Jewry faces numerous challenges. But just as certainly, as this report documents, the community possesses unusual and powerful resources to confront those challenges.

Toronto

Based on 1986 Statistics Canada census information, all census enumeration areas where at least 10 per cent of the population was of Jewish ancestry were identified. A random sample of all households in these areas was selected and contacted to determine if they were a Jewish household. The resulting sample represents an estimated 70 per cent of the community. Of the balance, who live in low Jewish density areas, 'Distinctive Jewish Name' households representing 18 per cent of the community were randomly selected for an interview, and households representing 12 per cent of the community were randomly selected from Federation lists.

Telephone interviews by professional interviewers were conducted with an adult over the age of 18 in 1400 Jewish households. A household was defined as Jewish if any family member currently identified themselves as Jewish. No persons in institutions, such as nursing homes, were interviewed for this study nor were persons without telephones. Interviews were conducted during the Spring and Summer of 1990. Of all known Jewish households contacted, 84 per cent completed the interviews.

Socio-demographic Overview

In June of 1991, the national Census included questions on religion and ethnic ancestry, and it will soon provide the most authoritative and comprehensive demographic information about our community. However, in order to provide a context for understanding the Jewish behaviour and attitudes of our community, it is necessary to start with some basic demographic information. Where data are available, we will compare our community with Jewish communities in the United States.

The Jewish community tends to live in identifiable areas in Greater Toronto. Nearly a quarter of the population (24 per cent) lives in Thornhill and portions of Richmond Hill. Another large area of concentration is along Bathurst Street between Steeles Avenue and Hwy 401 where 22 per cent of the population resides. Continuing south along Bathurst Street through the Lawrence Avenue area as far as Eglinton Avenue, we find another 11 per cent, and 12 per cent of the community lives south of Eglinton Avenue. An additional 15 per cent of the population lives in a large eastern area, which incorporates the York Mills/Bayview and Steeles/Leslie areas. Finally, 16 per cent of the community is scattered throughout the rest of Greater Toronto.

The Jewish community tends to concentrate in neighbourhoods that are located in identifiable areas of Greater Toronto. As will be noted, the Jewishness of a neighbourhood is related to other Jewish attributes. With respect to purely demographic characteristics, whereas about 30 per cent of the community lives in *low* Jewish density neighbourhoods, greater proportions of the never married (48 per cent), couples with no children (46 per cent), residents who were born in other parts of Canada (45 per cent), respondents aged 18-24 (53 per cent), respondents with graduate degrees or certificates (42 per cent), and fourth generation respondents (46 per cent), live in low Jewish density areas.

The *high* density areas, which contain about 25 per cent of the population, contain a greater proportion of those with household incomes under $20,000 (43 per cent), the widowed (39 per cent), empty nesters (37 per cent), those over 65 years of age (43 per cent), those with no more than a high school education (39 per cent), and first generation North Americans (37 per cent).

The rest of the households, approximately 45 per cent of the community, lives in *medium* Jewish density areas, which range from 9 per cent to 50 per cent Jewish. Living in these areas is a higher proportion of the households that report incomes above $150,000, couples with children in the household, those owning homes worth more than $750,000, and respondents in the 35-44 age range.

Most Toronto Jews are middle-class and upper middle-class. But many Jews have low or moderate incomes. The median household income reported by respondents is $55,000. Approximately one-fifth of the households report annual incomes of over $100,000. In spite of the apparent level of financial comfort the community has achieved, there are significant subgroups with serious financial difficulties.

Thus, although slightly over one tenth of the community reports household incomes below $20,000, there are groups whose proportion is two, three or four times as high. The elderly, the disabled, and single parents each constitute economically vulnerable groups. This is true not only in absolute but in relative terms. For example, respondents in the 35-44 age range are highly unlikely to report household incomes below $20,000, but nearly a third of all single parents in this age group are in this economic category.

The Jewish household comes in many forms. The average family size in our sample is 2.6 individuals per household. Even more than size, the composition of households is a key component in describing a community. A couple with children constitutes the largest category of households — 40 per cent of all households. A majority (62 per cent) of Toronto's Jewish population lives in such households. The next highest type of household is single Jewish adults living alone (24 per cent). Couples with children no longer living in the home, or 'empty nesters', constitute 20 per cent of all households. The smallest groups include couples without children (8 per cent), single parents (4 per cent), and miscellaneous other types (e.g. one parent with adult children in the household) contributing the balance (5 per cent) of all households.

Toronto is still largely a city of immigrants — 41 per cent of our respondents were foreign-born (and, among the married, 48 per cent of spouses). In comparison, among major American Jewish communities surveyed this past decade, the proportion of foreign-born ranged from 7 per cent (Boston, 1985) to 27 per cent (Miami, 1982). About 4 per cent of the respondents were born in Israel, 3 per cent in South Africa, 3 per cent in Great Britain, 5 per cent in the United States, and most of the remainder in Eastern Europe, including 5 per cent from the Soviet Union who arrived since 1970. Toronto is a truly cosmopolitan Jewish community and is composed of Jews from all over the world.

Among the 59 per cent of respondents who are Canadian-born, 66 per cent were born in Toronto, 15 per cent in Montreal, and the rest throughout Canada. Migration to Toronto continues, with 10 per cent of the foreign-born respondents and 12 per cent of foreign-born spouses arriving since 1985, and it should be expected that the population will continue to grow.

Distance from the immigrant experience is an important factor in understanding Jewish attitudes and behaviour. Generation is typically defined as:

• First generation: immigrant to North America
• Second generation: born in North America
• Third generation: at least one parent born in North America
• Fourth generation: at least one grandparent born in North America

The Greater Toronto Jewish community is heavily composed of respondents who are still relatively close to the immigrant experience. However, whereas two-thirds of the respondents are first or second generation North Americans, two-thirds of respondents between the ages of 18 and 34 are third or fourth generation. Thus, in anticipating future trends in the community, the experience of these later generations must be closely examined.

Jews are more likely to be owners rather than renters of their homes. Toronto, where 62 per cent reported owning their homes, is comparable to large American communities such as Philadelphia, Miami, San Francisco, and Baltimore. The Greater Toronto Jewish community shows very high rates of residential mobility, compared to most American Jewish communities. Approximately 15 per cent of Toronto's Jewish households have been at their current address for one year or less, 20 per cent for two to three years, while about 65 per cent have been at their current address more than four years, including 33 per cent who have been at their current address for ten or more years. These data reveal both the high growth rate of the Toronto Jewish community, as well as the propensity to move within the community.

Intermarriage rates are increasing. Of the couples in our sample, 84 per cent are composed of two persons who were born Jewish and are currently still Jewish or do not subscribe to another religion (the in-married). The balance, or 16 per cent of the couples, have one partner who was not born Jewish—6 per cent where the non-Jewish spouses now consider themselves Jewish (Jew by Choice) and 10 per cent where the spouse does not consider him or herself Jewish (mixed-marrieds). Thus, in the majority of intermarriages (65 per cent) the non-Jewish partner remains non-Jewish.

Intermarriage tends to increase with every succeeding generation throughout North America. For example, in the San Francisco Bay area, where the rate of intermarriage is high, rates of in-marriage declined from 79 per cent for the first generation Jews to 50 per cent for third generation, and to a low of 18 per cent for fourth generation. In Greater Toronto, while rates of in-marriage are strong among the first generation (91 per cent) and the second generation (92 per cent), the rates drop to 80 per cent of the third generation Jews, and drop substantially lower to 57 per cent of fourth generation Jews.

It is clear that intermarriage has been a growing phenomenon. Table 6 illustrates the degree of intermarriage taking into consideration when the marriage occurred. In the last thirty years intermarriage has increased tenfold from 3 per cent to 30 per cent of all couples. As we shall see, the intermarried households where both partners identify themselves as Jewish tend to be more similar to the in-married than the mixed married households. Perhaps

Table 6 *Per cent of couples in Toronto intermarried, by year of marriage*[a]

	PRE-1961	1961-1970	1971-1975	1976-1980	1981-1985	SINCE 1986	TOTAL
In-marriage	97	89	81	79	65	70	84
Jews by Choice	1	3	8	9	7	10	6
Mixed marriage	2	8	11	12	28	20	10

[a]Time period breakdowns include information about respondents currently divorced or separated

most significantly, all the in-married couples and those with a Jew by Choice identify all their children as Jewish, whereas only 39 per cent of the mixed couples do so.

These three subgroups tend to differ from each other in numerous ways. Mixed-married couples, where one partner is not identified as Jewish, tend to live in low Jewish density areas, are more likely to be fourth generation, and are less likely to identify with one of the major denominations or belong to a synagogue. The Jewish partner in such couples is less likely to manifest a range of Jewish ritual practices, Jewish friendships and organizational links, and ties to Israel than are other Jewish respondents.

Generally speaking, the couples where the non-Jewishly raised partner is now identified as Jewish are more similar to in-married couples than mixed couples in terms of Jewish religious practices but are closer to mixed couples in their organizational and friendship links and ties to Israel. Denominationally, these couples are also more likely to identify as Reform Jews. Interestingly, the Jewish educational background of those Jews who in-marry and those Jews in mixed relationships is not dramatically different, though the Jewish educational experiences and expectations of the children in these households are not equivalent.

Religion and Identity

Greater Toronto has a relatively high percentage of Jews who say that they are Orthodox or Conservative. Relatively small proportions of the Jewish population in most Jewish communities for which data are available identify themselves as Orthodox, with 10 per cent or less identifying themselves as such. Toronto, with 10 per cent of its respondents reporting that their households are Orthodox, is one of three communities with a high proportion identifying themselves in this manner. Baltimore, with 20 per cent, has the highest proportion of Jewish households identifying themselves as Orthodox.

Toronto, with 39 per cent of respondents identifying their household as Conservative, is also on the higher end of the range in North America. In many American communities, Jews are more likely (between 29 per cent and

52 per cent) to identify themselves as Reform than any other denomination. In Toronto, the proportion of respondents saying they are Reform (24 per cent) is lower than any US community for which we have data. First generation respondents are more likely to identify their households as Orthodox or as 'Just Jewish' than are other generations. The proportion of Reform Jews increases with distance from the immigrant experience. Reform is especially strong among 18- to 24-year-old respondents (41 per cent). Single parents are less likely to identify with a major denomination with the exception of Reform (30 per cent). One out of every four couples without any children classify themselves as Other.

A majority of Greater Toronto Jews do not currently belong to a synagogue. The proportion of Jews who say that they are members of a synagogue varies widely in the United States. For example, 33 per cent of the households in San Francisco report belonging to a congregation, as do 55 per cent of Baltimore's households. In Toronto almost half, 48 per cent, of the respondents report that their households belong to a synagogue. It should be pointed out that surveys tend to reveal much higher proportions of Jews who say they identify with synagogues than official synagogue records indicate, since respondents may report belonging to a synagogue if they attend sometimes, if they used to be members, or if they intend to join in the future.

Most Toronto Jews attend synagogue sometime, but few attend often. Among all the communities for which we have data, frequency of synagogue attendance seems to have increased in the latter part of the decade. Relatively low proportions of the population assert that they never attend synagogue; however, the more assimilated Jewish communities, such as San Francisco, find 24 per cent of the population never attending. In Toronto, over 90 per cent of all Jews report attending sometime during the year.

In comparison to communities in the United States, Greater Toronto shows relatively high proportions of households that light Sabbath candles, host or attend a seder, and observe *Kashrut*. Toronto appears average in households that light Hanukkah candles, and in respondents who fast on Yom Kippur. If we examine the different practices more closely, some interesting patterns emerge. Not surprisingly, Orthodox households have the highest rate of ritual observance. Conservative households tend to report percentages closer to the Orthodox than other groups, and Reform tend to appear between these two movements and the other groups. Those who never attend synagogue report relatively low levels of ritual observance. Notwithstanding their lower levels, it is still the case that one in five Jewish respondents who never attends synagogue services still fasts on Yom Kippur and one in three reports that their household attends or hosts a seder. Respondents who report that none or few of their closest friends are Jewish, are fourth generation, are single (except for the widowed), or who live in low density areas all have lower levels of ritual observance. Indeed, except for fasting on Yom Kippur, respondents with few Jewish friends have the lowest levels of ritual observance. This trend holds even if we look exclusively at households that have only Jewish respondents (i.e., no mixed marriages).

Single parents tend to be similar to never married and divorced or separated singles in their relatively low level of observance. The only exception is in lighting Hanukkah candles, where 61 per cent report lighting candles all the time. This is most likely due to the presence of children in the household. However, single parents still consistently report lower levels of observance than households with children and two parents present.

The Organized Community

Toronto Jewish Congress' Strategic Planing Report surmised that the nature, role, and functions of TJC are not well understood by the Jewish public. The Community Study asked respondents 'How familiar are you with the Toronto Jewish Congress?' Over 40 per cent of respondents claimed no familiarity with TJC and a further 25 per cent said they were not very familiar.

Among respondents who reported at least some familiarity with TJC:

- 55 per cent were judged by the interviewer to have difficulty in describing what TJC does
- 32 per cent correctly identified the central function of TJC
- only 10 per cent identified communal fund-raising as a function
- a large majority (73 per cent) of those who had an opinion thought that TJC was a local branch of the Canadian Jewish Congress

Since these questions were not asked of those who were unfamiliar with TJC, the overall picture confirms the suspicion that the awareness and knowledge of Toronto Jewish Congress by the community at large needs to be improved.

Jewish education remains strong in Greater Toronto. The community appears to take the Jewish education of its children seriously.

The vast majority of young children receive some form of Jewish education, with nearly one-half starting their school years in a day school or full-time Jewish context. At any point in time, 90 per cent of all children have received some form of Jewish education and 58 per cent are currently enrolled. Not surprisingly, a significant drop-off occurs in early adolescence. However, among 14- to 18-year-olds, fully 93 per cent have received some form of Jewish education. We can expect this trend to continue, since the parents of 86 per cent of pre-school children (including kindergarten children not in day school) expect their children to receive some form of Jewish education.

Certain subgroups of children are at least twice as likely not to receive any Jewish education. These include Jewish children of the mixed married, those not affiliated with one of the denominational movements, fourth generation households, and low income families.

Households were also asked to report on their help-seeking across a broad range of services that they might have needed within the preceding year. Of the 1400 households interviewed, 41 per cent indicated that they had sought some type of help. These households that needed help will serve as the basis of our analysis. For the one-third of these households that sought help for more than one type of service, the following analysis considers whether they contacted, utilized, or preferred a Jewish agency for at least one of their needs.

In seeking help, 52 per cent of households indicated that they preferred that the type of service they sought be provided by a Jewish agency. Across the spectrum of generations, the newer the Canadian the higher the preference (61 per cent first generation — 28 per cent fourth generation).

A majority, or 58 per cent of the households who sought help, report contacting a Jewish agency for at least one of their needs. Those reporting household incomes below $30,000 were more likely to contact a Jewish agency (65 per cent, 85 per cent of those who had only one need). Households north of Steeles and northern Metro again show relatively high levels of contact (74 per cent and 71 per cent respectively), as do Orthodox Jews (79 per cent) as well as the newer generation of Canadians (66 per cent first generation — 47 per cent fourth generation).

Families with young children report relatively high rates of help-seeking for their specific needs. A very high proportion, or 86 per cent of the households that contacted a Jewish agency utilized one for at least one of its needs. Interestingly, recent immigrants, who were most likely to prefer and contact a Jewish agency, were less likely (72 per cent) to utilize a Jewish agency for any of their problems.

People with disabilities are one of the few groups for which the study sought to identify and to pursue specific individual information for everyone in the household. The disabled were defined as those with any kind of physical, mental, or other health disability or condition for at least six months which limits employment, education, or daily activities. Five per cent of the Jewish population has a disability and of this group 36 per cent require special assistance.

Fifty per cent of the disabled individuals rely on family or personal financial resources to finance their special needs. Twenty-five per cent of the disabled have household incomes below $20,000.

The relationship between disability and income appears to be a function of age. A disproportionate number of elderly are in the lower income category and 58 per cent of the disabled are 65 years of age and older. The younger disabled, however, are also most likely to fall in the lower income category. Disabled individuals tend to live alone (30 per cent) or with just one other individual (47 per cent). Those living alone are less likely to report needing special assistance.

Not only do they represent a significant proportion (14 per cent) of the population, but those 65 years of age and over tend to require a significant level of assistance. In addition to the needs noted earlier, we also sought to assess the level of help provided by respondents to any of their elderly parents living in the area. Forty-four per cent of households in which the respondent was under 65 have at least one elderly parent living in the Greater Toronto area. Of these respondents with elderly parents, 33 per cent report providing some kind of regular care to a parent. Twenty-five per cent of respondents with elderly parents report that their parents are receiving care on a regular basis from someone other than the respondent of their spouse. In more than half of the cases where the parent is receiving from the respondent, additional care is also received from outside the home. The older the respondent the more likely that their parents are receiving care from others.

Three out of every four households report making a contribution to a Jewish philanthropy or charity. Close to 60 per cent report making a contribution to United Jewish Appeal.

Greater Toronto places relatively high among North American communities in the proportion of households that contribute. An equivalent proportion of the community's households that give Jewishly report making a gift to a non-Jewish charity. Of those who do give, the majority are giving less than $500 annually per household. Combined with those who do not give at all, a sizeable proportion (68 per cent) of Jews give either nothing or less than $500 per year to all Jewish philanthropies, including United Jewish Appeal (72 per cent).

Although giving is strong throughout the community, there are differences in various groups' tendencies to contribute. Respondents who are younger, those reporting lower levels of income, single adults, those who have immigrated within the last ten years, and those living in the 'Rest of Greater Toronto' area all report lower than average tendencies to contribute. Households that identify with Conservative and Orthodox movements are higher than average contributors. Reform households are average and those who do not identify with a major denomination are below average in their tendency to give. Respondents who have never been to Israel and households with one non-Jewish spouse have a lower tendency to contribute. Generally speaking, the less identified the household with the Jewish community, either religiously or organizationally, the lower the tendency to give.

Israel

There is a very strong support for Israel among Toronto Jews. Almost two-thirds of all respondents have visited Israel at least one time, including:

- 53% of 18- to 24-year-olds
- 62% of 25- to 44-year-olds
- 57% of 45- to 54-year-olds
- 71% of 55- to 64-year-olds
- 65% of 65- to 74-year-olds
- 69% of those over age 75

Compared to Jewish communities in the US, Toronto has by far the highest proportion of Jews who have visited Israel, more than 20 per cent higher than the next closest city. In addition, over half of those who have visited Israel have done so more than once.

Third and fourth generation Jews (one-half) are less likely than first and second generation Jews (two-thirds) to have visited Israel. Jewish respondents who are affiliated with communal institutions are more likely to have visited Israel. Over two-thirds (70 per cent) of respondents who belong to a synagogue or to a Jewish organization (and 80 per cent of those belonging to both) have visited Israel, compared to 51 per cent of those who belong to neither.

In terms of 'feelings of closeness' to Israel, of those with all or almost all of their friends Jewish, 65 per cent report feeling very close to Israel. Conversely, among respondents who indicate few or none of their friends are Jewish, only 22 per cent feel very close to Israel and almost half (48 per cent) feel distant from Israel.

Self-identified Orthodox and Conservative Jews are far more likely than other respondents to say that they feel close to Israel. In addition, only 1 per cent of Orthodox Jews and 11 per cent of conservative Jews say they feel distant from Israel, compared to 25 per cent of those who identify as Reform, 18 per cent who say they are 'Just Jewish', and 35 per cent of those who identify as 'Other'. In-married (56 per cent), conversionary (30 per cent), and mixed married (19 per cent) all differ in their reporting of feeling very close to Israel. Feeling distant from Israel is relatively high among mixed marriage couples (37 per cent) and less so among conversionary (27 per cent) and in-married (12 per cent). First and second generation Jews are far more likely (69 per cent and 50 per cent) respectively, to say that they feel very close to Israel than are third and fourth generation Jews (33 per cent and 24 per cent respectively).

Conclusion

This 'First Look' reveals a Jewish community that is relatively vibrant and sound. A high proportion of youth receives Jewish education, our links with Israel are strong, and the giving to Jewish philanthropies is generous. While there is always room for improvement, the overall picture is positive.

What the report also reveals is a community that is still, to a significant degree, an immigrant community. The majority of the population are first and second generation Canadians.

This raises a crucial question: how much of the success with Jewish education, the commitment to Israel and to *tzedaka* — obligatory charity — are by-products of our relative closeness to the European experience? Will the community be able to maintain its commitment to Jewish continuity and to Jewish values among the third and fourth generations and beyond?

Table 7   Demographic characteristics of the Montreal sample, national CRB survey
        (total sample: 352 people)

Sex:		Ethnic Extraction:	
Males	49.3%	Sephardim	19.9%
Females	50.7%	Ashkenazim	74.8%
Age:		Education:	
18–29 years	17.7%	Less than High School	12.9%
30–44 years	36.2%	Finished Sec V Cert.	16.3%
45–54 years	18.6%	College/Technical School	18.2%
55 +	27.5%	University Training	52.7%
Marital Status:		Individual Income:	
Married	65.1%	Under $25,000	56.8%
Single	21.0%	$25,000–$49,000	21.6%
Divorced/Separated	6.5%	$50,000–$99,000	14.8%
Widowed	7.4%	$100,000 +	6.8%
Birth Place:		Occupation:	
Canada	53.7%	Professional/Admin.	25.5%
Eastern Europe	15.8%	Sales	11.1%
Morocco	11.5%	Office	10.1%
Israel	4.7%	Owners/Self-employed	8.4%
Other	13.1%	Not working	30.1%

Montreal

Mobility and Politics

Most Montreal Jews think they will be living in Quebec in five years. About sixty per cent of respondents believe they will be living in this province in five years, 19.8 per cent say elsewhere, and a significant minority (21.1 per cent) claim they are unsure or do not offer a response. Of those who say elsewhere, 49.2 per cent specify a different province, followed by the US (23.2 per cent), Israel (17.4 per cent), and other countries (10.1 per cent). The great majority of those who mention another province specify Ontario (84.4 per cent). Specific groups more inclined to see themselves as not living in the province within five years include young adults, singles, the university-trained, Ashkenazim, and those with English as a mother tongue.

When asked to identify reasons for either remaining or leaving the province of Quebec, 72.9 per cent say the political situation is an important factor. About 66 per cent say the economic situation is important, followed by anti-Semitism (65.2 per cent), language policy (53.4 per cent), re-joining family (35.2 per cent), and better education elsewhere (28 per cent). The political situation is rated very important more often by Ashkenazim (51.6 per cent) than Sephardim (38.7 per cent). Ashkenazim are also much more concerned about language policy (33.1 per cent) than Sephardim (13.1 per cent). The issue of better education elsewhere seems to be somewhat more important for Sephardim than Ashkenazim, as are economic issues, anti-Semitism, and re-joining family.

In terms of constitutional changes for Canada, most people prefer a revised federalism that maintains the power of the central government. Only about seventeen per cent of those surveyed favour the current federal system, whereas 45.1 per cent prefer a revised federalism that maintains the power of the central government; 15.5 per cent a revised federalism decentralized in favour of all provinces; 1.8 per cent a revised federalism decentralized in favour of Quebec only; 3.3 per cent Sovereignty Association for Quebec; and 1.2 per cent complete independence for this province. About 12 per cent are not sure, and 3.4 per cent offer no response.

Culture/Religion Identity

There is a high level of bilingualism among Montreal Jews. About three-quarters of the sample is fluent or conversant in *French*. More specifically, 39.8 per cent of respondents claim they are completely fluent, and 38.1 per cent have a conversational knowledge of French. Sixteen per cent can only speak in simple sentences, whereas 6.1 per cent cannot speak at all. Seventy-three per cent of Ashkenazim claim they are fluent or conversant in French.

Younger people seem more proficient in French than their older counterparts. About 55 per cent of those 18-29 years are totally fluent, compared to 37.7 per cent between 30-44 years, 40.6 per cent between 45-54 years and 28.6 per cent above 55 years.

The great majority of the sample (91 per cent) is totally fluent in spoken *English*, whereas 6.1 per cent can converse adequately, but not fluently. About 69 per cent of Sephardim are completely fluent in English.

A significant minority of Montreal Jews are proficient in spoken Yiddish or Hebrew. One of five respondents (21.6 per cent) is fluent in spoken *Hebrew*, whereas 14.7 per cent have some conversational skills, but are not fluent. More than 46.1 per cent cannot speak Hebrew whatsoever. Sephardim have a higher level of Hebrew speech fluency than Ashkenazim.

About 26 per cent of the total sample is fluent in spoken *Yiddish*, whereas 18.8 per cent can converse adequately, and 54.8 per cent can speak only in simple sentences or not at all. Yiddish fluency increases dramatically with age. Only 9.1 per cent of those between 18-29 are fluent, compared to 13.9 per cent for those 30-44 years, 23.3 per cent for those 45-54 years, and 51.2 per cent for those 55 + years.

A large percentage of Montreal Jews are members of synagogues. About 66 per cent of respondents are members of a synagogue, temple or congregation. This is a high figure, greater than Jewish communities such as Los

Angeles (26 per cent), San Francisco (33 per cent), Chicago (44 per cent), Washington (44 per cent), or Toronto (56 per cent). Attending synagogue on High Holidays and special occasions is the most common form of participation among Montreal Jews. Other groups in which synagogue attendance is particularly frequent include those between 30-44 years, 55 + years, married individuals, and Sephardim.

The Montreal community has a high proportion of Orthodox members. About 24 per cent of the sample consider themselves to be Orthodox Jews. This percentage of Orthodox is higher than that of other Jewish communities across the continent. For instance, it is greater than New York (13 per cent), Miami (11 per cent), Toronto (10 per cent), St Louis (8 per cent), Chicago (6 per cent), and Washington (3 per cent). Only Baltimore (20 per cent) seems to have a comparable percentage of Orthodox members.

Montreal Jews feel very close to their fellow Jews, tend to have Jewish friends, and prefer living in areas where all or most of their neighbours are Jewish. In terms of the closeness they feel toward other Jews, 68.4 per cent of the sample say to a great extent, 27.8 per cent to some extent, 0.7 per cent claim not at all, and 3.1 per cent are unsure or don't offer a response.

About 46 per cent of respondents say that all or almost all of their friends are Jewish, 35.5 per cent that most are Jewish, 14.7 per cent that some are Jewish, and only 2.5 per cent that few or none are Jewish.

In terms of the 'Jewishness' of their neighbourhood, 22.2 per cent of those surveyed say all or almost all of their neighbours are Jewish, 25.2 per cent that most neighbours are Jewish, 39.1 per cent some neighbours are Jewish, and 13 per cent none or few neighbours are Jewish.

The rate of intermarriage among Montreal Jews is very low relative to most other Jewish communities on the North American continent. According to the 1986 Canadian Census the rate of intermarriage among Montreal Jews is 13 per cent, a figure well below that of the general American community (approx. 32 per cent). The present survey has an 11.4 per cent intermarriage rate among respondents, compared to 15 per cent in Baltimore, 15.5 per cent in Phoenix, 17 per cent in Chicago, 20 per cent in Boston, 21.4 per cent in Cleveland, 30 per cent in Washington, 33 per cent in Dallas, and 40 per cent in San Francisco.

The intermarriage rates are highest among specific groups. Men are much more inclined (18.3 per cent) than women (4.4 per cent) to marry someone born outside the faith; Sephardic and Ashkenazi respondents are about equally likely to have mixed marriages. Orthodox (5.2 per cent) and Conservative Jews (8.9 per cent) are less inclined than Secular/Reform Jews (14.1 per cent).

Intermarriage is more prevalent among the well-educated and affluent; 15.7 per cent among university-trained versus 4.3 per cent with less education have mixed marriages. Those living in households with incomes of $40000 + are more likely to intermarry than those with less household income.

The above statistics group those spouses who have converted to Judaism with those that have not. Men, secular Jews, and the university-educated are more likely to be in marriages in which there has been no conversion. Montreal seems to be the only major city in North America where intermarriages with conversions outnumber those without conversions.

The Organized Community

A high percentage of Jewish Montrealers have memberships in Jewish organizations. The Montreal Jewish community has a long history of organizational development, and this is reflected in the high figures for affiliation among those sampled in this study. Almost half (45 per cent) say they belong to a Jewish organization.

A third of those surveyed actively volunteer for the organized Jewish community. When asked whether in the past 12 months they have volunteered at least once a month for a community organization, 31.2 per cent of those surveyed say yes, and 68.8 per cent say no or don't offer a response.

Volunteerism is much stronger among women (42.1 per cent) than men (20.1 per cent). Widowed/divorced persons are more apt to be volunteers (41.9 per cent) than single (20 per cent) or married (32.6 per cent) individuals.

The level of Jewish volunteerism in Montreal (31.2 per cent) is higher than that of Toronto (25.4 per cent), Dallas (32 per cent), Detroit (26 per cent), San Francisco (24 per cent), Baltimore (22 per cent), and the general American rate (21 per cent). About eight per cent of the sample say that in the past 12 months they had volunteered for a non-Jewish organization.

Almost two-thirds of respondents (59 per cent) claim to give some donation to the Combined Jewish Appeal (CJA), whereas 13 per cent say they don't, and 28.1 per cent offer no response. Of those who contribute, 43.5 per cent donate less than $100, 35.4 per cent between $100 and $499, 13.8 per cent between $500 and $2,499, and 7.2 per cent give $2,500 or more.

Those who say they contribute to CJA are more likely to be female, between 45-54 years, married individuals, Ashkenazim, and Conservative Jews. Those living in households with incomes above $80000 are much more likely to be contributors than those in households with incomes under $40000. Persons with some university training are more inclined to donate than those with less education.

The level of philanthropy among Montreal's Jewish households (58.9 per cent) is slightly lower than Toronto (60.1 per cent), but much higher than that of the general American community (45 per cent).

About 52 per cent of households contribute to Jewish causes other than Combined Jewish Appeal. Of those who do, 40.1 per cent donate less than $100, 36.8 per cent between $100 and $400, and 23.1 per cent $500 or more. Forty-seven per cent of the households sampled also contribute to non-Jewish causes. The average contribution is $398, or about half of what is donated to Combined Jewish Appeal.

Almost 24 per cent of respondents (83 people) say they have been the victims of anti-Semitic slurs, whereas 7.1 per cent (25 people) have been the victims of anti-Semitic discrimination at work or business, 5.4 per cent have encountered anti-Semitic discrimination in their education, 3.9 per cent discrimination in finding a job, and 0.7 per cent discrimination in finding housing.

In terms of the level of anti-Semitism respondents feel there is in Canada, about 15 per cent say a great deal, 64.6 per cent say some, and 18.6 per cent a little. Females, persons 55 +, widowed/divorced persons, those with a high school certificate or less, and Orthodox Jews are more likely to claim there is a great deal of anti-Semitism in Canada. When asked whether anti-Semitism has increased or decreased in recent years, 61.1 per cent of the sample believe is has increased, 3.4 per cent that it has decreased, 26.7 per cent say it has stayed the same, and 7.3 per cent are unsure.

About 80 per cent of Montreal Jews say there is a great deal or some anti-Semitism in Canada, and the figure is 79.2 per cent for Toronto. Twenty-four per cent of Montreal Jews have been the victims of anti-Semitic slurs, compared to 21.2 per cent in Toronto. Finally, 36.5 per cent of Montreal Jews feel completely accepted in Canada compared to 38.1 per cent of Toronto Jews.

Most Montreal Jews feel close to Israel. About 83 per cent of those surveyed feel very or fairly close to Israel, whereas 13.4 per cent feel very or fairly distant, and 3.2 per cent are unsure or do not offer a response. The great majority of respondents (89.7 per cent) strongly or somewhat agree that caring about Israel is a very important part of being a Jew; 6.2 per cent strongly or somewhat disagree, and 4.2 per cent are unsure or do not respond.

There is a high frequency of visits to Israel among Montreal Jews. More than 70 per cent of respondents say they have been to Israel at least one time: 25.1 per cent once, 13.7 per cent twice, 8.8 per cent three times, and 22.9 per cent four or more times. Twenty-seven per cent say they have never gone, and 2 per cent do not respond.

★   ★   ★

The overall results of this study place the Montreal Jewish community as a leader in terms of quality of life, Jewish identity and affiliation, philanthropic and volunteer activity, and identification with the state of Israel. Immediate action needs to be taken to ensure its continuity so that Jewish Montrealers will continue to benefit from the highest quality of Jewish life in North America.

part two

Anti-

Semitism

Introduction

Robert J. Brym

Writing in the aftermath of World War II, Jean-Paul Sartre (1965 [1948]: 143) pointedly remarked that, 'contrary to a widespread opinion, it is not the Jewish character that provokes anti-Semitism but, rather, . . . it is the anti-Semite who creates the Jew.' Of course, anti-Semitism is not *all* that creates the Jew. Emotionally satisfying Jewish cultural experiences and frequent personal and professional associations with other Jews also contribute to the cohesiveness of Jewish communities. But Sartre correctly recognized the important role played by anti-Semitism in generating Jewish communal strength. Where anti-Semitism is weak — in medieval China or contemporary North America, for example — large segments of the Jewish community typically assimilate.

Anti-Semitism has not always been a minor force in the life of the Canadian Jewish community, and it has not yet been eradicated. Particularly in the 1930s, the ills of the era were often blamed on the Jews. The collapse of capitalism during the Great Depression provoked strong opposition on the left, and the Jews were increasingly blamed for the evils of capitalism, of communism, or of both. It was a conveniently plastic myth that could be stretched and distorted to fit the 'facts' and cloak deep uncertainties. Jews could be viewed simultaneously as Rothschilds and Trotskys, as capitalist exploiters and communist corrupters. Hence the coexistence, for example, of the *achat chez nous* boycott against Jewish businesses in Quebec and the campaign of Catholic unions to associate socialism with the Jews and thus check the spread of socialist influence on the *Québécois* working class.

It was in Quebec that organized fascism was most successful. A journalist by the name of Adrien Arcand published newspapers, held rallies, and recruited thousands of Blueshirts in his *Parti National Social Chrétien*. But anti-Semitism was by no means restricted to that province. One wing of the Social Credit party in Alberta espoused all the usual anti-Semitic propaganda about the imminent danger of a Jewish conspiracy to dominate the world. Swastika clubs were formed in Ontario. And between Hitler's rise to power in 1933 and the outbreak of World War II in 1939, Canada distinguished itself by accepting fewer European-Jewish refugees per capita than any other Allied country (Abella and Troper, 1982) save one: Newfoundland (Bassler, 1988). In the 1930s, anti-Semitism was state policy in Canada and Newfoundland.

In this section we reprint an article that well illustrates the nature of Canadian anti-Semitism in the 1930s. Cyril Levitt and William Shaffir transport us to the baseball diamond at Toronto's Christie Pits, where, on a fine mid-August evening in 1933, a banner emblazoned with a swastika was unfurled in order to enrage and provoke the Jewish team and its supporters. It worked. The largest and most violent non-labour unrest in the city's history ensued, as thousands of people (some reports say as many as 10,000) rioted, some wielding bats and lead pipes.

That was 60 years ago. What is the state of Canadian anti-Semitism today? No serious commentator doubts that the situation has greatly improved. After the Holocaust and the Eichmann trial, anti-Semitism became increasingly associated in the public mind with the worst evils of Western civilization. The West had an open love affair with Israel (at least until 1967). In the early 1970s, Canada's multiculturalism policy enshrined respect for ethnic pluralism and subsidized its expression. Canada became a more secular society and its citizenry more highly educated. Nearly three decades of unparalleled prosperity and rapid growth lowered job competition and rendered immigration a non-problem. Little wonder that in such circumstances anti-Semitism waned.

The new atmosphere is nowhere more evident than in Canadian Jews' contemporary attitudes towards Jewish immigration and in the actual drift of government immigration policy since World War II. Thus, by the 1970s and 1980s Canadian immigration policy was clearly biased *in favour* of Jewish immigration from the Soviet Union (Basok, 1991). And, not surprisingly, a 1979 survey conducted in Toronto among a representative sample of over 1,800 Jews, Germans, Ukrainians, Italians, Portuguese, Chinese, and West Indians showed that only 13 per cent of Jews considered present laws too restrictive in allowing other Jews to immigrate to Canada. By contrast, proportionately three times that many members of the six other large ethnic minorities surveyed—37 per cent—felt that current laws made it too difficult for members of their ethnic groups to immigrate to Canada (calculated from Breton, 1990: 204).

Nonetheless, 'dislike of the unlike' (as Salo Baron once called anti-Semitism) persists, virulently on society's fringes and in muted form at its core. Tiny groups of white supremacists, Ku Klux Klan members, unreconstructed Nazis, and young skinheads occasionally make the news with some rally or act of vandalism that shocks the public, both Jewish and non-Jewish. Several individuals—Malcolm Ross in New Brunswick, James Keegstra in Alberta, Ernst Zundel in Ontario—achieved notoriety in the late 1970s and 1980s for promoting the idea that the Holocaust never took place. Calls for the destruction of the State of Israel, although usually masked as anti-Zionism, are often driven by a deep anti-Jewish animus.

In the excerpt from their book on Zundel reprinted here, Gabriel Weimann and Conrad Winn masterfully analyse the results of a survey they conducted in order to determine how Canadians were affected by the trial of one of the country's most infamous hate-mongers. They make at least one surprising discovery: the trial increased Canadians' sympathies toward Jews. They also offer a provocative speculation: the trial may have nonetheless promoted disbelief in the reality of the Holocaust on the part of Canadians. If true, this adds weight to the claim of Alan Dershowitz (1991: 171-2) and others that Jews benefit little, and may in fact be harmed, by prosecuting anti-Semites.

In this section's final article, Robert Brym and Rhonda Lenton analyse the results of another recent survey. They show that while anti-Jewish sentiment in Canada is no longer widespread, Quebec stands out as the only province with a large Jewish population and a stubborn, relatively high level of anti-Semitism. They see reason for some concern in these findings, especially if Quebec gains independence (Brym and Lenton, 1992). Together with Weimann and Winn's survey, this suggests that anti-Semitism in Quebec and the rest of Canada, however diminished, is likely to galvanize the Jewish community for some time to come.

References

Abella, Irving and Harold Troper
  1982 *None is Too Many: Canada and the Jews of Europe, 1933-1948* (Toronto: Lester and Orpen Dennys)

Bassler, Gerhard P.
  1988 'Attempts to settle Jewish refugees in Newfoundland and Labrador, 1934–1939', *Simon Wiesenthal Center Annual* 5: 121-44

Basok, Tanya
  1991 'Soviet immigration to Canada: The end of the refugee program?' in Tanya Basok and Robert J. Brym, eds, *Soviet-Jewish Emigration and Resettlement in the 1990s* (Toronto: York Lanes Press): 141-57

Breton, Raymond
  1990 'The ethnic group as a political resource in relation to problems of incorporation: perceptions and attitudes', in Raymond Breton *et al.*, eds, *Ethnic Identity and Equality: Varieties of Experience in a Canadian City* (Toronto: University of Toronto Press): 196-255

Brym, Robert J. and Rhonda L. Lenton
  1992 'Anti-Semitism in Quebec: Reply to Langlois', *Canadian Journal of Sociology* 17, 2: 179-83

Dershowitz, Alan M.
  1991 *Chutzpah* (New York: Simon & Schuster)

Sartre, Jean-Paul
  1965 *Anti-Semite and Jew*, trans. George J. Becker (New York: Schocken)
  [1948]

The Swastika as Dramatic Symbol:

A Case-Study of Ethnic Violence in Canada

Cyril Levitt

and William Shaffir

A review of the literature on social unrest reveals that many scholars attribute rebellious or riotous behaviour to the actualization of predispositions rooted either in the personality of the individual or in the social structure.[1] Thus, as Herbert Blumer notes, 'they assert that social unrest is but a reflection of personality instability or an expression of acute structural strains on the existing social order.'[2] While such analyses have identified the important determinants of collective behaviour, they have only paid limited attention to the process by which such behaviour is shaped. Attention to this process necessitates an examination of how people define and interpret the stream of events unfolding in their experience. As the literature has shown, social unrest does not suddenly emerge fully formed, but undergoes a process of growth and development.[3]

In identifying the more vital features affecting the maturation of social unrest, Herbert Blumer draws attention to the role of dramatic events which serve as the nucleating points in their formation:[4]

> It is the dramatic event which incites and focalizes predispositions, and brings them to bear on a concrete situation; which shocks, arouses, enlivens, and shakes people loose from their routines of thought and action; which catches collective attention and stirs imagination; . . . which incites heated discussions and initiates intense interaction; and which stimulates the novel proposals and the impulsive tendencies that are so characteristic of social unrest.

The centrality of the dramatic event in the unfolding of social unrest is, of course, not unique to Blumer's formulation of collective behaviour. Others have also emphasized its significance. For example, Smelser claims that 'it is nearly always a dramatic event which precipitates the outburst of violence',[5] and provides the generalized beliefs with concrete and immediate substance.

The significance of the dramatic event lies in the fact that it serves as a central turning point affecting the career route of the social unrest. It brings into sharper focus the existing social arrangements, arouses passions of moral indignation, and rallies persons to redress some perceived injustice collectively. The object recognized as the turning point must be defined by the participants as something qualitatively different from what has occurred up to that point in the unfolding of events.

This paper examines the role of the swastika emblem in fomenting the virulent antagonism between Canadian Jews and Gentiles which culminated in the Christie Pits riot in the summer of 1933.[6] It focuses specifically on the dramatic event in the development of the riot — the sudden appearance of the swastika symbol along Toronto's eastern beaches and, about two weeks later, at a baseball game in Willowvale Park (commonly known as Christie Pits). Toronto's Jews had been made fully aware by both the city's English-language newspapers and the Yiddish daily (*Der Yiddisher Zhurnal*) of the savage Nazi persecution of Jews in Germany and of the symbolism of the swastika. They were also aware of overt anti-Semitic prejudices in Canada but had not considered such manifestations to be a serious threat to their safety or to their very existence, until the swastika was displayed provocatively in Toronto.

In referring to those objects which are the focal points of 'the impulses, feelings, and imagery of . . . people',[7] Blumer fails to distinguish between those objects which have passive symbolic value and those which have a highly-charged meaning for some groups. We suggest that dramatic symbols are best understood as objects which denote beliefs, ideas, or ideals that are capable of arousing intense feeling, emotion, passion, or energy. Admittedly, a merely formal symbol may become dramatized under certain conditions, just as a dramatic symbol may be demoted to passive status or even, under extreme conditions, robbed of its symbolic value completely.[8] For instance, the Japanese flag, once a dramatic symbol of treachery in the United States, is now trotted out and flaunted in public as a symbol of technological, scientific, and economic achievement. The symbols of the civil rights movement in the United States, which occasioned riots in the American South during the early 1960s, are now looked upon with indifference or occasionally only with passive disapproval. The dramatic symbol is highly contextual in nature, a lightning-rod of collective sentiments and shared emotions not for all time, but in specific circumstances and particular conditions. New dramatic symbols come into being and pass away quickly. Others, such as the German swastika, break dramatically upon the world historical stage and remain charged for long periods with strong collective sentiments.

In their well-known study of the so-called 'Zoot-suit' riots in Los Angeles in 1943, Turner and Surace claim that most symbols, even those we call dramatic ones, are ambiguous; that is, they evoke conflicting images.[9] It is precisely such ambiguity which serves as an inhibiting feature in collective behaviour. It is as if the countervailing images act as a brake upon that behaviour which is not generally sanctioned by the community at large. It follows, therefore, that if the symbol's ambiguity is resolved, then an important restraining feature on extreme collective behaviour will have been removed. As the authors assert: 'symbols which are unambiguous in their connotations permit immoderate behaviour toward the object in question. In the absence of ambivalence toward an object there is no internal conflict to restrict action.'[10]

In our case-study of ethnic violence, the swastika became stripped of its ambiguity, in part by the collective action surrounding its appearance in public in the weeks preceding the outbreak of the riot at Christie Pits. As an alarmed Jewish community confronted the new and heightened significance assumed by the swastika as a dramatic symbol of Nazi anti-Semitic persecutions, it unmasked the weak cover adopted by members of a swastika-bearing organization who had claimed that the emblem was nothing more than a good-luck charm associated with Indian tribes who had once lived in the area.[11]

In this paper, we first give a brief description of the prevailing anti-Semitism in Toronto which had alerted the Jewish community to be on guard against victimization. We then show how the city's English-language newspapers and the Yiddish daily published detailed reports about the plight of German Jews at the hands of Nazis, whose emblem was the swastika. We next describe how the establishment of Swastika Clubs in Toronto alarmed the city's Jews and how they attacked those who wore a swastika badge or sweatshirts displaying the emblem. We then describe how the unfurling of a white large blanket displaying a black swastika at a baseball match (where one of the teams was predominantly Jewish) triggered off a riot, and we conclude with an examination of the other factors which incited the rioters.

According to the Canadian Census of 1931, there were 45,305 Jews in Toronto in that year; they accounted for 7.2 per cent of the total population of the city, excluding the suburbs. In no area of Toronto did the Jews constitute a majority of the residents, but 30.5 per cent of the inhabitants in Ward 4 were Jewish, as were 18.6 per cent of those who lived in Ward 5 (where Christie Pits was situated). On the other hand, the number of Jews in Ward 8 (which included the eastern beaches area) was very small, accounting for under one per cent (0.08 per cent) of the ward's residents. Only 18,612 of Toronto's total Jewish population of 45,305 were born in Canada. Most of the Jewish immigrants had come from Poland and Russia and Yiddish was the mother tongue of the overwhelming majority (95.54 per cent) of Jews in Canada in 1931. The majority of those gainfully occupied in Toronto were wage-earners in small factories and shops producing and selling articles of clothing or furs while others were mainly retailers of dry goods or street hawkers.

Toronto Jews were often treated as undesirables. Stephen Speisman has shown that in contrast to earlier anti-Semitism in Toronto, which was typically expressed in actions against individuals, by 1933 a blanket condemnation of Jews had emerged.[12] There were restrictive covenants prohibiting the sale of some plots of land or houses to prospective Jewish buyers and the fact that the courts upheld such practices was ready confirmation for Canadian Jews that they could be discriminated against with impunity.[13] They were also unwelcome in some summer resorts where hotels had signboards boldly stating: 'Patronage exclusively Gentile'.[14] Indeed, a number of people we interviewed specifically recalled signs, located in various parts of Toronto and its outskirts, stating: 'No Jews or Dogs Allowed'. The effects of anti-Semitism were most severely felt in employment. It was practically impossible for Jews to get jobs as sales staff in any of the big department stores, and very few Jews were hired by the banks and financial institutions (it was standard practice in those days to ask for the applicant's religion on the employment form). Very few Jews worked for Ontario or Toronto Hydro or for government departments. One interviewee told us that a relative of his obtained a job in a company known for its discriminatory hiring practices by writing 'Protestant' in the space reserved for religion on the application form. Her boss discovered that she was Jewish (she was absent on the major Jewish holidays), and she was summarily dismissed. Another recounted that, after applying for a job at one of the major department stores in Toronto, he saw the personnel manager crumple his application form and throw it in the waste bin only moments after assuring the applicant that this application would be given 'careful attention'. The relative absence of Jews in specific professional and occupational groupings in Toronto has been explained in part by the restrictions placed upon Jewish applicants, candidates, students, and professionals. Speisman stated in his study of Toronto Jewry:[15]

> From the 1930s through the Second World War, Jews found it difficult to enter certain professions. . . . Jews could study law, medicine and dentistry only on a *numerus clausus* basis, and many a worthy Jewish student had to seek his livelihood in other pursuits. At the University of Toronto School of Dentistry, a dexterity requirement was a favourite ploy for keeping Jewish students out; the small number who made it into the program often found themselves subjected to open abuse by anti-Semitic professors. Graduates of the University of Toronto Medical School found that their prestigious diplomas could not obtain internships for them, so an entire generation of Jewish medical students emigrated to the United States seeking hospital posts to hone their craft. Canada did not want them.

The difficulties encountered by Jews in the professions were not confined to any particular region of Canada. In Regina, Saskatchewan, for instance, the General Hospital was informed in 1934 by the superintendent that a Jewish radiologist was unacceptable to the staff and to the public, and that physicians with Anglo-Saxon sounding names were preferable, even at a higher salary, to Drs Teitlebaum and Friedman. Indeed, any analysis of anti-Semitism in Canada during the early 1930s must emphasize both its scope and intensity. Although frequently camouflaged as nationalism, particularly in the Province of Quebec, and disguised and justified in terms of rising unemployment and economic uncertainties, the effects of the anti-Semitism for the Jews were unmistakably clear. Increasingly stereotyped as 'radical, disloyal, unbelieving, domineering, cosmopolitan, and otherwise as being a danger to Canadian society',[16] Jews encountered growing prejudice and discrimination because of their religion or ethnicity. The consequences of this had their most serious impact during the 1930s, as officials in the highest reaches of Canadian government, succumbing to various internal pressures, pursued a systematic policy of barring Jewish refugees from entry into Canada, thus ensuring their deaths at the hands of the Nazis. More than ever, Jews had reason to believe that anti-Semitism was stitched into the very fabric of Canadian society.[17]

The summer of 1933 revealed to Toronto Jews that some of their Gentile fellow-inhabitants felt profound hatred and contempt for them when the swastika emblem was publicly displayed and those who sported it shouted 'Heil Hitler' along the eastern beaches and later in Willowvale Park. Although the swastika symbol was not unknown in the city (for example, Rudyard Kipling's books in the public library bore the swastika on the title-pages), by the middle of 1933 the hooked-cross emblem had acquired notoriety as the badge of the Nazis and sinister connotations for Jews.

The Newspapers: Toronto Learns about the Swastika in Germany

In 1933, the newspaper was the prime source of national and international news for the majority of people. News broadcasts on the radio consisted of little more than newspaper items read verbatim. There were four daily English-language newspapers in Toronto in 1933: two morning papers, *The Daily Mail and Empire* and *The Globe*, and two afternoon/evening papers, *The Toronto Daily Star* and *The Evening Telegram*. In addition to these mass circulation dailies, the Jewish community of Toronto had its own daily Yiddish paper, *Der Yiddisher Zhurnal*. Other Yiddish daily newspapers, published in New York and Montreal, were on sale in Toronto and reported on matters affecting Jews in Canada and other parts of the world. *The Toronto Daily Star* had the largest sale of all the English-language dailies in the city (its circulation was about 215,000) and it was also the newspaper most frequently read by Jews. Together with the *Zhurnal*, it supplied Toronto Jews with horrifying reports of Nazi atrocities and frequent references to the swastika emblem which became invested with connotations of degradation, terror, and physical violence against Jews.

In a front-page story of its 13 February 1933 edition, the *Zhurnal* reported a speech by a Nazi deputy and stated: 'Kube, deputy in the Prussian parliament, says that Jews have polluted Germany like bedbugs. The only way to smoke them out is to drive them out.' No great leap of imagination was required to reach the conclusion that if Jews were 'like bedbugs' then the most efficient remedy was extermination. The editorial in that same issue stated that German Jews who believed Hitler's promise to punish those who

insulted any recognized religion were naïve and indulging in wishful thinking. It pointed out that on the very day that Hitler publicly proclaimed his
determination to protect established religious groups, the Nazis were staging
a pogrom against Jews in Gresfeld and it recommended:[18]

> The Central Verein of German Jews should stand by its former resolution to
> deploy self-defence organizations over the whole country, wherever there
> are Jewish centres. This would be more effective than all the decrees which
> Hitler might publish taken together.

A few days later, on 24 February, the *Zhurnal* published a report from
Germany under the headline: 'Jews Will Hang from Lampposts, Promises
Nazi Leader if a Hair on Hitler's Head is Touched' and quoted the threat: 'If a
hair is touched of any leader of the Nazi government, we will give a signal for
a general massacre of Jews which will only be halted when not a single Jew is
left alive'.[19] The Jewish Telegraphic Agency and German Jews fleeing the Nazi
terror and seeking refuge abroad provided further evidence of anti-Semitic
outrages. The *Zhurnal* of 23 March reported harrowing details under a
prominent headline which stated: 'Nazi Atrocities Beyond Human Imagination. Murderers, Torturers Unhindered. Jews Kidnapped and Beaten to
Death. Every Night a Tortured Jew Abandoned in Berlin Cemeteries. Those
Left Behind Alive Forced to Sign Statement that They Were Well-Treated.'[20]

Reports of atrocities in the *Zhurnal* were not as numerous in April as they
had been in February and March, largely owing to the newspaper's preoccu-
pation with reports of protests against the Nazi terror and of the efforts of
Toronto Jewry to aid their German-Jewish brethren. Nevertheless, some
incidents of physical violence against Jews in Germany were reported
throughout the month. On 7 April a *Zhurnal* headline stated: 'German Jew
and His Wife Dead Fleeing Kidnappers'.[21] Later that month the *Zhurnal*
reported more cases of kidnapping as well as instances of German Jews who
had abandoned all hope and had committed suicide. It also revealed that
German Nazis were organizing pogroms in Poland and Romania while the
violence was unabated in Germany. A man who sought refuge in Holland
revealed that Nazis had entered a synagogue in Gelsenkirchen looking for
any concealed weapons and arrested Jews whom they took to prison and
severely tortured, according to a report in the *Zhurnal* of 20 April. Four days
later, it published the account of a Jewish Telegraphic Agency correspondent
who had witnessed the plight of the German Jews at first hand after secretly
going to Berlin:[22]

> Not Berlin proper, not America, and not even the countries which border on
> Germany can have an exact notion and paint for themselves a complete
> picture of what is truly happening in Germany. The insults, the tortures, the
> awful hopelessness, the absolute helplessness of the Jews in Germany today
> are indescribable. I personally have found the Jewish situation far worse,
> infinitely more horrible than I imagined, far worse than even the worst
> reports, and I've just arrived here. Everything which was shocking in the

very first days of Hitler's coup d'état remains absolutely true to this very day. . . . Jews are continuing to disappear all the time and the whereabouts of their remains is unknown. Often they are found in the morgues.

There were further reports of violent attacks against Jews in Germany during the following months and on the first day of August the *Zhurnal* reported a 'bloody pogrom' in Berlin and quoted proclamations that described Jews as 'poisonous snakes'. The swastika was now the official emblem of the Nazi Party and a leaflet was distributed in Berlin stating:[23]

. . . The swastika, the official government emblem . . . 'Kill the Jews. Free yourselves from them once and for all!' There are two kinds of anti-Semitism. One, of a higher kind, limits Jewish power through laws. The other, lower kind, kills Jews. The latter is perhaps a dreadful kind, but it brings the best results because it ends for all time the Jewish question by exterminating them.

Some months earlier, in March 1933, *The Toronto Daily Star* had already carried reports of the swastika's association with Nazi anti-Semitic actions. One of its correspondents in Germany described how he saw 'a parade of hundreds of children, between the ages of seven and 16, carrying the swastika and the old imperial colours, and shouting at intervals: "The Jews must be destroyed".'[24] Two days later, the same newspaper had a front-page story under a headline which stated: 'Nazism Embodies Ideal Followed by Ku Klux Klan: Extreme Nationalism, Hatred of All Aliens Common to Both Orders: Nordics Superior'. Its reporter commented:[25]

Curiously enough, the Swastika or Hooked Cross, Hakenkreuz, the Nazi symbol, was an emblem much in evidence in the Ku Klux Klan lodges and in the parades of the order in days gone by. . . . A man without a program save hatred, ignorance and vulgarity is driving a great and disillusioned people to perdition. This is a pessimistic prognosis, yet I am afraid, although I hope not, that history will bear me out in this assertion.

A few days later, and again on its front page, *The Toronto Daily Star* published a report from Germany which stated that Pastor Dr Mieneke of Soldin had declared to his congregation: 'Christ himself was a Hitlerite. The Christian cross and the swastika belong together.'[26] On 15 April the newspaper published a photograph of Nazi Brownshirts wearing swastika badges. On 28 April, the front page of the same daily claimed that Jews who had fainted under torture were 'revived for further torture' in Germany and that a Polish Jew, whose name was printed in full, 'was carried into a cellar by uniformed men and beaten. They pulled the hair of his beard out and shaved a swastika on his head. He was then beaten again in time to the music of a piano.'[27]

There can be no doubt that by midsummer 1933 the swastika was seen by Toronto Jews as the symbol of infamous and inhuman Nazi anti-Semitism and it is not surprising that when it was publicly flaunted in the city, they were incensed. On the other hand, the members of Toronto's newly-formed

Swastika Clubs were still claiming with pretended innocence that the emblem was merely a good-luck sign and that it was openly displayed on Rudyard Kipling's books which could not be said to be in any way associated with Naziism.

Swastikas at the Beaches

On the first two days of August 1933, headlines in Toronto's English-language newspapers announced the establishment of the Swastika Clubs in the city and reported that the members of this new association had organized their first parade up and down the boardwalk from Balmy Beach to Wood-bine Avenue. *The Toronto Daily Star* did not hesitate to label the clubs as a Nazi organization and its issue of the first of August carried a headline which stated: 'Nazi Organization Seeking to Oust Non-Gentiles Off Beach'. On the following day, *The Evening Telegram* printed a similar headline: 'Hundreds Don Swastikas in Drive to Rid Beaches of Undesirable Persons' and the additional information that: 'Toronto "Swastikas" Arouse Jews'. On the same day, *The Globe* reported: 'Police Halt Possible "Swastika" Clash' while *The Daily and Empire* stated: 'Balmy Beach Dance Hall Closed to Avert Swastika Row. Nazi Parade Tours Boardwalk Singing Anti-Jewish Dog-gerel.'

On the first of August, after signs had been posted in and around the Balmy Beach Canoe clubhouse announcing the formation of the Swastika Clubs, clubhouse officials and members expected Jews to demonstrate their anger. The appearance of a large contingent of young Jewish men on that day alarmed the club officials, especially since some of the members, anticipating a confrontation, had armed themselves with broom handles and lacrosse sticks. The police officer on the beat notified No. 10 Police Station and an Inspector, accompanied by a sergeant and several officers, appeared shortly afterwards and cleared the grounds. The Swastika Clubs' sympathizers showed no resistance and dispersed in a more or less orderly manner, but they returned to the Balmy Beach clubhouse, where they gathered and stood in a circle for some time. On the Inspector's advice, the Commodore of the Balmy Beach Canoe Club halted the dance in progress in the ballroom and called upon those present to disperse and leave the clubhouse to avoid trouble. About four hundred people who were in the dance hall sang 'God Save the King' to the orchestra's accompaniment and left.

Der Yiddisher Zhurnal of 2 August announced: 'Nazi Organization Formed in Ward 8 to Drive Jews Away From Beaches'. According to *The Evening Telegram*, the Swastika Clubs were based 'on the line of the famous Hitler brown shirts in Germany and six local branches have already been established in Toronto's east end, boasting a membership of more than four hundred'.[28] On the evening of the first day of August, about a hundred members and sympathizers of the Swastika Clubs wearing swastika badges paraded down the boardwalk of the eastern beaches, chanting the following words to the tune of 'Home, home on the range':

> O give me a home, where the Gentiles may roam,
> Where the Jews are not rampant all day;
> Where seldom is heard a loud Yiddish word
> And the Gentiles are free all the day.

Tensions around the Beaches area originated in the south-eastern part of the city, a section miles from the Jewish residential area. Toronto's eastern beaches and parks were a favourite picnic area for thousands of Jewish immigrants who could not afford to buy or rent summer cottages and who did not have the means to travel to summer resorts (many of which, in any event, did not welcome Jews). The customs, food, and language of the weekend visitors were different from the prevailing norms in that area of the city, an area whose population was overwhelmingly of British descent. Its distance from the city centre, as well as its well-delineated boundaries, made it resemble a British village where the presence of outsiders was immediately noticeable. Residents of the Beaches were disturbed at the increasing presence of outsiders and their seeming disregard for 'proper' behaviour. 'You couldn't find a place to sit down on the bench or on the park land', one Beach resident recalled. 'And there were branches torn off these young trees . . . and half-eaten food, peels, candy wrappers strewn all over the place. And this was your area where you were living and you would come down here and see all that every Monday morning. No wonder people were annoyed.' Each of the English-language daily newspapers quoted from conversations with area residents who complained that the beach and park were being transformed every weekend into a picnic ground. The local residents, they claimed, had difficulty keeping their lawns clear of these strangers and were inconvenienced by parked cars that blocked their driveways. They also considered that using cars as dressing-rooms for bathers was indecent and intolerable. Though 'outsiders' visiting the beaches included members of the city's various ethnic minorities, resentment was focused entirely on the presence of Jews. A former Beach resident whom we interviewed remarked: 'There probably were other ethnic groups too. You couldn't pick out whether this person was Polish or that person was Jewish or what they were. But somehow or other the anger seemed to be aimed at the Jews.'

After that first march, the Swastika Clubs announced that they intended to stage a similar parade along the same boardwalk on the following Sunday. While the name 'Jew' was nowhere specifically mentioned in any of the organization's announcements or flyers, Toronto Jews were convinced of the Swastika Club's anti-Semitic character and objectives. They maintained that the epithet 'obnoxious visitors', which first appeared in a notice posted on Balmy Beach Canoe Club's bulletin board, was aimed specifically at them. The Balmy Beach clubhouse, a private social club catering to the area's residents, had displayed a notice on its bulletin board headed 'Join the Swastika Club' and stating:[29]

> Residents . . . of the Beaches are not a little perturbed at the recent influx of obnoxious visitors to Kew Gardens and surrounding territory on Saturdays and Sundays. Have you the courage to outwardly indicate your disapproval? If so, join the Swastika Club . . . There are no fees. The club badge may be obtained on payment of twenty-five cents . . . PLEASE WEAR YOUR BADGE WHENEVER YOU ARE ON THE BOARDWALK . . .

The clubhouse had served as the 'storm centre of the campaign' of the Swastika Clubs, according to *The Toronto Daily Star* which reported that posted on the clubhouse were large signboards bearing the swastika emblem and the words 'Heil Hitler'.[30] Notices of the Swastika Clubs' objectives were also posted on a bulletin board in front of the clubhouse which was situated in the boardwalk area itself.[31] According to *The Daily Mail and Empire* of 2 August, a large cardboard sign bearing the swastika and the words 'Heil Hitler' had been displayed on the door of the clubhouse but was removed by the club officials, who also removed the notices and signs that members of the Swastika Club had posted both on the clubhouse and in the immediate area on 1 August.

Convinced that the epithet 'obnoxious visitors' applied to them as Jews, some sixty to seventy 'sturdy Jews', as *The Toronto Daily Star* of the second of August described them, came to the beach *en masse* at about 9.30 p.m. Arriving by truck and car from the Spadina area of the city where they had congregated, they marched down Kew Beach Avenue and paced the boardwalk to the Balmy Beach clubhouse, where the swastika signs had been posted. Members of the Balmy Beach Canoe Club had learned of the proposed invasion of their clubhouse grounds, and the signs were removed before the Jewish contingent arrived. Reporting on the arrival of the Jewish group, *The Toronto Daily Star* quoted Al Kaufman who led them:[32]

> As soon as we got to the club grounds we mingled with those who appeared to be members of the club and at the same time looked for emblems of the Nazi organization. We couldn't find any. If we had we would have torn them off and if there had been any trouble I think we could have taken care of ourselves.

The Toronto Daily Star's item continued as follows: 'Kaufman and his "gang" paraded in small groups up and down five streets close to the clubhouse property, looking for Nazi emblems but reported that they couldn't find any trace of one.'

When leaders of the Swastika Clubs were interviewed, they claimed that their choice of emblem had no political significance, that it was selected 'as it symbolizes fraternity and good luck'. One of them added that the Balmy Beach area had once been a camping ground for the Iroquois Indians to whom the swastika was a good-luck sign and he pointed out that there once was a Swastika girls' basketball club in the area.[33]

The mayor of Toronto, William Stewart, attempted to foster an atmosphere of calm and reason. In a statement issued on the first day of August, at midnight, he declared that alleged Hitlerism and reported demonstrations at the eastern beaches would be thoroughly investigated by the police. Toronto, the mayor insisted, would never tolerate any group that attempted to take the law into its own hands. His statement read in part:[34]

> Let it be understood with the utmost clearness that we administer our laws through the police courts, and not through private groups, clubs or demonstrations. We have an abundance of British ideals which our people might emulate and follow: we need no inspiration from foreign sources and foreign isms, but simply a proper respect for law and order and British traditions. . . . We must follow British tradition, the British idea, in Toronto: the organizations or the political organisms of foreign lands do not need to be adopted, used, or aped in this country.

He stated that he was always ready to meet various interest groups, in order to reduce tensions and solve any problems, including representatives of the League for the Defense of Jewish Rights (which officially represented the Jewish community), representatives of the Swastika Clubs, and residents of the Beaches area. He personally appealed to all parties in the conflict for calm and reason and warned that those not heeding his considered advice should be prepared to accept the legal consequences of their actions. He added: 'We have gone through a long depression, and the sun is shining on the noon of a better day. Any demonstration that might cause ill-feeling would be regrettable. . . .'[35]

The most serious confrontation on the beaches occurred on Sunday 6 August, when the Swastika Clubs staged their second parade along the boardwalk with the members sporting swastika badges made of nickel with a red swastika cross impressed on them; several of the young men wore sweatshirts with a black swastika emblem. The parade started in the late afternoon and by early evening the members had marched up and down the boardwalk from Kew Gardens to Balmy Beach. *The Toronto Daily Star* reported on the following day, under a headline stating: 'Beaches in Turmoil as Swastika Emblem Incites Near Riots':[36]

> Sullen clouds of tense racial feeling, brooding over the east end waterfront for days, burst during the weekend and enveloped, in a series of clashes and near riots, thousands of Torontonians who flocked to the beaches for pleasure. . . . Trouble was in the air, and it required only the appearance of the Swastika sign to make it all too actively tangible. Throughout the turmoil, the small swastika badge, emblem of the rapidly growing club, bobbed and eddied as gangs of non-Gentiles, incensed by Hitlerism which they charged it symbolized, pounced on wearers. They tore sweat-shirts on which the sign was emblazoned from the backs of youths, and forced them to seek shelter in nearby houses.

A few days later, on 11 August, the same newspaper announced in a banner headline: 'Swastika Clubs Will Give Up Emblem'. Both the name and the badge of the clubs were to be abandoned and a new club was to be established with similar objectives under the title of 'The Beaches Protective Association'.

Clearly, the Swastika Clubs had been perceived by Toronto Jewry as an organization which aimed to foster virulent anti-Semitism in Canada and to promote Nazi principles. The clubs were short-lived—from the first to the eleventh of August—but their existence under the umbrella of the swastika for those few days caused very serious misgivings not only to the Jewish inhabitants but also to the authorities. Toronto's mayor had commented: 'It would not take long to start a conflagration in the city that you couldn't put out in a day.'[37] As we shall see below, his fears about the conflagration were justified on the evening of 16 August.

The Swastika at Christie Pits

The swastika, which had disappeared entirely from the eastern beaches district by 11 August, reappeared suddenly at Willowvale Park (Christie Pits) on the evening of 14 August. During a junior softball quarter-final game, in which Harbord Playground (a predominantly Jewish team) met St Peter's (a predominantly Catholic team), a huge swastika sewn in white cloth on a black pullover was unfurled in the final innings. According to *The Daily Mail and Empire* of 15 August, only small sections of the emblem had been unfurled from time to time 'amid much wisecracking, cheering and yelling of pointed remarks'. But according to both that paper and *The Evening Telegram*, when the Harbord team tied the score in the ninth inning, St Peter's fans unfurled the whole pullover with the emblazoned swastika—hoping thereby to spur their team to victory. On the other hand, according to *The Toronto Daily Star* of the same day, those who hoisted the swastika flag to the accompaniment of 'Heil Hitler' were a local gang. Whether the wavers of the banner were or were not local hooligans, the appearance of the swastika was seen as a deliberate attempt to provoke the Jewish supporters of the Harbord team, by displaying the Nazi emblem. After the end of the game, which was won by Harbord Playground, those holding the swastika flag raised it high and members of the gang swarmed on to the field, chanting their 'club yell' again and surrounding members of the Jewish team, according to the same newspaper. Though spectators expected that the situation on the playing field would result in fisticuffs, between supporters of the two teams, an uneasy calm prevailed.

At some time during the night of 14 August, a large swastika and the words 'Heil Hitler' were painted on the roof of the Willowvale Park clubhouse, after the attendants had left the grounds at ten o'clock—so that the vandals could not be identified. On the following morning, the Parks Commissioner announced that the swastika and the words 'Heil Hitler' would be obliterated and the matter turned over to the police. (*The Toronto Daily Star* of 15 August supplied more details of the incident and revealed that those guilty were a few members of the Pit gang, the gang that frequented Willowvale Park.)

On Wednesday evening, 16 August, Toronto experienced one of the worst non-labour riots in its history;[38] it was triggered by the flaunting of the swastika, according to *The Daily Mail and Empire*:[39]

> Widespread disorder raged over the vast area of Toronto streets for hours last night when rioting broke out following the display of the swastika emblem on a white quilt at a baseball game in Willowvale Park.
>
> The disturbance became largely racial in character, bands of Gentiles and of Jews apparently taking up opposing sides in the battle. As far as could be deemed, no arrests took place arising from the disorders, the police apparently devoting their major attention to breaking up the several serious mêlées which developed, in which hundreds appeared to be fighting at once.
>
> Cries of 'The Swastika! The Swastika!' rose in various parts of the park as soon as the taunting emblem made its appearance.
>
> In one confused mass, in sections of the crowd, more than 3,000 surged across the park and over the hill toward the emblem. Fighting broke out as Jews recognized Gentiles.

The Toronto Daily Star reported:[40]

> While groups of Jewish and Gentile youths wielded fists and clubs in a series of violent scraps for possession of a white flag bearing a Swastika symbol at Willowvale Park last night, a crowd of more than 10,000 citizens, excited by cries of 'Heil Hitler!' became suddenly a disorderly mob and surged wildly about the park and surrounding streets, trying to gain a view of the actual combats, which soon developed in violence and intensity of racial feeling into one of the worst free-for-alls ever seen in the city.
>
> Scores were injured, many requiring medical and hospital attention. . . . Heads were opened, eyes blackened and bodies thumped and battered as literally dozens of persons, young and old, many of them non-combatant spectators, were injured more or less seriously by a variety of ugly weapons in the hands of wild-eyed and irresponsible young hoodlums, both Jewish and Gentile.

Der Yiddisher Zhurnal's account was more moderate and put the blame for the violence squarely upon the swastika bearers, calling them Nazis:[41]

> Greater police detachments were called upon last evening in Willowvale Park on account of a fight which erupted between young Nazis and young Jews, and which threatened to assume a serious character. It was expected that the same gang which on the previous Monday incensed the Jewish players by displaying a swastika along with shouts of 'Heil Hitler' would once again attempt to cause trouble. And so it was . . .
>
> All was quiet until the end of the game, which the Gentile team won. As the crowd was dispersing, a group of Gentile boys celebrated the victory by

yelling insults at the Jews and they unfurled an old blanket, on which was painted a swastika.

After the Monday game, supporters of the Harbord Playground team had announced that they would be back in force for the return match on the following Wednesday. One Harbord fan reportedly told *The Toronto Daily Star*: 'We are not going to make trouble, but if anything happens we will be there to support our players'; the 'Willowvale Swastikas' (as that newspaper referred to the swastika bearers) were aware of that intention and they also mustered their supporters.[42] The predicted trouble was not long in erupting. Even before the game began, one Gentile spectator was reported to have required medical attention. The 'Swastika supporters' claimed that while they were cheering for the St Peter's team, a crowd of Jewish youths arrived and ordered them to be silent. 'Whatever the cause', *The Toronto Daily Star* of 17 August reported, there followed

> . . . a swiftly-ending free-for-all, with an unidentified swastika supporter requiring medical attention, the result, it is claimed, of a blow from a club, while one of the Jewish leaders was thrown down the hill into a cage back of the batter's box.

In the second inning, a second fracas occurred. It started in a section where a Jewish group was seated on the rising ground above the north-west diamond on which the game was being played; about thirty 'Willowvale Swastikas' yelled in unison 'Heil Hitler' close to where about a thousand Jewish supporters of the Harbord Playground team were positioned on the elevated site. Infuriated, the latter rushed towards those who had provoked them and a fight ensued in the course of which a spectator was struck with a sawn-off piece of lead pipe. A newspaper report the following day stated: 'Batons, lead pipes and other weapons were swinging freely'.[43]

The game was temporarily suspended while many of the spectators gathered around the battling groups. When play resumed, there were more yells of 'Heil Hitler' during the third inning and again violence erupted with supporters rushing to assistance of both sets of combatants. The police restored order and the game proceeded without further serious unrest until the end, when the St Peter's team won by 6-5. It was almost dark by then and before the crowd had dispersed there suddenly appeared at the top of the hill a large white blanket bearing a startling black swastika. *The Toronto Daily Star* reported that when the emblem was flaunted, 'a mild form of pandemonium broke loose'[44] and *The Evening Telegram* stated: 'In a moment all was turmoil'[45] and added that 'the sign stood out visible to the entire crowd and acted like a red rag to a bull';[46] the Jewish supporters immediately raced towards the hill, intent on capturing the hated Nazi banner and 'the swastika, the swastika' could be heard 'for blocks away'.[47] The 'Willowvale Swastikas' tried to repel the attack and very quickly the battle intensified. *The Globe* reported:[48]

The assault upon the swastika wielder was the signal for a general inrush of Gentile youths, who plied baseball bats and fists in a wild riot. By the time police reserves arrived the battle had gradually moved over to Bloor and Clinton Streets, where some serious casualties occurred, and where, it is alleged, bottles for the first time became legitimate weapons. From this battlefront, it is said, many injured limped away or were assisted to their various homes.

All four English-language newspapers and the Yiddish daily gave a great deal of space the next day (17 August) to their reports of the riot under alarming headlines. Those of *The Daily Mail and Empire* stated:

Scores Hurt as Swastika Mobs Riot at Willowvale
Mayor Promises Immediate Probe of Disturbance
Thousands Caught Up in Park Mêlée
Gang Wielding Lead Pipes and Bats Sweep Streets, Bludgeoning Victims

The Globe was more restrained:

Swastika Feud Battles in Toronto Injures 5
Fists, Boots, Piping Used in Bloor Street War
'Heil Hitler' Is Youth's Cry
City in Turmoil

The Toronto Daily Star claimed that Dennis Draper, Chief of the Toronto Police Department, had been advised earlier by the Parks Department that the baseball game would merit special police attention (but Mr Draper denied being warned that anything resembling a riot might occur):

Draper Admits Receiving Riot Warning
Six Hours of Rioting Follow Hitler Shout
Scores Hurt, Two Held

The Evening Telegram's headline stated:

Report Gunmen Here to Slay Swazis
Communists Incite Riot Police Authority States
Jewish Toughs Began Trouble Says Witness

while *Der Yiddisher Zhurnal* stated:

Swastika Attacks Give Rise to Great Panic in the City
Mayor Stewart Agrees to Take Swift Steps Against Nazis
Draper Asked to Report

If the swastika had not been flaunted at Willowvale Park, the Christie Pits riots would probably not have occurred. The deliberate display of a Nazi symbol was an irresistible provocation to the Jewish contingent because it was the final straw which broke the comparative restraint of those who had been subjected to less strident forms of anti-Semitism.

Conclusion

In his article entitled 'Civil Disorder Participation: A Critical Examination of Recent Research', McPhail successfully argues that in focusing on the 'states' or attitudes of individuals as causal variables in collective disorder, insufficient emphasis is placed on the conditions in the immediate surroundings which may contribute to the violence of a confrontation. In the Christie Pits riot, there were several factors which contributed to the affray apart from the flaunting of the swastika. First, whereas the police were present in considerable numbers at the Beaches, and were thus able to keep the crowds moving, they were conspicuously absent at Willowvale Park when the riot started despite warnings that trouble was anticipated. Second, in the earlier disturbances at the Beaches, young Jews could not quickly summon reinforcements since the Jewish area of the town was at that time some distance away; by contrast, Christie Pits was then on the edge of a Jewish enclave in Toronto. Third, as McPhail and Miller have noted,[49] an important condition for the initiation of civil disorder is the presence of a large number of people with a period of uncommitted time at their disposal;[50] the first baseball game drew large numbers of supporters of both the Jewish and Gentile teams. Fourth, after describing the violence at that game, the newspapers publicized the intention of the Jewish supporters to return in force for the second game in anticipation of trouble; that report must have spurred the leaders of the Gentile faction to muster their own reinforcements. Fifth, the attitudinal difference between the Jewish immigrant generation and their offspring in terms of reacting to the rising tide of anti-Semitism meant that the latter were less likely to be as accommodating as their parents to anti-Jewish sentiments and behaviour. Lacking their parents' memories and experiences of the anti-Semitism in eastern Europe, the young Jews who reacted physically to the swastika provocation considered their response to be entirely appropriate. By contrast, their parents' generation generally believed that the Gentile authorities, including elected officials and the police, could be entrusted to deal with the problems posed by the swastika and that they would responsibly fulfil their official duties. Negotiation with the Mayor's office as well as with representatives of the Swastika Clubs was the chosen route of Jewish officialdom, an approach which was judged decidedly unattractive by young Jewish men who relied instead on physical confrontation.

It was evident that the display of the swastika in Toronto in the summer of 1933 was a deliberate attempt by some young Gentiles to insult and provoke their Jewish contemporaries. Their pretence that the swastika was merely a good-luck symbol might have been more credible if its display had not been often accompanied with chants of 'Heil Hitler'. After the Christie Pits riot, Mayor Stewart banned the display of the swastika in public in the interest of 'peace, order and good government'.[51] The riot provided ample evidence that the younger generation of Toronto's Jewry would not meekly tolerate excessive forms of anti-Semitic abuse without resorting to violence. David Rome has commented[52] that a refugee from tsarist Russia, who was

> accustomed to the hostile glance of the passerby and the official, is not as likely to be injured by a similar meeting in Montreal. But his son who was taught in school and by his juvenile reading the decent expectations of western European and American equality, whose life is less tightly limited even by the invisible ghetto walls — this generation is likely to be stunned even by a static measure of hostility, especially when sensitized by shocking happenings overseas which can be readily transposed to his country.

Mayor Stewart's ban on the public display of the swastika in Toronto might have seemed an infringement of the civil liberties of the individual but there is a Canadian tradition of taking quick and firm action to avert the likelihood of collective violence and Mayor Stewart's decision accorded with that tradition.[53]

Notes

[1] See, for example, Richard A. Berk, 'The Controversy Surrounding Analyses of Collective Violence: Some Methodological Notes' in James F. Short, Jr and Marvin E. Wolfgang, eds, *Collective Violence* (Chicago, 1972): 112-18; Nathan S. Caplan and Jeffrey M. Paige, 'A Study of Ghetto Rioters', *Scientific American* 219, 2 (1968): 15-21; Kenneth B. Clark and James Barker, 'The Zoot Effect in Personality: A Race Riot Participant', *Journal of Abnormal and Social Psychology* 40, 2 (April 1945): 143-8; L. Festinger, A. Pepitone, and T. Newcomb, 'Some Consequences of De-individuation in a Group', *Journal of Abnormal and Social Psychology*, 47, 1 (April 1952): 382-9; Kerner Commission, *Report of the National Advisory Commission on Civil Disorder* (Washington, D.C., 1968); G. LeBon, *The Crowd*, (London, 1952); Stanley Lieberson and Arnold R. Silverman, 'The Precipitants and Underlying Conditions of Race Riots', *American Sociological Review* 30, 6 (December 1965): 887-98; William R. Morgan and Terry Nichols Clark, 'The Cause of Racial Disorders: A Grievance Level Explanation', *American Sociological Review* 38, 5 (October 1973): 611-24; A. Oberschall, *Social Conflict and Social Movements* (Englewood Cliffs, N.J., 1973); Jerome H. Skolniek, *The Politics of Protest* (New York, 1971); and Seymour Spilerman, 'The Causes of Racial Disturbances: Tests of an Explanation', *American Sociological Review* 36, 3 (June 1971): 427-42.

[2] Herbert Blumer, 'Collective Behavior' in Joseph B. Gitler, ed., *Review of Sociology: Analysis of a Decade* (New York, 1959): 127-58.

[3] See Herbert Blumer, 'Social Unrest and Collective Behavior' in Norman K. Denzin, ed., *Studies in Symbolic Interaction: An Annual Compilation of Research* (Greenwich, Conn., 1978): 1-54; Carl Couch, 'Collective Behavior: An Examination of Some Stereotypes', *Social Problems* 3 (Winter 1971): 310-22; Kurt Lang and Gladys Engel Lang, 'Collective Behavior Theory and the Escalated Riots of the Sixties' in Tamotsu Shibutani, ed., *Human Nature and Collective Behavior: Papers in Honor of Herbert Blumer* (Englewood Cliffs, N.J., 1970): 94-110; Clark McPhail, 'Civil Disorder Participation: A Critical Examination of Recent Research', *American Sociological Review* 36, 6 (December 1970): 1058-73; Clark McPhail and David Miller, 'The

Assembling Process: A Theoretical and Empirical Examination', *American Sociological Review* 38 (December 1971): 721-35; Enrico L. Quarantelli, 'Emergent Accommodation Groups: Beyond Current Collective Behaviour Typologies' in Tamotsu Shibutani, ed., *op. cit.*: 111-23; Neil J. Smelser, *Theory of Collective Behavior* (New York, 1963) Ralph H. Turner and Lewis K. Killian, *Collective Behavior* (New York, 1972); Ralph H. Turner and Samuel J. Surace, 'Zoot-Suiters and Mexicans: Symbols in Crowd Behavior', *American Journal of Sociology* 62 (1956): 14-20; and S. Wright, *Crowds and Riots: A Study in Social Organization* (Beverly Hills, 1978).

⁴Blumer, *op. cit.*: 17.

⁵Smelser, *op. cit.*: 16.

⁶This paper is based on research for a wider study which has been published in book form: Cyril Levitt and William Shaffir, *The Riot at Christie Pits* (Toronto, 1987).

⁷Blumer, *op. cit.*: 17.

⁸Turner and Killian, *op. cit.*: 48, come close to drawing this distinction in explaining the difference between cognitive and mystical symbols. In their view, 'the symbols most likely to gain currency in collective behavior are mystical rather than cognitive. They invest the object of the crowd action with an aura of infamy, of tragedy, or of nobility.'

⁹See Turner and Surace, *op. cit.*: 50.

¹⁰*Ibid.*

¹¹According to the 1988 edition of *The New Encyclopaedia Britannica*, the 'swastika as a symbol of prosperity and good fortune is widely distributed throughout the ancient and modern world. The word is derived from the Sanskrit *svastika*, meaning "conducive to well-being". . . . In 1910 a poet and nationalist ideologist Guido von List had suggested the swastika as a symbol for all anti-Semitic organizations; and when the National Socialist Party was formed in 1919-20, it adopted it. On September 15, 1935, the black swastika on a white circle with a crimson background became the national flag of Germany.'

¹²See Stephen A. Speisman, *The Jews of Toronto: A History to 1937* (Toronto, 1979): 318-19.

¹³See Lita-Rose Betcherman, *The Little Band* (Ottawa, 1982): 50-1.

¹⁴See Arnold Ages, 'Antisemitism: The Uneasy Calm' in Morton Weinfeld, William Shaffir, and Irwin Cotler, eds, *The Canadian Jewish Mosiac* (Toronto, 1981): 387.

¹⁵See Speisman, *op. cit.*: 318-19.

¹⁶See Yaacov Glickman, 'Anti-Semitism and Jewish Social Cohesion in Canada' in Rita M. Bienvenue and Jay E. Goldstein, eds, *Ethnicity and Ethnic Relations in Canada: A Book of Readings*, 2nd edn (Toronto, 1985): 267.

¹⁷For an extensive discussion of anti-Semitism in Canada during the 1930s, consult the following sources: Irving Abella and Harold Troper, *None is Too Many* (Toronto, 1933); Ages, *op. cit.* N. 14 above: 383-95; Lita-Rose Betcherman, *The Swastika and the Maple Leaf* (Toronto, 1975), and *The Little Band, op. cit.*; Glickman, *op. cit.* N. 16

above: 263-84; David Rome, *Clouds in the Thirties: Antisemitism in Canada 1929-1939*, sections 1-13 (Montreal, 1977); and Speisman, *op. cit.*

[18]*Der Yiddisher Zhurnal*, 13 February 1933: 1.

[19]*Ibid.*, 24 February 1933: 1.

[20]*Ibid.*, 3 March 1933: 1.

[21]*Ibid.*, 7 April 1933: 1.

[22]*Ibid.*, 24 April 1933: 1.

[23]*Ibid.*, 1 August 1933: 1.

[24]*The Toronto Daily Star*, 27 March 1933: 1.

[25]*Ibid.*, 29 March 1933: 1.

[26]*Ibid.*, 5 April 1933: 1.

[27]*Ibid.*, 28 April 1933: 1.

[28]*The Evening Telegram*, 1 August 1933: 1.

[29]*The Daily Mail and Empire*, 2 August 1933: 1.

[30]*The Toronto Daily Star*, 2 August 1933: 1.

[31]*Ibid.*: 11.

[32]*Ibid.*

[33]*The Daily Mail and Empire*, 2 August 1933: 1.

[34]*Ibid.*

[35]*The Evening Telegram*, 2 August 1933: 1-2.

[36]*The Toronto Daily Star*, 7 August 1933: 1.

[37]*Ibid.*, 9 August 1933: 1.

[38]Estimates of the size of the crowd in the Pits that evening ranged from 600-15,000 as reported by *Der Yiddisher Zhurnal* of 18 August; *The Toronto Daily Star* of 17 August reported that 10,000 people were in the park on the night of the riot, while *The Daily Mail and Empire* placed the figure at 'more than 8,000' in its 17 August edition. Realistically, it is likely that at least 2,000 to 3,000 were in the park when the riot broke out. Of these, probably no more than several hundred actively participated in the physical violence, although many other undoubtedly shouted encouragement to one side or the other.

[39]*The Daily Mail and Empire*, 17 August 1933: 1.

[40]*The Toronto Daily Star*, 17 August 1933: 1.

[41]*Der Yiddisher Zhurnal*, 17 August 1933: 1.

[42]*The Toronto Daily Star*, 17 August 1933: 1.

[43]*Ibid.*: 3.

[44]*Ibid.*: 1.

[45]*The Evening Telegram*, 17 August 1933: 1.

[46]*Ibid.*

[47]*Ibid.*

[48]*The Globe*, 17 August 1933: 1.

[49]Clark McPhail and David Miller, *op. cit.*: 725.

[50]*Ibid.*: 726.

[51]See *The Daily Mail and Empire*, 17 August 1933: 1. This resulted in some embarrassment for a number of the city's organizations. In a story entitled 'Must Not Flaunt Swastika Is Warning Of Boy Scouts', *The Toronto Daily Star* reported on 18 August, on its front page, that Toronto Boy Scouts' headquarters warned all recipients of the Scouts' 'Thank You Badge'—a swastika cross surmounted by the fleur-de-lys, given to friends of scouting for some exceptional deed—'against flaunting the badge in public until the current feeling against the Hitler symbol has died down'. The Toronto Library Board had to decide what to do about the swastika emblems decorating the thousands of Kipling volumes in their public libraries. It was decided not to remove the emblem. Toronto motor-cycle police unwittingly defied the Mayor's ban on the emblem since they were unaware that the swastika was stamped on the keys to the lockers at the police motor-cycle depot.

[52]See David Rome, *op. cit.*, Section 3: 10.

[53]See Kenneth McNaught, 'Violence in Canadian History' in John S. Moir, ed., *Character and Circumstance* (Toronto, 1970): 66-84.

Hate on Trial: The Zundel Affair,

The Media, Public Opinion in Canada

Gabriel Weimann

and Conrad Winn

The Impact of the Trial

The central purpose of this study has been to assess whether the trial produced a 'boomerang' effect. For a major boomerang effect to have occurred, a large proportion of Canadians ought to have been aware of the trial. The preceding chapter (of *Hate on Trial*) showed that only half of Canada's inhabitants were aware of the trial. Noting the kinds of people who were aware of the trial as opposed to those who were not, the chapter pointed to the possibility that the trial may not have affected public opinion in the way feared by many commentators.

Our survey contained several questions designed to measure the impact of the trial on respondents' feelings. The single most direct question was the following: '*Has the Zundel trial made you feel more sympathetic or less sympathetic towards Jews?*' A similarly worded question was also asked in order to help reveal how attitudes towards Germans might have been affected. Asking people if a major event changed their feelings about a group of people is not a perfect way of finding out if the event did in fact change their feelings. For example, people who were sympathetic to Jews from the outset might report becoming more sympathetic as a result of Zundel whereas in fact they may have simply remained highly sympathetic as before. People hostile to Jews may report no change in affection since, from their perspective, the Holocaust denial voiced in the courtroom justified their long-standing animosity. In spite of the limitations of our survey question, the answers to this question can be revealing. We had at our disposal some ways of circumventing the weakness of the question, as we shall show in a moment.

According to the testimony of our respondents, the trial did not affect the feeling of most people but was much more likely to increase than to decrease sympathy for Jews. Half (47 per cent) of the respondents said that their feeling towards Jews remained unchanged. One-fourth (26 per cent) reported that they did not know how their feelings were affected while one fourth (24 per cent) said that they became more sympathetic. Only a negligible number (2 per cent) reported the reverse effect, i.e., becoming less sympathetic to Jews (see Table 1).

It is possible that some of those who reported no change in their sympathy for Jews as a result of the trial were simply too unaware of the trial to be affected by it. To explore this possibility, we focused on those who were well informed about the case, i.e., those who knew why Zundel was convicted. The proportion of all Canadians who did not know how their feelings were affected by the trial was one-fourth as contrasted with only 2 per cent among those who followed the trial (Table 1). It is not surprising that those who did not know about the trial tended not to know how the trial had affected their feelings. Indeed, the fact that virtually all of those who knew why Zundel was convicted knew how their feelings had been affected suggests that asking respondents about the reason for the conviction was an effective way of identifying those whose feelings were influenced by the event.

Respondents were more apt to say that they became more sympathetic to Jews if they followed the trial than if they did not. The proportion who reported becoming more sympathetic to Jews was 34 per cent among people who were aware of the trial as compared to 24 per cent among Canadians as a whole. Whether or not people were aware of the trial, the proportion saying that they had become less sympathetic to Jews remained negligible.

Given that Canadians said that they were much more likely to feel more favourable towards Jews as a result of the trial, how did the trial affect their attitudes towards Germans? To see if the trial had affected attitudes towards Germans, interviewers asked respondents the following question, 'Has the Zundel trial made you feel more sympathetic or less sympathetic towards Germans?' Once again, most people said that their views remained unchanged or that they did not know how their views had changed. But, among those reporting a change, far more people reported becoming less sympathetic rather than more sympathetic (14 per cent vs 4 per cent). The tendency to become less sympathetic towards Germans was especially strong among those who were aware of the trial. Among Canadians who knew why Zundel had been convicted, virtually everyone reported knowing how the trial had affected his/her feelings towards Germans. The largest group continued to report no change in feelings. But, among those whose feelings had changed, the anti-Germans outnumbered the pro-Germans by a ratio of three to one (16 per cent vs 5 per cent).

To summarize to this point, the largest group of Canadians reported no change in feelings towards Jews or Germans. The relative proportion of 'no changes' and 'don't knows' diminished sharply as we focused on those Canadians who could recall what the trial was about. Many newspaper commentators feared that Zundel would be successful in his avowed goal of using the courtroom as a platform for disseminating hate against Jews. *In fact, he was more successful in disseminating animosity against Germans.* Among

Table 1 Attitudes towards Jews and Germans after the Zundel Trial (in per cent)

CHANGE IN SYMPATHY TOWARDS JEWS		CHANGE IN SYMPATHY TOWARDS GERMANS	
ALL RESPONDENTS (N = 1045)	KNOWLEDGEABLE RESPONDENTS (N = 527)	ALL RESPONDENTS (N = 1043)	KNOWLEDGEABLE RESPONDENTS (N = 526)
more 24	more 34	more 4	more 5
less 2	less 3	less 14	less 16
same 47	same 61	same 54	same 75
dk 26	dk 1	dk 28	dk 4

respondents reporting a change of sympathy, 92 per cent reported an *increase* in sympathy for Jews while 79 per cent reported a *decrease* in sympathy for Germans. (See Table 1.)

The animosity against Germans aroused by the trial is explained partly by the fact that Zundel himself was a German national and partly by the fact that responsibility for the Holocaust rested mainly with the German state. Zundel made no secret of his identification with and love for Germany. This fact may go some distance in accounting for the increase in anti-German sentiment among the Canadian public. Had a survey asked Canadians the same question after the conviction of the Canadian-born James Keegstra, it might have shown that Keegstra's conviction aroused less anti-German feeling.

The way in which the mass media reported both the trial and Holocaust news unrelated to the trial may have contributed to anti-German feeling as well. The media focused on the death camps and on the role of the German state in their creation and operation. With the notable exception of the CBC *Journal*'s special series on the Holocaust collaboration of Vichy France aired in 1984, the media generally avoided a discussion of the role of the Axis powers, the peoples conquered by them, and the behaviour of the Allies. The absence of a cross-national perspective may have left innocent media consumers the mistaken impression that anti-Judaism was mainly or exclusively a German problem. Futhermore, the absence of historical perspective may have left some media consumers with the impression that anti-Judaism began with the birth of the Nazi party.

The relative absence of cross-national and historical perspective in Holocaust stories results from the customary methods of operation of the press and television. Both media focus on recent, discrete events, rather than an unfolding process of events which may have taken place sometime ago. Newspapers attract readers by offering clearly written reports on the essential facts of yesterday's news, not by offering comprehensive accounts of complex events which took place decades earlier. Television news attracts viewers, especially the marginal clients for news, by offering dramatic visual

Table 2   Changes in Sympathy towards Jews by Province (column percentages)

	NFLD	NS	NB	QUE.
More sympathetic	13	20	20	17
Less sympathetic	7	0	0	1
Same — not affected	13	60	33	35
Don't know	68	20	48	47
Column Total	100%	100%	100%	100%
(N)	(31)	(30)	(40)	(264)

footage, not by offering profound and therefore long-winded analyses of complex phenomena. It is difficult for broadcasters and newspapers seeking mass audiences to offer the same degree of comprehensiveness, subtlety, and therefore objectivity which may be expected of university history courses.

Attitudes towards Jews — Who Changed?

What kinds of people became more sympathetic to Jews and what kinds were unaffected by the trial or became less sympathetic? Although few in number, those who became less sympathetic to Jews are relatively easy to describe. Those few who reported becoming less sympathetic were similar in profile to those kinds of people who were most apt to be unaware that the trial took place. In the category of people who became less sympathetic were francophones, people of limited education, young people, and respondents living in Newfoundland or Alberta. We are unable to say how the increased negative feelings among a minority of Albertans may have been related to the difficulties in Eckville. Ex-history teacher James Keegstra and his friends may have succeeded in disseminating their racist views among a minority of Albertans. Or, Keegstra and his friends may have reflected a facet of Alberta's once strong Social Credit movement. A Social Credit fringe group had occasionally produced a bizarre mixture of anti-Communist, anti-capitalist, anti-secular, anti-Jewish, and anti-Catholic rhetoric.[1]

Those respondents in our national survey who reported becoming more sympathetic to Jews were similar to those who were aware of the trial in that they tended to be English-speakers and residents of British Columbia, Saskatchewan, or Ontario. Residents of these three provinces tended to follow the trial and, whether or not they followed the trial, tended to become more sympathetic to Jews (see Table 2). Elderly people (those over 60), high school graduates, and women tended also to become more sympathetic. Although women were less informed of the trial than men, women reported becoming more sympathetic to Jews than did men.

People who said that their feelings about Jews remained unchanged tended to be males, younger than 60 years old, anglophones, university educated, and residents of Alberta and Nova Scotia. The unchanging response of

ONT.	MAN.	SASK.	ALTA	BC	ROW TOTAL
28	25	32	20	35	25%
2	3	4	7	0	2%
53	43	60	59	53	47%
17	30	4	14	12	26%
100%	100%	100%	100%	100%	100%
(369)	(40)	(50)	(99)	(122)	

university graduates makes sense since these people were most apt to be well informed about the Holocaust before the trial began. Even those university graduates who were not previously informed might not wish to reveal that their feelings had changed and thereby acknowledge indirectly that they had not been terribly knowledgeable before.

The Impacts of the Eichmann and Zundel Trials

The impact of the Eichmann trial on sympathy for Jews reveals some similarity with the Zundel trial. Neither conviction produced a 'boomerang' or negative effect. Virtually the same numbers of Canadians and Americans reported that their feelings remained unchanged — 46 per cent vs 47 per cent. The same percentage — 2 per cent — reported becoming less sympathetic to Jews in each case. Half of the respondents in both cases said that their feelings had remained unchanged by events. In the Zundel case, we showed that almost all of those whose feelings had been unaffected by the trial were those who had been unaware of the trial. Perhaps in the Eichmann case, too, those who were unmoved were unaware.

One difference between the two trials is that the Americans were more apt than the Canadians to indicate sympathy for Jews — 37 per cent vs 24 per cent. The greater indication of sympathy for Jews in the Eichmann case may stem from the nature of the defendant. Eichmann planned and administered murder on a vast scale. He was a major actor in history. To say that he was a mass murderer does not do justice to the magnitude of his evil. Zundel was a minor publicist and propagandist. At his worst, it can be said of Zundel that he sought to create a climate of opinion in which the murder of Jews would be viewed as justifiable.

The greater sympathy elicited by the Eichmann trial may also stem from differences of national cultures. Jews and Judaism have long occupied a slightly less pejorative place in American culture for reasons having to do with the religious roots of early Pilgrim settlement. The Puritans were fugitives from religious persecution who identified with other victims of religious oppression. As 'Old Testament' men and women, the Puritans saw themselves as early Israelites fleeing the oppression of Egypt's Pharaoh. For the Puritans, Europe was Egypt. The Atlantic ocean was the Sinai desert. America was the promised land, Zion, the new Jerusalem. The Puritans, it may be remembered, were the theological descendants of Oliver Cromwell, under whose rule England readmitted Jews after a long period of exclusion. Cromwell's supporters contemplated adopting Hebrew as England's national language and returning the sabbath to Saturday. The Puritans of New England searched throughout the Old Testament or Hebrew Bible for ways of giving meaning to their experience. At the Continental Congress in 1776, Benjamin Franklin proposed for the Great Seal a portrait of Moses dividing the Red Sea and the Pharaoh drowning while Thomas Jefferson proposed a portrait of the children of Israel struggling through the wilderness.

The Hebraic theological roots of early America led to laws and practices which made life in America somewhat less oppressive for Jews than in Europe. Rhode Island and other states settled by the Puritans led in the granting of equal voting and citizenship rights to Jews. By the middle of the nineteenth century, the United States government was the principal international spokesman for oppressed Jewish minorities in central and Eastern Europe. A century before Presidents Jimmy Carter and Ronald Reagan would ask the Kremlin to permit Russian Jews to emigrate, Washington was asking the Czar to bring an end to pogroms (massacres). In the nineteenth century, a significant minority of American Protestants were active proponents of Zionism.[2]

Before dwelling at too great a length on the possible cultural differences between the two countries, it is important to realize that English Canadians are not as different from Americans as our survey data seem to imply. The main reason why only 24 per cent of Canadians reported an increased sympathy for Jews is the relative lack of sympathy for Jews among French Canadians. As many as 37 per cent indicated increased sympathy in the American study as compared to 31 per cent among respondents in the English-speaking provinces and 17 per cent in Quebec. We shall return to a discussion of French-speaking Canadians later in our analysis.

Anti-Judaism Before and After the Trial

Above, we examined the attitudinal impact of the Canadian trial by analysing the changed sympathies of respondents as reported by the respondents themselves. Yet, it is an axiom in the social sciences that people should not always be believed. Respondents may not be conscious of how their feelings have changed. Alternately, they may be fully aware of their feelings and consciously choose not to tell the truth. In order to overcome the liability of relying on what respondents tell us, we resorted to an additional method.

Our survey asked respondents the following question: '*Would you say that Jews have too much power, just enough power, or not enough power in Canada?*'

Asking this question after the trial enabled us to see if the trial had made a difference in the magnitude of anti-Judaism because the very same question had been asked before. The League for Human Rights of B'nai Brith had set out to study anti-Judaism in Canada during the early 1980s. In 1983 and again in 1984, the League carried out nation-wide surveys with samples of 2011 and 2038 people.[3]

Table 3 compares the responses of Canadian adults to the very same question in the years 1983 and 1984, before the trial, and in 1985, just after the conviction. Such a year-to-year comparison is one of the better ways to measure the trial's overall impact because it is more immune to misleading answers by respondents. The risk of asking people at one point in time how they had felt in the past is that they may not remember their previous feelings with much accuracy. The three years of data support the main thrust of our earlier contention, namely that the trial did not increase the magnitude of anti-Jewish feeling in Canada.

The distribution of anti-Jewish opinions did not change significantly from 1983 to 1984 or from 1984 to 1985. In 1985, the proportion of people who thought that Jews held too much power appeared to increase by three percentage points, from 12 per cent to 15 per cent. However, this change is within the range of sampling error or chance variation. The apparent increase in anti-Judaism in 1985 may be more apparent than real. The increase of 3 per cent may be too small to deserve mention just as the decrease of 2 per cent in the previous year may also be too small to be interpreted as more than a sampling accident. The fact that 12-15 per cent of the Canadian people are anti-Jewish may be alarming, but this proportion appears stable and unaffected by the Zundel trial.

In September 1985, after both the Zundel and Keegstra trials, the League for Human Rights of B'nai Brith carried out its regular annual survey of ethnocentricism. The survey found that 16 per cent of Canadians perceived Jews to be too powerful. The September 1985 figure of 16 per cent is 1 per cent higher than our March 1985 figure, 4 per cent higher than in 1984, and 2 per cent higher than in 1983. The 15 per cent-16 per cent figures for 1985 may be interpreted in a number of different ways. First, the 15 per cent-16 per cent figures for 1985 may be only chance variations of no fundamental importance. Secondly, the 15 per cent-16 per cent figures in 1985 may be short-term fluctuations, reflecting the momentary irritation of some Canadians at the relatively high volume of Jewish news in the media. Thirdly, the 15 per cent-16 per cent figures may reflect an actual increase in hardcore anti-Jewish prejudice in 1985, whatever the reason for this increase. Fourthly, the 15-16 per cent figures may reflect an increase in hardcore anti-Jewish prejudice brought about by the hate trials.

Our analysis suggests that either the 15 per cent-16 per cent figures are chance variations or that a few Canadians were driven to express anti-Jewish prejudice by their irritation at the volume of Jewish news in the media. The League for Human Rights' September 1985 survey yielded evidence that

Table 3 Annual Changes in Perceived Power of Jews, 1983-85 (in per cent)

	TOO MUCH POWER	JUST ENOUGH POWER
1983	14	50
1984	12	56
1985	15	51

Source: For 1983 and 1984 data, *The Review of Anti-Semitism in Canada, 1984.*

hardcore prejudice remained stable during the year. Respondents were asked if they would vote for a Jewish candidate of their favourite political party. The responses in autumn, 1985 were almost identical to those given in 1984.[4] Our own data suggest futhermore that the Zundel trial did not increase anti-Jewish prejudice. Those respondents who followed the trial were less prejudiced than those who did not. Among those respondents reporting that their feelings about Jews were affected by the trial, an overwhelming majority reported becoming more sympathetic.

The proportion of Canadians who believe that Jews have too much power is comparable to current American figures. In the mid-1960s a national US study reported that 11 per cent of respondents believed that Jews are too powerful. This was a marked decline from the 44 per cent of Americans who thought that Jews were too powerful in the late 1940s, shortly after the Holocaust.[5]

The 12-16 per cent of respondents who believe that Jews are too powerful is comparable to the findings on this subject which were unearthed by Goldfarb Consultants, the survey research firm.[6] Martin Goldfarb's firm conducted a national survey in 1984 on behalf of the Canada-Israel Committee to determine attitudes towards Jews, Israel, and the Middle East. Given 1000 respondents, the questionnaire included questions on the perceived influence of Jews in business, politics, the media, government, and a category called 'wealth and resources'. The proportion of Canadians who felt that Jews have too much power varied from 11 per cent to 22 per cent depending on the field. Eleven per cent believed that Jews have too much influence in the media and government as compared to 12 per cent in politics, 19 per cent in wealth and resources, and 22 per cent in business.

Holocaust Denial

Another method of measuring the impact of the trial is to explore if Canadians are beginning to doubt whether the Holocaust took place as described in official government documents and in the studies conducted by scholars. Readers may recall that Zundel used the prolonged trial to cast repeated doubt on the Holocaust. Day after day, in court, the unbelievable questions were repeated. Did the Holocaust really happen? Did six million really die?

Table 4 Knowledge of the Trial and Doubts about the Holocaust (in per cent)

AGREE THAT SIX MILLION DIED		HOLD JEWS BLAMELESS	
knowledgeable of the trial (N = 527)	not knowledgeable of the trial (N = 525)	knowledgeable of the trial (N = 527)	not knowledgeable of the trial (N = 525)
61	40	70	50

Were there gas chambers? Did smoke come out of the chimneys? Could zyklon B (i.e., cyanide) really kill people? These questions were central to Zundel's leaflet, *Did Six Million Really Die?*, and his many other publications. They were raised in the courtroom by the defendant's lawyer, Douglas Christie, and then reported coast-to-coast in the Canadian media.

One of the purposes of raising doubts about the Holocaust was simply to make the case that it had not occurred or that the conventional understanding was enormously exaggerated. Another conceivable purpose of raising doubts about the Holocaust was to arouse the hostility against Jews, to suggest that they fabricated the whole event for personal gain or to suggest that whatever misfortune they actually did experience was of their own doing. We asked the following question: *'Do you think that the persecution of the Jews was mostly their fault, partly their fault, or not all their fault?'*

A large minority chose an apparently neutral or a clearly unsympathetic answer to this question. *Only 60 per cent of Canadians held Jews blameless for their dispossession and murder during World War II.* As many as 16 per cent said that it was 'partly' their own fault. Almost one-fourth—23 per cent—stated that they did not know how to apportion responsibility.

We also sought people's views about the magnitude of casualties. The question was worded as follows: *'According to official estimates six million Jews were killed in the Holocaust. Do you think this estimate is too high, about right, or too low?'*

Once again, a large minority chose an apparently neutral or clearly unsympathetic answer. *Barely half of Canadians agreed that six million Jews actually died.* Fifteen per cent believed that the estimate was too high. Another 28 per cent indicated that they did not know. These are indeed unpleasant findings, but they are not a consequence of the Zundel trial.

We compared people who were aware of the trial and people who were not with respect to how they assigned responsibility for the Holocaust and how they felt about the estimate of six million. Table 4 shows that people who were aware of the trial were *less* likely to express anti-Jewish views. The proportion of Canadians who agreed that the official estimate of six million deaths was right was only 40 per cent among those unaware of the trial but as high as 61 per cent among those who were aware. Those who either blamed Jews or believed that fewer than six million died were apt to be unable to

Table 5 *Holocaust Doubts after Eichmann and Zundel Trials*

	AFTER EICHMANN TRIAL — TOTAL US SAMPLE	AFTER ZUNDEL TRIAL — TOTAL SAMPLE	AFTER ZUNDEL TRIAL — ONLY THOSE AWARE
Jewish Persecution			
partly Jews' fault	30	16	18
mostly Jews' fault	+2 = 32	+1 = 17	+1 = 19
not all Jews' fault	53	60	70
don't know	15	23	11
	100%	100%	100%
Official Estimate of Six Million is			
about right	36	50	61
too high	42	15	13
too low	13	6	7
don't know	9	28	19
	100%	100%	100%

explain why Zundel's trial took place. Those Canadians who believed that reports about the Holocaust were exaggerated and who therefore were potentially most receptive to Holocaust-denial propaganda held their views before the trial took place. Those most receptive to Holocaust-denial propaganda were not affected by the trial because they were unaware of it.

A comparison with the Eichmann trial shows that Canadians today are more informed about the Holocaust than were Americans in the 1960s. Table 5 shows that Americans were more likely than Canadians to hold Jews responsible for their misfortune and more likely to believe that the estimate of six million is exaggerated. Thus, 32 per cent of Americans held Jews at least partly responsible as compared to only 17 per cent among Canadians. As may as 42 per cent of American respondents in the American study believed that the six million estimate was too high as compared to only 15 per cent among Canadians.

How can the greater willingness of Americans to blame Jews and to underestimate their human losses be reconciled with the evidence, discussed earlier, that Americans were more apt to report increased sympathy? On the one hand, a larger *majority* of Americans expressed feelings of increased sympathy. On the other hand, a larger *minority* of Americans than Canadians blamed Jews for their own misery and underplayed the loss of life. One possible explanation is that the American people are more polarized on the Jewish question as they often are on other questions. The greater polarization of the American respondents is one of a number of possible explanations for the different findings in the two studies. However, given the smaller size of the American sample of respondents and the fact that the American study was not national in scope, excessive effort should not be devoted to account-

Table 6 How Many Canadians Now Believe that We Should Question the Record of the Holocaust? (in per cent; N = 1043)

almost none	a few	many	don't know
23	30	13	33

ing for differences between the two countries which may be more apparent than real.

The 'Climate of Doubt'

One of the paradoxes in the analysis of public opinion is that people may hold one opinion but believe—incorrectly sometimes—that other people hold another opinion. In elections, candidates can often give an impression of greater support than they actually have by the intensive use of campaign signs and the clever use of the mass media. To this point, we have shown that Canadians did not become more anti-Jewish as a result of the trial and its 'one million dollars of free publicity'. They did not begin to doubt the record of the Holocaust as a result of the urgings of the proponents of Holocaust denial. Among Canadians aware of the trial, fewer people said that they did not know how many Jews were killed and more people accepted the conventional record of the period. However, do Canadians believe that their fellow citizens also see the world as they do?

We asked respondents the following question: '*The media have talked a lot about the doubts and questions raised by Mr Zundel over the past few weeks. In your opinion, are there a few Canadians, many Canadians, or almost no Canadians who now believe we should seriously question the historical records of this period?*' Table 6 portrays the distribution of responses to this question.

Most respondents feel that at least *some* other Canadians now have doubts. Thirteen per cent believe that 'many' people have doubts. As many as 30 per cent believe that 'a few' have doubts. Thirty-three per cent do not know if other people have doubts. Fewer than one out of every four respondents—23 per cent—express the view that 'almost no one' doubts the existence of the Holocaust.

It is difficult to know with confidence if the trial caused people to attribute doubts about the Holocaust to their fellow citizens. An ideal way of ascertaining whether the trial caused the doubts would be to compare our findings with reported doubts in national surveys carried out before the trial. However, previous national surveys did not ask Canadians if they thought that other people had doubts about the existence of the Holocaust. The existence of death camps was not widely debated in the media before Ernst Zundel was charged in the courts.

Our own data suggests that people were led to attribute doubts to other Canadians as a result of the trial. We compared the responses of those who knew what the trial was about with the responses of those who did not. *Those who knew why Zundel was convicted were almost twice as likely to attribute doubt to other people as those who did not know why he was convicted, even though people who knew why he was convicted were much less likely to harbour doubts about the Holocaust themselves.* The proportion of respondents who thought that either 'a few' or 'many' Canadians would now have doubts about how the Holocaust occurred was as high as 55 per cent among those informed about the trial and only 31 per cent among those who were uninformed.

When this finding is matched with our previously reported findings, we are able to create the following portrait of the overall impact of the trial. The trial increased somewhat public knowledge about the Holocaust and engendered greater sympathy for Jews while, at the same time, it led people to believe that their neighbours were moving in the opposite direction.

Of course, we cannot be totally and absolutely certain that the trial itself prompted people to believe that their neighbours now doubted the Holocaust. Canadians who were aware of the trial were not a cross-section of society. Readers will remember that Canadians knowledgeable of the trial tended to be English-speaking, well educated, older, male, and residents of British Columbia, Ontario, Saskatchewan. Perhaps people who were knowledgeable of the trial were pessimistic people who normally attributed doubt to other people or perhaps they were thinking about people with less education than themselves. We tried many varieties of statistical analysis to see if we could find any evidence for explanation for attributing doubt other than the trial. But we could find no such evidence. People who were knowledgeable of the trial were in fact more likely to believe — incorrectly — that more Canadians now doubt the historical record of the Holocaust. The fact that our more informed respondents were apt to distrust their neighbours' ability to think helps to explain why the journalists and experts were so certain that the trial would be a propaganda coup for neo-Naziism.

Not all of the respondents aware of the trial were equally certain that the trial would engender doubts in the minds of their neighbours. The more pro-Jewish respondents showed a slight tendency to be more confident of their neighbours. Most respondents (61 per cent) held Jews blameless for their victimization. Only 16 per cent said that Jews were 'partly at fault' and only 1 per cent said that they were 'mostly at fault'. Among Canadians who held Jews entirely blameless, 28 per cent said that no one would doubt the record of the Holocaust. The corresponding figures were 20% and 13% among people who held Jews partly or wholly responsible. Half of our respondents (51 per cent) thought that the accepted estimate of six million casualties was correct. Those who accepted the estimate were more likely to think that no one now doubts the record of the Holocaust than were those who thought the estimate too high (30 per cent vs 18 per cent).

At first glance, the fact that the trial made people misjudge their neighbours may seem unimportant. As long as the trial increased the public's understanding of the cataclysm, does it matter that people now think that their fellow citizens are moving in the opposite direction? The simple answer is that it does matter. It matters because people do not like to live in social isolation. People may fear being rejected socially or even being disadvantaged at work as a result of expressing unpopular beliefs. Initially, people who hold views which they perceive to be unpopular minority opinions may hesitate to share these views in public. Eventually, they may moderate their views or lose interest in the subject. People who belong to the initial minority may be emboldened to express their views more often and with greater enthusiasm as they observe the reticence of the majority. People who initially have no strong opinion may gradually adopt the views which they hear expressed more often and which they perceive to be the most popular and therefore the most convincing. As a result of these processes, opinions which were once held only by a minority can in due course become the opinion of the majority.[7] In the particular case of the Zundel affair, if people continue to believe — for the moment, wrongly — that their neighbours acquired doubts about the Holocaust, more and more doubts would be expressed about the Holocaust and the 'revisionist' perspective would eventually prevail.[8]

The dangers of the 'climate of doubt' are real. When people think that their neighbours have begun to doubt the official record of the Holocaust, they may begin to express doubts themselves. Our data show that Canadians who hold Jews blameless for the calamity are less apt to perceive their fellow citizens as doubters than do Canadians who blame Jews. How can we explain the link between blaming Jews for the Holocaust and believing that more Canadians now doubt the record of that period? It is possible that once people decide to hold Jews responsible for their victimization, they then jump to the conclusion that other people must also have reservations about the accepted view of this chapter in European history. However, it is also plausible that many people decide to hold Jews responsible after concluding that increasing numbers of Canadians are questioning the official record of this period.

In election campaigns, the 'bandwagon effect' is the term used to describe how some voters cast their eyes about to discover which train will reach the station first and, then, jump aboard. Politicians use lawn signs, television commercials, and declarations of support from known personalities to persuade voters that their train is going to reach the station first. The mass media tell people which politicians are winning and which opinions are prevailing. The media are less influential on contemporary and local issues such as highway construction, where the average citizen can readily observe whether more roads are needed. But the media are vital in issues such as the Holocaust which are far removed geographically and historically from the life experience of the average Canadian.

★ ★ ★

The trial of Ernst Zundel and the attendant publicity did not succeed in persuading Canadians of the virtues of Holocaust denial as feared by newspaper columnists, civil libertarians, Jewish leaders, and others worried about bringing him to trial. The trial did not penetrate very broadly into the mind of the public. Our single national survey yielded evidence that Canadians became more sympathetic to Jews. Respondents were much more likely to report becoming more sympathetic to Jews rather than less, especially in the case of respondents who were aware of the trial. Presumably, people who were already sympathetic or emotionally neutral before the trial became more sympathetic after. People aware of the trial were more likely to accept the historical record of the period and were more likely to hold Jews blameless for their persecution. But people aware of the trial were more likely to think that their neighbours now had doubts about the Holocaust. A comparison with surveys conducted in 1983 and 1984 shows that the ranks of the prejudiced hardcore grew little, if at all. According to the data, if the prejudiced hardcore grew slightly, this was likely not a result of the Zundel trial.

Ironically, the propensity to deny the Holocaust was strongest among those unaware of the trial and therefore predated Zundel's intensive media exposure. The fact that anti-Jewish attitudes, including Holocaust denial, existed before the trial suggests that the broader sources of anti-Judaism in society should be explored.

Notes

[1] C.B. MacPherson, *Democracy in Alberta* (Toronto: University of Toronto Press, 1962): 283-4 and Michael B. Stein, *The Dynamics of Right-Wing Protest* (Toronto: University of Toronto Press, 1973): 49-50. In September 1985, after Keegstra's trial in Alberta, the League for Human Rights conducted a national survey to measure anti-Jewish and other ethnocentric sentiments. The survey results provided some evidence that the trial increased slightly anti-Jewish sentiments in that province. Respondents were asked, as in previous League surveys, if they would be willing to vote for a candidate for office who happened to be Jewish. Canadians as a whole were willing in 1985 as in 1984 to vote for a Jewish candidate, but Albertans were slightly less willing. Albertans were no less willing in 1985 than in 1984 to vote for candidates of other ethnic minorities. Our appreciation to Professors Stephen Scheinberg and Taylor Buckner for drawing this to our attention. A report on the September, 1985 dataset is to appear in a forthcoming issue of *The Review of Anti-Semitism in Canada*.

[2] For an extraordinary account of the Biblical appeal of Zionism for American Protestants from John Adams to Harry Truman, see Peter Grose, *Israel in the Mind of America* (New York: Alfred A. Knopf, 1984).

[3] See H. Taylor Buckner, 'A Study of Canadian Attitudes towards Jews, Italians, and Poles — A Preliminary Comparative Analysis, 1983 and 1984', *The Review of Anti-Semitism in Canada: 1984* (Downsview: League for Human Rights of B'nai Brith, 1985): table 7.

[4] Our appreciation to Professor Taylor Buckner, Professor Stephen Scheinberg, and Arthur Hiess for this information.

[5]See Gertrude J. Selznick and Stephen Steinberg, *The Tenacity of Prejudice: Anti-Semitism in Contemporary America* (New York: Harper and Row, 1969) and Nathan Perlmutter and Ruth Ann Perlmutter, *The Real Anti-Semitism in America* (New York: Arbor House, 1982).

[6]Goldfarb Consultants, 'Perception of Jews, Israel and the Middle East', a research report prepared for the Canada-Israel Committee (May, 1983).

[7]The West German pollster, Elizabeth Noelle-Neuman, has termed 'spiral of silence' the process by which a vocal minority opinion supplants a silent majority opinion. See her 'The Spiral of Silence: a Theory of Public Opinion', *Journal of Communication* (1974): 43–51 and her 'Return to the Concept of Powerful Mass Media' in H. Egushi, ed., *Studies of Broadcasting* (Tokyo: Nippon Hoso Kyokai, 1973).

[8]The League for Human Rights' national survey conducted in September 1985 provide evidence that the Keegstra trial also contributed mainly to a climate of doubt rather than to a direct increase in anti-Jewish prejudice. Compared with responses to the League's 1984 survey, the September 1985 survey showed that Canadians were as willing to vote for a Jewish candidate for office. Only fractionally more respondents said in September 1985 than the previous year that Jews were too powerful. The major change in September 1985 was how respondents perceived their neighbours. Far fewer thought that anti-Judaism was in decline in 1985 than had thought so the year before. When asked how media coverage of the Keegstra trial had affected public sentiment, more respondents declared seeing an increase in anti-Jewish feelings than a decrease. Our appreciation to Professor Taylor Buckner for this information.

The Distribution of Anti-Semitism in Canada in 1984

Robert J. Brym

and Rhonda L. Lenton

Who is an anti-Semite? The press reports today's Jewish cemetery desecrations by skinheads, the trials of Holocaust deniers, and various anti-Jewish actions on the part of other fringe groups (e.g., Arnold, 1989; League for Human Rights, 1990; Wilson, 1989). Historians document the past extent of anti-Semitic policies and practices in government institutions and popular movements (Abella and Troper, 1982; Betcherman, 1975). But there are few contemporary analyses of the social geography of anti-Semitism in Canada, telling us exactly how strong anti-Semitic feeling is in various categories of the population (Brym, 1989: 49; but see Buckner, 1991). The following synopsis helps fill that gap in our knowledge. It is based on the results of the 1984 Canadian National Election Study, which was administered to a random sample of 3,377 Canadians.

Among many other questions, respondents were asked to indicate on a scale ranging from 0 to 100 their feelings towards Jews. They were told that a score of 0 represents the most negative attitude possible and a score of 100 represents the most positive attitude possible. Analysis of the data shows what may for some be surprisingly warm feelings towards Jews on the part of Canadians. Some 86 per cent of Canadians held positive or neutral attitudes towards Jews; only 14 per cent held negative attitudes. The median score for Jews on the 101-point scale was 70. This means that half the Canadian population held opinions above that point and half the Canadian population held opinions below that point. Canadian Jews were less well liked than Canadians of English origin, towards whom only 6 per cent of the population held negative attitudes. But they were better liked than Canadians of French origin, towards whom 15 per cent of the population held negative attitudes.

In some categories of the population the percentage of people who disliked Jews was above the national figure; in others it was below. Let us consider in detail the social distribution of the 14 per cent of Canadians who disliked Jews.

Let us look first at the provincial distribution of anti-Semitism. As can be seen in panel A of Table 1, the three provinces with the highest levels of anti-Semitism were Newfoundland, New Brunswick, and Quebec. In those three provinces negative feelings towards Jews were expressed by between 21 and 29 per cent of the population. On the other hand, and perhaps surprisingly, Alberta was the *least* anti-Semitic province: 7 per cent of its population disliked Jews.

The cynic might feel that the finding for Alberta must be invalid. Surely, he or she will claim, Albertans were downplaying their anti-Semitism in the wake of the bad press generated by the Keegstra affair. But the cynic will then have to explain why New Brunswickers did not engage in a similar exercise in the light of the bad press generated by the Ross affair.[1] The New Brunswick case suggests that no collective cover-up was taking place. A more plausible — albeit mundane — explanation for the low proportion of anti-Semites in Alberta is that the province's population is relatively affluent, highly educated, non-Catholic, and non-French. As we shall see, these are some of the main factors associated with low levels of anti-Semitism in Canada.

Consider first the anti-Semitic influence of Catholicism and its relative strength in different provinces. In Canada as a whole, 9 per cent of Protestants but more than twice that many Catholics disliked Jews in 1984 (see Table 1, panel B). Accordingly, four of the five provinces with the highest proportion of people who disliked Jews were also the provinces with the highest proportion of Catholics. And in eight of the ten provinces, anti-Semitism among Catholics was higher than anti-Semitism in the provincial population as a whole (see Table 1, panel C).

It is important to note, however, that it was mainly Catholics of French origin who accounted for the tendency of Catholics to be more anti-Semitic than Protestants. Thus Table 1, panel D, shows that 10 per cent of Catholics who spoke only English at home disliked Jews. That is 4 per cent below the national figure for all Canadians. In contrast, 24 per cent of Catholics who spoke only French at home displayed such attitudes: nearly twice the national figure.[2] The latter figure was identical for Quebec considered alone.

It is also significant that, depending on how religious they were, Catholics of French origin varied in their anti-Semitic attitudes. One might expect that anti-Semitism would increase with the religiosity of French-origin Catholics. But the data reveal precisely the opposite pattern. Some 21 per cent of very religious Catholics who spoke only French at home expressed negative attitudes towards Jews, compared to over 35 per cent of irreligious Catholics who spoke only French at home. For Quebec considered alone, the respective percentages were even more divergent: 20 per cent of very religious French Catholics in Quebec and 37 per cent of irreligious French Catholics in Quebec disliked Jews (see Table 1, panel E).[3] (Hereafter for the sake of brevity we refer to Quebec Catholics who spoke only French at home as *Québécois*.)

This fascinating pattern of anti-Semitic attitudes suggests that there were not one but two anti-Semitisms in French Canada in 1984. The first, traditional form of anti-Semitism was stimulated by the anti-Jewish preachings of the Catholic Church. Of course, the overwhelming majority of French-origin Catholics live in Quebec where, historically, the cultural

Table 1 Percentage of Canadians with Negative Attitudes Towards Jews, 1984

A. BY PROVINCE (N = 2,679)

Nfld	PEI	NS	NB	Que.	Ont.	Man.	Sask.	Alta	BC
29	15	13	23	21	10	13	16	7	11

Chi-square = 70.6, d.f. = 9, p $<$ .001

B. BY RELIGIOUS PREFERENCE (N = 2,302).

Catholic 19   Protestant 9

Corrected chi-square = 40.2, d.f. = 1, p $<$ .001

C. BY PROVINCE FOR CATHOLICS (N = 1,247).

Nfld	PEI	NS	NB	Que.	Ont.	Man.	Sask.	Alta	BC
44	24	5	23	22	14	20	10	7	17

Chi-square = 30.5, d.f. = 9, p $<$ .001

D. BY HOME LANGUAGE FOR CATHOLICS (N = 1,124), QUEBEC ONLY IN BRACKETS (N = 525).

English only 10 (0)   French only 24 (24)

Corrected chi-square = 36.0, d.f. = 1, p $<$ .001 (for Quebec only, corrected chi-square = 6.5, d.f. = 1, p $<$ .01)

E. BY RELIGIOSITY FOR CATHOLICS WHO SPOKE ONLY FRENCH AT HOME (N = 633), QUÉBÉCOIS ONLY IN BRACKETS (N = 498).

Not very religious 35 (37)   Fairly religious 23 (24)   Very religious 21 (20)

Chi-square = 6.5, d.f. = 2, p $<$ .05 (for Québécois only, chi-square = 6.5, d.f. = 2, p $<$ .05)

F. BY PROVINCIAL PARTY PREFERENCE FOR QUÉBÉCOIS (N = 341).

Liberal 25   Parti Québécois 25

Corrected chi-square = .002, d.f. = 1, not sig. (p $<$ .95)

division of labour between Jews and Québécois undoubtedly formed an important basis for anti-Semitism. In the Montreal garment industry, for example, many workshops and factories owned by Jews employed Québécois workers. But the historical record demonstrates that the Catholic Church also played a highly influential role in fostering anti-Semitism by charging the Jews with deicide and arguing that Christianity supercedes Judaism. That role was particularly evident in Quebec until the reforms of the Second Vatican Council, which opened in 1962.

What is the social basis of the second, secular form of anti-Semitism among Québécois? One hypothesis is that the Quebec nationalist movement is an important carrier of anti-Jewish feeling. Some Québécois may deeply resent the resistance of most of Quebec's Jews to Quebec nationalism. Moreover, in their survey of the social bases of the 'yes' vote in the 1980 Quebec referendum, Blais and Nadeau (1984) found that supporters of sovereignty-association tended to be lapsed Catholics of French origin. However, the results of the 1984 National Election Study lend no support to the view that Quebec nationalists were more anti-Semitic than non-

Table 1 Percentage of Canadians with Negative Attitudes Towards Jews, 1984

G. BY POLITICAL SELF-PERCEPTION (N = 1,681), QUÉBÉCOIS IN BRACKETS (N = 272).

Left 12 (21)   Centre 10 (13)   Right 11 (26)

Chi-square = .75, d.f. = 2, not sig. (p ⟨.7) (for Québécois, chi-square = 4.6, d.f. = 2 , not sig. p = .1)

H. BY INTERACTION OF RELIGIOSITY WITH POLITICAL SELF-PERCEPTION FOR QUÉBÉCOIS (N = 272).

Less religious left 26   Mixed religious centre 12   More religious right 22

Chi-square = 4.2, d.f. = 1, p ⟨.02

I. BY SCHOOLING (N = 2,677), QUÉBÉCOIS IN BRACKETS (N = 498).

Less than high   At least some high   At least some tech   At least some
school 26 (40)   school 14 (22)   school 14 (22)   university 7 (14)

Chi-square = 62.2, d.f. = 3, p ⟨.001 (for Québécois, chi-square = 16.2, d.f. = 3, p = .001)

J. BY FAMILY INCOME (N = 2,190), QUÉBÉCOIS IN BRACKETS (N = 425).

⟨$15,000 21 (30) $15–25,000 17 (20)   ⟩$25,000 11 (24)

Chi-square = 31.5, d.f. = 2, p ⟨.001 (for Québécois, chi-square = 2.3, d.f. = 2, not sig. p = .3)

K. BY SEX (N = 2,679).   Male 15   Female 12

Corrected chi-square = 4.9, d.f. = 1, p ⟨.03

Notes: 1. Percentages are rounded off to the closest whole number.
         2. The expected frequency is less than 5 for 1 of the 20 cells in panel A and 6 of the 20 cells in panel C.
         3. Provincial weights were used for Quebec-only calculations. National weights were used for all other calculations.

nationalists. Thus supporters of the two main provincial political parties—Liberal and Parti Québécois—were equally likely to express negative attitudes towards Jews, even though the latter is the champion of Quebec nationalism (see Table 1, panel F). In addition, people who said they voted 'yes' in the 1980 referendum were *less* likely than 'no' voters to be anti-Semitic (although not statistically significantly so at the .05 level).

A second hypothesis is that secular anti-Semitism among Québécois is related to being situated on the left wing of the political spectrum. That may seem an odd speculation given that anti-Semitism is generally associated with the right. But those familiar with the history of socialism know that there is in fact a long (although in general less violent) tradition of anti-Semitism on the left as well (Lichtheim, 1973; Wistrich, 1975). Since its origins in early nineteenth-century France, one current of socialism has associated Jews with the worst evils of capitalism and denied them any right to an independent existence, either as an ethnic group or a nation. Perhaps some form of that attitude has been passed from Fourier to Marx to the secular Québécois left.

No relationship between political self-perception and level of anti-Semitism was found for Canada as a whole (see Table 1, panel G). But in

Quebec considered alone the story is different. Only 13 per cent of Québécois who thought of themselves as being in the centre of the political spectrum expressed dislike of Jews. That was below the national figure for all Canadians. However, 26 per cent of right-wing Québécois and 21 per cent of left-wing Québécois expressed negative attitudes towards Jews. The relationship between political self-perception and anti-Semitism did not quite reach statistical significance at the .05 level, but that is influenced by the fact that the number of respondents represented in Table 1, panel G, is small (n = 272). It is unlikely that the relationship between political self-perception and anti-Semitism for Québécois was due to chance.

Table 1, panel H shows that there was an interaction between political self-perception and religiosity for Québécois. Simplifying somewhat, we may divide the Québécois into a less religious left, a more religious right, and a mixed religious centre. Anti-Semitism was high in the first two groups and low in the third. Chi-square for the relationship between anti-Semitism and the interaction of religiosity with political self-perception was significant at the .02 level despite the small number of people represented in Table 1, panel H (n = 272).[4]

However, the effects of Catholicism and political self-perception in Quebec by no means constitute the whole story of anti-Semitism in Canada in 1984. In fact, a multiple regression analysis not reported here demonstrates that social class was a somewhat more powerful cause of anti-Semitic attitudes than was religion: irrespective of religion, the lower one descends the socio-economic hierarchy of Canadian society the more anti-Semitism one finds; and occupying a low socio-economic position is rather more likely to make one anti-Semitic than being a Catholic. Thus, turning to Table 1, panel I, we see that over a quarter of Canadians with less than grade 9 education disliked Jews. As educational attainment increased, the proportion of people who disliked Jews declined, falling to 7 per cent among college graduates. Similarly, more anti-Semitism was associated with low family income (see Table 1, panel J). That is why the 4 provinces with the highest proportion of people who disliked Jews were among the 5 provinces with the lowest per capita income.

Interestingly, the negative relationship between family income and anti-Semitism, and the negative relationship between education and anti-Semitism, were affected by controls for union membership and NDP vote. Low education and low family income both continued to be statistically significantly associated (at p < .01) with high anti-Semitism for Progressive Conservative and Liberal voters and for people who were not members of trade unions. However, for NDP voters and union members, there was no statistically significant relationship (at the .05 level) between either family income and anti-Semitism or education and anti-Semitism. One may infer that, in Canada as a whole, sympathy for the NDP and union membership mitigated anti-Semitic feeling among the poorer and less-educated: people with low levels of formal education and low family incomes who supported the NDP or were union members tended not to be unusually anti-Semitic.[5]

Finally, it should be mentioned that sex was also associated with dislike of Jews. All else the same, men were more likely than women to dislike Jews (see Table 1, panel K).[6]

The preceding analysis allows us to conclude that in 1984 the incidence of anti-Semitism in Canada varied from one category of the population to another. Provincially, anti-Semitism was strongest in Newfoundland, New Brunswick, and Quebec. More men than women, more people with low than high socio-economic status, and more Catholics than Protestants, were anti-Semitic.

However, these observations are subject to a number of qualifications. Supporting the NDP and being a union member cancelled out the negative association between socio-economic status and anti-Semitism. Among Catholics, anti-Semitism was strongest among people of French origin. Among Catholics of French origin, it was strongest among the irreligious. And among Québécois, high levels of anti-Semitism were particularly evident on the less religious left and the more religious right.

We may also conclude that the overall level of anti-Semitism is quite modest in Canada as a whole. The only populous province with a relatively high level of anti-Semitism and a large Jewish population is Quebec. Moreover, one is entitled to be optimistic about the long-term outlook, at least outside Quebec. Specific events in the Middle East that are perceived by some to cast an unflattering light on Jews, and downturns in the domestic business cycle, will undoubtedly ignite sporadic increases in the anti-Semitic feelings of Canadians. But in the long term it is likely that anti-Semitism will decrease as Canadians become more affluent and better educated.

In Quebec the situation is more complex. In Table H, only 25 per cent of Québécois were found in the mixed religious centre category, where the level of anti-Semitism is 2 per cent below the national figure. But three-quarters of Québécois were found in the more extreme categories. In the less religious left category, where 21 per cent of Québécois were located, anti-Semitism was 57 per cent higher than the national figure. And in the more religious right category, where 54 per cent of Québécois were located, anti-Semitism was 86 per cent higher than the national figure. It is certainly possible that as Québécois become better educated and more secularized the level of anti-Semitism in Quebec will drop. The problem, however, is that secularized Québécois have a home waiting for them on the left — a home that is scarcely more hospitable for the Jews than is the more religious right.

Notes

[1]James Keegstra and Malcolm Ross were school teachers, in Alberta and New Brunswick respectively, who gained notoriety in the late 1970s for promoting updated versions of *The Protocols of the Elders of Zion* in their classrooms. *The Protocols*

was allegedly written by a coterie of Jews in 929 B.C. and outlines their purported plan to achieve world domination—most recently by means of controlling the world's liberal and communist movements and its major capitalist institutions, especially the banks and the mass media. Keegstra and Ross were both tried for promoting hatred. See, for example, Ross (1978) and, on the Canadian extreme right in general, Barrett (1987). On *The Protocols*—a document first forged by agents of the Czarist secret police in 1905, translated into English in 1920, and popularized by the Nazis in the 1930s—see Valentin (1936).

[2]Note, however, that Catholics in Newfoundland, who are English-speaking, were twice as anti-Semitic as French-speaking Catholics in Canada as a whole (see Table 1, panel C). For valuable historical insight on anti-Semitism in Newfoundland, see Bassler (1988).

[3]In Canada as a whole there was no statistically significant relationship between anti-Semitism and religiosity at the .05 level. Nor was there a statistically significant relationship between anti-Semitism and religiosity in Canada as a whole for either Catholics or Protestants considered alone.

[4]The categories for Panel H were created as follows. Left, centre, and right were assigned values of 1, 2, and 3, respectively. Not very religious, fairly religious, and very religious were assigned values of 1, 2, and 3, respectively. Five new categories—2 through 6—were then created by adding together the two sets of values $(1 + 1 = 2; 2 + 1$ and $1 + 2 = 3; 1 + 3, 2 + 2,$ and $3 + 1 = 4; 2 + 3$ and $3 + 2 = 5; 3 + 3 = 6)$. Categories 2 and 3 were then collapsed, as were categories 5 and 6, to yield Panel H. Less religious left is thus comprised of not very religious left and centre plus fairly religious left; mixed religious centre is comprised of fairly relgious centre plus very religious left plus not very religious left; and more religious right is comprised of very religious centre and right plus fairly religious right. The results were identical for a multiplicative model. There was no similar interaction for Canada as a whole; for n = 1,667, chi-square reached only 5.2 (d.f. = 2, p. 1).

[5]Yet, as noted, no relationship was discovered between political self-perception and level of anti-Semitism for Canada as a whole. The reason: Preferring the NDP and being a union member were not highly correlated with perceiving oneself as a leftist.

[6]Surprisingly, age was not statistically significantly associated with level of anti-Semitism at the .05 level.

References

Abella, Irving and Harold Troper
    1982 *None is Too Many: Canada and the Jews of Europe, 1933-1948* (Toronto: Lester and Orpen Dennys)

Arnold, Janice
    1989 'New kind of anti-semitism gaining acceptability', *Canadian Jewish News* (2 March: 22

Barrett, Stanley
  1987 *Is God a Racist? The Right Wing in Canada* (Toronto: University of Toronto Press)

Bassler, Gerhard P.
  1988 'Attempts to settle Jewish refugees in Newfoundland and Labrador, 1934–1939', *Simon Wiesenthal Center Annual* 5: 121–44.

Betcherman, Lita-Rose
  1975 *The Swastika and the Maple Leaf: Fascist Movements in Canada in the Thirties* (Toronto: Fitzhenry and Whiteside)

Blais, André and Richard Nadeau
  1984 'La clientèle du OUI', pp. 321–34 in Jean Crête, ed., *Comportement électorale au Québec* (Chicoutimi: Gaetan Morin)

Brym, Robert J.
  1989 'The rise and decline of Canadian Jewry? A sociodemographic profile', in Edmond Y. Lipsitz, ed., *Canadian Jewry Today: Who's Who in Canadian Jewry* (Downsview: JESL Publications): 37–51

Buckner, H. Taylor
  1991 'Attitudes towards minorities: seven year results and analysis: June 1990'. Paper presented at a conference on Anti-Semitism Around the World, sponsored by the League for Human Rights of B'nai Brith Canada, Montreal

League for Human Rights of B'nai Brith Canada
  1990 *Audit of Anti-Semitic Incidents 1990* (Downsview, Ontario: B'Nai Brith Canada)

Lichtheim, George
  1973 'Socialism and the Jews', in *Collected Essays* (New York: Viking): 413–57

Ross, Malcolm
  1978 *Web of Deceit* (Moncton: Stronghold Publishing)

Valentin, Hugo
  1936 *Anti-Semitism Historically and Critically Examined* (New York: Viking)

Wilson, Deborah
  1989 'Anti-semitism on the rise in Canada, B'nai B'rith says', *Globe and Mail* (14 March): A15

Wistrich, Robert S.
  1975 'Marxism and Jewish nationalism: the theoretical roots of confrontation', *Jewish Journal of Sociology* 17: 43–54

The authors would like to thank Jim Curtis, Graham Lowe, Jim Richardson, and Michael Shalev for helpful comments on a draft of this paper. The paper is based on data from the 1984 National Election Study, which was funded by the Social Sciences and Humanities Research Council of Canada. The data were made available by the principal investigators: Ronald D. Lambert, Steven D. Brown, James E. Curtis, Barry J. Kay, and John M. Wilson. They are not, however, responsible for the analyses and interpretations offered here, which are solely our responsibility.

part three

Culture

Introduction

William Shaffir

In order for any ethnic group to survive, it must impart its culture to successive generations. Though variously defined, culture consists of those conventional understandings that characterize the members of a particular group. In each group there are common understandings concerning the meaning of various objects and the proper ways in which they are to be handled. As well, there are shared values and norms of conduct—how various categories of people are to be approached and what may or may not be done with reference to them. Culture is not passed through the genes but is created by people and perpetuated in social interaction.

Among the components comprising an ethnic culture, sociologists have included a high degree of loyalty and adherence to certain basic institutions such as the family, religion, and language; distinctive folkways and mores; customs of dress, art, and ornamentation; and a sense of common descent, real or imagined. Of this variety, which features are most significant in helping to preserve the ethnic group's distinctive identity? In the view of many contemporary students of ethnicity, these include a common cultural tradition as a distinct subgroup within the larger society (Herberg, 1989; Isajiw, 1979).

In order to preserve its distinctive culture, the ethnic group must resist the assimilative influences of the surrounding host society. To the extent that members of the ethnic minority abandon their ethnic culture in favour of the dominant or 'official' culture, their behaviour is characterized by a process of assimilation. Assimilation can take the form of absorption into an established or dominant ethnic group, or of multiple groups amalgamating to form a new society and national people, as in the idea of a 'melting pot'. Above all, assimilation is centred around a search for identity and meaning.

In order to offset surrounding societal influences which may not merely transform the group but ultimately result in its dissolution, the ethnic community may establish a set of institutions to help meet its members' needs and requirements. Much like other ethnic groups, the Canadian Jewish community is no exception in its need for institutions. Indeed, the struggle for Jewish survival in the Diaspora is partly the story of the success—or failure—of Jewish social and political institutions in linking Jews to their community, helping them adapt to their surrounding environment, and sheltering them from both assimilation and hostile threats in their host societies. Of the many institutions, or cultural forms of expression, that Canadian Jewry has developed, the contributions in this section highlight religion, language, education, and Canadian-Jewish literature. Raymond Breton (1964) has coined the term 'institutional completeness' to characterize the extent to which an ethnic group possessed organizations and institutions developed by and for the members of that ethnic culture. Generally, such organizations and institutions parallel those of the wider extra-ethnic community that serve the public at large. Breton offered the specific example of parallel educational structures, one serving all segments of the city or region, and the other developed and controlled by members of a particular ethnicity and oriented toward the teaching of ethnic content—language, history, religion, and such. Comparatively speaking, the Canadian Jewish community measures very favourably along the institutional completeness continuum.

Insofar as religion involves the establishment of a system of beliefs and rituals and the formation of an organization of believers, it can be included under the rubric of culture. In this respect, a religion can be seen as a social institution that includes both a body of ethical principles, laws, and rituals as well as an organization, staffed by religious professionals and others, that structures the religious life of members of the faith and channels their participation in it. Judaism in Canada plays both roles for many Jews: its beliefs and values give meaning to individuals' lives, and its rituals, particularly those associated with the life cycle, loom large in the experience of most Canadian Jews.

As various research has documented, however, the role of Judaism in both the public and private lives of its adherents has changed (Cohen, 1988; Goldscheider and Zuckerman, 1984). As the environment and the existential features of Jewish life were altered, religious ritual and ethnic identity also shifted and even changed. Indeed, much like other ethnic groups in Canada, successive generations of Canadian Jews identify with and relate to religious ideas and practices differently from their parents' generation.

An important exception to this general principle are the Hassidic Jews who, in many respects, refuse to make concessions to the enticements of the secular world and live their lives as did earlier generations. Shaffir's selection in this section focuses on the Tasher Hassidic sect for whom, as for all Hassidic Jews, Orthodox Judaism lies at the core of their existence and serves as the basis around which all other aspects of their lives are organized. While religious observance is on the decline for Canadian Jews, Hassidic Jews continue to be characterized by their meticulous observance of Jewish law. Although constituting but a small percentage of Montreal Jewry, the Hassidic population in that city has increased dramatically over the very period during which the city's Jewish population has declined. Unlike their urban counterparts, the Tasher left the city and established their community in the Laurentian mountains north of Montreal. In his contribution, Shaffir describes the institutional network established by this community which has enabled it to expand, as well as to shape and control the behaviour of its residents.

If culture may be regarded as a system of symbols, and language as one of the most salient elements in that system, we can expect a parallel between ethnic language retention and changes in ethnic cultural content and practice. Language represents a basic mode of collective social identity and can serve as an important prerequisite to ethnic community participation (Handlin, 1951; Shibutani and Kwan, 1965). However, language is best seen as only one aspect of cultural survival and, while a desirable cultural attribute, it is not an absolute prerequisite for preserving the ethnic group's culture. This very point, among others, is captured in Davids' selection on Yiddish in Canada. Using data from the 1981 Census of Canada and earlier Censuses, Davids shows that Yiddish — once the predominant daily language of Canadian Jewry — is rapidly declining in general usage among Canadian Jews in the 1980s and can be expected to experience a continuing shrinkage in the years ahead. Ironically, despite their attempts at segregating themselves from the organized Jewish community, spoken Yiddish remains the living vernacular for Hassidic Jews, for whom the language is used both for purposes of communication and of insulation. Davids' analysis of the changes characterizing the identification of Yiddish as the mother tongue of Canadian Jews (96 per cent in 1931 but only 11 per cent in 1981) reflects their assimilation into the larger society. As importantly, however, it underscores the reality that for Canadian Jews language is only one dimension around which their cultural identity is organized.

To help impart particular features of the culture to the young, ethnic groups with the requisite resources have established their own schools. The Jews are an excellent case in point. Virtually every Canadian city with a sizeable Jewish population has a Jewish day school and, for students enrolled in the public school system, an afternoon Jewish school. Indeed, larger Jewish communities such as Toronto and Montreal can each boast a multitude of Jewish educational facilities reflecting various shades of the religious and cultural spectrum. Focusing their analysis on the intersections between the Jewish education system and the Jewish polity at the local level in Montreal, Weinfeld and Zelkowitz examine several dilemmas facing that city's Jewish education system. After brief consideration of the Montreal context regarding Jewish education, and the feasibility or desirability of universal Jewish education, the authors reflect on whether following a decade and a half of expansion in Montreal's Jewish day schools, a period of consolidation and review is now required. More to the point, they question whether the day schools are truly Jewish, or just schools for Jewish children?

References

Breton, R.
  1964 'Institutional Completeness of Ethnic Communities and the Personal Relations of Immigrants', *American Journal of Sociology* 70: 193-205

Cohen, S.M.
1988 *American Assimilation or Jewish Revival?* (Bloomington: Indiana University Press)

Goldscheider, C. and A. Zuckerman
1984 *The Transformation of the Jews* (Chicago: University of Chicago Press)

Handlin, O.
1951 *The Uprooted* (New York: Grosset & Dunlap)

Herberg, E.N.
1989 *Ethnic Groups in Canada: Adaptations and Transitions* (Scarborough, Ont.: Nelson Canada)

Isajiw, Wsevolod
1979 'Definitions of Ethnicity', *Ethnicity* 1: 111–24.

Shibutani, T. and K.M. Kwan
1965 *Ethnic Stratification: A Comparative Approach* (New York: Macmillan and Company)

Separation from the Mainstream in Canada:

The Hassidic Community of Tash

William Shaffir

Everett C. Hughes, writing about the many small societies not yet swept out by the broom of our industrial and urban civilization, reflected: 'How long will it take to mop them up, no one knows. The process seems to be going on rapidly now, but it will probably last longer than any of us would predict.'[1] The persistence of Hassidic groups, and indeed their growth, in North America has shown their capacity for survival.

Hassidim are ultra-religious Jews who live within the framework of their own centuries-old beliefs and traditions and who observe Orthodox law so meticulously that they are set apart from most other Orthodox Jews. Even their appearance is distinctive: the men bearded in black suits or long black coats with black hats over side curls; women in high-necked, loose fitting dresses, with kerchiefs or traditional wigs covering their hair. They are dedicated to living uncontaminated by contact with modern society except in accord with the demands of the work place and the state. They do not, for the most part, own radio or television sets nor do they frequent cinemas or theatres. They dress and pray as their forefathers did in the eighteenth century, and they reject Western secular society which they regard as degenerate. They do not, however, constitute a uniform group but are divided into a number of distinctive communities, each organized around the teachings of a particular *rebbe* or charismatic religious leader. In spite of their differences, all attach great importance to preventing assimilation by insulating their members from the secular influences of the host culture—a theme commonly encountered in ethnographic studies of such communities.[2]

An examination of Hassidic institutional life in Montreal reveals that far from diminishing in numbers (either through defections or on account of a lower birth rate), the Hassidic groups in the city flourish and are regarded both as attractive and viable by their respective followers. They pursue their Torah-based way of life with the same vigour and determination which characterized previous generations of their sects. In his analysis of the confrontation between *Haredim* (an extremely Orthodox sect) and the modern city, Menachem Friedman argues that, quite paradoxically, the urban centre has been largely responsible for the renaissance of such groups:[3]

In the setting of the big city, the haredi ghetto provides a solid territorial base for the various subgroups in the community. It enables the Haredim to maintain an independent culture which can borrow selectively elements from the surrounding culture, and to maintain a large measure of internal social control. The modern city thus affords the chance to sustain the haredi voluntary community in a dialectical balance of isolation from, and mingling with, the rest of the population.

That argument applies to various Hassidic groups in Montreal and other modern cities. However, although some Hassidim have been very successful at making use of conditions in large urban centres by pointing to the aliena- tion, crime, and drug and alcohol abuse afflicting many of the residents, and inviting a comparison with the Hassidic style in their own enclave, others have chosen to literally distance themselves further by moving to a more rural-like setting.[4] In 1963, for example, 18 households of Tasher Hassidim moved from Montreal to Boisbriand, about 18 miles away. One of the community's administrators explained: 'What we have is precious to us and our teachings tell us that when you have something precious, you build a fence around it the better to protect it.' A farmer's field of some 130 acres had been acquired in 1962; the supply of electricity was arranged through Hydro Quebec while provisions for running water and sewerage were co-ordinated through the Boisbriand municipality.

The name 'Tash' is derived from a little town in Hungary near the Czech border where the great-grandfather of the present Tasher *rebbe* began gather- ing Hassidim round him about a century ago. The Boisbriand community can now boast that it has the only Tasher Yeshiva in North America; the Tash groups in the United States only have two small synagogues, one in Wil- liamsburg and one in Boro Park. The Boisbriand Tasher Hassidim were enabled to move away from Montreal (where they had lived in close proxim- ity to other Hassidic groups since 1951, when their *rebbe* came from Hungary to Canada) by the loan of half a million dollars from the federal government's Central Mortgage and Housing Corporation. The community promptly built a Yeshiva, a synagogue with accommodation for 1,000 persons, a ritual bath, classroom space for boys and girls, offices, 18 bungalows for the *rebbe* and senior staff members, dormitories, and a kitchen and cafeteria.

I was told that the decision to move away from Montreal was apparently taken to escape the deteriorating moral climate of the city:

> Unfortunately the streets of today's society are a negative influence. . . . So it was only the foresight of the clever people [the *rebbe* and his closest followers] that felt that the streets are getting worse and worse and if we don't move now, it'll be too late. We won't have even what to move for.

In 1987, the Tasher settlement had about 115 households and some 70 yeshiva students; the majority of the latter were local residents while others had come from Montreal and New York. The total population numbered about a thousand souls. The older members were mainly immigrants from Hungary and Poland, of Tasher background, who came to Canada after the Second World War. In recent years, a number of the *rebbe*'s New York followers joined the Boisbriand community because of both their leader's charismatic appeal and the ideal geographic setting. The demand for extra housing was satisfied in part by successful negotiations with the federal and the provincial governments to designate part of the Tasher settlement as eligible for public housing subsidies, in order to accommodate households with a limited total income. The Tasher also receive financial assistance from their followers and sympathizers.

Although the Tash community is officially apolitical, it seems that exception may be made in the interests of good relations with the federal government and with the government of the Province of Quebec. The community's administrators proudly display the many letters of congratulations received by the Tasher *rebbe* from the highest ranking politicians of the country. The *rebbe* is said to have supported the aspirations of the Parti Québécois and to have influenced large numbers of Jews to vote for that party. Moreover, the Tasher named one of their streets 'Place Nov. 15' to commemorate the PQ's 1976 victory on that day. But the federal government was equally rewarded: in April 1979, a new street was officially inaugurated in the Tash settlement; it was called 'Place André Ouellet' in honour of the federal minister of Public Works who helped to approve a grant for a Tash housing complex in the settlement. The Minister and several politicians accepted the *rebbe*'s invitation to attend the ceremony. Three months later, an employee of the Tasher was reported to have told a Toronto daily newspaper: 'We are grateful to the PQ government. This is the best Government Jews have ever had in Quebec'.[5]

The Tasher apparently were not content with their stringent measures to distance themselves from the surrounding secular culture. That same year, 1979, they attempted to obtain separate municipality status for their Boisbriand settlement, with all the rights and privileges such a status entailed. Thus, paradoxically, in order to achieve a greater degree of officially sanctioned autonomy they had first to become more closely involved in provincial politics.

In his paper, I begin by outlining this interesting chapter in the community's history. I then examine the Tasher stress on the importance of geographical isolation; the community's attempt to achieve self-regulation and self-sufficiency in that isolation; and the organization and supervision of secular studies. The data were collected over a number of years since 1970, when I was employed by the Tasher for a brief period; and I have maintained regular contact until the present time, mainly through participant observation and informal interviews.[6] An earlier version of this article was sent to the Tasher and their comments enabled me to correct a number of factual errors.

'A Strange Bid for Autonomy'

In 1979, in what one magazine article headlined as 'A Strange Bid for Autonomy',[7] the Tasher submitted an application to the PQ government of Quebec for full municipal status, including the power to turn their religious rules into bylaws. *Maclean's* reported:[8] 'Here was Quebec's government, obsessed with the primacy of the French language and culture, hand-in-hand with a Yiddish-speaking enclave where, according to tradition rooted in the history of Eastern European Jewry, married women must shave their heads and boys and girls must never touch until they are paired for marriage by matchmakers.' However, there was a precedent for the creation of such a municipality. A few decades earlier, the Roman Catholic monks at the abbey in Saint-Benoit-du-Lac, in the Eastern Townships, had been allowed to make the abbey lands into a municipality and they still enjoyed that status when the Tasher made their bid.

At first, it seemed that the Tasher were not likely to encounter serious opposition. Indeed, their achievement of separate municipal status would have apparently served the interests of various parties. For the Tasher, it would provide not only religious autonomy but also an industrial tax base and the right to issue municipal bonds. For the wider municipality of Boisbriand, there would be a settlement of a tax dispute, as we shall see below. The provincial government, on the other hand, burdened with a reputation for anti-Semitism, saw in the plan a way to demonstrate its ready tolerance of Jews; and quick to appreciate the public relations value of the proposal, it made the following statement in the August 1979 issue of *Quebec Update*,[9] an official newsletter for American business leaders published in New York, under the heading of 'Hassidic Community Wins Government Help':

> The Quebec government will help about 400 Hassidic Jews of the Tashever sect form their municipality north of Montreal in Boisbriand. There are about 1,000 Hassidim in Canada and most of them are in Montreal. It will be the first time that Hassidic Jews have formed their own municipality in Canada thus enabling them to pass laws and regulations in keeping with their own traditions. Boisbriand voters will be asked to approve the plan this autumn and then a bill will be introduced into the Quebec National Assembly to set up the town. The Quebec government currently finances 80 per cent of the operating costs of Jewish private schools in Quebec as it does for private schools of other denominations.

When the Tasher settled in the Boisbriand area in 1963, they sought to have their community declared tax exempt as a religious institution. The municipality agreed to do so in respect of some of their buildings but claimed that part of the open land was being retained for speculative purposes and therefore taxed it. This dispute over the real estate status of part of the community's lands eventually reached the Supreme Court of Canada in 1965, which ruled in favour of the Boisbriand municipality and ordered the Tasher to pay $300,000 in back taxes. They paid only $57,000.

Later, in 1979, while still owing back taxes to the municipality, the Tasher mounted a new effort to secure a tax-exempt status for their community. Their case was heard in Quebec's Provincial Court and their plea was successful. They then stated that they would settle the outstanding sum they owed the municipality of Boisbriand after they achieved separate status. The provincial government consented to grant such a status provided the plan was approved by the Boisbriand municipality. Meanwhile, the Hassidim had obtained the support of the mayor and most of the municipal councillors. The *Globe and Mail* of 27 July 1979 reported the mayor as saying: 'They should have their own municipality. They live a totally different life. It's like another world.' It was proposed that the residents of the total area of Boisbriand would express their views through a referendum—the cost of which, an estimated $15,000, would be borne by the Tasher. The latter appeared confident that they would be granted a municipal charter within a matter of months.

At that stage, however, newspapers catering to both English-speaking and French-speaking readers intervened. *The Gazette*, Montreal's English-language daily, claimed in an editorial in July 1979 that the Hassidim's problems were rooted in matters of taxation; and added that even if they overcame those difficulties, there was a further matter to consider:[10]

> Neither would they be able to guarantee their own majority in the new town. They could not, under the Charter of Human Rights, make residence conditional on religion, and since Boisbriand is right on the road between Montreal and Mirabel Airport, the future may well bring an influx of new people who would leave the Hassidim with the same minority position they now find trying.

The editorial concluded: 'The best bet would seem to be to organize as a cultural and religious community, as the Hutterites have done successfully in Alberta and as the Hassidim themselves have done already if not entirely to their own satisfaction.'

Two months later, in September 1979, Montreal's French daily, *La Presse*,[11] published a lengthy article headed, 'Does Quebec want to legalize the creation of a city-ghetto?' The Tasher were described as 'the most intransigent' of the Hassidic groups residing in Quebec while the provincial government, in its wish to appear tolerant of cultural minorities in general and of the Jewish community in particular, 'could risk committing a grave historical error'. The author stressed the difference between a natural grouping of citizens of the same faith or culture and a ghetto sanctioned by civil law and then proceeded to ask: 'Does Quebec want to be the first modern country to have the honour of creating a Jewish city and legalizing a ghetto?' There might be unforeseen and regrettable consequences of setting such a precedent:

> What would the government do should the same request come from the Apostles of Infinite Love, Jehovah's Witnesses or a group of Catholics that

would decide to establish a city where divorcees would be excluded. . .? Or again, if the Italian community of Saint-Leonard decided to separate and to form a new municipality with a cultural base?

Shortly after the publication of that article, the mayor of Boisbriand withdrew his support of the Tasher's application for a separate municipal charter. In the 3 October 1979 issue of a weekly newspaper — *Voix Des Milles-Iles* — he was reported to have stated that the *La Presse* article was the last straw that broke the camel's back. There were informal meetings with Boisbriand residents at the Town Hall, described as 'an oral poll', which led the municipal administration 'to come out against the request for separation'. The Mayor declared that the file was closed and added: 'I can assure you that the citizens of Boisbriand are greatly relieved.'

The hostility of Boisbriand's municipal council and of many residents was apparently exacerbated by the presence of outsiders, immediately after the publication of the *La Presse* article, who claimed to be conducting a public opinion survey on the subject. The Tasher denied allegations that they had commissioned such a survey — which, for the most part, revealed that Boisbriand residents were indifferent to the Hassidim's request. As for the mayor and the town council, they decided against implementing their earlier decision to have a referendum. A Jewish weekly, *The Canadian Jewish News* of 15 October 1979, published an interview with the mayor who was reported to have said: 'We already spent too long on this question. . . . The citizens of Boisbriand are totally against this idea.' Some informed observers, however, were of the opinion that the town council's decision sprang from the fear that a Hassidic municipality would attract industry and would soon be transformed into a town with its own economy in competition with that of Boisbriand.

In the event, the failure to secure a municipal charter does not seem to have been a severe blow for the Tasher. They have been attempting to reach a settlement on the taxation dispute and meanwhile they have acquired additional acreage adjacent to their settlement. Indeed, they were hopeful in 1986 that the Boisbriand Town Council would pass rezoning legislation enabling the community to erect new buildings on land designated for agriculture. Apparently, that was one of the main reasons why they wanted to acquire separate status — in order to rezone the land for the construction of housing units — and it now seemed that they might succeed in their aim. However, perhaps it was a sour grapes reaction which prompted an administrator of the Tasher to comment to me, 'If I was offered a municipality today, I'd think twice before I'd say "Yes".'

The Importance of Geographical Isolation

A pamphlet published by the Tasher in English — 'The Story of Tash' — made the following statement:

While Tash seeks to imbue its members with a set of specific religious attitudes and values, it also generates a moral climate that ensures its members will comply with the social and ethical standards the community believes ought to be cherished and upheld by the larger society. It is precisely in this area that Tash is proud to deviate from some of the major trends in contemporary society such as delinquency, divorce, drug and alcohol abuse. These social ills are unheard of because the society is strong. Quite simply, no one in Tash need turn to these things. Each chassid is basically content with who he is; he knows his life holds meaning and purpose.

For the Tasher, the realization of such meaning and purpose is more readily achieved in a secluded setting, where the members of the community, and especially the younger generation, can be carefully shielded from exposure to undesirable influences.[12] That does not mean, however, that the technological achievements of modern society must also be rejected. Indeed, by 1983 the Tasher's central administrative office boasted computer equipment which several individuals manipulated with considerable skill. What they reject are many of the values and beliefs of the secular culture which are in direct opposition to the principles of a Hassidic way of life. The younger generation must be taught to live according to the highest principles of Orthodox Judaism. A Tasher told me:

> That's made very clear to them that there's an outside world which we're not supposed to follow. Of course they are aware [of the outside world]. They see things and they're taught that these are not the right things. . . . I mean everybody is going to end up in the outside world to a certain extent.

The Tasher of Boisbriand are not the only Hassidic group in North America to have deliberately chosen geographical isolation. A number of other Hassidic groups have organized enclaves and communities in suburban or semi-rural areas.[13] A Tasher cited a comment by Maimonides that people are very influenced by their surroundings; and since that is so, a proper environment must be secured at all costs:

> We would give away quite a lot of blats [pages] of gemooreh [Gemara] in exchange for avoiding certain influences. Had you given me the option of having the yeshiva in town that my son would be able in a year's time to learn 100 blat gemooreh in exchange for coming here and learning only 50 blat, there's no question I'd choose the 50 blats. I'd even choose 10 blats instead of 100.

Such an attitude is in sharp contrast to that adopted by other Hassidim who live in Montreal and who believe that they can protect their children in an urban environment by pointing to many of the evil ways of delinquent children in surrounding areas and thus confirming the superiority of the Hassidic life-style. For the Tasher, it is difficult enough to bring up children as devout and law-abiding Jews without having the additional burden of constantly ensuring that they are not influenced by the behaviour of modern city dwellers. One of them told me that even in such an area as Williamsburg, in

Brooklyn, where Hassidic Jews are concentrated, his children would be exposed to many things which he would not want them to see—things 'which don't exist' in the Boisbriand enclave. Another Tasher told me of the problems encountered when he went with his son into a department store for the first time:

> And my son said, 'Look at this', and I said, 'You're not allowed to look. She's not modest dressed. Don't look.' We went by a television, '*Tattee* [Dad] look. Look, look, he's jumping.' 'Don't look, the television is not for you to look.' He doesn't have so much to fight with [at Tash] because he doesn't see it. . . . So it's not so hard for him to fight. A boy [in Montreal] who's going every day to *cheder* [religious school] and is going by a Radio Shack and the television is out there with the big screen, every day he has to turn around.

The same sentiments were echoed by another young father who said that if he took his son to Montreal he constantly asked him to avert his eyes from what was exhibited in the shop windows and in the street. In the end, his son was likely to say in exasperation: 'So what should I do? Should I close my eyes? A car will come and knock me down.' In the Boisbriand enclave, on the other hand, he would not see the obscene covers of the magazines on newsstands in Montreal, he would see nothing that was evil in the streets. He would not even know what drug addiction is because he would never have seen a drug addict; and he would not know about such crimes as murder, because none took place in the Tash settlement. His son would not have to ask himself, 'Should I be good or should I be bad?' because he would have been taught and would have seen mainly what is good.

It is not only young children who might be led astray by the ways of the big city. A Tasher told me of the harmful influences which some modern magazines might exert on gullible Hassidic women in Montreal: a woman will pick up a woman's magazine because she has seen something on the cover about a piece of furniture she is thinking of buying; then she will read the magazine and find that it is quite interesting; 'so tomorrow she's going to buy another one and the week after she might buy a more interesting one. This all goes in a chain. . . . If I would live in a city, I wouldn't guarantee that I wouldn't become the same.' But there was no such temptation in Boisbriand. Moreover, I was told that the secluded location of the Tasher ensures not only the moral but also the physical welfare of children. They can play without risk of danger in the streets and at meal times all a mother has to do is go out and call them home. She can attend her household duties without having to check constantly that her children have not strayed too far. Tash parents, furthermore, do not have to be concerned about their children's playmates, as urban dwellers must in order to guard against harmful influences. In the Tash enclave, the role models for the young are provided by the resident adults and it is claimed that the physical security which prevails makes it possible to achieve the spiritual richness of life in the community. A Tasher explained:

I don't have to be very concerned if my kid leaves school at 5 o'clock or 6 o'clock to know exactly where he was till 7 o'clock. I'll assume he was playing in the snow because there's no place to go. Had I lived in town, I'd have a real problem. And there are people in town who would pick up their kids from school and they would take them home and they would be locked indoors. . . . Someone can succeed with the same objectives as we do but their social life is the one that suffers. We have more *gashmeeus* [social life] even though we don't have to lose on our *ruchneeus* [spiritual life].

Self-regulation and Self-sufficiency

The only street leading into the community (Avenue Beth Halevy) winds around a partially unfinished building—the girls' school—as well as a playground and several bungalows before ending at the *Oir Hachaim* Yeshiva complex. The main street of the settlement is semi-circular in shape and is lined with rows of duplexes; and there are two other small streets. The environment is austere; both the interior and the exterior of the Yeshiva—the centre of spiritual and social life in the community—could benefit from a fresh coat of paint. A prefabricated structure serves as the younger boys' school—the older ones study in the Yeshiva—and while a similar structure was available for the girls, a new girls' school has neared completion and is already in use. The community maintains two ritual baths: one for the men, which is located in the Yeshiva, while the women's *mikveh* is in a separate building. One supermarket stocks a variety of food products and household supplies for the everyday needs of the residents.

The men are mainly engaged in religious-oriented occupations (as teachers, ritual slaughterers, and *kashrut* supervisors) and in study in the *kollel* (advanced Tamudic academy) for which the participants receive a financial subsidy. In addition, a few individuals have developed commercial enterprises in such areas as printing, textiles, silk-screening, lumber, automatic sprinkler systems, and *shtreimel* (a round fur hat made of sable worn by married men on the Sabbath and other religious holidays) manufacturing. None of the women is gainfully employed outside the settlement. About 15 to 20 of them are involved in some teaching capacity in the girls' school, but only a few of them have had some formal teacher training before settling in Tash. A Tasher woman is the principal of the girls' school and while overseeing the secular studies assumes primary responsibility for the Jewish curriculum.

In Tash, as in other Hassidic communities, the *rebbe* in every way is the leader of his flock and that fact is central in the organization of the group. His followers turn to him for advice not merely on spiritual and ethical problems but also on a wide range of practical matters—moving to another location, taking a new job, planning an overseas trip, or even consulting a doctor. The *rebbe* is revered as a *tsaddik* (righteous person) and is believed to have special qualities of insight; his people therefore turn to him for guidance 'in the uncertain areas of life rather than in the clearly defined domain of the law'.[14]

Decision-making in the Tash community is theoretically vested in an advisory committee consisting of seven members (males), of which two or three are appointed by the *rebbe* and the remainder elected by adult males in the community. Before the election, which is held in the *Bays Medresh* of the Yeshiva, a slate is drawn up, slips of paper with the names of the candidates are distributed to those gathered, and secret balloting takes place. In practice, however, decision-making is the domain of the charismatic leader, the *rebbe*, alone. The seven who serve on his committee, I was told, are men 'he feels he can trust that they know what he wants'. The responsibilities of the elected members include those matters which are not the primary concern of the *rebbe*, such as an extension to the playground, for example, or modifications to the time-table of the community's bus service to Montreal.

A set of bylaws, established by the *rebbe*, governs the behaviour of all the residents; and each adult, whether male or female, must agree to abide by these bylaws before taking up residence in the settlement. Anyone who transgresses may be liable to eviction. What follows is a translation of these bylaws from a document in French prepared by the Tasher in 1979 for Quebec's Provincial Court in connection with their bid for autonomy:

> No book, newspaper, or magazine is permitted in the buildings of the community, unless their content is in conformity to Orthodox Judaism.
>
> All members of the community must attend religious services, three times per day, at the synagogue.[15]
>
> No radio, television, record, or cassette is allowed in the buildings of the community.
>
> No member of the community may attend the cinema or be present at any theatrical performance under the penalty of immediate expulsion.
>
> All women residing in the community must dress in accordance with the Orthodox laws of modesty, as follows:
>
> All dresses must be at least four inches below the knees, no trousers or panty-hose may be worn by young girls 3 years of age or older.
>
> [Married women's] Hair must be completely covered 24 hours a day, by a kerchief or by a wig which is no longer than the nape of the neck.
>
> It is forbidden for men and women to walk together in the street.
>
> Men and women must be separated by a wall, at least 7 feet high, when attending any gathering of a social or religious nature.
>
> All food consumed in the buildings of the community must conform to the dietary laws of the Code of Laws and be approved by the Chief Rabbi [*rebbe*] or his second-in-command.
>
> No car may be driven by a woman or by an unmarried man.[16]

The members must submit any interpersonal conflict to the arbitration of the court established by the Chief Rabbi.

The Sabbath day must be observed in strict conformity to Jewish law.

Members must study the Bible and other religious text for at least two hours daily.

The above by laws are permanent and cannot be amended by a democratic vote of the residents. One of the latter explained:

You don't have no choice. He [the individual] had a choice. When he came here he knew that this is what he will eat. This is what we're cooking and this is what we will eat. . . . Therefore, it's not like we're making votes and we voted this and this and a minority is not happy. Everybody who comes here knows what he will get.

In some other secluded Hassidic communities (such as Kiryat Yoel in Monroe, upstate New York, established by the Satmar Hassidim), the residents may own their housing units; but in Boisbriand the majority of the available accommodation is owned by a legal entity representing the Tasher *rebbe* and the households rent their dwellings. This policy permits the *rebbe* to select newcomers to the settlement and enables him to retain complete control of community politics and spiritual direction.

All communities which aim to live in isolation must find ways to satisfy the everyday needs of their members by providing a range of structures and services which would lessen dependence on outsiders and achieve a high degree of 'institutional completeness'.[17] The Tasher are no exception. One of their pamphlets states that after acquiring 130 acres of land in 1962, the community built a synagogue, a religious college (Yeshiva), dormitories, and 18 houses in 1963. No expansion occurred until 1970, when three more houses were built; these were followed by a prefabricated structure in 1971 to serve as the young boys' school; a women's ritual bath in 1972; 18 apartments in 1974; a matzo bakery and a slaughterhouse for kosher meat and poultry in 1975; a supermarket in 1976; a further 78 apartments during 1977-78; a children's playground (divided in two, one for boys and one for girls) in 1979; and in 1980 a school for young girls and a *kollel* for married men. But despite the availability of a plentiful supply of arable land, the Tasher do not grow any of their food.

Medical care so far has required members to go outside the confines of their settlement. Women are free to select the physician of their choice and give birth in the hospital with which their physician is affiliated. The Tasher did employ a visiting paediatrician who came for half a day each week, but does so no longer for reasons beyond their control. They wish to have a visiting dentist also but since they cannot guarantee a fixed income they have yet to appoint such a practitioner. On the other hand, the Tasher maintain a fully-equipped ambulance, including a cellular telephone; it is staffed by several members, one of whom has paramedic qualifications. They have also recently acquired an incubator; and some of the residents can now analyse the results of throat cultures. Meanwhile, it is necessary to leave their enclave if they must visit a doctor or a dentist; and so far, no attempt has been made to interfere with a person's choice of medical or dental practitioner. A bus service linking the settlement to Montreal is provided; it completes the return trip (35 minutes each way) three times daily during the week. As a rule, yeshiva students are permitted to use the bus by themselves—but reluctantly, for fear that they will see in the city manners and behaviour which are not in keeping with strict religious observance. The bus is also used by those who wish to make necessary purchases of items not available locally, such as clothing and electrical appliances.

Finally, the Tasher so far have no provisions for local burial; they make use of an Orthodox funeral parlour in Montreal. Nevertheless, the members of the community are proud of the high degree of self-sufficiency they have achieved. I was told: 'I think we're the most independent community. . . . If we would be put into a blockade . . . the basics we have here.'

The Organization and Supervision of Secular Studies

A Tasher pamphlet printed in English states:

> The Tasher community is living proof that one need not have advanced degrees in secular studies in order to succeed. Although the yeshiva and girls' school do teach French, English, mathematics and other secular subjects, the Rebbe does not place too much emphasis on these.

Like other Hassidic groups, the Tasher maintain that secular education threatens their traditional values; and in order to shield their children against its potentially harmful influences, which they believe to have affected Jewish children in lay schools, they run their own schools where secular classes are closely supervised to ensure that the pupils will not see any conflict with the contents of their religious studies.[18]

The secular programs in the two Tasher schools (one for boys and one for girls) which have about 160 pupils each are narrowly defined and do not fully comply with the requirements of the provincial authorities. The boys are instructed in French and English in reading, writing, and arithmetic for approximately two hours on weekday afternoons by outside teachers; the latter are fully qualified and work in the settlement to supplement their income. The aim is that the pupils will become proficient at writing a business letter, at communicating in English and French, and at mastering basic arithmetic.

The girls have secular classes for about three and a half hours every weekday and the languages of instruction are French and English, but all notices on the bulletin board are in Yiddish. The emphasis is on home economics; the natural sciences are not taught but there are courses in history and in geography. The fact that the girls are engaged for almost twice as long as the boys in secular classes is defended on the grounds that, first, the boys must have the minimum amount of diversion from their religious studies: they might become attracted to secular subjects to the detriment of their religious learning; and second, that girls will require practical skills later in life: 'They have to be able to understand much more of the outside world and what goes on because they're the people who'll be building the home, doing the shopping and everything else.'

The Tasher are convinced that education, whether religious or secular, is too important a matter to be dictated, or controlled, by outsiders. They have long refused any school subsidies from the government because they do not wish to comply with the obligations entailed.[19] They claim that in an interview with government officials, they said bluntly: '. . . we are Jews. We live as Jews. We will die as Jews. If you tell us we cannot continue our education the way we want it . . . then we have news for you. Either we're going to leave Quebec or we're going into shelters like in Russia, in basements.'

Like other Hassidim, the Tasher carefully screen the secular material used for teaching. Stories told to the children must not have 'ultra-modern' views. When I enquired about what kind of story they would consider harmful, one of their administrators gave as an example a tale about a Jewish boy who was a pupil in a non-Jewish school. The boy was eventually accepted for the baseball team; and on one Saturday they came to pick him up to play on that day but his father refused to let him go. My informant commented:

> Now that's a game that we think a boy shouldn't have on his mind, that he could go out and play baseball on *Shabbess* afternoon. . . . I'm not saying that that's the worst example of a story that might be passed. But there are stories that have sex in them, and things like that which are totally out.

The particular techniques used to screen the secular material vary according to the predilections of the individual charged with that responsibility. One such person used to censor photographs which showed women immodestly dressed or ink out in black pen sections of a photograph he thought reprehensible. Another one was more tolerant and explained that he thought it stupid to ink out the pictures of a little girl because she was not wearing socks, when it was clear from the context that the girl was a Gentile:

> Our kids are aware that the *goyim* do not dress the way we dress. . . . I mean, if you're reading a story about *goyim* then you know that *goyim* don't wear socks. As long as it's not a mini skirt or anything like that, it's O.K. I mean, everybody knows what they look like. I mean, it's no use blacking anything out. . . . You see, going to a very strong extreme causes problems.

Those employed to teach secular studies are specifically instructed about the constraints within which they must conduct their work. This is particularly the case for teachers in the girls' school where the curriculum is co-ordinated in a more formalized manner than is the case for the boys' secular studies. Teachers not only receive verbal instructions from the principal concerning the rules and regulations by which they must abide, but, in addition, proscriptive topics of discussion and methods of teaching are distributed to them in written form. For example, the written instructions to the English staff listing the rules and regulations specify:

1. All textbooks and literature to be used by the students in class or at home for extra-curricular activities, etc. must first be approved by the principal.
2. No stencil or photo copy of any other book may be used without the principal's approval.
3. Students are not permitted to go to the library nor is the teacher permitted to bring into the school, for the students, such books.
4. No newspaper or magazine may be read in school or hung up. Students are not permitted to read the above at home either.
5. No record or tape may be used in the classroom without the approval of the principal.
6. No extra subjects, books, magazine supplement or other information which is not on the required curriculum of the school may be taught.
7. For extra credit work or for class projects, etc., students should not be told to write away for such material. The teacher should supply them with the material with the principal's approval.
8. No discussions on boyfriends.
9. No discussions on reproduction.
10. No discussion about radio, TV or movies.
11. No discussion about personal life.
12. No discussion on religion.
13. No discussion about women's lib.
14. No homework on Thursdays.

The absence of homework on Thursdays is to enable the girls to help at home with preparations for the Sabbath. This particular regulation is irrelevant for the boys, however: they are never given any homework relating to secular studies.

The above instructions provide a clear picture of the stringent measures taken by the Tasher to ensure that their schoolchildren do not become acquainted with (or, worse still, become attracted to) the ways of those who do not faithfully adhere to their strict Hassidic life-style.

Conclusion

When I asked a Tasher administrator whether he thought that his community was a success, he replied that it obviously was, since the girls were modestly dressed, the boys all had earlocks, and all the men were bearded, and there was nothing offensive on sale in the local supermarket or on view in the streets. The settlement, he asserted, was 'a big success'. This sentiment was echoed by all those whom I interviewed. It was admitted that there was the odd case of deviant behaviour but such instances of rebellion or disaffection were said to be very rare and to pose no real threat to the norms of the community. The Tasher fiercely cherish their geographical isolation and they have learnt to screen carefully students who apply to study at their yeshiva; for if those young men come from metropolitan New York, they might have acquired habits or modes of thought which would corrupt the strictly reared native residents.

In her study of nineteenth-century communes, R.M. Kanter[20] noted two of the most serious problems they faced, which were factors leading to their eventual dissolution: the erosion of their membership, and a mounting scepticism about the realization of the ideals which had been the basis of their communal existence. In contrast, the Tasher so far are increasing in number, largely because of a high birth rate while defections are virtually non-existent, and the members, including the younger generation, appear to be quite content with their life-style and attracted to the values they have been taught to respect.

Paradoxically, it is precisely the high birth rate and the negligible amount of defections which may endanger the future of the community: within a few years, when the present teenagers marry and have children in turn, there will be an urgent need for the provision of extra accommodation and services. That, in turn, will require the infusion of considerable financial resources and it might then become necessary to approach the provincial government as well as the mainstream Jewish community—two bodies with which the Tasher have so far carefully controlled their involvement. On the other hand, the isolated setting of the community may help to shield it against the effects of such intrusions.

It will be interesting to see how the present *rebbe*, born in 1923, or his successor in title will face the challenge when it comes.

Notes

[1]Everett C. Hughes, *Where People Meet* (New York, 1952): 25.

[2]See, for example, Jacques Gutwirth, *Vie Juive Traditionnelle: Ethnologie d'une Communauté Hassidique* (Paris, 1979); Jerome Mintz, *Legends of the Hasidim* (Chicago, 1968); Solomon Poll, *The Hassidic Community of Williamsburg* (New York, 1962); Israel Rubin, *Satmar: An Island In The City* (Chicago, 1972); and William Shaffir, *Life In A Religious Community: The Lubavitcher Chassidim In Montreal* (Montreal, 1974).

[3]Menachem Friedman, 'Haredim Confront the Modern City' in Peter Y. Medding, ed., *Studies In Contemporary Jewry* (Bloomington, 1986): 74-96.

[4]Two examples of such relocation include New Square and Kiryat Yoel, the communities established by the Squarer and Satmar Hassidim respectively. The former, founded in the mid-1950s and incorporated in 1961, under the leadership of the Squarer *rebbe*, is located near Spring Valley, about a quarter of an hour's drive from the centre of New York City. Kiryat Yoel, situated outside Monroe in Orange County and incorporated in 1977, is a self-sufficient community where individuals own their homes and includes factories, schools, shops, and medical facilities.

[5]*Globe and Mail*, 27 July 1979: 2.

[6]An earlier article reported briefly on the Tash attitude to secular education: William

Shaffir, 'Hassidic Jews and Quebec politics', *The Jewish Journal of Sociology* 25, 2 (December 1983) 105-18.

[7]'A Strange Bid for Autonomy', *Maclean's* (November 1979).

[8]*Ibid.*

[9]*Quebec Update* 2, 31 (August 1979): 1.

[10]'Separatism in Boisbriand', *The Gazette*, 27 July 1979: 7.

[11]'Quebec veut-il légaliser la création d'une ville-ghetto?', *La Presse*, 29 September 1979: 4.

[12]The following view, published in *Di Yiddishe Heim* (vol. 20, p. 21) by a Hassidic woman from Lubavitch, also expresses the Tasher's opinion: 'Everyone today is so nutrition conscious. There are many tempting foods available, but we know they are really junk foods. . . . We cannot be any less aware of what we allow to enter our children's minds. We must be aware that what we give them provides the best nourishment for their souls — full of spiritual vitamins and minerals, not super-ficially tasty yet full of harmful chemicals and additives.

'To expect to stop all secular activity is unfortunately unrealistic. But at least we should be more aware of the potential harm involved, of how vigilantly we must supervise all of our children's activities'.

[13]In spite of efforts to guard against the intrusion of undesired outside influences, the process of assimilation has greatly altered much of the environment in which Orthodox Jews, including Hassidim, function in North America. See Gershon Kranzler, 'The Changing Orthodox Jewish Family in the Context of the Changing American Jewish Community', a paper delivered to the convention of the National Council for Jewish Education, Washington, DC, 1977, and Egon Mayer, *From Suburb to Shtetl: The Jews of Boro Park* (Philadelphia, 1979).

[14]See Jerome Mintz, *op. cit.*: 89. For a discussion of the role and influence of the Hassidic *rebbe*, see also Israel Rubin, op. cit., and William Shaffir, *op. cit.*

[15]Concerning this bylaw, a Tasher explained: 'We don't really have a regulation that says somebody must *davn* [pray] three times a day, because that's like saying somebody must be a Jew. For the court we had to explain everything.'

[16]I was told that this bylaw pertains to persons under the age of twenty.

[17]See Raymond Breton, 'Institutional Completeness of Ethnic Communities and the Personal Relations of Immigrants', *American Journal of Sociology* 70, 2 (September 1964): 193-205.

[18]See Solomon Poll, *op. cit.*: 37-51; Rubin, *op. cit.*: 137-56; and William Shaffir, 'The Organization of Secular Education in a Chassidic Jewish Community', *Canadian Ethnic Studies* 8,1 (1976): 38-51.

[19]See William Shaffir, 'Hassidic Jews and Quebec Politics', *op. cit.*: 115.

[20]Rosabeth M. Kanter, *Commitment and Community: Communes and Utopia in Sociological Perspective* (Cambridge, Mass., 1972): 139-61.

Reflections on the Jewish Polity and Jewish Education

Morton Weinfeld

and Phyllis Zelkowitz

This essay will explore several intersections between a system of Jewish education and a Jewish polity, at the local level. These reflections flow out of our recent involvement as directors of several studies of the Jewish education system in Montreal, focusing on systemic or communal characteristics rather than on evaluations of individual schools. Several of the dilemmas facing the Jewish education system of Montreal are illustrative of ambiguities of private responsibilities of Jewish citizenship and public responsibilities on the part of the community. Depending on the uniqueness of the Montreal situation, these dilemmas may have implications for other diaspora communities.

What follows is more a policy discussion paper than analytical social science. The discussion is geared at a framework or level which sociologists call, after Merton, 'the middle range' — between abstract grand theory and excessively empirical micro-sociology.

As will be suggested below, based on enrolment figures, the emerging view in the Montreal Jewish community is that Jewish day schools are a kind of public school system of the Jewish community. They are not seen as élitist private schools selected by parents in an individualistic manner for their children. The principle of communal responsibility has been generally accepted, as it is elsewhere.

This means that Jewish education is seen more and more as a communal rather than individualistic investment, and certainly not as a luxury, frill, or individual item of consumption. Most of the research literature on the consequences of Jewish education has been micro-sociological in nature and design, looking at various level of Jewishness for each individual, related to amounts of prior Jewish education. This approach de-emphasizes the insight of human capital analysis in which the society as a whole benefits from investments in education. In other words, parents ought not to be expected to bear the full brunt of the cost of their children's education; it seems in the interest of the polity to maximize the educational attainment of as many children as possible.

It is crucial to understand key differences between education in the general polity and Jewish education in the Jewish polity.

In both, the returns to education are both economic and non-economic.

The former are measured in higher incomes for the more educated (including the paying of more taxes), as well as productivity gains which benefit everyone. The non-economic gains are harder to measure, but include dimensions of moral behaviour, cultural development, tolerance, adherence to democratic norms, better health and consumer behaviour, etc.

The Jewish day school is an investment which yields comparable returns. The economic return derives from the quality of the secular education which those schools provide. For most Jewish parents, particularly non-Orthodox, this education must be at least comparable to that available in the public sector, as it is a requisite for entry to college and the achieving of stable careers. This in turn will lead to graduates earning higher incomes which will afford them the means to contribute to the Appeals which sustain the Jewish polity. It is important to emphasize this point. The secular program of studies, therefore, becomes practically as meaningful as the Judaic program for the long-term survival of a local community. The two are not working at cross-purposes. In other words, educational, occupational, and professional success will benefit the Jewish polity as well as the individual.

The non-economic benefits are of course crucial to Jewish schools. These benefits are the foundation for subsequent Jewish identification, and they consist equally of experiential dimensions which strengthen the bond with Judaism and the Jewish people, and cognitive dimensions which equip graduates with the requisite information to practise, appreciate, and live out those commitments.

Yet there are several key differences between education in the general and the Jewish polities. In the former, the state permits both a public and private school system to coexist. In general, the state funds public schools fully, while funding private schools either in part or not at all (depending on locale). School attendance is compulsory and universal up to the mid-teenage years. In the United States, over 85 per cent of children attend the public school system.

Second, attendance at public school is free, paid from general tax-based revenues of one form or another. Indeed, in some polities such as the United States, where richer school districts may provide better quality education than poorer districts, legislative efforts attempt to equalize expenditures.

Third, public schools are under the direct control of central education bodies, whether of a local or state/provincial level. In Quebec, secular programs of study are determined rigorously by the provincial Ministry of Education, affecting curriculum, materials, evaluations, etc.

As a result, public schools, directly or indirectly, socialize students into the values and attitudes deemed appropriate in the general polity, or the local community. This is accomplished through a variety of classes in subjects like civics, citizenship, social studies, sex education, religion or moral reasoning, history, as well as all sorts of extra-curricular or special activities. Occasionally this leads to minor conflicts, as when a group of parents may object to a textbook, or to a book found in the school library. But the normative principle is that since the community — usually incarnated as elected school board officials or appointed superintendents — pays the bills, it must oversee what goes on in the schools.

Using as a primary focus the Montreal system, we note, by contrast, that thee is a two-tiered 'public' system: day schools and supplementary schools. Neither is, in theory, free. Attendance in either case is voluntary. And the principle of school autonomy dominates over any notion of centralized control or supervision, at least in the Judaic sector.

In light of these characteristics, two important issues facing the Jewish polity in the field of education are: 1) the feasibility of approaching universal, maximal Jewish education; 2) the degree and viability of communal (e.g., federation) *laissez-faire* regarding school curriculum or orientation.

The Montreal Context

By any relative or absolute standard, Montreal boasts a well developed and diverse system of Jewish education. Unlike most American communities, the emphasis is on day school education. As of 1984-85, there were over 6,600 children aged 5 to 17 (excluding nursery) enrolled in Jewish day schools, from kindergarten to grade 11, the end of high school. There are ten day schools in the system, with several schools operating multi-branch facilities. The ideological spectrum of these day schools is broad, ranging from a large Yiddishist, semi-secular school descended from the populist *folkshule* model (and where Yiddish is indeed one of the four languages of instruction), to a traditional Hebraic, to Conservative, to neo- or modern Orthodox, to Hassidic schools and yeshivas. The overall budget of the day school system is about $26 million per year.

Using census and enrolment data, one can estimate that for 1981 the Jewish day schools enrolled about 66 per cent of the eligible primary school-age Jewish population and about 28-30 per cent of the Jewish secondary school-age population. These are extremely high proportions by any diaspora standard.

In addition, there is a supplementary Jewish education system, with nine schools which in 1984-85 involved about 1,800 students, almost exclusively of elementary school age. These included about 1,000 who attended afternoon supplementary schools, usually affiliated with synagogues, and 800 in supplementary classes offered in certain public schools to interested Jewish students. Over the past twenty years the day school system has seen sustained growth, while the supplementary school system has declined in size.

Day school growth in Montreal has been fuelled by forces similar to those which have operated in the US: perceived decline in the public schools, and fears of drugs or promiscuity. In addition, it has been relatively affordable. Not only has tuition been relatively low (see below), but these fees have been in large part tax-deductible.

Historically, the Jewish day schools have long championed their autonomy and have resisted any perceived encroachment upon their independence. This autonomy has been sustained by the fact that, until recently, the schools have not had to rely on the local Jewish community for financial support. This was because the Province of Quebec, beginning in 1970, granted 'Associate' status as public schools to those Jewish schools falling within certain guidelines (in practice these have had to do with teaching a required number of hours per week in French). Such schools have been eligible for per-pupil subsidies of more than 50 per cent of the cost of education (at one point these percentages were higher). Thus parental tuition fees must meet the costs of the Judaic curriculum alone, and fees have remained lower than comparable fees in the United States or other Canadian provinces.

In recent years, the Montreal federation, the Allied Jewish Community Services (AJCS), has become increasingly involved and sensitive to the importance of Jewish education. In the mid-1970s, a new agency, the Jewish Education Council (JEC), was created to serve as a coordinating umbrella agency serving the needs of all the schools (day and supplementary) in Montreal, and as a link between schools and the AJCS. The JEC consists of lay board, with wide representation, and a professional staff of educators and educational advisors. In addition, the JEC administers the Educational Resource Center (ERC) which is active in curriculum development, in-service training and professional development, and has a library of audio-visual equipment and materials and a sound studio. The JEC and ERC are funded by AJCS.

The Jewish day schools felt the need for an organization devoted exclusively to their needs and as a liaison with education officials of the Province of Quebec. This organization, the Association of Jewish Day Schools (AJDS), is funded directly by day school subventions and has at times dealt directly with AJCS (bypassing the JEC) on relevant matters.

During the 1980s, several trends have posed new financial problems for the schools. The percentage of per pupil costs supported by the government grants to the day schools has declined steadily, while costs have increased. All individual Jewish schools have set aside scholarship assistance funds for Jewish parents who cannot meet full tuition fees (about $2,500 per year per child). In some schools, a day school education may be received gratis for those truly in need. Over the years, average tuition fees have been rising steadily to meet this developing shortfall on a cost–plus basis, with the surplus used for scholarship aid (i.e., with the wealthier parents paying full fee in effect subsidizing other parents). Yet the point has been reached where the day schools are becoming increasingly reluctant to raise tuition fees; nor will they turn away needy students. They are therefore now turning for the first time in any major sense to the AJCS for a larger measure of fiscal relief, whether as scholarship aid or via some other formula. The AJCS, on the other hand, is wary of embracing a large commitment to the schools without sufficient accountability.

The Non-Elitist Character of Jewish Day Schools

With almost two-thirds of maximal enrolment at the elementary level, the Jewish day school system of Montreal can no longer be considered a private school system, but has become, in effect, a public school system of the Jewish community. The Jewish day schools are no longer élite institutions in these senses:

1. They in no way cater to a financial élite. The tuition costs, while much higher than in public schools, are well below those of the other private day schools in Quebec, which receive no provincial subsidies and which as a result teach fewer hours of French. In addition, financial aid is available to needy parents. As a result, there is a heterogeneous student population within each school, measured by social class. However, it is also the case that schools vary in the relative degree to which they attract low income students, determined by their residential location, the amount of aid available, and their general image in the community.

2. They in no way cater to a Jewish élite, measured either by parental Jewish background or parental Jewish commitment. The student bodies of non-Orthodox day schools may well include large minorities, and in some cases majorities, of children whose homes are minimally Jewish. This poses both problems and opportunities for the day schools.

A major dilemma is that in many cases the Jewish child receives little support in the home environment for the Judaic objectives of the day school. Often the two work at cross-purposes, and in any event the conflict makes the realization of school objectives very difficult. On the other hand, a possible opportunity is that a process of reverse socialization is often found in which children socialize their parents Jewishly via school activities and influences, through peers, etc. Thus the school may become a major focus and source of Jewish identity for the marginal parent.

Another problem is that many of these marginal Jewish parents are least committed to Jewish education and most likely to leave the Jewish system for an alternative, either public or private. These parents set limits on how 'Jewish' the school may be. Disgruntled parents have withdrawn children from day schools. The complaints have to do with perceived inadequacies in the secular program, or in English, or in lack of discipline. Some parents resent the 'normalization' of the Jewish day schools; they prefer an authentically private school.

The concern with keeping enrolments up as a source of state funding and as a status/prestige symbol is a dominant one. Yet the focus on numbers may deflect from a concern with higher quality, effective Jewish education.

3. The Jewish schools are no longer élite institutions intellectually or socially. In earlier days the impression in Montreal was that students in the day school system were be definition above average in cognitive ability, as

they had to be able to follow a dual English-Hebrew curriculum. Thus a strong weeding-out process took place through the grades. What has happened is that while high quality students remain in abundance in the Jewish day schools, substantial numbers of students whose abilities are average or less are now there. The prevailing thrust is not to weed these students out but to attempt to provide support and encouragement, where feasible, to enable them to remain in the system.

In addition, the Jewish day school population now includes numbers of children from homes which are economically disadvantaged, from single-parent families, etc., who have problems requiring the extensive use of social workers and other helping professionals. Both these trends add to school costs.

4. The Jewish day schools are not élitist in terms of their physical plant. They are, on the average, less attractive and spacious than the private schools and most public schools. Some of the schools are severely overcrowded and require renovation or replacement.

The Feasibility or Desirability of Universal Jewish Education

The importance of Jewish education to the future survival of diaspora Jewish communities has become an article of faith among Jewish communal leaders, often attaining motherhood status. Communities have monitored the numbers of enrolled Jewish students with a conviction of 'the more the better'. This conviction rests on research that Jewish education tends to have a positive effect on the Jewish identification of students in later life, independent of other factors such as family background. These relationships may not be as strong as we might like, or as immediate or linear, but they are logical, though different types of education may have different impacts. More important for students from minimally Jewish families, an intensive Jewish education may be the only hope for future communal involvement or identification. This is said despite the fact that it has become fashionable to denigrate the education-identification relation because it is too difficult to estimate precisely.

Yet even in a very Jewish community like Montreal, the vast majority of the Jewish population is non-Orthodox and the majority of children in the day schools, specifically in the elementary grades, are from non-Orthodox families. As indicated before, many of these families have a lukewarm commitment to Jewish education and feel that the Judaic studies are the least important component of the curriculum.

If we assume that the community accepts a human capital approach to Jewish education, then there is an interest in maximizing the number of Jewish children receiving the most intensive Jewish education. Yet schools will then include a large body of parents uninterested in intensive Jewish education but who see it as a necessary evil. Moreover, many Jewish parents might waver on the issue, requiring coaxing or incentives from the community or the school to enrol their children.

Just as membership in the Jewish polity is voluntary, so is the decision to opt for a Jewish day school. The decision is made by the family of the child. To what extent can and must the Jewish community move to entice marginally committed parents to enrol their children? On the one hand, the community is reluctant to victimize a child, to deny a Jewish education because some parents — even among those who can afford it — do not think it is worth the cost or the effort. On the other hand, it must be asked what the presence of a large mass of such Jewish students does to the affective and attitudinal Jewish education in a day school. Indeed, this is precisely the type of problem which has long afflicted supplementary Jewish education in North America — a clientele of relatively disinterested students from minimally committed homes, where the Judaic goal for the parents is a bare minimum rather than an enriching maximum.

Expansion of Jewish day school education into non-Orthodox population in a community will introduce less committed students into the system. Schools may well become financially dependent on retaining these marginal students. Ideally one hopes that such students, and perhaps even their families, may be transformed by the day school experience. But the other possibility is that such an eventuality might have a negative fallout potential. This has been a criticism levelled at some of the Jewish day schools in Montreal; the peer pressure and student cultures of the school tend to denigrate the importance of Judaic studies and Jewish commitments.

Just one example: A large (right-wing Conservative) day school has been trying without success to discourage parents from holding their young children's birthday parties in non-kosher venues and on Shabbat. Parties held at McDonald's on Saturday are commonplace. One party was held Saturday morning at a video arcade; another at noon on Shavuot in the parents' (non-kosher) home. The Board of this school has refused to insist that parents obey their guidelines on children's birthday parties for fear of antagonizing some parents. Some parents indicated they chose this school precisely because it was not Orthodox and therefore cannot understand the fuss.

Thus, in some of the Montreal day schools at present we find two conflicting sub-groups of parents; those wishing to de-emphasize the Judaic program (i.e., reduction in hours) and a smaller minority who may want a more intensive program, in a more positively Jewish environment.

For too long the concern in the Montreal Jewish community has been the quantitative growth of day school enrolment. It may well be opportune to shift the emphasis to more qualitative concerns and to invest resources, both human and material, in maximizing the effectiveness of the Jewish instruction and in striving for excellence in teaching. It is clear that the dominant peer-group culture in the two largest Jewish high schools in Montreal (with a majority of non-Orthodox families) is perhaps negligibly different from that culture which can be found in non-Jewish public schools attended by Jewish teens. Patterns of comportment and of dress are comparable, as are tastes in music or life style. Patterns of sexual behaviour and drug and alcohol use or abuse are also reportedly comparable to those prevailing in public high schools attended by Jews in Jewish areas. The traditional view was that those activities would be less prevalent in a Jewish day school. Summer trips to Israel held mid-way in the high school career (at a fee of $4,000 per student) are highly popular. While for many students these trips concretize the meaning of Israel and are positive Jewish experiences, for others they offer primarily an opportunity for experimentation and fun away from parental supervision.

The Jewish schools in Montreal and the communal bodies which support them have yet to come to grips with the implications of this intra-school diversity. It is not clear that every Jewish child can benefit equally from an intensive day school education. It may even be possible that substantial numbers of uncommitted students may undermine the effectiveness for those who are more committed. At some point an equilibrium must be reached between potential positive and negative consequences of expansion into the perimeters of the community. That equilibrium may have been reached in Montreal — short of universal attendance.

If the past decade and a half was a period of expansion in Montreal day schools, it may be that what is required now is a period of consolidation and review. Are day schools truly Jewish schools, or just schools for Jewish children?

Ideological Diversity in Jewish Education: E Pluribus Unum?

As indicated above, the Jewish education system in Montreal contains a great deal of diversity both between and within schools. This is a trait which differentiates this system from public school systems in the polity. Those schools usually promote one form of citizenship, have a uniform curriculum, and attempt to promote comparable visions of the moral world. Indeed, these public schools scrupulously avoid any religious entanglements, at least in the United States, and in systems such as the Protestant School Board of Greater Montreal. Even the Montreal Catholic School Boards are not very Catholic, and the thrust in school reform in Quebec is to move completely away from religious to linguistic demarcations of school jurisdictions.

Jewish day schools are in an anomalous position. While the secular curriculum is under the rather rigid control of the provincial education authorities, the conditions with regard to the Jewish curriculum, despite Hebrew as a common denominator, are essentially anarchic. Schools fervently guard their own autonomy, and are supervised only by the lay school boards as to the content of the Judaic curriculum.

The policy of the JEC and the AJCS on this has been basically one of decentralization and *laissez-faire*. The JEC and the ERC provide service and modest funding to all affiliated day schools in a non-judgemental manner. Thus, within the JEC umbrella at present we find, for example, a Workman's Circle supplementary school (to the left of the mainstream Jewish People's School) and several Hassidic day schools or yeshivas, at least one of which, along with the Bundist school, might be considered non-Zionist and where modern Hebrew or Israel are absent from the curriculum.

The question that arises is to what extent the Jewish polity would define within its public interest and fund Jewish schools which are anti-Zionist, non-Zionist, anti-Israel, anti-Hebraic, anti-religious, or quasi-racist (à la Meir Kahane).

In the Montreal Jewish community, the vocally anti-Zionist Satmar Hassidic day school is not included within the umbrella of the JEC and receives no funding. In part this is because they have not approached the JEC, but were they to do so it is likely they would not be accepted. The JEC monies, like those of all federation agencies, come from the funds collected annually by the Combined Jewish Appeal, which relies largely on Israel needs as a basis for the campaign. Using communal funds to support such a school might be too controversial.

The decentralized, relativistic, and tolerant approach by most Jewish federations also may be problematic for achieving the goal of unity among the Jewish people. The divisions among the Jewish people in Israel and in the diaspora are becoming increasingly salient: religious vs secular, Zionist vs non-Zionist, Orthodox vs non-Orthodox, Sephardi vs Ashkenazi. In Montreal, the Jewish schools in what has been defined here as the public school system of the Jewish community certainly reflect and perpetuate these distinctions.

It is also likely that Jewish school systems may not be able to remain aloof from possible escalations in the conflict between Orthodox and non-Orthodox subgroups in the community on the 'who is a Jew' question. Federations collect money from the entire Jewish community and may use portions of that money for Jewish education. It is probably the case throughout North America that Jewish schools, particularly day schools, are more religious or traditional in orientation (or more Orthodox) than the community at large. It is certainly the case that among big givers and lay leaders in most communities (as is the case in Montreal), the more religious or strictly Orthodox, while present, are under-represented.

Federations, or the big givers who sustain them, may come to question the allocation of the community funds (i.e., their own money) to Orthodox schools which refuse to recognize their status as Jews in cases involving divorce, intermarriage, or conversion. Moreover, the Orthodox establishment in Israel might also taint Orthodox schools in the diaspora, in the eyes of federations and givers, because of the former's stance on 'who is a Jew' and related controversies in Israel.

Since Jewish schools will increasingly play a role in Jewish socialization, and since patterns of socialization may shape future perceptions of legitimate status as a Jew, federations interested in promoting Jewish unity may need to involve themselves in the content of the schools which they fund. This may be needed to avoid future fragmentation of the polity, assuming that such fragmentation would be highly problematic. (This is an assumption. A reading of Jewish history reveals many cases of communal fragmentation, not all of which have been counterproductive. Nor is it clear that communal unity is desirable as an end in itself or as a measure for other objectives.)

Can Jewish federations indeed remain agnostic about the ideological, cultural, or curriculum orientation of Jewish schools which approach them for financial and other assistance? The stance of neutrality implicity assumes that all ways of being Jewish are equally valid. This may be true philosophically, but not communally. In addition, the diverse Jewish traditions and subcultures which are respected in some schools may be ultimately an impediment to achievement of effective Jewish communal unity.

Do central, communal organizations have a role to play in maintaining and even boosting enrolment in day schools? While each school in Montreal has jealously guarded its autonomy, it is difficult for an individual school to bear the costs of services which are increasingly demanded by parents: special programs for learning disabled or gifted children, computers, enrichment in the arts and sciences. Professional development, curricular innovation, and program evaluation are other areas where a central body can serve to promote educational quality and thereby work to retain children within the day school system. However, it is essential that the constituent schools cease to view each other as competitors, but rather as partners in Jewish socialization.

In Montreal, school autonomy continues to make individual schools sceptical of the intentions of the JEC and reluctant to submit to community discipline or planning regarding the establishment of new schools or fundraising. Indeed, the traditions of autonomy are so strong that some schools have used them to reject the notion of a Jewish community high school which might result from some form of merger or federation between the two largest day school systems, saving resources.

Conclusion

One of the truisms in the sociology of education is that it is difficult, if not impossible, to isolate public school systems from the society and polity which reflect and fund those schools. This has often led to conflicts between educators who have favoured educational autonomy, individualism, and training for independent thinking, and politicians concerned with the social consensus, political control, and social stability.

When Jewish schools were truly private, divorced from the mainstream communal organizations, these problems did not arise. However, if the trend towards greater communal (centralized) funding and coordination of schools continues, they will become more and more public institutions, responsible to the community, not just to sub-groups of parents and educators. The requirement of financial accountability of schools by itself invites some measure of political involvement. Moreover, a Jewish polity concerned with future survival and communal cohesion may be unable to continue policies of relative detachment from the goals, orientations, and content of Jewish schools.

Yiddish in Canada: Picture and Prospects

Leo Davids

The Jews driven out of central Europe centuries ago took with them the language spoken in their former homelands. Settling in Poland–Lithuania (where they were generously welcomed at that time), the non-Mediterranean Jews quickly formed concentrated communities that turned the German brought with them into Judaeo-German or 'Judisch-Deutsch', now generally known as 'Yiddish'. Since then, it has remained the general common tongue among Jews in Eastern Europe.[1]

What, then, is this language? It is basically mediaeval High German which was enriched with Hebrew and other borrowings (from the Slavic tongues, mainly) and was — as it still is today — written in Hebrew characters, which provided the only alphabet known to all Jews. Thus, spoken Yiddish remained more or less understandable to those of German speech, but written Yiddish was closed to anyone not able to read Hebrew writing. The non-German vocabulary (generally in the realm of religion where many Hebrew terms were naturally used) was also incomprehensible to gentiles. This tongue had become the lingua franca for Ashkenazic (North-European or Non-Mediterranean) Jews well before the modern era arrived, and has persisted as a major Jewish language into recent years. However, other Jews (from North Africa, the Near and Middle East) do not speak Yiddish; it is not a universal Jewish tongue.

As a result of the great Jewish emigrations from Eastern Europe, intensifying after 1880 and continuing to some significant extent even in the post-Holocaust years, Yiddish was transplanted to North and South America, and to other new areas of substantial Jewish settlement. This exposed living Yiddish to new borrowings (from English, especially) which have been blended in during the past few decades, and also enabled Yiddish to survive the destruction of European Jewry during the 1940s (Orenstein, 1981; Thiessen, 1973).

The survival of Yiddish henceforth, not in literature but as a spoken tongue, is open to doubt. Eastern Europe, given the high average age among Jews now living there, and other factors, is not likely to sustain any sort of Jewish culture in the long term, much less keep Yiddish alive into the next century. Thus, the further history of Yiddish is being created in its linguistic 'colonies', especially in the United States and Canada. This essay will focus on the current status and near-future prospects of Yiddish in Canada, using 1981 Census information to see how popular Yiddish remains, to review trends in its use by Canadian Jews, and to speculate about where Yiddish is likely to be, quantitatively, in the 1990s.[2]

The Linguistic Faithful

The group most faithful to Yiddish is the Hassidim. Often labelled 'Ultra-Orthodox', these Jews strive to change nothing in their pious way of life, but to keep from the contaminating influence of the secular world by maintaining their ancestral traditions entirely; e.g., retaining their black garments, style of haircuts (see Isaacs, 1977; Mayer, 1979; Shaffir, 1981), and obviously not speaking the host society's language among themselves. As they once used Yiddish to keep Polish or Russian out of their homes and 'hearts', they use it still to avoid the language of the majority. Their commitment to Yiddish, thus, is not a matter of historical accident but is today an ideological commitment resting on a religious motivation (see Korn, 1981; Poll, 1965; Landmann, 1962).

Describing a very large Hassidic sect, those who follow the vehemently anti-Zionist *Rebbe* (teacher-pastor) of Satmar (a town in Hungary), Rubin (1972) tells us:

> . . . in their combating of undesirable outside influences, Satmarer tend to . . . exclude grammar, either Hebrew or Yiddish, from the curriculum of both boys' and girls' schools, and modern Hebrew is actually a forbidden language, not only in the school but outside as well. . . . with the establishment of modern Hebrew schools with a Zionist orientation which concentrate specifically on language, omission of the latter has become an element of the official Satmarer ideology. (146)

We can now better understand why 'the Hebrew text is translated into Yiddish, which continues to be the daily language in Satmar' (Rubin, 1972: 145). Any other tongue could threaten the European history-oriented cultural purity of the community. In general, Rubin's account also applies, with little qualification, to all other sects of Hassidim (Poll, 1965; Isaacs, 1977). They insist on Yiddish, rejecting all other languages for use within the community although, for business with outsiders, a Hassid has to know other languages.

The Canadian Realities

What do the statistics show us about Yiddish in Canada? How widespread was its use among Jews here, and what is the recent situation as Jews have become integrated into Canadian society for longer and longer periods of time?

Table 1 shows a dramatic decline from Yiddish as the standard, unchallenged mother tongue of Canadian Jews in 1931 (with 96 per cent having been raised with it) to its 'specialty' status in 1981, when only 11 per cent of Canadian Jews

Table 1 Jews and Yiddish Mother Tongue in Canada, 1931-1981

	YEAR					
	1931	1941	1951	1961	1971	1981
Total Jews (Religion)[a]	155,700[a]	168,600	204,800	254,400	276,000	296,400
Yiddish Mother Tongue Population	149,500	129,800	103,600	82,400	49,900	32,800
Yiddish Mother Tongue as Percentage of Total Jews	96%	77%	51%	32%	18%	11%

[a]Numbers are rounded to the nearest 100.
Sources: Statistics Canada, Census Reports on Religious Denominations and on Mother Tongue (for 1981, see Cat. No. 92-902 and 92-910).

Table 2 Regional Concentration and Loss of Yiddish in Canada, 1961 and 1981

	MARITIME PROVINCES	QUEBEC	ONTARIO	THE WEST & NORTH	TOTAL
1961 YMT[a]	950 (1.2%)	35,850 (43.5%)	32,450 (39.4%)	13,200 (16.0%)	82,450 (100%)
1981 YMT	200 (0.6%)	12,400 (37.9%)	15,000 (45.8%)	5,150 (15.7%)	32,750 (100%)
1961-81 Percentage Decline[b]	78.9%	65.4%	53.8%	61.0%	60.3%
1981 YLH[c]	20 (0.2%)	5,400 (50.7%)	4,300 (40.2%)	950 (9.0%)	10,650 (100%)

[a]Yiddish Mother Tongue
[b]As a proportion of that region's 1961 number (e.g. the 750 lost in the Maritimes are 78.9% of the 950 counted as YMT in 1961)
[c]Yiddish Language of the Home
Sources: Dominion Bureau of Statistics, 'Mother Tongue' Report of the 1961 Census, Catalogue No. 92-549 (= Bulletin 1.2-9); Statistics Canada, "Mother Tongue" Report of the 1981 Census, Catalogue No. 92-902 (Table 1); and "Home Language" Report of the 1981 Census, Catalogue No. 92-910 (Table 6).

reported it as their mother tongue. Until the 1950s, as is evident from Table 1, the majority of Jewish children in Canada were reared speaking Yiddish, but their later abandonment of it was so massive that, as our later data will show, in the 1980s very few Jews learn Yiddish in childhood as their first language. However, some study Yiddish in school and may be able to speak it (see Thiessen, 1973: 51) without showing up in the Census.

It should be remembered that the shrinkage in the number of Yiddish speakers that we are examining in this paper proceeds in the context of overall Jewish demography in Canada (and the world). Overall Jewish numbers are now generally in a no-growth condition, as has been pointed out elsewhere (Davids, 1981, 1983). This bodes poorly for the future of a language spoken only by a single ethnic group, and receiving very little reinforcement from current immigration. Likewise, the leadership of French Canada is concerned about the survival of its language, which is a similar situation although on a far larger scale, and one may view the recent Quebec language laws as a response to the weakening demographic situation of francophones in the past two decades (Lachapelle and Henripin, 1982: 300-20; Beaujot and McQuillan, 1982: 193-7; Laurin, 1977).

Table 2 indicates the locations of Yiddish decline in Canada, i.e. the provinces or regions where the shrinkage of Yiddish Mother Tongue (YMT) is faster or slower. In turn, this helps us predict where Yiddish, in coming years, is more likely to remain evident in contrast to places where it is already defunct as a spoken language.

Table 2 shows us a trend toward concentration in Montreal and Toronto, as the peripheral regions lose YMT population and thus no longer have a viable speech community for Yiddish to survive in. By 1981, as is evident in the table, the two Jewish centres, with a combined Jewish population of about 220,000, had lost many Yiddish speakers but had retained a YMT population of over 27,000, which constitutes 83.7 per cent of Canada's total YMT population; that percentage was just a little higher than the 1961 figure of 82.8 per cent. However, the rest of Canada shows continuing declines in this respect—from 17.2 per cent of all YMT (over 14,000 people) in 1961, to 16.3 per cent (but only 5,000 people) in 1981.

Considering the percentage declines in each region, Table 2 shows that the steepest losses between 1961 and 1981 occurred in the Maritimes (79 per cent fewer YMT people), followed by Quebec's shrinkage of 65 per cent. Other evidence suggests that net emigration of Jews from those parts of Canada (see Statistics Canada, 1981 Census Report No. 92-907, Table 2) has aggravated the YMT decline due to high mortality in the generally old population involved. In contrast, Ontario's Jewish immigration gains during this 1961-1981 period have moderated its YMT shrinkage (54 per cent) somewhat, but few Yiddish speakers enter Canada today, as Jews come from predominantly other linguistic backgrounds and internal migrants are overwhelmingly of English Mother Tongue. These trends will likely continue in the current decade.

Table 3   Yiddish Mother Tongue vs Yiddish Home Language in Canada, 1971 and 1981[a]

	TOTAL JEWS	YMT[b] POPULATION	YLH[c] POPULATION	YLH AS % OF JEWS	YLH AS % OF YMT
1971	276,000	49,900	26,300	9.5%	53%
1981	296,400	32,800	10,650	3.6%	32%

[a]All figures are rounded to the nearest fifty.
[b]Yiddish Mother Tongue
[c]Yiddish Language of the Home
Sources: Statistics Canada, 'Mother Tongue' (Cat. No. 92-902) from the 1981 Census; 1971 Census of Canada, Vol. 1, Part 4 (Table 10); and Report 92-910 from the 1981 Census (Tables 1 and 6).

Looking further at the Maritimes data in Table 2, we see that the total YMT population had shrunk to 200 people in 1981, suggesting that Yiddish is virtually defunct in that area. Outside Ontario and Quebec, it is only Manitoba's Winnipeg that retains some vigour as a Yiddish centre, but it too has lost—between 1961 and 1981—at least half of its former YMT strength.

Recent censuses have also inquired about language usually spoken at home, which indicates the *next* generation's mother tongue but need not be the same as the mother tongues of today's adults. In Canada, the use of English at home is generally increasing (1971 vs 1981) at the expense of all non-official languages (see Henripin, 1974: 37-8). This new kind of information—not available prior to 1971—gives us additional perspectives on the changing fortunes of Yiddish, as we examine Yiddish Language of the Home (YLH) in addition to YMT trends. We begin to do this in the lower part of Table 2, and focus on it directly in Table 3.

To conclude our discussion of regional changes in Yiddish, in light of the distinction between those who know the language (YMT) and those who still use it normally (YLH) in private life, we note in Table 2 that the 1981 Yiddish-speaking population (YLH) is much smaller than the YMT total: 10,650 for YLH compared to 32,750 for YMT. But the regional concentration in YLH is very evident, suggesting the emerging outlines of the 1991 picture from our present data. Looking at the Montreal plus Toronto YLH population, we find (in Table 2) 90.9 per cent of Canada's total, leaving a mere 9.2 per cent in the rest of Canada. Winnipeg's YLH total is reduced to hundreds, compared to the many thousands in previous decades, while in all the Maritimes together there are only 20 YLH respondents, so that Yiddish is now dead there as a domestic language. The total disappearance of YMT people east of Montreal is just a matter of time, as the remaining old YMT population passes from the scene. The Canadian West is probably not far behind, in contrast to the apparent durability of the Central-Canada YLH population.

Table 3 shows us the rapid decline in current use of Yiddish—measured by

YLH totals—compared with the slower decline of YMT population. While the ten-year interval (1971-1981) brought a decline of 17,100 people in Canada's YMT total, which is 34 per cent fewer than at the earlier Census, the YLH decline of 15,700 was fully 60 per cent of the 1971 at-home speakers. Whereas in 1971 the majority (53 per cent) of YMT Canadians continued to speak Yiddish at home, by 1981 fewer than one in three of the YMT population were counted among the YLH group. The figures in Table 3 thus mean cessation of use by those who know the language, not just dying-off of its aged speakers.

Also visible in Table 3 is the disappearance of Yiddish as a common tongue among Jews. Whereas 1 in 10 was a Yiddish speaker (9.5 per cent) in 1971, that had dropped to one in 28 Jews by 1981 (3.6 per cent). This is very clear evidence of Yiddish having almost become a 'dead language,' known and studied by specialists but not a folk tongue any longer. As a survey respondent wrote to Prof. Thiessen, nearly 20 years ago (1973: 89):

> When eastern Europe was destroyed, Yiddish lost its geographical base, and though enclaves may continue to exist in Mea Shearim, Williamsburg, Montreal and Rio, the end is in sight. Sure, we have Yiddish courses in our universities. These are attended by students whose parents left them culturally rootless, and who are searching for their Zaida (grandfather) and the shtetl (ghetto). For them it is a therapy. . . . For those with the long view, Yiddish is an episode like Alexandria, or Spain, and is destined for the limbo of Aramaic and Ladino.

It is difficult to disagree with this assessment.

Impact on Jewish Cultural Life

There are many Yiddish boosters (Boraisha, 1981 [1946]: 47; Fishman, 1981: 4 and Landis, 1981; Rudin, 1976; Thiessen, 1973: 37-41) who claim that the abandonment of Yiddish will mean grave losses for Jewish identity and culture, but this thesis may be hard to sustain on a more objective examination.

One line of pro-Yiddish argument sees it as the essential international bond of world Jewry. Has Yiddish not served, this group says, as the common denominator linking Jews of different countries but of East European origin (Patai, 1971: 126-8)? Will the loss of this language, then, mean the loss of the international Jewish community?

What has been happening, over the past few decades, is the replacement of Yiddish by Hebrew as the normal communication medium among serious Jews, or the really 'Jewish Jews'. Rather than leaving a true void, the passing of Yiddish might be said more easily to permit construction of an intangible bridge linking Israel with Diaspora Jewry—modern spoken Hebrew. At the same time, young Jews from Buenos Aires, New York, and Antwerp are increasingly using Hebrew (often perfected during an educational sojourn in Israel) to speak with one another.

Speaking Yiddish is generally understood in the literature (e.g., Wirth, 1975 [1928]: 181-5), to be a very important indicator of fidelity to shtetl culture in all its ramification; thus, replacement of Yiddish by German (in pre-Holocaust Europe) or English (in North America) is taken to mean that modernization has taken place, and the speaker no longer functions within the mental and social framework of the highly isolated, very religious and traditionalist culture of East-European Jewry (see Heilman, 1981). Yiddish speech is a symptom, however, not a cause, of Jewish knowledge and commitment, but many writers apparently confuse these and promote the daily use of Yiddish believing that this medium guarantees the survival of Yiddishkeit; i.e., a distinct Jewish community, culture, and lifestyle.

It should also be remembered that the use of Yiddish for literary purposes (rather than for translation of prayer books and other sacred works on behalf of the poorly-schooled) does not go back much earlier than 1850, and its adoption then was a blow to those who wished to revive Hebrew for expressing modern Jewish creativity. It is, thus, not at all clear that Yiddish is the best medium for Jewish writing, or that the latter will now be impoverished by a shift to Hebrew (and English, for that matter). We cannot pursue this issue any further here, but it is considered elsewhere (Orenstein, 1981).

Prospects for Spoken Yiddish

What remains to be considered is the fate of Yiddish among Hassidim, who are no doubt an increasingly major component of that remaining YLH group we still found in 1981, which will show up in later censuses as an 'endangered species' just hanging on. No longer a general Jewish tongue, Yiddish is becoming a specifically Hassidic medium, which will tend to cut Hassidim off from other Jews who no longer use it. This development makes of Yiddish an identity-card for Hassidim which may have vital functions internationally (as Hassidim resident in different countries meet), but at the local level Yiddish is merely an alternative to local host-society languages. That is, Montreal or Parisian Hassidim may speak French to each other, or Yiddish; Brooklyn Hassidim can choose English or Yiddish; and Jerusalemites have a Hebrew or Yiddish option. Yiddish speakers today all have communication alternatives; thus their use of Yiddish is a constant choice, an ongoing act of value-guided fidelity to tradition.

It is inconceivable, one might argue, that Hassidim should use English or French—thus Yiddish is safe among them! However today's reality is not guaranteed indefinitely, and here we are trying to project linguistic patterns ten, even twenty years in the future. While Yiddish is secure now among Hassidim everywhere, we cannot be so sure about the future (cf. Jochnowitz, 1981: 737).

Interestingly, a close look at the 1981 YLH data indicates that Yiddish has not only lost many YMT Jews in their adulthood, but has also gained a few who were not YMT children but now report use of the language in their own homes. (Perhaps this is just a pious fantasy in some cases.) Many of these must, no doubt, be 'Baalei Teshuva' (late-starting or 'born again' Jews, who turn to Orthodox belief and practice after being part of the secular majority); if such penitents whole-heartedly adopt a Hassidic lifestyle, they are likely to also learn Yiddish and use it at home.

According to the 1981 Census report on language use (92-910, Table 1: 1-7), Yiddish is home language for 8,180 people of YMT, but the total YLH population is, as we saw above (Tables 2 and 3), over 10,600 people. Thus, subtracting 8,180 YMT Canadians who are also YLH respondents from the 10,635 YLH total (No. 92-910, Table 6: 6-5), we find 2,455 converts to Yiddish, i.e., people of other mother tongues now speaking Yiddish at home. This group is surprisingly substantial; these 2,455 people are fully 23 per cent of Canada's 1981 YLH total. Nevertheless, during the 1980s Yiddish will undoubtedly continue to lose more speakers than it gains, in line with the 1971-1981 trends shown in Table 3, above.

Self-report data on language use may include some wishful thinking or pro-underdog inaccuracies, as Charles (1948: 86) hypothesized many years ago, in considering fertility data among Jewish women: 'Possibly among the Canadian—and British—born, the statement of Yiddish mother-tongue indicates Jewish sentiment rather than the actual use of this language in the home.' In more recent years, it seems even more reasonable to be a little sceptical about the validity of such language statistics, without rejecting them altogether.

A great contemporary scholar of retention and evolution in Yiddish (in both its linguistic and sociological aspects), J.A. Fishman (1980: 482-3) writes:

> If I could pick the populations to monitor more closely . . . I would select ultraorthodoxy in the USA and in Israel. . . . The appearance of a non-Yiddish speaking orthodoxy must have a very definite impact on the phenomenology of Yiddish among Yiddish speaking orthodoxy, both in the USA and Israel. . . . In both countries ultraorthodoxy is beginning to accept and to enact national (citizenship) roles, to interact more with nonorthodox Jews as well as with non-Jews, to be more exposed to standard printed Yiddish. . . . All of these social processes, ongoing in different ways, have differential consequences for Yiddish.

These remarks indicate, in contrast to most of the literature, an awareness of the still-evolving contemporary fate of Yiddish—a feature of Jewish life not static or eternal, but continuing to reflect the demographic, educational, and inter-group contact factors of contemporary Diaspora Jewry. Fishman touches here on many of the de-isolating factors that may be making the empirical/descriptive content of work by Poll, Rubin, and others—which we looked at earlier—obsolete in another generation or so. (See the description of 'Linguistic Assimilation' in Patai, 1971: 369-71.)

One fact in favour of Yiddish is the generally high natural increase (i.e., surplus of births over deaths) among Hassidim, who frown very strongly on birth control and abortion and have large families. As Rubin (1972: 123) tells us:

> couples strive to have children as soon as possible . . . age differences of a year or so between siblings are rather common. The current tendency in Satmar is toward large families.

Similarly, Isaacs (1977: 191) writes:

> . . . they are hurrying to repopulate the world with Hassidim. It is said that the Hassidic population of Brooklyn . . . is doubling every five years. . . . Hassidic families of 10, 12 or more children are not unusual. For the older Hassidim, these often are second families, the first ones having been killed in Europe.

Although Mayer's data (1979: 101) suggests much lower total fertility, the literature agrees that this part of the Jewish community is 'doing well' demographically, with substantial natural increase, and almost doubling every five years. Thus, Yiddish remains secure at present, in a minimal way, wherever there are Hassidim.

Theoretically speaking, one may ask why it should be the Hassidim who preserve Yiddish today, although they almost all have a fine working knowledge of classical Hebrew (and Talmudic Aramaic), while the secular and socialist 'Yiddishist' groups—so powerful in earlier years—have largely disappeared. Aside from a purely demographic explanation, in which high Hassidic fertility leads to cultural survival (in contrast to the low fertility of the Jewish majority), the literature rarely addresses this question. If Yiddish is so unimportant to most Jews, what is its special charm for the ultra-Orthodox?

Weinreich's (1981: 107-11) and Birnbaum's argument (1979: 13-14, 18-23) that Yiddish arose out of German, in the first place, and has further diverged from it during the past 400-600 years because of the East Ashkenazic Jews' religiously motivated desire for separateness (which produced their ghettos and thus their distinctive language) provides the key, evidently. Now, just as then, Yiddish is a symptom or product of rejecting the surrounding culture, its values and vernacular, in order to preserve the community's role as a sacred-spiritual group, and keep Jews a 'Kingdom of priests and a holy nation' (Exodus 19: 6); otherwise, Jews then could have quickly adopted Polish, Ukrainian, or what have you, and Yiddish would have long ago disappeared. Wirth's analysis (1975 [1928]: 268-89) of ghetto dynamics leads to the same conclusion. Therefore, massive secularization 'killed' Yiddish for most Jews (Birnbaum, 1979: 35-8), but the essential thrust of Hassidic commitment in daily practice is the devoted self-segregation that appreciates precisely the limited currency of Yiddish and holds on to it as a tool for just this purpose (see Rubin, 1972: 145-6 and Fishman, 1981: 10-11).

Conclusion

The result of our discussion, then, allows us to predict that in 1991 and after, the Census will reveal a continuing shrinkage of YMT population (as many older speakers pass away) but perhaps a stabilization of YLH; also, the percentage of YMT who are YLH people should begin climbing again, as the Hassidim of Canada doggedly speak Yiddish among themselves and with their children, becoming a small but not a declining population that will report—even if not always so accurately—that they are of Yiddish Mother Tongue *and* use Yiddish, ordinarily, as Language of the Home. If present language retention and fertility trends persist, these would be the statistical consequences evident in the 1991 and 2001 Censuses of Canada.

One cannot, however, extrapolate indefinitely. We do not know a number of crucial variables, including future Hassidic fertility patterns (perhaps a reaction, currently, to Holocaust losses or a sign of recency of immigration), and language choices that will be made by Canadian-born Hassidim (now not so numerous, but becoming an increasing proportion of the population), who *do* speak English, and often French in Montreal. Nor is it clear that we will never see massive emigration to Israel among Hassidim. Will there be as much travel and correspondence between Hassidim in different linguistic areas—keeping Yiddish vital as the common language—as there has been for the past few decades, or will Hassidic communities meet their needs locally and thus have less and less need of Yiddish? (Canadian English is *not* associated with pogroms. Will it eventually be accepted for daily use by Hassidic children?) If any of these variables shifted substantially, then the protected Yiddish sanctuary we have discovered might disappear again, perhaps by mass migration to Hassidic centres in Israel.

Fishman's (1980: 487) assessment is worth quoting here:

> Nevertheless, increasing reverence of Yiddish seems to be setting in, with increasingly favourable attitudes, side by side with decreasing utilization of the language.

Although he is depicting the Israeli linguistic scene, North American Ortho-dox circles are in a similar position. Ultra-Orthodox circles may follow, a little later—or perhaps much later. (See Fishman, 1981: 11-12, 46-8; Jochnowitz, 1981.)

As Orenstein (1981: 311-12) and others point out, Yiddish scholarly and literary activity continues to flourish in the major centres of Jewish culture, but it is hard to envision future conferences or publications on a large scale, if no one comes to hear and understand, or if there are no readers. The universities, having added Yiddish to their linguistic pantheon (Weinreich, 1965), will no doubt keep research and professional communication about Yiddish going for the foreseeable future, and there is still a nostalgia market for popular books (like Feinsilver, 1980 [1970]).

An emerging phenomenon begotten from the great in-group respect for

Yiddish, while actual speaking decreases, is Judaeo-English, or 'Yinglish'. Although the literature may not label it as such, observers of the non-Hassidic Orthodox scene (e.g., Helmreich, 1982: 148), have described the contemporary linguistic norm among American-born Talmud students, which is a heavily Yiddish-flavoured and Hebrew-laden argot very similar to Yiddish itself, but without the German and Slavic material. It is a result of the same kind of high isolation that Wirth (1975 [1970]: esp. Chap. XIV) and others talked about in explaining the emergence and maintenance of a strong Jewish culture in the Diaspora, and this tongue has important psycho-social functions for 'modern Orthodox' Jews today (Heilman, 1981: 246-50). In future, some of the scholarly attention that was focused on Yiddish may be redirected to this new area of Judaeo-English, which has no literature but no doubt thousands of quite unself-conscious speakers. Although not using much of its vocabulary they carry on the intimate spirit and music of Yiddish (see Feinsilver, 1980 [1970]: Chap. III).

Notes

[1]Works on the history of Yiddish are abundant; one major scholarly monograph is Landmann, 1962, another is the translation of Max Weinreich's history (1980). Brief overviews are provided by Birnbaum, 1979; Boraisha, 1946/1981; Herzog, 1978, and Thiessen, 1973.

[2]American data are not so easy to obtain and to turn into time-series tables, so we will not attempt to depict the US situation, although it is similar to Canada's.

References

Beaujot, Roderic and Kevin McQuillan
  1982 *Growth and Dualism* (Toronto: Gage Publishing Co.)

Birnbaum, Solomon A.
  1979 *Yiddish: A Survey and a Grammar* (Toronto: University of Toronto Press)

Boraisha, Menahem
  1981 'The Story of Yiddish', *Jewish Spectator* 46, 3 (Fall 1981): 40-7.
  [1946]

Charles, Enid
  1948 *The Changing Size of the Family in Canada* (Census Monograph No. 1). Ottawa: Dominion Bureau of Statistics, 1941 Census of Canada.

Davids, Leo
  1981 'The Family: Challenges for Survival' in *The Canadian Jewish Mosaic*, ed. by M. Weinfeld *et al.* (Toronto: John Wiley): 97-112.

———
  1983 'Jewish Demography: A Brief Overview of the Current World Situation', paper presented at Plenary Assembly of Canadian Jewish Congress (Montreal, May 1983).

Feinsilver, Lillian M.
1980   *The Taste of Yiddish* (New York: A.S. Barnes & Co. [1980 reprint])
[1970]

Fishman, Joshua A.
1980   'The Sociology of Yiddish After the Holocaust: Status, Needs and Possibilities' in *The Field of Yiddish*, ed. by Marvin I. Herzog *et al.* (Philadelphia: Institute for the Study of Human Issues): 475-98.

────────

1981   *Never Say Die! (A Thousand Years of Yiddish in Jewish Life & Letters)*. (The Hague: Mouton Publishers)

Heilman, Samuel C.
1981   'Sounds of Modern Orthodox[y]: The Language of Talmud Studies' in J.A. Fishman (ed.) *Never Say Die* (The Hague: Mouton): 227-53.

Helmreich, William B.
1982   *The World of the Yeshiva: An Intimate Portrait of Orthodox Jewry* (New York: Free Press)

Henripin, Jacques
1974   *Immigration and Language Imbalance* (Ottawa: Information Canada)

Herzog, Marvin
1978   'Yiddish' in *Jewish Languages: Theme and Variations*, ed. by Herbert H. Paper (Cambridge, Mass.: Association for Jewish Studies): 47-58.

Isaacs, Stephen
1977   'Hassidim of Brooklyn' in *A Coat of Many Colors*, ed. by Abraham D. Lavander (Westport, Conn.: Greenwood Press): 189-94.

Jochnowitz, George
1981   'Bilingualism and Dialect Admixture Among Lubavicher Hassidic Children' in J.A. Fishman (ed.) *Never Say Die* (The Hague: Mouton): 721-37.

Korn, Yitzhak
1981   'Yiddish and Hassidism', *Jewish Frontier* 48 (Oct.): 13-15, 18.

Lachapelle, Rejean and Jacques Henripin
1982   *The Demolinguistic Situation in Canada* (Montreal: Institute for Research on Public Policy)

Landis, Joseph C.
1981   'Who Needs Yiddish?' in J.A. Fishman (ed.) *Never Say Die* (The Hague: Mouton): 349-64.

Landmann, Salcia
1962   *Jiddish: Das Abenteuer Einer Sprache* (Olten: Walter Verlag)

Laurin, Camille
1977   *Le Français, Langue du Québec* (Montreal: Editions du Jour)

Mayer, Egon
1979   *From Suburb to Shtetl: The Jews of Boro Park* (Philadelphia: Temple University Press)

Orenstein, Eugene
1981 'Yiddish Culture in Canada, Yesterday and Today' in *The Canadian Jewish Mosaic*, ed. by M. Weinfeld *et al.* (Toronto: John Wiley): 293-313

Patai, Raphael
1971 *Tents of Jacob: The Diaspora—Yesterday and Today* (Englewood Cliffs, N.J.: Prentice Hall)

Poll, Solomon
1965 'The Role of Yiddish in American Ultra-Orthodox and Hassidic Communities', *YIVO Annual of Jewish Social Science* 13: 125-52.

Rubin, Israel
1972 *Satmar: An Island in the City* (Chicago: Quadrangle Books)

Rudin, Neil
1976 'Yiddish Literature: A Path to Ethnic Awareness', *Tradition* 16, 1 (Summer): 77-82.

Shaffir, William
1981 'Chassidic Communities in Montreal' in *The Canadian Jewish Mosaic*, ed. by M. Weinfeld *et al.* (Toronto: John Wiley): 273-86.

Thiessen, Jack
1973 *Yiddish in Canada: The Death of a Language* (Leer: Schuster Verlag)

Weinreich, Max
1980 *History of the Yiddish Language* (Translated from the 1973 original by S. Noble) (Chicago: University of Chicago Press)

———

1981 'The Reality of Jewishness Versus the Ghetto Myth' in J.A. Fishman (ed.) *Never Say Die* (The Hague: Mouton): 103-17.

Weinreich, Uriel
1965 *College Yiddish*, 4th ed. (New York: YIVO Institute)

Wirth, Louis
1975 *The Ghetto* (twelfth impression, 1975) (Chicago: University of Chicago
[1928] Press)

The author acknowledges the financial support of Multiculturalism Canada, and the constructive criticism of reviewers in the manuscript's earlier versions.

part four

Intercommunal

Relations

Introduction

Morton Weinfeld

Jewish life in Canada, as in any diaspora community, inevitably involves social interactions whose complexities extend beyond simple anti-Semitism. Indeed, Jews have both influenced and been influenced by their environment. Whether the issue is the deeply personal dilemma of intermarriage, or the formal relations among ethnic organizations and the government, or the informal economic networks in which Jews act, the patterns of Jewish behaviour reflect the evolving context of intercommunal relations.

In the New World, these relations have enjoyed an ease often absent in the Old World, marked with its history of political, and bloody, anti-Semitism. While anti-Semitism in Canada and the United States remains a fact of life, its manifestations and context are different. Within the environment of societies which are free, democratic, built on waves of immigration, and without the same rigidities of class and culture, the range of Jewish-Gentile relations was very wide.

In North America, as opposed to Europe, the Jewish rung in the ethnic or racial hierarchy was determined in part by the status of the pre-existing aborginal groups, as well as non-white immigrants. Jews, as white Europeans, benefited. In addition, the pre-existing conflict in Canada between the English and French meant that Jews became a kind of third solitude within the Canadian mosaic, and certainly within Montreal.

Canada defines itself as a multicultural society, with the concept enshrined — if somewhat ambiguously — in section 27 of the Charter of Rights and Freedoms. Canada offers two main policy objectives in the area of ethnicity: equality of opportunity without discrimination on the basis of origin, and the possibility of retaining and valuing a particular ethnic cultural heritage. It is unfortunate that even assuming the best intentions of politicians, the sad sociological truth is that these two objectives have a real zero-sum aspect. The more a group or individual tries to maximize the retention of a particular ethnic culture, the less likely that they will also be able to maximize socio-economic achievements.

Yet Jews, more than any other group, have somehow been able to fashion a workable synthesis from these two contradictory objectives. Jews enjoy high educational and economic status, while boasting high levels of communal organization and identification: the best which is feasible of both worlds (Breton *et al.*, 1990). As a result, other ethnic groups seek to emulate Jewish communal achievements in Canada.

Relations between Jews and the external community or communities vary between poles of segregation and integration. This may be determined in turn by the acceptance of Jews in various regions of Canada, and by the degree to which Jews share common characteristics, or common objectives, with other groups. At times communities will seek formal cooperation. A case in point is the tripartite collaboration on the constitutional debate developed by the organized Jewish, Italian, and Greek communities in Quebec.

In 'The Jews of Quebec: An Overview', Morton Weinfeld analyses the socio-cultural situation of Quebec's Jewish community, where the degree of isolation has been more pronounced than that of Jewish communities elsewhere in Canada. This isolation is rooted in historic language differences, given the anglicization of the early Jewish community. It continues to be manifested in the general federalist leanings of Jews, and most other Quebec anglophones and allophones, in the face of rising Quebec nationalism and the possibility of independence. The demonization by some Québécois of Mordecai Richler, and the varying responses to this demonization and to his new book, O Canada, O Quebec, by individual Jews and communal leaders, underscores this tension. The breakdown of these boundaries, a process which began in the post-war years, remains a formidable challenge.

In their review of Jewish-Ukrainian relations in Canada in the post-war period, Harold Troper and Morton Weinfeld compare these relations to the periodic hostilities which erupted in eastern Europe. The Canadian environment has served to dampen the historic volatility, routing it through the constraints of liberal democratic politics. Nevertheless, their analysis also reveals how the old wounds of history — specifically the role of Ukrainians as alleged collaborators in the Holocaust — may be resurrected within modern policy contexts and play a role in shaping communal agendas and identities.

A relatively under-researched area of ethnic activity is that of the ethnic community as an economic resource. Some recent studies have examined specific types of ethnic economic activity, (e.g., Light and Bonacich, 1988; Breton et al., 1990, ch. 4). Earlier work in this area suggested that such activity would be concentrated among immigrants, and would entail a kind of 'mobility trap' harming subsequent life chances (Wiley, 1967). Yet the evidence from Morton Weinfeld's study of the Jewish sub-economy in Montreal suggests that this intra-group Jewish economic behaviour may last beyond the immigrant generation and need not be associated with weaker economic performance.

Nothing can define the degree of inter-group relations more than intermarriage. Social scientists can interpret intermarriage in one of two ways. On the one hand nothing is a better barometer of acceptance by the majority group; on the other hand, it may also endanger the continued existence of the group itself. Jewish outmarriage is far lower than the rates for comparable ethnic and religious groups in Canada. Yet this is cold comfort for Jewish religious and communal leaders, who see in the clearly rising rates of inter-marriage the danger of extinction.

There exists little sociological consensus as to the precise causes of inter-marriage, at either the micro (individual) or macro (societal) level. It is also unclear whether intermarriage should be seen as a simple cause or conse-quence of assimilation, or indeed as a neutral event caused by multiple forces and capable of multiple outcomes and interpretations. In their analysis of Canadian intermarriage patterns, Robert Brym, Michael Gillespie, and A.R. Gillis focus attention on the role of structural demographic patterns, rather than anomie, in explaining inter-provincial variation in Jewish intermarriage. They reveal that Jewish outmarriage is more likely where the Jewish popula-tion is smaller and the proportion of North American-born, and North American in-migrants, is higher.

References

Breton, Raymond, Wsevolod W. Isajiw, Warren E. Kalbach, and Jeffrey G. Reitz
  1990 *Ethnic Identity and Equality: Varieties of Experience in a Canadian City* (Toronto: University of Toronto Press)

Light, Ivan and Edna Bonacich
  1988 *Immigrant Entrepreneurs: Koreans in Los Angeles. 1965-1982* (Berkeley: Univer-sity of California Press)

Wiley, Norbert
  1967 'The Ethnic Mobility Trap and Stratification Theory', *Social Problems* 15: 147-59

The Jews of Quebec: An Overview

Morton Weinfeld

The Jews are a small minority within Quebec; but the Québécois are an equally small minority within a predominantly English-speaking continent. To understand the situation of Jews in Quebec, it is thus important to recognize that we have here not a classic minority–majority relationship, but rather one between two groups, each of which is deeply marked by minority traits. Before presenting a brief overview of the Jewish community in Quebec, it might be worthwhile to note some of the points of similarity between Jews and Québécois. For it is one theme of this essay that the relation between Jews and non-Jewish francophones in Quebec has yet to overcome social and psychological barriers sustained by the dual insecurities involved.

Both Jews and Québécois are groups that have been obsessed with survival, in both its quantitative and qualitative forms. One consequence of this has been a deep concern for rates of fertility and natural increase, determinants of group size. A second consequence has been the development of institutional supports for defending the group against external threats. Thus Jewish communal organizations, which can be seen as decision-making bodies at the head of a Jewish 'polity',[1] are alert for signs of anti-Semitism and defend Jewish interests. The Quebec government likewise has as one of its objectives the defence (and expansion) of the rights and interests of the French collectivity.

A third consequence of this obsession with survival is the fear of attrition through cultural assimilation, i.e., the erosion of a group's knowledge of and commitment to its own culture. For Québécois, the dominant fear currently is of linguistic assimilation, away from the French language; for Jews, it is a drift away from Jewish religious and cultural behaviour and from ties with the community. For both groups, specific languages play central roles in maintaining the group, albeit in very different ways. While French is the language of daily use for Québécois, Yiddish and Hebrew for Jews have come to assume symbolic importance, as languages associated with religious ritual, familial history, and group celebrations.

Both groups share parallel histories of minority struggle and perceived victimization, including a common exclusion by a dominant Anglo-Saxon group from key economic and social sectors in Quebec. This has made communication between the two groups almost impossible. To some extent, victimized groups develop compassion for other victimized groups. In Quebec, this compassion has been shifted. Québécois may perceive Jews as successful or powerful, and thus are unaware of the fragility of this condition or the insecurity which it masks. Jews perceive francophones as a dominant political majority controlling government in Quebec, unaware of the resentments and frustrations of a conquered people. Each has had its own agenda for survival, its own baggage of travail and sorrow in which there is little room for compassion for the suffering of the other. For both Jews and Québécois, the motto 'Je me souviens' rings true; however, they are remembering very different histories — one remembers Auschwitz, the other, the Plains of Abraham.

Brief Demographic Outline

As is the case for most minority groups in Quebec, to speak of the roughly 100,000 Jews in Quebec is to speak really of the Jews of Montreal.[2] Montreal Jews tend, in general, to reside in geographically limited areas — usually in west-end sections with significant Jewish populations — and not scattered throughout the province as a whole, or even the many sections of Montreal which are predominantly francophone. What has captivated Montreal Jewry about their city is its cosmopolitan, as well as its intensively Jewish, character. The Jewish neighbourhoods — with their bakeries and butchers, parks, playgrounds, delicatessens, cinemas, synagogues, Jewish schools, and other communal institutions — combine with the appeal of the downtown core, Lac-aux-Castors park, old Montreal, and the Laurentian mountains where Jews used to vacation (before Florida swept the province, Jew and Gentile alike), and other selected spots, to cement the tie of Montreal Jews to their city. It is this unique ambience that is captured historically in some of the fictional reconstructions of Mordecai Richler's St Urbain Street. It can be found today in the streets and shopping centres of Jewish neighbourhoods several miles to the west of St Urbain Street. Thus, to the extent that the true historic character of Quebec lies outside the Montreal metropolis — in smaller cities, towns, villages — Montreal Jews have had very little contact with it.

Even within Montreal, Jewish residential segregation continues to be very high, as it is for most other minority groups in the city. For example, a 1978 survey of Jewish household heads in Montreal found nearly one-third of Montreal Jews concentrated in the Snowdon-Côte-des-Neiges area of Montreal, with a further 18 per cent in Côte-St-Luc.[3] Other areas of relative Jewish concentration are the largely English-speaking communities within Hampstead, St-Laurent, Chomedey-Laval, Notre-Dame-de-Grace, Westmount and the Town of Mount Royal. Virtually no Jews live east of Boulevard St-Laurent.

The Jews of Montreal are an aged group, compared to most other groups in the province; indeed the aging of Diaspora Jewry is a common trend. The main reason for this aging is the low fertility rate of Jews, historically and at present, where Jewish reproduction seems near zero population growth. The aging population will mean that communal institutions may have to scram-

ble desperately to recruit new people for membership and leadership positions, and funds for their maintenance.

Like all minority groups in Quebec, the Jewish community includes a
large proportion of foreign-born members. As a rule of thumb, we can
estimate that just about one-half of the Jewish adults in Quebec were born in
North America. (The comparable figure in the United States would be about
80 per cent.) This high proportion of immigrants reflects migration processes of the pre-war and post-war period (including Holocaust survivors), as
well as more recent waves of immigrants from the Soviet Union, Israel, and
North Africa. Jewish immigration to Quebec has slackened in recent years.
Since immigrants are often young adults, the lower immigration rates may
add to the high age level of the Jewish population.

Who are the Jews?

The Jews in Quebec, like Jews in any Diaspora community, do not fit neatly
into one simple category. There are a number of analytically distinct components of Jewishness, with a variety of definitions of who is a Jew. These
various bases of Jewish identity make analysis of the Jewish group somewhat
more complex than that of other minority groups.

Jews as a Religious Group

Perhaps the dominant perception of Jews is as a religious group—one bound
together by common beliefs and religious practices. For a large part of Jewish
history, certainly through most of the 2,000 years since the Roman dispersion of Jews in the first Christian century, this perception may have been true.
Belief in one faith, in the God of the Torah, in the Torah as the word of God,
and rigorous observance of Jewish religious laws (e.g. *kashrut* or dietary laws)
was the normal pattern, though certain variations emerged within the framework of orthodox, Rabbinic Judaism.

Today, however, religious Judaism is fragmented into four main branches:
Orthodox, Conservative, Reform, and Reconstructionist.[4] The latter three
are newer branches, each attempting to modify Orthodox Judaism in harmony with the intellectual, social, and practical constraints of modern life.
These four branches of Judaism often conflict with each other, particularly
the Orthodox group, which sees itself as the guardian of authentic Judaism
and thus denies the legitimacy of the other denominations. Each denomination is structurally and politically independent—there is no equivalent of the
Papacy in Judaism.

In Montreal, roughly 41 per cent of adult Jews identify themselves as
Orthodox, 35 per cent as conservative, and 9 per cent as Reform, with the
remainder not identifying themselves with any of these three branches.
Montreal Jews, like Jews throughout North America, are not frequent
synagogue-goers. Twenty per cent of Montreal Jews claim they *never* attend

synagogue, and another thirty per cent *only* attend on the major holidays of Rosh Hashanah and Yom Kippur. Of those who attend, two-thirds attend Orthodox synagogues. Moreover, it seems that many Montreal Jews who hold membership in congregations do so for family or sentimental reasons — but not to attend services regularly.[5]

Religion, however, is more than regular synagogue attendance. Montreal Jews tend to demonstrate their religiosity (at least in comparison to American communities) in other ways. It was found that 93 per cent attend a Passover seder, 80 per cent refrain from eating bread on Passover, 81 per cent fast on Yom Kippur and light Hanukkah candles, 61 per cent light Sabbath candles, and 46 per cent claim to observe *kashrut*, dietary laws at home.[6]

The religiosity of Jews is also demonstrated in observance of Jewish life-cycle rituals: circumcision of the newborn male child; bar and bat mitzvah ceremonies at puberty; intensive marriage celebrations; and the *shiva* ritual of mourning for the death of a family member. In addition, the extensive development of a private network of Jewish day schools — in which close to half the school day is devoted to Jewish subjects such as Bible, Talmud, Hebrew (or Yiddish) language and literature, Jewish history and philosophy — can be considered a manifestation of the traditionalism, if not religiosity, of Montreal Jewry.

The role of religion in the life of Quebec Jews is, in summary, more of periodic symbolic importance rather than continuing, regular involvement. Yet, one can argue that it is the very infrequency of Jewish religious partici-pation that invests in each specific ritual of practice observed, an above-average emotional or psychological importance. Moreover, the religious rituals or holidays observed most regularly are those functional to the goal of survival, while requiring the least inconvenience. They tend to be infrequent (in contrast to daily requirements such as *tefillin* or weekly requirements like strict Sabbath observance), child-centred (helping to socialize the young), or parallel to Christian holidays in timing and practice (e.g., gift-giving at Hanukkah).

Jews as an Ethnic Group

Jews are more than a religious group — they are in some ways a people, a nation, or in sociological parlance, an ethnic group. The ancient Hebrews were a nomadic tribe, before they received the Torah, and even in the Kingdom of Israel, Jews were defined (by themselves and others) as a nation with political sovereignty. There are many sociological definitions of 'ethnic group', yet Diaspora Jews share many of the characters of such groups no matter how defined: Jewish language(s) and culture(s); a sense of common origin and history; a sense of communal bond; a tie to a given territory (Israel); and in the words of psychologist Kurt Lewin, an interdependence of fate.

This sense of peoplehood was generally translated into communal struc-tures throughout the Diaspora, with an entrenched tradition of welfare institutions for the poor, the sick, and the elderly, supported from charitable donations by community members. (Charity, clearly, was more a moral *obligation* to the Jewish community than an act of kindness or love, as in the Christian traditions.)

This ethnic dimension is ironically rooted in the religious (Orthodox) definition of who is strictly a Jew — any person born of a Jewish mother. Thus there is an element of biological descent in the ethnic dimension. The emphasis on maternity dates back to ancient times when one could mistakenly identify paternity (as in cases of rape). An additional justification for the maternal definition is the presumed socializing role played by mothers rather than fathers for the young child. The point is that this biological definition, for Orthodox Jews, takes precedence over any other characteristics such as beliefs or behaviours; even the most non-observant, irreligious Jew is still a Jew, yet a person who was not born of a Jewish mother (or a person who converted to Judaism under a non-Orthodox auspices) is not considered Jewish according to most Orthodox Jewish leadership.

Any discussion of Jewish peoplehood in Quebec must include a description of the two major ethnic subgroups of Jews: Ashkenazim and Sephardim. Ashkenazim (the word means Jew from *Ashkenaz*, or ancient Germany) are essentially European Jews and their North American descendants. Ashkenazim speak Yiddish, a language based on medieval German and incorporating elements of Hebrew as well as Slavic languages. They in turn can be divided into German and Eastern-European Ashkenazim (from Poland, Russia). At one point substantial conflict existed in North America within this group, between the more upper-class German Jews (many affiliated with Reform Judaism) who had emigrated in the nineteenth century, and the poorer, more traditional East-European masses who emigrated at the turn of the century, fleeing Russian anti-Semitism and poverty. Today Ashkenazi Jews constitute the vast majority (over 95 per cent of Diaspora Jewry); only in Israel are they a minority, comprising 40–45 per cent of the Jewish population.

The second Jewish group is called Sephardim, from the Hebrew word for Spain, *Sepharad*. Sephardic Jewry today is, in fact, an amalgam of Jews from Spain (the original Sephardim) who dispersed into Southern Europe, Asia Minor, and North Africa, and what may be called Oriental Jews from communities in North Africa, Yemen, and Iraq which pre-dated the Spanish Expulsion by centuries. The largest group within Sephardic Jewry today consists of Jews from Morocco, Tunisia, and Algeria, all of which were French protectorates prior to independence. Sephardic Jews have their own authentic languages — Ladino, a form of Judeo-Spanish, and Judeo-Arabic. They differ from Ashkenazim in that their Gentile cultural environment, and often their lingua franca, was a matrix of Islam and Arabic, as opposed to the Christian (in its various forms) European influences on Ashkenazi Jewry. Sephardic Jews have distinctive religious rituals, customs, and practices, along with different languages and histories.

Quebec Jewry today differs from all other North American Jewish communities in its large proportion of North African or francophone Jews, estimated at between 15,000-20,000.[7] Of course, not all francophone Jews are Sephardim; many from France or Belgium are Ashkenazi. Moreover, not all Sephardim are North Africa or francophone; some are Syrian, Egyptian, or Iraqi Jews. Yet the vast majority of Sephardim in Montreal are both North African (essentially, Moroccan) and francophone.

The Sephardic Jews are a predominantly post-1945 immigrant group. Their arrival posed a dual problem of integration for the Montreal Jewish community. Not only where these Jews of different background (influenced by Islam, French, and Arab culture), but they tended, like the East European immigrants before them, to be relatively poor. Moreover, with swarthy complexions and black hair, they were often distinguished from the fairer, anglophone Jews. The reception of the local community to these newcomers ranged from concerned generosity (many of those immigrants were, in fact, refugees from actual or threatened intolerance) to apathetic indifference, to open distrust and hostility. The latter emotion perhaps reflected a paternalistic sense of superiority over these 'Arab Jews' as well as a politically motivated suspicion of the francophone dimension. Their French fluency was seen as a magnet drawing the North Africans into the still largely alien francophone majority, away from the traditional anglophone-Jewish orientation.

Yet, despite mutual tensions, the current situation is one of greater mutual respect and cooperation among the anglophone and francophone Jews. The processes of immigrant adaptation are largely over, and North African Jews have begun to entrench themselves in the middle class, in business and the professions. At the same time, the North African community succeeded in establishing its own institutional structure—a religious authority with a Moroccan Chief Rabbi, a school and an umbrella social and cultural agency called the Centre Sépharade du Québec. In addition, francophone Jewish representation has been increasing on the boards of most other Jewish communal agencies.

Jewish Culture

For many Jews, familiarity with elements of a Jewish cultural repertoire, with greater or lesser ties to religion or peoplehood, is the foundation of Jewish identity. Jewish culture, like culture generally, can be divided into high culture—literature, art, music, scholarship; and popular culture—the elements of lifestyle such as food, dress, mannerism, speech, social custom, folklore, humour—typical of the average member of the group.

Jewish languages play a role in both. Yiddish, the language of Ashkenazi Jews, is no longer a language of common daily use, except for elderly immigrants and clusters of ultra-orthodox Hassidic groups. Yet passive knowledge of Yiddish remains high. In 1971, 21,000 Quebec Jews claimed Yiddish as their mother tongue—the language they first learned and can still understand. The language also plays an important symbolic role, with key words or phrases used as code words to establish a special bond or rapport during communication. Jewish fiction, Jewish jokes, songs, curses, and cuisine make ample use of Yiddish terms in this way. At the same time, scholarly interest in Yiddish literature remains strong, legitimized by the acclaim accorded to the writings of I.B. Singer and the presence of Yiddish in university or Jewish Studies programs.

Hebrew is the second Jewish language; its role in the life of Quebec Jewry is on the rise. While it, too, is unlikely to be a primary language of use, it is strengthened by its role as the language of the Judaic religion — most Jewish children are taught some elements of Hebrew, and in Montreal, with the extensive network of Jewish schools as well as summer camps in which some Hebrew is used, it is likely that Hebrew will supplant Yiddish as the major Jewish language. Hebrew is also important as a bridge with the state of Israel. Not only do many Montreal Jews have Hebrew-speaking relatives or friends living in Israel, but Hebrew songs and dances have become standard features of Jewish festivals and entertainment. Finally, the substantial number of Israelis who have settled in Quebec in recent years, represents a living source of strength for the Hebrew language.

The prevalence of both Jewish languages is seen in the 1978 survey; we find 13 per cent who claimed to speak, and 45 per cent who claimed to read Hebrew 'very' or 'fairly' well; 59 per cent claimed to speak, and 37 per cent claimed to read Yiddish 'very' or 'fairly' well. With one-half of Jewish children attending private Hebrew day schools, the proportion speaking Hebrew should certainly increase in the future.[8]

Yet culture is more than language. One can argue that Jewish culture is now manifested in subtle ways, as part of an identifiable Jewish style. A visit to a Jewish delicatessen or bakery may illustrate this. Some Jews might argue the distinctiveness of Jewish humour. Others see significance in the abundant artifacts of Jewishness: *chais* or Stars of David worn on chains around the neck, *mezuzot* affixed to doorways, Israeli or Jewish paintings on the wall, even ostentatious patterns of dress called typically Jewish, yet in fact common to all *nouveau riche* groups.

More profoundly, we have a complex of values which, though rooted in Jewish tradition, are now considered general, secular characteristics. An example is the supposed priority which Jews place on harmonious family life, on responsibility to spouse and (aged) parents, pre-marital chastity (for females) and marital fidelity; and the particular emphasis on sacrifice for and protective nurture of the children. However, the import of modern life has been felt in the Jewish family as well, as seen in the rising Jewish divorce rate, and the discovery of abusive situations in Jewish families.

Another value is that of communal obligation in the form of charitable contributions. While it is fashionable to deride the meaning of Jewish philanthropy, its significance becomes apparent in comparisons with other groups. Jews give disproportionately more to Jewish and non-Jewish charities alike.

The latter donations may be motivated by the subconscious hope of buying acceptance or security. Some would argue that Jewish giving reflects an internalization of the Jewish responsibility to the less fortunate of all kinds. The 1978 study found that 87 per cent of the sample claimed to have contributed to the Combined Jewish Appeal in the past year. While this was probably an exaggeration, CJA records themselves suggest that two-thirds of Jewish households make some contribution. The median contribution lies in the $50-99 range; in Canada as elsewhere, the major donations flow from the 'big givers'.[9]

Certainly, the contributions of 'big givers' (often informally publicized) can be explained, in part, by the substantial application of organized pressure. *Noblesse oblige*, duty, and the search for communal recognition and praise are as important. Even more difficult to explain are the thousands of average donations from middle-income Jews. Nor can we explain the generosity which many Jews reserve for special philanthropic projects (e.g., a specific Israeli university or welfare institution) or for dramatic events like the Six-Day War of 1967.

Another example of the secularized cultural value is the Jewish commitment to and excellence in educational or scholarly pursuits. The present evidence of relative Jewish educational achievement is striking, beginning with average IQ scores to grade scores in various school levels, to completed college-level degrees. Even within academia, American studies attest to the prominence of Jews in the front rank.[10] This record of achievement, which cuts across all areas of endeavour—the sciences, the humanities, the professions—certainly contributes to what Ernest van den Haag has called 'the Jewish mystique', and has led to an accepted assumption that Jews tend to value intellectual achievement more than most groups. There is no denying the evidence, in Quebec as in elsewhere, of the levels of Jewish education achievement. In 1978, roughly 43 per cent of Montreal Jewish household heads had had at least some post-secondary education, roughly twice the Canadian level for persons aged 15 or over.[11]

'Jewish genius', as typified by Freud, Chomsky, Durkheim, Marx, Lévi-Strauss, or Einstein is another dimension of this mystique, which has interested non-Jewish scholars for some time. Most analysts link this unique element of original creativity to the marginality of Jewish intellectuals, who break from their formal religious tradition (Spinoza in this regard was perhaps the first modern Jewish intellectual), coupled with some idea of the transmutation of traditional Jewish Talmudic learning applied in the secular realm.[12]

Finally, in the United States, Jews, and through them the Jewish experience, have played an integral role in the development of contemporary American culture, at the 'high' and the popular level. Writers such as Saul Bellow, Philip Roth, and Bernard Malamud are celebrated novelists, among America's finest. Arts such as theatre and film are equally infused with Jewish talent, with such names as Neil Simon and Woody Allen as two examples.

And Jews play a predominant role in television, as producers, writers, directors, and even as actual characters. What this means is that Jews play a role in shaping mainstream American views — they are becoming less and less marginal. A farmer in rural Iowa or auto worker in Detroit can enjoy on his TV screen Jewish comics on 'the Johnny Carson Show' or situation comedies written by 'New York liberal' Jews.

In Quebec, there is no such interaction between Jews and mainstream francophone culture. The creative artists in the media are primarily francophone. Jewish creativity in Quebec (e.g., Mordecai Richler, Leonard Cohen, etc.) has been almost entirely in English. Even today, French-language artists are largely unfamiliar with Jewish life in its many dimensions. As a result, the French-language population receives little exposure to the Jewish community and its culture. This cultural alienation has played a large role in reinforcing a sense of Jewish marginality in Quebec.

Segregation

One indicator of Jewish identification is the pattern of social interaction which Jews display. In their informal social networks, among friends, neighbours or acquaintances, and perhaps surprisingly, even in economic activities, we find high degrees of Jewish social and economic segregation. Classical sociologists used to assume that this type of behaviour was inevitably a response to exclusionary behaviour on the part of the majority group, especially in regard to economic segregation. Yet contemporary evidence and analysis must conclude that some of this segregation is voluntary. Many Jews, consciously or unconsciously, signify their identification by socializing with other Jews.

In 1978, almost 90 per cent of adult Montreal Jews agreed that 'all or most' of their friends were Jewish, and 53 per cent agreed that among people in their neighbourhood, 'all or most' were Jewish. And more than one-third admitted that 'all or most' of their business associates were Jewish (employers, partners, employees, customers, suppliers, clients, etc.). While Jews are by no means unique in this tendency to group self-segregation, the extent of it lends some objective support to the frequent characterization of Jews as clannish or cliquish. Jews do stick together, and not only because of Gentile anti-Semitism. Factors like the laws of *kashrut*, as well as proscription against intermarriage, play some role. It is also possible that certain recreational pastimes, such as heavy social drinking, are more common among non-Jews than Jews, though the oft-remarked-upon tradition of Jewish sobriety, if not abstinence, has been changing dramatically. As might be expected, social segregation tends to be greatest among older, less-educated, English-speaking Jews.

Jewish economic segregation is also widespread, with only 30 per cent of Montreal household heads employed by essentially non-Jewish firms — the majority is either self-employed or works for wholly or largely Jewish-run concerns. What is interesting is that this Jewish economic segregation seems equally prevalent among foreign-born and native-born, and religious and less-religious Jews. Moreover, there seems to be no difference in the occupational status or income of Jews deeply involved in this 'Jewish sub-economy' and those less involved.[13]

Israel

Israel, as both a political reality and as an idea, plays an important role in the lives of Quebec Jews. It is often difficult for non-Jews to understand the bond between Israel and Diaspora Jews. Part of the attachment is a subliminal residue of the centrality of Zion in the Jewish liturgy and in the Jewish Holy Scriptures. Yet, there is more. In the post-Holocaust era, Israel symbolizes for many Jews the triumph of Jewish aspiration in the face of complete despair, an ego-boosting alternative to the historic image of the weak, suffering Jew. Israel is one way for the Jew to comprehend the incomprehensible—the destruction of European Jewry. Secondly, practically all Jews—Ashkenazi and Sephardi alike—have personal ties to Israel via relatives and friends, and thus have a direct personal stake in Israel's security and prosperity.

Quebec Jews demonstrate their ties to Israel in myriad ways. Philanthropy to Israel is one. Sixty per cent of the total CJA contribution is sent to Israel, and only 29 per cent of Montreal contributors feel that more of the CJA receipts should go to local needs. Secondly, 60 per cent of Jewish household heads have visited Israel, and 45 per cent, more than once. Israel, through emissaries of Zionist causes and the state, maintains an organization devoted to the goals of facilitating Jewish immigration to Israel, as well as defending Israel's case to both the Jewish and non-Jewish public. Another indicator of the tie to Israel is seen in the type of news stories which Montreal Jews follow. Forty-seven per cent find news on the Middle East (i.e. Israel) most interesting, followed by 26 per cent indicating 'Quebec news' and 20 per cent, national (Canada) news.[14]

This emotional, financial, and political involvement in Israel's fate poses two current questions: first, given the fact that the state has been successfully created, that most Diaspora Jews show no intention of emigrating to Israel (the classical Zionist vision), and that 90 per cent of Montreal Jews feel one can 'be a good Jew' without moving to Israel, what are the unique, specific roles which Zionist organizations play in the Diaspora? For example, the sophisticated defence of Israel's case in the political arena is handled by the Comité-Québec-Israel, a professional lobby, independent of Zionist organizations.

A second problem is the working out of the proper relationship between Diaspora Jews and Israel, in terms of mutual criticism and possible dissent from Israeli policy. Because of the tremendous pressures ranged against Israel, including the armed Arab states, the Soviet bloc and most of the Third

World — sustained by Arab petro-dollars and the threat of energy blackmail in collaboration with oil companies — Diaspora Jews have become reluctant to criticize Israeli policies in public. The fear has been that such criticism might be misinterpreted as anti-Zionist, which for many Jews is, in its de facto consequence, little more than a dressed-up, pseudo-intellectualized anti-Semitism. Israel, from its perspective, has insisted on unfailing support for its policies from Diaspora Jews, arguing that Jews not living in Israel, and thus not faced with the dangerous realities and consequences of Israel's decisions, ought to defer to Israel's judgement.

While Jews in Quebec are solidly committed to Israel's survival, it appears that a re-thinking of the Diaspora-Israel tie and the legitimacy of constructive criticism is taking place in some circles. Yet this does not detract from the major aspect of the relationship: the commitment to, even love for, the Jewish state, and the concern for its security and development.

In the early twentieth century, the Zionist movement encountered, from both hostile Gentiles and sceptical or fearful Jews, the charge of potential dual loyalty. It was feared that Jewish citizens of Diaspora countries might become suspect citizens, with a prior loyalty to the new Jewish state. The contemporary version of the dilemma is the need for Jewish defenders of Israel's cause to harmonize this advocacy with the foreign and domestic interests of the host country. For most liberal democratic societies, this poses few if any problems.

First, it is recognized that this fear of 'dual loyalty' is an anachronistic relic of the days of the nation-state. The only loyalty owed by Jews or any citizens to the democratic state is obedience to its laws and acceptance of legal duties and obligations. Within these conditions, it is the legitimate right of any group of citizens in a representative democracy (Jews concerned for Israel, Poles concerned for Poland, conservationists concerned for the environment) to petition and attempt to influence the policies of their government. Second, most Western societies have been strong supporters of Israel's rights to security and survival, for moral, political, and geo-strategic reasons. (In a society such as France, however, which has changed since 1967 from its previous firm support for Israel, the Jewish community has experienced particular unease.) Third, the Jewish commitment to Israel has not prevented Jewish communities from contributing, disproportionately in many ways, to the economic, cultural, scientific, and political health of the Diaspora host societies, and it should not in the future.

The Jewish Polity

Sociologists have described the role of voluntary organizations as a medium for expression of Jewish identity. The old saying of 'for every two Jews, three organizations' captures this tendency to organize which typifies Jewish life. Using the term of Raymond Breton, Jews are an 'institutionally complete' ethnic group. The Jewish community provides a wide array of social institutions meeting welfare, health, social, cultural, recreational, athletic, religious, and educational needs for its members. While all ethnic groups boast a network of such institutions, financed in large part by voluntary donations or fee-for-service within the community, and which by definition parallel the public-institutional networks provided by the state, the Jewish network is perhaps the most extensive.[15]

The roots of the organized Jewish community lie both in the tradition of Jewish collective responsibility in Europe, and in the anti-Semitism which Jews faced in North America in a variety of settings, from hospitals to social clubs. This led Jews to develop their own institutions in response.

Several observers have used the term 'polity' to describe this facet of Jewish life. Through their financial contributions, a form of voluntary taxation, the Jewish community supports a range of services for its members and, through a variety of procedures of varying degrees of democracy, selects individuals for positions of authority.

The two dominant communal structures in Montreal are the Allied Jewish Community Services (AJCS), and the Canadian Jewish Congress, Quebec Region (CJC).

These Jewish institutions come into contact at various points with the external governmental authorities. Many Jewish welfare organizations receive funding from the provincial government, in recognition of the 'public character' of these services (e.g., the Sir Mortimer B. Davis Jewish General Hospital, or Jewish Family Services, a social welfare agency). It should be noted that the facilities or services of these agencies, whether the YMHA, the Jewish Public Library, the Saidye Bronfman Centre, the Hillel student organization, are available to *any* member of the public. Even more important, Jewish Day Schools receive over 50 per cent subsidies per pupil from the Quebec Ministry of Education, once they have met government requirements regarding hours of French-language instruction.

The AJCS combines the functions of fund-raising (via the Combined Jewish Appeal) with administration and co-ordination of the more than twenty welfare and cultural agencies in its jurisdiction. Each agency, and AJCS itself, is administered by professional staff and by lay boards of individuals appointed from the community at large and, occasionally, from the specific constituency which the agency serves. This objective description of the political process hides the powerful roles of a handful of wealthy contributors who exercise influence — directly or indirectly — whether they actively hold formal positions of authority. This influence is not used for day-to-day routine but for key decisions of general importance or for setting broad, communal priorities.

The CJC has been called the Parliament of Canadian Jewry. Its major executive officers are elected through a process of representative group-democracy in which voters are allocated to the various Jewish organizations in accordance with their membership. Among its duties, Congress is responsible for representing the Jewish community to the federal or provincial governments in

Canada in any matters of concern to the community, ranging from proposals for a new Canadian constitution to that of Soviet Jewry. There is overlap in responsibility for domestic issues between AJCS and CJC, and over the years, power and influence have gravitated from the CJC to the AJCS.

Like the AJCS, power within Congress affairs often resides in a few wealthy individuals (though the role of wealth is greater at AJCS than within the CJC) who may be in contact with elected officers or professional staff.

The degree to which these two dominant organizations are responsive to the needs of the Jewish community, i.e., are open to change initiated from 'below' or are open to a cross-section of communal participation, is a matter of some debate. Though strict procedures of formal electoral democracy are not observed, democratic outcomes often ensue. For example, the Montreal Jewish communal leadership has been prodded successfully on certain issues, such as increasing the importance of Jewish education, or a vigorous adoption of the cause of Soviet Jews, which originated from within the community (notably younger, more militant Jews). Indeed, the Jewish élite has often co-opted insurgent grass-root movements, by integrating those involved into the mainstream community. This strategy is far from Machiavellian: it represents a chronic shortage, facing the Jewish community, of persons with the talent and motivation to volunteer their services for communal work.

On balance, the organized Jewish community probably fares no better — and nor worse — than does the Canadian or Quebec state in terms of qualitative democracy. In other electoral systems, the theoretical safeguards of political rights are strong, but in practice they often fall short of the mark. Voting rates are low, and even for voters, the majority confines its political participation to the quinquennial ballot. The Jewish polity, while weaker in democratic *process*, may in its rough fashion compensate with a reasonable degree of responsiveness. While far from ideal, the Jewish polity and its Canadian counterparts at the federal, provincial, and municipal level are comparable in their output and grudgingly acceptable for their members. The 1978 survey found that only 16 per cent felt that the leadership of the Jewish community represents the interest of 'a few Jews', 50 per cent, 'most Jews', and 34 per cent, 'all Jews'.[16]

At the level of the individual Jew, we know that for some, activism within Jewish organizations plays an important, ego-satisfying role. Almost 80 per cent of Montreal Jews are regular or occasional readers of the Jewish press in Canada; 48 per cent claim membership in at least one Jewish voluntary organization (e.g. B'nai B'rith, Hadassah, YMHA), and 54 per cent claim to attend at least one yearly lecture, discussion, or artistic performance sponsored by the Jewish community.[17]

Socioeconomic Profile of the Community

The Jewish community in Montreal is a wealthy one, by any comparative or absolute yardstick. In the 1978 survey, more than 55 per cent listed their occupation as either manager-administrator or professional-technical; more than 13 per cent reported family incomes of greater than $50,000. Yet, high average levels of wealth mask a reality which includes many poor Jews — by one estimate, one sixth of Montreal Jews. For example, the 1978 survey found roughly one-quarter of respondents claiming annual family incomes of less than $10,000.[18]

While Jewish poverty is found among the unemployed (6 per cent of the 1978 sample), immigrants, female-headed households, and the middle-aged, the bulk of Jewish poverty is concentrated in the aged. Many of these were members of the fairly large Jewish working class in Quebec of the 1920s and the 1930s. Others are elderly post-war immigrants. However, it is safe to assume that as generations pass, the middle-class nature of the Jewish community will become more prevalent. (By 1978, only 8 per cent of household heads listed skilled labour as their occupation.)

It is this relative affluence of the Jewish community that creates the foundation of organized Jewish life. Moreover, research reveals that Jewish wealth, as measured by income, is explicable by factors such as education or had work. Indeed, Jews in Quebec had to overcome economic discrimination (mainly from the wealthy Anglo-Saxon élite) in a struggle for economic success, and in transformation from its early, working-class character.

Some Jewish intellectuals in Quebec (as elsewhere), usually marginal to the mainstream community or highly assimilated, are ill at ease with this new relative affluence. For some, its very existence signifies a betrayal of a Jewish left-wing heritage and early socialist sympathies. Jewish life today is thus stereotyped as a barren, materialistic, middle- and upper middle-class suburban one, and as an obstacle rather than pace-setter in fundamental social reform.

Some of these Jewish intellectuals or artists lament the passing of the immigrant, Yiddish, working-class generation, and hold a nostalgic, often exaggerated vision of the communal warmth and social solidarity which is assumed to have existed then.

Yet this transition to middle- and upper middle-class status, in Quebec and elsewhere, is linked to the question of whether Jews in North America have become relatively more conservative. The question is of interest given the long record of Jews (as individuals and as a community) in support of left-wing or liberal causes and reform. American public opinion polls consistently have found Jews the most opposed to censorship, outspoken in favour of welfare legislation, freedom of speech to Communists and in favour of rights to birth control, sex education, and abortion, and equal rights for all minorities. In Quebec, Jews played a role in the trade union movement, and in opposing the anti-democratic elements of the Duplessis regime. The historic voting record also shows Jews voting disproportionately for the main liberal parties, whether Democrats over Republicans in the US, or Liberals over Union Nationale in Quebec.

The Jewish political dilemma has always been to reconcile their economic interests in a free market place with their political interest as a small, insecure, vulnerable minority in protection for individual rights. One way to understand the strong Jewish support for federalism and the Liberal party nationally and provincially is to recognize that Jews believe that these options best safeguard their interests on both counts. This theme is developed in the following sections.

Jews and the Quebec Environment

The Jewish response to life in Quebec is a paradox. On one hand, Jews prosper economically and enjoy full religious freedom and state support for Jewish schools and other institutions. According to the 1971 census, Jews were the most bilingual of Quebec's anglophone groups, with 44 per cent claiming to speak French; the 1978 survey found 52 per cent who speak French 'very or fairly' well, and 30 per cent who use French 'exclusively, primarily or as often as English' at work. Moreover, reflecting the trends to French immersion in education in the Jewish schools, 64 per cent claimed their children spoke French 'very or fairly' well. Surveys in the 1960s found Jewish Montrealers in strong support of French language rights in Quebec, and in sympathy with the French efforts to retain their culture and resist assimilation.

Yet on the other hand, Quebec Jews have lived for decades in near total isolation from Québécois life, with few social or political contacts. In this way Quebec was more European than North American, and the Jewish ghetto-like existence approximated conditions existing in Eastern Europe at the time of the mass immigration. This isolation (only slightly less from the Anglo-Saxon than from the French community) may have had beneficial results regarding Jewish cultural vitality. Part of this isolation emerged as a by-product of the integration of Jews into the anglophone linguistic and cultural community (even if social interaction, such as marriage, was kept low).

Fear of anti-Semitism has also contributed to this isolation. Of course, anti-Semitism was and is no stranger to anglophone Quebec, yet it differed from the French variety. The former represented the snobbish élitism of the economically powerful—it was for the most part 'polite' anti-Semitism; the latter was more populist in nature, reflecting the resentment of the economically disadvantaged, with more physicality and potential for violence—the anti-Semitism of the mob. In many ways, the Jewish economic position in Quebec was that of a classic middleman minority, often occupying roles as small shopkeepers, traders, businessmen, or professionals. Jews would often be visible to the francophone working-class person, and thus might inherit some of the rage felt against the dominant, yet inaccessible or invisible Anglo corporate élite. And, as a few Jewish families (e.g., Bronfman, Steinberg) began to expand business operations, the image of widespread Jewish economic power emerged. In this way, French anti-Semitism resembled that directed by Blacks against Jews in the US, or by Ukrainian peasants against Jews in seventeenth-century Ukraine (where Jews often managed the estates of absentee Polish landlords and thus had most direct contact with the Ukrainian masses). As professionals or merchants, Jews were visible. Yet throughout the period of Quebec development, real corporate and financial power was in non-Jewish, Anglo-Canadian or American hands.

To understand Jewish fear of anti-Semitism, one must not only take into account the historical record of Quebec society, but supra-national events such as the Holocaust. At present, perhaps 20-25 per cent of Montreal's adult Jewish population are post-war immigrants, survivors of the Holocaust. These Jews cannot help but remain forever alert to the possible dangers; moreover, many other Ashkenazi Jewish adults either lost family during the tragedy, or helped fight the Nazis in the Allied Armies. Thus, the memories of the Holocaust linger on; inevitably, they colour perception of current events. Moreover, for many Jews, to survive the Holocaust and to emigrate to North America was to escape 'Europe', or the old world, and come to a different *New World*, where the historical baggage of European society, its nationalism, ideologies and class conflicts from which Jews suffered would not exist.

The historic record of anti-Semitism in Quebec, like its current manifestation, compares well with that of Western Europe, but certainly differs from the US. Influenced by the conservatism of the Catholic Church, Quebec in the 1920s and 1930s through to the end of the Duplessis era maintained an anti-Semitic tone reflected in official or semi-official statements, various newspapers, and social movements. Anti-Semitic journals flourished, and economic boycotts against the Jews were launched. Nationalistic movements such as the Bloc Populaire included elements of anti-Semitic ideology and action. Just before and after the Second World War, Adrien Arcand and his small band of Nazi sympathizers orchestrated protests against the Jews. More important, opposition from Quebec played a key role in influencing the Liberal government of Mackenzie King to maintain restrictions on the admission of Jewish refugees from Europe during the 1930s.

It should be noted that attitudes towards Jews in other parts of North America were not much better. (An old Jewish 'joke' defines an anti-Semite as a person who hates Jews more than necessary.) Apart from the occasional brawl or act of vandalism, Jews have not suffered from physical violence—no lives were lost because of anti-Semites in Quebec.

The current situation in Quebec is even more paradoxical. Objectively, finding concrete evidence of anti-Semitic discrimination—acts directed against Jews leading to some loss or penalty—is like finding a needle in a haystack. Jews enjoy complete freedom of religion in Quebec. Jewish day schools receive generous per-capita grants from the province (unheard of in the United States); universities of both languages support the academic study of Judaica; government cultural agencies, both federal and provincial, assist Jewish cultural or research projects through various programs. Quebec has passed comprehensive human rights legislation, enforced by a Human Rights Commission, which acts, along with federal legislation, to protect Jews from all forms of discrimination.

Moreover, despite the widespread talk of latent anti-Semitism and paranoia, which surfaced in both print and electronic media around the time of the Parti Québécois victory, survey data do not support a claim that Jews perceive substantial amounts of anti-Semitism in the province. For example, in 1978 only 11 per cent claimed there was 'a great deal' of anti-Semitism, while 14 per cent found none. While 28 per cent thought there was more in Quebec, 16 per cent thought there was more in the rest of Canada. Moreover, half the sample had no *personal* experience of anti-Semitism in Quebec (though 85 per cent believes that at least a bit exists in Quebec).[19]

This survey does not prove that no anti-Semitic prejudice (attitude) exists on the part of Gentile Quebeckers. For example, a recent survey found 64 per cent of French Québécois (37 per cent of English Quebeckers) who agreed that Jews had 'too much power over business in Quebec'.[20]

How can one link this data on anti-Semitism to the well-known near-total opposition to most forms of aggressive nationalism in Quebec, notably to independence/sovereignty association in any form, and to the Parti Québécois? One answer may lie in the concept of a 'new anti-Semitism' which has replaced the older, more blatant form historically experienced by Jews. One can define this new anti-Semitism (and one can debate the appropriateness of the term) as indifference or opposition to perceived Jewish issues or concerns, rather than opposition to Jews *per se*. Many Jews feel that with blatant anti-Semitism no longer fashionable (if not illegal), the major problems are acts with anti-Semitic *consequences*, regardless of whether the motivations are anti-Semitic. Jews oppose Quebec nationalism not because of anti-French sentiment, or because of a perceived anti-Semitism: rather, the by-products of nationalism (including possible constitutional change in the direction of greater autonomy for Quebec) can be considered as detrimental to long-term Jewish needs and objectives. When asked in 1978 to list possible reasons why they might emigrate from Quebec, Jews listed 'the possibility of anti-Semitism' far below factors such as general or personal economic issues, general political conditions, disagreement with government objectives, and language legislation.

The Jewish position on the national question in Quebec is rather uniform. Jews are federalists (in 1978, 64 per cent supported 'revised federalism' and 35 per cent supported status quo federalism); 98 per cent indicated support for the provincial Liberal party. In the 1981 election return for the largely Jewish (and anglophone) riding of D'Arcy McGee, the liberal MNA captured 97 per cent of the vote. Yet, it should be clear that along with this support for federalism, Jews as individuals and as an organized community have been among the leading advocates of equality and fair treatment for francophones throughout the country, and have endorsed recognition of French as the major official language in Quebec.

For many years, Jewish communal agencies have been emphasizing French competence in their operations, and prominent Jewish-owned enterprises such as Steinberg Ltd have been model corporations in their rapid francization (indeed, some elements of the anglophone community have criticized such firms as being too eager to comply).

Certainly, a few individual Jews do not share the federal communal consensus. By and large, these are intellectuals and professionals, usually marginally affiliated (if at all) with the mainstream Jewish community or its institutions. Some observers have claimed increasing support for either the Parti Québécois and/or sovereignty-association on the part of younger Jews, notably Sephardic francophone Jews. Reliable evidence on this issue is unavailable. Several Jews have achieved certain prominence as supporters of sovereignty-association and the Parti Québécois; indeed, the Parti Québécois, with a strong democratic tradition, continues to seek support from Jews and all other non-French Quebeckers. No doubt, several active professionals within the organized Jewish community, and also in continual contact with the Parti Québécois, have developed attitudes of cooperation and respect. While in most cases, their philosophies fall short of embracing ultimate nationalist political goals, there is minority sentiment favouring greater adaptation to Quebec society and involvement in governmental, quasi-governmental organization and political parties in the province. On balance, however, one concludes that the strong majority of the mainstream Jewish community remains opposed to the Parti Québécois and its fundamental political objectives. Why?

The fears individual Jews have of nationalism of any kind are easy to understand—they have often been its victims. Jews, always marginal, fear that language facility alone may not compensate for the proper ethnic pedigree—origin as 'un vrai Québécois'. The frequent references in Quebec to the 'collectivity', to group rights, alienate Jews who have through force of tradition embraced the classic liberal model of equal citizenship regardless of group ties, in which individuals, not groups, are the ultimate beneficiaries of rights and freedoms. Thus, the greater diversity of Canada, with its three broad ethnic divisions of English, French, and all others, is more appealing as a point of reference than the relatively more homogeneous Quebec. Jews also fear an interventionist state acting in behalf of a francophone collectivity that might encroach on areas usually associated with the private affairs of citizens, such as leisure, recreation, or culture. Government regulations in areas such as advertising, the movie industry, or the news media may stir fears of possible censorship and restriction of individual liberties.

It is ironic that Quebec society is itself becoming more ethnically and linguistically heterogeneous at this very time, due to the recent influx of Third World immigrants. Quebec has to a great extent reversed its historic xenophobia, and has ostensibly embraced multi-cultural principles in rather the same way as the federal liberal government in Ottawa. Some efforts are underway not only to assist minority groups in retention of their ancestral culture, but to open doors (including the francophone public service) to greater participation to all allophones, including Jews. We do not yet know how much of this participation will materialize; sociological experience tells us that minority groups may well set their own limits as a safeguard to retention of their group identity.

Along with nationalism are economic worries. Some Jews feel that any move towards Quebec sovereignty might be associated with general economic decline and flight of capital and investment. Moreover, periods of economic dislocation or uncertainty have historically been dangerous for Jews specifically. Other Jews might be sceptical about an independent Quebec's commitment to free enterprise, or may fear future expansion of the role of the state (*étatisme*) in regulation of commerce or the professions, or in the increase of the comparatively high tax rates on the middle and upper middle classes.

The continued francization of the provinces also raises worries. It should be noted immediately that there is nothing inherently Jewish about the English language; Jews can certainly live Jewish lives in Paris. Yet on the North American continent, English is the lingua franca of the Jewish community. Montreal has historically relied on American-trained Jewish professionals, including rabbis, to staff its institutions. Francization of the Jewish community may lead to a certain marginalization of Montreal from the rest of continental North American Jewry, losing its élan as a Jewish cultural centre in the New World.

The francization of the Jewish day schools has proceeded steadily, with ever increasing amounts of the school day devoted to studies in French. There is no doubt that the French competence of Jewish children is increasing. Yet Jews, who take a continental approach to the economic mobility possibilities of their children, recognize the need for English competence as a key to such success. And geographic mobility is becoming a central feature of highly-educated labour in modern, post-industrial societies. The community has thus been debating whether the francization of the Jewish schools has led (or needs to lead) to a weakening of English language instruction or effective teaching of Judaica.

A final concern of some Quebec Jews, which would rise only given actual sovereignty, lies in the domain of foreign affairs. The importance Jews attach to Israel's security has been described. Within this context, the Jewish community has evolved foreign affairs positions which emphasize not only support for Israel, but opposition to Soviet expansionism, to Arab military preparedness, and to Third World nations who inevitably adapt pro-Arab and anti-Israeli positions, for ideological or economic reasons. Many Jews wonder what kind of foreign policy might emerge in a sovereign Quebec, *vis-à-vis* East-West relations, and the Middle East. A greater tilt towards the Arab states, or neutralism *à la* France, would represent a dramatic change in the political climate in which Jewish concern for Israel's basic survival would be expressed.

Towards the Future

The Jewish future in Quebec, looking toward the 1990s, remains uncertain. There has been a steady stream of departure of younger Jews from the province, a flow pre-dating the 1976 victory of the Parti Québécois. It is difficult to know how many have actually left. In 1978, about one-third of the adult (over 18) children of older Montrealers had left the city. While few persons in Montreal had specific plans to leave, it was clear that any drastic changes in the political climate might lead to a jump in Jewish emigration. For example, 70 per cent of Jews under the age of 40 claimed they 'definitely or probably' would leave Quebec should a 'referendum show clear support for independence'.[21]

The 1981 census reveals that the Jewish population in Quebec is about 7.5 per cent less than in 1971, from 110,000 to about 102,000.[22] This population decline results not only from emigration as births, deaths and in-migration also play a role. In Ontario by comparison, Jewish population has increased from 125,000 to 148,000. The future size of the Jewish community in Quebec will decline, due as much to low Jewish fertility rates, common throughout the continent, to the high proportion of aged in the Jewish population, and to a slowdown in Jewish immigration to Quebec or to emigration. This rapid aging of the Jewish community in Quebec, coupled with its smaller size, will pose severe problems for the Jewish community. Fund-raising will have to be done from a smaller base, and the welfare needs of the aged will make greater claims on the Jewish budget. At some point, the Jewish community may have to undergo a fundamental, painful rationalization of services. Priorities will have to be established with great care.

For some time, the conventional wisdom among Jewish communities has been that communal services in traditional areas such as welfare, health, and poverty would be gradually assumed by the state. The Jewish community would concentrate its communal role in areas such as Jewish education, cultural programming, and youth work. However, a survey of communal preferences revealed, perhaps surprisingly, that public support was high for *Jewish* health care services, or care for the aged. Perhaps a Jewish ambience was still considered important for potential users of such services. The task of the Jewish community to satisfy all the articulated needs with restricted funds will be formidable.

In many ways, the triumph of the Parti Québécois in 1976, and again in 1981, forced Quebec Jewry to come to grips with its own attitude to Quebec. There are obviously many features of life in Montreal which Jews find attractive, and indeed make Montreal one of the most attractive locations for Jews anywhere on the continent. The quality of life for all citizens in Montreal compares well with other cities. To this, Jews can add a generally comfortable economic position and a robust cultural and communal life. Yet, perhaps for the first time, Jews may feel the pressure to begin a serious dialogue with other Québécois. The Jewish community will continue to be vigilant in its own behalf, pursue its interests, and champion those fundamental principles of democracy, freedom, and individual liberty which it holds dear. As the community continues to francize, cracks in the Jewish and French solitudes may appear, much as they have between the Jewish and Anglo-Saxon group. Mutual veils of ignorance and barriers of distrust may be lifted.

Signs of adaptation abound. Amidst the talk of exodus one hears of Jews buying houses and sinking roots, and even of Jews returning to Montreal after having lived elsewhere. While the outcome of this encounter cannot be predicted, it is doubtful that the splendid isolation of the past will be recaptured. A new era in the history of the Jews in Quebec is about to unfold.

Notes

[1]For a detailed discussion of the concept of a Jewish polity, see Daniel J. Elazar, *Community and Polity: The Organizational Dynamics of American Jewry* (Philadelphia, 1976).

[2]According to the 1981 census, 102,355 people in Quebec identified their religion as 'Jewish'. Over 90,000 selected 'Jewish' alone as their ethnic origin; many others selected a multiple origin, such as 'Jewish' and 'European'. The 1991 census is expected to reveal a decline of 10 per cent or more.

[3]The statistics cited here, and many others in this essay, unless otherwise indicated, are taken from a survey of household heads reported in Morton Weinfeld and William W. Eaton, *The Jewish Community of Montreal: Survey Report* (Canadian Jewish Congress and Allied Jewish Community Services: Mimeo, 1979): 86. More recent data on Montreal Jewry are presented in the chapter "An Overview of the Canadian Jewish Community" in this volume.

[4]For a discussion of religious Judaism in Canada, see Stuart Schoenfeld, 'Canadian Judaism Today' in M. Weinfeld *et al.*, eds, *The Canadian Jewish Mosaic* (Toronto, 1981): 129-50. For a general overview of contemporary Jewish life in Canada, see M. Weinfeld, W. Shaffir and I. Cotler, eds, *The Canadian Jewish Mosaic* (Toronto, 1981).

[5]Weinfeld and Eaton, *The Jewish Community of Montreal*: 34-5.

[6]*Ibid.*: 36.

[7]There is no consensus on the number of francophone and/or Sephardic Jews in Quebec. For a review of the history and characteristics of this sub-community of Jews, see Jean-Claude Lasry, 'Une diaspora francophone au Québec: Les Juifs Sépharades'. *Questions de Culture* (Migrations et communautés culturelles), vol. 2 (Institut Québécois de recherche sur la culture, 1982): 113-38.

[8]Weinfeld and Eaton: 46.

[9]*Ibid.*: 40-1.

[10]For a review of traits of achievement of American Jewish academics, see S.M. Lipset and E.C. Ladd, 'Jewish Academics in the United States' in Marshall Sklare,

ed., *The Jew in American Society* (New York, 1974): 255-88. In general, the two-volume anthology by Marshall Sklare, ed., *The Jew in American Society* and *The Jewish Community in America* (New York, 1974) provides a good overview of American Jewry today.

[11]Weinfeld and Eaton: 26.

[12]For a critical review of the relationship between Jewish educational success and the Jewish religious tradition, see Miriam K. Slater, 'My Son the Doctor: Aspects of Mobility Among American Jews', *American Sociological Review* (June 1969): 359-73.

[13]Morton Weinfeld, 'The Ethnic Sub-economy: Explication and Analysis of a Case Study of the Jews in Montreal', in this volume, p. 218.

[14]Weinfeld and Eaton: 46-7.

[15]See Harold M. Waller, 'Power in the Jewish Community', in M. Weinfeld *et al.*, *The Canadian Jewish Mosaid*: 151-70.

[16]Weinfeld and Eaton: 47.

[17]*Ibid.*: 47.

[18]*Ibid.*: 28.

[19]*Ibid.*: 58.

[20]From a privately funded survey on ethnicity in Quebec conducted by the author.

[21]Weinfeld and Eaton: 62.

[22]The figures represent people who declared themselves Jews by religion.

Jewish-Ukrainian Relations in Canada

since World War II and the Emergence

of the Nazi War Criminal Issue

Harold Troper and

Morton Weinfeld

History, according to D.V. Grawronski, 'is the interpretive study of the recorded fact of bygone human beings and societies, the purpose of which is to develop an understanding of human actions, not only in the past but for the present as well'.[1] But as historians know full well, historical understanding grows out of continual dialogue between the historian and his sources, between the mind set of the historian and the interpretive weight given a particular set of facts. E.H. Carr notes, quite correctly, 'facts of history cannot be purely objective, since they become facts of history by virtue of the significance attached to them by the historian'.[2] Thus, historical interpretation is dynamic, shifting according to the evidence examined and the questions asked of that evidence. What history reveals depends on where one digs for evidence and where one digs may well depend on the questions one wants answered.

The definition of an ethnic group involves a sense of shared history, real or imagined. For both Jews and Ukrainians the flow of events which constitutes each group's shared history is not imagined. But interpretation of those events is grounded in different if overlapping understandings of the past and how those understandings are applied to the cause of ethnic cohesion today.[3]

More to the point, Jews and Ukrainians in Canada share a common geographic origin in Eastern Europe. They do not share a common historical understanding. The divergence in community historical perspective is not just a result of different interpretations given to evidence but to the larger framework of understanding within which evidence is examined. The central assumption of Ukrainian historical self-awareness remains that Ukrainians have been an oppressed people dispossessed of sovereignty, struggling for national self-realization against the power of foreign imperial might—Polish, Austro-Hungarian, Russian, German, Soviet—and their local agents. This *Nasha Pravda*—community truth—and the sense of mission it engenders is essential to understanding the Ukrainian community in its Canadian diaspora. Thus, the community historical narrative is critical to the future survival of the Canadian Ukrainian community.

If Jews in Canada also place priority on group survival and commitment to community, their group historical narrative—rooted in the same Eastern European soil—is very different. For Jews the historical legacy is not one of suppression of national aspirations. Far from it. The Jewish story is of an ever descending spiral of anti-Semitism leading almost inevitably to the Holocaust.

Ukrainians and Jews play a role in one another's narratives. To Ukrainians, Jews were in the Ukraine but withheld commitment to its sovereignty. They were not rooted to the land but to their own marginality. Whether for profit or security, Jews joined the camp of those suppressing the legitimate aspirations of Ukrainian peoplehood. They served as middlemen between the Ukrainian people and their oppressors. They were the tax collectors, liquor dealers, innkeepers, estate managers, and moneylenders who benefited from the oppression of the Ukrainian majority.

Jews, on the other hand, picture themselves as history's victims, squeezed between the power of an oppressive regime and the violence of local peasants. The ground was forever shifting under their feet. Jews yearned for a security where they could live and work peacefully in those few areas open to them. But rare was the Jewish generation which did not know the edge of the sword.[4]

These divergent perspectives are critical in differentiating Jewish and Ukrainian understanding of specific past events. Like ghosts stalking the landscape of historical memory, these visions haunt Ukrainian and Jewish worlds today. Let us explore several examples. For Ukrainians, for example, the 1648 rebellion led by Bogdan Chmielnicki is an early chapter in the ongoing Ukrainian struggle for national self-determination. That the rebellion ultimately failed does not detract from the place Chmielnicki has achieved in the pantheon of national heroes, a visionary who bequeathed his nationalist dream to later generations of Ukrainians. For Jews, however, Chmielnicki's name is cursed. His rebellion is recalled as a wholesale slaughter for Jews perhaps second only to the Holocaust itself. Chmielnicki is recalled as the spiritual forefather of Hitler.[5]

In the same vein, for Ukrainians, the flickering light of an independent Ukraine glowed briefly with the short-lived Ukrainian National Republic, 1917-1921. Here was a glorious national rebirth smothered in its infancy by crushing Soviet power. The Petliura government, we are told, sought not only to realize the aspirations of the Ukrainian people but also to ensure the security of a minority Jewish population. It legislated an end to discrimination and welcomed full Jewish participation in the state while encouraging Jewish communal continuity.

Once again, Jewish historical memory differs. The Petliura regime is associated with pogroms and the years in which the central regime passed model Jewish legislation but was unable or, more likely, unwilling to enforce its own edicts. By inaction, the government gave silent approval to wholesale attacks on the Jews. The Petliura years, therefore, are not recalled as a moment of enlightenment but a black mark in the annals of a people—yet another step down the road to the Holocaust.[6]

The era of World War II also divides Jews and Ukrainians. For Jews, the Holocaust could not have happened without the wilful participation of local populations. Nowhere, many Jews hold, was that participation more readily given than in the Ukraine. Nowhere was the local population matched in brutality. Nowhere does the local population share so great a responsibility for the murder of millions. The Nazis only gave licence to long-standing Ukrainian anti-Semitism.

The Ukrainian narrative is different. Horrible as the Jewish fate was, at least Jews knew the enemy to be Naziism. For Ukrainians, squeezed between Soviet and Nazi oppression, trying to keep from being ground to dust by one or the other, choices had to be made. For some, active or passive collaboration with the Nazis gave more promise of physical and national survival than with the dreaded Communists to whom Jews looked for salvation. If some Jews collaborated with the Soviets against their Ukrainian neighbours, a few Ukrainian 'criminals', it is conceded, even participated in the Holocaust. But others risked their own live to save Jews. They were led in spirit and deed by Ukrainian Catholic Metropolitan A. Sheptytsky. Sheptytsky instructed his Church officials to hide Jews, issued pastoral letters against Ukrainian cooperation in anti-Jewish actions and protested directly to Himmler. This, Ukrainians note, is far more than was done by the Vatican.[7]

Even in Canada, thousands of miles and now more than a generation removed from Ukraine, these two separate and incompatible historical narratives shape the self-definition of diaspora Ukrainian and Jewish polities. For Ukrainians and Jews, the two most survivalist ethnic communities in Canada, the inheritance of historical pain—for Ukrainians the denial of a legitimate homeland and for Jews the experience of physical annihilation of the Holocaust, the last act in an age-old anti-Semitic drama—is a cement which helps to bond respective community members together. Nor can it be denied that if the historical narrative is now blurry in detail, the sense among both Ukrainians and Jews in Canada that each was an architect of the other's suffering remains deeply ingrained.

In Canada's liberal democracy, old world antipathies may still lie deep within group consciousness, but it is increasingly unacceptable to articulate these sentiments publicly. Ukrainian and Jewish historical grievances toward one another have seldom received public airing nor have they been a source of inter-ethnic conflict until recently. For the most part Jewish and Ukrainian communities have remained two solitudes.

The separateness of the two communities is, in part, a reflection of their separate immigration processes. While Ukrainians and Eastern European Jews alike entered Canada after the turn of the century, each found a separate niche. Until World War II Ukrainians remained predominantly a rural, western people; Jews congregated in the cities of eastern Canada. While there was Ukrainian contact with Jewish merchants on the Canadian prairies or Jews with Ukrainians in the teeming immigrant north-end of Winnipeg, institutional contact was rare.

In the wake of World War II the character of both communities changed. The shock of the Holocaust, the integration of newly arrived survivors into the community, the continuing decline of anti-Semitism in the larger civic culture, widespread economic prosperity, professionalization, social mobility and the rebirth of a Jewish national state in Israel with which Canadian Jewry identified, reshaped and re-invigorated Canadian Jewish life. Today, Canada's almost 300,000 Jews, about 66 per cent Canadian-born, enjoy the highest standards of living of any Canadian group and support the most complete network of intra-ethnic organizational structures in Canada.

The post-war era also reshaped Ukrainian-Canadian life, with the census currently recording approximately 750,000 persons of full or partial Ukrainian descent. Post-war arrivals, largely Displaced Persons, brought with them an ideological fervour and nationalist commitment far greater than that which awaited them in Canada. Once settled in Canada they renewed the communal tie to, and concern for, the Ukraine. Many adhered to a strong and singularly ideological mission, a militant anti-communism combined with a strong attachment to Ukrainian nationalism and a continuity of Ukrainian culture.

These post-war arrivals settled in the large urban centres of eastern Canada but through their organizational skill and dedication to their nationalist cause, they soon influenced if not dominated the organizational outlook of the entire Canadian-Ukrainian community. Their agenda, to a greater or lesser degree, became the agenda of the larger community.[8]

Both Jews and Ukrainians remain concerned with group survival across generations. While Jews are undergoing some slippage, assimilation is far more advanced among Ukrainians. Ukrainians find it more difficult than Jews to encourage the now more than 90 per cent Canadian-born Ukrainians to assume the burdens of community concerns let alone retain Ukrainian language loyalty or endogamy. Nevertheless, while Jews by almost any measure demonstrate comparative success at intergenerational survival, Ukrainians in Canada come second only to Jews.

But to the committed, Ukrainian slippage is a concern especially as declining linkage to the community may represent a twilight for the Ukrainian national cause. Any threat to that cause is to be opposed. In 1985 the very integrity of the community, the good name it could pass on to the next generation, and the sanctity of its nationalist struggle seemed under attack. The issue of Nazi war criminals in Canada had surfaced and a smouldering historical legacy of Jewish–Ukrainian antipathy from the old world suddenly reignited in the new. But the issue of Nazi war criminals is one that has smouldered since the 1950s.

No single incident illustrates the longevity of this problem so well as that of the controversial Halychyna Division. Late in 1943, as the Nazis sought to stem the tide of Soviet advance from the east, Berlin authorized the organization of a Ukrainian Waffen S.S. unit. By the time the Division was ready for duty in 'counter insurgency' for which it had been trained, the military needs of the eastern front took precedent. In 1944 the unit was deployed to confront seasoned Red Army troops. At the Battle of Brody the Division was decimated. Of the almost 11,000 Halychyna who went into combat, barely 3,000 survived as combat ready troops. The Nazis, now in full retreat, brought the rag-tag Halychyna back to division strength by collecting into its ranks other Ukrainians, including those who had served the Nazi occupation forces in various capacities and now retreated westward with them. But before the reconstituted Halychyna could be again tested in major conflict, the Division surrendered en masse to the British.[9]

In prisoner-of-war camps in northern Italy the Division underwent routine security investigation. It received a clean bill of health. Soviet authorities also attempted to induce the Division to return to Ukraine; almost to a man, Halychyna members refused. Claiming they were not Nazis but Ukrainian nationalists who had enlisted both to fight the hated Russians and in anticipation of becoming the bulwark of the Ukrainian army of an independent Ukrainian state they dreamed would arise Phoenix-like out of the ashes of war, they were not prepared to go back to a Soviet Ukraine. The nationalist fires still burned.

As a Nazi military unit the Halychyna was ineligible for Displaced Persons status and as members of an S.S. unit, all were also ineligible for most overseas resettlement programs. The unit was transferred to Britain where its existence came to the attention of the Ukrainian community in Canada. After assuming responsibility for the comfort needs of the men, the community quietly lobbied the Canadian government to grant members of the Division admission to Canada. At first the government resisted for as former members of the notorious S.S., Halychyna members were expressly barred admission to Canada. But in July 1950, as Canada was opening its door even wider to immigration from Europe, especially that of Displaced Persons, the Canadian cabinet exempted the Halychyna from regulations prohibiting the entry of former S.S. members.[10]

The Canadian Jewish community was stunned. The organizational umbrella of Canadian Jewry, the Canadian Jewish Congress, protested the government's move as a moral outrage. While the Congress had no specific information of Halychyna wartime activities, it reminded the government that the S.S. was officially designated by the Allies as a criminal organization.

Given the mass murder of Polish and Ukrainian Jewry and the hands-on role played in that systematic death by the entire S.S. and its local collaborators, there was no doubt among Congress leaders that the Halychyna, too, had blood on its hands.[11] The government, taken aback by the vehemence of the Jewish reaction and a rush of negative press coverage, offered a small compromise. It would temporarily forestall admission of Halychyna members to allow Congress to present hard evidence of criminal acts against individual Halychyna members.

Congress welcomed the delay, but at first took the position that it should be sufficient to show that the Halychyna, as an integral part of the S.S., made up entirely of volunteers, forfeited eligibility for immigration into Canada. The government would have none of it. The Cabinet had already ruled the Halychyna was to be treated as an exception to the blanket prohibition against the admission of S.S. members to Canada. If individuals were to be prohibited entry, government wanted evidence of criminal acts perpetrated by those individuals who only then would legally be barred. Congress tapped every source available. It came up empty. Perhaps because of the poor state of available records in the early 1950s or because there was no wrongdoing on which to gather evidence, the Jewish network produced neither evidence implicating the Halychyna as a unit in specific criminal acts nor evidence against individual Halychyna members. Out of patience with Jewish requests for further delays and under continued pressure from the Ukrainian community, the government authorized immigration to proceed.[12]

The Canadian Jewish Congress had been defeated but not converted. Doubts persisted. Many Jews believed that among Halychyna members admitted and the tens of thousands of Eastern European D.P.s entering Canada at the same time, including many Ukrainians, were many unrepentant Nazi sympathizers if not outright war criminals. Spokesmen for the Ukrainian community, in turn, saw Jewish agitation as little more than age-old Ukrainian baiting. As Ukrainian organizational life in Canada became ever more nationalist and anti-Soviet, so too accusations that Jews would stop at nothing to undermine the Ukrainian national cause grew more shrill.

For years, relations between Jewish and Eastern European communal organizations in Canada remained, at best, cool, formal and distant. Those with Ukrainians were even more so. During the 1950s and 1960s, periodic eruptions served only to further charge the atmosphere. In 1957 for example, Ukrainian nationalist leader Andreii Melnyk was scheduled to come to Canada to celebrate the twenty-fifth anniversary of his movement's founding. The editor of an independent Winnipeg Jewish newspaper lashed out against the visit as one 'famous in Poland as a ruthless anti-Semite' and an active Nazi agent involved in the ruthless murder of Ukrainian Jews.[13]

As the editor's charges spilled into the public press, the Ukrainian community leaders responded in anger. Fearing the Melnyk visit would be spoiled and, indeed, their national cause placed under a cloud of suspicion, they demanded an apology.[14] Holocaust survivors bristled at the very notion of an apology and Congress leaders again scrambled to determine whether or not there was any truth behind the accusations against Melnyk. If there was truth the charge would stand. If, however, no proof were available there would have to be an apology, no matter how unpalatable the prospect. No incriminating evidence was forthcoming and, in the end, the editor was forced to retract his accusation and issue a formal apology.[15]

The Melnyk incident receded into memory. There are only a few similar incidents, but not because Jews and Ukrainians in Canada found common cause for cooperation. Rather, it was because institutional relations were so restrained that even negative contact was rare. Throughout the 1960s each community, uneasily aware of the other, kept its distance.

In the 1970s some movement, if one-sided, developed for rapprochement. Tentative efforts to bridge the gulf of historical suspicion and mistrust separating Jewish and Ukrainian communities in Canada began, largely at Ukrainian initiative. In part this initiative proved a reflection of demographic shifts in the two communities. A new generation of Canadian-born, urban, educated Ukrainian and Jewish professionals were gradually making their weight felt within their respective community councils. Some, especially Ukrainians, were ready for detente. This is not to argue the younger leaders were immune to the old world antipathies. This is not the case. Nor is it to argue that the older generation of leaders readily stepped aside in favour of the new. This was also not the case. But in both communities, notably within the Ukrainian community, there were those who saw much to gain from better relations.

Perhaps Ukrainian moves toward bettering relations with Jews grew in part out of fear that Ukrainians were being made historical villains. Ukrainian historical self-definition painted their people as oppressed, dispossessed, and victimized people. Theirs was a glorious if so far unsuccessful struggle for national self-realization against all odds. If this was the community's *Nasha Pravda* (community truth), it was also running headlong into the western world's understanding of the Holocaust and the history of European anti-Semitism which preceded the Holocaust. Increasingly, the Ukrainian historical drama was lumbering under the weight of a publicly accepted historical experience that seemed transfixed on Jewish suffering. Not only did Ukrainians see their national struggle ignored, their litany of suffering overlooked, but they also resented Ukrainians being made the villains of Jewish and western historical narrative. The more the Holocaust captured the public and scholarly historical imagination, the more Ukrainians saw their every spark of hard-won and short-lived national self-assertion dismissed as a pogromist's licence to murder Jewish men, women and children. Ukrainian heroes were vilified as collaborators and murderers in someone else's historical epic. To a Ukrainian community struggling to keep group identity alive, to retain community pride and commitment, to encourage continuity from generation to generation, this challenge to its historical sense of self had to be met. Denial of the Holocaust was out of the question.

But, if common cause could be made with the Jewish community in areas of mutual interest—the future of interethnic relations in Canada, the Soviet question, joint approaches to government—the historical heat could be turned down.

It is not unreasonable to assume, from the Ukrainian community's perspective, that there was also ample social and economic reason to enlist Jewish cooperation in areas of joint concern. For Ukrainian-Canadians increasingly active in community institutional affairs there was much to learn from the Jews. After all, Jews had been living as a diaspora minority for two millennia. The Ukrainian diaspora, by contrast, was barely a century old. What is more, Jews had blazed a path through North America urban business and professional life for others to follow. By the 1970s, as more Ukrainians were making their way along this same path, one-to-one contacts with Jews increased as did appreciation of the model of Jewish mobility in North America.

What is more, Jews seemed to have succeeded in carving a place for themselves in urban North America without sacrificing commitment to Jewish continuity. On the contrary. As individual Jews built a socially, economically, and politically secure place for themselves in North American society, Jewish communal life thrived. The Jewish polity was active and took pride in both cultural enrichment in North America and the growth of a Jewish national homeland in Israel. Israel's electrifying victory in the 1967 Six-Day War further served to energize Jewish communal life in the diaspora.

All this was not lost on the Ukrainian community. The very idea that after two thousand years of statelessness diaspora Jewry celebrated the rebirth of their homeland stood as a beacon of hope to Ukrainian diaspora dispossessed of an independent homeland. Thus, on the individual and communal level there was indeed much to learn from the Jews. The time seemed appropriate. There was a precedent. If Israelis and Jews could make an accommodation with Germany and Germans, why not with Ukrainians? What is more, some Ukrainians believed they could offer Jews reciprocity in forgiveness. Ukrainians, after all, believed they had much to forgive the Jews.

But nothing could be further from the Canadian Jewish consciousness than the notion that Ukrainians had historical grievances against the Jews. The very idea would be greeted with disbelief in Jewish circles. Nor did most Jews understand, let alone sympathize with, problems of Ukrainian ethnic continuity. Canadian Jews knew little or nothing of the agony of the Ukrainian experience, whether in the Ukraine or in the diaspora. If anything, Canadian Jewish leaders believed the Ukrainian community was now among the most politically powerful ethnic community voices in Canada—if not through its organizational strength then by sheer weight of numbers.

Jewish leaders, judging their own institutional clout, felt repeatedly frustrated in their lobbying of government. They could not make headway on such basic Jewish agenda items as anti-boycott legislation, legislation to prohibit foreign firms or governments from demanding discrimination against Canadian Jews or other Canadian citizens as a precondition of a business most often in the Middle East.[16] At the same time there seemed to be a growing strength of Ukrainian political will. Was it not Ukrainian pressure which delivered up the federal government's policy of multiculturalism promising financial and political support to ethnic continuity in Canada? That was an achievement the Jewish polity, for all its supposed influence, could not match. If Jewish communal leaders needed any more proof of the surging strength of the Ukrainian polity it came on 9 October 1971. The very day after the government's formal announcement of its Multicultural-ism Policy in the House of Commons, the Prime Minister flew off to Winnipeg to address the Tenth Tri-Annual Congress of the Ukrainian Cana-dian Committee (UCC), the Ukrainian Canadian umbrella organization. In is banquet address, he personally congratulated the Ukrainian Canadian com-munity for its key contribution in reshaping Canadian social policy. Multi-culturalism was a Ukrainian victory. But the content of the Prime Minister's keynote address, full of the platitudes such an occasion demands, was obvi-ously less important than the fact of his presence. By *reporting in* to the UCC, so to speak, he lent credence to the notion that a new era of ethnic political influence, most importantly Ukrainian influence, was dawning.[17]

Better inter-ethnic relations, no matter how anxiously encouraged by some Ukrainians or thought to have some positive benefits by some Jewish leaders, were not easily achieved. Modest efforts at better relations were begun in Winnipeg where the Jewish community was dwarfed in number and political weight by their fellow Ukrainian Winnipegers. Even in Toronto, seat of Ukrainian nationalist sentiment, several efforts at bridge-building were started. In the autumn of 1974, for example, a young lawyer and head of the UCC in Ontario approached fellow lawyer Sidney Harris of the Congress executive in Toronto and Ben Kayfetz of the Congress' Toronto staff. The three went out to dinner. 'Our discussion', Kayfetz recorded, 'ranged across the whole spectrum of Jewish–Ukrainian concerns. We touched, of course, on the animosity and suspicion that persists in certain quarters on both sides. It was felt this might be to some extent a form of generation gap which may diminish in the course of time.' In the meantime, it was agreed, informal contacts, like their private dinner, should continue in spite of the negative feelings such contacts might generate among militant factions in both communities.[18]

Hostility could be generated even on an issue where the two communities might be expected to find common ground for cooperation, like Soviet violation of human rights. The Jewish community's official position called for Soviet adherence to the freedom of religion and freedom to migrate, as set down in the Soviet Constitution. Congress officials, in 1974, felt it quite in keeping with this position to support publicly those demanding the release of imprisoned Ukrainian activist Valentin Moroz. But even this symbolic gesture of unity with one whose imprisonment touched the conscience of humanity raised the ire of some in the Jewish community, predominantly Holocaust survivors, for whom historical memories of the Jewish experience in Ukraine remained fresh.[19] Whatever one might tell them about Moroz, his personal or political views, or his incarceration, was irrelevant. It was enough that a Jewish statement of support for Moroz's human rights made common cause with Ukrainian Canadian nationalist organizations which some Jews regarded as little more than a collection of unreconstructed fascists and Nazi sympathizers.[20]

Ironically, the Moroz statement was credited with stilling some of the more strident anti-Jewish voices in the Ukrainian community. Alex Epstein, a Toronto Jewish lawyer and self-styled Sovietologist with contacts in the organized Ukrainian community, repeatedly tried to find common ground for the two ethnic polities. He welcomed the Moroz statement as a good first step by a Jewish community leadership which previously avoided anything but cautious distance from the Ukrainian community. Ukrainians, Epstein wrote Congress, 'were deeply moved by this expression of sympathy and support from the Jewish community'. It was a gesture, he continued, which could not but help 'young and liberal' leadership then coming to the fore, 'in stifling anti-Semitic remarks and statements made by other Ukrainians'.[21]

As a follow-up to Congress' Moroz initiative, Epstein arranged another dinner, this time between Toronto Congress leaders and Walter Tarnopolsky, a well-known law professor and pro-Moroz activist. Although Tarnopolsky held no formal position in the Ukrainian community structure, he was 'well regarded by them. They seek his advice on political and communal questions, as one of their leading intellectuals.'[22] Tarnopolsky was not an unknown to Toronto Jewish leaders. His prominence in the Canadian Civil Liberties Association cemented his friendship with several like-minded Jewish civil libertarians also active in Canadian Jewish Congress affairs.

A 1975 dinner meeting, hosted by the Jewish leaders, was held at a fashionable Russian restaurant in downtown Toronto. As waiters in Eastern European folk costumes buzzed about, discussion was light, cordial yet frank. There was no agenda and except for agreeing on a second meeting to be hosted by Ukrainian leaders nothing concrete was accomplished.[23]

The follow-up dinner, three months later, in an equally elegant but this time Chinese restaurant, brought out a large contingent of Ukrainian community leaders. Again nobody had any fixed agenda for the egg-roll diplomacy. As heaping dishes of Chinese food were passed around the table, informal but guarded conversation ranged over various topics. Dinner ended with no suggestions made as to joint actions or programs.[24] But again all agreed such meetings were useful in breaking the ice. Unspoken was a disquieting awareness that there remained vocal and important constituents in both camps who would attack any cooperative effort, no matter how tentative, as tantamount to consorting with the devil.

Nevertheless, new lines of contact had been opened. If the mood was not one of mutual trust, at least Ukrainian participants believed a useful foundation now existed on which to build. Several other Ukrainian efforts to reach out to the Jewish community followed, including an unprecedented 1978 invitation to Rabbi Gunther Plaut, the high-profile President of the Canadian Jewish Congress and newly appointed member of the Ontario Human Rights Commission, to address an important Ukrainian gathering.[25] His address, as chance would have it, fell the very week that the NBC mini-series *Holocaust* was telecast across North America. Plaut did not shy away from the historical legacy which clouded Ukrainian-Jewish relations in Canada and his comments were well received. Perhaps, as he concluded in a report to Congress, there was now a more congenial mood for better relations— certainly within sections of the Ukrainian community and perhaps among the Jewish leadership as well.[26]

One issue, however, would eventually derail these modest steps toward better working relations—the problem of Nazi war criminals. The existence of Nazi war criminals in Canada had long been a concern of the Canadian Jewish Congress. Beginning with the entry of Halychyna Division members in 1951 and mass immigration of Displaced Persons, Canadian Jews were convinced that some—nobody knew exactly how many—Nazi activists, collaborators, and war criminals had secreted themselves in Canada. Efforts to enlist government cooperation in exorcising these people from Canada or interesting the larger Canadian public in the issue failed. Pressed on the problem, Canadian authorities had but one response—they lacked a legal framework for action. Many suspected the government just did not care. It was an issue easily ignored. There was no ground-swell of public outrage supporting the Jewish demand. The Holocaust, it seemed, was a Jewish memory and the war criminals a parochial Jewish concern.[27]

Nevertheless, slowly through the 1960s and into the 1970s, the problem of alleged Nazi war criminals in Canada notched itself higher and higher on the Canadian Jewish agenda. And as the Holocaust joined the rebirth of a Jewish state as the twin pillars of modern secular Jewish identity, anger at the very idea that alleged Nazi war criminals in Canada should go unpunished grew deeper. A series of events served to heighten this concern. In May 1960 the State of Israel announced the apprehension of Holocaust mastermind Adolf Eichmann. His trial in Israel for 'crimes against humanity' and under Israeli law 'crimes against the Jewish people' exposed Jew and non-Jew alike to the reality of the Holocaust as no other event had done. The trial was a crucial first step in turning the Holocaust from a private Jewish agony into part of the western historical legacy—an event of monumental proportions destined to preoccupy historians, moral philosophers, and the conscience of mankind. After the Eichmann trial, thoughtful people could no longer dismiss the Holocaust as a momentary excess of a few extremists run amok; it was now documented as the centrepiece of a political and racial ideology with deep historical roots, an ideology that commanded the loyalty of millions. But loyalty was not enough. The Holocaust was a labour-intensive venture and could not have been conducted without the wilful cooperation of a seemingly endless supply of those ready to assist—German and non-German alike.[28]

In 1964, shortly after Eichmann had been executed, world Jewry, including Canadian Jewry, was galvanized by the news that the West German statute of limitations would soon stop all war crimes prosecution in Germany. Canadian Jewish leaders prevailed on the Canadian government to intercede with West German authorities. Lester Pearson, the Canadian Prime Minister, was reminded that Canada had 'no statute of limitation whatever for crimes involving murder, or for that matter, other homicidal crimes'. The Prime Minister agreed. Canada lent its voice to the world outcry. West Germany responded with a ten-year moratorium on implementation of its statute of limitations in the case of war crimes. Canadian Jewish leaders noted the sad irony that it was easier to get Canadian officials to protest the possible legal sanctuary of Nazi war criminals in West Germany than to act against any alleged Nazi war criminals in Canada.[29]

A further jolt to Canadian Jewish consciousness came in 1965 when a small band of self-styled Canadian Nazis organized a series of public outdoor rallies in Toronto and Montreal. The tiny band gathered in a Toronto park replete with Nazi regalia and swastika flags. Both the press and television gave these home-grown Nazis and their racist sloganeering wide publicity. Jewish community reaction was swift. With the support of civic, media, church, and labour leaders, the Canadian Jewish Congress demanded appropriate legal action from civic authorities. But for some Jews this was not enough. Thousands of Holocaust survivors in Canada had come of age. They now constituted an important voice in Jewish community life. Few questioned their moral authority. Survivors organized counter-demonstrations which occasionally spilled over into violence.

As exaggerated rumours of budding national neo-Nazi threats percolated through Jewish circles, youthful Jewish self-defence groups sprang up. One self-defence group, N3, named for Newton's Third Law—for every action there is an equal and opposite reaction—joined with survivors to confront the neo-Nazis. Later, the N3 refocused on the problem of Nazi war criminals in Canada.[30] Newly founded survivor organizations moved under the Canadian Jewish Congress umbrella. They easily won support of plans to ensure memorialization of the Holocaust, Holocaust education in the schools, and renewed pressure on government to deal with any and all Nazi war criminals in Canada.[31]

In 1967 Canadian Jewry again confronted a Holocaust—not as an historical event but as a distinct possibility. In the two weeks between the Egyptian closure of the Straits of Tiran and the advent of hostilities, Canadian Jewry feared the worst. Could it be that for the second time in a century—no, a quarter century—a major Jewish community would face annihilation? Could there be a second Holocaust with the world again ready with eulogies but no help? The lightning victory of Israeli military power removed the immediate threat. But the 1967 experience jolted Canadian Jewry as no other post-war event. The sense that it could happen again cemented the bonds between Canadian Jewry, Israel, and the memory of the Holocaust. Renewed demands that Nazi war criminals living in Canada be brought to justice followed naturally.

Thus, by the early 1970s, the circle was completed. The issue of Nazi war criminals in Canada became an important agenda item for organized Canadian Jewry. But all efforts to engage the government in efforts to investigate and rid Canada of war criminals failed. Efforts to build a broad coalition of Canadian groups in support of action against Nazi war criminal also failed. It was possible to rivet public attention on a specific issue—the Eichmann trial, or the media hype around the telecast of *Holocaust*—but that interest could not be sustained. Canada had long been an insecure nation, focused inward, concerned with national unity and a fragile collective identity. The issue of Nazi war criminals was just too foreign, too filled with images better forgotten, and too disassociated from the prosperous civil calm which characterizes Canada to engage the larger Canadian civic culture in a crusade against alleged Nazi war criminals in Canada.

In the United States, Jewish lobbying on specific war criminal cases had more impact. Beginning with the modest publicity attending the 1973 deportation to West Germany of Hermine Braunsteiner Ryan, the 'mare of Maidanek', American immigration and justice officials started down the road which led in 1979 to the Office of Special Investigation within the US Department of Justice. The OSI was mandated to search for Nazi war criminals in the United States and, through a process of denaturalization and deportation, remove these persons from the United States. Canadian Jewry, observing the American initiatives, demanded no less of Canada.[32]

Even as the Nazi war criminal issue engaged Jewish organizational attention in the 1970s, Canadian-Ukrainian spokesman continued to press for a rapprochement with their Jewish counterparts, to transcend the historical antipathies deeply ingrained in each community's vision of the other. But the Holocaust emerged again and again to bedevil even casual contact between the Jewish and Ukrainian communities in Canada. As OSI investigations began to focus on several post-war Ukrainian immigrants in the United States, Canadian-Ukrainian leaders picked up no signals that their own government would follow the American lead. But Jewish lobbying continued to be a source of worry.

In the spring of 1977, several Congress officials in Toronto lunched with leaders of the Toronto-based World Congress of Free Ukrainians, again at the instigation of Alex Epstein. The mood was cordial but strained. Informal discussion ranged over a broad series of topics but eventually and for the first time focused in on the Jewish community's efforts to force the government's hand on Nazi war criminals. The Secretary-General of the Ukrainian organization assured his Jewish luncheon partners 'that his organization would not knowingly harbour war criminals and he was interested in seeing a positive policy on this question enacted'.[33] The pledge seemed unequivocal. It took very little, however, to test the pledge. Several months after the pleasant luncheon, an anonymous flyer was mailed to Ukrainian organizations across Canada. It requested information on one Ivan Solhan (Sovhan), said to have been a ranking Ukrainian police official accused in the death of several hundred Jews. Solhan was thought to be living in Canada. 'It is hoped', the flyer stated, 'people in Ukrainian circles will be able to find Solhan.' The flyer requested that any information be sent to Simon Wiesenthal's documentation centre in Vienna. It was signed 'a concerned Canadian'.[34]

Perhaps smarting at the suggestion that Ukrainian organizations could snap their fingers and deliver up Nazi war criminals, the Secretary-General angrily wrote to Ben Kayfetz who had attended the recent lunch meeting. The letter affirmed the 'bond of friendship between the two communities' and the cooperation of Ukrainians 'in bringing to justice any individual who has been responsible for premature murder whatever his racial or national origin, whatever his political or ideological motives'. But the assurance was not without an accompanying caution. There had been, it was noted, 'a number of mistaken accusations against innocent individuals which were legally challenged and withdrawn'. The flyer smacked of the same slander; but this time the victim of the accusation could not defend himself. The accuser remained nameless. Hinting that the Canadian Jewish Congress was either behind the flyer or knew who was, it was demanded that henceforth Jewish officials communicate directly and openly with 'the numerous central organizations of our community in the world, rather than by anonymous channels'.[35]

Kayfetz was as appalled at any notion the CJC was behind an anonymous flyer as he was amazed anyone could believe the Jewish community was so tightly organized that a word from Congress could rein in those circulating the flyer. This monolithic vision was as far from true of the Jewish community as it was of the Ukrainian. Furthermore, in a memo to Congress leaders, he wondered if the protest was not just a little disingenuous. The offending flyer was amateurish but it was not an accusation of guilt. It was a request for information—information necessary to avoid the very kind of false accusations Ukrainians protested. As to the ringing declaration of support for bringing war criminals to justice—Kayfetz was now obviously sceptical. 'On reading of the letter, I see it is something less than that.'[36]

While American-Ukrainian community spokesmen rose to the challenge of the OSI, their Ukrainian-Canadian counterparts saw little on the Canadian horizon to indicate they would soon be subject to the same type of investigations. Certainly the Jewish lobbying effort was having no more luck in the late 1970s and early 1980s than had been the case in the early 1950s. In essence, the Jewish argument was, as it had always been, grounded on the moral necessity of government action. The Jewish community repeatedly pressed public officials that it was immoral that those who willingly participated in crimes the likes of which the world had never previously witnessed—crimes against humanity itself—should find safe haven in Canada. It was an affront to the memories of millions who had been murdered and to every Canadian combatant who had put his or her life on the line to defeat Naziism. It offended Canadian fidelity to justice and the rule of law.

To Jewish delegations and petitions and to protest resolutions and personal representations, the government's answer was equally consistent. Much though the government might want to take the initiative in acting against any alleged Nazi war criminals in Canada, there was a problem. Opinion from the government's legal advisors remained that there was no legal framework under Canadian law, no workable legal remedy, which would allow for government action. What this meant, in effect, was that without a legal framework to deal with alleged Nazi war criminals in Canada, there was no justification for police investigations of individuals, or for court proceedings. After all, Canadian police act against individuals when Canadian laws are broken but if no Canadian law was broken, there was no reason to issue orders to Canadian police to follow up on information about alleged Nazis in Canada. The courts also had no basis for action.

One door remained open. Canadian Jewish leaders were told that if another country requested the extradition of a Canadian resident the Canadian legal and administrative machinery could swing into action. But, here too, there were limits. Canada would not initiate. It responded to the application of a second state. Furthermore, not all countries were equally welcome to apply. The list of countries with which Canada had negotiated extradition treaties is far from complete and it was unlikely in the extreme that Canada would respond positively to a request for extradition on capital crimes from countries like the Soviet Union where the system of justice is incompatible with that of Canada. Consequently, although the door was open to extradition, it was only open by a crack.[37]

After years of attempting to sway government by pointing to the moral injustice of alleged Nazi war criminals living freely in Canada, in the late 1970s the Canadian Jewish Congress gradually shifted gears. While the case for doing what was right was not dropped, in the late 1970s the Jewish polity set out to challenge the government's longstanding position that there was no remedy in Canadian law. The CJC determined to show there was not one but a series of legal options available to government. In so doing they also hoped to prove, as if it needed proving, it was not lack of legal remedies but lack of political will which left the Nazi war criminals so long immune to Canadian justice.

Yet this begs a key question. Why, more than thirty-five years after the war's end, with the Holocaust ever more integrated into the western historical narrative, with Canadian Jewry in high profile component of the Canadian social mosaic, with individual Jews in previously undreamed-of positions of power, prestige, and responsibility, with the organization of Canadian Jewish lobbying the envy of other ethnic communities — why was there such a lack of political will on the part of the government?

The answer is of several parts. The Liberal Party Government of the day was very much the creature of its leader, Pierre Trudeau. The degree to which he took a personal interest in the details of the war criminal issue has yet to be spelled out in detail.[38] But there is little doubt that Trudeau, though a student of history, drew a sharp line between the past and the present. Trudeau, who opened the window of opportunity to Jews in public service as no other prime minister had ever done — appointing a Jew to be Chief Justice of the Canadian Supreme Court, appointing three Jews to his last cabinet, appointing a Jew as the Canadian Ambassador in Washington, peppering his personal advisory staff with Jews — showed little patience for the special pleading of the Jewish polity or that of other ethnic lobbying groups. He neither opposed ethnic continuity nor rejected the right of any group to petition government for relief of grievances. But the Canadian interest came first, and as far as Trudeau was concerned, few if any singularly ethnic interests were at one with the national interest. On the issue of war criminals, if Trudeau gave the matter much thought, it was likely as a parochial Jewish concern engaging little broader support and an issue, if pursued, likely to be divisive of national harmony.

But how so? One can only speculate as to whether the Prime Minister and his advisers felt tackling the war criminal issue head on would only serve to dredge up the complicity of previous governments, prominent individuals and institutions in the admission and perhaps harbouring of Nazi war criminals. This remains to be shown. More to the point, the Prime Minister, and old hand at Canadian politics, surely understood that pursuing the issue of war criminals could well inflame inter-ethnic tensions in Canada. If national harmony was essential, if building a new consensus for federal unity his goal, then the potentially divisive and ethnically parochial Nazi issue would best be avoided. Setting Jews and Eastern Europeans, notably Ukrainians, on a collision course — even in the name of justice too long delayed — was not in the national interest. But the issue of the Nazis would not go away and the Jewish community seemed ever more determined to make its case, a legal case, more forcefully. In the spring of 1982, as Congress officials were preparing a comprehensive legal brief on Nazi war criminals, their cause received several unexpected boosts.

As the Congress brief was being redrafted, Albert Helmut Rauca, a 73-year-old suburban Toronto man, was taken into custody by the Royal Canadian Mounted Police (RCMP) on a West German extradition warrant. He stood accused of direct involvement in the murder of thousands of Lithuanian Jews during World War II. Congress leaders were delighted by the Rauca extradition proceedings. Not only did it promise the removal from Canada of an accused Nazi mass murderer, but it also focused national attention on the problem of Nazi war criminals in Canada as nothing had been done before. Ironically, however, the Rauca hearings forced Congress to withhold from government the brief it prepared outlining legal remedies under Canadian law. Underlying the Congress brief were arguments in support of trying war criminals in Canada. At the time Rauca's lawyer was also arguing that there were legal options for domestic prosecution of his client. Until they were used, he opposed his client's extradition to West Germany. Rather than have Congress face the embarrassment of seemingly supporting Rauca's legal arguments against extradition and for trial in Canada, the Congress brief was held back pending a final determination of Rauca's legal fate.[39] Meanwhile, Congress staff in Toronto made their knowledge of foreign archives and other war crimes related material available to the Justice Department lawyer acting for the Crown in the extradition proceedings.[40]

The tumult over the Rauca proceedings raised the possibility that other wanted Nazi war criminals were living comfortably in Canada. In late August, 1982 *Today Magazine* published an article about Harold Puntulis who, like Rauca, had lived quietly in suburban Toronto for many years. Puntulis, also like Rauca, reportedly participated in the murder of thousands of Jews and gypsies in the Baltic during World War II. The Puntulis story was not new to Jewish leadership. His was among the more notorious cases Congress officials repeatedly and unsuccessfully brought to the attention of federal authorities in the hope of action. But Puntulis escaped justice forever; he died peacefully only a few weeks before the *Today Magazine* article was published.[41]

Public sensitization to Nazi war criminals received another jolt in September, 1982. As the Rauca trial continued, *None Is Too Many* was published. The book, a scholarly study of the Canadian response to the plight of European Jewry before, during, and after the Holocaust, did not directly address the question of Nazi war criminals entering Canada. It did, however, detail the rigid Canadian rejection of Jewish refugees during the long night of Nazi terror. In this, *None Is Too Many* inadvertently set up a contrast between the conscious Canadian refusal to offer sanctuary to the victims of Nazi brutality and a growing realization that Canada may have given haven, perhaps unknowingly, to their Nazi murderers after the war. This best seller and the wide publicity it received left many to wonder at the shame of past Canadian immigration policies. It further stiffened the resolve of Canadian Jewry to demand action.[42]

Perhaps because of the heightened public consciousness, perhaps because Jewish legal arguments were having the desired effect, perhaps because Trudeau, slumping in popularity polls, gave every sign of stepping down and his ministers were now jockeying for support in a leadership race all expected soon, there seemed a softening in the government's rigidity on the Nazi war crimes issue. Guarded hints were dropped that the government might, just might, be prepared to test Canadian law by bringing charges against several documented Nazi war criminals in Canada. Jewish leaders interpreted the hints of test cases as nothing less than a commitment.[43]

Before the Liberal government's resolve could be tested, Canadian voters delivered a crushing blow to Liberal Party futures. On 17 September 1984, Prime Minister Brian Mulroney was sworn into office with the largest majority ever awarded a Canadian government. For the Jewish polity the change in government was troubling. Trudeau may have had little sympathy for the Jewish agenda, but the Jewish polity had a long history of access to his government. Indeed, Jews tended to support the Liberal Party and Trudeau's own parliamentary seat was in a heavily Jewish area of Montreal.

Mulroney was another thing again. Congress leadership had limited connections with the new Conservative machine and Mulroney was a largely unknown commodity. Only one Jew sat on the new government benches. On the other hand, Ukrainians and other eastern Europeans were traditionally strong backers of the Conservative Party. A number of Ukrainian-Canadians and others of Eastern European descent were elected to parliament under the new government's banner and several were included in the Mulroney cabinet. Who would speak for Jewish interests?

The Jewish establishment felt locked out.[44] But oddly, while they had no access, perhaps because they had no access, it was possible for those at the margins of organized Jewish life to influence government. This proved to be the case with Sol Littman, a retired journalist who had covered the Rauca trial for Canadian television. After parting company with the Canadian Broadcasting Corporation (CBC), he published a book on the Rauca affair, *War Criminal on Trial*. During his research he visited the Wiesenthal Center in Los Angeles and eventually became the Center's Canadian representative.

Even before his book was published, Littman was already a source of controversy within Ukrainian circles. Preliminary to his book on the Rauca trial and extradition, he published an article in *Saturday Night* largely drawn from his manuscript. In this teaser for the forthcoming book, Littman explored Canadian government complicity in the post-war admission of alleged war criminals into Canada. To illustrate his point, Littman pointed a finger at Halychyna Division members. If Division members were understandably shy about being discussed in the context of an article on Nazi war criminals, they were livid at Littman's assertion that the Division was assigned guard duty at concentration camps and participated in putting down the 1943 Warsaw Ghetto uprising, at the cost of thousands of Jewish lives. While questions still remained to be answered about the activities of individual Halychyna members before they joined the Division, Halychyna members protested their unit was never involved in anti-Jewish actions. Indeed, the Warsaw Ghetto uprising was over before the Halychyna was organized. A slander suit was filed against *Saturday Night*. The offending sentences were expunged from the final published text of Littman's book which contains the publisher's note, 'Material in this book appeared in somewhat different form in *Saturday Night* magazine'.[45]

Littman and the Simon Wiesenthal Center he represented in Canada were clearly outside the formal umbrella of the Canadian Jewish Congress. But the election of a Mulroney Conservative government in December, 1984, which left Congress out in the cold, provided a new opening for Littman. Even as Congress representatives requested and were denied a meeting with

Mulroney's new Minister of Justice, Littman, robed in the mantle of Wiesenthal's name, requested and was granted a meeting with the Minister. As Congress looked on bewildered, Littman, accompanied by several spokesmen for the California-based organization, arrived in Ottawa. The meeting, Littman recalled, was productive. Uninformed on years of Congress lobbying of a reluctant government on the issue of Nazi war criminals in Canada and unaware of the previous government's seeming promise to take several test cases to court, the Center pressed its own agenda. The test cases on which Congress had pinned so much hope did not come up in the discussion. The Minister reassured the Wiesenthal Center delegation he was well aware of their concern and hinted some plan of action was in the offing.[46]

Littman was again in Ottawa several weeks after his initial meeting with the Justice Minister when he received an urgent call from the Simon Wiesenthal Center's California headquarters. The Center, he later explained, had obtained documents under American freedom of information legislation indicating, among other things, that in 1962 a Dr Joseph Menke applied to the Canadian embassy in Buenos Aires for admission to Canada. His request was referred to the Canadian visa control office in Cologne, Germany which, in turn, requested information on Menke from Allied intelligence authorities in Europe. According to the documentation, Canadian authorities were advised that Joseph Menke was a known alias used by the notorious Dr Joseph Mengele, the wanted Nazi war criminal who conducted barbaric medical experiments on inmates at Auschwitz concentration camp.

Littman tried to follow up the information. He checked with both the Canadian Immigration Service and the RCMP. Neither divulged any record of the Menke application or whether or not the application had been rejected. Littman, incorrectly concluding that the Menke who applied to enter Canada and Mengele were one and the same and fearing that the mass murderer had actually come to Canada, wrote the Prime Minister on 20 December 1984. A copy of the letter was also sent to the Minister of Justice. In his letter Littman offered no doubt that Mengele had indeed tried to enter Canada. He also charged that Canadian authorities were at best negligent both in not keeping tabs on the case and not advising Allied authorities of Mengele's whereabouts at the time. 'This', he cautioned the Prime Minister, 'leaves us with the frightening possibility that Mengele may actually be living in Canada today.'

> If this possibility seems too incredible to credit, let me remind you that former S.S. Master Sergeant Helmut Rauca who was responsible for the death of 9,200 innocent men, women and children in one afternoon, arrived in Canada as an immigrant in 1950 and lived here totally undisturbed until he was finally tracked down by the RCMP in 1982.

On behalf of the Simon Wiesenthal Center, Littman demanded a release of all documentation and 'an immediate investigation, ordered at the highest level' into the Mengele affair:

The dimension of Mengele's crimes, and the legacy of his 400,000 victims, demand that no stone remain unturned in the quest to bring this man, who is the personification of evil, before the bar of justice. Only a thorough investigation ordered by your governmentcan [sic] ascertain what role Canada played in the bizarre case of Joseph Mengele.[47]

While Littman awaited a reply, a second meeting with the Minister of Justice was hastily arranged at which time Littman raised the Mengele story. The Minister was not particularly moved by the Mengele revelations but indicated again that something was in the offering. He refused to be more specific.

Almost four weeks after sending Mulroney his letter, Littman was informed from the Wiesenthal Center that the *New York Times* now had the file from which Mengele's alleged Canadian connection had been pulled. Rather than see the Canadian angle get lost in a larger *New York Times* story, Littman called a press conference in Toronto for 10 January 1985. He told reporters he would reveal the contents of his Mulroney letter.[48] He also filled in the *New York Times* on his Mengele accusations.[49]

The media smelled a good story. *Maclean's Magazine*, jumping the gun, phoned the Prime Minister's Office in an effort to find out what was in Littman's letter. Littman later learned the Prime Minister's Office was taken by surprise. Not only did they not reveal what was in the letter, they also seemed never to have heard of it. According to Littman, a mad scramble to find the letter ensured. It was apparently misplaced in the wave of Christmas greetings that flooded the Prime Minister's Office during holiday week. Just before his scheduled press conference began, Littman was summoned to the phone. A Mulroney aide apologized for the delay in answering the now located letter. It was hinted that Littman postpone his press conference until after the Prime Minister considered the letter's contents, but Littman refused. He released his letter and the accompanying documentation to the press. The story made headlines the following Monday and was even carried in the *New York Times*.[50]

The flurry of media controversy generated by the Littman accusations caught the Prime Minister's Office off guard. Stumbling around for an appropriate response — a response that would keep the Mulroney government on the side of the angels, distance it from accusations of indifference to the Nazi war criminal question being levelled against the previous Trudeau government, and perhaps grant the new government a cooling-off time while appearing to take decisive action — Mulroney latched upon the idea of a judicial inquiry. On 7 February 1985, the Prime Minister announced that respected Quebec Superior Court Justice Jules Deschênes had agreed to conduct an inquiry into the presence of Nazi war criminals in Canada, including Mengele, and to determine if any remedy existed in Canadian law to deal with them.

The Mulroney caucus and cabinet were surprised. Some huddled together discussing the political fallout which might result.[51] Congress leaders also reacted with disbelief. They had never pressed for a Deschênes-like inquiry. They had not gotten close enough to Mulroney or his cabinet to press them on anything. While the Mulroney initiative was welcomed publicly, Jewish leaders privately were very uneasy. They did not know what Mulroney was up to. What about the long-awaited and some felt promised test cases? Were they a dead issue?[52] While it would be wrong to credit the Mengele letter with being the only factor influencing the Mulroney government to establish the Deschênes Commission, it was the most public factor. Wide publicity given the Mengele letter ensured that in the public mind it was Littman, not years of Congress lobbying, that forced the government's hand.

The Deschênes Commission and, more particularly, Littman's supposed role in its establishment, galvanized the organized Ukrainian community. Littman was already identified as a Ukrainian baiter. To many, Littman's earlier allegations against the Halychyna Division were part of a larger attack on the integrity of the entire Ukrainian diaspora. He spoke of fully 3000 Eastern European war criminals in Canada.[53] In tarring the reputation of individual Ukrainian-Canadians as Nazi war criminals, he was accused of also damning the entire community for supposedly sheltering war criminals for decades. Nor was Littman initially seen as a loose cannon on the Jewish deck—a spokesman for the fringe Wiesenthal Center. To many he was a stalking horse for the Canadian Jewish establishment, saying publicly what most dared not to say themselves.[54]

Surprisingly, the Mulroney government was caught unawares and unprepared for the eruption of Jewish-Ukrainian tension. For most in government, as for most Canadians, the term 'Nazi' conjured up an Eichmann or a Mengele, not a low-level non-German police official, concentration camp guard, or local bureaucrat. When Ukrainian organizations reacted to the Deschênes Commission as signalling an attack on the Ukrainian diaspora, the government pondered the fallout at the ballot box.

Other results were also predictable. Those few channels open to Ukrainian-Jewish dialogue dried up. Whatever good will had slowly and painstakingly accrued through years of hesitant efforts to bridge the gulf between Jewish and Ukrainian polities in Canada, mostly at Ukrainian initiative, evaporated almost over night. The Jewish community thrown headlong into the Deschênes process confronted a Ukrainian community increasingly convinced they were going to be the victims of an organized smear campaign, a community under siege. As the Deschênes Commission began its deliberations the gulf between Ukrainians and Jews in Canada grew wider. Old wounds inflicted far away and long ago were re-opened.

Notes

[1] D.V. Grawronski, *History: Meaning and Method* (Glenview, Ill.: 1969): 3.

[2] E.H. Carr, *What Is History*, 2d ed. (London: 1986): 114.

[3] For a discussion of the definition of ethnicity, see Wsevolod W. Isajiw, 'Definitions of Ethnicity', *Ethnicity* 1 (1974): 111-24.

[4] For a discussion of the historical self-understanding of both Jewish and Ukrainian policies and the place each allots to the other, see Howard Aster and Peter J. Potichnyj, *Jewish-Ukrainian Relations: Two Solitudes* (Oakville, Ont.: 1983).

[5] Alternate Ukrainian and Jewish historical discussion of the 1648 rebellion is the topic of Frank E. Sysyn, 'The Jewish Factor in the Khmel'nyts'kyi Uprising', unpublished paper.

[6] Historians continue to debate the Petliura government and its Jewish policy. The issue was a matter of heated exchange in the pages of *Jewish Social Studies*. Taras Hunczak, 'A Reappraisal of Symon Petliura and Ukrainian Jewish Relations, 1917-1921', *Jewish Social Studies* 31 (1969): 163-83; Zosa Szajkowski, '"A Reappraisal of Symon Petliura and Ukrainian and Jewish Relations, 1917-1921": A Rebuttal', *Jewish Social Studies* 31 (1969): 184-213; 'Communications', *Jewish Social Studies* 32 (1970): 246-63. The exchange with added documentary material was published in Taras Hunczak, *Symon Petliura and the Jews: A Reappraisal* (Toronto: 1985).

[7] The historiography of the Holocaust as it touches Ukraine continues to grow. A useful overview of World War II in the larger sweep of Ukrainian history is available in Paul R. Magocsi, 'Ukraine: An Introductory History', unpublished manuscript. No discussion of the Holocaust in Ukraine can ignore Philip Friedman, 'Ukrainian-Jewish Relations During the Nazi Occupation', *Yivo Annual of Jewish Social Science* 12 (1958/59): 259-98, which is the starting point for much later analysis. The failure of Jews, notably Yad Vashem in Israel, to accord Sheptytsky his due as a 'righteous gentile' still rankles. See Shomon Redlich, 'Sheptytsky and the Jews', *Jerusalem Post*, 21 December 1985.

[8] Lubomyr Y. Luciuk, 'Searching for Place: Ukrainian Refugee Migration to Canada after World War II' (unpublished PhD thesis, University of Alberta, 1984).

[9] Literature in English on the Halychyna Division, also known as the Galicia Division, is spotty at best. See, for example, Basil Dmytryshyn, 'The Nazis and the SS Volunteer Division "Galicia"', *American Slavic and Eastern European Review* 15 (1956): 1-10; Wasyl Veryha, 'The "Galicia" Ukrainian Division in Polish and Soviet Literature', *Ukrainian Quarterly* 36 (1980): 253-70; Richard Landwehr, *Fighting for Freedom: The Ukrainian Volunteer Division of the Waffen-SS* (Silver Spring, Md.: 1985); Myroslav Yurkevich, 'Galician Ukrainians in German Military Formations and in the German Administration' in Yury Boshyk, ed., *Ukraine During World War II: History and Its Aftermath* (Edmonton: 1986): 67-87.

[10] The Ukrainian-Canadian lobbying effort on behalf of the Halychyna and community support for the Division is detailed in Bohdan Panchuk, *Heroes of Their Day: The Reminiscences of Bohdan Panchuk*, Ed. by Lubomyr U. Luciuk (Toronto: 1983).

[11]Canadian Jewish Congress Papers, CJC Archives (hereafter referred to as the CJC Papers), Ukrainian Galician Division Papers, 1950-1951 (Galician Files), Memorandum of Rosenberg to Hayes, 30 June 1950; Telegram of Bronfman to Harris, 4 July 1950.

[12]CJC papers, Galician Files. Memorandum of Rosenberg to Hayes, 'Halychyna Division', 26 July 1950; Memorandum of Rosenberg to Hayes, 'Halychyna Division', 23 October 1950; Hayes to Harris, 2 August 1950; Harris to Hayes, 6 November 1950; Harris to Bronfman, 7 November 1950; Memorandum of Hayes to National Executive, 10 January 1951.

[13]*Jewish Post*, 2 May 1957.

[14]British United Press Dispatch, 4 May 1957.

[15]CJC Papers, Andre Melnyk Files. Frank to Hayes, 10 May 1957; Memorandum of Kayfetz to Hayes, 17 May 1957; Frank to Hayes, 16 May 1957; Kochan to Fenson, 31 May 1957; Canadian Jewish Congress Archives, Toronto, Catzman Papers. Memorandum of Kayfetz to Hayes, 'Meeting with officers of Ukrainian National Federation', 14 May 1957; *Jewish Post*, 23 May 1957.

[16]Yaacov Glickman, 'Political Socialization and the Social Protest of Canadian Jewry: Some Historical and Contemporary Perspectives', in Jorgen Dahlie and Tissa Fernando, eds, *Ethnicity Power and Politics in Canada* (Toronto: 1981): 123-50.

[17]National Archives of Canada (NAC), Louis Ronson Papers (Ronson Papers), vol. 4, file 7. 'Note for Remarks by the Prime Minister to the Ukrainian-Canadian Congress, Winnipeg, Manitoba, October 9, 1971.'

[18]NAC, Ronson Papers, vol. 4, file 7, Memorandum of Levy to Ronson, 'Ukrainian Contacts with JCRC', 5 August 1971.

[19]Similar sentiment abounded in the American Jewish community. See Abraham Brumberg, 'Poland and the Jews', *Tikkun* (July/August, 1987): 15-20, 85-90.

[20]Canadian Jewish Archives, Toronto (CJC-T), J.C. Hurwitz Papers, File July-December, 1974, Memorandum of Kayfetz to Hurwitz Papers, File Ukrainian Canadians, 9 September 1974; File July-December, 1974. Minutes, JCRC, Toronto, 11 September 1974, 6-8.

[21]CJC-T, J.C. Hurwitz Papers. File July-December 1974. Epstein to Kayfetz, 5 November 1974.

[22]CJC-T, Hurwitz Papers, File January-June 1975, Memorandum of Kayfetz to Pearlson and Hurwitz re: 'Ukrainian-Canadians', 4 February 1975.

[23]NAC, Ronson Papers, vol. 4, file 7, Memorandum of Kayfetz to Harris *et al.*, 25 March 1975.

[24]CJC-T, J.C. Hurwitz Papers, File January-June 1975. Memorandum of Kayfetz to Harris *et al.* re: 'Continuing Conversations with Ukrainians Leadership', 15 April 1975; Report on Ben Kayfetz, re: 'Meeting with Ukrainians', 3 June 1975.

[25]NAC, Plaut Papers, CJC Ukrainian-Jewish Dialogue, 1977-78. Bardyn to Plaut, 31 January 1978; Kayfetz to Plaut, 15 February 1978; Plaut to Bardyn, 17 February 1978; Plaut to Bardyn, 7 March 1978.

[26]*Canadian Jewish News*, 28 April 1978; *Globe and Mail*, 22 April 1978; NAC, Plaut Papers, CJC Ukrainian-Jewish Dialogue, 1977-78 — Confidential Memorandum of Plaut, 'Visit of Rabbi Plaut and Address to Ukrainian Professional and Business Club of Toronto, 20 April 1978', 24 April 1978.

[27]See for example, CJC-T, Catzman Papers, Confidential Memorandum of Kayfetz to Catzman *et al.*, 5 September 1958; Kayfetz to Finestone, 23 September 1958.

[28]Hannah Arendt, *Eichmann in Jerusalem: A Report on the Banality of Evil* (New York: 1964), and Gideon Hausner, *Justice in Jerusalem* (London: 1967).

[29]CJC Papers, Submission to L.B. Pearson. Memorandum of Saalheimer to Gelber, 27 March 1964; Prinz to Rusk, 2 March 1984; Garber to Martin, 13 April 1964; Hayes to Couts, 1 October 1964; Bronfman to Pearson, 14 October 1964.

[30]Interview with Max Chirofsky, 21 May 1986, Toronto.

[31]Interview with Ben Kayfetz, 9 August 1986, Toronto.

[32]American and international action against Nazis is considered in Tom Bower, *Blind Eye to Murder: Britain, America and the Purging of Nazi Germany; A Pledge Betrayed* (London: 1981); Charles R. Allen, *Nazi War Criminals in America: Facts, Action; The Basic Handbook* (New York: 1985); Adalbert Rückerl, *The Investigation of Nazi War Crimes, 1945-1978; A Documentation* (Heidelberg: 1979); Rochelle G. Saidel, *The Outraged Conscience: Seekers of Justice for Nazi War Criminals in America* (Albany: 1984); Allan A. Ryan, *Quiet Neighbors: Prosecuting Nazi War Criminals in America* (New York: 1984).

[33]NAC, Plaut Papers, CJC National JCRC, Memoranda (Pt. 1), 1977. Memorandum of Kayfetz to Plaut *et al.* re 'Ukrainians,' 18 August 1977.

[34]NAC, Plaut Papers, vol. 4, file 7. Flyer entitled 'Nazi Crimes in Przemyls' (Poland), n.d.

[35]NAC, Plaut Papers, CJC National JCRC, Memoranda (Pt. 1), 1977. Shymko to Kayfetz, 8 August 1977.

[36]NAC, Plaut Papers, CJC National JCRC, Memoranda (Pt. 1), 1977. Memorandum of Kayfetz to Plaut *et al.* re 'Ukrainians', 18 August 1977.

[37]In his report on Nazi war criminals in Canada, Justice Jules Deschênes reviews the legal opinions accepted by the government and their flaws. Commission of Inquiry on War Criminals, *Report, Part I: Public* (Ottawa): 1986: 85-239.

[38]Some light may be shed on this question with the final release of *Nazi War Criminals in Canada: The Historical and Policy Setting from the 1940s to the Present*, prepared for the Deschênes Commission of Inquiry on War Criminals by Alti Rodel.

[39]Interview with David Matas, 29 March 1986, Toronto. For a study of the Rauca case, see Sol Littman, *War Criminal on Trial: The Rauca Case* (Toronto: 1983).

[40]CJC, Silverstone Papers, War Criminal Correspondence, 1982. Memorandum of Narvey to Amerisinghe, re: 'Documents in Soviet Archives', 19 August 1982.

[41]Jeff Ansell and Paul Appelby, 'The War Criminal', *Today Magazine*, 28 August 1982.

[42]Irving Abella and Harold Troper, *None Is Too Many: Canada and the Jews of Europe, 1933-1948* (Toronto: 1982).

[43] Interview with David Matas, 29 March 1986, Toronto; interview with Milton Harris, 10 May 1986, Toronto; Milton Harris Papers, War Crimes File, MacGuigan to Kaplan, 8 December 1983.

[44]Milton Harris Papers, War Crimes File. MacKay to Raphael, 13 November 1984; Crosbie to Raphael, 19 November 1984; Raphael to Harris, 21 November 1984; Harris to Granovsky, January 1985.

[45]Sol Littman, 'Agent of the Holocaust, The Secret Life of Helmut Rauca', *Saturday Night*, July 1983: 11-23; Littman, *War Criminal on Trial*: iv.

[46]Interview with Sol Littman, 21 January 1986, Toronto.

[47]Commission of Inquiry on War Criminals, Documents, Littman to Mulroney, 20 December 1984.

[48]Interview with Sol Littman, 7 May 1987, Toronto.

[49]Interview with Arthur Meighen, 25 May 1987, Toronto.

[50]Interview with Sol Littman, 22 October 1986. Toronto. *Toronto Star*, 23 January 1985; *New York Times*, 23 January 1985.

[51]Interview with Jeff Norquay, 21 March 1986, Ottawa.

[52]CJC, Silverstone Papers. Deschênes Commission Press Releases, Newspaper Clippings. CJC Press Release, 'Canadian Jewish Congress President Says War Criminal Commission Not Enough'. 7 February 1985.

[53]Commission of Inquiry, *Report*: 245-48.

[54]CJC-T, JCRC Papers, Ukrainian File. Epstein to Satok, 11 February 1985; Satok to Epstein, 13 February 1985; interview with John Gregorovich, 8 April 1987, Toronto; interview with Roman Serbyn, 18 February 1986, Montreal.

The Ethnic Sub-Economy:

Explication and Analysis of a Case Study

of the Jews of Montreal

Morton Weinfeld

Social scientific analyses of the relationship between minority group status and economic achievement have generally described and explained negative consequences for such groups in plural societies. The economic victimization of minority groups is due primarily to active discrimination on the part of the dominant group(s), and may range from attempted extermination (in which case economic penalties are of secondary importance), expulsion, concentration (on reservations or in ghettos), or legal discrimination (as in apartheid laws) to more subtle forms of 'illegal' discrimination in employment or wages and institutional discrimination which reduces opportunities. All such discrimination will adversely affect the economic performance of a minority group and its members (Sowell, 1975).

Indeed, implicit in the phrase 'equality of economic opportunity' is a notion of a single, complex economic system in which all individuals should be able to participate to the full extent of their abilities, extracting a fair economic reward. That reality departs from this image has been amply demonstrated in studies of ethnic and racial stratification (Duncan and Duncan, 1968; Farley, 1977) and in Gordon's (1964) construct of the 'ethclass' in which minority group status practically coincides with (usually inferior) social class. Furthermore, as argued by current critiques of neo-classical labour economics, there are 'dual' or 'split' labour markets in which minorities, as well as other workers, are relegated to non-competitive, low-paying jobs in depressed economic sectors (Bonacich, 1972; Cain, 1976).

A second type of economic victimization may result unintentionally from the voluntary actions of minority groups, who limit their economic activities and relations to members of their own groups. Immigrants arriving in reasonably open societies tend to seek initial employment through networks of contact within an existing ethnic community (Anderson, 1974). Ethnic economic segregation may have the advantage of linguistic familiarity, congenial work atmospheres, absence of 'red tape', recognition of the employees' cultural or religious needs, and a perceived greater job security, all reinforced by ties of origin, family relationships, or sense of communal obligation.

Nevertheless, the consequences of such 'voluntary' economic segregation are seen as negative, penalizing minorities by locking them into an 'ethnic mobility trap' (Wiley, 1967) in which rewards or opportunities are less than those available in the mainstream economy. Such behaviour inevitably produces less than full participation in post-industrial society (Porter, 1975) and penalizes not only the immigrants, but their descendants as well.

In opposition to the prevailing view, theoretical and empirical studies have identified certain groups for whom minority status may have positive economic consequences. These minority groups tend to be disproportionately represented as self-appointed entrepreneurs, who eventually achieve, for themselves or their children, a certain measure of relative economic success, notwithstanding the fact that at given points in their occupational careers, many of them struggle near or at the poverty line.

Light (1979) has reviewed three sets of theoretical explanations for the high degree of self-employment among Jews, Asians, and other minorities: (1) the cultural theory of entrepreneurship, in which the cultural values or social institutions of an ethnic heritage are seen as functional for successful enterprise; (2) middlemen minority theories, which emphasize the solidarity of sojourning minorities linked to a homeland; and (3) the disadvantage theory, which sees the trend to self-employment as a rational response to various forms of discrimination in the labour market.

All three approaches have been used to explain Jewish economic behaviour, particularly business success and occupational mobility, in various societies (Eitzen, 1971; Glazer, 1958; Rosen, 1959; Slater, 1969; Sombart, 1969; Strodtbeck, 1958). This paper will not adjudicate among these three approaches. Indeed, it would seem that the debate about the reasons for differing propensities among minority groups for self-employment may be losing its salience as an important contemporary sociological puzzle. The proportions of North Americans self-employed has been steadily diminishing, comprising 6.7 per cent of American non-farm workers in 1973. Moreover, the self-employed do not earn more than wage earners (Light, 1980: 31).

In addition, we note the increasing heterogeneity of the self-employed category. Not only is there substantial variation in the scale and income of businessmen, but the rise of a new middle class of educated independent professionals along with the classic entrepreneurial middle class complicates the meaning of the self-employed status. The old self-employed small businessman usually needed hard work, savings, business acumen, and pluck; the self-employed professional relies on educational achievement and recognized credentials.

Third, and related, is the growth in high status salaried occupations, whether as managers in large firms or as professionals in public or quasi-public bureaucracies (Bell, 1973). Such occupations bring greater rewards in prestige and income than do most self-employed occupations, and have become increasingly popular among Jews, Asian minorities, and other historic middlemen groups.

Thus, a label such as middleman minority may be descriptively misleading, ignoring the increasing occupational diversity found within minority groups. For example, Bonacich (1973) describes the high concentration of Jewish retailers in Stamford, Connecticut in the 1930s as evidence of the Jewish tendency to middlemen minority status even within a modern industrial setting. Yet, at the same time there were large numbers of working class Jews in nearby New York, as well as a growing number of salaried Jewish professionals.

Many analyses of the economic conditions of minorities contain fragmentary evidence, usually ethnographic, of the presence and use of economic networks operating within a given group. This study represents a beginning effort to systematically and quantitatively explicate the concept of the ethnic sub-economy, using the case of Jews in Montreal. The term 'ethnic sub-economy' can be applied to any minority group — ethnic, religious, racial, linguistic in a plural economy. Jews can be considered as a religious and/or ethnic group.

The Ethnic Sub-Economy

The 'ethnic sub-economy' can be defined as a network of economic relationships which may link employees, employers, consumers, buyers, and sellers, of a specific ethnic group or minority. The image is one of a parallel economy. It need not be limited to one class, or one economic sector, or to one spatial area in a given urban setting. An ethnic sub-economy may exist regardless of the conditions of immigration of the group, attitude to the homeland, and degrees of hostility facing the group. The existence of an ethnic sub-economy may be established by tracing the relative frequency of economic transactions ethnic members have within and without their own group. Thus, members of an ethnic group can participate to a greater or lesser extent in the ethnic sub-economy. The boundaries are set behaviourally, not geographically. The ethnic sub-economy will include its own markets for labour, capital, goods, services, and information, which may parallel those existing in the 'mainstream' economy.

The ethnic sub-economy can be considered a general case, to include any configuration of ethnic economic behaviour. Whether economic advantage or penalty accrues to participants in the sub-economy must be established empirically. The concept can describe an economically successful middleman minority, an immigrant enclave, or a depressed racial ghetto. An ethnic sub-economy may have a greater working-class or greater middle-class dimension; yet, it is conceived as a vertical social phenomenon, existing across social classes. Indeed, like the mainstream economy, its social class composition and industrial base may change over time.

The notion of an ethnic sub-economy is similar in some respects to the concept of a 'cultural division of labour' by Hechter (1978). Just as a societal division of labour may be more or less 'hierarchical' or 'segmental', so may a sub-economy vary as to the class composition or the occupational-industrial concentration of its members. Hechter, however, posits a causal model in which ethnic solidarity is dependent on, among other things, high levels of intra-group interaction (including economic transactions). The data presented below suggest, however, that the relation between ethnic solidarity, variously defined, and frequency of intra-group economic interaction, may be more complex (or subtle) at the microsociological level of analysis.

An ethnic sub-economy would be relatively self-contained in the range of its economic activity. Whereas the 'middleman minority', by definition, fulfils intermediary economic functions, linking ethnic groups or economic sectors, the ethnic sub-economy might be conceived as a potential total economy in miniature. Economic relations outside the group would be relatively infrequent (though, of course, they could not be eliminated) for those whose primary economic activity was within the group.

Studies of immigrant or minority groups often reveal forms of intra-group economic activity. Immigrant social histories are replete with such data (Howe, 1976). Sowell (1975) and Nelli (1967) argue that what is here called an ethnic sub-economy is an asset only for immigrants in ethnically stratified societies, easing the processes of initial adaptation and economic integration. They suggest that minorities should abandon their ethnic economic base following the passing of the immigrant generation.

Evidence for the existence of ethnic sub-economies can be seen in the structure of urban housing markets. Ethnic groups in Toronto report that they rent or buy housing predominantly from persons of the same ethnic origin (Weinfeld, 1977). A detailed study of rental housing in Montreal identified ethnic networks which operated in various neighbourhoods to promote exchanges of labour and information and to influence landlord-tenant relationships (Krohn et al., 1977). One study of the business élite in Quebec noted the marked tendency for large firms owned by Jews to recruit primarily Jewish persons for senior management positions (Sales, 1979: 136-8). Another study of Montreal's Italians found them to be likely to work for or with other Italians (Boissevain, 1970: 21).

This study presents and analyses data concerning the economic behaviour of a random sample of Jewish household heads in Montreal. The objective is to attempt to establish the degree to which a Jewish sub-economy exists, and to begin an initial examination of some of the characteristics of one such sub-economy.

The analysis is focused within the Jewish group and is not concerned with relative Jewish over- or under-representation in certain economic classes or sectors. Rather, the aim is to identify the pattern of intra-group economic behaviour, and address the following questions: (1) What are the dimensions of the Jewish sub-economy in Montreal? (2) To what extent is this an 'immi-

Table 1   *Occupational and Income Distribution of Jewish Household Heads in Montreal*

CENSUS OCCUPATIONAL CATEGORIES	CURRENT/LAST/USUAL		
	OCCUPATION %	FAMILY INCOME	%
Managers and administrators	43.0	Less than $10,000	26.0
Professional and technical	12.3	10,000–19,999	24.9
Clerical	13.2	20,000–29,999	16.4
Sales	11.4	30,000–49,999	19.4
Service	1.8	50,000 +	13.3
Skilled labour	7.9		
Other	10.2		100.0
Not reported	—		
	100.0		

grant' phenomenon; i.e., does it persist beyond the immigrant generation? (3) To what extent is participation in the Jewish sub-economy in Montreal associated with disadvantage, such as a perception of anti-Semitism, or with positive factors such as a 'preference' for dealing with Jews or a high degree of religiosity which might channel interactions to other Jews? (4) To what extent is participation in the Jewish sub-economy associated with either economic benefits or losses for the participants?

Methods and Sample

The data were collected from a 1978 survey of 657 Jewish household heads in Montreal.[1] The sample was generated by creating a 'master list' of Jewish households in Montreal and sampling randomly within the list. The master list eventually included an estimated 85 per cent to 90 per cent of all Jewish households in Montreal compared to census figures. A questionnaire containing 332 questions was administered to each subject in the form of a one-hour interview.

Table 1 presents the occupational and income distributions for the sample. The variance is substantial, particularly as regards the distribution by family income. Thirty-seven per cent of the respondents were self-employed; 29.6 per cent were college graduates (bachelor, masters, doctorate, or professional degree).

Size and Shape of the Jewish Sub-Economy

Three questions were available from the survey questionnaire to ascertain the degree of individual participation in the Jewish sub-economy. They provide some indications of the dimensions of the phenomenon itself. The distributions for these questions are presented in Table 2.

Respondents were asked several questions about the 'company, institution or organization you work with'. We see that 24.4 per cent indicated that Jews comprised the majority of the customers or clients of this firm or organization. In addition, 69.8 per cent of the respondents indicated that the 'majority of the executive management' was Jewish. (This latter figure includes those who were self-employed, either in business or the free professions. In fact, 33 per cent of the sample work for other Jews.) In other words, only 30.2 per cent of the sample were employees of non-Jewish firms or organizations.

More generally, respondents were asked to identify what proportion of their 'business associates' were Jewish. As we see from Table 2, 35 per cent of the respondents indicated that 'all or most' of their associates (partners, suppliers, employees, employers, customers/clients, colleagues, etc.) were Jews. Only 6.2 per cent indicated they had no business association or contacts with Jews. Bearing in mind that Jews represent only four per cent of the Metropolitan Montreal population, according to the 1971 census, this is a substantial amount of concentration.[2]

Studies of immigrant life and histories of Jewish economic integration suggest that firms operating in an ethnic sub-economy would be smaller (small shopkeepers, craftsmen, retailers, etc.) than those operating in the large scale mainstream economy. The respondents were divided into two groups: those whose firm/organization employed fewer than 50 employees, (64 per cent) and those, 50 or more (36 per cent). Of the former, 38.9 per cent identified all or most of their business associates as Jews, compared to 25.2 per cent of the latter (large firms). While those involved in smaller enterprises were, therefore, more likely to be participants in the ethnic sub-economy, we still find that significant numbers of those in large enterprises were also participants.

Participation in the Jewish Sub-Economy and Length of Residence in Montreal

Participation in an ethnic sub-economy, according to an assimilationist perspective,[3] should be more typical of immigrants than of native-born members of an ethnic group, and of more recent immigrants compared to those who arrived earlier. This view would be based not only on a hypothesized pattern of preferences, but on the supposition that structural barriers, e.g., knowledge of the host language and majority group hostility, and thus exclusion from full economic participation, might be greater for (more recent) immigrants.

Table 3 presents the trend on generational participation in the ethic sub-economy. Generation is measured as foreign-born (first generation), those native-born, but with both parents foreign-born (second generation), and those with at least one parent native-born (third generation or above). The

Table 2 *Ethnic Background of Majority of . . .*

	I. CLIENTS/CUSTOMERS[a]	II. EXECUTIVE[a]/MANAGEMENT (INCLUDES SELF-EMPLOYED)	III. BUSINESS ASSOCIATES . . . [a]	
	%	%		%
English Canadian	20.0	13.8	None are Jewish	6.2
French Canadian	21.6	6.5	Few are Jewish	20.3
Jewish	24.4	69.8	Some are Jewish	38.5
Other/Combination	34.0	9.9	Most are Jewish	23.5
			All are Jewish	11.5
	100.0	100.0		100.0
	N = 539	N = 550		N = 548

[a]Excludes respondents indicating 'don't know' or 'not applicable'.

Table 3 *Length of Residence in North America by Participation (per cent) in the Ethnic Sub-Economy*

INDICATORS OF PARTICIPATION FOR ALL RESPONDENTS

| | ETHNIC BACKGROUND OF MAJORITY OF | | | | | AMONG MY BUSINESS ASSOCIATES . . . ARE JEWS | | |
| | CUSTOMERS/CLIENTS | | EXECUTIVE MANAGEMENT | | | | | |
GENERATION	JEWISH	NON-JEWISH	JEWISH	NON-JEWISH		NONE OR FEW	SOME	MOST OR ALL
First	19.8	80.2 (N = 263)	69.2	30.8 (N = 276)		32.7	33.5	33.8 (N = 260)
Second	29.3	70.7 (N = 174)	75.6	24.4 (N = 180)		21.5	38.2	40.4 (N = 186)
Third +	28.3	71.7 (N = 97)	60.6	39.4 (N = 94)		19.6	52.0	28.4[a] (N = 102)
YEARS IN CANADA			FOR FOREIGN-BORN RESPONDENTS					
less than 25	21.5	78.5 (N = 94)	54.8	45.2 (N = 98)		44.6	27.3	28.2 (N = 95)
25–44	24.3	75.7 (N = 80)	77.1	22.9 (N = 86)		30.6	38.9	30.5 (N = 78)
45 +	23.0	77.0 (N = 89)	74.6	25.4 (N = 92)[a]		18.2	36.4	45.5 (N = 87)[a]

[a] Chi-square significant at $p < .05$. The reader will note that in those cases of significant differences in the generational patterns, the direction of the differences in no case conforms to the assimilationist expectation, that of decreasing levels of participation in the Jewish sub-economy with higher length of residence in North America.

data show no linear decrease in participation for the different generational groups.[4] For example, for the third generation, 28.3 per cent have primarily Jewish customers/clients, 60.6 per cent work for themselves or other Jews, and 28.4 per cent indicate that all or most of their business associates are Jewish.

A similar finding arises in comparing immigrants resident in Canada for different periods of time. The foreign-born respondents are divided into three roughly equal groups: those in Canada for fewer than 25 years, those resident for 25-44 years, and those in Canada for 45 or more years. There is no evidence of any decrease in participation in the Jewish sub-economy moving, from the 'greeners' (more recent immigrants) to the old-timers.

The data suggest that in no way can the Jewish sub-economy in Montreal be considered a phenomenon of (recently arrived) immigrants. A similar finding can be inferred from data provided by Light (1979: 34), which indicates only a marginal difference, from 158 to 150, in the self-employment rate per 1,000 employed, comparing foreign-born and native-born of Russian stock (largely Jewish) in the United States.

Anti-Semitism, Religiosity, and Participation in the Jewish Sub-Economy

Participation in the Jewish sub-economy is not limited to (more recent) immigrants. An alternate correlate of participation might be the perception of anti-Semitism. Those respondents who believe that non-Jews are basically anti-Semitic might seek to avoid any economic consequences of this anti-Semitism (note: all that is required is a perception of anti-Semitism, rather than a first-hand encounter with it or other objective evidence of its existence). Alternatively, more frequent participants might come to believe, perhaps as a rationale for their behaviour, in the prevalence of higher levels of anti-Semitism.

The data in Table 4 suggest that there are no significant differences in participation between those respondents perceiving more anti-Semitism and those perceiving less (see Appendix, p. 233 for a discussion of the index of perceived anti-Semitism). For example, of those who perceive *little* anti-Semitism, 21.8 per cent have Jews as a majority of customers, 68.1 per cent work for themselves or other Jews; the corresponding percentages for those perceiving *much* anti-Semitism are 26.6 per cent and 70.9 per cent. Thus fear of anti-Semitism does not seem to be systematically associated with participation in the Jewish sub-economy.

An alternative voluntaristic factor associated with participation might be religiosity. As Howe (1976) has described, some of the early immigrant workers in the needle trade in New York enjoyed the relative freedom to observe the Sabbath and holidays as a result of working for a Jewish employer. Moreover, the demands of a Jewish community for religious products or services (kosher food, Hebrew teachers, etc.) would create employment and business opportunities for religious Jews. Such an explana-

Table 4 Proportions of Respondents of Selected Characteristics (per cent) by Nature of Participation in Jewish Sub-Economy

	INDICATORS OF PARTICIPATION						
	CUSTOMERS/CLIENTS MAJORITY		EXECUTIVE MANAGEMENT		AMONG MY BUSINESS ASSOCIATES....ARE JEWISH		
	JEWS	NON-JEWS	JEWS	NON-JEWS	NONE OR FEW	SOME	MOST OR ALL
A. Perceived Anti-Semitism							
Low	21.8	78.2 (N = 252)	68.1	31.9 (N = 270)	28.5	39.4	32.1 (N = 274)
High	26.6	73.4 (N = 244)	70.9	29.1 (N = 247)	24.0	37.4	38.6 (N = 276)
B. Religiosity							
Low	28.1	71.9 (N = 167)	66.7	33.3 (N = 171)	23.3	44.2	32.5 (N = 172)
Medium	20.9	79.1 (N = 177)	66.8	33.2 (N = 190)	28.7	36.2	35.1 (N = 188)
High	24.1	75.9 (N = 170)	76.0	24.0 (N = 175)	27.4	35.4	37.1 (N = 175)
45 +	23.0	77.0	74.6	25.4	18.2	36.4	45.5
C. Prefer doing business with Jews							
Disagree strongly or somewhat	19.2	80.8 (N = 329)	67.7	32.3 (N = 365)	28.5	43.7	27.7 (N = 375)
Agree strongly or somewhat	35.6	64.4 (N = 160)[a]	73.9	26.1 (N = 165)	21.6	27.2	51.2 (N = 145)[a]

[a]Chi-square significant at $p < .05$.

tion would correspond to the 'special consumer demands' theory of ethnic enterprise for Oriental or European immigrants (Light, 1972: 11-15). Thus, we might expect participation in the Jewish sub-economy to be greater for more religious Jews.

Table 4B presents data that indicate no difference between more or less religious Jews in their participation in the Jewish sub-economy (see the Appendix for a description of the index of Jewish religiosity). Among the least religious third of the respondents, there are 32.5 per cent with all or most of their business associates Jews, 66 per cent self-employed or working for other Jews, and 28.1 per cent with primarily Jewish customers. The percentages for the most religious third do not differ significantly. Clearly, the Jewish sub-economy survives due to factors other than the religiosity of its participants.

Apart from a religious motivation, Jews may simply prefer to have economic dealings with other Jews due perhaps to custom, language (Yiddish or Hebrew) similarities, or similar cultural sensibilities. Respondents were asked to indicate degrees of (dis)agreement with the statement: 'I prefer doing business with an establishment that I know is owned by Jews'. Those with greater agreement might be expected to be greater participants.

The data in Table 4C indicate that Jews agreeing with this statement are indeed more likely to have a majority of Jewish customers or clients, and to indicate that all or most of their business associates are Jews. There is no significant difference in proportions self-employed or working for other Jews. Thus, we have here some evidence (for two out of three indicators) that respondents' preferences are associated with participation in the Jewish sub-economy. Yet the minority tendencies are also quite striking. For example, of those Jews who do *not* prefer doing business with other Jews, we find 19.2 per cent with primarily Jewish customers and 27.7 per cent with Jews as most or all of their business associates.

Costs and Benefits of the Jewish Sub-Economy

Are participants in the Jewish sub-economy economically better or worse off when compared to Jews active in the mainstream economy?

Three measures of economic performance are analysed: occupation, intra-generational mobility, and income. Occupation is measured by the Blishen score, an index of socioeconomic status computed for various occupations (Blishen, 1968). Intra-generational mobility is measured as the difference in Blishen scores between respondents' first full-time job in Canada and their present (or last, usual) job. Income represents total family income.

Table 5 presents the data in tabular form. Looking at all three indicators of socio-economic achievement and all three measures of participation in the Jewish sub-economy, we find a consistent pattern (nine chi-squares) of no significant difference (at $p< .05$) in economic achievement between those respondents with greater and those with lesser degrees of participation in the

Table 5 *Economic Achievement and Economic Segregation (per cent)*

	BUSINESS ASSOCIATES WHO ARE JEWS			ETHNIC ORIGIN OF MAJORITY OF CLIENTS/CUSTOMERS		ETHNIC ORIGIN OF MAJORITY OF EXECUTIVE MANAGEMENT	
	NONE OR FEW	SOME	ALL OR MOST	NON-JEWISH	JEWISH	NON-JEWISH	JEWISH
Occupation							
High	43.2	47.0	51.4	45.3	49.2	46.8	45.7
Low	56.8	53.0	48.6	54.7	50.8	53.8	54.3
	100.0	100.0	100.0	100.0	100.0	100.0	100.0
	(N=132)	(N=197)	(N=173)	(N=384)	(N=128)	(N=160)	(N=372)
Intra-generational Mobility							
High	45.5	46.4	45.0	47.8	34.4	40.0	47.2
Low	54.5	53.6	55.0	52.2	65.6	60.0	52.8
	100.0	100.0	100.0	100.0	100.0	100.0	100.0
	(N=132)	(N=196)	(N=173)	(N=383)	(N=128)	(N=160)	(N=371)
Income							
High $20,000 +	50.0	63.2	52.5	52.9	52.7	57.2	50.2
Low $20,000	50.0	36.8	47.5	47.1	47.3	42.8	49.8
	100.0	100.0	100.0	100.0	100.0	100.0	100.0
	(N=121)	(N=171)	(N=160)	(N=338)	(N=112)	(N=145)	(N=313)

ethnic sub-economy. We find no evidence of either economic costs or economic benefits associated with participation in the Jewish sub-economy.

Correlation and regression analysis (not presented in tables) were used to isolate the independent effects of participation in the Jewish sub-economy on economic achievement. The sample was divided into foreign-born and native-born respondents on the assumption that different processes might be at work for these two groups. The zero-order correlations confirmed the cross-tabular findings for both foreign- and native-born. (Participation in the Jewish sub-economy was measured by the proportion of respondent's business associates who are Jewish [Table 2, Section III]. The correlations were .07, .04, and .01 with occupation, mobility, and income for foreign born, and were .10, .05 and .03 for the native-born. None of these are substantial in magnitude or significant statistically.)

A regression analysis controlled for the effects of age, sex, years in Canada (for the foreign-born), and education of the respondents for the same three dependent measures: occupation, mobility, and income. In the income equations, spouse's labour force status (employed or unemployed) and respondent's occupation were also included as variables. Interaction effects of economic segregation and both years in Canada and education were estimated as well.

In none of the six equations (three each for native- and foreign-born) does the standardized beta for the effect of segregation on economic achievement attain statistical significance. The same is true for interaction effects. Those variables which are significant and which explain the major part of the variance in occupation, mobility, and income are sex, age and education of respondents. In no equation does economic segregation (entered last) explain more than 0.1 per cent of the variance. The major finding would seem to be that reported economic segregation plays an insignificant role in the economic achievement of our respondents.[5]

Discussion

It seems that a large number of Jews in Montreal participate, in varying degrees, in the communal economic system. The measures used in this study have been conservative. For example, respondents who answered that the *majority* of their customers were Jews were identified as participants; those with a large *minority* of Jewish customers (30 per cent, 40 per cent) were excluded, in the analytical categories. (Remember that Jews represent only 4 per cent of the population of Metropolitan Montreal.) From the data in Table 2, we might estimate that between one-quarter and one-third of the respondents were almost exclusively economically active within the Jewish sub-economy.

To be sure, anyone with direct or indirect familiarity with North American urban life is aware of the existence of ethnic residential and commercial concentrations. In addition to a linguistic, English-French, division in

Montreal, we find there are clearly identifiable Jewish, Italian, and Greek areas, as well as a Chinatown and a black area. What is difficult is to account for individual decisions to participate in such sub-economies.

Participation in the Jewish sub-economy of Montreal cannot be explained by the factor of immigration, by perception of anti-Semitism, or by religious correlates. Respondents who 'prefer' dealing with other Jews are slightly more likely to participate. Yet, there are more participants in the Jewish sub-economy who do *not* prefer business dealings with Jews than there are those who do. Finally, there seem to be neither economic costs nor benefits associated with participation. Though it was not examined, it seems likely that a (mis)perception about relative economic payoff cannot explain the participation either. Stated differently, participation in the Jewish sub-economy is distributed randomly over occupational and income groupings.

The question remains: Why do many Jews in Montreal concentrate their economic activity among other Jews? The phenomenon might be explained by generational transmission, and the convenience of adopting inherited patterns of economic activity. Immigrants may pass on to second and third generations, established economic networks, which are no worse than any other new ones. Inertia may maintain them. The phenomenon may reveal weaknesses in the impersonal, universalistic assumptions of both neo-classical economics and functional sociology. Ascription persists, and may be functional in modern industrial societies (Mayhew, 1968). One subject for systematic investigation might be the role of the extended family in minority groups as a mediating agent in contemporary economic activity which could, of course, solidify the tie to the ethnic sub-economy.

Other explanations might include the role of residential distributions. Residence or the location of a respondent's workplace in the 'Jewish' area might be associated with participation in the Jewish sub-economy. At a macro-sociological level, objective discriminatory forces may help channel some Jews into the Jewish sub-economy. (This factor is distinct from the microsociological, subjective perception of anti-Semitism, analysed above.)

Several lines of research suggest themselves. Comparative research might establish the generalizability of the concept of ethnic sub-economy through quantitative studies of different minority groups in a number of settings. Certain environments may be more or less conductive to the existence of ethnic economic systems.

Of interest to sociologists might be the relation of participation in the ethnic sub-economy to other dimensions of ethnic life, such as the social cohesion of the group, residential or territorial segregation, political mobilization, patterns of cultural assimilation, inter-group conflict, and even intra-group conflict.[6] In this study, the religious variable examined covers only one facet of ethnic identification. It may be that other forms of communal solidarity play a role. Indeed, one might attempt to unravel whether participation in an ethnic sub-economy is more likely cause or effect of such solidarity.

Of interest to urban economists would be details regarding ethnic consumption patterns, participation in the housing markets, links between manufacturing, wholesaling and retailing operations, membership in professional associations, the giving and receiving of credit, the use of information networks, and the occupational and sectoral profile of participants in the sub-economy.

Another line of research might lead to the development of a political economy of minority groups. Some minority groups, such as the Jews, are characterized by a wide array of political and social institutions and formal organizations. Groups vary in their 'institutional completeness', or the degree to which needs of members may be met through institutions and resources indigenous to the group, such as welfare organizations, churches, newspapers, social and cultural clubs, etc. (Breton, 1964). In the Jewish case, the degree of institutional completeness and the proliferation of local, regional, and national organizations is so great, the term 'polity' has been used to describe the Jewish community (Elazar, 1976). An ethnic polity consists of the voluntary, representative or quasi-representative organizations which are involved in decision-making and the provision of services.

Minority groups differ in the degree to which they may be organized, internally, as a polity. The ethnic sub-economy may be considered as the economic analogue to the ethnic polity. Activity in both is voluntary and may be independent of economic (or political) participation in the mainstream societal systems. One might speculate as to the relation between the establishment of a successful ethnic polity and the extent of participation in the ethnic sub-economy.

A more complete elaboration of the workings of an ethnic sub-economy would include treatments of both 'public' and 'private' sectors. This paper has focused on the private sector of the Jewish sub-economy. The public sector of the ethnic sub-economy would be sustained through the pattern of philanthropic contributions or fee for services used to support welfare institutions, churches, and other cultural, social, or political institutions (these revenues could also include government grants). The funds would be used in part to employ communal public servants. Some portion might also be reallocated to other, perhaps more needy, members of the group. In the Jewish case, the public sector of the Jewish sub-economy is considerable. For example, Elazar has estimated a total Jewish communal budget of $2 billion in the United States (1976: 293-313).

Using standard economic measures, it might be possible to obtain from survey data, or in other ways, quantitative estimates of the size of an ethnic sub-economy, including both public and private sectors. One might compute average and total revenues for participants, as well as other economic indicators, such as rates of return, productivity, economic growth, etc.

Analysis of the bases of economic power of élites within any minority group — whether within or without the sub-economy — may be useful in understanding the dynamics of intra-communal politics. One might ascertain whether the links between power and wealth operative within minority communities flow through the sub-economy or through the mainstream economy. Journalistic accounts (Newman, 1979) might be supplemented by systematic scientific studies.

Appendix

I. Perceived Anti-Semitism

Responses to the following two questions,

1. Do you feel there is prejudice against Jews in Quebec?
>   Yes, a great deal.
>   Yes, some.
>   Yes, a bit.
>   No, none.

2. 'Anti-Semitism' is a problem in this city.
>   Strongly agree.
>   Agree somewhat.
>   Don't know.
>   Disagree somewhat.
>   Strongly disagree.

were combined into an additive ordinal index of perceived anti-Semitism (correlation of .47, alpha reliability coefficient of .64), which was used in subsequent analyses. (The index of perceived anti-Semitism ranges from a low of 2 to a high of 9, with a mean of 5.78 and a standard deviation of 1.90.) Scores between 2 and 6 were recorded as low, those 7–9 as high.

II. Religiosity

An ordinal, additive index of religiosity was computed from responses to:

1. Apart from wedding or bar-mitzvahs, how often do you attend synagogue religious services?
>   Never.
>   Primarily on the High Holidays.
>   Primarily on the major Holidays.
>   On major Holidays and some Sabbaths.
>   All Sabbaths and Holidays.
>   Daily.

2. Is it all right for Jews to marry non-Jews?
>   Strongly agree.
>   Disagree somewhat.
>   Don't know.
>   Agree somewhat.
>   Strongly disagree.

3. How well do you read Hebrew?
   Very well.
   Fairly well.
   With some difficulty.
   With great difficulty.
   Not at all.

4. The number of the following six rituals observed by the respondent:
   Take part in a Passover seder.
   Keep kosher at home.
   Light Sabbath candles.
   Fast on Yom Kippur.
   Refrain from eating bread on Passover.
   Light Hanukkah candles.

The index of religiosity ranges from a low of 4 to a high of 22, with a mean of 14.2 and a standard deviation of 4.4. The inter-item correlation is .42, the alpha reliability coefficient is .74. The index is recoded with values of 4-11 low, 12-16 medium, and 17-22 high.

Notes

[1] For a thorough review of the sampling procedure, see Weinfeld and Eaton (1979). The survey had been commissioned as a means to facilitate community planning by the Allied Jewish Community Services and the Canadian Jewish Congress in Montreal.

[2] This degree of intra-group economic interaction within the Jewish group may not be atypical for other ethnic groups in Montreal. Impressionistic evidence suggests that the English and French, as well as smaller groups such as the Italian and Greek, might also operate in part, at least, within the ethnic sub-economy. One of the prerequisites for the existence of an ethnic sub-economy (as opposed to a middle-man minority) might be a minimum threshold size of the group in order to satisfy the specialization and differentiation needed in any economic system. The Jewish population of Montreal, 109,000 according to the 1971 census, would seem to be sufficiently large, as would the other groups listed above.

[3] According to this perspective, all forms of participation in the host society should increase with the transition from the immigrant to the native-born generation. Residential dispersion, more complete acculturation, higher educational attainment, would all contribute to making an ethnic group member more comfortable in competing economically with those outside the group, for positions not tied to the origin group itself. This would represent a form of structural assimilation, as described by Gordon (1964).

[4] In this case, and in subsequent tabular analyses, findings of statistically insignificant differences (at $p < .05$) will be noted. Of course, one cannot prove 'the null hypothesis'. Finding insignificant chi-square values in a specific sample does not

theoretically rule out significant differences in other samples. Thus, we present the findings here as suggestive, though of strong substantive interest. Their value is reinforced by the cumulative pattern of insignificant or unexpected relationships.

[5]See note 4. The same argument applies for statistically insignificant beta co-efficients.

[6]Smaller sub-economies may exist *within* minority groups. Thus, Hassidic Jewish sects may exhibit patterns of economic segregation from other Jews as well as from the economic mainstream.

References

Anderson, Grace
   1974 *Networks of Contact. The Portuguese in Toronto* (Waterloo: Wilfrid Laurier University Press)

Bell, Daniel
   1973 *The Coming of Post-Industrial Society* (New York: Basic Books)

Blishen, Bernard P.
   1968 'A Socio-Economic Index for Occupation in Canada' in Blishen *et al.*, *Canadian Society* (Toronto: Macmillan)

Boissevain, Jeremy
   1970 *The Italians of Montreal*. Studies of the Royal Commission on Bilingualism and Biculturalism (Ottawa: Information Canada)

Bonacich, Edna
   1972 'A Theory of Ethnic Antagonism: The Split Labour Market', *American Sociological Review* 37: 547-59

———
   1973 'A Theory of Middlemen Minorities', *American Sociological Review* 38: 583-94.

Breton, Raymond
   1964 'Institutional Completeness of Ethnic Communities and the Personal Relations of Immigrants', *American Journal of Sociology* 70: 193-205

Cain, Glen G.
   1976 'The Challenge of Segmented Labor Market Theories to Orthodox Theory: A Survey', *Journal of Economic Literature* 14: 1214-57

Duncan, Beverly and Otis Dudley Duncan
   1968 'Minorities and the Process of Stratification', *American Sociological Review* 33 (June): 356-64.

Eitzen, Stanley D.
   1971 'Two Minorities: The Jews of Poland and the Chinese of the Philippines' in Norman Yetman and C. Holy Steele, eds, *Majority and Minority* (Boston: Allyn and Bacon): 112-38.

Elazar, Daniel J.
  1976 *Community and Polity: The Organizational Dynamics of American Jewry* (Philadelphia: Jewish Publication Society)

Farley, Reynolds
  1977 'Trends in Racial Inequalities: Have the Gains of the 1960's Disappeared in the 1970's', *American Sociological Review* 42: 189-208

Glazer, Nathan
  1958 'The American Jew and the Attainment of Middle-Class Rank: Some Trends and Explanations' in M. Sklare, ed., *The Jews* (New York: The Free Press)

Gordon, Milton
  1964 *Assimilation in American Life* (New York: Oxford University Press)

Hechter, Michael
  1978 'Group Formation and the Cultural Division of Labor', *American Journal of Sociology* 84: 293-318

Howe, Irving
  1976 *World of Our Fathers* (New York: Basic Books)

Kessner, Thomas
  1977 *The Golden Door* (New York: Oxford University Press)

Krohn, Roger G., Berkeley Fleming and Marylyn Manzer
  1977 *The Other Economy: The Internal Logic of Local Rental Housing* (Toronto: Peter Martin)

Light, Ivan
  1972 *Ethnic Enterprise in America* (Loss Angeles: University of California Press)

———

  1979 'Disadvantaged Minorities in Self-Employment', *International Journal of Comparative Sociology* 20: 31-45

Mayhew, Leon
  1968 'Ascription in Modern Societies', *Sociological Inquiry* 38: 105-20

Nelli, Humbert S.
  1967 'Italians in Urban America: A Study of Ethnic Adjustment', *International Migration Review* 1: 38-55

Newman, Peter C.
  1979 *The Bronfman Dynasty* (Toronto: McClelland and Stewart)

Porter, John
  1975 'Ethnic Pluralism in Canadian Perspective' in Nathan Glazer and Daniel P. Moynihan, eds, *Ethnicity* (Cambridge: Harvard University Press)

Rosen, Bernard
  1959 'Race, Ethnicity, and the Achievement Syndrome', *American Sociological Review* 24: 47-60.

Sales, Arnaud
1979 *La Bourgeoise Industrielle au Québec* (Montréal: Les Presses de l'Université de Montréal

Slater, Miriam
1969 'My Son the Doctor: Aspects of Mobility Among American Jews', *American Sociological Review* 34: 359-73

Sombart, Werner
1913 *The Jews and Modern Capitalism*. Translation by M. Epstein (New York: Franklin)

Sowell, Thomas
1975 *Race and Economics* (New York: David McKay)

Strodtbeck, Fred L.
1958 'Family Interaction, Values and Achievement' in M. Sklare, ed., *The Jews* (New York: The Free Press)

Weinfeld, Morton
1977 'Determinants of Ethnic Identification of Slavs, Jews, and Italians in Toronto.' PhD thesis, Harvard University.

Weinfeld, Morton and William Eaton
1979 *The Jewish Community of Montreal: Survey Report* (Montreal: Jewish Community Research Institute [Canadian Jewish Congress])

Wiley, Norbert
1967 'The Ethnic Mobility Trap and Stratification Theory', *Social Problems* 15: 147-59

Financial assistance from the government of Quebec (Department of Education: FCAC program) is gratefully acknowledged.

Anomie, Opportunity, and the Density of Ethnic Ties:

Another View of Jewish Outmarriage in Canada

Robert J. Brym

Michael W. Gillespie

A.R. Gillis

Outmarriage and the Cohesion of Ethnic Groups

It is not hard to see why rates of outmarriage are often used to measure ethnic group cohesion. Group solidarity seems little affected when casual and contractual ties are forged between members of different ethnic groups. But when bonds of great intimacy span ethnic lines, those who do the crossing erode group boundaries, signifying that they place relatively low value on the socio-cultural integrity of their ethnic group.

The degree to which low rates of outmarriage are viewed as important for ethnic solidarity varies from one group to another. However, there is little doubt that for Canadian Jews low rates of outmarriage are important. For example, in a study of University of Manitoba students, Driedger (1975: 160) found that Jews emphasize inmarriage as a 'cultural identity factor' more than do all other ethnics in his survey (French, German, Ukrainian, Polish, British, and Scandinavian). Actual rate of outmarriage reflect this. Jews have long had among the lowest rates of outmarriage of all ethnic groups in the country (Kalbach, 1974: 7) and the Canadian rate is among the lowest of all Jewish communities in the world outside Africa and Asia (Bachi, 1979: 34).

Rates of outmarriage among Jewish Canadians do vary widely from one province to another. For example, in 1971 the outmarriage rate ranged from a high of 57 per cent in New Brunswick to a low of 8 per cent in Quebec. Werner Cohn (1976) set out to explain these provincial variations in *The Canadian Review of Sociology and Anthropology* several years ago.[1] He argued that the social milieu in which individuals find themselves may vary in degree of social cohesiveness or social solidarity. This social web of solidarity acts, on the one hand, as a source of restraint, keeping the individual from an otherwise excessive pursuit of strictly personal ends, and, on the other hand, as a source of protection, affording the individual assurance that he is not alone in the world, that the social group will succour and support him. (1976: 91)

Cohn makes it clear when he uses the terms 'social solidarity' and 'social cohesiveness' (or their opposite, 'anomie') that he refers to a cultural, normative or, as Durkheim would put it, moral phenomenon. He suggests that various norms, including endogamy, will be strongly supported where social cohesiveness is high, but will be breached more frequently in less cohesive, more anomic social environments. In short, Jewish outmarriage results from anomie. Cohn argues that outmarriage rates vary from one province to another with other indicators of anomie: suicide, rape, cannabis use, crime, divorce, deaths attributed to mental diseases, and in-migration of North Americans. He sees all of these phenomena as symptoms of the breakdown of group cohesion and control.

This paper critically examines Cohn's findings and his explanation of them. We argue that his analysis suffers from severe methodological flaws which lead him to overstate the impact of anomie on exogamy. Because of this, attention is deflected away from opportunity structures as predictors of outmarriage. We argue that a *structural* explanation of outmarriage is more fruitful than the anomie theory.

The major methodological problems with Cohn's analysis concern his unit of analysis, his weighing of cases, and the significance of his anomie measures as correlates of outmarriage. We examine these issues first.

Unit of Analysis: Host System or Ethnic Community?

Cohn uses provincial-level data on various indicators of anomie to draw inferences about the Jewish community of each province. However, whether anomie in the host society reflects anomie in the Jewish or any other ethnic subsystem is unclear. An anomic ethnic community can, after all, exist in a host society which is high in solidarity. And an anomic host society can contain ethnic subsystems which are high in solidarity. Schermerhorn (1970) and others note that ethnic assimilation is a function of the states of *both* the ethnic and host systems, which may vary independently in their levels of solidarity and orientations to control, exogamy, and other dimensions of assimilation.

In view of this, indicators of anomie based on the province as the unit of analysis may obscure important differences in levels of anomie between the host system and the ethnic communities it contains. That is, the levels of analysis in Cohn's data and in his arguments are incongruent, and an aggregation-disaggregation effect may have produced ecologically fallacious conclusions (see Robinson, 1950).

Weighting and Regional Variation

Cohn tries to show that variation in rates of outmarriage between the Jewish populations in each province result from provincial variations in anomie. Yet he notes that 'whenever I report a correlation between outmarriage and other variables, or between any two variables . . . Each case was weighted by a factor representing its population' (1976: 94, n. 2). This procedure allows three provinces—Ontario, Quebec, and British Columbia, all of which have relatively large populations—to exert a large effect on any relationships discovered. After weighting, the remaining provinces contribute little to any correlations.

Weighting is often appropriate when we want the characteristics of a sample to more closely match the characteristics of a population; weighting enables us to infer relationships about the population from relationships in the sample with greater confidence. But if, like Cohn, one already has population data at hand and wants to discover something about inter-provincial variations in the population, weighting produces a distorted image of actual differences between the units of analysis.

Anomie and Outmarriage

If outmarriage is a product of anomie, other measures of the concept used by Cohn should be correlates of Jewish outmarriage. However, the unweighted data clearly show that rates of outmarriage are only weakly correlated with rates of suicide, crime, divorce, rape, and cannabis use (see Table 1). The r's range from .11 to -.39, offering no support for Cohn's view that anomie produces Jewish outmarriage. Not only are the correlations weak, but in four out of five cases they are in the wrong direction.

Two other measures of anomie used by Cohn—the number of people who died from mental diseases per 100,000 population, and the percentage of Jews born in other provinces or the US—are different. They are strong correlates of outmarriage (r's = .53 and .78, respectively) and in the predicted direction. If we focus on the correlations among the seven indicators of anomie, we see that these latter two are distinct from the other five which, indeed, appear to measure a single dimension. If we regard the first five measures as more valid indicators of anomie, then the obvious inference to be drawn from the correlation matrix is that Jewish outmarriage and anomie are in fact unrelated.

What are we to make of the two exceptions to this pattern? We will discuss the positive correlation between North American Jewish in-migrants and outmarriage when we examine the social structures underlying some of the correlations in Table 1. Our *ad hoc* interpretation of the correlation between outmarriage and deaths due to mental diseases is that it is accidental. The death rate from mental diseases is only moderately or weakly associated with the five conventional measures of anomie used by Cohn (r's = .17 to .50),

Table 1 Zero-Order Correlation Matrix: Jewish Outmarriage, Anomie Variable and Structural Variables, Canadian Provinces, 1971

	OM	EN	LS	LP	MI	ME	SU	CR	DI	RA	CA
OM	1.00	—	—	—	—	—	—	—	—	—	—
EN	-.92	1.00	—	—	—	—	—	—	—	—	—
LS	-.86	.94	1.00	—	—	—	—	—	—	—	—
LP	-.73	.83	.92	1.00	—	—	—	—	—	—	—
MI	.78	-.62	-.56	-.44	1.00	—	—	—	—	—	—
ME	.53	-.52	-.26	-.11	.56	1.00	—	—	—	—	—
SU	-.39	.57	.67	.54	.09	.17	1.00	—	—	—	—
CR	-.08	.16	.26	.23	.45	.49	.77	1.00	—	—	—
DI	-.16	.32	.47	.43	.37	.34	.85	.88	1.00	—	—
RA	-.09	.16	.31	.25	.45	.43	.73	.89	.92	1.00	—
CA	.11	.15	.26	.35	.61	.50	.76	.83	.83	.76	1.00

OM = Jews who married non-Jews as a percentage of all Jewish brides and grooms
EN = ratio of Jews born in Europe to Jews born in North America
LS = natural log size of Jewish community
LP = natural log population of province
MI = percentage of Jews in each province born in another Canadian province or the USA
ME = deaths attributed to mental diseases, rate per 100,000 population
SU = deaths attributed to suicide, rate per 100,000 population
CR = convictions under the criminal code of Canada
DI = divorce, rate per 100,000 population
RA = rape offences per 100,000 population
CA = cannabis offences per 100,000 population
Sources: Calculated from data in Cohn, 1976: 92-3, 97, 100: *Perspectives . . .*, 1974: 264.

while the five conventional measures are all highly intercorrelated (r's = .76 to .92). In view of this it is unlikely that the rate of death due to mental diseases actually reflects anomie. We cannot think of plausible *ad hoc* explanations of why it is related to outmarriage (r = .53). We suspect that it is simply due to chance, a suspicion given some support by the results of an F-test ($F_{1,7}$ = 2.73. p > .05).[2]

Structure and Opportunity

Cohn's case for a strong positive association between outmarriage and anomie has little support. Also, his argument is weak for excluding two potentially important independent structural variables. They are: 1) the number of Jews in each province; and 2) the ratio of European-born to North

American-born Jews per province. Variants of both have been recommended as explanations for inter-provincial differences in rates of Jewish outmarriage (see, for example, Rosenberg, 1963: 64-9; Weinfeld, 1981: 372).

Consider first the question of community size. We suggest that rates of outmarriage are products of the density of contacts among members of a local ethnic community. Density of contacts should not be confused with population density in the demographic sense; by density we mean *frequency* and *duration* of interactions per person in a population, not number of people per unit of geographical area. As far as the relationship between size and frequency of interactions is concerned, it should be noted that in large Jewish communities like those in Toronto and Montreal, which are more likely to be 'institutionally complete' (Breton, 1964), Jewish Canadians have a relatively large number of potential spouses in their ethnic age cohort. There are more social contexts and institutions within which courtship can be fostered. Also, more people can act formally or informally as 'go-betweens' for potential spouses. In contrast, members of small Jewish communities, like those in Halifax or Saskatoon, have few potential marriage partners in their ethnic age cohort. Because of this, there is greater pressure to go outside the ethnic group to marry. The situation regarding go-betweens and courtship contexts is analogous.[3] In short, expected interaction frequency, and therefore opportunities for intermarriage, increase proportionately and linearly with community size.

However, the expected *duration* of interactions varies *inversely* and linearly with community size. This is because individuals have finite amounts of time to devote to social interactions. It follows that the more interactions they have, the less time is available for each.

Since density of ties is a function of both frequency and duration of interactions, and since frequency and duration vary in opposite ways with community size, we may reasonably expect, following Mayhew and Levinger (1979: 88, 91, 96), that size will have diminishing effects on density of ties, i.e., there will be a *non*-linear relationship between size and density (and therefore between size and rate of outmarriage). Specifically, we expect outmarriage to decrease as the natural log of Jewish community size increases. In fact it does, with $r = -.86$ (see Fig. 1). There is no linear relationship between size and outmarriage, but this is no reason to dismiss size as a cause of outmarriage, as Cohn does.

A second important determinant of the presence of Jewish marriage opportunities is the ratio of European-born to North American-born Jews in each province. The proportion of European-born Jews in a community is largely a function of that community's attraction for Jews who arrived from Eastern Europe between the beginning of the century and the onset of the Great Depression or in the years immediately following the Second World War.[4] Most Jews who arrived during these periods went to Montreal, Toronto, and Winnipeg partly for economic reasons (these communities were growing rapidly and provided abundant opportunities for earning a

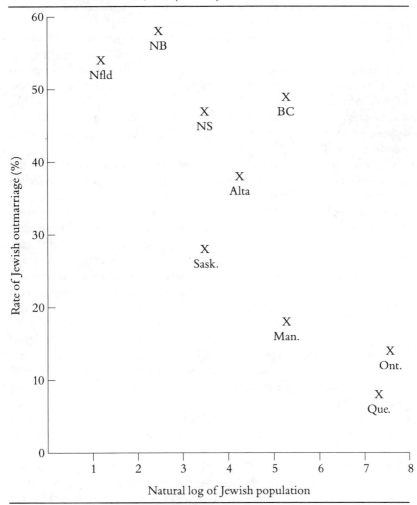

Figure 1   *Rate of Jewish Outmarriage by Natural Log of Jewish Population Size,*
Canadian Provinces, 1971 (r = –.86)

livelihood). Friendship and kinship ties also drew them there, as did the well-developed Jewish institutional superstructure (these were the largest Jewish communities in Canada, even in 1900). In a sense, the influx of Eastern European Jews to these cities reflected the size and institutional completeness of their Jewish communities. At the same time, vigorous Eastern European Jewish immigration ensured the growth of both community institutions and the Jewish population base, as well as other conditions that facilitate inmarriage. So there may be a reciprocal relationship (in the causal sense) between the proportion of European-born Jews and the density of social ties in a community. Since outmarriage should be lowest where the density of ties among ethnic group members is highest, it is not surprising to find that the correlation between the ratio of European-born to North American-born Jews and the rate of outmarriage is very high ($r = -.92$).

Strong social pressure encouraged Eastern European Jewish immigrants to stay within the boundaries of the Jewish community. Relatives, friends, and Jewish employment agencies provided jobs. Because they typically knew no English when they arrived, immigrants were inclined to live near, and interact and do business with, other Jews. Anti-Semitism, especially in the 1930s, also buttressed group cohesion. As with other ethnic groups, the declining importance of these forces over time has heightened tendencies towards assimilation and outmarriage (Reitz, 1980).

However, the story is *not* the same for those Jewish immigrant groups who did not require or were not offered as much assistance by the established Jewish community. For example, French-speaking North African Jews in Montreal have been largely excluded (and have excluded themselves) institutionally, linguistically, and in terms of friendship, kinship, and residential concentration from the English-speaking Jewish community of the city. Arriving since the late 1950s, largely without benefit of strong Jewish institutional or group support, they form a virtually separate ethnic enclave about 15 per cent the size of the English-speaking Jewish community. Not surprisingly, therefore, the North African Jews of Montreal have an outmarriage rate over four times higher than English-speaking Montreal Jews (Lasry and Bloomfield-Schachter, 1975: 272). Broadly analogous cases probably include the Czech and Polish Jews who emigrated to Canada after 1968 and perhaps the Russian Jews who started arriving in 1971 (Zaslavsky and Brym, 1983) as well as Jews who have migrated from other Canadian provinces or the US.

As noted earlier, Cohn argues that a strong positive association between outmarriage and proportion of North American in-migrants reflects the impact of anomie. Presumably, these in-migrants frequently outmarry because they do not believe in the norm of endogamy. That may be true. But it is at least equally plausible that these people outmarry for structural reasons. They are almost certainly relatively young and highly assimilated Jews who do not require much support from the established Jewish community in order to make their way in the world. Because of their weak ties to the Jewish community, outmarriage should be high where the proportion of North American in-migrants is also high. In fact the correlation between these two variables is .78.

Conclusions

We have argued that the opportunities Jews have for outmarriage (as measured by the proportion of North American in-migrants among Jews in each province, the ratio of European-born to North American-born Jews in each province, and the size of each province's Jewish community) explain inter-provincial variations in the rate of Jewish exogamy. We have questioned the importance of anomie as an explanation of these variations, and supported our argument by demonstrating the existence of strong correlations in the predicted directions between our three independent variables and rates of outmarriage.

We nonetheless have few illusions about the conclusiveness of our argument. Multiple regression equations and structural equation models may be used to *illustrate* more precisely the relationships posited here.[5] But further research, conducted with smaller units of analysis and using many more cases, must be undertaken before our viewpoint can be accepted with a higher degree of confidence.

Notes

[1]Given the urban concentration of the Jewish population, provinces are not ideal units of analysis. Although data on less aggregated units would be preferable, it must be borne in mind that 1) the purpose of our paper is to reanalyse Cohn's provincial-level data, and 2) less aggregated data are not available.

[2]Some readers might question the use of tests of significance when the nine provinces constitute the population of cases in which we are interested. Such a question reflects the widespread misunderstanding that the *only* purpose of statistical inference is to generalize from a sample to a population. Another use is to see whether the results of a particular analysis could simply represent the chance distribution of the stochastic component terms associated with each of the cases. This question arises whether the cases analysed consist of the entire population or a sample. Our use of statistics to answer this question is similar to their use in social or social-psychological experiments, in which there is (or should be) no attempt to conceive of the subjects as a sample of some larger population. The main differences is that in experimental research the statistical properties of the stochastic component necessary for valid statistical inference are, to some extent, guaranteed by the nature of the design, whereas in non-experimental research, such as ours, the existence of these properties is usually assumed.

[3]For a more general discussion of the importance of community size on the emergence and survival of ethnic and other subsystems see Blau, Blum and Schwartz, 1982; Brym, 1984; Fischer, 1976; Mayhew and Levinger, 1979.

[4]Few Jews who arrived before 1900 are still alive; there was little Jewish immigration during the Depression and war years. Since the post-war period there have been relatively few European Jewish immigrants of the type described here.

[5]A multicollinearity problem prevents us from including any more than two of our independent variables in the multiple regression equation. Doing so yields $Y^\star = .30X^\star_1 - .75X^\star_2$, where Y is the rate of outmarriage, X_1 is the proportion of North American in-migrants, and X_2 is the ratio of European-born to North American-born Jews ($R^2 = .94, F_{2,6} = 44.22, p < .001$).

We used LISREL (Joreskog and Sorbom, 1978) to construct a structural equation model including all three independent variables and avoiding multicollinearity problems. The chi-square associated with the model is 1.34, which, for the four degrees of freedom we incurred, indicates an extremely good fit of the model to the data. The model is reported in detail in Brym, Gillespie, and Gillis, 1982.

It should also be noted that we intended to incorporate in our discussion and in our model two other structural variables — occupational concentration and mean SES of ethnic communities — because they have been found to predict rates of outmarriage very well in the US (Hechter, 1978), and ethnic group cohesion moderately well in Canada (Reitz, 1980). From a special census tabulation of Jewish males by occupation in each province for 1971, mean SES was calculated using the standard Blishen and McRoberts (1976) scale, and occupational concentration using a formula recommended by Hechter (1978: 303, n. 11). However, the scores did not correlate with rates of outmarriage as expected. Outmarriage and mean SES are weak correlates $(r = .17)$. For outmarriage and occupational concentration, $r = .74$, which is strong but in the opposite direction from that predicted.

Reitz (personal communication) recommends that a measure of the *difference* between an ethnic group's mean SES and the mean SES of the surrounding population might be a better predictor of outmarriage and is more consistent with his theory as well as Hechter's. As a crude test of that argument we rank-ordered the Jewish communities of each province on the basis of mean SES, rank-ordered each province in terms of per capita income plus transfer payments minus taxes for 1970 (Phillips, 1978: 10), and for each province subtracted the Jewish community's rank from the province's rank. Those differences for each province were then rank-ordered, as were the provincial outmarriage rates. The Spearman rank-order coefficient of correlation between these two ranking was .82, which is strong, but again in the opposite direction from that predicted. That is, the greater the rank difference between the ranked vertical economic location of a province's Jewish population and the ranked vertical economic location of a province's entire population, the higher the rate of outmarriage. Alternatively, one might examine the absolute differences between each Jewish community's rank and each province's rank, rank-order those differences and correlate them with ranked rates of outmarriage. Doing so yields a Spearman's rho of .35, which is considerably weaker but still in the opposite direction from that predicted.

At least for Canadian Jews in 1971, then, these independent variables do not predict outmarriage as expected. Canadian Jews in 1971 may be exceptional from the viewpoint of Hechter and Reitz. On the other hand, our measures may be inadequate: it could reasonably be argued that we ought to be analysing SES and occupational concentration only for urban areas (in which almost all Jews reside) rather than for entire provinces.

References

Bachi, Roberto
  1979 ha-mashber ha-demografi shel tfutzot ha-gola. (Jerusalem: sifriyat shazar, ha-ma-khon l'yehadut zmanenu, ha-universita ha-ivrit birushalayim.) [Hebrew: The Demographic Crisis of the Diaspora Communities.]

Blau, Peter M., Terry C. Blum and Joseph E. Schwartz
  1982 'Heterogeneity and intermarriage', *American Sociological Review* 47: 45–62

Blishen, Bernard R. and Hugh A. McRoberts
  1976 'A revised socioeconomic index for occupations in Canada', *Canadian Review of Sociology and Anthropology* 13: 71-9.

Breton, Raymond
  1964 'Institutional completeness and the personal relations of immigrants', *American Journal of Sociology* 70: 193-205.

Brym, Robert J.
  1984 'Cultural vs structural explanations of ethnic intermarriage in the USSR: a statistical reanalysis', *Soviet Studies* 36: 594-601.

Brym, Robert J., Michael W. Gillespie, and A.R. Gillis
  1982 'Anomie, opportunity, and the density of ethnic ties: another view of Jewish exogamy in Canada'. Structural Analysis Programme Working Paper #36. University of Toronto, Department of Sociology.

Cohn, Werner
  1976 'Jewish outmarriage and anomie: a study in the Canadian syndrome of polarities', *Canadian Review of Sociology and Anthropology* 13: 90-105.

Driedger, Leo
  1975 'In search of cultural identity factors: a comparison of ethnic students', *Canadian Review of Sociology and Anthropology* 12: 150-62.

Fischer, Claude
  1976 *The Urban Experience* (New York: Harcourt, Brace, Jovanovich)

Hechter, Michael
  1978 'Group formation and the cultural division of labour', *American Journal of Sociology* 84: 293-318.

Joreskog, K.G., and D. Sorbom
  1978 LISREL IV: Analysis of Linear Structural Relationships by the Method of Maximum Likelihood (Chicago: International Education Services)

Kalbach, Warren E.
  1974 'Propensities for intermarriage in Canada as reflected in the ethnic origins of native-born husbands and wives: 1961 and 1971'. Paper presented at the annual meetings of the Canadian Sociology and Anthropology Association (Toronto).

Lasry, Jean-Claude, and Evelyn Bloomfield-Schachter
  1975 'Jewish intermarriage in Montreal, 1962-1972', *Jewish Social Studies* 37: 267-78.

Mayhew, Bruce H., and Roger L. Levinger
  1979 'Size and density of interaction in human aggregates', *American Journal of Sociology* 82: 86-110.

Perspectives Canada
  1974 Ottawa: Statistics Canada.

Phillips, Paul
  1978 *Regional Disparities* (Toronto: James Lorimer)

Reitz, Jeffrey G.
 1980 *The Survival of Ethnic Groups* (Toronto: McGraw–Hill Ryerson)

Robinson, William S.
 1950 'Ecological correlations and the behavior of individuals', *American Sociological Review* 15: 351–7.

Rosenberg, Louis
 1963 'Intermarriage in Canada 1921–1960'. Pp. 57–81 in Werner J. Cahnman, ed., *Intermarriage and Jewish Life: A Symposium* (New York: The Jewish Press and the Jewish Reconstructionist Press)

Schermerhorn, Richard
 1970 *Comparative Ethnic Relations* (New York: Random House)

Weinfeld, Morton
 1981 'Intermarriage: agony and adaptation' in M. Weinfeld, W. Shaffir, and I. Cotler, eds, *The Canadian Jewish Mosaic* (Toronto: John Wiley and Sons): 365–82

Zaslavsky, Victor and Robert J. Brym
 1983 *Soviet-Jewish Emigration and Soviet Nationality Policy* (London: Macmillan and New York: St Martin's Press)

part five

Politics

Introduction

Robert J. Brym

Ethnic communities typically consist of different classes, religious denominations, parties, and other groups. These collectivities usually hold diverse views about how the community should be governed and about how the community's external relations should be managed. Politics express the more or less stable reconciliation of these distinct views by means of a whole host of mechanisms set up to establish community agendas and make authoritative decisions.

Politics are typically marked by consensus and conflict. But what makes the political life of Canadian Jewry unusual is that consensus and conflict are so neatly compartmentalized. Internally, the community is deeply divided and its divisions are clearly visible to group members, especially in Toronto. But the face which the community presents to the outside world is one of abiding harmony.

A 1979 survey of major ethnic minority groups in Toronto convincingly demonstrates that these are not airy generalizations. The survey compared representative samples of Jews, Germans, Ukrainians, Italians, Portuguese, Chinese, and West Indians (n = 1,841). The researchers discovered that Jews were nearly twice as likely as members of the other six large minority groups to perceive two or more deep cleavages in their respective communities. Specifically, 61 per cent of Jews, but only 33 per cent of other minority group members, perceived two or more divisions in their communities that 'very much' or 'somewhat' divided their groups internally. Some 64 per cent of Jews thought that the division between rich and poor was a serious cleavage, followed closely by the 63 per cent who thought that religious divisions represented important fissures. Forty-three per cent of Jews thought that the origin of their co-ethnics in different regions or countries significantly divided the community. And 29 per cent of Jews felt that political differences divided their community very much or somewhat — still 2 per cent more than the corresponding percentage for the six other ethnic groups combined (calculated from Breton, 1990: 244). Nor are these results specific to 1979. As Daniel Elazar and Harold Waller note in their recent historical and institutional analysis of the governance of Canadian Jewry, 'the history of the [Toronto] community has been marked by rivalry and disunity' (Elazar and Waller, 1990:165, 205-24; for the somewhat contrasting Montreal case, see 118 ff.).

Although in the 1979 survey the Jewish group was the most frequently perceived as highly disunited by its members, it was also remarkably united in its support for its leaders, who make binding decisions for the community and represent it to the outside world. In Toronto, Jews were more likely than Germans, Ukrainians, Italians, Portuguese, Chinese, and West Indians to know their community leaders personally, to have contact with them at least occasionally, and to be at least somewhat informed about their activities. Jews were also more likely than members of other ethnic minorities to feel that their community leaders were concerned with community problems and interests, and to feel that their leaders made a big effort to win community approval for their actions. Jews were more likely than other minority group members to disagree with the statement that politicians do not take their ethnic leaders seriously. They were also more likely to disagree with the statement that their leaders do not have enough connections with important people in business and government to achieve results for the community (Breton, 1990: 231, 234, 238). The overall picture which emerges from these data is that, by and large, Toronto Jews (and, one assumes, Jews elsewhere in Canada) support their community leaders' representations to the outside world and think of their leaders as accessible, concerned, and effective. They are certainly more likely to share that opinion than are members of other ethnic minorities about their community leaders.

Politically speaking, then, the Canadian-Jewish community is Janus-faced: it displays a high level of external consensus despite exhibiting a high level of internal disharmony. That is no small feat. How is it achieved? Undoubtedly, the abundant resources available to the community play an important role in the construction of consent. The Jewish community is relatively affluent, it systematically recruits leaders from a pool of comparatively highly educated people, and over the years it has, under the aegis of the Canadian Jewish Congress, established what is probably the most highly articulated and centralized organizational infrastructure of any minority ethnic group in the country apart from the French. All these resources—material, leadership, and organizational—can be and are effectively employed to maintain a united front in community dealings with the outside world. We gain a clear sense of how this is achieved from Harold Waller's article in this section. Waller bases his summary of the inner workings of Canadian Jewish political life on his award-winning twenty-year study of the governance of Canadian Jewish communities (Elazar and Waller, 1990).

Jewish communal solidarity also has deep social-psychological underpinnings anchored in persecution anxieties and feelings of non-acceptance by majority Canadians. Group unity is maintained in response to the widespread perception of a hostile world. Consider how Canadian Jews express their central value: support for the State of Israel. In their contribution to this section, David Taras and Morton Weinfeld undertake a comparative analysis of Canadian and US Jews' political activities *vis-à-vis* Israel. They show that support for Israel takes different forms in the two countries. The Canadian approach is quieter, more philanthropic, and more ideological. The American approach is more open, more variegated, and relies to a greater degree on lobbying government officials. Taras and Weinfeld suggest that the muted Canadian approach is at least in part the product of fear and insecurity.

The 1979 survey of ethnic groups in Toronto again helps elucidate the point. Minority group respondents were asked whether they felt easily accepted by majority group members as neighbours, while majority group respondents (n = 497) were asked whether they easily accepted specified minority group members as neighbours. The same questions were asked about acceptance as relatives. Significantly, Jews were the least likely of all minority groups to feel easily accepted both as neighbours (22 per cent) and relatives (8 per cent)—this despite the fact that fully 89 per cent of majority Canadians said they were ready to accept Jews as neighbours easily, and 77 per cent said they were ready to accept Jews easily as relatives. In fact, the discrepancy between what majority Canadians declared as their feelings and the minority group members' feelings of acceptance was by far the greatest in the case of the Jews (calculated from Breton, 1990: 200).

The Jews' long history of persecution helps us understand why Canadian Jews today perceive hostility and non-acceptance far in excess of what actual conditions would seem to warrant. More to the point, these perceptions make it a relatively easy matter for Canadian-Jewish communal leaders to create consensus. For example, ever since the Israeli invasion of Lebanon in 1982 a significant minority of Canadian-Jewish Zionists has been highly and publicly critical of Israel's relations with the Arab world in general and the Palestinians in particular (Brym, 1983). Yet the mailing list of Canadian Friends of Peace Now has not yet grown beyond 2,000 households, in part because of the opposition of the Jewish communal leadership to the idea of trading land for peace. The Peace Now line is that its brand of dissent is in Israel's best interest; the official community line is that any dissent aids the Jews' enemies. So far in Canada, the official line prevails to a much greater degree than in the world's two largest Jewish communities, the US and Israel, partly because Canadian-Jewish leaders possess a near monopoly on communal resources and partly because Canadian Jews exhibit an elevated sense of distrust.

Consistent with the above argument, an examination of political party preferences suggests that Canadian Jews desire accommodation above all else. In his article reprinted here, Jean Laponce analyses Canadian-Jewish party preferences by combining the results of 235 Gallup polls conducted from 1953 to 1983. This yielded a representative sample of over 2,300 Canadian Jews and 216,000 non-Jews. His most important finding is that Jews were much more likely than Protestants and somewhat more likely than Catholics to support the party that dominated Canadian politics since the arrival of most Jewish immigrants and acted as the principal agent of their political socialization in Canada: the Liberals. The Liberals were supported by nearly 63 per cent of Jews between 1953 and 1983, compared to 58 per cent of Catholics and 32 per cent of Protestants. Laponce also found that Jews were more likely to vote NDP than one would expect on the basis of their socio-demographic characteristics. One may speculate, however, that recent Canadian-Jewish experience has mirrored that in the US: the vestiges of Jewish trade unionism and socialism waned in the 1980s, as support for the new governing party, the Conservatives, increased.

References

Breton, Raymond
  1990 'The ethnic group as a political resource in relation to problems of incorporation: perceptions and attitudes', in Raymond Breton et al., eds. *Ethnic Identity and Equality: Varieties of Experience in a Canadian City* (Toronto: University of Toronto Press): 196–255

Brym, Robert J.
  1983 'Israel in Lebanon', *Middle East Focus* 6, 1: 14–19

Elazar, Daniel J. and Harold M. Waller
  1990 *Maintaining Consensus: The Canadian Jewish Polity in the Postwar World* (Lanham, MD: University Press of America)

The Canadian Jewish Polity:

Power and Leadership in the Jewish Community

Harold M. Waller

The Jewish community is a political system. Of course, there are obvious differences between it and nation states or other governmental units; most important, the latter can compel compliance from persons within their bounds whereas the Jewish community is decidedly a voluntary system. Nevertheless, the Jewish community acts as a government in a limited sphere for persons willing to submit to the discipline of membership and accept its decisions as binding.

Any examination of the community must deal with the way in which those decisions are made and with the people who make them: in short, with power. Social scientists have dozens of definitions of power; a useful working one is the ability to accomplish goals. Within a given system, who are the people most capable of achieving their goals? What techniques do they use to do so? What consequences do the distribution of power and the methods of decision-making have for the whole society?

Power cannot be separated from finances because many of the key decisions in the Jewish community, as in most political systems, deal with such matters. In fact, it can be argued that taxing and spending are the most important activities of community governing bodies because the amounts available and the manner in which they are allocated largely determine the scope and nature of the community's activities. And although the Jewish community cannot use legal compulsion to collect money from its members, it is possible and useful to view its general fund-raising as a form of taxation.

The Jewish Political System

Since biblical times, Jews have viewed political systems in terms of groups formed by consensus through compacts or agreements. Within such a group, the concept of equality was traditionally paramount, but the notion of the divine source of law limited the use of democratic principles and forms. One historian noted that Jewish regimes have had 'aristocratic tendencies that often have degenerated into oligarchic patterns of rule', although infrequently degenerating into autocracy.[1] In other words, in the traditional view, people were entitled to equal treatment but not equal participation in what is now called the political process.

Historically, another principle guiding Jewish politics was a commitment to bargaining as a key method of decision-making. This brought cooperation and consensus, which were deemed preferable to conflict and divisiveness, and gave less value to voting *per se*. Such an approach was the result of the idea of a society based on a covenantal relationship between man and God, which implied obligations on both sides.[2]

In modern times, these traditional Jewish views of political systems led to the establishment of federal models of organization whereby disparate groups can affirm common interests and goals without relinquishing their own identities. In other words, the 'new' communal federation, which has become so important in North America in recent decades, is really a manifestation of consensus and covenant, a form of relationship basic to the political culture of the Jewish people for millennia.[3]

North American Jewry also inherited what one observer has called the 'political tradition of aristocratic republicanism'[4] from its forebears in Europe, where leadership was usually based on scholarship, wealth, or social class. The utility of Judaic learning for leaders declined in America, where the authoritative interpretation of religious questions was not as important as in Europe, but the custom of entrusting communal responsiblities to the wealthy and well-born persists, with certain modifications that have enlarged the pool of potential leaders.[5]

Such emphasis on the economic power and social status of leaders can, of course, raise questions about the nature of governance. If the élite confuses its own interests with those of the community at large, power can become significantly concentrated in the hands of an oligarchy. Fortunately, the Jewish community usually balances this tendency with a general distrust of centralized power and fear of abuse of the masses,[6] an attitude that is particularly strong among American Jews. The result is that the political process in the Jewish community of the United States has evolved into a 'trusteeship of givers and doers'.[7] Wealth and status are not the only means of entering the leadership; some individuals are self-selected on the basis of their ability and their willingness to assume responsiblilty.

In Canada today, power in the Jewish community may be observed at three levels: countrywide, local, and sublocal. The last refers to individual congregations or to chapters of some national organizations and is not of great interest here. The other two are closely related. Most national organizations are based upon local units; the general route to power at the national level is through a base in a local organization. It is highly unusual for someone to achieve power and importance nationally without a strong local base. Therefore, the best way to study power in the Canadian Jewish community is to look first at the local communities, especially the two large ones, Toronto and Montreal. The analysis can then be extended to the countrywide process.

One difference in the countrywide Jewish community structures of Canada and the US is the existence in Canada of a fair degree of centralization. The Canadian Jewish Congress (CJC) was established in 1919 to represent all Canadian Jews and their various organizations to governments, foreign Jewish bodies, and the outside world in general. As a result, Canadian Jews are accustomed to the notion of unified representation in a way that American Jews are not. For some years now the CJC has faced encroachment from other countrywide bodies, notably the federations collectively through the National Budgeting Conference (NBC) and the Canadian office of the Council of Jewish Federations, B'nai Brith Canada (BBC), and the Canadian Zionist Federation (CZF), though the last has diminished in effectiveness over the past five years. Still, the idea of communal unity is taken seriously and generally respected.

At the local level between about 1975 and 1985, the situation was compli-cated by competition between the CJC and the local federations for the dominant role in community affairs. For some time now the evolution of the community has been in the direction of an increasing role for the federations, based largely on the resources available to them, the greater dynamism of their activities and key leaders, and the fact that they have emerged as the local governments of the Jewish community.[8] In a system where most power is local, this is quite important. For the most part, the countrywide bodies rest upon a base of local affiliates. Although they may have national officers and boards, the people who occupy such positions normally come out of the local affiliates, with CJC being an important exception. Certainly this is true with the federations, which have NBC as their national body. In effect, NBC responds to the interests of the local communities, even when performing such obviously national tasks as allocating funds to CJC, to Israel-oriented groups, or for the settlement of immigrants.

Inevitably, as the federations enhanced their importance, they began to challenge CJC as the premier organization in Canadian Jewish life. Eventually a *modus vivendi* was worked out in which Congress would retain its nominal position as the representative body of the community, dealing in particular with the outside world and cultural and educational issues. The federations, which arrived on the scene much later than Congress, represented a response to the health, welfare, and more recently educational needs of the commu-nity. They developed out of a desire to unify, coordinate, and fund the complexity of the services that the community demanded. By the 1970s they had broadened the scope of their activities to encompass general community planning and policy-making, a move directly related to their dominance in the realms of fund-raising, budgets, and spending. Furthermore they became specialists in dealing with governments, an increasingly important task for the community. It was essential for the community to adapt itself to the growing scope of general governmental activity, which was impinging on matters traditionally under community control. The federations became the crucial link between Canada's Jews and their governments on matters relating to the community in a collective sense. Thus it was not surprising that the federations began to challenge the primacy of Congress, especially since they often exhibited more drive, vitality, and relevance than did local CJC affiliates.[9] The result was a reassessment of the roles of the major organizations, at least in the larger cities. The Winnipeg and Toronto communities each decided to merge the local CJC operation with the local federation, preserving at least the appearance of a centralized structure.

Because of the tradition of centralization, political power tends to be concentrated primarily in those organizations that have the broadest scope. Today these are the CJC, its regional groupings, the federations, the NBC, and BBC. Other organizations, such as Zionist groups, fraternal bodies, educational and cultural institutions, and synagogues are generally too specialized to provide their activists with access to community-wide power. Individuals who aspire to positions of leadership generally have to become involved in either the local welfare federation or the local CJC affiliate (or even both) at a fairly early stage in their careers. By succeeding at ever-increasing responsibilities, some reach the higher levels of these organizations and begin to be involved in national activities; eventually they may be recruited to leadership positions at that level too.

Leaders at the Local Level

Toronto and Montreal, which are home to nearly three-quarters of Canada's Jews, understandably dominate countrywide Jewish affairs. Their local political systems are elaborate and highly developed, based on an array of organizations and service agencies. Access to true power, however, is generally limited to those with links to the decision-making process in those organizations whose policies and actions determine the most important factors that affect the lives of Jews within their jurisdiction (insofar as these matters are within the control of the Jewish community at all). In effect, this limitation restricts real power at the local level in Toronto to those who can influence or control decisions in the Jewish Federation of Greater Toronto and in Montreal to those who can affect the actions of Allied Jewish Community Services (AJCS). To a lesser extent, access to power is possible through either the Ontario or Quebec regions of CJC as well.

Although social scientists can show that an élite runs these groups, they, like all Jewish organizations, are constantly looking for new 'leadership material'. Generally, potential leaders are brought into an organization by those already involved, although some people may simply volunteer for responsible work in fund-raising or a community agency. Jewish organizations rarely hold mass public elections for officers and members of governing boards. CJC is the notable exception, electing its national officers at a triennial plenary assembly with perhaps 1,000 voting delegates representing virtually all Jewish organizations in the country. In addition to the election of national officers and other leaders, the regions of CJC hold elections at around the same time for their officers and members of the executive.

A recruit who succeeds in his or her assigned tasks and appears to fit in well with the rest of the group receives increasingly important assignments. AJCS and the Toronto federation invite talented newcomers to participate in leadership training programs. Often major fund-raising campaign responsibilities are a prelude to an important decision-making position.

Hard work and dedication are always keys to advancement. Nevertheless, the system gives a definite preference to the affluent. In the first place, the well-to-do simply have time for unremunerated activity, a phenomenon that has been widely observed in the general literature on political participation. Moreover, the selection process helps to create and perpetuate an élite because it is highly dependent upon the personal, professional, and business connections of those already in power. Disproportionate numbers of communal leaders come from certain business fields or the legal profession. But that situation may be changing, following demographic changes in the community. There is little doubt the occupational distribution is shifting, as it did a generation or more ago in the United States. This is likely to lead to an increase in the proportion of professionals, educators, and academics in the leadership, with a corresponding decline of business people.

In both Montreal and Toronto, many professions, including medicine, dentistry, academia, and the rabbinate, have not been well represented.[10] Moreover whole social, economic, and religious groups tend to be neglected. The poor, especially the elderly poor, are certainly left out of leadership positions. Women were certainly neglected until about 15 years ago. Since then there has been a concerted effort to involve women at the highest levels of decision-making, with women assuming the major countrywide and local positions. It would appear that gender is no longer a barrier to community leadership positions. Even though men predominate on the various boards and committees, the trend is clearly toward equal opportunity for women.

Another issue is peculiar to Montreal, which has had a significant proportion of Sephardic Jews, mainly from Morocco, in the community since the 1950s. Yet the major leadership positions remain in the hands of Ashkenazic Jews. This has been a sensitive issue for some time, as efforts to involve Sephardim at the higher levels of community leadership have not been successful in producing continuity of personnel or leaders for the community at large. Instead, it appears that the Sephardim have concentrated on their own communal organizations, which have become quite vigorous. At times the issue of the Sephardim comes to the fore, such as the period at the beginning of the 1990s when some Moroccan leaders publicly questioned the community's routine opposition to Quebec nationalism and especially the province's language policy. The suggestions that the French-speaking Sephardic Jews might be more understanding of the aspirations of the Québécois helped to drive a wedge into a community that valued unity very highly. Ever since the election of the secessionist Parti Québécois in 1976, the question of the community's appropriate stance with respect to nationalism has been one of the key underlying issues for the Jews. Generally, however, the leadership has preferred that the debate on that issue remain private because of its delicacy, especially since they do not want the Jews, or a portion of the Jews, to be identified or regarded as disloyal to Quebec. In any event, efforts have been made to stress the diverse composition of the community and to increase the use of French in the conduct of community business. But this effort has not succeeded in integrating the Sephardim fully into the community political process.

The method of recruitment tends to tilt the power structure towards older rather than younger people, a bias that is reinforced by the controlled process of advancement. Only in unusual cases does a young person skip stages and move up to the top quickly.

Formal positions in the organizations are not, however, the only basis for power in the Jewish community. Individuals with valuable political resources (wealth, prestige, expertise, and so on) are able to influence the political process. Indeed, the nature of the Jewish political process lends itself to decision-making out of the public eye, a fact that works to the advantage of those who do not hold formal positions of power.

Historically, the best Canadian example of behind-the-scenes power was the late Samuel Bronfman, whose support was for years an essential element for any successful undertaking in the Montreal Jewish community. Though he at times held organizational leadership positions, his status was built on a combination of factors: he headed the wealthiest family in the community, and his personality and commitment enabled him to stand head and shoulders above other community leaders. After his death in 1971, no single person was able to assume a dominant position in the Montreal Jewish community, but several individuals, mainly men of means, became key actors independent of the official positions that they held.

Toronto has never had a leader comparable to Bronfman. As a result, its tradition is one of plural leadership and perhaps a bit more openness than Montreal's. Even so, a few leaders in the city command respect and deference regardless of their titles.

The Reichmann brothers, Albert, Paul, and Ralph, became the wealthiest Jews in Toronto during the 1980s, though they became seriously overextended early in the 1990s. When they were doing well, they were extremely generous with selected charitable causes, generally emphasizing right wing Orthodox religious and educational institutions throughout the world. They tended not to devote much effort to mainstream Jewish community fund-raising in Toronto, thereby foregoing possible leadership roles. Thus their influence in Toronto was limited to indirect influence through the institutions that they financed. They had little impact on the countrywide Jewish community.

Another group playing a role in the political process is the community professionals, the people who actually run the organizations. As those bodies have become increasingly professionalized in recent years, opportunities for careers in the Jewish civil service have multiplied. Jewish federations now require sophisticated managerial tools and administrative techniques.[11] Opportunities thus exist for Jewish civil servants to establish themselves as separate political entities, distinct from both the leaders and the grass roots, and to receive prestige and high status in the community. Simply by virtue of intimate everyday involvement in the affairs of an organization, a professional is in a better position to pull the levers of political power than most lay people, to influence policy without in a formal sense making it. The professional with sharp bureaucratic skills may even dominate an organization without the volunteer leaders being aware of the fact. He or she has an excellent opportunity to structure the policy choices available to the lay leaders and otherwise to run operations as he or she thinks best for the organization.

The very influence of popular, highly competent professionals can also be a problem if it becomes a source of tension between professionals and lay leaders. As communities become more tightly run by the federations, the potential power of the professionals grows. The exact balance between them and the lay leaders depends upon such factors as the professionals' expertise, control of information, and, of course, competence, and the lay leaders' assertiveness, knowledge, and political ability, as well as the personalities involved.

The Exercise of Political Power

Any decision-making process must be viewed in the context of the persons who have the power and the means they use to reach decisions. In the Jewish community, the traditional methods are those that lead to consensus. Accommodation has a much higher value than does winning by a strictly democratic vote. This sort of accommodation begins with the process of choosing the decision-makers. The composition of the formal statutory body affects the outcome of decisions in any organization. Most Jewish organizations are set up so that current leaders, in effect, choose their own successors. Careful selection and controlled advancement of newcomers can ensure that voting does not get out of hand.

Several other factors constitute a check on democratic forms. One is the custom of key members of the élite discussing an issue before the official body debates it. Studies in both Toronto and Montreal show that persons in contact with the decision-making process are well aware of this practice, whether they are part of the élite or not. A discreet meeting allows the leaders, elected or otherwise, to work out a position that reflects a certain amount of negotiation but can be presented publicly with a reasonably united front. The members of the statutory body to which it is brought may or may not realize that they are ratifying a decision made elsewhere.

Another factor that affects the distribution of power in the community dovetails with the system's use of accommodation and behind-the-scenes negotiations. This is the community's financial dependence on the relatively few wealthy families who contribute such a large proportion of its funds. Whether or not the representatives of these families hold official positions of responsibility, their desires must be important in any realistic decision-making process. Although fund-raisers can pressure the wealthy to donate large sums, ultimately contributions are voluntary. The community cannot compel contributions in the way that a government can levy a tax. The ever present, if implicit, threat of refusing to contribute (or contributing at a significantly lower level) in the future gives substantial weight to the preferences of the 'big givers'.

Despite these behind-the-scenes pressures, studies show that the formal committees or boards are not mere rubber stamps. Although the key people can shape decisions, they cannot afford to push things through against the wishes of public boards, a consideration that results in a type of élite accommodation. This gives the process more openness than might otherwise have been expected. As one researcher has pointed out, the common concerns and interests of the élites give a certain overall predictability to decision-making, but there is also fragmentation and competition sustaining democratic tendencies.[12]

One problem here lies, of course, in the decision-makers' perceptions of community needs. Any group that is not adequately represented within the élite must campaign very energetically in order to persuade the decision-makers of the correctness and desirability of a position outside their usual point of view. It can be done, however, particularly if the campaigners are able to enlist the support of the community service professionals, who are placed so that they can facilitate grass-roots participation in community decision-making, if they wish to do so. In Montreal, for example, social workers (with some support from academics and others) stimulated a group of poor and aged Jews to mount a pressure campaign that persuaded the leaders of AJCS to fund Project Genesis, a service for the aged poor. The group did not succeed easily or without rancour, but the funding was forthcoming.

Another grass-roots issue on which the Montreal élite walked a tightrope but finally decided to avoid controversy involved that city's Jewish day schools. Traditionally they had received no general community funding. During the 1960s, they faced increasing financial difficulties and, like many private schools in the province, managed to obtain per-pupil grants from the Quebec government. (By the late 1980s, AJCS, through the Jewish Education Council, had decided to provide substantial additional funding to offset the cost of scholarships.) During the early 1970s, however, the Liberal provincial government tied continuing provision of money to conversion of the schools' secular programs to a French language curriculum, even though the bulk of the students spoke English as their mother tongue. When the Parti Québécois took power in 1976, it increased admissions barriers and added so many curriculum constraints that many parents, students, and educators saw compliance as creating schools that no longer met the needs they perceived.

Consequently, the day schools turned to AJCS for political support and for financial aid.

Neither was forthcoming at the time. The AJCS leaders made it clear that they would refuse to take a strong stand against the government, partly because they perceived being in open opposition to government policies as undesirable for the Jewish community and partly because the big contributors to the annual campaign were simply not interested in increasing their gifts in order to ameliorate the problems of the day schools. Yet grass-roots pressure compelled the originally indifferent leaders to take some responsibility for the day schools. Having done that, however, they were able to nudge the schools to an accommodationist posture, despite the serious misgivings of many parents and educators.

All of these considerations show that decision-making—and hence power—in Jewish communal life rests mainly with an élite. They take their trusteeship seriously, assuming leadership roles out of a sense of responsiblilty and even obligation. Other groups in the community can reach them, albeit with difficulty. One primary goal of their decision-making process is to avoid open controversy. This reinforces the existing tendency toward discreet accommodation.

During the early 1970s, when social scientists examined the Jewish élites of both Toronto and Montreal, control of each community's affairs rested in the hands of no more than sixteen or twenty men. These were almost all well-educated, successful businessmen or professionals, in their sixties or seventies, residents of affluent sections of town, members of select synagogues and private clubs. Some of them were related to each other through marriage. Many were personally wealthy. With them, though not quite of them, stood a very few top Jewish civil servants in each city, men whose jobs and personalities combined to give them enormous influence in community affairs. These people constituted the Jewish establishment. There is constantly talk about broadening the base of communal leadership by bringing new people in. During the 1970s the main noticeable shift was to include some relatively younger men. During the ensuing decade, however, there was a marked increase in the involvement of women, the Orthodox, and some quite young people.

The élite is not really a closed group, but entry is closely controlled, so unless a powerful insurgent group arises, the élite can perpetuate itself. The likelihood of replacing the present élite is small, because the group now in control includes most of the wealthy Jews who care about Jewish life. Any change in political control would prove a futile gesture unless the larger contributors to the fund-raising campaigns accepted it.

The Smaller Communities

Of the Canadian Jewish communities outside Toronto and Montreal, only Winnipeg, Ottawa, and Vancouver have more than a few thousand members, so Jewish life in them is not nearly as complex and organized as it is in the two large cities. Nevertheless, whereever there are at least several hundred Jews, there is usually an organized Jewish community, usually some sort of council affiliated with the CJC.

Size precludes the possibility of any of the smaller communities offering the wide range of services that Toronto and Montreal provide. Thus the scope of decisions to be made is relatively narrower, and the political stakes in Jewish community life are not as high. Identification with Israel, however, is an effective motivating force among nearly all Canadian Jews, and the raising of substantial amounts for it and whatever local activities exist is ample justification for energetic fund-raising organizations. Moreover, the establishment of the National Budgeting Conference, comprising representatives of the federation or community council in each of Canada's eleven largest cities plus the United Israel Appeal, assured the smaller communities of some role in determining national spending priorities. So there are some consequential stakes for the decision-makers in the organizations of the smaller communities.

In general, the exercise of power in the smaller centres follows the patterns already observed in Toronto and Montreal.[13] However, there are some differences. For example, in Ottawa the key body is the Vaad Ha'ir, with heavy synagogue representation. Virtually all community activities are at least coordinated through the Vaad, making Ottawa one of the most highly organized communities in Canada. Much of the membership of the Vaad is long-term, which gives a great deal of stability to community governance but also inhibits the emergence of new leadership. Many of the other aspects of leadership and decision-making resemble those in the two large Canadian cities, especially the existence of a relatively small group of wealthy families with disproportionate influence. The formal holding of an office is not essential to the exercise of political power, and the realities of the sources of community funds weigh heavily on the decision-making process.[14]

Winnipeg, once an unusually vibrant Jewish community, if never a large one, has seen its population level off and then start to decline during the past thirty years. Much of the explanation for the demographic change has been the desire of young people to seek greater economic opportunities in larger centres, particularly Toronto or perhaps Vancouver. The voluntary leaders are the key political actors, and usually have been successful businessmen or lawyers. They come together in what can be regarded as a multiple-element oligarchy, with each element having its own sources of power and no one element able to dominate.

In contrast to Winnipeg, Vancouver's community has been growing for some time, especially since 1971. As a result, more of the population is relatively new than in most other Canadian communities, especially with immigration from abroad at low levels. Surprisingly, there has been considerable continuity of leadership, with a relatively small group of people, usually affluent, dominating. The nature of the community is such that the leaders do not depend on the professionals to the same extent as in other cities and thus put in a considerable effort of their own.

The National Level

As a highly organized community, Canada's Jews have long emphasized a national presence. The trend in communal life, however, has been towards increased power for the welfare funds, which are local organizations, with the resulting anomaly that national organizations are overshadowed politically by local ones. This trend has particularly affected the CJC because it has no independent sources of financing but depends on money raised by the fund-raising arms of the local federations, especially those of Montreal and Toronto. The result has been two major developments: the merger movement in the larger communities, with the exception of Montreal, and the granting of authority to the NBC to routinize the allocation of funds to national organizations.

The creation of the NBC and its subsequent operations have provided Canadian Jewry on a countrywide basis with at least some aspects of a government for the community as a whole, thereby implcitly challenging the hegemony of the CJC to speak for it. CJC continues to take stands on matters of public concern and to pursue issues such as the prosecution of war criminals, defence against anti-Semitism, and the preservation of national unity. NBC dominates in the control of funds for countrywide organizations that do not have their own fund-raising capacity. This includes Congress, Jewish Immigrant Aid Services, and the Canada-Israel Committee and other Israel-oriented groups. Control over funds also means that NBC exercises oversight with regard to those organizations, evaluating their performance and programs. Inevitably control over funds has come to mean some control over the use of funds, making NBC a major shaper of the direction of community policy at the countrywide level. Internally, NBC determines how much money will remain in the local federations (all of the campaigns are local), how much will go to Israel through the United Israel Appeal, and how much will thus be available for the national organizations. Subsequently it makes allocations to the specific organizations from that last pool. The membership of NBC largely reflects the local federations, so that the initial decisions regarding the amounts to be kept in the local communities and to be sent to Israel essentially determine how much is available at the national level, but cannot be made without regard for the needs of the local communities. As those needs have become more pressing, due first to inflation, then to the concerns of the schools, and finally to declining revenue because of bad economic conditions, the local federations have been badly squeezed. Their perceptions of their own financial predicaments inevitably have an impact on their attitudes toward the issues that face NBC. NBC does try to operate by consensus, but there is little doubt that the interests of the Toronto and

Montreal federations carry the greatest weight, making their representatives among the most powerful people there.

Despite all this, there is an important difference between politics at the national and local levels that is related to financial concerns. Most of the issues at the local level revolve around funding, budgetary allocations, service programs, and the like. At the national level, however, leaders are often concerned with issues that involve ideas rather than money; this makes it possible for different kinds of people to gain power there than would be the case locally. As a result, the national leadership is more heterogeneous and perhaps a bit more representative. Patterns of recruitment and advancement are more varied and perhaps more open. Spirited electoral battles are not unknown in national organizations, whereas they are rare at the local level. In addition, Congress, which is still one of the most important national organizations, has traditionally been more open to lawyers, intellectuals, and professionals than are the business-oriented dominant local bodies. Moreover, although it could once operate on its own, the CJC is now essentially dependent upon accommodations worked out with other national bodies; these are ususaly based on some kind of élite agreement. A major focus of activity at the national level for the past twenty years has been Israel and attendant issues. The community endeavours to speak with one voice on matters related to Israel, normally through the vehicle of the Canada-Israel Committee (CIC), which is sponsored by CJC, CZF, BBC, and the local federations. Concern for Israel does bring Canadian Jews together, yet it has also been a divisive issue, both organizationally and substantially. The attempt to operate a body that reflects the views of several other bodies is difficult under any circumstances; in the atmosphere of organizational conflict and competition that is so common in Canadian Jewish life, this is especially challenging. Debates over the approach and effectiveness of CIC have occurred on many occasions; the last led to a reorganization toward the end of the 1980s. The result was a more decentralized structure, with greater power to local committees, which perforce would have to work closely with the federations. Between the influence of the federations on the local CIC activities and the role of the federations with respect to the national CIC, it is clear that the federations now have a most important voice in CIC policy-making, further reinforcing their growing importance in Canadian Jewish life.

Substantive matters involving Israel have been a source of conflict during the past decade, especially as Jews who dissented from Israeli government or Canadian Jewish community policy became more open and vociferous in expressing their views. This conflict has been particularly evident in Toronto, where Canadian Friends of Peace Now is most active, and where extremist fringe groups manage to garner some media publicity. By making public pronouncements or by running advertisements articulating its position, the Peace Now group appeared to be challenging the community's official position that the CIC and its constituent organizations spoke on behalf of all

Canadian Jews. A concrete manifestation of conflict concerned a conference held at Montebello, Quebec, in 1988, in which delegations of Canadian Jews and Canadian Arabs met to discuss Middle East issues. When news of the meeting got out, a major conflict erupted, especially over the composition and selection of the Jewish delegation, which had been put together by the organizers rather than CIC and appeared to be heavily weighted toward Toronto sympathizers with the Peace Now position. Eventually the opposition of the CIC and other community organizations led to the cancellation of a scheduled second meeting. The whole episode left a considerable amount of bitterness between the Peace Now people and the mainstream of the community.[15]

In general, success at the countrywide level for an individual depends to a large extent on his or her effort and effectiveness. He or she usually builds on the base of a strong local organization, but occasionally personal characteristics are sufficient. Financial status does not seem to be quite as important as at the local level, although one should not minimize its importance. It would appear that the nature and scope of politics at the countrywide level differs somewhat from that at the local level. Thus it is possible for a person to function primarily in national affairs without spending a lot of time at the local level, but that is relatively rare.

Another major factor in entering politics at the national level is home town. Toronto and Montreal make up so large a part of the national Jewish community that their people have generally dominated the political process. Periodically, this situation breeds resentment in other regions, but the sheer size of the two cities and the location of key offices in one or both make it difficult for people from elsewhere to function effectively, though modern communications techniques have improved that situation somewhat. For some time, Montreal was the source of most key national leaders, but the trend for the last fifteen years has definitely been toward Toronto. This is due to the dynamic growth of the Toronto community, coupled with the steady population decline of the Montreal community in response to the political and economic changes occurring in Quebec. With so many young adults having left Montreal, the prospects for a further decline of importance are great. On the positive side for Toronto, it has emerged as the national leader in trade and commerce and has benefited in terms of population growth from Jews moving from Montreal, from some western cities, and from some smaller centres in Ontario. Moreover, the existence of a unified community structure in Toronto provides a more solid organizational base than does the dual structure in Montreal.

Concluding Observations

In perspective, the distribution of power within the Canadian Jewish community reflects a certain tension between traditional oligarchical tendencies and the democratic impulse of the modern era. The fact that community organization and policies are not the most important considerations of most Jews, however, limits pressure for democratization. Most Jews simply do not make the effort to participate politically, although some may complain about political outcomes. Democratization does become an important issue from time to time, but no permanent constituency is concerned about it. Generally the structure is sufficiently flexible so that those who complain loudly enough about a lack of democracy can be brought into the process. Given the elaborate nature of community structures and the complexity of the political process, a few new people cannot bring about major changes from within unless they are able to find allies among the more established players.

The trend in Canadian Jewish life is towards increasing importance for the federations, although the existence of a national organization such as the CJC provides some balance. The socioeconomic élite that dominates the federations and hence Jewish political life does not govern arbitrarily and is conscious of its trusteeship for the interests of the entire Jewish community. But the extent to which it actually responds to grass-roots sentiments varies, depending on the issue and what is at stake.

One of the clearly observable trends in recent years, with significance for the exercise of political power, is the increasing professionalization of the civil servants and lay leadership, as well as the Jewish organizations themselves. This is evident in most of the bodies involved in communal governance, such as the federations, NBC, CJC, and BBC. Leadership recruitment and training programs are now helping to identify a new generation of men and women, born in Canada, who are taking over the positions of power from the old line leadership. These people are more attuned to the utilization of the same organizational and managerial techniques and processes employed in other kinds of large organizations. The combination of a new generation of leaders that shares the backgrounds and educational experiences of the professional leadership has contributed to what amounts to a revolution in the way in which Jewish bodies are run.

As a result of the convergence of the interests and orientations of the newer lay and professional leadership, the organizations are likely to come to resemble bodies in the general society that share the same dominant secular professional culture, a departure from the business-oriented attitudes of the past. Furthermore, one can expect that both lay and professional leaders will reflect the effects of better Jewish education and leadership development programs with the result that they will approach cultural, intellectual, and religious matters somewhat differently than their predecessors did.

It is no secret that the present system is not well equipped to cope with dissent. The leaders prefer consensus politics and are uncomfortable when faced with active opposition. Organized dissent is, in fact, rare, although individual dissenters do emerge occasionally. They are often coopted into the system, a practice that can inject new ideas into it without endangering basic values. In the future, however, one can expect increased pressure to open up the decision-making process to a greater degree. Younger people, with their experience in other large organizations, are accustomed to a more open style of decision-making. Thus, although the tendency to defer to insider groups persists, there is likely to be a movement toward more transparent policy formation in the future. Undoubtedly this will create certain tensions within the organizations, which will have to be accountable to the rank and file of the community that contribute to the campaigns while remaining responsive to the big givers who provide the bulk of the community's revenue.

Jewish community politics in Canada is hardly a closed system, but it is not entirely open either. It functions quite well most of the time in delivering services and representing the interests of its constituency. It errs most often in favour of efficiency at the expense of formal democracy.

Notes

[1] Daniel J. Elazar, 'Some Preliminary Observations on the Jewish Political Tradition', Workshop in the Covenant Idea and the Jewish Political Tradition, working paper no. 10 (Ramat Gan: Department of Political Studies, Bar-Ilan University, 1978): 11.

[2] Daniel J. Elazar and Stuart A. Cohen, *The Jewish Polity: Jewish Political Organization from Biblical Times to the Present* (Bloomington: Indiana University Press, 1985): 8–11.

[3] See Bernard Susser and Eliezer Don Yehiya, 'Prolegomena to the Study of Jewish Political Theory', Workshop in the Covenant Idea and the Jewish Political Tradition, working paper no. 8 (Ramat Gan: Department of Political Studies, Bar-Ilan University, 1978): 16.

[4] Daniel J. Elazar, 'The Kehillah', Workshop in the Covenant Idea and the Jewish Political Tradition, working paper no. 6 (Ramat Gan: Department of Political Studies, Bar-Ilan University, 1977): 19.

[5] See Charles S. Liebman, 'Dimensions of Authority in the Contemporary Jewish Community', *Jewish Journal of Sociology* 12 (1970): 35–6.

[6] See Ernest Stock, 'In the Absence of Hierarchy: Notes on the Organization of the American Jewish Community', Study of Jewish Community Organization, working paper no. 3 (Philadelphia: Center for the Study of Federalism, Temple University, n.d.): 4.

[7] Daniel J. Elazar, *Community and Polity: The Organizational Dynamics of American Jewry* (Philadelphia: Jewish Publication Society of America, 1976): 336.

[8] Daniel J. Elazar and Harold M. Waller, *Maintaining Consensus: The Canadian Jewish Polity in the Postwar World* (Lanham and Jerusalem: University Press of America and the Jerusalem Center for Public Affairs, 1990): Ch. 2.

[9] Elazar and Waller, Ch. 4.

[10] Toronto has had some exceptions in the last category; Rabbis Gunther Plaut and Jordan Pearlson achieved major community leadership positions.

[11]The increasing status of the professionals and the relative scarcity of able candidates have resulted in very generous remuneration for the top people.

[12]Yaacov Glickman, 'The Organization and Governance of the Toronto Jewish Community', mimeographed (Toronto, 1974): 98, 100.

[13]Elazar and Waller, Ch. 10–17.

[14]Zachariah Kay, *The Governance of the Jewish Community of Ottawa*, Canadian Jewish Community Reports no. 6 (Philadelphia: Center for Jewish Community Studies, Temple University, 1974): 22.

[15]For a fuller discussion of the controversy over the Montebello meeting see Harold M. Waller, 'The Montebello Mystery', *Viewpoints* (Israel) 76 (1 August 1988).

Left or Centre? The Canadian Jewish Electorate,

1953-1983

J.A. Laponce

While the electoral cleavages between Protestants and Catholics are well documented in countries as diverse as Germany, the Netherlands, Switzerland, Great Britain, Australia, and the United States,[1] the cleavages between Jews and Christians are less well known, and even in countries where empirical evidence is available, studies of the Jewish vote often rest on data that are local rather than national in scope and which are, in nearly all cases, based on small samples.[2]

A set of Canada-wide surveys of an unusually large size—nearly a quarter of a million respondents—permits us to add Canada to the very few states where the party preferences of Jewish voters have been analysed, and enables us to test—with more controls than those allowed by the much smaller American and Australian data sets—the theory that Jewish electors prefer left-wing parties.

We have four main reasons for wanting to do this analysis. First, the Jewish vote is, *per se*, interesting to study if only because Jews are highly politicized. They are, in Lipset and Raab's words, 'politically hyperactive'.[3] Yet, there is to date no nation-wide study of their party preferences in Canada. Second, the studies of the Jewish electorate that have been done outside Canada have generated—possibly because of the lack of firm evidence—a rich set of theoretical explanations, richer than that used to explain the Catholic or the Protestant vote.

Third, a better understanding of the linkage between religion and politics requires that we go beyond the study of political contrasts among major denominations, since minority feeling—a factor that interacts often with religious beliefs—is likely to be more pronounced in a democracy when the group is relatively small.

And fourth, as a binational state, Canada offers an ideal setting for the cross-national comparison of dispersed minorities, such as Canadian Jews, that are located within different cultures.

I shall first review the major theories intended to explain the Jewish vote outside Canada before using some of them as guides to the analysis of the Canadian electorate in the period 1953-1983. I conclude that the Jewish vote is best explained by combining left-right and centre-periphery explanatory models as well as by distinguishing the notion of a cultural from that of a political centre.[4]

Explaining Jewish Preferences for the Left

Studies of the Jewish vote in prewar Poland and Czechoslovakia as in contemporary Australia, Great Britain, France, and the United States have shown that specific issues, candidates, and circumstances can occasionally shift it to the right or at least to the centre-right. These studies, however, leave the overwhelming impression that if social class and occupation are held constant, Jewish voters are markedly inclined to the left.[5]

This inclination has generated a variety of explanations, some emphasizing factors internal to the Jewish faith and culture, and others relying on external variables relevant to non-Jewish dominant groups and host societies.[6] Lawrence Fuchs attributes a preference for the left to *Jewish values*: the valuing of education that makes Jews more likely to follow the lead of intellectuals who support causes of the left more often than those of the right; and the valuing of charity and non-asceticism that lead to a claim for reforms and justice now rather than to a trust in the Divinity to set things right eventually.[7] A similar argument underlies Moses Rischin's and Nicholas Berdyaev's assumption of a natural attraction of Judaism to either socialism or Marxism.[8]

Gerhard Lenski and Seymour Martin Lipset argue that *status discrepancy* plays a role in determining the partisan orientation of Jewish voters. As high achievers, Jews are more sensitive than low achievers to any dissonance between their role in society and the status given them by the socially and culturally dominant group. That dissonance leads them more frequently than low achievers to a protest vote against the powers that be — typically a vote for the left — even by those who are close to or even part of the power élite.[9]

Arthur Liebman proposes another explanation internal to the Jewish community, namely, the historical experience of a transition from *ghetto to universalism*. Liberalism, which was associated since the eighteenth century with both universalism and pluralism, enabled Jews of the Enlightenment to reject the cultural ghetto where they feared religious orthodoxy would keep them. It permitted them as individuals to act as equals on the world stage while allowing them to maintain their cultural distinctiveness.[10]

Like Liebman's explanation, the so-called *accommodation theory* combines psychological and historical factors, but the factors are different. Heinrich Heine, when he remarked 'As does the Christian, so does the Jew', summarized the injunction of Jeremiah to the Jews of Babylon to the effect that the peace of the city of exile was their peace and that the law of the country of exile was their law.[11] In its contemporary form, Heine's statement takes the form of the 'accommodationist' interpretation adopted in part by Lipset, Akoka, Rabi, and Schnapper and Trudel[12] which expects Jewish communities of the Diaspora to express and often to magnify the political norms of their host communities. Since United States politics have been dominated in the twentieth century by the Democratic party, American Jews would be expected to concentrate their votes on the Democrats; since French politics has had, for a long time, a left-wing bias, one should expect that French Jews will prefer left- to right-wing parties; and so on in Australia, Britain, or Canada. If one accepts the accommodationist interpretation, one should also expect that when dominant host groups shift from left to right, so do the Jews, after a certain time lag.

Among external factors, *anti-Semitism* is, not surprisingly, the most often cited, usually to explain a preference for the left as well as occasional deviations.[13] Werner Cohn associates the tradition of left voting, whether in Europe or in North America, to the cleavages created by the French Revolution of 1789 and to the French, German, and Austrian revolutions of 1848.[14] The parties of the left then espoused the cause of democracy, liberalism, equality, civil rights, and change, while the parties of the right, though not necessarily anti-Semitic, were on the side of traditionalism, clericalism, and other non-egalitarian ideologies where anti-Semitism had found its preferred political niche. According to this explanation, if Jews are more inclined to vote for the left than their class or occupation would lead one to expect, it is because the right rejected their support for religious, nationalistic, or other political reasons, whereas the left welcomed or at least accepted it.

Foreign policy, particularly in the form of *concern for Israel*, has been added recently to the older anti-Semitism variable. In their simplest form, the 'anti-Semitism' and 'concern for Israel' explanations predict that Jews will support the most pro-Jewish or pro-Israel parties or at least those that are the least antagonistic. These explanations do not imply an a priori left preference but usually lead to the finding that left-wing parties have been more open to Jews and more pro-Israel than right-wing ones, with the major exception of postwar England.

The comparison of democratic and non-democratic systems leads Medding to reinterpret the explanations of Liebman, Lipset, and Cohn by introducing the *nature of the regime* as an intervening factor. The Jewish vote, argues Medding, will deviate as little as necessary from the norms of the society (left or right) but will deviate according to whether the threat to Jewish interests is perceived as coming from below or from above in the social hierarchy.[15] The tendency to support the left, and in particular the centre-left, is not seen as a universal characteristic of Jews but as a characteristic of Jews in liberal regimes where the threats or potential threats to Jewish cultural and economic interests come from above.

Finally, one must add to this set of specific factors an explanation meant to apply to cultural minorities in general; namely, parties of the left are more likely to support the concerns of non-dominant ethnic communities including those of Jews outside Israel.[16]

Formulating Hypotheses for Canada

What would these assumptions and explanations lead one to predict in the Canadian case? Should Jews be expected to give above-average support to the New Democratic Party, the Liberals, or the Conservatives? For the 1953–1983 period covered by our data, the three main federal parties were not markedly distinct in their policies *vis-à-vis* Israel except during the first Suez crisis when the Conservatives were more supportive. The 1979 promise by Prime Minister Joe Clark to move the Canadian embassy from Tel Aviv to Jerusalem was quickly rescinded and thus should not be expected to hold long-term consequences in favour of the Conservatives.[17] As for anti-Semitism, it is not obviously and visibly linked to any one of the three major federal parties. There may, however, be some justification for equating the 'threat' posed by French Canadians, especially Quebec independentists, to the alleged 'threat from below' posed by American Blacks that is sometimes used to explain a decline in Jewish support for the Democrats.[18]

Taking into account Canadian circumstances, none of the previous explanations except possibly that of Medding would lead us to expect a preference for the Conservatives. Nearly all theories lead us to expect verification of the 'usual' Jewish inclination toward the left. But should that inclination be more favourable to the Liberals or to the NDP?

That status discrepancy theory predicts a preference for the left but, since we lack measures of the intensity of the assumed discrepancy, does not allow us clearly to allocate that vote either to the Liberals or to the NDP. Similarly, the 'ghetto to universalism' explanation predicts a preference for the left but does not help in allocating that preference. Fuch's and Cohn's interpretation would predict that the NDP will receive proportionately more Jewish support than the Liberals, since the New Democrats' egalitarianism is more pronounced than that of the other two parties.

The accommodationist theory suggests an hypothesis distinguishing clearly the left from the centre-left and favours the Liberals rather than the NDP. The Liberals have dominated Canadian politics since the arrival of most Jewish immigrants, and have acted throughout that period as the prime agency of political acculturation.[19] We should expect them to receive proportionately greater support from Jews than from Christians. Higher support than from Protestants? Certainly. Higher support than from Catholics? Very likely, but less clearly so, since Catholics, like Jews, are likely to have the attitudes of a minority which desires integration.

The very limited empirical evidence originating from Canada supports theories that predict a Jewish preference for the NDP and the Liberals over the Conservatives, but does not indicate clearly whether such preference benefits primarily the Liberals or the New Democrats. Using a nation-wide survey, Mildred Schwartz reports 'oversupport' for the NDP and to a lesser extent for the Liberals, and a corresponding 'undersupport' for the Conservatives;[20] but, on the basis of a survey that excludes Quebec, Gagne and Regenstreif report oversupport for the Liberals and undersupport for both the NDP and the Conservatives in the same period.[21]

These uncertainties and contradictions justify the formulation of four separate hypotheses distinguishing left from left-of-centre preferences: (H1) Jews are more likely than Protestants to support the NDP; (H2) Jews are more likely than Catholics to support the NDP; (H3) Jews are more likely than Protestants to support the Liberals; and (H4) Jews are more likely than Catholics to support the Liberals.

Data

In no country outside Israel do Jews account for more than 1.5 per cent of the total population, except in the United States where they are 2.6 per cent.[22] Identifying and analysing their electoral behaviour is thus difficult and costly. Typically, in Canada as in France and Australia, commercial and academic election surveys use samples that comprise too few individuals to allow for the analysis of small groups. A large national survey of 3,000 Canadian electors, for example, would include about 40 Jewish respondents. A more common sample size of 1,500 would reduce this number to about 20.

Short of drawing an extremely large sample, there are four major ways to address this problem of N's. The first is offered by the snowball sampling technique. A hard-to-find respondent leads the interviewer to a similarly hard-to-find person (a friend, relative, or acquaintance) who leads to another person, and so on until the desired sample size is reached. A study by Benayoun of the Jewish vote in Toulouse employed this technique, which is a source of uncontrollable biases and very costly when the target population is dispersed territorially.[23] Second, one can use the sounder methodology employed by Corbeil and Delude to study francophones outside Quebec.[24] A large random sample reached by telephone was used to identify a sub-group of French-speakers, the only one to be interviewed later. Third, one can oversample if the group to be oversampled is highly concentrated geo-graphically. Like the Corbeil-Delude screening technique, oversampling would in the case of Canadian Jews be a very expensive solution since the Jewish population is not sufficiently concentrated geographically.[25]

There remains a fourth possibility: merging data from existing surveys where the wording of the questions remains the same over time. Fortunately, the question on religious preference used by Gallup (CIPO) has remained unchanged since the early 1950s.[26]

By merging 235 surveys from the period 1953-1983, a total sample of 218,738 respondents, 2,312 of whom mentioned a party prefernce and indi-cated their religion to be Jewish, was obtained.[27] This combined sample will enable us to control for more than one intervening factor while correlating party preference and religious self-identification; unfortunately, the intensity of religious practice or feeling could not be measured. Such a measure, used in the Michigan surveys of the American electorate, appears very rarely in the Canadian Gallup questionnaires.

Findings

Three of the four hypotheses pass the first test, that correlating religion and party preferences for the sample as a whole (see Table 1). The hypothesis that fails, H1, expected Jews to be more likely than Protestants to support the NDP. They are not. Even with frequencies in such an unusually high range, the x^2 test of the difference between Protestants and Jews did not come close to statistical significance. The three other hypotheses are sustained, but with unequal vigour. Jews are markedly more likely than Protestants to support the Liberals, and markedly less likely to support the Conservatives; but the difference between Jews and Catholics, while statistically significant (p < .05), is a relatively small four percentage points.[28]

The two similarities that appear in Table 1 — Jews are like Protestants in the support they give to the NDP, but not much different from Catholics in the support they give to the Liberals — is confirmed, although qualified, in Figure 1 when we control for time and region.[29] Outside Quebec, the similarity between Jews and Catholics is accentuated in that their NDP and Liberal plots almost coincide and their Conservative patterns have much in common. In the Canadian case Heinrich Heine's statement must be reworded to read: 'as do the Catholics, so do the Jews' (or vice versa).[30]

In Quebec the picture differs. Irrespective of the level of support for the Créditistes, the percentage of Jews favouring the Liberals has been higher than that of Catholics since the mid-1950s. In English Canada, Jews are like Catholics, while in Quebec they are more Catholic than the Catholics. Why does such a high proportion of votes favour a single party? Why the Liberals? We shall return to these questions, but suffice it to say that the time and regional controls indicate that Quebec should be analysed separately.

Longitudinal controls which identified the party in power showed little effect on the party preferences of Jews. Variations were more pronounced when we controlled for the party leading in the polls, but did not justify breaking the sample into separate periods.[31] We may thus apply regional and socio-demographic controls to the whole sample and retain the advantage offered by a large number of cases.

Controlling for Socio-demographic Categories

Catholics, Protestants, and Jews are very unevenly distributed geographically and socially. While 56 per cent of Canadian Catholics in the sample reside in Quebec, only 33 per cent of Jews and 3 per cent of Protestants do so; while 35 per cent of Catholics and 25 per cent of Protestants live in families with at least one trade unionist, only 15 per cent of Jews do so. While 34 per cent of Jews had attended university, only 14 per cent of Protestants and 9 per

Table 1 Religion and Party Preference, 1953-1983 (in percentage)[a]

	CCF/NDP	LIBERALS	CONSERVATIVES	SOCIAL CREDIT/ CRÉDITISTES	LABOUR PROGRESSIVE	OTHER	(N)
Protestants	17.1	32.3	45.9	4.2	0.2	0.4	(78,167)
Jews	17.0	62.5	18.5	1.0	0.5	0.6	(2,312)
Catholics	12.0	58.1	22.1	6.2	0.4	1.3	(66,461)
Totals	14.8	44.4	34.7	5.0	0.3	0.8	(146,940)

[a]Source of data in this article is J.A. Laponce and Laine Ruus, *Merged File of the Canadian Electorate*, University of British Columbia data bank. Equalizing the weight of each half-decade does not produce any sizeable variation. For the NDP, Liberals, Conservatives and SC, the weighted statistics (each half-decade having the same weight) are respectively: Protestants 16.7, 35.2, 43.6, 5.1; Jews 16.2, 63.9, 17.6, 1.1; Catholics 10.5, 59.2, 21.6, 7.0. The widest variation (Protestant-Liberal) is under three percentage points. Unless mentioned otherwise, the article uses the unweighted sample.

cent of Catholics had; while 19 per cent of Jews were ranked as wealthy in the 1950s (the measure disappeared in subsequent surveys), only 5 per cent of Protestants and 4 per cent of Catholics were so classified. While 76 per cent of Protestants and 70 per cent of Catholics lived in urban centres, 96 per cent of Jews did so.

Some of these differences do not affect the overall averages reported thus far while others, such as those resulting from the place of residence, need to be controlled to ascertain whether Jewish support for the Liberals and the NDP is attributable to ethno–religious factors rather than simply to patterns of socio-geographical concentration. The controls introduced in Tables 2 and 3 permit such a test.[32]

Preferences in Quebec

Separating Quebec from the rest of Canada enhances some of the contrasts noted earlier, but reduces others. In Quebec, Jews were markedly *more* Liberal than either Catholics or Protestants so that in all subgroups of Table 2 the Jewish Liberal score exceeds that of Catholics. Jews in Quebec were also *more* likely than Catholics to support the NDP, the only exception being respondents with secondary education. The difference in NDP support between Jews and Protestants is less pronounced: Jews were more likely than Protestants to support the NDP in only 9 of the 15 categories in Table 2. Data on parties of the right confirm what we observed on the left, since in all cases except in the category 'white collar' Jews were *less* likely than Catholics to support the Conservatives and in all cases *less* likely than Protestants to support that party.

If one is prepared to define the left as composed of Liberals and New Democrats and the right as composed of Conservatives and Social Credit/ Créditistes, then in all categories of Table 2 Jews appear more leftist than either Catholics or Protestants.[33] But if one establishes a left–right separation between the NDP and all other parties, the hypothesis of a Jewish inclination to the left is no longer universally confirmed. In short, the last three hypotheses, H2, H3, and H4, are once again sustained, but H1 is not.

Preferences outside Quebec

In all cases Jews outside Quebec were less likely than Protestants to support the Conservatives or the combination of Conservatives plus Social Credit by a considerable margin. In most cases Jews were more likely than Protestants to support the NDP (markedly so among the university-educated, trade unionists and professionals), but the overall difference is not large. The first and third hypotheses are thus by and large confirmed. However, the striking pattern of Table 3 rests in confirmation of the remarkable similarity of Jewish and Catholic preferences. While Quebec Jews were more likely than Quebec Catholics to support the Liberals and the NDP, outside Quebec the difference

Figure 1 Party Preferences of Catholics, Jews and Protestants, 1953–1983
       (in percentages)

1. CCF/NDP outside Quebec

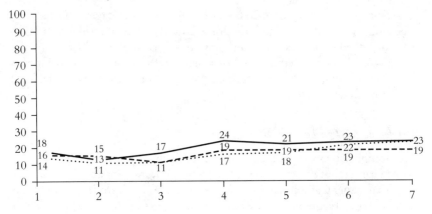

3. Liberals outside Quebec

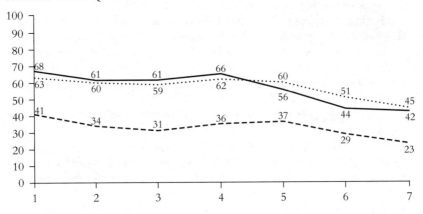

5. Conservatives outside Quebec

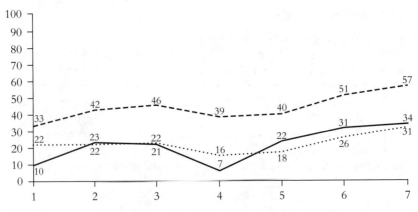

2. CCF/NDP in Quebec

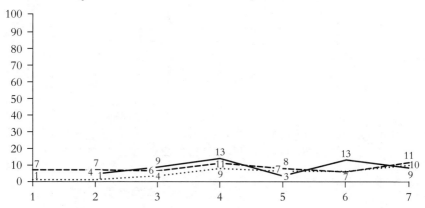

4. Liberals in Quebec

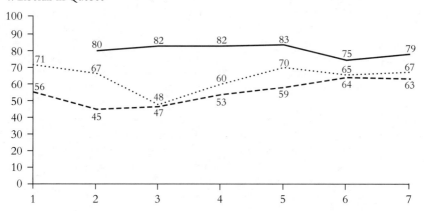

6. Conservatives in Quebec

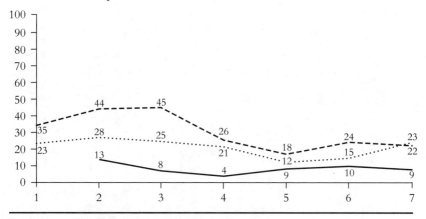

Key: ········· Catholics, ⸺⸺Jews, − − − − Protestants.
Note: Seven time points are as follows: 1 = 1953–1954; 2 = 1955–1959; 3 =1960–1964;
4 =1965–1969; 5 = 1970–1974; 6 = 1975–1979; 7 = 1980–1983. All N's exceed 45 with the
exception of Jews in Quebec in 1953–1954 whose preferences are therefore not reported.

Table 2 Party Preferences in Urban Quebec, 1953-1983

	CCF/NDP			LIBERALS			CONSERVATIVES			CRÉDITISTE		
	Protestant	Jewish	Catholic	Protestant	Jewish	Catholic	Protestant	Jewish	Catholic	Protestant	Jewish	Catholic
Males	9[a]	12	9[a]	58[a]	75	60[a]	31[a]	9	19[a]	1	1	9[a]
Females	8	7	6	62[a]	83	67[a]	29[a]	10	17[a]	1	1	8[a]
Anglophones	8[a]	11	7[a]	61[a]	77	74	30[a]	11	16[a]	—	1	2
Francophones	12	11	8	59	67	63	18	14	18	5	2	9
Union family	13	21	10[a]	57[a]	76	58[a]	27[a]	1	18[a]	2	1	11[a]
Non-union family	7	9	6[a]	61[a]	79	66[a]	31[a]	10	18[a]	1	1	7[a]
Primary education	8	7	3	53[a]	80	62[a]	34[a]	10	21[a]	3	1	12[a]
Secondary education	8	7	9	60[a]	83	64[a]	30[a]	7	16[a]	1	1	8[a]
University education	8[a]	16	15[a]	61[a]	70	62[a]	28[a]	17	18[a]	—	1	2
Professionals[b]	7[a]	22	13[a]	58	70	69	34[a]	8	13[a]	—	—	3
Executive/management	6	6	5	56[a]	85	68[a]	36[a]	8	17[a]	—	1	6[a]
White collar	7	10	7	58[a]	72	67[a]	33[a]	18	17	—	—	7[a]
Blue collar	8	13	6[a]	57[a]	72	58[a]	31[a]	7	18[a]	1	4	15[a]
Under age 40	10[a]	15	9[a]	62[a]	69	61[a]	25[a]	13	17	1	2	9[a]
Over age 40	6	6	5	58[a]	85	65[a]	34[a]	7	19[a]	1	—	8[a]

[a] p(χ^2) ≤ .05 when either Protestants or Catholics are compared with Jews.
[b] Occupational data are for the period 1953-1979 only.

Table 3 *Party Preferences of Urban Respondents outside Quebec, 1953-1983 (in percentages)*

	CCF/NDP			LIBERALS			CONSERVATIVES			SOCIAL CREDIT		
	Protestant	Jewish	Catholic	Protestant	Jewish	Catholic	Protestant	Jewish	Catholic	Protestant	Jewish	Catholic
Males	20	20	22	31[a]	55	53	44[a]	23	23	4[a]	1	2[a]
Females	17[a]	22	18[a]	32[a]	55	58	47[a]	21	22	4[a]	1	2
Anglophones	19	21	20	32[a]	55	52[a]	46[a]	22	26[a]	3[a]	1	2[a]
Francophones	20	10	16	37[a]	71	67	36[a]	19	15	5	—	2
Union family	30[a]	40	27[a]	29[a]	38	51	36[a]	18	19	4[a]	1	2
Non-union family	14[a]	17	15	33[a]	58	58	49[a]	23	25	4	1	2
Primary education	21	20	21	29[a]	55	55	43[a]	23	19	6[a]	1	3[a]
Secondary education	19	19	21	31[a]	57	54	46[a]	22	23	3[a]	1	2
University education	13[a]	23	15[a]	38[a]	55	56	47[a]	20	27[a]	2[a]	—	1
Professionals[b]	13[a]	23	11[a]	41[a]	59	63	42[a]	17	23	3[a]	—	1
Executive/management	10	13	10	38[a]	67	64	46[a]	18	22	5[a]	—	3[a]
White collar	14	17	13	37[a]	57	64	44[a]	22	21	4	3	2
Blue collar	25	29	23[a]	32[a]	52	56	37[a]	16	18	5[a]	1	3
Under age 40	21[a]	24	21[a]	34[a]	53	54	40	20	23	4[a]	1	2[a]
Over age 40	17	17	18	30[a]	57	57	49[a]	24	23	4[a]	1	2[a]
Maritimes	10	7	13	39[a]	62	55	50[a]	31	31	1	—	1
Ontario	19	20	20	34[a]	58	61	46[a]	21	18	1	—	1
West	21	23	22	27[a]	48	43	43[a]	25	30[a]	9[a]	2	6

[a] $p(x^2) \leq .05$.
[b] For period 1953-1979 only.

either disappears or is so reduced as to become far less significant than the overall resemblance. In Quebec, Jews and Catholics were separated by less than 6 percentage points in only 24 of 60 (40 per cent) paired comparisons; outside Quebec, this occurs in 86 per cent of the cases (62 of 72 comparisons in Table 3).

A summary picture of these similarities and differences is given in Quebec by the image of three bell-shaped curves lined along a left-right axis with their apex in the Liberal party; one of the curves, representing Jewish preferences, is much higher and narrower. By contrast, outside Quebec there are only two such curves — one for Protestants with its apex in the Conservative party and the other for both Catholics and Jews with its apex in the Liberal party.

Predictive Models of the Jewish Vote

Applied one at a time, the controls in Tables 2 and 3 had the advantage of offering an overall picture with enough cases to ensure that the differences observed were based on sufficient N's. However, such a pedestrian approach to the correlation between religion and party preference has the disadvantage of not allowing for interaction among a sufficient number of predictors.

To obtain such interaction we applied log linear analysis to the factors of Tables 2 and 3 that covered the whole period and obtained a simplified model by eliminating the factors with low coefficients and withdrawing the factors that produced empty cells in the matrix. Only four variables remained at the end of this process: religion, trade union membership, province of residence, and level of education (see Table 4).

The log linear analysis verifies most of the previous observations, but qualifies some of them and invites — an invitation we shall eventually decline — that we push the analysis beyond the simple testing of our hypotheses toward the testing of the theories on which the hypotheses were based. The models of Table 4 show that when trade union membership and education are accounted for, Jewish party preferences were (a) markedly different from those of Protestants in Quebec as well as in English Canada; (b) distinct from those of Catholics but more so in Quebec than in English Canada where they are as likely to support the Conservatives and only slightly less likely to support the Liberals. The models also show that the odds of voting Liberal as a result of Jewish religious affiliation are much higher in Quebec than in the other provinces, a finding that confirms previous observations.

The qualification introduced by the log linear analysis is as follows: all four hypotheses are confirmed except in the case of Jews outside Quebec, who were slightly less likely than Catholics to vote Liberal. However, the interaction of 'Jewish' and 'no university education' changes the sign of the coefficient with the odds increasing from .86 to 1.04. In one respect, the models are clearer than the results noted previously. In all cases, Jews appear more

Table 4 Preferences of Urban Respondents, 1953-1983 (saturated log linear models)[a]

	CCF/NDP		LIBERAL		CONSERVATIVE	
IN QUEBEC	JEWS + CATHOLICS	JEWS + PROTESTANTS	JEWS + CATHOLICS	JEWS + PROTESTANTS	JEWS + CATHOLICS	JEWS + PROTESTANTS
1. Main effect	.16[c]	.83[c]	2.19[c]	2.35[c]	.09[c]	.11[c]
2. Jewish religion	1.12	1.19[c]	1.44[c]	1.34[c]	.45[c]	.38[c]
3. Union family	1.44[c]	1.57[c]	.84[c]	.87	.64	.57[c]
4. No university	.58[c]	.71[c]	1.33[c]	1.26[c]	.75[c]	.82
5. 2 + 3	1.13	1.04[c]	1.00	.95	.62	.69[c]
6. 2 + 4	.90	.74[c]	1.31[c]	1.40[c]	.75[c]	.68[c]
7. 3 + 4	.88	.85[c]	1.09	1.06	.91[c]	.98
8. 2 + 3 + 4	.89	.93	1.11	1.14	—[b]	—[b]
OUTSIDE QUEBEC						
1. Main effect	.56[c]	4.80[c]	1.00	.65[c]	.30[c]	.47[c]
2. Jewish religion	1.28[c]	1.29[c]	.86[c]	1.34[c]	.95	.60[c]
3. Union family	1.53[c]	1.59[c]	.80[c]	.82[c]	.85[c]	.84[c]
4. No university	1.06	1.08	.99	.93	.92	.97
5. 2 + 3	1.10[c]	1.05	.88[c]	.87[c]	1.01	1.04
6. 2 + 4	.88[c]	.87[c]	1.04	1.12[c]	1.04	.99
7. 3 + 4	1.09	1.11[c]	.93	.94	1.03	.97
8. 2 + 3 + 4	1.07	1.06	.98	.97	.98	1.01

[a]Only respondents indicating a party preference are included.
[b]Insufficient cases.
[c]$p \leq .05$.

likely to support the NDP once trade union membership and education are taken into consideration. In short, we verify the expected tendency of Jews to support the left rather than the right: in the NDP column the four odds of Table 4 are positive, in the Liberal column three out of four are positive, and in the Conservative column the four are negative.

Beyond confirming what the theories led us to expect, do these findings also allocate explanatory power to any of the theories? If Jews vote for parties of the left and centre, do they do so because of status discrepancy, anti-Semitism, charitable ethos, a desire to integrate, or minority status? This question requires that we operationalize each of the theories in such a way that they can be hooked together by some form of regression. I tried to do so but abandoned the attempt for lack of appropriate data, as illustrated by the two following examples. Consider first the status inconsistency explanation. Let us assume that such inconsistency is more pronounced among university-educated Jews, particularly among the small number of them who are trade unionists; and let us also assume that status inconsistency in these groups leads to higher levels of NDP support. If so, the interaction of religion and education, as well as of religion and union membership in Table 4 should produce a systematic pull of the Jewish vote to the left. Such a pull appears in favour of the CCF/NDP but, disturbing for the theory, the odds of voting Conservative are not changed by the interaction of religion and education outside Quebec when we compare Jews to Catholics. Were the original assumptions correct? Is the level of perceived status inconsistency related to professional and educational status? That remains to be shown.

Consider now the accommodation theory. How should we, with the data at hand, operationalize it? Should we expect established Jewish élites to set the political integration pattern or should we expect the less affluent, the less educated to be more eager to integrate? The first assumption seems preferable but we lack empirical support for either. The interaction between religion and *lower* education in Table 5 shows positive odds of voting Liberal (the party favoured by the accommodation interpretation) but, contrary to our expectations, university education has the effect of polarizing toward the left and right, away from the centre. Should we thus reject the accommodation theory, or question this operationalization of it? The second opinion is the more reasonable.

Discussion and Conclusion

The analysis leaves us with four major observations: (1) Jews are more likely to vote NDP than either Catholics or Protestants, controlling for trade union membership, level of education and professional status; (2) Jews are much more likely than Protestants to vote Liberal; (3) Jews are more likely than Catholics to vote Liberal in Quebec, but not in English Canada; and (4) Jews are overwhelmingly Liberal, particularly in Quebec.

This last observation may well be the most significant. Use of the Auto-

Table 5 *Preferences of Urban Jewish Respondents, 1953-1983 (log linear results)*

	CCF/NDP	LIBERALS	CONSERVATIVES
Main effect	.25	1.54	.17
A. Union family	1.72	.72	.86
Non–Union family	.58	1.39	1.16
B. No university education	.72	1.24	.92
University education	1.40	.81	1.08
C. English Canada	1.50	.60	1.66
Quebec	.67	1.67	.60
D. Interaction	1.20	.90	—
B and C	.83	1.11	—
L²	3.60	5.17	5.88
(N)	(2,182)	(2,182)	(2,182)

ªFor each party model, the residual consists of a preference for the other parties. For example, the NDP residual is a preference for either the Liberals, Conservatives or Social Credit/Créditistes. Reading the cell entry in row A of the first column, 1.72 represents an odds of 1.7 to 1 that a respondent living in a family with at least one trade union member will prefer the NDP to the other parties, all other factors in the model being equal. None of the categories in the three party matrices had Ns less than 30 and all the cells of the NDP and Liberal matrices had expected values greater than five. In two cells of the Conservative matrix (12%), the expected values were less than five. Levels of significance between .10 and .35 were selected to reduce the probability of Type I and Type II errors, as recommended in David Knoke and Peter Burke, *Log-linear Models* (Beverly Hills: Sage, 1984), 31.

matic Interaction Detector to ascertain the lowest Jewish preference for the Liberals produced a low 48 per cent in Quebec, although the splits went as far as seven successive branchings.[34] The 'low' of 48 per cent was recorded among blue-collar workers under 40 years of age. Outside Quebec the percentage went much lower (26 per cent), but this required the unusual combination of being a professional and a trade union member. In short, Jews are more inclined to support the left, whether defined as the NDP or the NDP and Liberals combined. Their dominant electoral characteristic, how-ever, rests in a high level of Liberal support, and in a far greater political resemblance to Catholics than to Protestants.[35]

Let us now return to the question of why, *vis-à-vis* Liberal support, Jews would be more Catholic than the Catholics in Quebec, yet like Catholics in the support they give not only to the Liberals but to the Conservatives and the NDP as well outside Quebec. It will be easier to answer these questions if we add a few more: Why do Protestants, Jews, and Catholics prefer the Liberals to any other party in Quebec while Catholics and Jews diverge from Protestants in the rest of the country? More generally, why are Jews on the political side of Catholics not only in Canada but also in the two predomi-nantly Protestant democracies for which we have good statistics on the Jewish vote, the United States and Australia? And why is it that in France, the only Catholic democracy for which we have reliable data, Jewish voters are *not* on the side of practising Catholics but on that of Protestants?[36] The answer suggested by these questions bypasses the specificity of religious beliefs and may well rest in the combination of two lay factors: a group's minority status and its desire for integration.

Minority status inclines to the left but the desire for integration prevents diverging to the political peripheries. It is thus not so much the left as the centre-left that is preferred: the left for redress, the centre for integration. In Quebec, Jews are a double if not a triple minority: a religious minority within the Canadian state, and a religious and linguistic minority within Quebec society.[37] Consequently, one should expect the cleavage between Jews and the host community to be deeper, not only because the religious and linguistic factors of differentiation reinforce each other, but also because the Québécois, being a minority in the North American as well as the Canadian contexts, have more sharply defined defensive group boundaries.

Bloc voting is a normal electoral strategy for minority groups.[38] Being a minority, Catholic Québécois concentrate their votes; being even more of a minority, Jews in Quebec concentrate their votes even more. But why should the latter vote as a bloc for the very party so strongly supported by Catholics? At this point the accommodationist interpretation suggests that in democratic countries of immigration such as Canada and the United States, a centre-left political party — the Democrats in the United States, the Liberals in Canada — become agencies of integration to the nation as well as vehicles for a redress of wrongs caused by or attributed to the established cultural and social order.

These parties become particularly attractive to the groups and communities that are not at the cultural core, that are not part of the dominant historical stream of the society — groups that may have been persecuted or harassed or subject to discrimination (Jews in Canada, Protestants and Jews in France) or conquered (Indians and French Canadians) or may have a race, religion, language, or national origin that identifies them as foreigners for a much longer time than those who share the distinguishing characteristics of the socio-cultural élites. Such parties become the parties of minorities, to the extent that when Protestant anglophones in Quebec felt threatened by a new Québécois assertiveness and, by way of consequence, developed minority feelings, they too turned to the Liberals.[39]

Distinguishing political from cultural centres of influence, distinguishing the control over taxes and budgets from the control over integrating national symbols, particularly those associated with the creation and survival of a nation through history, thus appears essential to understanding electoral cleavages and party systems in multi-ethnic societies. In such societies, the political system may well be dominated by the party of the minorities (if only because of the magnitude of immigration), while the cultural centres of power may remain in the traditionally dominant social group.[40]

The disjunction between the political and the cultural may explain why groups which have achieved high levels of education and which have been economically and socially successful (such as Protestants in France, or Jews in Canada, France, and the United States) continue to react to their marginality in the religio-cultural domain, a marginality embedded in psychological structures with deep historical roots.

Notes

[1] For a summary of the impact of the denominational factor as well as a guide to the literature on the Catholic and Protestant vote in Germany, the Netherlands, Australia, Britain, Canada, and the United States, see the relevant chapters in Richard Rose, ed., *Electoral Behavior* (New York: Free Press, 1974). For Switzerland, see Jürg Steiner, *Amicable Agreement versus Majority Rule: Conflict Resolution in Switzerland* (Chapel Hill: University of North Carolina Press, 1974).

[2] See footnote 5 for specific references.

[3] The term, used by Lipset and Raab to describe American Jews, has validity beyond the United States. See Seymour Martin Lipset and Earl Raab, 'The American Jews, the 1984 Elections, and Beyond,' *Tocqueville Review* 6 (1984): 411.

[4] The left-right dimension is ordered in this discussion as follows: NDP/CCF, Liberal, Conservative, Social Credit/Créditiste. On the applicability of the left-right dimension to the comparison of European and North American party systems see, among others, Samuel Barnes and Max Kaase, eds, *Political Action: Mass Participation in Western Democracies* (Beverly Hills: Sage, 1979); Ronald Inglehart, *The Silent Revolution: Changing Values and Political Styles Among Western Publics* (Princeton: Princeton University Press, 1977); Ronald Inglehart and Hans Klingemann, 'Party Identification, Ideological Preference, and the Left-Right Dimension among Western Mass Publics', in Ian Budge, Ivor and Dennis Farlie, eds, *Party Identification and Beyond* (London: Wiley, 1978): 243-73; and J.A. Laponce, *Left and Right: A Topology of Political Perceptions* (Toronto: University of Toronto Press, 1981).

For the applicability of that dimension to Canada see also Ronald D. Lambert, 'Question Design, Response Set and the Measurement of Left-Right Thinking in Survey Research', *Canadian Journal of Political Science* 16 (1983): 135-44; David Elkins, 'The Perceived Structure of the Canadian Party System', *Canadian Journal of Political Science* 10 (1974): 503-24; and Ronald D. Lambert, James E. Curtis, Steven D. Brown, and Barry J. Kay, 'In Search of Left/Right Beliefs in the Canadian Electorate', *Canadian Journal of Political Science* 19 (1986): 541-63. For qualifiers and criticisms see John F. Zipp, 'Left-Right Dimensions of Canadian Federal Party Identification: A Discriminant Analysis', *Canadian Journal of Political Science* 11 (1978): 251-77; and R.L. Ogmundson, 'A Note on the Ambiguous Meaning of Survey Research Measures Which Use the Words Left and Right', *Canadian Journal of Political Science* 12 (1979): 799-806.

[5] A survey of the Jewish vote in Romania, Poland, Hungary, Austria, South Africa, Latin America, the United States, Britain, Australia, France, and Czechoslovakia is presented in Peter Medding, 'Toward a General Theory of Jewish Political Interests and Behaviour', *Jewish Journal of Sociology* 19 (1977): 115-44. For the United States, see Gerhard Lenski, *The Religious Factor* (Garden City: Anchor Books, 1963); Lawrence Fuchs, *The Political Behavior of American Jews* (Glencoe: Free Press, 1956);

Lawrence Fuchs, 'American Jews and the Presidential Vote', *American Political Science Review* 49 (1955): 385-401; Werner Cohn, 'The Politics of American Jews', in Marshall Sklare, ed., *The Jews: Social Patterns of an American Group* (Glencoe: Free Press, 1959): 614-26; Mark R. Levy and Michael S. Kramer, *The Ethnic Factor: How America's Minorities Decide Elections* (New York: Simon and Schuster, 1972); Arthur Liebman, 'The Ties that Bind: The Jewish Support for the Left in the United States', *American Jewish Historical Quarterly* 66 (1976-77): 285-321; Stephen D. Isaacs, *Jews and American Politics* (Garden City: Doubleday, 1974); Arthur Liebman, *Jews and the Left* (New York: Wiley, 1979); Lipset and Raab, 'The American Jews, the 1984 Elections, and Beyond,' *Tocqueville Review* 6 (1984): 401-19.

For Britain, see Geoffrey Alderman, 'Not Quite British: The Political Attitudes of Anglo-Jewry', in Ivor Crewe, ed., *British Political Sociology Yearbook* vol. 2 (London: Croom Helm, 1975), 141-9; and Geoffrey Alderman, *The Jewish Community in British Politics* (Oxford: Clarendon Press, 1983).

For France, see C. Ysmal, 'Stabilité des électorats et attitudes politiques', in Jacques Capdevielle *et al.*, *France de gauche, vote à droite* (Paris: Presses de la Fondation nationale des sciences politiques, 1983); Dominique Schnapper and Solange Trudel, 'Le vote juif en France', *Revue française de science politique* 33 (1983): 933-61; Jacky Akoka, 'Vote juif ou vote des Juifs? Structure et comportement électoral des Juifs en France', *Pardès* (1985): 114-37.

For Australia, see Peter Medding, 'The Persistence of Ethnic Political Preferences: Factors Affecting the Voting Behaviour of Jews in Australia', *Jewish Journal of Sociology* 13 (1971): 17-39; Peter Medding, ed., *Jews in Australian Society* (Melbourne: Macmillan, 1973); William Stewart Logan, 'Australian Government Middle East Policy and the Domestic Jewish Vote: An Exercise in Electoral Geography,' *Australian Journal of Politics and History* 28 (1982): 201-17.

For Canada, see Jack Jedwab, 'Uniting Uptowners and Downtowners: The Jewish Electorate and Quebec Provincial Politics, 1927-39', *Canadian Ethnic Studies* 18 (1986): 7-19; and Mildred Schwartz, 'Canadian Voting Behavior,' in Rose, ed., *Electoral Behavior*: 543-618.

[6]The best overviews of the various theoretical explanations of the Jewish vote are in Medding, 'Toward a General Theory of Jewish Political Interests and Behavior', and Liebman, *Jews and the Left*.

[7]Fuchs, *The Political Behavior of American Jews*; Liebman, *Jews and the Left*. Lipset and Raab ('The American Jews') agree that the tradition of charity and the obligation of the community to help the individual lead Jews to support liberal causes.

[8]See Nicolas Berdyaev, *The Russian Revolution* (Ann Arbor; University of Michigan Press, 1961); Moses Rischin, *The Promised City: New York's Jews, 1870-1914* (New York: Harper, 1970); and Liebman, *Jews and the Left*: chap. 1.

[9]Seymour Martin Lipset, *Political Man* (New York: Anchor, 1963): 256; and Lenski, *The Religious Factor*. See also Robert Michels, *Political Parties* (Glencoe: Free Press, 1915): 275-6.

[10]Liebman, *Jews and the Left*.

[11]Wladimir Rabi, 'Le vote juif en question', *L'Arche* (1973): 32-8.

[12]Lipset, *Political Man*; Akoka, 'Vote juif ou vote des Juifs?'; Rabi, 'Le vote juif en question'; Schnapper and Trudel, 'Le vote juif en France.'

[13]See works cited above in notes 1 and 5.

[14]Cohn, 'The Politics of American Jews'.

[15]See Medding, 'Toward a General Theory of Jewish Political Interests and Behavior'; Liebman, *Jews and the Left*; and Lipset, *Political Man*.

[16]Donald L. Horowitz, *Ethnic Groups in Conflict* (Berkeley: University of California Press, 1985); and Laponce, *Left and Right*.

[17]The promise was made on 25 April 1979, during the federal election that led to a short-lived Conservative government. Gallup polls record the following distribution of Jewish support for the Conservatives in the months preceding and following that promise: February, 17 per cent (N = 53); May, 17 per cent (N = 42); and June, 22 per cent (N = 44). For Catholics, the distribution was February, 17 per cent; May, 14 per cent; and June, 21 per cent. Because of the small N, these statistics are given merely as tentative evidence of the lack of impact of the promise.

The October 1956 Suez Crisis produced a major disagreement between the CCF and the Liberals, on the one hand, and the Conservatives on the other. The latter criticized the government for not having supported the British intervention. The debate appears, however, not to have produced any shift in the Jewish electorate. Gallup polls record the following levels of party preference in July 1956, September 1956, October 1956 and May 1957: support for the Liberals by Jews was 73 per cent, 62 per cent, 68 per cent, 75 per cent; and by Protestants was 39 per cent, 40 per cent, 38 per cent, 33 per cent. Support for the Conservatives by Jews was 18 per cent, 12 per cent, 14 per cent, 17 per cent; and by Protestants was 36 per cent, 35 per cent, 41 per cent, 45 per cent. These percentages, like those given above, should be read with caution since the number of Jewish respondents was very small, 22, 34, 22, and 24, respectively. The Canadian debate over Suez was centred on the British rather than the Israel action. See James George Eayrs, 'Canadian Policy and Opinion during Suez', *International Journal* 12 (1987): 98-108; and James H. Aitchison, 'Canadian Foreign Policy in the House and on the Hustings', *International Journal* 12 (1987): 273-87.

[18]On Black-Jewish relations in the United States, see Medding, 'Toward a General Theory of Jewish Political Interests and Behaviour'; Louis Harris and Bert Swanson, *Black-Jewish Relations in New York City* (New York: Praeger, 1970); and William Schneider, Michael D. Berman, and Mark Schultz, 'Bloc Voting Reconsidered: Is There a Jewish Vote?' *Ethnicity* 1 (1974), 345-92.

[19]J.A. Laponce, 'Ethnicity, Religion and Politics in Canada', in Mattei Dogan and Stein Rokkan, eds, *Quantitative Ecological Analysis in the Social Sciences* (Boston: MIT Press, 1969): 187-216.

[20]The exact N cannot be determined from Schwartz's tables but must be closer to 50 than 60.

[21]'Over' and 'under' support were measured in relation to the overall distribution of party preferences in the whole sample. See Wallace Gagne and Peter Regenstreif, 'Some Aspects of New Democratic Party Support in 1965', *Canadian Journal of*

Economics and Political Science 33 (1967): 529-50; and Schwartz, 'Canadian Voting Behavior'. Courtney and Smith's study of federal-provincial split voting in Saskatoon indicates less split voting for the Liberals than the NDP (only nine Jewish respondents). See John Courtney and David Smith, 'Voting in a Provincial General Election and a Federal By-election: A Constituency Study of Saskatoon City', *Canadian Journal of Economics and Political Science* 33 (1966): 339-53.

[22]In the state of New York, Jews represent 10.6 per cent and in the city of New York 24 per cent of the total population. Outside the United States, the major concentrations of Jewish populations, measured in percentage of the total population, are as follows: Israel, 83.7; Venezuela, 1.4; Canada, 1.3; France, 1.1; Argentina, 0.9; Hungary, 0.9; USSR, 0.7; United Kingdom, 0.6; Australia, 0.5; South Africa, 0.4; Belgium, 0.3; Switzerland, 0.3.

[23]Chantal Benayoun, *Les Juifs et la politique: l'élection de 1978 à Toulouse* (Paris: CNRS, 1983).

[24]Yvan Corbeil and Camille Délude, *Etudes des communautés francophones hors Québec* (Montréal: CROP, 1982). One can also, as do Medding and Waller and Weinfeld, rely on Jewish directories although this technique poses difficult control-group problems. See Harold Waller and Morton Weinfeld, 'A Viewpoint Survey of Canadian Jewish Leadership Opinion', *Viewpoints*, 8 October 1987; and Medding, 'The Persistence of Ethnic Political Preferences'.

[25]Jews are not a majority in any electoral district, although they approach it in Quebec's Mount Royal (48 per cent). Two other ridings in Ontario have more than 20 per cent Jewish voters: St Paul (23 per cent) and Willowdale (29 per cent); three more have at least 15 per cent (Outremont in Quebec, 18 per cent; Don Valley East, 18 per cent, and Eglinton, 16 per cent, in Toronto). These districts account for only 30 per cent of Canada's total Jewish population.

[26]The question reads, 'What is your religious preference?' The itemization of the code of these answers was changed in 1978 to (1) Protestant, (2) Jewish, (3) Roman Catholic, (4) other, (5) no religious preference/not stated, from (1) Protestant, (2) Jewish, (3) Roman Catholic, (4) other and no religious preference/not stated. The change of code does not affect the comparison of Protestants, Catholics, and Jews but it does prevent the comparison of the religious to the 'no religion' vote.

The Gallup surveys do not include questions on ethnic identification other than those regarding language and religion. Ideally, one would like to have a measure of both religious and cultural Jewish self-identification. The 1981 Canadian census indicates a high correlation between the answers 'Jewish' to the question on religion and to that on 'ethnic origin': 94.2 per cent of those who said their ethnic origin was 'Jewish' gave 'Jewish' as their religion; 3.6 per cent said they had 'no religion'; and 2.2 per cent indicated a Christian denomination.

[27]The total number of respondents per half-decade was as follows: 11,842; 14,979; 18,308; 15,473; 16,472; 38,732; 31,134. For each of these half-decades, the number of Jewish respondents mentioning a party preference was as follows: 235, 179, 270, 333, 273, 565, 457. The variations in political preferences across time periods were not such as to justify weighting by decades or by party in office. All the statistics and N's reported in the analysis are based on the unweighted sample.

[28]Unless otherwise indicated, the statistics presented in this article are based on those respondents who indicated Catholic, Jewish, or Protestant as their denominational preference and who mentioned a preference for either the CCF/NDP, Liberals, Conservatives, or Social Credit/Créditistes. Undecided responses were as follows: Jews, 19.6 per cent; Protestants, 21.0 per cent; and Catholics 25.6 per cent.

[29]Data from half-decades for each of the partisan categories can be obtained from the author. The widest variation occurs in the relative support given to the Liberal party by Catholics and Jews. The rise of the Créditiste movement was a historical test to which Jews and Catholics responded differently. It shifted the Catholic vote to the right but had little effect on the Jewish vote.

[30]It would be interesting to study the party preferences of Jews during the period of very low Liberal support in the polls in 1986–87, a period that is not part of our data set and not available for secondary analysis at the time of writing.

[31]Distinguishing four situations, (a) Liberals in power (b) Conservatives in power (c) Liberals ahead in the polls and (d) Conservatives ahead in the polls, shows the following variations in the percentage of Jews preferring the NDP (a) 17.5 (b) 15.5 (c) 17.0 (d) 16.8; for the Liberals (a) 63.0 (b) 64.4 (c) 65.5 (d) 49.5; and for the Conservatives (a) 18.6 (b) 19.6 (c) 15.3 (d) 32.5. Translating these percentages into indices of oversupport or undersupport, where 100 signifies a Jewish percentage identical to the sample percentage, indicates a systematic but slight oversupport for the NDP (112, 127, 110, 106), a major oversupport for the Liberals (138, 151, 138, 145), and a systematic undersupport for the Conservatives (54, 52, 49, 69).

[32]Five of the six categories cover the entire period while the one concerning profession covers only part of the period.

[33]The classification of the Liberals as left of centre is debatable. The electorate views the Liberals as clearly to the left of the Conservatives, but gave them in 1979 an average location of 4.30 on a 7-point left-right scale (while locating the NDP and the Conservatives at 3.16 and 4.77, respectively). However, the same electorate classifies the Liberals to the left of centre of their 'ideal' party: 4.30 compared to 4.37 in 1979, 4.37 compared to 4.56 in 1968, and 4.42 compared to 4.64 in 1965. See Lambert, 'Question Design, Response Set and the Measurement of Left–Right Thinking in Survey Research'; and Elkins, 'The Perceived Structure of the Canadian Party System'. Alford, who had originally merged the CCF and Liberals into a single left category, decided subsequently to separate them in his analysis. The degree to which the Liberals are to the left is less important to our analysis than their being located between the NDP and the Conservatives on the spatial dimension. See Robert R. Alford, *Party and Society: The Anglo-American Democracies* (Chicago: Rand McNally, 1963); and Robert Alford, 'Class Voting in the Anglo-American Political Systems', in Seymour Martin Lipset and Stein Rokkan, eds, *Party Systems and Voter Alignments* (New York: Free Press, 1967): 67–93.

[34]In a free split the AID program selects the variable that maximizes the difference between the two groups to be formed by the split. The only restriction on the splitting was that no group be less than 40 cases.

[35]The greater proximity to Catholics appears in American surveys as well. On the tendency of the vote of American Jews to shift somewhat to the right in the 1970s

and 1980s while remaining closer to Catholics than Protestants, see among others Alan M. Fisher, 'Realignment of the Jewish Vote', *Political Science Quarterly* 94 (1979): 96-116; Milton Himmelfarb, 'Are the Jews Becoming Republican?' *Commentary* 72 (1981): 27-32; and Steven M. Cohen, *American Modernity and Jewish Identity* (New York: Tavistock, 1983).

[36]Alain Greilsammer attributes the left inclination of French Protestants to three factors: minority status, support for the secular state established by the Revolution of 1789, and the opposition between Catholics and Protestants in their choice of candidates for election. See Alain Greilsammer, 'Sociologie électorale du Protestantisme français', *Archives des sciences sociales des religions* 49 (1980): 119-45. A survey by *Le Point* indicated that in 1977 the voting preference for the left were as follows: Catholics 23 per cent, Protestants 45 per cent and Jews 56 per cent. The survey was restricted to respondents practising their religion.

[37]See Morton Weinfeld, 'La question juive au Québec', *Midstream* (1977): 20-31; Morton Weinfeld, William Shaffir, and Irwin Cotler, eds, *The Canadian Jewish Mosaic* (Toronto: Wiley, 1981); Morton Weinfeld, 'Le milieu juif contemporain au Québec', in *Juifs et réalités juives au Québec* (Québec: Institut québécois de recherche sur la culture, 1984): 53-81; David Rome, 'Jews in Anglophone Quebec', in G. Caldwell and E. Waddell, eds, *The English of Quebec: From Majority to Minority Status* (Quebec: Institut québécois de recherche sur la culture, 1984), 159-75; and Louis Le Borgne, 'Les Juifs de Montréal: entre l'Europe et l'Amérique', *Conjoncture* (1983): 119-30.

[38]See Horowitz, *Ethnic Groups in Conflict*; J.A. Laponce, *The Protection of Minorities* (Berkeley: University of California Press, 1960); and J.A. Laponce, 'Assessing the Neighbour Effect on the Vote of Francophone Minorities in Canada', *Political Geography Quarterly* 6 (1987): 77-87.

[39]Here I speculate beyond the data because I lack psychological measures of insecurity. This interpretation, however, is supported by the fact that Quebec Protestants increased their support for the Liberals in the second half of the 1990s (see Figure 1).

[40]Interpreting the Jewish vote in terms of minority status coincides with interpretations of the Catholic vote. See John Meisel, 'Religious Affiliation and Electoral Behaviour: A Case Study', *Canadian Journal of Economics and Political Science* 22 (1956): 481-96; Lynn McDonald, 'Religion and Voting: The 1968 Federal Election in Ontario', *Canadian Review of Sociology and Anthropology* 6 (1969): 129-44; and Richard Johnston, 'The Reproduction of the Religious Cleavage in Canadian Elections', *Canadian Journal of Political Science* 18 (1985): 99-113.

I am grateful to Ivan Avakumovic, Sandra Burt, Werner Cohn, Jean Crête, David Elkins, Virginia Green, Richard Johnston, Seymour Martin Lipset, and Peter Woolstencroft for their comments on an earlier version of this article and grateful also to the anonymous referees for the *Journal* whose critical comments were very helpful. I shall disappoint some of them for having tried but abandoned, for lack of appropriate data, the regression analysis that they had suggested.

Continuity and Criticism:

North American Jews and Israel

David Taras and

Morton Weinfeld

The Canadian and American Jewish communities, while sharing much common ground, are products of distinct historical, social, and political circumstances. Each community has been shaped by and has had to adapt to the forces, rhythms, and patterns of nations which have had substantially different attitudes towards ethnic and religious minorities. In Canada, where there are sharp differences and competing visions about national identity and considerable regional, linguistic, and psychological barriers to the forging of a strong national consciousness, ethnic and religious minorities have been encouraged to some degree to maintain their traditional cultures. This commitment was enshrined in the multicultural policies fashioned by the federal government in the 1970s and 1980s. In the United States, where there is fervent patriotism and a fulsome sense of national mission and destiny, minorities must convert to American political beliefs, to what Samuel Huntington has called the 'American creed'.[1] At the same time they struggle to keep the fabric of their community's life intact against the powerful tide of vast homogenizing American culture.

Yet the two communities have been profoundly transformed by the monumental events of contemporary Jewish history: the Holocaust, the emergence of the state of Israel, and the wars and dramatic events of the Middle East conflict. A strong identification with Israel has reshaped Jewish life in North America and given North American Jews a new political agenda: advocacy on behalf of Israel.

The centrality of Israel rests on a number of foundations. First, establishment of the state of Israel has erased the shame and desolation of homelessness. With no country of their own for almost two thousand years, Jews were outcasts and supplicants, constantly uprooted and continually victimized. During the Holocaust many Jews were left stranded with no country to take them in. The current 'ingathering' of Soviet Jews reinforces for North American Jews the necessity of having Israel as a sanctuary to turn to, should the roof fall in on their own lives. Second, Israel gave communities that were divided by sectarian differences and swept up by forces of assimilation a common Jewish experience. In particular, it provided a means for non-observant Jews to con-nect with a Jewish experience. As Solomon Schecter once remarked, Zionism's strength was 'that it could be all things to all men'.[2] A third factor was that in the exuberance that followed Israel's victory in the 1967 Six-Day War, Israel assumed mythic proportions for some Jews. The raid on Entebbe in 1976 and the air strike against Iraq's nuclear reactor in 1981 enhanced Israel's image as strong and self-reliant. By identifying with what were seen as heroic deeds in response to extraordinary challenges, people could be lifted out of the ordinar-iness of their daily lives. Lastly, Israel touches deep religious impulses. It represents a return to places that are sacred in Judaism and encourages among believing Jews the conviction that a 'covenantal' relationship exists between God and the land of Israel. Israel is at once a place of national restoration and sanctuary and of religious renewal and inspiration.

This paper describes the historical, social, and organizational differences between the Canadian and American Jewish communities, how the two communities lobby their respective governments on behalf of Israel, and the changing nature of the relationship of the two communities to Israel. Although charitable contributions are an important expression of pro-Israel activism and concern, this article focuses on the political dimension of North American Jewry's relationship to Israel. The Palestinian uprising in Israel's occupied territories (the Intifadah), which has raged since December 1987, has changed some elements of Israel-diaspora politics. The essential unde-rpinnings of the relationship, the strong bonds of affection and need that tie North American Jews to Israel have, however, remained unchanged.

By examining pro-Israel lobbying by and attitudes towards Israeli policies in the two communities, we demonstrate that American Jews have been more self-assured and assertive than Canadian Jews. This self-confidence may stem from the fact that the American community is older, larger, and better integrated than its Canadian counterpart. It may also be that each group has learned to adapt to the social and political values which dominate in its particular country. Seymour Martin Lipset has argued, for instance, that there is greater deference to authority in Canada and a 'habit of obedi-ence'.[3] As James Bryce pointed out many years ago, 'the sentiment of defer-ence to legal authority, planted deep in days when that authority was regarded with awe as having an almost sacred sanction, has lived on into a time when the awe and sacredness has departed'.[4]

Social and Cultural Differences

Comparing the Canadian and American Communities

Any analysis of the respective attitudes and involvements of Canadian and American Jews regarding Israel must be grounded in an understanding of the different historical, demographic, and socio-cultural features which characterize the two communities. The essential difference is that Canadian Jews identify more strongly as Jews than their American counterparts. They speak more Yiddish or Hebrew, provide their children with more years of Jewish education, are far more likely to identify with religious Orthodoxy and much less likely to identify with Reform, practise a greater number of religious rituals, have lower rates of intermarriage, contribute more generously on a per capita basis to Jewish and Israeli charities, are more likely to have Jewish friendship networks, and are more likely to have visited Israel and to express concern for Israel's welfare. Table 1 presents some quantitative measures of these differences, taken from two 1981 sample surveys of American Jews (one national and one from the New York area) and a 1979 study of Jewish heads of households in Montreal. Although one might not be able to generalize entirely from Montreal to all of Canada, the sample is nevertheless an interesting barometer of Canada-wide trends.

These differences affect the tenor of Jewish public life. American Jews are more widely integrated into American politics and culture. Currently 38 out of 535 members of the United States Congress are Jewish. There are only 5 Jews among the 295 members of Canada's House of Commons. On the whole, the works of Canadian Jewish artists and writers are more likely to deal with Jewish themes, and from a more knowledgeable base, than are the works of American Jews.[5] One can also argue that Canadian Jews have not influenced popular culture in Canada to the extent that American Jews have been able to shape American humour, music, television, and films. In the United States, Jews are defined, and usually define themselves, as one of the triumvirate of great American religions.[6] In Canada, Jews are defined by themselves and by other Canadians—indeed by the Canadian census itself—as both a religious and an ethnic group. This heightened salience of the ethnic dimension blends well with the Canadian multicultural ethos and reinforces the cultural distinctiveness of Canadian Jews.

These differences between the two communities can also be discerned from demographic variables which do not deal strictly with Jewish characteristics, but which reflect the pattern within which the communities must exist. The census count of the Canadian Jewish population in 1986, including people who reported an ethnic origin only partly Jewish, is 344,000, compared with an American estimate, derived from local surveys, of 5.8 million.[7] We might note the importance of these differentials in absolute numbers: the American Jewish community boasts large size, economies of scale and organization, and the possibilities for greater feeling of communal security, particularly in light of its concentration in major urban areas. In percentage terms, Canadian Jews comprise roughly 1.4 per cent of Canada's population whereas American Jews comprise 2.5 per cent of the population of the United States.

Even these differences in absolute and relative percentages understate the greater sense of minority status among Canadian Jews. While close to 75 per

Table 1 Cultural characteristics of American and Canadian (Montreal) Jews (%)

	UNITED STATES NATIONAL[a]	NEW YORK AREA (1981)[b]	MONTREAL (1979)[c]
Denominational Identification			
Orthodox	6	13	41
Conservative	26	36	35
Reform	26	29	9
Other (incl. none, secular)	32	23	15
Ritual Observances			
Light Sabbath candles	22	39	61
Attend Passover seder	77	87	93
Light Hanukkah candles	67	74	81
Fast on Yom Kippur	54	64	81
Observe Kashrut at home	15	26	46
All/Most friends Jewish	61	—	87
Belong to a congregation	51	41	68 (of those who attend)
Have visited Israel	37	37	60
Have considered settling in Israel	—	18	22

Sources:
[a]Steven M. Cohen, 'The 1981–1982 national survey of American Jews', *American Jewish Yearbook, 1983* (New York: American Jewish Committee, 1983): 89–110.
[b]Paul Ritterband and Steven M. Cohen, 'The social characteristics of the New York Jewish community', *American Jewish Yearbook, 1984* (New York: American Jewish Committee, 1984): 128–61.
[c]Morton Weinfeld and William W. Eaton, *A Survey of the Jewish Community of Montreal* (Montreal: Jewish Community Research Institute, 1979).

cent of Canadian Jewry lives in Toronto, Montreal, and Vancouver, at 4.2, 3.2, and 1.4 per cent respectively, Jews cannot be said to constitute a truly significant proportion of the population in any of those metropolitan centres. These percentages are far lower than the comparable estimated figures for New York and northern New Jersey, Los Angeles, Miami/Fort Lauderdale, Philadelphia, Boston, and Washington. It should also be noted that American Jewry has migrated out of the northeastern enclave in the period since World War II to a much greater extent than Canadian Jews have moved out of the Montreal–Toronto concentrations into the west.[8] The smallness of the Jewish Canadian population, both absolutely and relatively, may well contribute to a greater insecurity with respect to status and an increased feeling of marginality. Equally important, Canadian Jews are more likely to be foreign-born and thus one generation closer to the traumatic experiences of the Old World: 32 per cent for Canadian Jews compared with 17 per cent for American Jews. The longer exposure to the modern

Table 2   Views of young Jewish communal leaders, professors, and rabbis on the Middle East (1976)

		TOTAL %	RABBIS	PROFES-SORS	YOUNG LEADERS MONT-REAL	YOUNG LEADERS TOR-ONTO
QUESTION						
Canadian Jews should publicly criticize Israeli policies and actions.	NO	36	29	36	36	38
	YES	56	65	59	57	44
Israel should offer Arabs territorial compromise in the West Bank in exchange for peace.	YES	60	68	72	55	46
Israel should maintain permanent control of West Bank	YES	28	28	19	29	40
Israel should offer to share rule over West Bank with Jordan and Palestinians	YES	47	51	65	34	40
Palestinians have a right to a home in the West Bank if Israel is not threatened	YES	58	57	64	56	53
Israel should place a moratorium on further West Bank settlement	YES	54	54	65	52	40
Israel should talk to the PLO if it renounces terrorism and recognizes Israel	YES	72	78	80	71	61
Canada should not have any contact with the PLO until it recognizes Israel	YES	79	84	78	77	82
Jewish campaign contributions should be used to elect Israel's friends	YES	70	73	69	66	76
The Jewish community should work to build alliances with other ethnic and religious groups	YES	90	84	92	88	91
An effort should be made to get more Jews to run for political office	YES	74	68	73	75	76
The Jewish community organizations should work on both Jewish issues as well as issues of concern to all Canadians	YES	90	94	88	92	89

Source: Harold Waller and Morton Weinfeld, 'A *Viewpoints* survey of Canadian Jewish leadership opinion', *Viewpoints* 15, 4 (1987) (supplement to *Canadian Jewish News*, 8 October 1987): 1–3.

influences of the New World may explain the higher levels of education among American Jews and (along with historic differences in the relevant law) the higher divorce rate.

The foundations of the Canadian Jewish community were laid, relatively speaking, with the mass migration from Eastern Europe at the turn of the century. The earlier German Jewish migrations of the mid-nineteenth century played a far greater role in the history of American Jews. That migration wave, imbued with the more modern norms of Reform Judaism, differed from the traditionalism of the East Europeans who came later. Moreover an openness to America — some might say, to assimilation — typified the institutions built by German Jews in the United States to a far greater extent than did those the community built in Canada. Even within the East European Yiddish-speaking mass migration of the turn of the century, we find subtle yet nonetheless revealing Canadian-American differences. The foundations of the mass migration to the United States were laid in the last two decades of the nineteenth century, before the full bloom of various nationalist Jewish ideologies in Europe. A greater proportion of the immigrants to Canada, by contrast, arrived in the first two decades of the twentieth century, bringing with them a greater heritage of Bundist (Jewish cultural nationalism) and Zionist ideas which they transplanted to North America. These ideologies, whatever their differences, shaped Jewish national and cultural expression in Canada. American Jews, however, were stamped with more assimilationist, internationalist, and socialist ideologies, which proved more fertile soil for a rapid Americanization.[9]

Canada also had proportionally larger influxes of Holocaust survivors after World War II, both in the immediate postwar years and from Hungary in 1956, compared with the United States. The survivors were experienced in Jewish traditions (though not all practised) and in Jewish ideological debates. Many knew Yiddish and Hebrew. Most important, they were staunchly committed to Israel's survival as a natural reaction to the horrors of Nazi persecution. Criticisms of Jews and of Israel were seen to be motivated by or contributing to anti-Semitism. A subsequent wave of North African Jewish immigrants to Montreal shared this trait of strong and unabashed support for Israel's security.

If the stronger sense of Jewishness among Canadian Jews is rooted in the differences in the immigration sequences, both past and present, then one can hypothesize that as the period of mass migration recedes, the characters of the Canadian and American Jewish communities may converge. However, other analysts might claim that the differences reflect enduring national disparities stemming from the broader societal patterns of the melting pot and the mosaic. One can argue that unlike the situation in the United States, in Canada there are forces, laws, and policies which tend to reinforce ethnic identities and cultures and that this Canadian distinctiveness will persist. For example, the strict separation of church and state in the United States precludes government finding for religious — including Jewish — schools. The absence of such a constitutional separation in Canada has led to government funding of Jewish schools in several Canadian provinces. Government multicultural programs and the ethos of multiculturalism have become important features of the Canadian landscape. There are no American parallels to the inclusion of multiculturalism in the Canadian Charter of Rights and Freedoms and the establishment of a ministry of state for multiculturalism. Canadian Jews are as prosperous as American Jews and as well represented in business and professional élites. Classical anti-Semitism is muted in both countries. Yet Canadian Jews may feel less secure, less integrated, and less willing to be assertive in their relations with government because of the demographic and contextual features we have described.

Lobbying for Israel: AIPAC and CIC

Any discussion of the link between the Canadian and American Jewish communities and activism on behalf of Israel must begin with an exploration of the political environment of ethnic group lobbying in the two countries. Canada, even more than the United States, has been ambivalent about according interest or lobby groups full legitimacy as actors on the political stage. Yet interest groups, particularly those not directly tied to business or labour, have proliferated since the 1960s, and within the roster of these voluntary groups, the number of those representing minorities has grown even more proportionately.

Lobby groups generally are tarred with the label 'special interest', suggesting that somehow their activities distort the political process and obscure the national interest. Such a view, to be sure, is only one perspective. In the countervailing view, the lobbying process, representing citizens petitioning their government, is at least as valid a part of the democratic process as voting at regular intervals. Ethnic lobby groups face the additional challenge of avoiding the charge of conflict of interest or, to put it more directly, of dual loyalty. Thus, while economically based interest groups are deemed to be acceptable, ethnic interest groups, with their connotations of foreign entanglements and extra-territorial ties, are allegedly too particularist and may be thought to undermine national interests. To some public servants in Canada, the Jewish community's intense concern about Canadian policy in the Middle East may well seem an irritant.[10] In the United States such involvement is more accepted, perhaps because of the size of the American Jewish community and the long (though now weakening) tradition of ethnic coalition politics nourished through the Democratic party, but in Canada it is relatively novel.

Of all ethnic groups in North America, perhaps none takes politics and foreign affairs more seriously than does the Jewish community. In Canada, it is likely that other minority groups will emulate the activism of the Jewish community on foreign policy issues, particularly those groups whose homelands remain involved in contentious wars or civil strife. This will open up the democratic process, but will make foreign-policy making far more cumbersome than in the past.

Although the two Jewish communities have developed similar institutions for lobbying their respective governments on behalf of Israel, the American community has been far more vigilant, aggressive, and successful than has the Canadian community. The American Israel Public Affairs Committee (AIPAC), which was founded under a different name in 1951, is one of the most feared and powerful lobbies in Washington. It is run by an executive committee made up of the presidents of thirty-eight major American Jewish organizations. It has been able to secure large amounts of American foreign aid for Israel including the turning of loans into grants, to block routinely the sale of American arms to Arab countries while ensuring sales to Israel, and to reward its political friends and punish its enemies. Even when AIPAC lost its battle to prevent the sale of the AWACS (airborne warning and command systems) to Saudi Arabia in 1981, the Reagan administration was forced to make substantial concessions to Israel in order to win the necessary votes for the deal in Congress.

The Canada-Israel Committee (CIC), which was established in 1967, is based on a sometimes shaky alliance of the Canadian Jewish Congress (CJC), the Canadian Zionist Organization, and the fraternal organization, B'nai Brith. Its board of directors also includes representatives from the United Israel Appeal and Jewish community councils across Canada. While successful in some instances, the CIC suffered several bruising defeats during the 1970s and 1980s. It was unable to spur passage of federal legislation preventing the application in Canada of the Arab economic boycott against Israel (a similar law was passed in the United States with little fuss), to hold Joe Clark to his 1979 promise to move the Canadian embassy in Israel to Jerusalem, or to sway Canadian policy during Israel's invasion of Lebanon in 1982 or during the intifadah. In a recent study of the reactions of Middle East interest groups to Canadian government decisions made from the October War of 1973 to the intifadah, David Goldberg found that the CJC was the least 'satisfied' of all the groups involved in Middle East policy-making.[11]

The differences in the success of the two lobbies may be attributable in large part to the political environments within which they operate. Because the United States is a world power which plays a major diplomatic, military, and economic role in the Middle East, AIPAC sees itself as engaged directly in the struggle for Israel's survival. Weapons deliveries, economic and military aid packages, and tilts in the American diplomatic position can all affect the balance of power in the Middle East. Israel, in turn, depends on AIPAC's muscle. By contrast, Canada has only been a marginal player on the Middle East chessboard and its actions, while often symbolically important, cannot affect the power equation in the region.

Another crucial difference in the political environments of the two countries is that power in the American system is highly decentralized and diffused, with influence over policy spread across a number of competing agencies and departments in the executive branch and a myriad of congressional committees. Presidential decisions can be overturned or vetoed by the Congress as was the case when a letter signed by seventy-six senators 'exploded' President's Ford's plans to reassess Middle East policy in 1976 or when the Reagan administration's plan to sell arms to Saudi Arabia was blocked by both houses of Congress in 1986.[12] Most important, perhaps, races for political office are far more expensive to wage in the United States than in Canada, and politicians are far more dependent on co-ordinated contributions from individuals and political action committees (PACs). During the 1988 congressional elections in the United States, the average incumbent senator raised $4.3 million and races for the House of Representatives were won at an average cost of $427,117 per seat. Members of Congress spend much of their time in the relentless pursuit of campaign funding. According to one estimate, senators 'must raise $14,000 a week, every week, for six all-consuming years' to be able to bankroll a campaign for re-election. House members must harvest at least $4,000 a week in campaign contributions during their two-year terms.[13] United States campaign spending laws, enacted in 1974, specify that individuals can only give $1,000 to any one candidate, but they and their family members are allowed to donate $5,000 each to a political committee. Although PACs can only give $15,000 to one candidate in each election, with primaries, runoffs, and the general election each counting as separate elections, several PACs usually form a close alliance to support a candidate of their choice.[14] In Canada, members of parliament are held in check by tight party discipline and the cabinet controls the policy-making process. Campaign spending laws are also much more restrictive. During the 1988 federal election in Canada, the spending ceiling for candidates running in an individual constituency was $46,900.[15] The CJC thus has fewer points of contact and a limited opportunity to involve itself directly in the electoral process.

AIPAC operates according to the elementary rules of politics: the views and actions of office holders must be monitored constantly; friends are to be rewarded, and opponents isolated. This is how one former Senate aide described AIPAC's repertoire:

> If you vote with them, or make a public statement that they like, they get the word out fast through their own publications and through editors around the country who are sympathetic to their cause. It's an instantaneous reward with immediate positive feedback. . . . Of course, it works in reverse as well. If you say or do something they don't like, you can be denounced or censured through the same network. That kind of pressure is bound to affect a senator's thinking, especially if they are wavering or need support.[16]

AIPAC is adept at applying pressure on members of Congress through their constituents, campaign workers, or financial contributors to their campaigns. Action and reaction can be swift. Lee O'Brien describes how on one occasion Representative Thomas Downey expressed doubts about voting for a foreign aid package for Israel because he had been receiving mail from his district protesting the amount of money being spent on foreign aid. Two days later, he received 3,000 telegrams from constituents asking him to vote for aid for Israel. He promptly voted in favour of the foreign aid bill.[17]

The American Jewish lobby's real clout comes from its ability to direct campaign contributions to congressional candidates through PACs. Although AIPAC is not (despite its name) a political action committee, there are at least seventy pro-Israel PACs.[18] Campaign contributions from pro-Israel PACs were probably decisive in defeating two of Israel's principal critics in Congress: Illinois Representative Paul Findly who lost in 1982 and Charles Percy, chairman of the Senate Foreign Relations Committee, who went down to defeat in 1984. Percy had been instrumental in spearheading the sale of the AWACS to Saudi Arabia. According to one source, pro-Israel PACs contributed over $320,000 to Percy's opponents in the Illinois Senate race, and Michael Goland, a California developer with ties to one pro-Israel PAC, spent over one million dollars in an 'independent' media campaign against him.[19] AIPAC's executive director, Tom Dine, described what had taken place: 'All the Jews in America, from coast to coast, gathered to oust Percy. And the American politicians — those who hold public positions now, and those who aspire — got the message.'[20]

By contrast, the CIC's efforts are somewhat anaemic. While the Canadian lobby does the same contact and education work as its American counter-part, it does not possess the same resources, impetus, or tools. The CIC meets regularly with cabinet ministers, tries to win friends among members of parliament, monitors government activity, sponsors tours by parliamentarians to Israel, and organizes an annual dinner and study conference. Its diligence and sophistication have often been remarked upon. Yet the CIC is not heavily immersed in election politics. The Jewish lobby does not have a political fundraising network at its fingertips and shies away from partisan political activity. The concern of Canadian Jews for Israel is expressed mainly through philanthropy — by contributions to charities through the United Israel Appeal and investments in Israel Bonds — rather than through politics. The question is whether Canadian Jewry's lower political profile is the result of a political system that provides interest groups with fewer points of access and in which there is less at stake in terms of directly influencing Middle East events, or whether it is the product of fear and insecurity. It may be that the multicultural environment that allows Canadian Jews to have a greater affinity for Israel also inhibits the community from acting assertively within the wider Canadian political arena.

The Intifadah and the Limits of Dissent

We have mentioned earlier that Canadian Jews are more Jewish and identify more strongly with Israel than their American counterparts. Not surprisingly, therefore, the responses of the two communities to the intifadah that has raged in Israel's occupied territories since December 1987 have been quite different. While criticism and dissent have been rife in both communities, there seems to be greater caution and restraint among Canadian Jews.

What have been the reverberations within the Canadian Jewish community in the wake of the intifadah? In the absence of reliable survey evidence, the best sources of information are the official pronouncements of the major Jewish communal bodies, notably the Canada-Israel Committee and the Canadian Jewish Congress, and the reports on relevant incidents in the *Canadian Jewish News* (*CJN*). The *CJN* plays a key role in Canadian Jewish life, particularly in Toronto and Montreal, and indeed many Canadian minority groups find it a model of what an ethnic community newspaper should be. To be sure, the *CJN* has its share of critics, who have argued that the paper represents the communal establishment and thus under-reports dissent in the community. Lacking any comprehensive survey of Jewish popular opinion on the Middle East, or rigorous content-analysis studies, however, one cannot know if any systemic bias exists. In fact, a review of the *CJN* over the past two years does reveal some reporting of dissident events and intra-communal debate. Historically, Canadian Jews have strongly supported Israel. Both in public and privately, the mainstream communal organizations and leaders have generally espoused views supportive of the Israeli government of the day. Dissenting views were to be found outside official mainstream organizations or were expressed by various leaders speaking as individuals.

Yet almost all differing views were expressed *within* the Jewish community and media rather than to the general public. Paid ads critical of Israeli policy, whether in the Toronto *Globe and Mail* or the *CJN*, were few and far between. Op-ed articles written by Canadian Jews critical of Israeli policy would appear occasionally, but these inevitably reflected individual opinions and were never penned by leaders of mainstream Jewish organizations.

Beginning with the Israeli military action in Lebanon in the early 1980s, expressions of scepticism began increasingly to be heard within the community, though they were still generally voiced internally.[21] In a sense the precondition for growing dissent had been set with the election victory of the Likud party of Menachem Begin in 1977. A large majority of Canadian Jewish activists (as was also true of American Jews) had been nourished on a Labour party model of Israeli Zionism and were uncomfortable with the apparent militancy, right-wing nationalism, and rhetorical style of Likud. A survey of scholars, rabbis, and young communal leaders conducted in 1987 found that territorial compromise was favoured in exchange for peace. Seventy-nine per cent of those surveyed felt that Canada should not have any contact with the Palestine Liberation Organization (PLO) until it recognized Israel, but 72 per cent indicated that Israel should talk to the organization if it renounced terrorism and recognized Israel. Surprisingly, 56 per cent believed that Canadian Jews could express public disagreement with Israeli policies and actions[22] (see Table 2).

Following the outbreak of the intifadah, intra-communal debate seemed to grow, with an increasing polarization between left and right. A case in point was the dialogue between Jewish and Arab Canadians held at Château Montebello in April 1988, sponsored by the Canadian Institute for International Peace and Security (CIIPS). The two-day seminar, planned and held in secret, brought together 15 Arab and 15 Jewish Canadians, chosen to represent a cross-section of opinion. Many Canadian Jews expressed serious reservations over the entire enterprise. It was claimed that the Jewish delegates did not reflect the existing range of Canadian Jewish opinion, but rather one skewed towards criticism of Israeli policy. Some mainstream Canadian Jewish leaders, such as Sidney Spivak of the CIC, claimed to have attended only as individuals and not as representatives of their organizations. Others claimed that Jewish delegates spent more time in dialogue (and debate) with each other where differences of opinion are less pronounced than with the Arab delegates. In short, the fear of a 'sell-out' of Israel through an event manipulated by the Canadian government underlay many of these concerns. Moreover, Montebello was seen as part of a continuing attempt by the Mulroney government to move Canadian policy away from a pro-Israeli position. The Montebello controversy spawned hostile reactions among Canadian Jews and led, *inter alia*, to the creation of the Montreal-based Canadian Institute of Jewish Research (CIJR), which placed a full-page ad opposing Montebello in the *CJN*.[23]

A scheduled second meeting at Montebello was 'postponed' because of the protests of Canadian Jewish leaders and developments in the Middle East.[24] CIIPS remained determined to play an active role in the Middle East debate, however, and sponsored a November 1989 symposium in conjunction with the United Nations Association of Canada. Unlike the Montebello conference, this meeting was open and also did not pretend (consciously or unconsciously) to represent mainstream Canadian Jewish opinion. The National Council of Canada-Arab Relations, Canadian Friends of Peace Now, and the Near East Cultural and Educational Foundation were involved in the meeting. The CIC, of course, protested vigorously.

As the intifadah persisted, debate over Israel's reaction to it and the peace process in general seemed to intensify within the Canadian Jewish community. The organized community, as reflected in the public statements of the CJC and the CIC, linked the end of the intifadah to Arab acceptance of the Israeli peace plan of the day. Yet opponents of Israeli policy seemed to take the offensive. The pages of the *CJN* in late 1989 featured exchanges of letters between supporters of Peace Now and the CJC's president, Les Scheininger. Milton Harris, who had been president of the CJC from 1983 to 1986, called publicly for greater Israeli flexibility on meeting with PLO representatives. In January of 1990, Harris clashed publicly with Moshe Ronen, chairman of the CJC's national executive committee, on the TV Ontario program, 'Speaking Out'. (The disagreements between the two Arab Canadians on the panel were muted.) In February, Scheininger debated Middle East issues with

Michael Marrus, a University of Toronto historian and a member of Canadian Friends of Peace Now, at a packed meeting at Holy Blossom Temple in Toronto. Both events were covered prominently in the *CJN*.[25]

The fact that an equivalent body to Peace Now has not emerged among Arab Canadians may have had some influence on Canadian Jewish attitudes. The point is often made, usually by critics of Israeli policy, that the range of debate on the Middle East among diaspora Jews, certainly Canadian Jews, is far narrower than that in Israel itself. This is unquestionably true. Many Jews in Canada and elsewhere accept an internalized self censorship regarding Israel, arguing that life-and-death decisions affecting Israel ought to be made by Israelis alone. Many fear that even well-meaning criticism of Israel may be used by anti-Semites or by extreme opponents of Israel as a weapon to delegitimize Israel in the world community. Hard-line positions and emotional rhetoric from Arab Canadian spokesmen would certainly make it less likely that Canadian Jews would want to criticize Israel openly in public forums or in media appearances. Thus, the absence of a partner in dialogue may have had an effect on the public emergence of the debate among Canadian Jews on recent Israeli policy.

Thus, by 1990, we find a situation in which the leaderships of the CJC and the CIC continue, in their official pronouncements, to support Israeli government positions. Increasingly, however, Jewish communal criticism of these positions is being voiced in public. Criticism by Canadian Jews on matters of Israeli policy (excluding that from splinter groups on the extreme left) ought not to be confused with weakened support for the elemental security and survival of Israel, however. In the reported words of Michael Marrus at the Holy Blossom debate: 'All of us Jews in Canada are firm supporters of Israel and its people. Support is woven into our very being as Jews.'[26]

American Jews remain emphatically supportive of and attached to Israel. Nonetheless, since 1982 they are no longer willing to hold back criticism of Israeli government policies. Prominent American Jewish leaders, important national Jewish organizations, and American Jewish opinion have been willing to break the long-standing taboo on criticizing Israel's actions. As the historian, Jacob Neusner, has written:

> We do, however, sense a sea change nowadays. Relationship between American Jewry and the state of Israel, once marked by our submission to their dictates, have so changed that, in not a few aspects of shared discourse, we take the unfamiliar role of the self-confident party and they the equally strange role of uncomfortable one. We are telling them precisely what we think, even when they do not want to hear it.[27]

The floodgates of dissent were blown open by Israel's invasion of Lebanon in 1982 and the massacre of Palestinians in the Sabra and Shatila refugee camps by Israel's Christian allies. Rabbi Alexander Schindler, president of the Union of American Hebrew Congregations, Howard Squadron, a past president of the Union of the Conference of Presidents of Major American

Jewish Organizations, and Rabbi Arthur Hertzberg, a vice-president of the World Jewish Congress, were unrelenting in their criticism. Schindler argued that public dissent was now required and warned that 'if either the Israeli leaders or the institutions of American Judaism suppress honest dissent and smear the dissenters, I predict that the Jewish people will be spiritually impoverished and Israel's cause intolerably diminished'.[28]

There is no equivalent in Canada to left-wing Jewish magazines such as *Moment* and *Tikkun* which provide an outlet for expressions of dissent on almost all aspects of American Jewish life.[29] Since the outbreak of the intifadah almost every issue of both magazines has contained articles which criticize or debate Israeli policies. *Moment*'s editor, Leonard Fein, is a strong and frequent critic of Israeli policy, and his practice has been to present readers with opposing viewpoints.[30] For instance, the September 1988 issue featured a debate between Mark Heller (pro) and Daniel Elazar (against) on 'A Palestinian State: Thinking the Unthinkable', and the March 1989 issue offered a similar debate on 'The West Bank as a Military Asset — How Important?'.[31] *Tikkun* has been more relentless and militant in its criticism. For example, the September and October 1989 issues contained four articles on the pathology of occupation. Then, in December 1989. *Tikkun* sponsored a major conference in New York which was attended by hundreds of people from the Jewish left. The proceedings were published over several issues. Two hundred prominent American Jews associated with *Tikkun*'s educational arm, the Committee for Judaism and Social Justice, signed an ad which appeared in the *New York Times* during the visit of the Israeli prime minister, Yitzhak Shamir, to the United States in April 1989. The ad's headline read: 'No, Mr Shamir. Don't assume that American Jews support your policies toward the Palestinians.' The text stated: 'Many American Jews, loyal supporters of Israel, do not support the suppression of the Palestinian people and the continued occupation of the West Bank and Gaza. You do not have a blank check from American Jewry to continue these policies.' The ad called upon Israel to begin negotiations with the PLO and not to rule out the possibility of a Palestinian state. It cited recent polls that indicated that 58 per cent of American Jews would support direct negotiations with the PLO.[32]

As with Canadian Jews there is concern among American Jews about the limits of dissent and the form it should take. The deepest misgivings are about whether criticism will play into the hands of Israel's enemies. Robert Alter has observed:

> There is a kind of immorality in American Jews giving any Israeli government an automatic blank check when they care deeply about the future of the Jewish state and see things that seriously disturb them. . . . I think considerable vigilance must be exercised to ensure that the time, place, and manner of the criticism do not conspire to make it an instrument that can be turned against Israel's most vital interests.[33]

On the other hand, Leonard Fein of *Moment* believes:

> Given the venomous glee with which Israel is attacked by its enemies, one understands the disposition of Israel's friends to refrain from all criticism. But the price of that abstention is grievously high: in time we ourselves lose the ability to know whether our restraint is substantial or tactical. Though we may begin be seeking to insulate Israel from criticism, we end by viewing Israel as beyond criticism.[34]

A survey of officials of major Jewish organizations released in January 1990 found that 73 per cent approved of discussions between the Israeli government and the PLO if it 'recognizes Israel and renounces terrorism'. Forty-six per cent believed that Israel should offer to talk with the PLO 'with no pre-conditions'. Territorial compromise in the West Bank and Gaza was favoured by 76 per cent of those surveyed. Fifty-nine per cent supported the idea of eventual Palestinian independence, although 78 per cent also believed that 'the PLO was determined to destroy Israel'.[35] In addition, 77 per cent admitted that they had privately criticized Israel's actions during the intifadah.[36]

So while American Jews are now in the midst of a heated debate over Israel's policies and have begun to air these differences, major Canadian Jewish organizations still seem to be trying to keep the lid on criticism, although there is evidence that this attitude is changing.

Conclusion

Israel is integral to the spiritual and cultural identity of North American Jews, and Canadian and American Jews remain firmly committed to defending the interests of the state of Israel. During times of crisis both communities can be depended on to mobilize resources and exercise whatever political muscle is at their disposal on behalf of Israel. The problem, however, is that there is now considerable confusion about what is in Israel's best interests. With the Israeli government and public deeply divided over peace initiatives, settlements in the occupied territories, what to do to dampen the intifadah, and whether to negotiate with the PLO, North American Jews have been caught up in the frenzy of debate and disagreement. Even as AIPAC and the CJC continue to advocate unflinching support for Israel, the communities they represent are increasingly divided about what the 'bottom line' for the preservation of Israel's national security should be.

The nature of pro-Israel politics differs considerably in the two North American communities. American Jewry has been at once more aggressive in defending Israel's interests and more willing openly to debate what those interests are. It must be remembered, however, that the willingness of American Jewry to criticize Israel is a relatively new phenomenon that began in a meaningful way only with the Lebanon war of 1982. Canadian Jews seem to be more cautious, both in lobbying Ottawa and in entering the political debate on Israel's future. A closer affinity with Israel may explain their reluctance to challenge Israeli policies although the temperature of debate seems to be heating up among Canadian Jews. There are other explanations for the different outlooks and responses of the two Jewish communities. The earlier immigration of American Jews, their larger numbers, the general acceptability of ethnic lobbying in the United States, and the openness and accessibility of the American political system may contribute to a self-confidence among American Jews that their Canadian counterparts seem to lack. It may also be that the two North American communities have taken on the colouring of the national cultures within which they live. Canadian Jews may have remained deferential to authority whether in Canada or in Israel, while American Jews have assertively proclaimed their rights in a country that has allowed ethnic lobbying to flourish. These differences may narrow in the future as fewer of the Canadian Jewish community are foreign born, as its members become more confident, and as the political system becomes more open.

Notes

[1] Samuel Huntington, *American Politics: The Promise of Disharmony* (Cambridge, MA: The Belknap Press of Harvard University Press, 1981). See also Seymour Martin Lipset, *Continental Divide: The Values and Institutions of the United States and Canada* (Toronto: C.D. Howe Institute and Washington: National Planning Association, 1989).

[2] Quoted in Samuel Halperin, *The Political World of American Zionism* (Detroit, MI: Wayne State University Press, 1961): 279.

[3] Seymour Martin Lipset, 'Revolution and counterrevolution: The United States and Canada' in Eli Mandel and David Taras, eds, *A Passion for Identity: An Introduction to Canadian Studies* (Toronto: Nelson Canada, 1988): 70.

[4] Quoted by Lipset in *ibid*: 70.

[5] See 'Jewish culture and Canadian culture' in Morton Weinfeld, William Shaffir, and Irwin Cotler, eds, *The Canadian Mosaic* (Rexdale, Ont.: John Wiley, 1981).

[6] This denotes the 'triple melting pot' thesis in which ethnic distinctiveness was to be submerged within inclusive Protestant, Catholic, and Jewish denominations. See Will Herberg, *Protestant, Catholic, Jew: An Essay in American Religious Sociology* (Garden City, NY: Doubleday Anchor, 1960). The rediscovery of ethnicity in the United States since the 1960s does not negate the strong religious self-identity of American Jews compared with the ethnic self-identity of Canadian Jews.

[7] The American national estimates are based on extrapolations from local Jewish community surveys, which may vary among themselves in the screening questions used to identify, and count, Jews. While the Canadian census counts are not problem-free, they are far more reliable and valid than the American measures.

[8] Barry Kosmin, Paul Ritterband, and Jeffrey Scheckner, 'Jewish population in the United States, 1986', *American Jewish Year Book, 1987* (New York: American Jewish Community, 1987): 164-91.

[9]See Eugene Orenstein, 'Yiddish culture in Canada: yesterday and today' in Weinfeld, Shaffir, and Cotler, eds, *Canadian Jewish Mosiac*: 293-314.

[10]See John Kirton and Peyton Lyon, 'Perceptions of the Middle East in the Department of External Affairs and Mulroney's policy 1984-1988' in David Taras and David Goldberg, eds, *The Domestic Battleground: Canada and the Arab-Israeli Conflict* (Montreal: McGill-Queen's University Press, 1989): 186-206.

[11]David Goldberg, 'Keeping Score: From the Yom Kippur War to the Palestine uprising' in Taras and Goldberg, eds, *Domestic Battleground*: 102-22.

[12]Edward Tivnan, *The Lobby* (New York: Simon and Schuster, 1987): 89, 260.

[13]Tom Morganthau *et al.*, 'Checkbook politics', *Newsweek*, 2 April 1990: 32-3.

[14]See Larry Sabato, *PAC Power* (New York: Norton, 1984).

[15]Robert Matas, 'Add free labor to expenses of campaigns, panel urged', *Globe and Mail* (Toronto), 30 March 1990: A2.

[16]Quoted in Lee O'Brien, *American Jewish Organizations and Israel* (Washington: Institute for Palestine Studies, 1986): 175.

[17]*Ibid.*: 177.

[18]*Ibid.*: 183-8.

[19]Tivnan, *The Lobby*: 190-1.

[20]*Ibid.*: 191.

[21]At a private emergency briefing sponsored by the Canadian Zionist Federation during the Lebanese war, participants were presented with an analysis of events designed to maximize support for Israel. Many of those attending, while strongly sympathetic to Israel, were unimpressed.

[22]Harold Waller and Morton Weinfeld, 'A Viewpoints survey of Canadian Jewish leadership opinion', *Viewpoints* 15, 4 (1987) (supplement to *CJN*, 8 October 1987): 1-3.

[23]The CIJR is comprised of a group of professors united in their support for Israel's security, though not necessarily for all the policies of its government.

[24]For a review of Jewish communal reactions to the Montebello meetings, see *CJN*, 9 and 23 June 1988, and the *Suburban* (Montreal), 25 and 29 June 1988.

[25]*CJN*, 18 January and 8 February 1990.

[26]*Ibid.*: 8 February 1990.

[27]'American Jews and Israel — a symposium', *Commentary* 85 (February 1988).

[28]Tivnan, *The Lobby*: 175.

[29]However, *Viewpoints*, an independent intellectual bi-monthly supplement to the *CJN*, does deliberately seek out and publish lengthy articles from a wide spectrum of opinion.

[30]See, for instance, 'A New Zionism', *Moment* 14 (April 1989): 58-65.

[31]'A Palestinian state: thinking the unthinkable', *Moment* 13 (September 1988): 40-1; 'The West Bank as a military asset — how important?' *Moment* 14 (March 1989): 32-40.

[32]'No, Mr Shamir', *Tikkun* 4 (May/June 1989): inside back cover.

[33]'American Jews and Israel — a symposium': 25.

[34]*Ibid.*: 33.

[35]Steven Cohen, *Israel-Diaspora Relations: A Survey of American Jewish Leaders* (Tel Aviv: Israel Diaspora Institute, 1990): 8.

[36]*Ibid.*: 70.

part six

The Jewish

Family and the

Changing Role

of Jewish Women

Introduction

Morton Weinfeld

The Jewish family has long held a particular fascination for students of modern Jewish life (Sklare, 1971). Jewish tradition and folklore hold that there is a particular warmth and commitment found within Jewish families that is in some ways distinctive. An idealized vision of the Jewish family has been inherited from a blend of old-country memories and nostalgia for the immigrant generation, coming from the humour of Sam Levenson or Harry Golden, or more scholarly reconstructions (Zborowski and Herzog, 1962).

The evidence we have on both old-country Jewish families and those of the immigrant generation is more nuanced (Cohen and Hyman, 1986; Howe, 1976). On the one hand, alcoholism and related incidents such as child abuse or wife abuse were relatively rare. The care of children and the reverence for elders do seem to have been major features of Jewish family life, reflected in the evidence of universal male Jewish schooling, and subsequent Jewish educational and occupation success (Blau, 1974).

Yet any idealized image of the Jewish family was challenged by other evidence and interpretation. Immigrant Jewish families had to deal with juvenile delinquency and desertion. The poignant Yiddish letters to *The Forward* in New York, translated and published in the volumes of *A Bintel Brief*, described the turmoil within immigrant Jewish families, including intergenerational tensions. New waves of Jewish comedians and authors developed the stereotype of the 'yiddishe mameh' suggesting that maternal devotion could be excessive, perhaps neurotic, smothering, and ultimately counterproductive (for an early example see Wolfenstein, 1958). Extended Jewish families gave way to nuclear family forms; Jewish old age homes and retirement colonies in Florida became common alternatives to sharing a home or neighbourhood with aging parents.

New issues, many drawn from trends in families generally, have also emerged as elements for analysis within Jewish family life. These include increasing rates of intermarriage; the family as an agent of socialization; declining Jewish fertility rates; increasing rates of divorce; divorce and remarriage; homosexuality and voluntary singlehood; power relations within families, the challenge of feminism, and dual career families; the sharp increase in the proportions of Jewish elderly, and the sandwich generation facing the responsibilities of caring for aging or infirm parents. Jewish social scientists often analyse these trends by reformulating the age-old question: is it good for the Jews? Some see the trends as indicating demographic and indeed cultural decline, while others, more optimistic, see transformation and survival (Cohen, 1988).

In research on Jewish families, two tasks can be defined. First is the basic empirical task, attempting to measure and compare Jewish behaviours on these sorts of variables, with those of non-Jews. Second is the task of ascertaining whether any such differences flow from what can be termed Judaic cultural forces, or from social structural or demographic factors such as social class. In other words, do any distinctive Jewish family patterns represent anything uniquely Jewish, or are they some combination of immigrant and/or middle-class behaviour?

The three papers in this section address some of these important issues. Leo Davids presents a profile of the 1981 population of Canadian Jews (defined by religion). We note how skilful use of census data can shed light on general trends in Canadian Jewish fertility and marital status, as well as variation within the Jewish group. For example, looking at Yiddish-speaking Jews offers insights on Hassidic Jews, as does looking at fertility patterns of younger Jewish women.

Sheva Medjuck analyses the ways in which feminism poses challenges to traditional Jewish familistic patterns, and indeed to the organized Jewish community and to Jewish religious ritual. (For an early example of Jewish feminist writing, see Koltun, 1976.) The analysis includes use of 1986 data on the socioeconomic status of Jewish women. Medjuck analyses the relevance of feminist concerns to Jewish women, and elaborates a perspective in which these concerns can and should be integrated into mainstream Jewish life.

Carolyn Rosenthal directs our attention to the issue of Jewish intra-family relations, with respect to older Jewish women. We find that while on some measures the degree of intra-family Jewish contacts is greater than the average, on other measures there are no differences. Thus the old dichotomy of traditional vs. modern family forms may miss the subtlety of Jewish and other ethnic family patterns. Clearly, in this area, as in all the other areas covered by these three articles and mentioned above, further research is needed to capture the transformations in the Jewish family.

References

Blau, Zena Smith
   1974 'The Strategy of the Jewish Mother' in M. Sklare, ed., *The Jew in American Society* (New York: Behrman House): 165-88

Cohen, Steven M.
   1988 *American Assimilation or Jewish Revival?* (Bloomington: Indiana University Press)

Cohen, Steven M. and Paula Hyman
   1986 *The Jewish Family: myths and reality* (New York: Holmes and Meier)

Howe, Irving
  1976 *World of Our Fathers* (New York: Simon and Schuster)

Koltun, Elizabeth, ed.
  1976 *The Jewish Woman: New Perspectives* (New York: Schocken)

Sklare, Marshall
  1971 *America's Jews* (New York: Random House)

Wolfenstein, Martha
  1958 'Two Types of Jewish Mothers' in M. Sklare, ed., *The Jews: Social Patterns of an American Group* (New York: The Free Press): 520–34.

Zborowski, Mark and Elizabeth Herzog
  1962 *Life is with People: The Culture of the Shtetl* (first published 1952) (New York: Schocken)

Marital Status and Fertility

Among Sub-Groups of Canadian Jews

Leo Davids

Research on the demography of the Jews in Canada (and the United States) has firmly established today's situation with regard to fertility and population size. The historical change from a traditional, high-fertility population to an extremely modern one has been well documented by Louis Rosenberg (1939, 1959) and others (Henripin, 1972; DellaPergola, 1980; Davids, 1981) who show that Jews in Canada have moved within two or three generations to a situation characterized by late marriage, low fertility, and rising divorce (Davids, 1982). Whereas the earlier generations of Jews had very few never-married people, and almost all of them became parents of at least enough children to replace themselves, the younger age groupings of Canadian Jews, almost entirely born in Canada, are characterized by a high age at marriage and very low fertility, which is far below the population replacement level (Davids, 1985). This is the trend in almost all Jewish communities outside Israel (Bachi, 1976; Schmelz, 1984).

In this respect, work on the Canadian population scene today indicates that the Jews were 'ahead of their time' in moving toward negative population growth, since the general populations of the United States and Canada are now clearly moving in that direction (Statistics Canada, 1984: 73-9). In any case, this research has established the population scene for Canadian Jewry as a whole, but there have been few attempts, in recent decades, to go inside that totality so as to look at variations among different sub-groups of Jews. We shall find that Canadian Jewry is not homogeneous in the marriage and birth areas.

This was not the case when place of birth was a key variable in research on Canadian Jews, when many comparisons were made between Jews born in Europe, versus in Canada, and those coming from other places. It is argued here that interesting and important findings can be obtained on the condition of the Canadian Jewish population and on its probable future compositions by studying the major sectors within Canadian Jewry, but we must go beyond the traditional focus on place of birth and generational categories.

There has been some interest in looking at the population structure and variations within Canadian Jewry in recent times, but little literature. James Torczyner and associates (1984) have conducted some research (on behalf of the Council of Jewish Federations, Canadian Office) in this vein. That work focused on intermarriage, as well as economic and household structure characteristics. Our focus in the present paper is on the areas of linguistics and of fertility, and we try to avoid some of the definitional decisions that Torczyner *et al.* have become involved in. We prefer to take only those of Jewish religion as our encompassing category, rather than add to the persons of Jewish religion those of Jewish ethnic origin but of no religion, as has been done by Torczyner.[1]

Data Base

Whereas very few countries outside of Israel supply highly credible statistics on Jews, the Canadian Census provides an excellent resource for population research on Jews (see Millman, 1983; Davids, 1985). Some 300,000 Jews in Canada today are identifiable by religion, and in many cases by responses to Census questions concerning ethnic origin and languages.

When one has identified Jews through the religion response on the Census, it is simple enough to obtain many other characteristics of the Jewish population from the responses to the appropriate census questions. In this paper we will examine a number of findings obtained in this way from the Canadian Census of 1981 (with occasional reference to corresponding data from the 1971 Census, to show change over the ten-year period) and examine groupings within the Jewish population of Canada in terms of age or generation, and languages. We shall focus in particular on marriage and divorce, as well as the fertility or family-size variables, to assess the population 'health' of these groupings.

Language, as a basis other than age or geography, has recently been used in an *American Jewish Year Book* overview (Davids, 1985) to examine the Jewish population. One can compare Jews by city or generation, but in order to discover differences in the area of culture or group lifestyles, it is also necessary to study cultural variables which can differentiate substantial groupings within the total Jewish population. Census data on mother tongue and language spoken at home provide an opportunity to do that. We can than identify which sectors of Canadian Jewry are likely to increase in the coming decade, which are likely to shrink, and which seem to be holding their own.

In addition to a few published Statistics Canada reports from the 1981 Census (which are referred to in the tables), this paper examines certain tabulations prepared on special order with the aid of funding from the Social Sciences and Humanities Research Council of Canada, and the Ethnic Studies Research Program of Multiculturalism Canada. Where our tables do not list a Statistics Canada publication as source, the raw data come from these special tabulations prepared by the Census Customer Service branch of Statistics Canada.

The tables themselves have been selected and 'trimmed' to present their message clearly and with very little extraneous information. Therefore, it will be enough to sum up the principal message of each table in a few sentences.

Canadian Jewish Mother Tongues

Canadian Jews are overwhelmingly of English mother tongue, but there are still substantial groups of Jews who report other mother tongues; the most important of these, numerically, are Yiddish and French. Whereas the vast majority of Canada's English mother tongue Jewish population were born in Canada (as of 1971 and 1981), this is certainly not the case for the other language groups. There is a great difference between the substantial native-born percentage that we find in regard to Yiddish, French, and (to a much smaller extent) Hebrew, versus the situation for all other languages spoken by Jews in Canada. That is, Yiddish and French clearly have some vitality as Jewish spoken languages in Canada at the present time, and therefore show a substantial proportion of their mother-tongue adherents as having been born in Canada. Hebrew occupies a much weaker position in this regard, but still appears to have some kind of living speech community in Canada, thus over 1/8th of those reporting Hebrew mother tongue are Canadian-born.

All the other languages reported as mother tongues by Canadian Jews have 3 or 4 per cent Canadian-born speakers, while 96 per cent or so were born abroad. It is a straightforward inference that, since these languages are hardly spoken in Canada (among Jews) at all, the speakers are predominantly first-generation immigrants. Thus, one can hardly predict much of a future for languages such as Hungarian or Russian among the Jews of Canada (unless large numbers of new immigrants with those languages continue to arrive in future), but there are many Canadian-born Jews who speak Yiddish and French, which suggests that these languages may continue to be significant mother tongues among Jews for some time to come.

Marital Status and Age Groups

Table 2 includes both a comparison between marital status of Jewish and all Canadians in 1981 and a clear look at age of marriage for Jews in general as opposed to those of specific language groupings. Comparing the Canadian total percentages for single, married, etc., with those for Jews indicates immediately that the Jewish population is older, and therefore has fewer never-married people in it but a significantly higher percentage of people currently married or widowed. The percentage separated or divorced among the total (all-ages) Jewish population is slightly higher than that for all Canadians.

What the rest of Table 2 indicates is that 80 per cent of Jews aged 20-24 are single. Even among Jews aged 25-34 we find about 27 per cent never-married, which suggests increasingly later marriage among the Canadian Jewish population in 1981.

Table 1 Jewish Population,[a] by Mother Tongue and Nativity, Canada, 1981

MOTHER TONGUE	TOTAL	BORN IN CANADA	PER CENT NATIVE[b]
Total Jews	296,425	187,120	63.1
English	296,825	170,590	82.5
Yiddish	30,815	9,805	31.8
French	14,920	4,240	28.4
Magyar (Hungarian)	7,525	240	3.2
Hebrew	7,510	1,020	13.6
Russian[c]	5,915	175	3.0
All others	22,915	950	4.1

[a]Religious denomination criterion, not ethnic origin.
[b]Percentage of those reporting that mother tongue born in Canada (or, second column above as a proportion of the first).
[c]Another 810 Jews report 'Ukrainian' as their mother tongue, of which 145 are Canadian-born; are many of these, perhaps, exit-visa 'Jews' finding this useful as a tool to leave the USSR, but not really Jews at all?
Source: Statistics Canada, special tabulations from the 1981 Census of Canada.

Table 2 Marital Status for All Canadians vs Several Types of Jews, by Selected Age
Groups, 1981

		NEVER MARRIED		MARRIED		SEPARATED OR DIVORCED		WIDOWED	
Total Canada	N	10,736,100		11,478,710		970,590		1,157,670	
	%	44.1		47.2		4.0		4.8	
Total Jews	N	112,405		153,265		12,485		18,275	
	%	37.9		51.7		4.2		6.2	
Age 20-24	%	80.0		19.5		0.5			
Age 25-34	%	26.9		69.3		3.7			

		M	F	M	F	M	F	M	F
English mother tongue									
Age 15-19	%	99.4	99.1	0.5	0.9	0.1	—	—	—
Age 20-24	%	89.4	74.1	10.3	23.8	0.3	2.0	—	—
Age 25-34	%	36.4	22.1	59.0	70.1	4.7	7.7	—	—
Yiddish home language[a]									
Age 15-19	%	92.0	93.0	8.0	7.0	—	—	—	—
Age 20-24	%	46.0	26.0	50.0	74.0	4.0	—	—	—
Age 25-34	%	30.0	4.0	65.0	90.0	5.0	4.0	—	—

[a]These data are of limited reliability, due to very small sample frequencies; accept only as gross approximations.
Sources: Statistics Canada, Reports of the 1981 Census, Catalogue No. 92-901; and unpublished tabulations, with author's calculations.

However, if we compare those who report Yiddish as their home language[2] with the mainstream Jews of English mother tongue, we find that Yiddish-speaking younger Jews have a relatively much earlier marriage pattern by sex. Typically, among the Yiddish-speaking Jews (Table 2) 7-8 per cent are married even before age 20, and a majority of those in the 20-24 year group are already married. Among those of Yiddish home language, married females are fully 90 per cent of the 25-34 year group, and the proportions single are much lower than they are for all Jews or for those of English mother tongue. It also appears that the percentage separated or divorced among Jews of English mother tongue aged 25-34 years is quite high (about 6-7 per cent), while those of Yiddish home language in the same age range seem to be somewhat less likely to be separated or divorced. Nevertheless, due to the small number of Yiddish-speaking cases that constitute the basis for our percentages one should not make too much of them or their differences from those Jews of English mother tongue.

All in all, Table 2 suggests that Jews both have an older population than all Canadians, and are prone to late marriage. The small sub-population reporting Yiddish home language (which, we shall be arguing, represents primarily an ultra-Orthodox group) tends toward much earlier marriage, with almost all of that population already married (or in a situation of marriage dissolution) by the time they attain age 30 or so.

Table 3 gives us the highlights regarding age structure for Jews as compared with all Canadians, and for those of English mother tongue versus those who report speaking Yiddish at home currently. The child population (aged 0-14) for all Canada in 1981 was close to 23 per cent of the entire population, but it was not quite 18 per cent for Jews as a whole. Similarly, the percentage of seniors (aged 65 +) in Canada generally is about 9 per cent, versus over 16 per cent among the Jews. However, vast differences appear when we introduce the language factor in the same way as we did in Table 2. Jews of English mother tongue have a child and senior population very close to that of Canada as a whole; the senior population among English mother tongue Jews is slightly larger than it is for all Canada and the child population slightly smaller, but these differences are trivial. However, Jews of Yiddish home language have a very small child population and are mostly aged 65 and over; among those reporting Yiddish home language, the seniors constituted fully 55 per cent (Davids, 1984). If we had only the data in Table 3, we would assume that Yiddish home language is almost entirely a geriatric phenomenon and that Yiddish home language has no future in Canada at all. This impression is somewhat erroneous, as we shall point out when we examine further data.

The Yiddish-Speaking Young Families

Table 4 gives us a census-based measure of fertility for certain types of Jews. Since we do not have vital statistics data to report Jewish fertility as we have

Table 3 Children and Seniors, for All Canadians and Several Types of Jews, 1981[a]

		TOTAL	CHILD POPULATION (AGE 0-14)	SENIOR POPULATION (AGE 65 +)
Total Canada	N	24,083,500	5,474,200	2,184,600
	%		22.7	9.1
Total Jews	N	296,400	53,100	48,700
	%		17.9	16.4
English mother tongue	N	206,000	45,300	20,300
	%		22.0	9.9
Yiddish home language	N	10,500	1,100	5,800
	%		10.5	55.2

[a]Rounded figures.
Sources: Statistics Canada, Reports of the 1981 Census, Catalogue No. 92-901; and unpublished special tabulations (December 1983), with authors' calculations.

for all of Canada, we use approximations based on the census in the same manner as demographers (e.g., Henripin, 1972) have done in the past. The Table 4 picture is one of approximately 250-300 children aged 0-4 years per 1,000 Jewish women aged 15-44 but for those of Yiddish home language the number of children per 1,000 women is 3-4 times greater. This very surprising high fertility among those of Yiddish home language indicates that the picture based on the previous table regarding the demographic features of Canada's Yiddish-home-language population is misleading.

The only sensible reconciliation of the great preponderance of seniors among those of Yiddish home language, while at the same time we have found extremely high fertility, is that we have two quite separate subpopulations which share the fact that they are Jews of Yiddish home language.

Table 4 Women Aged 15-44, Among Selected Types of Canadian Jews, with Child-Woman Ratios, 1981[a]

	TOTAL	WOMEN 15-44	CHILDREN 0-4	RATIO OF CHILDREN 0-4 PER 1,000 WOMEN 15-44
Total Jews	296,400	64,250	17,900	279
English mother tongue	206,000	50,625	15,200	300
Yiddish home language	10,500	490	550	1,122
French-Spanish-Arabic mother tongue	19,400	5,225	1,350	258

[a]Rounded figures.

The larger group consists primarily of Jews who came from Eastern Europe in the early part of this century, who are in 1981 senior citizens, but who still speak their original mother tongue as their current home language. These people had high or moderate fertility during their child-bearing years, but within the 1981 total (of those of Yiddish home language) this older group had very few children enumerated together with them. The other sub-population of Yiddish speakers, however, consists of a young, small but high-fertility ultra-Orthodox group which has been discussed in my paper concerning Yiddish in Canada (Davids, 1984). This ultra-Orthodox population has high fertility, as indicated in Table 4, but is at the present time quite small in absolute numbers and therefore does not yet have a large impact on overall child versus senior proportions, if one looks at both groups with Yiddish home language together. In coming years, no doubt, this ultra-Orthodox group will rise in the pyramid and make the entire Yiddish home language population very different from how it appeared in 1981.

Based on these an other indicators in the Census, I would estimate Canada's total ultra-Orthodox (or Hassidic) population to have been some 2,500-3,000 souls in 1981, living in 600-700 households. These households would be almost entirely families, with an average size of four or more per home, larger than for all Canada and certainly than the average Jewish household size. In the near future, we must expect substantial growth among this group.

Canada's Sephardic Jews

We now turn to the Sephardic[3] population, which is growing larger than Canada's aged Yiddish-speaking group. By and large, these Jews came from Morocco, sometimes via Israel or another country (see Lasry, 1983). The French, Spanish and Arabic mother-tongue category appears in Table 4 for the first time, but does not indicate there anything noteworthy.

Table 5 enables us to take a good look at the Sephardic population, and to separate out those of French mother tongue from those of Spanish and Arabic mother tongue. Table 5 indicates that the Jews with Arabic mother tongue in Canada are quite a small population, with a total just over 1,500; in addition, they are a highly-aged population, recording over 10 per cent widows but a very small percentage of single, never-married individuals (i.e. children and youth). However, the Jews of Spanish mother tongue number close to 3,000 in Canada and those of French mother tongue are a still more vigorous group.

Indeed, the francophone Jewish population in Canada has a very healthy demographic profile, as shown in Tables 5 and 6. With a quite small widowed group but a large single (and child) population, the French mother tongue community is doing quite well now and its outlook is good for the foreseeable future. It is noteworthy that the percentages separated or divorced among those of French mother tongue are the same as, or slightly higher than, they are for all Canadian Jews. However, our tables indicate that the

Table 5 *Jewish Population, by Marital Status and Selected Mother Tongues, Canada, 1981*

MARITAL STATUS		TOTAL	FRENCH MOTHER TONGUE	SPANISH MOTHER TONGUE	ARABIC MOTHER TONGUE
Total	N	296,425	14,915	2,890	1,560
Never married	N	112,400	6,260	885	250
	%	37.9	42.0	30.6	16.0
Married now	N	153,265	7,420	1,790	1,070
	%	51.7	49.7	61.9	68.6
Widowed	N	18,275	545	120	160
	%	6.2	3.7	4.2	10.3
Separated	N	4,545	270	55	55
	%	1.5	1.8	1.9	3.5
Divorced	N	7,940	420	40	25
	%	2.7	2.8	1.4	1.6

French mother tongue Jewish population in Canada has excellent cultural prospects for survival, which was also shown in Table 1 (where we found that over 28 per cent of Jews reporting French mother tongue were Canadian-born).

Table 6 *Jewish Population, by Selected Mother Tongues: Total, Children and Seniors, Canada, 1981*

	TOTAL	FRENCH MOTHER TONGUE	SPANISH MOTHER TONGUE	ARABIC MOTHER TONGUE
Total Jewish population	296,425	14,915	2,890	1,560
Jewish children, 0-14				
Total	53,095	3,330	380	35
0- 4	17,920	1,210	130	5
0- 9	17,330	1,155	130	—
10-14	17,845	965	120	30
As per cent of their total population	17.9	22.3	13.1	2.3
As per cent of total Jewish children	100.0	6.3	0.7	0.1
Jewish seniors, 65 +				
Total	48,700	895	285	315
As per cent of their total population	16.4	6.0	9.9	20.2

Tables 5 and 6 depict the Spanish mother tongue group as demographic-ally quite traditional; it is also a much more aged group than the French. Those reporting Spanish mother tongue had a relatively small percentage of never-married people, as well as a much lower divorced percentage than for all Canadian Jews, or those of French mother tongue. The child proportion for the Spanish group, as shown in Table 6, is quite weak. Again, however, we must be careful not to read too much into percentages when the actual number of cases is so small.

What we can conclude from Tables 5 and 6 is that the Sephardic population of Canada (where we put together all Jews of French, Spanish and Arabic mother tongue) is primarily a French-speaking group, which may be due either to immigration patterns — where French was the original language abroad and has been retained in Canada — or to the fact that French is an official language in Canada and therefore has much more favourable condi-tions for schooling and language retention than is the case for the other languages. However that may be, one would not predict a bright future for Spanish among the Jews in Canada. One the other hand it appears that French is doing very well among those (in Montreal) who find French both fashionable and useful, and by no means a disadvantage as their children's mother tongue.

It is also useful to look more closely at marital status for young adults in the peak procreative years, in relation to recent concerns about mature 'singles' with concomitant low fertility. Table 7 presents marital status for all Canadian Jews versus Sephardim (i.e., those of French, Spanish, and Arabic mother tongue) in the 25-34 and 35-44 age categories. It shows that this Sephardic population has earlier marriage tendencies and less divorce than the majority Jewish community, and thus a better fertility potential.

However, small sub-groups in Table 7 show variations from the above favourable pattern — e.g., the high percentage of separated in the 25-34 age group of Spanish mother tongue. (With so few cases, these variations are of limited significance.)

Before concluding this examination of demographic prospects for the Sephardic population, note that the French-speaking Jews of Canada are heavily concentrated in the city of Montreal. Although Montreal also has a substantial population of Jews with Spanish mother tongue, the concentra-tion of Jews in that city is much greater for the French and Arabic than the Spanish group. As above, the Arabic mother tongue population is mainly concentrated in Montreal but is a small component of the Canadian Jewish community.

Specifically, 69 per cent of the Jewish population with Arabic mother tongue in 1971 lived in Montreal, while in 1981 something over 76 per cent of Canadian Jews reporting Arabic mother tongue were located there. A still greater concentration is the case for Jewish francophones, 77 per cent of whom were residents of Montreal in 1971 and just under 80 per cent in 1981. However, for those of Spanish mother tongue we find that just over 37 per

Table 7 *Jewish Population, by Selected Mother Tongue and Age Groups, and Marital Status, Canada, 1981*

MARITAL	TOTAL		FRENCH MOTHER TONGUE		SPANISH MOTHER TONGUE		ARABIC MOTHER TONGUE	
	N	%	N	%	N	%	N	%
AGE 25-34 YEARS								
Total	52,190	100.0	3,040	100.0	685	100.0	3,725	100.0
Never married	13,530	25.9	710	23.4	130	19.0	840	22.6
Married	35,225	67.5	2,150	70.7	510	74.4	2,660	71.4
Separated	1,415	2.7	65	2.1	35	5.1	100	2.7
Divorced	1,950	3.7	115	3.8	10	1.5	125	3.4
Widowed	70	0.1	—	—	—	—	—	—
AGE 35-44 YEARS								
Total	34,085	100.0	2,685	100.0	425	100.0	3,110	100.0
Never married	2,510	7.4	180	6.7	40	9.4	220	7.1
Married	28,050	82.3	2,305	85.8	380	89.4	2,685	86.3
Separated	1,265	3.7	90	3.4	5	1.2	95	3.1
Divorced	1,980	5.8	100	3.7	—	—	100	3.2
Widowed	280	0.8	10	0.4	—	—	10	0.3

cent lived in Montreal in 1971, while in 1981 only 35 per cent of Jews were residents there, while over 50 per cent (1,460 persons) lived in Toronto. This suggests that the westward movement of Jews which was noted in the late 1970s (Davids, 1985: 192) also led to a slight deconcentration of Spanish-speaking Jews from Montreal, but this certainly did not occur among those of French mother tongue.

In short, it seems clear that the favourable environment of Montreal both attracts francophone Jews and encourages French language retention among Jews there, while French-speaking Jews in Toronto or other Jewish centres outside of Quebec are no doubt far less likely to retain that language in the long run.

There is an unmeasured but substantial Sephardic component among those of Hebrew mother tongue in Canada. Although one can safely say that the origin of many Canadians reporting Hebrew mother tongue is North Africa (or the Middle East), we cannot specify how many of those with Hebrew mother tongue are of Sephardic origin. Nevertheless, it may be noted that about 34 per cent of those reporting Hebrew mother tongue in 1981 were residents of Montreal, which is very close to the Spanish mother tongue proportion. Thus, Montreal is the most important Sephardic centre in Canada. When we specify Jews of French mother tongue we find 80 per cent in Montreal, versus 20 per cent (including just over 2,000 in Toronto) throughout the rest of Canada.

Summary and Conclusion

Using religion and language data from the Canadian Census, with a few easily defended postulates regarding who speaks what, we have begun to map out the heterogeneous cultural composition of Canadian Jewry. What of the foreseeable future? What is likely to happen, demographically, during the next 10-25 years?

Briefly, it looks as if the major sub-groups we have examined in this paper will increase their proportions in the total Canadian Jewish community of a generation or so hence, while the mainstream Jewish population — of East European descent but now very 'Canadianized' — will lose ground both absolutely and relatively. This majority within Canadian Jewry shows all the demographic weaknesses that Schmelz (1984) and others have so clearly indicated in Diaspora Jewry: late marriage, low total fertility, high average age with a large (and rapidly growing) senior population, and consequently a diminishing parental group and net population shrinkage.

However, the ultra-Orthodox (i.e. younger Yiddish-speaking) and the francophone Sephardic groups we have focused on show excellent survival capacity (reinforced by high residential concentration) in their tendency to earlier marriage, higher fertility, few seniors, and good in-group retention of children born to them. In a few decades, the expansion of these groups will enhance Canadian Jewry's heterogeneity, and the consequent population shifts will no doubt have their internal educational, 'political', and other ramifications (see Schoenfeld and Davids, 1984).

It hardly needs stating that the strategies we have employed in this paper can and should be used for research on/with other groups and future censuses. This kind of research is very cost-effective and vital both for understanding the past developments which explain today's realities, and for indicating the likely trends of the hereby foreseeable future.

Notes

[1]If we include all those who report Jewish religion, whether synagogue-affiliated or 'practising' or not, but do not include others — which obviously encompasses all sorts of Jews — we save entanglement in some doubtful calculations while excluding few people who would consider themselves a part of the Canadian Jewish community and whose life (and demographic) choices are likely to have an impact on the shape of Canadian Jewry in future years. That is, one may reasonably assume that those not reporting Jewish religion are perhaps not so relevant to the future evolution of Canadian Jewry, as it is doubtful that their descendants will stay part of the Jewish population in Canada. While this assumption would not hold true in certain specialized instances, most notably the Jewish immigrants who have come during the 1970s and subsequently from the USSR (where Jewish ethnic origin may be the more appropriate criterion), it is safe to say that if a person of Jewish ethnic origin reports himself not to be of Jewish religion, then he — or his descendants — are likely to be outside the organized Jewish community.

[2]Rather than Yiddish mother tongue, which indicates a biographical-historical reality that may have no meaning today, we focus on home language and age to locate the currently traditional group, still involved with the *shtetl* (East European Jewish) culture.

[3]'Sephardim', in the narrow sense, are Jews of Spanish (or Portuguese) descent. Most references now use the term loosely or broadly to include all Mediterranean and Oriental Jews. That usage means not only those speaking Iberian languages, but Jews who may speak Arabic, French, Italian, Turkish, and other Near- or Middle-Eastern languages. It is impractical (for cost reasons) to research all of these.

References

Bachi, R.
   1976 *Population Trends of World Jewry*. Jewish Population Studies, No. 9 (Jerusalem: Institute of Contemporary Jewry, The Hebrew University)

Davids, L.
   1981 'The Family' in M. Weinfeld *et al.*, eds, *Canadian Jewish Mosaic* (Toronto: Wiley): 97–112

————
   1982 'Divorce and Remarriage Among Canadian Jews', *Journal of Comparative Family Studies* 13, 1: 37–47

1984 'Yiddish in Canada: Picture and Prospects', *Canadian Ethnic Studies* 16, 2: 89-101

1985 'Canadian Jewry: Some Recent Census Findings' in *American Jewish Year Book*, Vol. 85: 191-201

DellaPergola, S.
1980 'Patterns of American Jewish Fertility', *Demography*, 17, 3: 261-73.

Henripin, J.
1972 *Trends and Factors of Fertility in Canada* (Ottawa: Statistics Canada)

Lasry, J.-C.
1981 'A Francophone Diaspora in Quebec' in M. Weinfeld *et al.*, eds, *Canadian Jewish Mosaic* (Toronto: Wiley): 221-40

Millman, I.I.
1983 'Data on Diaspora Jewish Populations from Official Censuses' in U.O. Schmelz *et al.*, eds, *Studies in Jewish Demography* (New York: Ktav): 33-120

Rosenberg, L.
1939 *Canada's Jews: A Social and Economic Study of the Jews in Canada* (Montreal: Bureau of Social and Economic Research, Canadian Jewish Congress)

1959 'The Demography of the Jewish Community in Canada', *Jewish Journal of Sociology* 1, 2: 217-33

Schmelz, U.O.
1984 *Aging of World Jewry*. Jewish Population Studies, no. 15 (Jerusalem: Institute of Contemporary Jewry, The Hebrew University)

Schoenfeld, S. and L. Davids
1984 'Judaism' in M.L. Holten, ed., *Spirit of Toronto 1834-1984* (Toronto: Image Publishing Company)

Statistics Canada
1984 *Report on the Demographic Situation in Canada 1983. Supply and Services* (Ottawa: Statistics Canada, Catalogue No. 91-209E).

Torczyner, J.L. *et al.*
1984 *The Jewish Family in Canada 1981* (Toronto/Montreal: Canadian Jewish Congress and Canadian Office, Council of Jewish Federations)

The author gratefully acknowledges financial support for this research from Multiculturalism Canada and from the Social Sciences and Humanities Research Council of Canada.

If I Cannot Dance to It, It's Not My Revolution:

Jewish Feminism in Canada Today

Sheva Medjuck

There is probably not a Jewish feminist in Canada today who at some point or another has not been asked 'Is feminism good for the Jews?' When the question was first posed twenty years ago, Jewish feminists were indulgent and explained in painstaking detail that feminism was a major positive force in both secular and Jewish life and could contribute a new richness to Judaism. Not only have the voices of Jewish women not been heard, but also many members of the Jewish establishment are now blaming feminism for the 'crisis' in Jewish life. We shall argue in this article that feminism is not a threat to Jewish survival, a danger to be opposed, but rather a vital cause to be supported by the entire Jewish community.

For Jewish feminists, there has been a constant tension in our lives, an ongoing dissonance between our identities as Jews and our identities as women. For most Jewish feminists, there seems to be an inherent conflict between our interests as women and our interests as Jews (Schneider, 1985: 504). In the early years of the feminist movement, many Jewish women attempted to resolve this conflict by dismissing their Jewish identities and abandoning Judaism as hopelessly patriarchal and not worth the struggle. Increasingly, Jewish women are refusing to 'make the choice' between their commitment to feminism and to Judaism. We are no less Jews as feminists and no less feminists as Jews. We recognize that we must fight against the anti-Semitism of the feminist movement and the sexism of Jews and will not be denied our identity by either group. 'In the life of a Jewish woman there is not a Jewish self separate from a female self. Being a Jewish woman or a female Jew is a totality and all experience is filtered through that integrated reality' (Greenberg, 1986: 180).

There is certainly no doubt that Jewish women in Canada today share many of the same goals and aspirations as their non-Jewish sisters. Educational and occupational successes (see below) have 'resulted in Jewish women embracing feminism on a scale unparalleled by other ethnic groups' (Draper, 1983: 7). Jewish women, like many other minority women, however, have the added burden of trying to explain their loyalty to feminist principles to their own ethnic community, as if to support women's issues is somehow Jewish treason. Feminism does not threaten Judaism in any way. To the question 'Is feminism good for the Jews?' the answer is that it is *essential* for Judaism to continue to be relevant to our lives.

Jewish Women in Canada: Secular Advances

It is now common knowledge that in the past few decades Jews have taken full advantage of the educational and occupational opportunities available to them and have achieved considerable upward mobility. Occupational pro-files in the 1986 census indicate the occupational success of Jews. When, for example, Jewish occupational profiles are compared with Canadians who trace their ancestry to one of the two founding groups, the British, we see that only 13.3 per cent of British men are managerial, compared to 26 per cent of Jewish men; and only 8.2 per cent of British women are managerial compared to 14.1 per cent of Jewish women (Table 1). At the same time it is interesting to point out that labour force participation rates hardly differ between the two groups. Some 77.4 per cent of Jewish men and 58.6 per cent of Jewish women compared to 77.7 per cent of British men and 57.1 per cent of British women are in the labour force.

These data present a somewhat different picture if we compare the occu-pational achievement of Jewish women with that of Jewish men. The ratio of the percentage of Jewish men managers to the percentage of Jewish women managers is 1.8 (i.e., Jewish men are almost twice as likely as Jewish women to be managers). When we look at the same data for British men and women, we see that this ratio is only 1.6 (British men are slightly more than one and a half times as likely to be managers as are British women). On a comparative basis, therefore, British women are doing somewhat better than Jewish women when compared to men in their same ethnic group. On a more encouraging note, the gap between Jewish men and women in high status jobs has decreased considerably. In 1971, for example, Jewish men were over three times as likely to be managerial as were Jewish women (15.5 per cent compared to 4.7 per cent were managers) (Census of Canada, 1971), while by 1981 this ratio had shrunk to slightly less than two and a half (25.4 per cent compared to 10.4 per cent) (Torczyner, 1983: 20-1). Nevertheless, in 1986 almost one-third of Jewish women were still in clerical jobs. The 'distance' between Jewish men and Jewish women in terms of occupational achievement in 1986 is still considerable.

Jewish occupational achievement can, in part, be understood by educa-tional success. The 1986 census reports that 34 per cent of Jewish males and 23.8 per cent of Jewish females (over 15) had completed university. We can appreciate this figure by comparing it to the figures for those of British ethnicity—11.7 per cent of men and 8.4 per cent of women of British ethnicity completed university (Table 2). Jews are almost three times as likely to have university degrees as those of British ethnicity. However, we see a considerable gap between Jewish women and Jewish men. Jewish men are almost one and a half times as likely to have a university degree as Jewish

Table 1 Occupation by Sex, Jewish and British, 1986 Census 15 Years and Over
and in the Labour Force

| | JEWISH | | | BRITISH | | |
OCCUPATION	TOTAL	MALE	FEMALE	TOTAL	MALE	FEMALE
Managerial	20.8	26.0	14.1	11.1	13.3	8.2
Professional	28.9	28.1	30.1	16.8	13.2	21.3
Clerical	17.5	7.1	31.0	19.2	7.0	34.8
Sales	17.0	18.5	15.0	9.5	9.2	9.9
Service	5.4	5.0	6.0	12.4	10.0	15.6
Primary	0.7	1.0	0.4	5.7	8.2	2.4
Processing	1.4	2.0	0.5	4.9	7.0	2.1
Product fabr'ng	3.2	4.5	1.4	6.2	9.2	2.3
Construction	1.6	2.7	0.1	5.5	9.5	2.3
Other	3.5	5.0	1.5	8.8	13.4	3.0
Total	100.0%	99.9%	100.1%	100.1%	100.0%	100.0%

women. Jewish cultural norms reinforce the general societal discrimination against women and higher education. For example, the warnings of parents and grandparents to their Jewish daughters and granddaughters to be smart, but not too smart, lest we educate ourselves right out of the marriage market, are still fresh in our minds. (Does this mean that marriage is a job in which a PhD overqualifies you?) Nevertheless, compared to their non-Jewish sisters, Jewish women have achieved overwhelming educational success.

Not surprisingly, in light of the above, 1986 income data on Jewish men and women indicate a considerable distance between them. As Table 3 indicates, for those who have incomes, the median salary for Jewish men is almost twice that of Jewish women ($25,439 and $13,343 respectively).

Table 2 Education by Sex, Jewish and British, 1986 Census 15 Years and Over

| | JEWISH | | | BRITISH | | |
EDUCATION	TOTAL	MALE	FEMALE	TOTAL	MALE	FEMALE
< grade 9	9.3	8.8	9.7	11.2	12.1	10.5
Some High School	19.9	18.9	20.9	31.4	30.3	32.4
High School	10.5	8.5	12.4	12.7	11.1	14.2
Trade certificate	1.2	1.5	0.9	2.7	4.0	1.6
Other non-certificate	5.8	5.2	6.5	6.8	6.2	7.3
Other certificate	8.8	7.5	10.1	15.3	14.7	15.9
Some university	15.5	15.5	15.5	9.8	9.9	9.7
University	28.9	34.0	23.8	10.0	11.7	8.4
Total	99.9%	99.9%	99.8%	100.0%	100.0%	100.0%

Table 3   Income by Sex, Jewish and British, 1986 Census 15 Years and Over with Income

INCOME	JEWISH			BRITISH		
	TOTAL	MALE	FEMALE	TOTAL	MALE	FEMALE
< $15,000	43.2	33.2	54.1	52.1	38.6	66.4
15–19,999	10.0	8.1	11.9	11.1	10.2	12.0
20–24,999	8.5	7.9	9.2	9.2	9.9	8.5
25–29,999	6.9	7.2	6.6	7.5	9.7	5.1
30–34,999	6.0	6.9	5.2	6.2	8.9	3.3
35,000 +	25.2	36.8	13.1	13.8	22.5	14.6
Total	99.8%	100.1%	100.1%	99.9%	99.8%	99.9%
Average	28,609	38,055	18,703	18,688	24,160	12,929
Median	18,201	25,439	13,343	14,049	20,445	9,802
Standard error	206	374	132	15	25	12

Figures for these tables are calculated from data in *Profile of Ethnic Groups*, Census Canada 1986, CS 93-154, Statistics Canada, 1986.

Similarly, while 54.1 per cent of Jewish women have incomes of less than $15,000, only 33.2 per cent of Jewish men have such incomes. While Jewish women have incomes that are higher than their non-Jewish sisters, their incomes are still considerably less than that of Jewish men.

This very brief profile suggests that Jewish women, while not as occupationally mobile as their Jewish brothers, have nevertheless attained a fair degree of educational and occupational success. Almost 60 per cent (58.6) of Jewish women over 15 years of age are in the paid labour force. Married women continue their labour force participation after marriage as is indicated by an over 60 per cent labour force participation rate among married Jewish women. Jewish women are increasingly participating in the educational and occupational structures of the larger society. Although clearly affected by the discrimination against women found in the society as a whole, Jewish women have found considerable success both educationally and occupationally. What is the relationship between these secular successes and their lives as Jewish women?

Jewish Women and the Jewish Family

The Nuclear Family and the Jewish Woman

The increased educational aspirations, increased labour force participation, and career orientation of Canadian Jewish women have far outpaced changes in their status in the Jewish family. The family is the arena in which the conflict between Jewish women's educational and occupational aspirations and Judaism is most often played out. Feminism has been seen as a particular threat to the Jewish family because it forces us to re-evaluate the traditional male-female roles within the family. While many women experience enormous pressures from their increasing participation in the paid labour market and their virtually unchanging family responsibilities, this burden is especially difficult for Jewish women in that Judaism has put a very strong emphasis on the family's responsibility as the transmitter of Jewish values. While historically the Jewish family was seen as the haven from external oppression, currently in Canada it is seen as the primary mechanism to counter assimilation.

The 'family', however, in this context, is simply a euphemism for women's domestic labour. The alarmists in the Jewish community suggest that the women's movement has put the Jewish family under attack and as such an important vehicle for Jewish continuity is being eroded. Lost in all this panic about feminism undermining the foundations of Judaism, is any discussion of men's role in the family. As Schneider argues:

> Why all the emphasis *now* on the importance of family in Jewish life? With appropriate uneasiness, Jewish feminists suggest that the hue and cry is a reaction to the emergence of Jewish women into the labor force from their typical roles in the American [and as we noted above in the Canadian] family of the past forty years. . . . when Jewish men moved into the mainstream of American life from the 1920s to 1945, no one called a conference to examine how *their* actions were subverting the traditional Jewish male values of study and religious observance. (1985: 256)

As we noted above, Canadian Jewish men have achieved a high level of material success. The Jewish community prides itself on this success, particularly when juxtaposed against the anti-Semitism encountered along the way. However, it is curious that it is rarely pointed out that the success of Canadian Jewish men in the secular society has transformed their roles within Judaism. As Rela Geffen Monson suggests:

> [t]he father who was concerned with *kashrut* in the home, the quality and quantity of Jewish learning of his children and in their emotional, ethical and intellectual growth as Jews, was replaced by the one who provided the money so that secondary institutions and surrogate teachers and models could do this job for him, under the direction and coordination of the mother. (cited in Schneider, 1985: 282)

There is little doubt that in the majority of Canadian homes today, the role of the Jewish father has been severely altered. In the past, a Jewish father was responsible for the education of his children (or at least his sons) and was expected to socialize them to Jewish values. Even the Talmud states that the responsibilities of the Jewish father include teaching his son Torah and a trade (Kiddushin 29a). Historically, the Jewish father was a mentor, not necessarily a provider. This role of the Jewish father, however, virtually disappeared as more and more Jewish men refocused their energies to occupational and material success. Canadian Jewish fathers do not differ in any major way from non-Jewish fathers (Waxman, 1988: 60). As Rabbi Michael Gold succinctly summarizes the contemporary role of fathers: 'Fatherhood in modern life entails two major tasks: being a semen donor and a bread winner' (Gold, 1988: 85). While there is enormous concern among Jewish leaders about women's increasing labour market participation and its apparent consequences on Jewish family life, no parallel questions are being asked about Jewish men's responsibility for the Jewish home. The patriarchal nature of the Canadian Jewish community has simply assumed that Jewish women are primarily responsible for Jewish family life.

The discussion of the 'family' (i.e., women's domestic role) by Jewish leaders reaches its most fevered pitch when discussing the Jewish birth rate, a popular theme in almost every rabbi's sermons. Jewish women are often blamed for the falling Jewish birth rate. Rather than understanding these demographic changes in terms of the larger context in which they occur, this decline is frequently laid on the shoulders of women (or more correctly, in their wombs). The 'narcissism and self-centredness' of Jewish women is pitted against the needs of the Jewish community.

Most Jewish women have not abandoned the family in their quest for careers. However, there is a conflict between career aspirations and domestic responsibilities. Jewish women are having fewer children not because they have suddenly become narcissistic, but because the larger community (both Jewish and secular) has failed to provide any reasonable solutions to the conflict between home and labour-market responsibilities. Davids (1989: 56) concludes that

> Parenthood is not popular, it is looked down upon and barely tolerated by large segments of the public in western countries and generally in the developed world. It is important to recognize that Diaspora Jewry is very much part of the industrialized world in a psychological and cultural sense, and so this attitude toward parenting (versus other kinds of activities) shows up in an even more marked and definite way when we look at secular 'mainstream' Jewish behaviour in this area.

It is not that parenting is unpopular, but rather that it is increasingly difficult for women to combine child care responsibilities with the demands of the labour market. We cannot encourage Jewish women to be occupationally and economically successful without redefining their domestic responsibilities. Jewish women are expected to undertake more schooling, increased labour-force participation, longer work hours, more demanding and stressful jobs, etc. without any changes to the Jewish family. The burden on Jewish women is simply too overwhelming.

The socioeconomic realities of Jewish women's lives in Canada today require that solutions must be found in the community and not in the personal sacrifices of already overworked Jewish women. Why is the major burden of guilt and responsibility placed on Jewish women? Why are Canadian Jewish men not made to feel guilty for this decline in the birth rate? Are they not also parents? If the Canadian Jewish establishment really feels that the declining birth rate is a problem for continued Jewish existence, then why are men not to blame? Or indeed, why is the entire Jewish community not to blame for its failure to provide necessary services to Jewish families? Why are we not focusing our concern on the failures of Jewish education, or on the lack of services to Jewish families, or on the erosion of Jewish identity among alienated Jewish women (an issue which is almost always overlooked in these discussions)?

> Perhaps if it were clear to a whole generation of Jewish women that the men they'll marry will share the responsibility of parenthood and not just sit on committees or play racquetball, they'd view motherhood more auspiciously. (Schneider, 1985: 388)

While some analysts of Jewish demographic trends have suggested ways of countering declining birth rates in the Jewish community, rarely do these recommendations include a radical rethinking of the position of Jewish women within the family. For example, Davids (1989: 58) suggests that education (especially outreach) is important in population retention. In addition, he argues that Jewish bodies should provide support programs to make the stresses of parenthood in modern society easier to live with. These types of proposals do not address the concrete realities of Jewish women's lives. Without major rethinking of our cultural and social norms, women remain the primary caregivers to their families and as such carry the major burden of child care. We must not assign blame for low Jewish birth rates to Jewish women. As Canadian Jewish women increasingly participate in the paid labour force, we cannot expect them to continue to bear the full weight of family responsibilities. Canadian Jewish women are not the scapegoats for problems in the larger Jewish community. We cannot continue to bear all the guilt for problems that Jewish men and the Jewish community as a whole refuse to address. Family life cannot be built on a relationship which oppresses women. The time is long past when the entire community must share the *Angst* around Jewish family life.

Included in this *Angst*, we now also must consider the problem of domestic violence against women. The Jewish home is supposed to be a sanctuary but, unfortunately, we are confronted by Jewish domestic violence. At a recent presentation on the need for transition houses for Jewish women (Halifax, 1991) many in the audience were incredulous at Jewish wife abuse. The stereotype of Jewish men is that they make wonderful husbands who revere their wives. The reality is that for many Jewish women their homes have become places of terror. The Jewish community in Canada seems reluctant to acknowledge Jewish domestic violence, often in the mistaken belief that it will contribute to anti-Semitism. Jewish women's lives are risked in our concern over what our non-Jewish neighbours will think of us.

'Admitting a violation of "shalom bait"' (peace in the home) is an embarrassing *shanda* (disgrace)' (Gluck, 1988: 168).

Alternative Family Forms and Jewish Women

Jewish women who are not in traditional nuclear families find their status even more problematic in many ways than do their married sisters. Marriage is considered the normative state, and a single Jewish woman is often a nonperson in the Jewish community. She is often perceived as being in a holding pattern, waiting to marry. In and of herself, she is less than a legitimate person. The heroine of Gail Parent's *Sheila Levine is Dead and Living in New York* cannot even buy a single cemetery plot for herself in which her body can rest after she commits suicide because 'The problem is, dear, we don't cater to single people. All the plots are double' (Parent, 1973). Single Jewish women express profound alienation from the Jewish community. A single woman has little context in which to be a Jew. While single Jewish men are part of the community in that they count in any *minyan* (quorum of ten needed for communal prayer), for single Jewish women 'there's no ecological niche, no community, in which she can express her Jewish identity' (Schneider, 1985: 306).

Jewish widows often feel that their connectedness to Judaism is severed when their husbands die. In a study by Robin Siegal, one woman reported that her synagogue took away her seats after her husband died and gave them to 'a family' (Siegal, 1979). Single Jewish mothers, however, fare the worst of all single Jewish women. Rabbi Sol M. Roth, Honorary President of the (Orthodox) Rabbinical Council of America, wrote in 1982 that 'The synagogue must preserve standards. It is concerned with norms, and a "normal" Jewish life is not the single parent' (Roth, 1982). Single-parent families 'have a greater tendency to withdraw from synagogues and other Jewish institutions . . .' (Davids, 1981: 107). One may question whether they 'withdraw' or whether they are 'cast out of' the Jewish community. While other single Jewish women may be non-entities, single Jewish mothers are outcasts. If the Jewish community is, in fact, a community that serves all Jews, then it will have to redefine its 'couples only' orientation in ways that speak to all Jews irrespective of life style or living arrangement.

Obviously feminism does not offer a panacea for all the ills that affect the contemporary Jewish family. However, feminist principles provide an important ideological basis for transforming the patriarchal structure of the family and ensuring greater gender equality. Feminism has had a major impact on the lives of many Jewish women and on how they conceive of their relationships within the family. Failure to embrace feminist principles of gender equality in the family will lead to the continuing alienation of women from Judaism. Since Jewish survival depends to a large extent on the commitment of these women, feminist ideology must be incorporated into Judaism.

Canadian Jewish Women and Religious Law

With the increased participation of women in the larger secular society, the position of women in traditional Jewish law becomes increasingly problematic. As Blu Greenberg suggests:

> Today while secular society has opened up a new range of real roles and psychological expectations to women, the halakhic status and religious life of Jewish women remain circumscribed. It is like sitting in a stationary car alongside a moving one: the effect upon one passenger is a sense of moving backwards: upon the other, a sense of pulling away, of losing connection, of leaving behind. (1981: 5)

While there are numerous aspects of Jewish *halacha* (law) which create major problems for Jewish feminists (most particularly Orthodox Jewish feminists), perhaps the two which have received most widespread attention are the laws surrounding Jewish divorce (*get*) and the laws excluding women from being counted in the quorum of ten necessary for communal prayer (*minyan*).

Divorce

There is little debate that the laws with respect to the *get* are oppressive to Jewish women. According to Jewish law, a man may issue a divorce decree to his wife, but she cannot issue a divorce decree to her husband, although she must accept it for it to become final. The power is still in the husband's hands as only he can issue such a decree. One of the first studies of the impact of *get* conflicts in Canada was undertaken by B'nai B'rith Canada (B'nai B'rith, 1987). The study, using 25 lawyers and 7 rabbis from across Canada as respondents, sought to ascertain the degree to which the *get* was being used as a bargaining tool in Jewish divorce proceedings. The study cites cases in which husbands refused to grant a *get* unless their wives' family provided substantial monetary compensation and cases in which husbands would issue a *get* only if their wives withdrew all claims for any support. The study identified 311 cases in which there was conflict over the *get*, 48 per cent due to the *get* being used for spite or vengeance, and 28 per cent attributed to the *get* being used as a bargaining tool in maintenance and matrimonial property disputes. There was a delay in 202 cases because of the husband's refusal to grant a *get*, while 92 cases were delayed because the wife refused to consent to a *get*. Interestingly, 80 per cent of the cases reported by lawyers but only 61 per cent of the cases reported by rabbis were attributable to a man's refusal to grant a *get*. (Perhaps, the patriarchal structure of Jewish religious life alienates women from the Jewish establishment and thus they seek help with their *get* through lawyers rather than through rabbis. Men feel more integrated into synagogue life and more comfortable with rabbis, and hence seek help with their *get* problems from rabbis.)

Both the lawyers and the rabbis in the B'nai B'rith study seem to concur that women suffer far more from *get* conflicts (a recognition of little comfort to women trapped by their husbands). Among the rabbis, the situation was described as unjust, wherein the majority of women were given 'the short end of the straw' (1987: 15). Similarly, lawyers also note the enormous stress that the *get* puts on women. As one lawyer noted, women suffered the greatest emotional and social stress. Over 70 per cent of his Jewish female clients with *get* problems endure 'emotionally dramatic breakdown' as they cannot remarry.

In Canada, as elsewhere, Jewish women have had very little leverage in trying to convince recalcitrant husbands to grant them a *get*. Although, in some instances, rabbis and other members of the Jewish community have attempted to put pressure on the husband to grant a *get*, not surprisingly this strategy has been largely unsuccessful. Pressure from rabbis and other members of the Jewish community carries no particular sanctions and in a society such as Canada where most of the rewards come from the larger secular society, the power of the Jewish community is insufficient to convince these men to change their minds. Beyond this ineffectual social pressure, the religious establishment in Canada seems unwilling to intervene in the *get* issue in a way that would alleviate the grief experienced by these women.

In Canada the civil courts have been brought in to help resolve the issue of the *get*. In 1986 Ontario introduced legislation under the Family Law Act which required an applicant to file a statement indicating that they 'have removed all barriers that are within his or her control and that would prevent the other spouse's remarriage within that spouse's faith'. If a party fails to comply with this, and if the party is an applicant, the proceedings may be dismissed (as cited in B'nai B'rith, 1987: 8). Following this lead, the Canadian Government amended the Divorce Act (Chapter 18 was given royal assent on 12 June 1990 and proclaimed in force on 12 August 1990). This legislation allowed the divorce courts to require affidavits indicating that barriers to remarriage within the deponent's religion had been removed by the applicant and empowering the courts to dismiss any application for failure to comply with this requirement (An Act to Amend the Divorce Act, Chapter 18, section 2, subsections 2-4).

It is interesting to note that the civil courts do not see this involvement with the *get* procedure as interfering with religious law. In the Superior Court of New Jersey, Justice Minuskin ruled that the *get* is a release document from a contractual relationship devoid of religious connotation (180 N.J. Super 260, 434A. 2d, 665 [1981] as cited in Bleich, 1984: 265). The Canadian provisions indicate that it is the court that will determine if the spouse has genuine grounds of a religious or conscientious nature for refusing to remove barriers to remarriage (Subsection 4[a] and [b]). The Ontario legislation was based on the premise that the *get* is essentially a rescission of a contract whereby the parties themselves, not an ecclesiastic tribunal, execute the *get* (B'nai B'rith, 1987: 10). The *get* is simply a contract, not an expression of religious faith. If this argument has merit (as our various judicial systems seem to believe), then it is curious that the Jewish religious establishment is reluctant to interfere with the rules governing *get*. Surely, Jewish religious life would not in any way be compromised if the rules governing contracts were to be modified. It speaks rather harshly to the Jewish community's concern for women's lives, when Jewish women must turn to the civil courts in order to attempt to resolve the issue of *get*. The civil courts have gone where the Jewish establishment has feared to tread.

The minyan

The second most controversial issue with respect to Jewish women and religious law concerns the issue of participation in ritual services, especially the *minyan*. In Orthodox Jewish law a quorum of ten men is required for community prayer and thus community comes to be defined in terms of male participation only. While the Conservative, Reform, and Reconstructionist branches of Judaism have moved some way in counting women for the quorum, even in these cases the old baggage seems to survive. There are very few synagogues in Canada today in which women participate as full equals in all aspect of prayer. One Canadian woman expressed her dismay when, after being refused an *aliyah* (blessing over the Torah) by the rabbi (Conservative) at her nephew's Bar Mitzvah (even though she herself had her Bat Mitzvah at this very synagogue), she was instead afforded the honour of pouring tea at the luncheon that followed. On the Bar Mitzvah of her second nephew, she was, in fact, granted an *aliyah*, although she was the first woman to have participated in the services of this synagogue. Although this can be considered a step in the right direction, it would be nice 'to be at a service where the men are holding the babies and the women are holding the Torahs' (Schneider, 1985: 65). The exclusion that many Jewish women feel is exemplified by the comments of this Toronto Jewish woman:

> The synagogue I used to attend was the one in which my parents were married, my brothers celebrated their Bar Mitzvah, and I was named and married. When I was pregnant I told myself that if it were a girl I would find a more progressive synagogue because I wanted to assure my daughter greater equality in her Jewish life. My family was devastated. My grandfather, in an attempt to restore *shalom bait*, concluded that it was not so terrible. Since I would stay if I had a son, he and my father would still have the pleasure of sitting with him in synagogue, of seeing him *davening* (praying), of seeing him learn his Bar Mitzvah. I realized that implicit in this was that they would not really miss much if I had a daughter and left their synagogue because her participation in synagogue life was so minimal. This argument convinced me to change synagogues no matter the sex of my child. I wanted my child to understand equality. (personal communication, 1989)

When this issue of equal participation was raised at a Canadian conference of Jewish leaders, the standard response from many Jewish men was that women are *lucky* that they do not have the obligation to participate and did women really want to have to get up and run to *shul* (synagogue) at 7 o'clock in the morning. This response suggests that women are currently lying in bed to all hours of the morning. A great many Jewish women would gladly trade the peace and tranquillity, as well as the sociability, of a morning *minyan* for the chaos of trying to get husband and children and themselves dressed, fed, and off to work or school, or of an evening *minyan* rather than scurrying around trying to make dinner for a hungry family after having just returned from her paid job. It also assumes that Jewish men unfailingly fulfil this *mitzvah*. Of course, without gender equality in the home, in fact, women will not be able to be full participants in the *minyan*. It is hard to reach God in prayer when your baby is crying in your arms or your children are badgering you.

The problem of full participation in religious life can nowhere be better illustrated then in the saying of *Kaddish*, the memorial prayer for the dead. One Orthodox woman living in a small Canadian city retells the story of her father's *Kaddish*:

> I was only sixteen when my father died quite suddenly, leaving my mother to raise three daughters. When the men came for the *minyan* at our house during *shiva* (period of mourning), they chased my mother, my sisters, and me from the living room into the hallway during services. I was devastated. I was a mourner. What was I doing cowering in the hallway, while unknown men were saying the *Kaddish* for *my* father? At the *minyan* the following day I refused to leave the room. I stayed and said *Kaddish*, but they pretended I did not exist. I felt like an outcast. My mother, whose grief was inconsolable, was asked if she would like to hire a Yeshiva boy to say *Kaddish* for the year, since she *only* had three daughters. I felt abandoned by Judaism on that day. (personal communication, 1991)

The brilliant film, *Half the Kingdom*, by Canadian filmmaker Francine Zuckerman, documents a similar case of a Jewish woman who would not be deterred from going to the daily *minyan* to say *Kaddish* for her father, despite total hostility from the men. Finally, they hung a plastic shower curtain so they could separate her from the men (a *mechitza*). Displaying enormous courage and wit, she returned to the *minyan* with a matching shower cap on her head.

While this discussion has focused on issues of divorce and *minyan*, they are only examples of women's exclusion from Jewish life. These two specific issues are probably of more concern to Orthodox and to a lesser extent Conservative women than to Reform or Reconstructionist women. Nevertheless, despite the fact that the Reform and the Reconstructionist movements have theoretically accepted women's equal participation, the practice seems to contradict this acceptance. For example, although the Reform movement declared in 1846 that women were equal to men, and by 1922 women could enter the rabbinate (Joseph, 1981: 207), the number of women rabbis in Canada can still be counted on the fingers of one hand.

Jewish feminists in Canada, like their sisters everywhere, are demanding remedies. However, for many feminists, these simple remedies are only the beginning and they argue that a more radical, far-reaching restructuring of Judaism is required. It is not enough to raise young Jewish women to ponder whether they should be doctors, lawyers, or rabbis. Rather, the task is to make Jewish women's experience and perceptions a part of normative Jewish life. Granting women not only equal access, but also full equality in defining and shaping Judaism will serve to make it relevant to the lives of all Jews, regardless of gender, and will demonstrate Judaism's commitment to justice and equality. As Judith Plaskow argues, equal access should not be the whole feminist agenda, for equal access, in itself, will 'not touch the roots of our marginality or the foundations of our subordination':

> the Jewish feminists might argue that it is a matter of simple justice for Jewish women to have full access to the riches of Jewish life. But when a woman stands in the pulpit and reads [in] the Torah that daughters can be sold as slaves (Ex. 21: 7-11), she participates in a profound contradiction between the message of her presence and the content of what she learns and teaches. It is this contradiction that feminists must address, not simply by 'adding' women to a tradition that remains basically unaltered, but transforming Judaism into a religion that women as well as men have a role in shaping. (1990: xiv)

Jewish Women and Jewish Communal Life

Jewish women have been very active in Jewish communal life; however, their roles have been largely restricted to either women's organizations or to enabling roles. Within the synagogue, for example, women are to be found in the kitchen preparing the *Kiddish* for the men after *their* Sabbath *minyan*. While there are women's organization within the Jewish community that are critical in preserving and conserving Jewish life and in advancing Jewish causes, their work goes largely unrecognized by the larger Jewish community. Women are virtually absent at the decision-making levels of major Jewish organizations. One need only examine the Executive Councils of major Jewish organizations at both the national and regional levels to recognize that women are grossly underrepresented. Of Canadian Jewish Congress's twelve presidents, only one has been a woman (elected in 1986), and the senior levels of the organization are still largely male-dominated. While at the regional level there is an increased female presence, patriarchy is still very much in evidence. In one Canadian region, for example, two out of twenty executive members are women. In a climate where the support staff is continually referred to as 'the girls in the office' and hardly anyone understands why it is inappropriate to have a secretary's job description include 'making coffee for the Director', it becomes impossible to get women's issues on the agenda. At any meeting of Canadian Jews, at any level, women's concerns receive only passing attention and the patriarchal structure of the

Jewish community is never seriously addressed. There is never any analysis of gender inequality in Jewish communal life. As Schneider succinctly notes, 'the men have the power and the women are the classic "enablers", making it possible for men to use their power unfettered by such concerns as who'll serve the lunch' (1985: 462).

Conclusions

While Canadian Jewish women have begun to penetrate the occupational and educational institutions of the larger society and have often been in the forefront in demanding greater gender equality, their progress in Jewish life has lagged far behind their secular progress. To those who argue that feminism will divide the Jewish community, it is important to point out that Jewish women are already feeling alienated from the Jewish community, and that change is essential if we want to ensure women's future and equal participation in Jewish life. If Jewish women's voices are not heard, the Jewish community runs the risk of losing large numbers of young, well-educated, potential leaders. Feminists are working for changes to Judaism because we identify ourselves as Jews and as feminists, and refuse to choose between these identities. Jewish feminists are demanding to be feminists in the Jewish community and Jews in the women's movement. For too long, Jewish feminists who wish to live as Jews and as feminists have been forced into a divided existence. Jewish women have been a major force both within the women's movement and within the Jewish community, but many Jewish women are uncomfortable with their dual identities. Emma Goldman once remarked that 'if I can't dance to it, it's not my revolution'. Until recently, Jewish feminists have learned two separate and often disparate dances, one in the feminist community and one in the Jewish community. If we fail to combat sexism in Judaism, as well as anti-Semitism in the women's community, we cannot dance to the dance any longer, and we will continue to find ourselves alienated from both communities. The very survival of Judaism is threatened unless we seriously address this estrangement of many Jewish women from the Jewish community.

References

Bleich, David
  1984 'Jewish Divorce: Judicial Misconceptions and Possible Means of Civil Enforcement', *Connecticut Law Review* 16, 2 (Winter 1984)

B'nai B'rith Canada
  1987 *The Use of Get as a Bargaining Tool in Jewish Divorce Proceedings* (Downsview, Ontario: B'nai B'rith Canada)

Breitman, Barbara
  1988 'Lifting Up the Shadow of Anti-Semitism: Jewish Masculinity in a New

Light' in Harry Brod, ed., *A Mensch Among Men: Explorations in Jewish Masculinity* (Freedom, California: The Crossing Press): 101-17

Brod, Harry
1988 'Toward a Male Jewish Feminism' in Harry Brod, ed., *A Mensch Among Men: Explorations in Jewish Masculinity* (Freedom, California: The Crossing Press): 181-7

Brod, Harry (ed.)
1988 *A Mensch Among Men: Explorations in Jewish Masculinity* (Freedom, California: The Crossing Press)

Census of Canada
1986 *Profile of Ethnic Groups*. CS 93-154 (Ottawa: Statistics Canada)

_____

1971 *Occupations, by Sex*. CS 94-734, Vol.III, Part 3. Bulletin 3.3-7, 1975

Cohen, Steven Martin
1980 'American Jewish Feminists', *American Behavioral Scientist* 23, 4 (March–April)

Davids, Leo
1989 'The Canadian Jewish Population Picture: Today and Tomorrow' in Edmond Y. Lipsitz, ed., *Canadian Jewry Today: Who's Who in Canadian Jewry* (Downsview, Ontario: J.E.S.L. Educational Products): 52-9.

_____

1981 'The Family: Challenges for Survival' in M. Weinfeld, W. Shaffir, and I. Cotler, eds, *The Canadian Jewish Mosaic* (Toronto: John Wiley & Sons): 97-112.

Draper, Paula
1983 'The Role of Canadian Jewish Women in Historical Perspective' in Edmond Y. Lipsitz, ed. *Canadian Jewish Women of Today: Who's Who of Canadian Jewish Women* (Downsview, Ontario: J.E.S.L. Educational Products): 3-10.

Gluck, Bob
1988 'Jewish Men and Violence in the Home' in Harry Brod, ed., *A Mensch Among Men: Explorations in Jewish Masculinity* (Freedom, California: The Crossing Press): 162-73.

Gold, Michael
1988 'The Real Jewish Father' in Harry Brod, ed., *A Mensch Among Men: Explorations in Jewish Masculinity* (Freedom, California: The Crossing Press): 84-91

Greenberg, Julie
1986 'Seeking a Feminist Judaism' in Melanie Kaye/Kantrowitz and Irena Klepfisz, eds, *The Tribe of Dina* (Montpelier, Vermont: Sinister Wisdom Books): 180-6.

Greenberg, Blu
1981/5742 *On Women and Judaism: A View from Tradition* (Philadelphia: The Jewish Publication Society of America)

Joseph, Norma Baumel
1981 'Reflections on Jewish Feminism' in M. Weinfeld, W. Shaffir, and I. Cotler, eds, *The Canadian Jewish Mosaic* (Toronto: John Wiley & Sons): 205-20

Kaye/Kantrowitz, Melanie and Irena Klepfisz, eds
1986 *The Tribe of Dina* (Montpelier, Vermont: Sinister Wisdom Books)

1988/5748 *Lilith: The Jewish Women's Magazine* 19, 19 (Spring 1988/5748)

1989/5749 *Lilith: The Jewish Women's Magazine* 14, 2 (Spring 1989/5749) 7-10

Parent, Gail
1973 *Sheila Levine is Dead and Living in New York* (New York: Bantam)

Plaskow, Judith
1990 *Standing Again at Sinai: Judaism from a Feminist Perspective* (San Francisco: Harper & Row)

Province of Ontario
1990 An Act to Amend the Divorce Act (Barriers to Religious Remarriage). Chapter 18, sections 1-4. Assented June 12, 1990

Roth, Sol
1982 'The State of Orthodoxy', *Tradition* 20, 1 (Spring, 1982)

Schneider, Susan Weidman
1985 *Jewish and Female* (New York: Simon & Schuster, Inc.)

Siegal, Robin
1979 *When a Jewish Wife Becomes a Widow*. Hebrew Union College: M.A. thesis

Torczyner, Jim
1983 *The Dynamics of Canadian Jewry: An Emerging Profile of a Diverse and Challenging Community Agenda*. A paper prepared for the Council of Jewish Welfare Federation, Atlanta, Georgia, 17 November

Waxman, Chaim I.
1988 'The Jewish Father: Past and Present' in Harry Brod, ed., *A Mensch Among Men: Explorations in Jewish Masculinity* (Freedom, California: The Crossing Press): 59-73

Aging in the Family Context:

Are Jewish Families Different?

Carolyn J. Rosenthal

For most people, family relationships are of central importance throughout life, providing a source of meaning, companionship, and tangible help in times of need. Families may provide a sense of continuity with past and future through links to older and younger generations.

Family relationships are among the most enduring and long-term ties individuals form. Research has exposed as myths the formerly accepted notions that older people are abandoned by their families and isolated from them (Rosenthal, 1987; Bengtson *et al.*, 1990), that in the past older people were better treated by their families than they are today (e.g. Laslett, 1976), and that the elderly in other, less complex societies than our own are better treated by their families (Nydegger, 1983).

While these statements apply quite generally to contemporary Canadians, they may be especially true for Canadian Jews. Certainly, there exists a belief among many Jews and non-Jews that there is something 'special' about Jewish families, and that Jews value the family even more than other Canadians do. The purpose of this chapter is to explore these assumptions, drawing on a study of older Canadian women in which relationships with children were investigated. A second purpose is to set a broader context by examining features of contemporary families and the relationships between older parents and adult children.

Families, and relationships within families, do not exist in a vacuum. Like all social relationships, those of interest in this chapter must be viewed within a broader societal context. While culture is one factor that shapes relationships, and one that is of primary interest in this chapter, other factors also exert influence. One important factor is demography.

Aging Families in Demographic Context

The Aging of the Population

The extent to which aging has become a focus of public attention and concern is, to some degree, a reflection of broad demographic changes that have occurred in Canada. These changes are: an increase in the number and proportion of old people in the population; within the older population, an increase in the number and proportion of persons who are *very* old; and an increasing predominance of women in the older population. The two main causes of these changes are increased life expectancy (more people are living into late life) and decreased fertility (people are having fewer children). Changing immigration patterns also contribute to population aging.

The aging of the Jewish population in Canada mirrors the aging of the country's population as a whole, but the changes have been even more pronounced. Whereas 10.7 per cent of all Canadians are aged 65 or older, 15.2 per cent of Jews in Canada are in that age group. Among ethnic groups in Canada, only Latvians, Estonians, and Lithuanians have higher proportions of elderly. In 1986 there were 52,345 older Jews in Canada, out of a total Jewish population of 343,705 (Minister of Supply and Services Canada, 1989: 2-34).[1]

The proportion of older people in the Canadian population has risen dramatically over the past century, from 4.1 in 1881 to 10.7 in 1986 (Minister of Supply and Services Canada, 1988: 9). The number of older people in the population has grown from just over a quarter of a million people in 1901 to close to 2.7 million in 1986 (Minister of Supply and Services Canada, 1988: 23).

Birth rates in Canada have declined over this century, with the 'baby boom' being an aberration in an overall downward trend. The birth rate among Jews shows the same pattern of decline, but the birth rate is also notably low, compared to other groups (Anderson and Frideres, 1981: 184). While, in part, this may reflect cultural preferences, it also relates to the high educational and economic attainment of Jews compared to other groups, for these factors are typically associated with later child-bearing and fewer children.

Life expectancy of Canadians has increased approximately 27 years since 1900. Today, average life expectancy at birth is 73 years for men and almost 80 years for women. The difference in life expectancy between men and women points to another important demographic feature: among the older population, women predominate and this is increasingly so as one looks at older age groups. This gender imbalance was not evident until the 1960s, but within two decades, there were 124 women for every 100 men in the age group 56-79 and 184 women for every 100 men in the 80 and over age group (McDaniel, 1986: 41).

Population aging is also affected by immigration patterns. The large numbers of immigrants to Canada early in this century kept the overall population relatively young. Later on, however, as immigration rates declined, these immigrants added to Canada's aging population (McDaniel, 1986: 37). The massive Jewish immigration in the first three decades of this century had the same effect on the Jewish population. Between 1900 and 1930, Canada received 123,249 Jewish immigrants, while in the following 35 years the total was only 33,368 (Anderson and Frideres, 1981: 141-55; note, however, that this number does not include Jews who came to Canada after the war as 'displaced persons'). Although Canada may continue to receive Jewish immigrants, it is unlikely that future immigration will be substantial enough to change markedly the aging of the Jewish population.

Within the older population itself, there has been disproportionate growth in the very old segment. The proportion over age 80 grew from an almost negligible proportion in 1961 to almost 20 per cent in 1986 and is projected to rise to almost 25 per cent by the year 2001 (McDaniel, 1986: 43). The very old are of special interest because they are most likely to be frail and to need support and services. There is a higher proportion of persons aged 75 and over among Jews than among Canadians as a whole — 5.8 per cent, compared to just over 4 per cent. The high proportions of old people, and especially of very old people, among Jews makes more understandable the extensive concern in Jewish communities with providing services to the elderly. Because Jews tend to be concentrated in large cities, the needs of most Jewish elderly can be addressed through services organized by the Jewish community. Although elderly Jews are found in cities across Canada, they are concentrated in Toronto (41.4 per cent of Canada's Jewish elderly), Montreal (28.6 per cent) and Vancouver (5.5 per cent) (Minister of Supply and Services Canada, 1989: 2-34). Indeed, 92.8 per cent of all Canadian Jewish elderly live in the four provinces of Ontario, Quebec, British Columbia, and Manitoba.

The implications of population aging for families

The demographic changes in the population are changing the nature of family life. With declines in fertility and increases in life expectancy, families have more generations alive, and fewer people in each generation. This is especially true of Jews, because of their distinctively low birth rate. Even among today's elderly, while Jews are less likely to be childless than British or French elderly, childlessness is more common than among German, Italian, Polish, and Ukrainian elderly (Driedger and Chappell, 1987: 73). Most older Jews have one or two children, and they are less likely to have three or more children than are any of Canada's other major ethnic groups (Driedger and Chappell, 1987: 73). As well, because Jews have higher socioeconomic status, on average, than Canadians as a whole, and because higher socioeconomic status is related to longer life expectancy, Jewish families may be more likely to have living upper generation members.

Individuals are more likely to have parents alive than has ever been the case in history. Among Canadians born in 1860, when they reached aged 50 only 16 per cent had a surviving parent. For Canadians born in 1910, at age 50, 33 per cent had a parent alive. When Canadians born in 1960 reach age 50, 60 per cent will have a parent alive (Gee, 1990). It is possible that the figures may be even higher among Jews, given the relationship between socioeconomic status and longevity.

Women typically outlive their husbands, because women tend to live longer than men and, in addition, tend to marry men who are somewhat older than themselves. Within families, this means that the oldest generation often includes widows. Here, too, the impact of socioeconomic status on life expectancy may result in later age at widowhood among Jewish women, although, again, this is speculation.

The demographic changes in families may have both positive and negative consequences for families. On the positive side, the increased duration of family ties means that there is increased opportunity for adults of different generations to form close emotional bonds that grow over time. Parents and children may share as many as 50 years of life (Bengtson et al., 1990). Husbands and wives may share a similar length of time. Grandparents and grandchildren may share enough years that the relationship extends into the grandchild's adult years.

Because women live longer than men, women experience longer duration of ties with children and grandchildren than men do. And, because women are typically widows in the last years of their lives, if and when they need various types of social and emotional support, they turn to children, usually daughters, or to other sources, rather than to a spouse. Whatever the role demography has played, it is well documented that women are the 'linch-pins' in North American kinship systems (Rosenthal, 1985). Typically, the mother–daughter tie is the strongest family tie, aside from the marital bond.

When older people are widowed, they typically live alone rather than with a child or other relative, and Jewish elderly are no exception. Indeed, living with someone other than a spouse or a never-married child is less common among older Jews than among most other groups (Driedger and Chappell, 1987: 71).

The increased duration of family ties may also have negative aspects. Where family relationships have not been positive, prolonged duration may simply mean prolonged unhappiness and conflict. A second negative consequence is that more and more adult children experience their parent's living into frailty and needing care. This may be exacerbated by the trend toward fewer children, with the implication that there will be fewer middle-aged adults available to care for more frail elderly parents.

Aging in Jewish Families

In contrast to the large body of research on families in later life, relatively little research has focused on ethnic variations in aging families. In the existing literature, three models or views of aging in ethnic families are evident (Rosenthal, 1986). The first model equates ethnicity with culture, especially immigrant culture; with assimilation, ethnic differences are thought to diminish and gradually disappear. The second model views ethnic differences as resulting from social inequality. Many so-called ethnic differences would be seen, on closer examination, to be the result of economic factors rather than cultural traditions. The third model equates ethnicity with 'traditional' ways of thinking and behaving. This model is often implicit in research and is also a model that is found in popular culture. Because the assumptions underlying this model are often simply take for granted, they are somewhat 'hidden' from our understanding. For this reason, I decided to explore this model further.

The 'traditional' model of aging in ethnic families views families as falling, conceptually, on a traditional/modern continuum, and views ethnic families as 'traditional' (Rosenthal, 1983). The 'traditional' family is believed to be characterized by an emphasis on the importance of the family and the obligations of children toward parents, by extended kin ties, emotional warmth, closeness between generations, and frequent contact among members of all ages. In contrast, the 'modern' family is thought to be characterized by a focus on the rights of the individual rather than the importance of the family as a group, an emphasis on the nuclear rather than the extended family, independence of adult children from parents rather than the meeting of obligations to parents, emotional distance between generations, and infrequent contact between adult generations. This model would predict that as ethnic family members assimilate to the dominant culture, support for older people would decline.

We may rightly ask who exactly comprises the 'modern' family. It is generally assumed that North American families are 'modern' in the sense that they possess the characteristics attributed to the modern family type to an appreciable degree. Research, however, calls this assumption into question. For example, in both Canada and the United States, not only is there widespread support for the idea that families should care for their older members, but this support is even stronger in the young adult generation than in middle or oldest generations (Brody et al., 1984). Similarly, much of the research on the family life of older people may be viewed as failing to support the conception of the modern family type, at least in its extreme statement.

In order to understand ethnic differences in family life, it is necessary to investigate explicitly the traditional/modern distinction. To do this, we must specify who represents the 'North American' or 'modern' family. In this chapter, I use 'Anglos', specifically persons whose major ancestry is British, Scots, or Welsh, to represent the dominant North American or mainstream group. As well, research must distinguish between ethnicity as an element of social structure and ethnicity as culture, and must keep behaviour distinct from both. Thus, three dimensions—culture, structure, and behaviour—ought to be incorporated into research, and analysis of the relationship between any two must control for the effects of the third.

Relationships between Older Parents and their Adult Children

A comparison of relationships between older parents and adult children in Jewish and Anglo families may determine whether these relationships are really different in Jewish families. It should be noted that I am focusing on Jewish families of eastern European origin. The Anglo family was chosen for comparison because it is usually assumed to represent a family type that is very different from the Jewish family. Anglos are thought to typify the 'modern' western family. The emphasis on individualism and the nuclear family is thought to be reflected in independence of adult children from parents and in emotional distance and infrequent contact between adult generations.

In contrast, the Jewish family of eastern European origin is thought to represent the 'traditional' family type. Although little research has focused on the family relations of older Jews, research on earlier life stages suggests Jewish families have stronger ties and are more cohesive and closely knit (Balswick, 1966: 167). Farber *et al.* (1981) found young Jewish adults had more frequent contact with parents, in-laws and siblings than non-Jews did. Winch *et al.* (1967) found Jews had more kin (usually parents or siblings) living nearby than did Catholics or Protestants, and that this proximity was due to a wish to remain living near one another. However, more recent research indicates that low fertility among Jews limits the availability of kin (Thomas and Wister, 1984); this lessens the potential for Jews to have siblings living nearby. Research has found that Jewish families have more contact and give one another more assistance than Protestant or Catholic families do (Winch *et al.*, 1967). Wake and Sporakowski (1972) found middle-aged Jewish parents felt more strongly that children had various types of obligations to parents than Catholic or Protestant parents did. In sum, previous research suggests that Jewish elders would have more frequent contact, closer geographical proximity, and greater emotional closeness with children, and would feel more strongly that children owed obligations to parents than Anglo elders would.

To explore these comparative issues, a study was conducted of 58 Anglo women and 60 Jewish women living in Hamilton, Ontario. All the women were aged 60 or older, had at least one living child, and were living in the community. The Anglo women were interviewed as part of a larger study conducted in 1980 and comprised a sample that was representative of the population. The Jewish women were interviewed in a separate study, conducted in 1982. The Jewish sample was drawn from organizational lists and the Jewish community's telephone directory, a fairly complete listing of local Jewish adults.[2] The two studies used many of the same measures, making comparisons possible. Because the Jewish sample is not representative of all Canadian elderly Jewish women, the findings should be viewed as tentative only, and as limited to older women of eastern European origin.

The study focused on several dimensions commonly used to study relationships between older people and their adult children: the number of children older parents have and how geographically near or distant they are; frequency of contact between parents and children; how emotionally close parents feel toward children; and norms and attitudes parents hold concerning the obligations of children toward parents. Some of these dimensions refer to culture, some to structure, and some to behaviour. The first— availability and proximity of kin—refers to social structure. Norms refer to culture. Emotional closeness and contact refer to behaviour.

Cultural Contrasts

Jewish women in the study did not believe the general experience of aging was different because they were Jewish; only 15 per cent of the women felt ethnicity made a difference. In contrast, when asked whether the family life of older Jews was different, almost two-thirds felt being Jewish contributed to a better family life in old age. Many referred specifically to the emotional quality of relationships. Most commonly, they expressed the view that there was greater emotional closeness in Jewish families, especially as compared to Anglo families. For example, one Jewish woman said, 'The Jewish family is very different. It is closer and more caring than Anglo-Saxon families. . . . Other European groups are close, however.' Another woman said, 'Jewish families are close and their older people are more respected.'

Other perceived differences included more respect, care, and affection for older members of Jewish families. Some women believed older Jewish parents saw more of their children than Anglo elders did, either because of greater affection or because of the observance of ethnic-religious ritual. For example: 'Jewish families are closer. Children visit their parents. There's always a holiday or "simcha" to get together for.'

These quotations show that most elderly Jewish women believe their family life is better because they are Jewish, aside from any consideration of whether it is better by any objective measure. This may be useful in enabling these women to exempt themselves from what they may view as a poor quality of family life for older people in general. When their own situations do not fit their negative stereotypes, they view themselves as lucky and exceptional. On the other hand, these positive views of Jewish family life may set up high expectations that fail to be met in real life.

Another area of cultural difference has to do with attitudes and expectations concerning the obligations of children toward aging parents. Jewish women had stronger expectations about children's obligations to parents than Anglo women did. A majority of Jews but only a minority of Anglos felt grown children have an obligation to take care of elderly parents, and far more Jews than Anglos felt children should have legal responsibility for parents who can no longer care for themselves. Jews were more likely than Anglos to feel that adult children should keep in close contact with their parents. Jews were also more likely to feel that adult children who move far away are not being fair to their parents, although only a minority of Jews supported this statement. These differences persisted when differences in socioeconomic status and being Canadian-born versus foreign-born were taken into consideration, so they are, at least in part, an effect of culture *per se*.

Behavioural Contrasts and their Origins

The study then pursued the question of whether ethnicity makes a difference in behaviour. Do Jewish elders see more of their children than Anglo elders do? To answer this question, it is important to disentangle the effects of ethnicity from other factors which lead to greater parent–child contact. Such factors include: increasing age, poor health and widowhood of the parent; closer geographical proximity; greater numbers of children (the more children a person has, the more likely they are to live near an adult child); and socioeconomic status (lower SES is related to closer geographical proximity, more children and more frequent contact; greater contact in this case is connected to providing direct assistance, which is more common among lower SES groups). I controlled for the effects of these other factors, in order to determine whether Jewish women had more contact with their children and whether they felt they had closer emotional relationships with their children than Anglo women did.

The results showed there is a cultural tendency among Jews for greater contact with children, both in person and by telephone, than is found among Anglos. The most important factor leading to contact, however, was proximity. Not surprisingly, the closer parents and children live to one another, the more frequently they get together and the more often they speak on the phone. All else being equal, Jewish women were no more likely to live near their children than Anglo women were. However, the more children a person has, the greater the likelihood that a child will be living close to the parent. Thus, because Jewish women had fewer children than Anglo women (following a general tendency among Jewish women toward low fertility, as discussed earlier), this led indirectly to Jewish women living farther from their children than Anglo women. Although proximity had the strongest impact on contact, when Jews and Anglos living similar distances from their children were compared, Jews had more frequent contact with children than Anglos did. We are therefore entitled to conclude that Jewish culture increases frequency of contact with children, compared to Anglos.

In contrast to the findings on contact, elderly Jewish women did not feel more emotionally close to children than Anglo women did, when other factors such as age, widowhood, number of children, proximity, and health were taken into consideration. This was an ironic finding in view of the perceptions of Jewish women themselves that being Jewish is related to greater family closeness. Greater family size was related to less closeness, suggesting the emotional intensity of family relationships increases as family size decreases. Poorer health was also associated with less closeness, perhaps reflecting the negative impact of dependency on the emotional quality of parent-child relationships.

Are Jewish Families Different?

The study described above supported some common assumptions about Jewish families, but refuted others. Certainly, the study indicated that there are differences between Jewish and Anglo families in later life that are independent of such other important factors as socioeconomic status, marital status, age, and health. At the level of cultural meanings, 'the family' seems more central to Jewish than to Anglo women (Latowsky, 1971). Most Jewish women believe Jewish families are better for old people than Anglo families are. Jewish women feel more strongly that adult children have and should fulfil obligations to parents. They place heavy emphasis on the family and hold high expectations of their children.

At the level of behaviour, Jewish elders had more contact with their adult children. Behavioural differences such as this, however, must be viewed in relation to other factors. While it is true that Jewish elders had more contact with their children, even when the analysis controlled for structural factors, the most important contributor to frequent contact was the structural factor of living in close proximity. The complex way in which Jewish ethnicity affects contact illustrates the more general complexity of relating ethnicity to family life. The fact of being Jewish contributed to greater contact with children than if one were Anglo. However, being Jewish was also related to having fewer children, and this in turn was related to a lesser likelihood of living in close proximity. Thus, while being Jewish contributed in a direct way to more frequent contact, indirectly, through family size and proximity, it contributed to less frequent contact.

The study illustrated that the impact of ethnicity is not uniform across different domains of family life. Ethnicity affected contact but not emotional closeness. Again, complex inter-relations were at work. Jews had fewer children than Anglos and because parents with fewer children tend to be closer to their children than parents who have many children, it may indeed be the case that Jewish parents are closer to children—not because they are Jewish but because they have smaller families.

It will be recalled that one purpose of the study was to test the 'traditional/ modern' model of aging in ethnic families. The analysis showed that the 'traditional/modern' distinction is too simplistic to be useful. Neither the Jewish nor the Anglo group could be fully characterized as one or the other. Jewish families were more traditional with respect to norms and attitudes concerning how children should behave toward parents and in having more frequent contact with their children than their Anglo counterparts. However, they were not distinctively traditional with respect to patterns of emotional closeness or geographical proximity. These findings suggest that the 'traditional/modern' model may be misleading, clouding as many differences as it illuminates.

Ethnicity in Perspective: Other Issues in Aging Families

While the focus in this chapter has been on the impact of being Jewish on parent–child relations in later life, we ought to place ethnicity in perspective. Many issues in the aging ethnic family are important in all aging families. Ethnicity adds an ingredient.

In all families there is tension between change and continuity (Bengtson and Kuypers, 1981). Family efforts to preserve continuity are evident in 'kin-keeping' activities. For example, most families have someone who makes special efforts to keep family members in touch with one another (Rosenthal, 1985). A sense of family continuity is reinforced through the repetition of family rituals (Rosenthal et al., 1988). Some ethnic groups may have traditions that assist such continuity-enhancing devices, and indeed one might speculate that Jewish traditions are of this nature. Friday night dinners that provide weekly reunions for parents, children, and grandchildren are one such tradition. Passover, which brings the extended family together, is another. In perspective, however, it must be remembered that other groups have their own traditions. Anglos, the group used for comparison in the study described above, have Sunday dinner and Christmas, occasions that are important family times (Rosenthal et al., 1988).

Alongside continuity, change is ubiquitous in family life. One source of change is transitions such as marriage, divorce, retirement, and widowhood which are experienced by individuals but affect other family members. As the circumstances of parents and children change, so do the expectations that each generation holds of the other. For example, parents may expect different behaviours from a married as opposed to a single son. Analogously, children may change their expectations of a parent once the parent is widowed. Again, we may ask how ethnicity affects these changing expectations and negotiations between parents and children. One intriguing question for future research might be whether the transition to grandparenthood is distinctive in Jewish families. In particular, we might wonder what effect the increase in intermarriage in the child generation has on the role of the grandparents. It may be that intermarriage creates a more vital role for grandparents in that they become 'guardians of the heritage', so to speak. We might even wonder if some Jewish grandparents in this situation actually become more observant in order to pass on some Jewish heritage to their grandchildren. Other questions for future research include how Jewish families deal with a mother's transition to widowhood, how Jewish grandparents respond to divorce in the adult child generation, whether Jewish parents are less likely to relocate following retirement because of the pull of family ties, or whether Jewish elders have distinctive expectations of or reactions to their children with the onset of frail health and dependency. While we may have hunches regarding the answers to these questions, comparative data are very rare.

In all families, there are both similarities and differences in values between parents and children. The extent to which actual differences exist and to which they are perceived to exist influences parent-child relationships. Such differences may cause overt conflict or inner distress. Parents normally wish to pass on their values to their children. Children normally wish to establish their own identities. This may contribute to a tendency for children to hold somewhat different values than parents and to perceive generational differences as greater than they really are (Bengtson and Kuypers, 1971). Ethnicity may compound this more generally experienced situation in that parents may feel they must pass on the ethnic/cultural heritage or it will die out. Thus, the conflict in ethnic families related to assimilation is, in one sense, a sharpened version of expectable generational differences. On the other hand, these differences should not be overstated. Within families, continuity of values is more striking than differences (Bengtson et al., 1990).

Another universal issue in families as members age is the tension between autonomy and dependency (Bengtson and Kuypers, 1981). All aging families face the issue of growing parental dependency, whether real or anticipated. Parents and children have different perceptions of the meaning of dependency, the importance of autonomy, and the appropriate balance between the two. We may ask how ethnicity further complicates or facilitates resolving the inherent challenges and dilemmas. Ethnicity may have a cultural effect in that different generations may hold different expectations concerning appropriate behaviour. Alternatively, ethnicity may have an indirect effect through its relationship to economic resources. Parents who are economically disadvantaged need more assistance from children than parents who are well off financially. If we found lower levels of help from children of affluent Jewish parents, then we could hardly attribute this to cultural values, although at first glance that might appear to be the explanation.

A related issue is the need to avoid romanticizing families when studying the family life of older people. Families have negative as well as positive aspects. A strong endorsement of norms of family obligation, as found among Jewish elders in the study described in this chapter, indicates high expectations of children. However, high expectations may be accompanied by dissatisfaction among older parents if their expectations fail to be fulfilled. Similarly, we may think that 'more is better' when it comes to contact — that the more older parents see their children, the happier the parents will be. Yet studies find no association between morale and how often parents see their adult children (Lee, 1979). On the other hand, morale is related to relations with age-peers (Chappell, 1983), reminding us that the family is not the only important social arena in the lives of older people. It is, however, an important arena for most older people, and, as discussed earlier in this chapter, may be especially important in terms of emotional salience to Jewish elderly. In this respect, and in some others explored in this chapter, the answer to the question posed in the chapter's title seems to be a somewhat qualified, 'Yes, Jewish families are different.'

Notes

[1] The figures given in text were calculated by combining single-origin and multiple-origin responses regarding ethnic origins.

[2] In drawing the sample, assistance was sought from several people who were actively involved in Jewish community life. These included a rabbi and a former president of one of the large Jewish women's organizations. Using the telephone directory and the organizational lists, these informants identified all the women who met the sampling criteria. All names were known to at least one of the informants and thus the resulting list was presumed to be relatively accurate. Using the list of persons identified as eligible, sampling was done randomly.

References

Anderson, A. and J. Frideres
  1981 *Ethnicity in Canada: Theoretical Perspectives* (Toronto: Butterworths)

Balswick, J.
  1966 'Are American-Jewish families closely knit?' *Jewish Social Studies* 28: 159-67

Bengtson, Vern L. and J.A. Kuypers
  1971 'Generational differences and the developmental stake', *Aging and Human Development* 2: 249-60.

  _____

  1981 'Psycho-social issues in the aging family'. Paper presented at the 12th International Congress of Gerontology, Hamburg, Germany, July

Bengtson, Vern L., Carolyn J. Rosenthal and Linda Burton
  1990 'Families and Aging: Diversity and Heterogeneity' in R. Binstock and L. George, eds, *Handbook of Aging and the Social Sciences*, 3rd ed. (San Diego, California: Academic Press)

Brody, Elaine, Pauline Johnsen and Mark Fulcomer
  1984 'What should adult children do for elderly parents? Opinions and preferences of three generations of women'. *Journal of Gerontology* 39: 736-46

Chappell, N.
  1983 'Informal support networks among the elderly', *Research on Aging* 5: 77-99

Driedger, L. and N. Chappell
  1987 *Aging and Ethnicity: Toward an Interface* (Toronto and Vancouver: Butterworths)

Gee, Ellen
  1990 'The changing demography of intergenerational relations in Canada' in P. Conrad and V. White, eds, *Canadian Gerontological Collection VII. The Chang-*

ing Family in An Aging Society: Caregiving Traditions, Trends, Tomorrows?
(Ottawa: Canadian Association on Gerontology): 49-65

Farber, B., C. Mindel and B. Lazerwitz
  1981 'The Jewish American family' in C. Mindel and R. Habenstein, eds, *Ethnic Families in America* (New York: Elsevier): 350-85

Laslett, P.
  1976 'Societal development and aging' in R. Binstock and E. Shanas, eds, *Handbook of Aging and the Social Sciences* (New York: Van Nostrand Reinhold): 87-116

Latowsky, E.
  1971 'Family life styles and Jewish culture' in K. Ishwaran, ed., *The Canadian Family* (Toronto: Holt, Rinehart and Winston): 94-110

Lee, Gary L.
  1979 'Children and the elderly', *Research on Aging* 1: 335-60

McDaniel, Susan A.
  1986 *Canada's Aging Population* (Toronto and Vancouver: Butterworths)

Minister of Supply and Services Canada
  1988 *Canada's Seniors.* Catalogue No. 98-121

  1989 *Dimensions: Profile of Ethnic Groups.* Catalogue No. 93-154

Nydegger, C.
  1983 'Family ties of the aged in cross-cultural perspective', *The Gerontologist* 23: 26-32

Rosenthal, Carolyn J.
  1983 'Aging, ethnicity and the family: Beyond the modernization thesis', *Canadian Ethnic Studies* 15: 1-16

  1985 'Kinkeeping in the familial division of labor', *Journal of Marriage and the Family* 47: 965-74

  1986 'Family supports in later life: Does ethnicity make a difference?' *The Gerontologist* 26: 19-24

  1987 'Aging and intergenerational relations in Canada' in Victor W. Marshall, ed., *Aging in Canada: Social Perspectives*, 2nd ed. (Markham, Ontario: Fitzhenry and Whiteside): 311-42

Rosenthal, C.J., and V.W. Marshall
  1988 'Generational transmission of family ritual', *American Behavioral Scientist* 31: 669-84

Thomas, K. and A. Wister
  1984 'Living arrangements of older women: The ethnic dimension', *Journal of Marriage and the Family* 46: 301-11

Wake, S. and M. Sporakowski
1972 'An intergenerational comparison of attitudes towards supporting aged parents', *Journal of Marriage and the Family* 34: 42-8

Winch, R., S. Greer and R. Blumberg
1967 'Ethnicity and extended familism in an upper-middle-class suburb', *American Sociological Review* 32: 265-72

The author gratefully acknowledges the support of the Ontario Ministry of Health through a Career Scientist Award. The research in this chapter was supported through grants from the Social Sciences and Humanities Research Council of Canada and the Programme in Gerontology/Centre for Studies of Aging, University of Toronto.

part seven

Minorities

Introduction

William Shaffir

To outsiders especially, an ethnic group seems a homogeneous entity. While allowing for minor exceptions, members of the group are painted with broad strokes and characterized by stereotypes in terms of which the group is popularly defined. Jews and Gentiles alike have a stereotyped image of Canadian Jews as middle class, primarily of German or Eastern European background, concentrated in Montreal and Toronto, acculturated to the larger society's lifestyle and values, and led by males. While this generalization may be quite accurate for the bulk of Canadian Jewry, as a generalization, it excludes many particulars and many differences.

While the Canadian Jewish community can be differentiated from other ethnic groups in this country along a number of salient dimensions, it shares with others the fact that it, too, is internally differentiated. In fact, the larger Jewish community is best conceptualized as comprising a number of subgroups; each is distinctive, but together they make up a whole that is more than the sum of its parts. In fact, the community's diversity has been augmented recently by the arrival of immigrants from previously untraditional sources of immigration, including Israel, South Africa, and the former Soviet Union. While some of these groupings might approximate or even fit the stereotypes, others (for instance, the poor and the elderly, or recently-arrived Russian immigrants) are not part of the mainstream and hence often neglected in discussions and analyses of the Jewish community in Canada.

The Yiddish expression, 'Vee es kristlt zich, azoi yidlt zich' ('As the Christians do, so do the Jews'), can help us to better appreciate the Jewish community's diversity. While, perhaps, different from other ethnic groups in certain fundamental respects, the Jewish community is affected by the same forces that shape the larger society. As Québécois nationalism intensified in the 1960s and 1970s, so too has the Sephardic community been encouraged to steer a course that will enable its members to retain their distinctive heritages. And as poverty was 'discovered' in the 1960s, so, too, was it uncovered in the Jewish community. Jim Torczyner's contribution examines the persistence of invisible poverty among Canadian Jews. Most notably, the Jewish poor are likely to be elderly, women, and persons who live alone and who, as Torczyner argues, are precisely the populations that tend to be least visible. As he illustrates, because of the convergence of societal stereotypes, demographic characteristics, and changes in public and private service delivery, the Jewish poor become invisible to Jews and non-Jews alike.

Despite the many forms of Jewish cultural expression, the attachment of Canadian Jewry to the State of Israel is surely among the strongest and the most vibrant. As a body, Canadian Jews are sustained as Jews by the existence of the Jewish State, and the Diaspora and Israel have evolved a symbiotic, mutually reinforcing relationship. For most Canadian Jews, there exists a generalized support for the State of Israel and an attachment to it strong enough to play an important role in the consciousness of even those Jews who are relatively assimilated. Such a role generally includes some measure of financial support and, for a substantial minority, the occasional visit to Israel. For a small number, however, identification with Israel has been accompanied by a decision to settle there permanently. The article by Cyril Levitt and William Shaffir examines not only the circumstances propelling individuals to make *aliyah* but, as well, their rather painful decision to resettle permanently in Canada. Though few in number, such individuals share feelings of failure, guilt, and regret about their unsuccessful *aliyah* and, by their decision to attempt to live in Israel, stand apart from the mainstream of Canadian Jewry.

An examination of the Canadian census reveals that, over the decades, Jews have overwhelmingly settled in urban areas. In fact, Jews are more residentially concentrated than any other ethnic group in Canada. But not all Jews live in the large urban centres of the country. Unfortunately, there is a dearth of research on Jews scattered across the very small communities in Canada — specifically, how their lifestyle and identification as Jews may differ from that of their urban counterparts. Based on her research on the Jews of Atlantic Canada, Sheva Medjuck analyses the more typical forms of Jewish expression she encountered. Focusing on such concerns as the importance of the Jewish home, the role of the synagogue and the State of Israel, and friendship networks and other institutional supports, she concludes that the continued persistence of Jewish communities in the many small communities of Canada reflects both the tenacity and the salience of Jewish identity.

While the Jewish community is comprised of groups with differing ethnic origins, relations between them may be strained. Jean-Claude Lasry's paper focuses on the social integration and ethnic attitudes of North African Jews living in Montreal. Perhaps surprisingly, the results indicate that Ashkenazi Jews rate less favourably than French Canadians as colleagues and bosses. In terms of ethnic group preferences, Ashkenazi Jews rank last. This clearly reflects intracommunity tensions which, according to the author, are a composite of several influences, including linguistic differences and the incorporation of Arabic culture in the lifestyle of North African Jews.

Intracommunity tensions are also evident between Soviet-Jewish immigrants in Canada and the larger Canadian Jewish community, as Roberta Markus and Donald Schwartz show in their contribution to this section. The established community and the new arrivals have very different ideas — grounded in distinct historical experiences — about how the émigrés ought to express their Jewish identity. As a result of the failure of the established community to attract any more than a small minority of Soviet Jewish émigrés, Markus and Schwartz see a very real danger that Soviet Jews arriving in Canada may be lost to the community as they assimilate into the broader society.

A fairly substantial body of social science literature now allows us to conclude that the economic, social, political, and psychological boundaries of the Canadian Jewish community are shifting. The community is becoming increasingly heterogeneous: the bases of its members' self-identification as Jews, as well as the criteria used by others to identify Jews, are changing. On the other hand, a general consensus emerging out of the research literature is that Canadian Jewry is gradually assimilating into the larger society (Brym, 1989; Schoenfeld, 1989). We arrive at an interesting paradox: recognition of the community's diversity has been aided by the increasing acceptance of Jews in the larger society and their relative affluence. As the spectres of anti-Semitism and discrimination have become less threatening, the Jewish community has been able to direct much of its energies and resources inward and has thus become more aware that it is diversified. Simultaneously, its general affluence has led to an increase in the number of trained professionals and institutionalized services, further encouraging the identification of subgroups. Thus, the very forces encouraging assimilation on the part of some Jews facilitates identification on the part of others.

References

Brym, R.J.
　1989 'The Rise And Decline Of Canadian Jewry: A Socio-Demographic Profile' in E.Y. Lipsitz, ed., *Canadian Jewry Today: Who's Who In Canadian Jewry* (Downsview, Ont.: J.E.S.L. Educational Products): 37–51 (reprinted in this volume)

Schoenfeld, S.
　1989 'Jewish Identity In A Multicultural Canada: The Implications For Assimilation And Intermarriage' in E.Y. Lipsitz, ed., *Canadian Jewry Today: Who's Who In Canadian Jewry* (Downsview, Ont.: J.E.S.L. Educational Products): 92–8

Jewish Survival in Small Communities in Canada

Sheva Medjuck

Jews in Canada have been the focus of much study. Over the last number of decades there has been a growing awareness that there is a pressing need to better understand not only our history but also our present circumstances. Much of this work has as its task an analysis of the collective well-being of the Jewish community in Canada in the attempt to provide prognoses for the future. Unfortunately what is often left out of the analysis is any discussion of the thousands of Jews scattered across the many small communities of Canada. Their absence suggests at best a kind of benign neglect, at worst, an implicit statement that if Jews do not live in the large metropolitan centres of Canada, then they are insignificant to the understanding of Jewish life.

Both academic and non-academic literatures seem equally guilty of this major oversight. There are many excellent studies on the nature of Jewish life in Montreal or Toronto or Winnipeg. It is extraordinarily rare to find any literature whatsoever on Jews in Regina or North Bay or Chicoutimi or Yarmouth. Yet all these places have Jews who are actively part of the Jewish community but often feel overwhelmed by the sheer numbers of Jews in the larger centres. Against such odds it is difficult for them to get their story told.

In recent years there has been some attempts to rectify this situation, although these have certainly not been extensive enough. For example, after years of struggle, the Canadian Jewish Congress recognized that Jews in small communities may have unique experiences in their struggles to maintain their Jewishness, and therefore established the Small Communities Committee whose mandate it was to provide these communities the much needed support of Canadian Jewry. This recognition was very important symbolically for Jews living in small communities because it was a clear statement that they are an important part of the Canadian Jewish community and that their needs would at last be addressed in this forum. The Small Communities Committee also provides a newsletter to Jews in small communities which, among other things, includes information on the activities of these small centres. This provides not only a mechanism for communicating what these communities are doing but also formally illustrates that there are out there in all these scattered centres, active Jewish communities who, despite obstacles, are maintaining their Jewish identity and in many cases thriving.

The academic literature has by and large also neglected small-community Jews. While on occasion they are mentioned in passing in so-called national studies, they rarely receive more than a paragraph or two at the end of a lengthy discourse on Jews of Toronto or Winnipeg. My own work on *Jews of Atlantic Canada* was in large measure a response to the neglect of these small communities (Medjuck, 1987). It is difficult to appreciate the tensions and dynamics of ethnic survival in a community of ten or twenty or even a hundred Jewish households when one's reference is only to communities where there are 50,000 fellow Jews. One almost assumes that in some way or another Jewish communities of 50,000 or more will survive and flourish. It is not so obvious how disparate and widely scattered small communities survive. While the numbers of Jews in Saskatoon or Moncton or Corner-Brook do not collectively outnumber the number of Jews living in a few blocks of certain Toronto neighbourhoods, their Jewish identity is nevertheless as salient a part of their lives.

Much of the literature tends to critique Canadian Jews' lack of concern for their Jewish identity. While the problematic aspects for Jewish survival may be endemic to the Canadian Jewish community in general, they take on pandemic qualities in regions that are out of the mainstream of Jewish life as are the small communities of Canada. Firstly, in terms of Jewish support structure, most small communities lack well-developed organizational and communal facilities.[1] Secondly, there is not a strong ethnic presence in that there is no population concentration to provide clear visibility of the Jewish community. Normally, these small communities tend to be geographically distant from centres of Jewish concentration. Finally, in terms of the openness of the host society in which Jews live, Jews in small communities tend to be fairly well accepted and integrated into the large society. Indeed, because they are more likely to interact with their non-Jewish neighbours, they are often more integrated into the communities in which they live than are their co-religionists in large communities.

Jews continue to exist in such out of the way places as St John's, or Yarmouth, or Moose Jaw. While their survival may seem to some enigmatic, it should also be a source of pride for it illustrates the centrality that Jews in small communities give to their Jewish identity.

The Support Structure

When examining large Jewish communities one is struck by the extensive Jewish support systems, for example, the extensive network of synagogues, Jewish 'Y's, Jewish cultural centres, day schools, Jewish day care centres, etc. In small Jewish communities these systems usually do not exist. Indeed, for Jews living in the small Jewish centres of Canada, it is almost inconceivable that there are Jewish vegetarian societies, Jewish single-parent groups, etc. whose membership outnumbers their entire Jewish community. The abundance of resources of this nature almost takes on an exotic quality about it in a centre that has difficulty in having enough Jews to hold High Holiday services. The existence of relatively extensive Jewish institutional arrangements has functioned as a mechanism for survival. There exist religious, semi-religious, and secular organizations and institutions that provide various avenues for those who wish to maintain Jewish identity.

The role played by ethnic facilities in the mainstream of ethnic identity is relatively well institutionalized. Lenski (1961: 36-7) and Sklare and Greenblum (1967: 263) have pointed out that ethnic life has two major components: one that revolves around the group's religious institutions and a second, revolving around the communal, non-religious life of the group. Jewish organizational life can provide a secular alternative for Jews who have little religious involvement. Jews who live in the many small communities scattered across Canada do not have access to these type of institutions. Outside the major centres one does not find Jewish 'Y's, Jewish community centres, Jewish welfare agencies, Jewish day schools, or senior citizen housing.[2]

The structural basis for ethnic identification has been well recognized in the literature on ethnicity. Breton and Pinard (1964: 74-88) and Breton (1964) argue that there is both a cultural and a structural basis for ethnic identification. Structural factors, that is, the extent to which the ethnic group has its own structures to serve the needs of the group, are an important determinant of the ability of the ethnic group to maintain its membership against the processes of integration in the host society. An ethnic group that would be able to provide all such services would be considered by Breton to be institutionally complete; e.g., education, work, medical care, etc., can all be provided totally within the boundaries of the ethnic community. If a community can provide few or no services within the boundaries of the ethnic community, its membership is highly dependent on the host society. This may encourage integration in order to access these needed services. In the Jewish experience, the Jewish shtetl of Eastern Europe provides an example of an institutionally complete community. There was little need for Jews to go outside the boundaries of their community. These ghettos served to create a sense of ethnic solidarity critical to Jewish identification (Lewin: 1984). While no such model was transported to North America, there are differences in the abilities of various communities to be able to provide services to its membership. The Hassidic groups might represent the one extreme in their ability to maintain separate organizational and communal structures (Poll, 1969: 256; Shaffir, 1974: 175-9).

Communities like Toronto are in a much more advantageous position to provide to the members of the Jewish community at least some services. In Charlottetown, or Prince George, or Flin Flon, or Bathurst, it is necessary to seek all services within the structure of the host society. The degree of institutional completeness is non-existent. 'Large' small communities may be able to support some basic institutions. Normally all resources in such communities will be utilized to support a synagogue. While the existence of a synagogue provides an important structural support for the community, the situation is still problematic, particularly for non-religious Jews.

The Problem of Visibility

In addition to the lack of structural support, Jews in small communities lack collective visibility as members of an ethnic community. Jews in large centres, while still in a minority position, constitute socially visible significant ethnic groups. In small Jewish communities Jews often lack the numbers to constitute a socially visible minority. While the entire community might know that a particular store owner is Jewish, or that a certain doctor is Jewish, there is no recognition that these individuals are members of an ethnic group within the community itself (although their membership in the Jewish group in general might be recognized). It is uncommon to find Jewish residential ghettos in small communities. (Indeed, it is impossible to conceive of a residential ghetto when the entire Jewish population may be only a handful of Jews.) Jews in small communities do not have the ethnic neighbourhoods or the modern homogeneous suburbs that help maintain Jewish identity.

The Openness of the Host Society

Compounding the lack of resources and the absence of a socially visible ethnic presence, is the nature of the host community itself. While each region may have somewhat differing experiences, Jews today by and large tend to live in an environment that is both pluralistic and hospitable. While certainly this is a desirable situation in that it provides Jews the opportunity to live as free and full members of their society, in small Jewish population centres this openness takes on an added dimension. The relatively open nature of Canadian society encourages active participation in the structures of that society. A unique outgrowth of the more open nature of Canadian society is a particular form of absorption. Kallen, for example suggests that the 'adaptation of the Jewish home and synagogue to the prevailing norms of the host society has resulted in considerable loss of distinctive Jewish cultural content' (1977: 120). Without some attachment to a distinctive cultural and/or religious ethnic heritage, the issue of Jewish ethnic survival becomes problematic. In small communities, however, the very small population base complicates this participation in that these Jews participate not only in the relatively impersonal aspects of the larger society, such as politics and economics, but also in the more intimate areas such as friendship networks and kinship ties through intermarriage. The problem of preserving Jewish identity is compounded by the greater integration and potential assimilation that may occur in small centres. In my own study of Jews in Atlantic Canada, for example, Jews in this region were very well integrated into the larger society (particularly in terms of educational, occupational, and economic success). They were to be found on the membership lists of the country and yacht clubs. They participated in great numbers in community affairs including politics. Lacking Jewish communal structures, they tended to participate in the structures of the larger society.

The openness of the host society together with the small population base make it very difficult in small communities to maintain ethnic boundaries in the same way that Jews in large centres are able to do. An important key to any group's ethnic identity lies more in the ethnic boundaries that surround the group rather than the cultural matrix within the boundary, as Barth (1969) has argued in general and Kallen (1977) in particular with regards to the Jewish community in Toronto. Given the difficulties in defining and maintaining these boundaries, Jews in small communities have greater difficulties in maintaining the social parameters of ethnic identity.

These factors might lead to the conclusion that the prognosis for continued Jewish identity in small communities is particularly grim. However, despite all these problems and difficulties, Jewish life persists in many very small centres and that while the amorphous sense of identity may not be as strong or as well developed as some might wish, it appears to be present and not as weak as might be expected.

The Maintenance of Jewish Identity in Small Communities

Jewish identity in North America has come to be defined in a number of ways. Although among Jews themselves there may be disagreement about what or who or why is a Jew, there still exists an awareness of being Jewish, a commitment to belonging to that identity, however one may define it. For Jews in small communities, this ambiguity in the definition takes on a more problematic aspect because the restricted variety of available alternatives on which to attach one's Jewish identity. Nevertheless, despite the lack of structural supports, the lack of a visible ethnic presence, and the openness of the host society, Jews continue to identify as Jews in these communities.

Even in small communities Jewish identity remains a salient part of one's identity. My own research on Jews of Atlantic Canada helps to elucidate the processes by which Jews who lack the resources of their fellow Jews in large centres still are able to maintain a strong sense of Jewish identity. In this study various mechanisms for maintaining Jewish identity were examined in an attempt to understand the significance of each of these factors for Atlantic Jews.

The Importance of the Jewish Home

Jewish life in the home has traditionally played a most crucial role for the maintenance of Jewish identity. Much of Jewish religious life was customarily centred in the home. Home-oriented Jewish life is also less affected by outside influences. Practices with respect to the synagogue, for example, are more likely to be influenced by the type of synagogue in the community (or, indeed, if there is a synagogue at all). Because the home represents the most private domain, it is less susceptible to these outside influences.

The dietary laws, *kashrut*, for example, are well established within religious law. Their importance as a socio-cultural means of identity must not be overlooked. It is a daily reminder of one's religious orientation in that it invests the act of eating with enormous religious significance. It is important symbolically, for both Jew and non-Jew are aware that Jews do not eat certain prohibited foods. Thus one is defined both externally and internally by obeying the laws of *kashrut*.

For Jews in the small cities and towns of Atlantic Canada, while only 24 per cent actually claimed to keep a strictly kosher home and 10 per cent keep kosher outside the home, only 31 per cent indicated that they kept *no* kosher observances at all. Thus while only a few are strictly observant, over two-thirds maintain some practice (e.g. no pork products, meat and dairy food kept separate, etc.). When one considers the difficulty of trying to keep kosher in a region such as Atlantic Canada, which has no kosher butcher, no kosher bakeries, and where all products must be imported, then the importance of even tenuous observances takes on significant symbolic meaning. Also it should be noted that strict observance of the dietary laws for Jews in Atlantic Canada makes it impossible for one to eat outside one's home except in the homes of those fellow Jews who also keep strictly kosher. Given these factors it is particularly significant that so many of them do either keep kosher or make some attempt to do so. The keeping of some observances suggest a compromise between the desire to maintain an important link with one's Jewish identity and the demands of the secular society.

A similar type of compromise can be seen with the practice of the Sabbath. Again the Sabbath has a religious as well as symbolic importance. Jews and non-Jews alike know that Jews 'rest' on a different day. While maintaining a traditional Sabbath is practised by very few households, yet many homes observe some Sabbath practice. Well over half (58 per cent) of Atlantic Canada Jews indicated some form of home-oriented Sabbath observances as being always or sometimes done. For Jews in small communities to keep a strictly traditional Sabbath creates both difficulties and restrictions on one's activities. This problem is not restricted to Jews in small communities. For example, Elazer notes in his study of American Jewry that as full-fledged Americans, Jews mix with fellow Americans often to the detriment of Sabbath and *kashrut* (1976: 27). The problems faced by Jews in small centres, however, are much more pronounced. There are no Jewish residential ghettos. There is a small population base so that those who wish to remain a traditional Sabbath lack the numbers to reinforce one another. Keeping a strictly traditional Sabbath makes one not only different from non-Jewish neighbours, but also from one's Jewish neighbours. Despite these practical difficulties the importance of some form of Sabbath observances is clearly evident. Those things which can be done at home, without too much difficulty, and which would indicate the special religious and socio-cultural nature of the Sabbath, e.g. lighting Sabbath candles and saying the blessing over the wine (Kiddush), are practised by a relatively large number of Atlantic Jews.

Within the home, a similar process of adaptation can be identified with respect to the holidays of Passover and Hanukkah. Thus, for example, while fewer than half of Atlantic Canada Jews indicate that they use special dishes at Passover, most attend seders (special Passover dinners) and eat matzah (unleavened bread) (85 and 79 per cent respectively), the two major expressions of the holiday. Over three-quarters light Hanukkah candles. These findings suggest that an important factor in observing certain Jewish practices is the degree to which the activity intrudes upon everyday life in a secular society. Hanukkah candle lighting, seder observances, lighting Sabbath candles, and saying Kiddush have many practitioners. Activities such as maintaining a traditional Sabbath and keeping a strictly kosher home are practised by a very small number of people. They create restrictions on secular activities. In a region with a small Jewish population base certain practices are difficult to keep. There is potentially a conflict with the larger society. Keeping a traditional Sabbath or keeping kosher tends to isolate the Jew from the larger community. Hanukkah and Passover activities, occurring annually, are less isolating and are far more likely to be practised by the entire Jewish community. It is also significant to note that Passover occurs at roughly the same time as Easter and Hanukkah at the same time as Christmas. It would seem that these 'Jewish alternatives' (Sklare and Greenblum, 1967: 55) help the Jew more readily deal with Christian holidays and, thus, are more likely to be valued and more likely to be practised than those observances that alienate the individual from the general community.

As we have noted above, lacking the numbers it is often difficult for Jews to maintain certain home-oriented Jewish practices. Nevertheless, even in small communities, although they have clearly made accommodation to the demands of the secular society in which they live, Jews still observe those practices which can be easily accommodated to their situation. There remains an important symbolic affirmation of one's Jewish identity.

The Role of the Synagogue

More problematic than home-oriented behaviour is behaviour centred around the synagogue. Many very small Jewish communities do not have a synagogue and thus one of the major structural supports for Jewish identity is not available. For those communities that may have a synagogue, the synagogue plays an important role for the preservation of Jewish identity, a role that goes beyond the traditional religious one. Given the absence of other organizations, the synagogues that do exist in smaller communities have become the paramount conservers and preservers of Jewish ethnic identity and are forced to take on functions that secular communal organizations carry out in larger Jewish communities. Because the communities are so small, the existence of a synagogue provides a focal point for organized Jewish life. When one is forced to close because of a declining population, the Jewish community loses its major support system. In Atlantic

Canada, for example, the centrality of the synagogue is reflected in the high percentage of Jews who belong to a synagogue. Only 18 per cent do not belong to a synagogue. The vast majority of Atlantic Canada Jews indicated that the synagogue was important for maintaining their Jewish identity. This was further borne out by the fact that even among individuals who reside in communities where there is no synagogue, 60 per cent are affiliated with a synagogue in a neighbouring centre. This high rate of synagogue membership is exceptional when compared to large communities (Axelrod *et al.*, 1974; Schoenfeld, 1978: 220-1). However, Rose's study of small-town Jews in New York State (1969) notes that although most do not attend synagogue, three-quarters belong to a religious congregation. This high rate of synagogue affiliation indicates the lack of a wide range of other Jewish institutions to provide alternative ties to Judaism. Affiliation with a synagogue becomes one of the few ways that Jews in small centres can formally associate with fellow Jews. The synagogue has taken on a central role. This image of the synagogue is quite distinct from the image of the synagogue in large urban centres both in Canada and the United States. As Sklare and Greenblum (1967: 179) note: 'The synagogue in America has taken on the character of a voluntary association. It vies with other associations, both inside and outside the Jewish community for affiliation and involvement.'

This generalization, perhaps, is accurate for large urban centres but in smaller communities the synagogue is not simply another voluntary organization but rather, given the lack of well-developed institutions, a primary mechanism for maintaining identity. Lacking other institutions that allow small town Jews to publicly identify as Jewish, this high affiliation rate and the stress on the importance of the synagogue is not surprising. Even for the non-religious Jew who wishes to continue to maintain some sort of Jewish identity, the synagogue may be one of a few basic avenues available. Also, to belong to a synagogue creates no major conflicts with one's activities in a secular world. To belong to a synagogue causes little or no disruption in one's existence in the host society.

Not surprisingly, synagogue membership does not translate directly into synagogue attendance. For example, while only a small minority report going to a synagogue on a weekly basis, nevertheless synagogue attendance around the High Holidays is very high (80 per cent report going to synagogue during the High Holidays). Most Jews regard the High Holidays as the most significant religious event of the entire year. It is the Jewish religious experience *par excellence*. In addition, to set aside one day a year for Yom Kippur (or at most three days if one includes both Rosh Hashanah and Yom Kippur) interferes only minimally with one's secular life. It is less of a 'sacrifice' to daily activities than weekly Sabbath attendance where one must set aside a full morning a week. Retention of these holidays is, therefore, much easier for the Jew in a secular society. Jews in small communities participate extensively in the larger host society. For no Jew is it possible to restrict life solely to the Jewish community. Jews who wish to maintain some form of Jewish identity must somehow deal with the tension between the host society and the demands of Judaism. Attendance only at High Holidays harmonizes more with the host society than more frequent attendance. For the Jew in the small communities in Canada, whose life is of necessity integrated into that of the larger community, the dilemma is even more serious than for the Jew in large urban centres where one has more of an option to situate identity totally in a community of fellow Jews. No such option exists in smaller communities. The host society takes on a far more seductive quality. As one of our respondents notes:

> the synagogues are empty because parents have taken them (their children) to scouts, to swimming lessons, to guitar lessons. The kids are widely accepted into all the other activities and if they don't go skating, for example, on Saturday morning there is a social pressure — why didn't they go and the parents give in to the social pressure.

The State of Israel

Any discussion of Jewish identity would be incomplete without some reference to the State of Israel. The central role that identification with the State of Israel plays in the complex mix of contemporary Jewish identity has been well documented (see, for example, Goldscheider, 1974; Kallen, 1977; Kaplan, 1957; Medding, 1969; Sherman, 1960; Sklare, 1971). For Jews in smaller communities identification with Israel provides a mechanism for identification that is accessible to them despite their geographical location. In Atlantic Canada, for example, Jews express overwhelmingly positive attitudes towards the importance of Israel. While Israel and Zionism may serve as secular alternatives to religious identification for Jews in large urban communities (Kallen, 1977: 150), at least for Jews in Atlantic Canada it would appear that Zionism and support for Israel serve to reinforce other aspects of Jewish identification. Thus, for example, in Atlantic Canada, support for Israel and Zionism is positively correlated with synagogue membership and attendance. Synagogue members and attenders feel more intensely the necessity of supporting Israel than do non–members and non-attenders. Similarly, those who keep kosher or recite Sabbath Kiddush or light Sabbath candles, for example, are more likely to feel that support for Israel and Zionism is essential than those who do not keep these practices. It is clear that for Jews in the small communities in Atlantic Canada the various ways of defining oneself as Jewish tend to reinforce one another. In effect, the prejudice towards things Jewish seems not to limit itself to one aspect of Jewish identity but rather is very broad in scope. It may be, given the rather tenuous nature of Jewish existence in small communities. that Jews extend their commitment to all things Jewish simply to ensure the continued existence of a Jewish community.

Other Institutional Supports

The above discussion clearly illustrates that Jews in small communities have not abandoned the traditional mechanisms for Jewish identity but may have adapted them to their unique situation. In addition, Jews in small communities, recognizing the distinctive nature of their struggle against processes of assimilation and acculturation, often develop additional mechanisms for enhancing Jewish identity. For example, in Atlantic Canada, Camp Kadimah, a Jewish Zionist camp, has emerged as a direct consequence of the perceived need for additional supports for maintaining identity. Many of the respondents in our study stressed the importance of the camp for binding the communities together and for providing a sense of common identity for the children who attend. The camp is especially central for Jews from very small communities where there are few fellow-Jews and where children have little opportunity to socialize with other Jewish children.

The Atlantic Jewish Council represents another example of a unique response to the problems of maintaining Jewish identity in the small communities of Atlantic Canada. This Council serves all Jews in the region whether they live in the larger communities of Halifax and Moncton or in the small communities of Wolfville or Antigonish. It is simultaneously an umbrella organization for all the region's programs, entertainment, various celebrations of Jewish holidays, etc. In particular, it has tried to reach out to the very small and even unorganized Jewish communities. While the Atlantic Jewish Council has had some problems, its very existence had enhanced the quality and quantity of Jewish life in the region.[3]

Friendship Networks and Attitudes Toward Intermarriage

The home, the synagogue, and the State of Israel all function to help Jews maintain their identity. In addition, Jews in small communities appear able to provide their own self-help institutions as the creation of Camp Kadimah and the Atlantic Jewish Council attest. There are as well other noninstitutional mechanisms for maintaining Jewish identity. Many studies of Jewish identity and survival stress the fundamental role that friendship patterns play in this process. The informal community (Gans, 1974: 19) or 'associational Jewishness' (Sklare and Greenblum, 1974: 42), it is argued, promote group cohesion. Rose (1969) found that even for Jews in small towns, although over fifty per cent designated a Gentile as their closest friend, 30 per cent said they were 'more comfortable with Jews than non-Jews'. In our study of Atlantic Canada, Jews express the same preference. Three-quarters of them report that at least half of their closest friends are Jews. At the other extreme only two per cent report no close Jewish friends. What is particularly remarkable is that Jews constitute less than one per cent of the entire population. To the extent that 'associational Jewishness' is important for the maintenance of Jewish identity, Jews have another mechanism to enhance and ensure Jewish survival.

One issue of great concern in any discussion of the preservation of Jewish identity is intermarriage. While intermarriage rates are usually somewhat higher in the many small communities in Canada when compared to large urban centres, nevertheless, one still finds in these small communities a clear recognition that intermarriage is problematic for Jewish survival. Again in my own study of Atlantic Canada Jews, attitudes to intermarriage suggest that most Jews want their children to remain Jews and recognize the problems inherent in interfaith marriages. Over three-quarters of them agreed that intermarriage threatens Jewish survival. Similar findings were noted by Rose (1969) in his study of New York State small town Jews. Discouraging interfaith marriages and maintaining strong friendship networks with fellow-Jews are clear articulations of the importance that Jews in small communities place on their Jewish identity.

Conclusions

In a pluralistic society, such as Canada, ethnic identity, even in small communities, has not lost its saliency. In a society as open as Canada, the process of acculturation and absorption are inescapable. There is almost a seductive quality to the nature of the open society. There is, however, a 'line', tenuous as it might be, which is not crossed. Jews have been, and still are becoming, like their neighbours in the surrounding host society. Especially for Jews in small Jewish centres contact is too intense and unavoidable. Still ethnic identity, changing though it may be, persists. It is conceivable that given the nature of the modern industrial state, ethnic identity has taken on a new importance (Glazer and Moynihan, 1975: 1-26). In a society which is increasingly impersonal, ethnic identification may provide an important affective bond for individuals.

One could argue that precisely because the Jewish community is so small in the smaller centres, this sense of affective identification, this sense of belonging, may be enhanced. There is a strong sense of community in a city or town where you know every fellow-Jew and have more than likely participated in all their major life passages. Jews in these small centres have a sense of *gemeinschaft* (community) that is absent from many larger communities. Thee is an overwhelming sense of community when one enters the synagogue, for example, and is greeted by every person present. When someone is sick, or someone gives birth, or someone dies, the entire community participates in the sadness or the joy.[4] This sense of community is not generally appreciated by Jews who have not experienced it. A personal anecdote of a small-town Jew might serve to illustrate this difference.

A distant cousin of mine, living in New York, once called to ask me to help two of her friends who were planning to vacation in the Maritimes and were strictly kosher. When her two friends called, they made enquiries as where the good kosher bakeries were, and where they could buy ready-to-eat kosher meat products. Neither, of course, are available east of Montreal. Instead, I invited them to my home, fed them several meals, and sent them on their way with an enormous care package. As they were leaving, they asked me 'Why should a Jew live in such a God-forsaken place as the Maritimes?' My response was simple. 'Because in New York, they would think you totally mad to take in two strangers, provide several meals for them as well as a care package to take away, while in this community this is perfectly normal behaviour.'

This sense of community with fellow Jews tends to disappear in the more impersonal environment of large cities.

Some authors have argued that a Jew is a 'disturbed marginal man' (Stonequist, 1937) or an 'eternal stranger' (Simmel, 1950). The argument is that Jews are caught between two worlds—the demands of the majority culture and the demands of their Jewish heritage: as Park (1928) concludes, 'one whom fate has condemned to lived in two societies and in two, not merely different, but antagonistic, cultures'. This view of Jewish life, if true for Jews in large centres, should be even more accurate for Jews in small communities. However, we have illustrated in this discussion that such is not the case. Jews in small communities struggle to maintain their sense of Jewish identity by using whatever mechanisms they have available while at the same time they seem to have integrated into their communities. They participate in both cultures not as antagonistic forces but rather adapting to each in turn. Rose's (1969: 346) conclusion about the New York State small-town Jew may be equally valid in the Canadian experience:

> He enjoys the advantage of sharing two 'cups of life', and in a word, is bicultural. This duality (rather than marginality) causes the majority of respondents to come to agreement with one who stated: 'You see, we feel we have the best of both'.

A recollection from one of the respondents from our study of Atlantic Jews serves to indicate the ability of the Jew to live with the duality of his/her existence. He reported to us that in the community where he grew up there were enough children to have a small Junior congregation. After Sabbath services were finished, this group of youngsters would walk together in their suits with their *tallith* bags under their arms to go see the 1:15 movie matinee.

> Nice little Jewish boys with their suits and tallis bags every week 'very religiously' [in original] go to the movies. At 3:00 o'clock they would go to someone's home and watch television.

The respondent did not report this incident to illustrate any ambivalence or 'marginality' but rather to explain the fellowship (the 'chevra') that existed.

In light of the increasing concerns over the processes of assimilation that are occurring among Jews everywhere, it would be naïve not to be concerned about the major obstacles to Jewish survival that are present in small communities. Nevertheless, it is equally important to recognize the ways that many Jews in small communities are finding to deal with this crisis and to counteract threats to their Jewish survival. At times these struggles are lost, but the continued persistence of Jewish communities in the many small communities of Canada speaks to the tenacity of Jewish ethnic identity.

Notes

[1]While larger small communities may have some minimal structural support, e.g., a synagogue, nevertheless, these pale when compared to the extensive networks of structures found in large urban centres.

[2]It is necessary to recognize that to group all small communities together is equally problematic as even in small communities, there is a difference in the resources available. A community that is able to maintain a synagogue has a major resource that a community whose membership is too small to do so has not. Even in small communities with synagogues the ability to maintain the synagogue is usually somewhat precarious.

[3]One finds similar self-help efforts in all small communities. The first Jewish cemetery in the interior of British Columbia opened late in 1988. The community's next task is the building of a community centre in Kelowna.

[4]It may be argued that this sense of community, of *gemeinschaft*, is also felt in terms of belonging to the general community, not only the Jewish community. The strong sense of collective identification that one feels in small centres simply does not exist in large urban centres.

References

Axelrod, Morris, Floyd J. Fowler and Arnold Gurin
  1974 'The Jewish Community of Boston/Membership in Synagogues and Jewish Organizations' in Marshall Sklare, ed., *The Jewish Community in America* (New York: Behrman House, Inc.): 111-27

Barth, Frederik
  1969 *Ethnic Groups and Boundaries, The Social Organization of Culture Differences* (Bergen: University of Bergen)

Breton, Raymond
  1965 'Institutional Completeness of Ethnic Communities and the Personal Relations of Immigrants', *American Journal of Sociology* 70, 2

Breton, Raymond and Maurice Pinard
  1964 'Group Formation and Immigrants' in *Canadian Society* (Toronto: The Macmillan Company of Canada, Limited): 74-88

Devos, George and Lola Romanucci-Ross
  1975 'Ethnicity: Vessel of Meaning and Emblem of Contrast' in G. Devos and L.

Romanucci-Ross, eds, *Ethnic Identity: Cultural Continuities and Change* (Palo Alto: Mayfield Publishing Company): 363-90

Driedger, Leo
1978 'Introduction: Ethnic Identity in the Canadian Mosaic' in Leo Driedger, ed., *The Canadian Ethnic: A Quest for Identity* (Toronto: McClelland and Stewart Ltd.)

Elazer, Daniel J.
1976 *Community and Polity: The Organizational Dynamics of American Jewry* (Philadelphia: The Jewish Publication Society of America)

Gans, Herbert J.
1974 'The Origin of a Jewish Community in the Suburbs' in Marshall Sklare, ed., *The Jewish Community in America* (New York: Behrman House Inc.): 19-14

Glazer, Nathan and Daniel P. Moynihan
1975 'Introduction' in Nathan Glazer and Daniel P. Moynihan, eds, *Ethnicity: Theory and Experience* (Cambridge, MA: Harvard University Press)

Goldscheider, Calvin
1974 'American Aliya: Sociological and Demographic Perspectives' in Marshall Sklare, ed., *The Jew in American Society* (New York: Behrman House Inc.): 335-84

Greenblum, Joseph and Marshall Sklare
1958 'The Attitude of the Small-Town Jew Toward His Community' in Marshall Sklare, ed., *The Jews, Social Patterns of an American Group* (New York: The Free Press): 288-303

Isajiw, Wsevolod
1968-9 'The Process of Social Integration; The Canadian Example', *Dalhousie Review* 48, 4 (Winter): 510-20

Kallen, Evelyn
1977 *Spanning the Generations: A Study of Jewish Identity* (Don Mills: Longman Canada Ltd.)

Kaplan, Mordecai M.
1957 *Judaism as a Civilization* (New York: Reconstructionist Press)

Lenski, Gerhard
1961 *The Religious Factor* (Garden City: Doubleday and Co., Inc.)

Lewin, Kurt
1948 *Resolving Social Conflicts* (New York: Harper & Brothers)

Lipset, Seymour Martin
1974 'Intergroup Relations/The Changing Situation of American Jewry' in Marshall Sklare, ed., *The Jewish Community in America* (New York: Behrman House, Inc.): 312-13

Medding, P.Y.
1974 *From Assimilation to Group Survival* (New York: Hart Publishing Co.)

Medjuck, Sheva
1986 *Jews of Atlantic Canada* (St John's: Breakwater Press)

Park, Robert
1928 'Human Migration and the Marginal Man', *American Journal of Sociology* 33: 881-93

Poll, Solomon
1962 *The Hassidic Community of Williamsburg* (New York: The Free Press of Glencoe, Inc.)

————
1969 'The Persistence of Tradition: Orthodoxy in America', in Peter J. Rose, ed., *The Ghetto and Beyond* (New York: Random House)

Rose, Peter J.
1969 *The Ghetto and Beyond: Essays on Jewish Life in America* (New York: Random House)

————
1969 'Strangers in Their Midst: Small-Town Jews and Their Neighbours' in Peter J. Rose, ed., *The Ghetto and Beyond* (New York: Random House): 335-56

Schoenfeld, Stuart
1978 'The Jewish Religion in North America: The Canadian Experience (1870-1900)', *The Canadian Journal of Sociology* 3, 2 (Spring): 209-31.

Shaffir, W.
1974 *Life in a Religious Community: The Lubavitcher Chassidim in Montreal* (Toronto: Holt, Rinehart and Winston of Canada Ltd)

Sherman, C. Bezalel
1960 *The Jew Within American Society* (Detroit: Wayne State University Press)

Sherman, Muzafer and Carolyn W. Sherif
1956 *An Outline of Social Psychology* (New York: Harper & Brothers)

Simmel, Georg
1950 'The Stranger' in Kurt H. Wolff (trans.) *The Sociology of Georg Simmel* (Glencoe IL: The Free Press): 402-8

————
1969 'Ethnic Church and Desire for Survival' in Peter J. Rose, ed., *The Ghetto and Beyond* (New York: Random House): 101-17

————
1974 *The Jew in American Society* (New York: Behrman House Inc)

————
1958 *The Jews: Social Patterns of an American Group* (New York: The Free Press)

————
1974 (ed.) *The Jewish Community in America* (New York: Behrman House) and Joseph Greenblum

————

1974 'The Friendship Pattern of the Lakeview Jew' in Marshall Sklare, ed., *The Jewish Community in America* (New York: Behrman House Inc.): 42–66

————

1967 *Jewish Identity on the Suburban Frontier* (New York: Basic Books, Inc.)

Stonequist, Everett V.
1961 (1937) *The Marginal Man: A Study in Personality and Cultural Conflict* (New York: Russell and Russell)

The Persistence of Invisible Poverty

Among Jews in Canada

Jim Torczyner

The Jew is not a burden on the charities of the State nor of the city; these could cease their functions without affecting him. . . . A Jewish beggar is not impossible; perhaps such a thing may exist, but there are few men who can say that they have seen that spectacle.

—Mark Twain, 1899[1]

As we approach a third millennium, Jews are characterized as successful and self-reliant. They are perceived to have established an unsurpassed tradition of philanthropy and networks of community-subsidized services. In Canada, 25 per cent of the Jewish community have obtained a university degree. The corresponding figure for all Canadians is 8 per cent.[2] In the United States, Jewish household incomes are 50 per cent higher than national norms.[3] In 1987, Jews contributed more than $700 million to the campaigns of their federations.[4]

Notwithstanding these achievements, poverty remains a persistent and significant aspect of the Jewish communal experience. Earlier in this century, popular and scholarly literature portrayed the plight of waves of poor Jewish immigrants and the hardships they endured on the lower east side of New York or the Main in Montreal. Poverty and struggle characterized the early twentieth-century Jewish community, became part of American folklore, and was woven into the fabric of North American Jewish identity. But more Jews prospered and achieved distinction, and as they moved out of the old neighbourhoods, those who did not succeed became invisible to society at large and fellow Jews alike.

Only in the early 1970s as an outgrowth of the war on poverty did research rediscover the Jewish poor. Findings pointing to poverty rates of between 15 and 20 per cent were reported in Chicago in 1971,[5] in New York in 1973,[6] and in national United States estimates released in 1974.[7] Levine and Hochbaum synthesized these efforts in *Poor Jews: An American Awakening*. This volume included a chapter by Ann Wolf entitled 'The Invisible Jewish Poor'. These studies estimated that there were up to one million poor Jews in the United States and a quarter of a million in New York City alone.[8]

American studies of the Jewish community in general and its poor in particular have been hampered by a variety of factors. First, the United States census does not gather data on religious affiliation. Consequently, Jewish population estimates have been based on extrapolations from census data on mother tongue and country of origin, examinations of death records, affiliations with certain institutions, absences from public schools during Jewish high holidays, and on distinctive Jewish names. Samples are small because of the cost of special surveys, and these studies often used different definitions of Jewishness.[9]

Studies of the Jewish poor have posed other methodological problems as well. Groeneman found that Jewish respondents had the highest refusal rates of all religious and ethnic groups with regard to questions of income.[10] In addition, large numbers of the poor are not affiliated with the Jewish community. Several studies indicate that as few as 10 per cent of the Jewish poor are affiliated with Jewish agencies, and these are as clients.[11] Samples drawn from agency client lists, consequently, reflect a small proportion of the Jewish poor who, as service users, are not representative of those who do not avail themselves of communal services.

These few studies notwithstanding, however, there has been limited research interest in the Jewish poor. For many years, Jewish social scientists generally avoided research on the Jewish population, and scholars who were not Jewish did not find it appropriate to research Jewish issues. 'Insiders wanted to be universalists', observed Paul Ritterband, 'and outsiders felt inadequate in the company of insiders.'[12] Research regarding the Jewish poor elicited even less interest.

The Canadian Census

Because the Canadian census gathers information with regard to religion, ethnicity, and income, it is possible to correlate demographic characteristics of the Jewish poor. The data used here are derived from the 'long form' of the census which is administered to 20 per cent of the population. Responses are weighted, tested, and released for the entire population. The Canadian census has more than a 95 per cent reliability rate and the most recent data available from a long-form census are for 1981.

Jews can identify themselves in the census by religion, ethnicity, or both. All other information gathered by the census can be correlated with religious and ethnic identity. Some limitations arise from the lack of attitudinal and qualitative data. Others concern its timeliness given the ten-year gap between censuses and the multi-year process of data collection, storage, reliability testing, and preliminary analysis prior to the generation of specific data bases.

Despite these limitations, the Canadian census offers unique opportunities for research regarding the demography of both Canadian and United States Jewry. Studies reveal very similar demographic patterns among Canadian and United States Jews. In the first instance, the majority of members of these communities are only separated by a few hundred miles. Fifty-two per cent of American Jews live in the Northeast.[13] Two thirds of Canadian Jewry live in the eastern cities of Montreal and Toronto.[14] Norland and Freedman found that American and Canadian Jews experience similar social processes, and, as a result, Canadian census data could compensate for the limitations of the United States census.[15] In terms of actual demographic characteristics, Schmeltz and DellaPergola report that both Canadian and American Jews experienced a rapid and comparable increase in the proportion of divorced individuals and one-parent households.[16] Lastly, Rosenwaike's findings regarding Jewish elderly persons in the United States are analogous with Canadian findings.[17]

Thus, given the proximity and demographic similarity of Canadian and American Jews, Canadian census findings can be extended with some confidence to the United States scene as well. Inferences relating to the transferability of data regarding the Jewish poor must take into account generally higher rates of poverty in Canada on the one hand, and a wider health and social safety net on the other. The extent to which these two factors offset each other is unclear. Montreal data from the 1971 census suggests comparability. It found that 20 per cent of the Jewish community was poor, a percentage similar to the American studies cited earlier.[18]

Methodology

The development of a demographic profile of the Jewish poor had three purposes:
- to compare their salient characteristics with those of the Jewish community in general in order to identify those factors which distinguish them from the rest of the community.
- to compare these characteristics with the Canadian poor at large to determine the degree to which Jewish poverty mirrors the larger Canadian experience.
- to identify those demographic characteristics which contribute to the invisibility of the Jewish poor.

This research was guided by the following assumptions:
- Poverty levels are functions of macro-social and -economic forces and fluctuate in relation to them.
- These forces produce a disproportional allocation of resources, thus creating a poverty class.
- Particularly disempowered groups of people constitute a disproportionately high percentage of this poverty class (women, the elderly, unemployed, immigrants, single parents, etc.).
- Poverty levels in societal sub-groups (i.e. religious and ethnic groups) will mirror these overall trends and will be populated by similarly disadvantaged groups of persons.

• The extent to which poverty levels differ among particular sub-groups depends on the degree to which the demographic characteristics of the particular sub-group differ from overall, societal demographic characteristics.

To pursue this inquiry, ten tables, each with four sub-sections, were generated for 150 regions across Canada. These tables cross-tabulated Jewishness and income with 39 variables, grouped as follows: basic demographic data such as age and sex; living arrangements and family structure; education and labour force activity; and immigration patterns.

A uniform definition of Jewishness was created from the ethnicity and religious variables in consultation with major Jewish organizations across Canada: 'Jewishness is defined as those individuals who are Jewish by religion *or* Jewish by ethnicity where no religion is indicated.'[19]

Income was measured categorically and continuously. Three categories, below poverty, marginal, and above poverty were constructed by factoring Statistics Canada's poverty line for 1981, and adding a marginal category.[20] This poverty line varies according to family size and population density within a geographic region. Table 1 presents these income levels.

Findings

By the definition outlined above, 312,000 Canadians identified themselves as Jews in 1981. One out of six was poor or near poor: 14.4 per cent of Canadian Jews lived below the poverty line and another 2.5 per cent were marginal to it. The corresponding figure for Canada as a whole was almost 25 per cent.

Poverty is common among Jews in all Canadian regions. Poverty rates vary from a low of 11 per cent in Ottawa to a high of almost 30 per cent in New Brunswick and Newfoundland. In most instances, Jewish poverty rates follow general regional patterns.

The percentage of Jewish poor is high in parts of the country which have higher percentages of poverty and are low in regions with fewer poor. Jewish poverty rates nationally, however, are substantially lower (8 per cent) than the Canadian average. Thus, one partial explanation for the invisibility of the Jewish poor is that they are a minority within a minority. Of the close to 6 million Canadian poor approximately 50,000 are Jews. They form less than 1 per cent of all of Canada's poor. Table 2 presents poverty rates among Jews and all Canadians nationally and in selected regions in 1981.

Though fewer in number, 50,000 people who compose 17 per cent of the Jewish community are not an insubstantial number. Other factors explain their invisibility. Some of these relate to the demographic characteristics of the Jewish poor which reflect overall differential characteristics between the Jewish community and Canadian society as a whole. Most notably, the Jewish poor are likely to be elderly, women, and persons who live alone, and these populations are generally less visible than younger persons or families

Table 1   Statistics Canada Low-Income Lines — Estimates for 1981

	POPULATION OF AREA OF RESIDENCE				
	500,000 AND OVER	100,000– 499,999	30,000– 99,999	LESS THAN 30,000	RURAL
No. in Family					
1	$ 8,970	$ 8,519	$ 7,991	$ 7,388	$ 6,333
2	11,835	11,231	10,479	9,724	8,669
3	15,831	15,002	14,021	13,042	11,609
4	18,243	17,337	16,208	15,076	13,419
5	21,259	20,127	18,771	17,488	15,604
6	23,218	21,937	20,505	19,072	17,036
7 or more	25,555	24,198	22,616	21,032	18,771

with school age children. In 1981, 15.8 per cent of the Jewish community was 65 or older, and this figure is 75 per cent higher than the corresponding Canadian figure. This dramatic difference persists among those who are over the age of 75, and will continue, albeit in less dramatic fashion, in the foreseeable future as the 55–64 age cohort reveals similar, though less pronounced, trends. Table 3 synthesizes these findings to illustrate the essential differences in the age structure of both communities.

Poverty rates in the Canadian population as a whole exceed those of the Jewish community as every age level even though Jewish poverty rates rise and fall in relation to the overall Canadian pattern. Poverty rates among seniors and women, for example, are highest in both populations. A substan-

Table 2   Jews and All Canadians with Poor or Marginal Income Status, 1981

TOTAL N OF POOR IN CANADA = 5,876,870   TOTAL N OF POOR JEWS IN CANADA = 52,785

LOCATION	PER CENT OF JEWISH POPULATION	PER CENT OF ENTIRE POPULATION
CANADA	16.9	24.8
Newfoundland and New Brunswick	29.5	35.0
Halifax	16.3	21.0
Montreal	19.3	24.0
Ottawa	11.0	17.7
Toronto	15.0	18.2
Windsor	23.0	24.2
Winnipeg	16.7	22.3
Edmonton	20.7	17.4
Vancouver	15.5	18.4

Table 3   Age Structure of Jews and All Canadians, 1981

AGE	PER CENT OF JEWISH COMMUNITY	PER CENT OF CANADIAN POP.	PER CENT OF DIFFERENCES
0–15	18.5	22.9	+23.8
0–30	41.2	51.1	+24.0
55–64	11.8	8.9	–32.6
65+	15.8	9.0	–75.5
75+	5.1	3.0	–70.0

tially higher proportion of the Jewish poor, however, consist of the elderly in general, and women in particular. Three out of ten Jewish poor persons are over the age of 65—this is twice the percentage of the elderly in the Canadian poor population. As women tend to live longer than men and are less financially secure, they have higher rates of poverty; consequently, one out of three elderly Jewish women is poor. Table 4 provides comparative data on poverty rates by age, and by age and sex for people 65 years and older.

A second distinguishing feature which lends to their invisibility is the disproportionate percentage of the Jewish poor who live alone. One out of three Jewish poor persons lives alone. The corresponding figure for the Canadian poor population is one in five. Thus, despite the fact that a greater percentage of Canadians who live alone are poor, they account for a smaller percentage of the entire Canadian poor population. These rates of poverty among persons who live alone are much higher for women and the elderly in both populations. Table 5 presents these findings.

The younger the person, the more likely he will be male if he lives alone. The older one gets, the likelihood increases that the person living alone will be female. This relationship holds for both the Jewish and entire Canadian populations. Among Jews, however, a much greater percentage of those who live alone are elderly. They account for one third of all those who live alone; and elderly women themselves comprise 25 per cent of this population.

In Canada, one out of two persons who live alone is poor. These rates of poverty decline between the ages of 30-49. They then continue to rise steadily—increasing with advancing years. Three out of four elderly Canadians who live alone (75 per cent), live below the poverty line. The corresponding figure for the Jewish poor is 60 per cent.

These two distinguishing characteristics of the Jewish poor—the prevalence of the elderly and those who live alone—explain, in part, why the Jewish poor tend to be invisible. Creating mutually exclusive categories from these two variables, one accounts for half the Jewish poor and only one quarter of the Canadian poor.

These characteristics are closely associated with anonymity and invisibility. Less likely to be vocal with regard to one's needs or capable of negotiating complex bureaucracies, and more likely to live alone and without family

Table 4 Poverty by Age and Sex, Jews and All Canadians, 1981

	N	% OF ENTIRE POPULATION	% WHO ARE POOR	% OF ENTIRE POOR
CANADIAN POPULATION				
AGE				
0–14	5,444,795	22.9	27.6	25.8
16–64	16,211,290	21.1	58.6	58.6
65 +	2,141,255	9.0	42.4	15.6
SEX				
Male	11,625,235	49.5	22.8	45.6
Female	11,860,085	50.5	26.7	54.4
AGE & SEX				
M65 +	915,925	3.9	42.1	6.6
F65 +	1,221,235	5.2	48.2	9.1
JEWISH POPULATION				
AGE				
0–14	57,475	18.4	15.7	17.1
16–64	205,025	65.8	13.7	53.3
65 +	49,225	15.8	31.0	28.9
SEX				
Male	155,455	48.9	14.7	43.4
Female	156,280	51.1	18.9	56.6
AGE & SEX				
M65 +	23,200	7.4	23.7	10.4
F65 +	26,025	8.4	37.6	18.5

Table 5 Characteristics of Persons Living Alone, Jews and All Canadians, 1981

VARIABLE	CANADIAN POPULATION		JEWISH POPULATION	
	N	%	N	%
% of total population	2,376,085	10.1	40,785	13.1
% who are poor	1,234,505	52.0	17,625	43.2
% of total poor population	1,234,140	21.0	17,630	33.4
% of single poor who are female	765,168	62.0	11,425	64.8
% of single poor who are 65 +	462,665	37.5	8,215	46.6

or other social supports, the Jewish poor are often unnoticed because they interact less with other people. They become invisible to Jew and non-Jew alike.

Family Structure and Poverty

Data correlating marital status, family size, couple- and single-parenting with income and other demographic criteria point to the economic solvency of the traditional nuclear family. Husband-wife family persons constitute 80 per cent of the Jewish community, but only half of the Jewish poor. The same trend is evidenced in the Canadian community as a whole.

Complementing the data regarding the elderly and those living alone in the Jewish community, the Jewish poor, be they in husband-wife or single-parent families, have fewer children and smaller families than their Canadian counterparts. More than one in four low-income Canadians live in families which have three or more children. The corresponding figure for the Jewish poor is one in eight. This finding is consistent with the data (Table 2) which indicated that there is a 25 per cent higher percentage of children in the Canadian community than among Jews. Table 6 presents these findings.

In both the Canadian and Jewish community single-parent families are headed by women in almost all cases. They account for 16.5 per cent and 12.3 per cent of the poor respectively. In addition to the economic stress of single-parenting and the higher percentages of women among the elderly Jewish poor, women are economically disadvantaged at every age level.

Labour Force Activity and Poverty

While the evidence presented to this point helps to explain the invisibility of the Jewish poor, data relating to labour force activity partially counteracts this trend. Although the Jewish population had almost identical unemployment rates with all Canadians in 1981, and the unemployed constituted similar percentages of the poor in each community, a higher percentage of poor Jews worked (51 per cent vs 46 per cent). Similarly, a higher percentage of low-income Canadians were not in the labour force as compared to their Jewish counterparts (62 per cent vs 57 per cent). Clearly, the employed poor are likely to be more visible and have more frequent interactions than those who are not in the labour force. Table 7 identifies these differences among Jewish and Canadian poor with regard to labour force activity.

A closer examination of the characteristics of the working poor and the poor who are not in the labour force reveals that a greater percentage of poor men work than women. Although men represent less than half the poor, they constitute the majority of the working poor. These findings hold true for both the Jewish community and the Canadian population as a whole.

Many of the Jewish working poor, however, live alone or in husband-wife families without children (54 per cent). The corresponding figure among the

Table 6 Poverty and Family Structure, Jews and All Canadians, 1981

	JEWISH POPULATION			CANADIAN POPULATION		
	% OF ENTIRE POP.	% WHO ARE POOR	% OF ENTIRE POOR	% OF ENTIRE POP.	% WHO ARE POOR	% OF ENTIRE POOR
Unattached	13.1	42.3	33.4	10.1	52.0	21.0
Husband–wife families	79.1	12.0	51.8	80.1	19.0	58.6
Single parent families	6.5	32.0	12.3	8.1	50.7	16.5
Husband–wife 0 children	23.3	14.4	19.3	17.0	20.8	14.0
Husband–wife 1–2 children	39.6	9.2	21.0	46.6	15.2	23.9
Husband–wife 3 + children	17.3	11.6	11.5	23.0	23.4	20.7
Lone parent 1–2 children	5.4	31.6	9.9	6.0	47.7	11.1
Lone parent 3 + children	1.3	32.7	2.4	2.4	58.6	5.4

Canadian working poor is substantially lower (29.5 per cent). Conversely, a higher percentage of single-parent families and husband–wife families with three or more children who are poor are likely not to be in the labour force (26.8 per cent among Jews and 41.3 per cent among Canadians).

These factors associated with family structure help to explain why a greater percentage of poor Jews work. That is, poor Jews are more likely to live alone or in families with fewer children, and therefore may be more readily available for work than the greater percentage of single-parent families and families with three or more children among the Canadian poor. Paralleling these findings, three quarters of the Jewish poor who are not in the labour force are either less than 14 or over the age of 65. The corres-

Table 7 Labour Force Activity and the Poor, Jews and All Canadians, 1981

	JEWISH COMMUNITY[a]			CANADIAN POPULATION[b]		
LABOUR FORCE	% OF ENTIRE POP.	% WHO ARE POOR	% OF ENTIRE POOR[c]	% OF ENTIRE POP.	% WHO ARE POOR	% OF ENTIRE POOR[d]
Employed	51.0	11.2	31.9	46.2	13.6	17.9
Unemployed	9.3	19.1	10.5	8.9	28.2	10.1
Not in work force	39.8	24.5	57.6	45.0	34.2	62.0

[a]N = 312,060 [b]N = 23,485,320 [c]N = 52,785 [d]N = 5,824,080

ponding figure for the Canadian poor is two-thirds. That is, only on in four poor Jews who are not in the labour force are between the ages of 15 and 64; while one in three Canadian poor fit in this category. Table 8 compares the working poor and those not in the labour force by age, sex, and living arrangements.

Education, employability and poverty are closely related and further explain why a greater percentage of poor Jews work. Jews, at all income levels, are better educated than the Canadian population as a whole. One out of three Jews has less than a high school education while 50 per cent of all Canadians have not completed high school. Among the poor, less than half of the Jewish community (45.9 per cent) had less than a high school education. The corresponding figure among the Canadian poor is almost 2 out of 3 (64.6 per cent). Similarly, 15 per cent of all poor Jews have completed university. Among the Canadian poor, only 3.4 per cent have a university degree and only 8 per cent of all Canadians — irrespective of income levels — have graduated from university. Table 9 relates income levels to educational achievement.

The Jewish Poor: Immigrant and Native-born

Immigrants are more likely to be poor and are less likely to be able to access their rights than residents of longer duration and members of the cultural and linguistic majorities. It is certainly not surprising that a much smaller percentage of Jews are 'non-immigrants' (49.7 per cent) than the rest of the Canadian population (84.7 per cent). One in ten Jews immigrated to Canada in the decade prior to 1981. The corresponding figure for the Canadian population as a whole is less than one in twenty. Immigrants in the previous decade constituted three times the percentage of the Jewish poor than they did among the Canadian poor (17.6 per cent vs 5.6 per cent). Table 10 compares these patterns among Jews and the Canadian population as a whole.

Thus a variety of distinct demographic characteristics contribute to the invisibility of the Jewish poor. Fewer in number, a substantially higher proportion of the Jewish poor consist of the elderly in general, and women in particular. The far greater frequency with which the Jewish poor live alone or in smaller families with fewer children, along with the higher percentage of immigrants among them, contribute to their invisibility. These factors outweigh the countervailing influence of the increased percentages of poor Jews who work and their substantially higher levels of educational attainment.

Understanding the Invisibility of the Jewish Poor

The invisibility of the Jewish poor is only partially attributable to their demographic characteristics and societal stereotypes regarding Jews in general. During the past forty years, North American Jewry has undergone

Table 8 Poverty and Labour Force Characteristics, Jews and All Canadians, 1981

VARIABLE	JEWISH COMMUNITY			CANADIAN POPULATION		
	% OF ALL POOR[a]	% OF POOR WHO WORK[b]	% OF POOR NOT IN LABOUR FORCE[c]	% OF ALL POOR[d]	% OF POOR WHO WORK[e]	% OF POOR NOT IN LABOUR FORCE[f]
All	100	31.9	57.6	100	27.9	62.0
SEX						
Male	43.4	54.6	37.0	45.6	57.9	59.5
Female	56.6	45.4	63.0	54.4	42.1	60.5
AGE						
0-14	17.1	—	30.4	25.8	—	41.8
15-29	23.5	41.9	8.5	26.2	45.5	13.0
30-49	17.5	36.2	6.9	18.7	37.5	9.0
50-64	11.4	14.0	10.2	12.2	14.1	11.3
65+	28.9	6.6	44.0	15.6	2.9	24.9
LIVING ARRANGEMENTS						
Live alone	33.4	38.5	30.0	21.0	27.6	18.1
All husband-wife families	51.8	48.9	54.5	58.6	57.2	60.7
H-W 0 children	19.3	15.5	21.8	14.0	11.9	15.3
H-W 1-2 children	21.0	24.4	20.5	23.9	27.9	22.3
H-W 3+ children	11.5	9.0	13.8	20.7	17.4	23.1
All single parent families	12.3	10.5	13.0	16.5	12.3	18.2
SP 1-2 children	9.9	8.6	10.3	11.1	9.1	11.8
SP 3+ children	2.4	1.9	2.7	5.4	3.2	6.4

[a]N = 52,780 [b]N = 16,815 [c]N = 30,430 [d]N = 5,824,080 [e]N = 1,625,945 [f]N = 3,610,150

rapid mobility and unparalleled integration. These trends accompanied and produced dramatic changes in family and communal structures and in the relationships among Jews and between Jews and the wider society. It is these factors which have accentuated the alienation of low-income Jews from the mainstream of Jewish communal life.

In 1941, for example, 80 per cent of Montreal's Jews lived in the neighbourhoods which they first settled. Most worked in needle trade shops located near their residence.[21] This close proximity in the work place and in the neighbourhood gave impetus to grass-roots, communal activity. By 1940, the *Canadian Jewish Year Book* listed 44 Jewish labour organizations and local affiliates, three schools, four youth movements, and 20 sick benefit societies, all sponsored by the Jewish labour movement. Forty of Montreal's

Table 9 Education and Income,[a] Jews and All Canadians, 1981

CANADIAN POPULATION

ED. LEVEL	N	% OF POP.	% WHO ARE POOR	% POOR POP.
0–8	3,676,415	20.0	41.0	34.6
⟩8 and ⟨H.S.	5,119,745	27.9	25.5	30.0
H.S.	8,094,080	44.1	17.2	32.0
B.A.-M.A.	1,407,890	7.7	10.5	3.4
PhD	54,690	0.3	6.2	0.1
Total N	18,352,520			

JEWISH POPULATION

ED. LEVEL	N	% OF POP.	% WHO ARE POOR	% POOR POP.
0–8	31,300	12.3	34.0	24.0
⟩8 and ⟨H.S.	51,950	20.4	18.3	21.9
H.S.	105,990	41.7	15.8	38.5
B.A.-M.A.	61,380	24.1	10.4	14.7
PhD	3,710	1.5	6.2	0.5
Total N	254,330			

[a]Excluding children less than 15 and still in school.

Table 10 Immigration and Poverty, Jews and All Canadians, 1981

YEAR OF IMMIGRATION	CANADIAN POPULATION			JEWISH POPULATION		
	% OF ENTIRE POP.	% WHO ARE POOR	% OF ENTIRE POOR	% OF ENTIRE POP.	% WHO ARE POOR	% OF ENTIRE POOR
Non–Immigrant	84.3	24.9	84.7	63.7	13.3	49.7
Pre–1941	2.1	43.5	3.7	7.9	28.8	13.3
1941–50	1.1	21.2	1.0	4.0	19.7	4.6
1951–60	3.9	16.2	2.6	7.6	17.9	7.9
1961–70	3.8	16.1	2.5	7.2	17.6	7.5
1971–81	4.7	29.1	5.6	9.6	31.1	17.6

fifty synagogues were located within one mile of each other. St Urbain Street, later popularized by the novelist Mordecai Richler, housed six synagogues. As one Rabbi put it: 'everyone knew who was poor, and everyone knew who was pretending to be rich.'

By 1951, only 43 per cent of the Jewish community lived in these neighbourhoods. In 1971 the figures were further reduced to 6 per cent, and, by 1981, less than 5 per cent of the Jewish population resided in these areas.[22] As opportunities expanded, Jews prospered, moved, and integrated themselves into more affluent neighbourhoods. Some of the poor remained behind. Others moved to newer, working-class neighbourhoods. The poor were increasingly isolated, and their prime organizational vehicle, the labour movement, no longer expressed Jewish concerns. Few organizations represented the Jewish poor.

Success and stratification were accompanied by an erosion of other traditional, grass-roots, Jewish communal structures. Synagogues once served political, cultural, and social welfare functions in addition to their religious roles. While guiding religious practice, synagogues educated children, nursed the infirm, provided relief for the poor, buried the dead, raised funds, provided status to its leaders, and mediated disputes among its members.

Many religious, social, and recreational organizations became disengaged from direct contact with and service to the Jewish poor. Jewish organizations federated, relocated, and redefined their focus in light of the needs, resources, and interests of the majority of their members. Agencies and synagogues alike moved to the neighbourhoods which now housed the middle class majority, and while commitment to the poor remained, priorities increasingly reflected the needs of the majority.

These trends in population and organizational growth and movement led to the emergence of centralized federations as the prime fundraising and service delivery mechanisms of the Jewish community.[23] The benefits of improved fund raising, coordination of planning, and professionalization of service also engendered greater alienation among the Jewish poor. As services became centralized in the middle class communities, it became less possible to provide relief for the poor in their neighbourhoods. Lerner[24] and others report that federation services reach a minority of the poor because services have moved, outreach is lacking, and insufficient priority is given to them. Given these inevitable changes in community structure, the Jewish poor have little contact with other Jews.

Poor Jews are often alienated from the neighbourhoods in which they remained and the new residents who moved in. As those who prospered moved out, they were replaced by other immigrant, ethnic, and disadvantaged groups. New cultures, organizations, and lifestyles, unfamiliar if not inhospitable to the Jewish poor, often took up occupancy in the buildings which formerly housed the synagogues, libraries, and Jewish cultural institutions of a previous era. The remaining Jewish poor are often estranged from their new neighbours. One Montreal study conducted in an ethnically diverse, low-income community revealed that distrust of other residents' backgrounds impeded the development of tenants' associations. With regard to Jewish residents, non-Jewish tenants believed the broader societal myths that Jews looked after their own and were not as badly off as they appeared.[25]

As public agencies gradually adapted to their new clientele and introduced services, hired staff, and designed and then cut back programs to respond to them, less attention was directed to the needs of the Jewish poor who represented a small and dwindling—if not invisible—constituency. Their cultural needs became less understood, as agency personnel received little training concerning them, and as few people on the boards of public agencies represented them. Often agency personnel believed that better services were readily available in the Jewish community and that Jews looked after their own.[26] The Jewish poor—and the elderly in particular—unable to reach Jewish services, are often reluctant to seek help from public services because of fears regarding impersonal, bureaucratic authority, and because of cultural values regarding dependency in general, and seeking help from 'outsiders' in particular. One study found substantial numbers of the Jewish poor who did not avail themselves of services because 'they were too ashamed of being poor to utilize Jewish services, and too ashamed of being Jewish to make use of public services'.[27]

As a consequence of these changes the poor have become disconnected from the mainstream of Jewish organizational life as well as from the communities in which they live. They have become a minority among Jews because they are poor, and a minority among the poor because they are Jews. Despite substantial numbers, they are underserviced and underrepresented. Their demographic characteristics combined with societal stereotypes regarding Jews in general explain their invisibility.

Policy Implications

Outreach, advocacy, and organization are interventions which can be utilized to identify the Jewish poor and make contact with them, as well as to secure their entitlements and representation. Given the degree of isolation which poor Jews experience, indirect recruitment methods such as media broadcasts, community newspapers, and organizational referrals have not produced substantial numbers of previously unidentified poor. Direct contact, conducted by persons familiar with the cultural milieu of the Jewish poor and carried out through door-to-door canvassing has succeeded in identifying, advocating, and organizing large portions of this community.[28]

While identification with the Jewish community has been essential in order to recruit the Jewish poor and educate the public and its agencies about them, organizing efforts to affect their conditions of poverty or secure their representation have succeeded in situations where a multi-ethnic base has been established. That is, the Jewish poor have benefited from public campaigns which align their interests with those of other poor people. In Montreal, for example, Project Genesis, a community organization principally funded by the Jewish federation, elected a slate of candidates to the board of the public service agency which included a rabbi, a black community worker, and a Vietnamese immigrant. This organization, in coalition with a

Native Indian organization, advocated and secured a precedent-setting agreement extending welfare benefits to all homeless persons.[29]

These examples indicate that demographics and social context ought to inform social work intervention. Door-to-door recruitment by persons of the same cultural group is uniquely suited for a population of elderly and isolated persons who tend to live alone. Public advocacy counteracts invisibility, and alliance-building is a strategy of both necessity and choice for groups which are minorities among minorities.

Notes

[1] Mark Twain, *Collected Letters*, 1899.

[2] J. Torczyner, *The Jewish Family in Canada* (Council of Jewish Federations, 1984).

[3] Norman Fuehauf in *Jewish Philanthropy in Contemporary America* (North American Jewish Data Bank, 1988).

[4] Fuehauf, *op. cit.*

[5] Aviva Silberman, *Who Are the Jewish Poor?* (Chicago: The Ark, 1971).

[6] *New York's Jewish Poor and Jewish Working Class: Economic Status and Social Needs* (New York: Federation of Jewish Philanthropies of New York: 1973).

[7] Figures cited in Jerome M. Comar, 'Our Jewish Poor: How Can They Be Better Served' in Naiomi Levine and Martin Hochbaum, eds, *Poor Jews: An American Awakening* (New Brunswick: Transaction Books, 1974).

[8] Levine and Hochbaum, *op. cit.*

[9] *Kosmin, Ritterband, and Scheckner, 'Jewish Populations in the United States, 1987', American Jewish Year Book*, Vol. 88, 1988.

[10] S. Groeneman, 'The Potential of Market Facts Telenation Survey Methodology for Sampling American Jews' in *Towards a National Survey in 1990* (New York: Research Department, CJF, April 1988).

[11] See for example Penni Reichson-Kolb, 'Access to Social Service in the Jewish Community: Issues and Response', MSW thesis, McGill University School of Social Work, November 1978; J. Torczyner, *The Poor Among Us: Project Genesis Montreal*, 1976 and Ann G. Wolfe, 'The Invisible Jewish Poor', *The Journal of Jewish Communal Service* 48, 3 (1972): 259-65.

[12] Paul Ritterband, *Some Reflections on Jewish Social Science in the United States*, North American Jewish Data Bank, Council of Jewish Federations, 1986: 16.

[13] 'Jewish Populations in the United States, 1987', *American Jewish Year Book*, Vol. 88, 1988.

[14] Statistics Canada, Census Canada, Ottawa, 1981.

[15] Joseph Norland and H. Freedman, 'Jewish Demographic Studies in the Context of the Census of Canada' in U.O. Schmeltz, P. Glikson, and S. DellaPergola, *Papers in Jewish Demography, 1973* (Jerusalem, 1977).

[16]U.O. Schmeltz and Sergio DellaPergola, *Basic Trends in American Jewish Demography* (American Jewish Committee, 1988).

[17]Ira Rosenwaike, 'A Demographic Profile of the Elderly Jewish Population in the United States in 1970,' *The Journal of Aging and Judaism* 1987 (Spring-Summer).

[18]J. Torczyner, *The Poor Among Us*.

[19]Council of Jewish Federations, Toronto, 1984.

[20]The marginal category reflects the midpoint between one household size and the next below the poverty line. For example, if the poverty line was $4,000 for a family of two, and $6,000 for a family of three, the marginal line would be $5,000 for a family of two.

[21]Louis Rosenberg, *Population Characteristics of the Jewish Community of Montreal* (Canadian Jewish Congress, Montreal, 1956).

[22]*Canadian Jewish Year Book*, 1941.

[23]Daniel J. Elazar, 'Community and Polity: the organizational dynamics of American Jewry,' The Jewish Publication Society of America, Philadelphia, 1976.

[24]S. Lerner, 'The Jewish Poor: do we help? should we? can we?' *Journal of Jewish Communal Service* 61, 1 (1985).

[25]Robert Taylor, 'Factors Influencing People's Willingness to Join Tenants Associations', MA thesis, McGill University, Montreal, 1977.

[26]Phil Cohen, 'Battling Against Shylock's Legacy,' *Social Work Today*, United Kingdom, February 2, 1989.

[27]J. Torczyner, 'To Be Poor and Jewish in Canada' in Cotler *et al.*, eds, *Canadian Jewish Mosaic* (Toronto: John Wiley and Sons, 1981).

[28]Project Genesis, 'The Genesis File,' Montreal, 1985.

[29]Project Genesis has received national attention for its organization of the Jewish poor in coalitions with diverse ethnic groups since 1973. Its annual reports as well as media accounts document these and other interventions.

Sephardim and Ashkenazim in Montreal

Jean-Claude Lasry

Immigration has been the main source of growth in Montreal, as well as in the Canadian Jewish community as a whole. Since 1957 Maghrebian Jews have contributed to this growth but with much tension. (In Arabic, North Africa is called *Maghreb*, which means Occident.)

Moroccan Jews comprise the majority of the Sephardim who immigrated from the Maghreb to Montreal. For many of them, immigration to Canada was the third step in their immigration from Morocco. The first phase, *aliyah*, the 'ascent' to the Holy Land, was motivated by religious and spiritual reasons. Emigration to France, the second phase, was favoured because of its geographic closeness and the Maghrebian Jews' infatuation with French culture.

The third phase resulted, in a significant way, from the lobbying efforts the Montreal Jewish Community directed to the Federal Department of Immigration in the middle 1950s. Ironically, the linguistic peculiarity of North African Jews (the majority of whom spoke French as their mother tongue) did not seem to have at that time any significance for the Quebec English-speaking Jewish leaders. All Jews, whether they came from Turkey (where they spoke Ladino), from Russia or Hungary, had been dissolving linguistically in the North American anglophone 'melting-pot'.

In the 1960s, a conjunction of historical, political, and economic forces led the French Canadians to 'La Révolution Tranquille', which in turn gave rise to the Renaissance of Sephardic and Maghrebian Jewish identity in Quebec. The Montreal Jewish community had expected North African Jews to integrate linguistically as previous migrations had done. But it did not anticipate the deep changes occurring in French Canadian society: the affirmation of a national identity and of a desire to be and to find pride in being Québécois.

Within this spirit of French Canadian renewal, preservation of their Sephardic traditions became a leitmotiv of the North African leaders. This led to keen struggles with the established Jewish community, such as attempts to inhibit the emerging Maghrebian leadership of Montreal (Lasry, 1981; Centre Communautaire Juif, undated). Similar tensions have pervaded Ashkenazi-Sephardi relations in Israel, and they are reminiscent of relations between German and Russian Jews at the end of the nineteenth century in the United States.

The creation of a Sephardic francophone *landsmanshaft* was perceived as a threat by the Ashkenazim who wanted to preserve the anglophone mono-lith, which was more apparent than real, since over 40 per cent of the

Ashkenazim were born outside of Canada, and English was not their mother tongue (Rosenberg, 1965).

The object of this paper is to present a preliminary analysis of the social integration and ethnic attitudes of a sample of North African Jews living in Montreal, taking into account the history of intracommunity relations just sketched.

Subjects

A sample of 469 North African Jews living in the Greater Montreal area was surveyed in 1972, from a master list of more than 2,500 households, representing approximately 10,000 to 13,000 persons (probably the whole universe of North African Jews at the time). The master was composed of several community lists, supplemented by the similarly spelled names of other persons appearing in the telephone directory.

A random sample was stratified by length of residence in Canada, which ranged from to 2 to 15 years at the time of the study. Close to 70 per cent of the respondents had lived in Montreal for four years or more. The sample included 258 men and 211 women, of which 199 were couples. Ages ranged from 18 to 62.

Questionnaires

Interviewers of North African Jewish origin administered questionnaires to the subjects. The questionnaire, which required two hours to complete, addressed such dimensions as occupation, family relations, mental health, social relations, and attitudes (see for example, Lasry and Sigal, 1980, 1975; Lasry, 1980, 1977).

Respondents were asked to identify the groups in which they found the best colleagues, bosses, friends, neighbours, and children's friends. They were also asked to state whether they liked, disliked, or were indifferent to ten ethnic groups: Sephardim, French-Canadian Jews, non-Jewish English Canadians, Blacks, French, North African Jews, Mexicans, Israelis, and Ashkenazim.

Results

In general, respondents reported little difficulty in making friends in Montreal. Only one third met with some difficulty, mainly because of lack of time, and great distances. For most, the network of friends involved new acquaintances (met in Montreal) and very often relationships originating from North Africa.

The ethnic choices as to the best bosses, best colleagues, etc. were to be made among four main reference groups of Montreal: North African Jews, French Canadians, Canadian Jews, and non-Jewish English Canadians.

Table 1 *In Which One of the Following Ethnic Groups Does One Find the Best ...?*

ETHNIC GROUPS	COL-LEAGUES	BOSSES	FRIENDS	CHILDREN'S FRIENDS	NEIGH-BOURS
North African Jews	26%	6%	68%	21%	55%
	(19%)[a]	(4%)	(45%)	(15%)	(36%)
Canadian Jews	13%	22%	23%	75%	15%
	(10%)	(14%)	(15%)	(54%)	(10%)
French Canadians	46%	41%	8%	3%	25%
	(33%)	(26%)	(5%)	(2%)	(16%)
English Canadians	14%	31%	1%	1%	5%
	(10%)	(20%)	(1%)	(1%)	(4%)
Several groups, no answer	—	—	—	—	—
	(27%)	(36%)	(34%)	(27%)	(35%)
	100%	100%	100%	100%	100%
(N)	(362)	(361)	(480)	(191)	(199)

[a]Percentage including the category 'Several groups, no answer'.

The results of these choices appear in Table 1. Work relations indicate the degree to which French are liked: they are perceived as the best colleagues (46 per cent) and the best bosses (41 per cent). Non-Jewish English Canadians and other non-Jews are preferred over Canadian Jews as bosses (31 per cent vs 22 per cent). Canadian Jews are better liked as friends (23 per cent) rather than as neighbours (15 per cent). North African Jews are not liked as bosses (6 per cent), but preferred as colleagues (26 per cent) and chosen by the majority of respondents as friends (68 per cent) or neighbours (55 per cent).

The respondents report a completely different ethnic preference pattern for their children's friends. Three-quarters of them would prefer their children to choose Canadian Jews for friends; included in this figure are a third of the respondents who would rather have non-hyphenated Jews as friends for their children.

The answers to the second question on ethnic group preferences have been summed up in an Attraction Index, calculated by subtracting the 'Dislike' from the 'Like' percentages (Table 2). The group with the highest attraction score, as well as the highest percentage of expressed likes, is the respondents' own ethnic group, the *North Africans*. This preference is exactly contrary to that expressed by North Africans living in Israel. Shuval (1962, 1966) has shown that they reject themselves in Israel, and she explains this self-rejection by the internalization of the prevailing negative stereotype held by Israeli society towards North African Jews.

In Montreal, 'Sephardi'[1] is almost synonymous with North African Jews, who are an active and well-organized community (Lasry, 1981). That *Sephardim* is the second choice for North African Jews living in Montreal is then quite understandable.

Table 2 *Attitudes of North African Jews of Montreal[a] Toward 10 Ethnic Groups*

ETHNIC GROUPS	LIKE	DISLIKE	INDIFFERENT	TOTAL	ATTRACTION SCORE[b]
North African Jews	86%	4%	10%	100%	82%
Sephardim	75%	2%	23%	100%	73%
Israelis	70%	7%	23%	100%	63%
French Canadians	57%	9%	34%	100%	48%
Canadian Jews	53%	15%	32%	100%	38%
English Canadians	35%	9%	56%	100%	26%
Mexicans	28%	3%	69%	100%	25%
French	46%	21%	33%	100%	24%
Blacks	32%	11%	57%	100%	21%
Ashkenazim	36%	23%	41%	100%	13%

[a]N varies between 237 and 278.
[b]Differences between percentage of Likes and Dislikes.

Israelis have the third-highest attraction score. This score reflects the very high prestige enjoyed by the Israeli population among North African Jews living in the Diaspora, despite the socio-economic and socio-ethnic cleavage threatening the very structure of Israeli society.

The clear preference evidenced in the labour relations appears again for the *French Canadians*. They are more liked and less disliked than the *Canadian Jews*, whose attraction score is about 10 percentage points lower.

Four ethnic groups follow fairly closely, in terms of attraction: the *English Canadians*, the *Mexicans*, the *French*, and the *Blacks* (scores between 26 and 21). The attraction score of the French is quite low, despite a 'Like' score of 45 per cent, because the 'Dislike' score is almost the highest expressed (21 per cent). For North African Jews, French culture was the epitome of civilization. However, the French who settled in Maghreb held such colonialist attitudes that they elicited very hostile feeling from the North African Jews. This hostility was also fuelled by the chauvinistic and even racist attitudes the immigrants from North Africa experienced when they settled in France. The recent turnabout of France, ceasing to support Israel to become pro-Arab, roused further indignation.

The most salient point of Table 2 is the last portion attributed to the *Ashkenazim*. Their 'Dislike' percentage is the highest (23 per cent) while the percentage of 'Likes' expressed by our respondents toward them is among the lowest (36 per cent). This clear rejection of the Ashkenazim reflects deep intracommunity tensions which could lead to a schism in the Jewish community of Montreal, parallel to the one existing in Israel between Ashkenazim and Sephardim (Eaton, Lasry, Sigal, 1979).

This hostility toward the Ashkenazim was also evident in the questions about work relations. They had the highest rate of rejection as bosses and as colleagues. Perhaps, the fact that our respondents were not treated differently than the other non-Jewish employees by their Ashkenazi bosses could explain part of this hostility. Some even complained that their Ashkenazi boss would not take into account their Sabbath observance, which on the other hand was respected by their new French Canadian Catholic boss.

Table 2 also shows that the concepts of *Ashkenazim* and *Canadian Jews* are very clearly differentiated in the minds of our respondents. 'Ashkenazim' are perceived as immigrants with heavily accented English while 'Canadian Jews' are perceived as native-born, second-generation Canadians who speak unaccented English. As Canadian Jews take over from the European-born the controls of business and community affairs, community relations will most likely improve. This hypothesis is supported also by the choice of Canadian Jews for friends of the children. The North African Jews of Montreal have come to realize they could not establish social relations with the Ashkenazim, yet they do not despair of community peace. They wish Canadian Jewish friends for their children, hoping they will succeed where they failed: making friends with the other segment of the Jewish community.

Discussion

These factors may explain the patterns of intra-community relations in Montreal: the hostility expressed by old immigrants toward the newcomers, the Arabic cultural component of the North African Jews, and the linguistic differences.

The first factor is universal, occurring in every country of immigration. Old-timers, with their comfortable way of life and their assimilation to the host culture, are perturbed by newcomers who bring back memories of conditions the first settlers had worked hard to erase. Having most likely been discriminated against by the host population, the first settlers may now retaliate, with a certain degree of security since it all happens within the 'family'. This history of Jews settling in America is but a succession of immigrant waves interacting with each other. Each wave of immigrants wants to imitate and to be accepted by the previous one, which had become the Establishment (e.g., the Sephardic Grandees looking down on the German Jews, who treated the Russian Jews with condescension).

The second factor stems from the Arabic cultural component of the North African Jewish personality. Maghrebian Jews hold lifestyles, values, and attitudes which are very different from the Anglo-Saxon ones quickly adopted by the Canadian Jews. Those differences often lead the anglophone Jews to disbelieve the authenticity of the North African Jews' Jewishness and even to refer to them as Arabs, which is intended as an insult. (One such incident happened when a Moroccan choir gave a performance at the Pavilion of Judaism, during the 1967 Montreal World Exposition.)

Fortunately, this labelling seems to have disappeared today, possibly reflecting a different attitude of the North African Jews towards themselves.

Rather than feeling insulted, they seem to feel a certain pride in the Arabic dimension of their heritage. For example, many have come to know and love Arabic music in Montreal. Since 1974 the *Communauté Sépharade du Québec*, the planning and representative body of the North African Jews, has been holding an annual Sephardic Week, which emphasizes the Arabic dimension in art, customs, traditions, and folklore. This phenomenon does not seem peculiar to Montreal. It is happening also in the United States, in France, and even in Israel, where Cohen (1979) reports, 'Since Sadat's visit . . . , "Arab" is no longer an insult . . . so today we take "Arab Jew" as an identification to be proud of.'

The third factor, the linguistic difference, owes its importance to the political situation in Quebec. Since they spoke French, North African Jews have been perceived as a threat to the anglophone monolith of the Montreal Jewish community. In a Quebec that changed almost overnight to a society extremely conscious of its French culture and its future, the 'francophones' (as North African Jews are often referred to) were a thorn to the Establishment, demonstrating the necessity of mutation to French. That they communicate among themselves in French may have associated the North African Jews with the anxiety-provoking nationalistic aspirations of the Québécois. They were even held responsible for government French policies. For example, when the Ministry of Education forced the Jewish day schools to augment substantially their hours of French teaching, the cause of this 'calamity' was attributed by some anglophone Jews to Ecole Maimonide, the first Jewish day school where language of instruction was French (created by the North African Jewish leadership, in 1969).

Conclusion

The first factor, one inherent in the adaptation process of the successive waves of immigrants, disappears as the newcomers integrate into the community and join the Establishment. The second factor, the Arabic component of the North African personality, is changing from a tension-inducing factor to a source of pride. The linguistic difference, a deep divisiveness between North African Jews and the anglicized old timers, is also bound to disappear with time, as francization generalizes in Quebec and as its inevitability becomes certain. Some communal institutions have already carried out programs to promote the acceptance of francization. For some anglophone Jewish community leaders, North African Jews may slowly perceived as a blueprint of their own Jewish future in French Quebec.

At the attitude level, the marked preference of our respondents for 'Canadian Jews' rather than 'Ashkenazim' implies a clear distinction between both concepts. As Canadian Jews will take over from the European-born Ashkenazim the controls of business and community affairs, relations between them and North African Jews should improve. Selection of Canadian Jews as friends for the respondents' children supports this prediction.

Note

[1]We use the term 'Sephardi' and object to the ones coined by the Government of Israel, for instance 'from Asia-Africa' or 'Orientals', since those geographical labels negate the specificity of the Sephardi culture by covering about half the globe.

References

Centre Communautaire Juif
  n.d.   *Etre nous-mêmes: Histoire de la Communauté Juive Marocaine à Montréal (au travers de ses associations)*. Montréal: YM-YWHA & NHS (Young Men's Hebrew Association)

Cohen, Shalom
  1979   'Israel's Begin May be Losing Vital Support of Sephardis', *Washington Post*, 9 December

Eaton, W.W., Jean-Claude Lasry, and John J. Sigel
  1979   'Ethnic relations and Community Mental Health Among Israeli Jews', *The Israel Annals of Psychiatry and Related Disciplines* 17, 2: 165–74

Lasry, Jean-Claude
  1977   'Cross-cultural perspective on mental health and immigrant adaptation', *Social Psychiatry* 12, 2: 49–55

———

  1980   'Mobilité professionnelle chez les immigrants juifs nord-africains à Montréal', *International Review of Applied Psychology* 29, 1/2: 17–30

———

  1981   'A Francophone Diaspora in Quebec' in M. Weinfeld, W. Shaffir, I. Cottler, eds, *The Canadian Jewish Mosaic* (Toronto: Wiley): 221–40

———

Lasry, Jean-Claude and John J. Sigal
  1975   'Durée de séjour au pays et santé mentale d'un groupe d'immigrants', *Canadian Journal of Behavioral Science* 7, 4: 339–48

———

  1980   'Mental and Physical Health Correlates in an Immigrant Population', *Canadian Journal of Psychiatry* 25: 391–3

Rosenberg, L.
  1965   *La Communauté juive au Canada de 1931 à 1961: changements dans les traits caractéristiques de la population*. Montréal: Congrés Juif Canadien, Bureau de la Recherche Sociale et Economique

Shuval, Judith T.
  1962   'Emerging patterns of ethnic strain in Israel', *Social Forces* 40, 4: 323–30

———

  1966   'Self-rejection among North African immigrants to Israel', *The Israel Annals of Psychiatry and Related Disciplines* 4, 1: 101–10

Soviet Jewish Émigrés in Toronto:

Ethnic Self-Identity and Issues of Integration

Roberta L. Markus

and Donald V. Schwartz

Since 1971, more than 250,000 Jews have emigrated from the Soviet Union. The expectation among North American Jews was that these Jews would have strong Zionist commitments and would resettle in Israel. This occurred during the 1971-73 period when the number of Soviet Jewish émigrés who did not settle in Israel ('drop-outs') was insignificant. However, since 1974 an increasing proportion of Jews leaving the Soviet Union have opted to migrate to North America and an indeterminate number have left Israel to settle in the United States and Canada. By 1983, more than 75,000 former Soviet Jews had resettled in the United States and over 8,000 had chosen to settle in Canada. Of these, approximately 6,000 have come to Toronto.

The resettlement challenges posed by Soviet Jewish émigrés in Toronto (housing, food, emergency medical care, employment and subsistence or supplementary living allowance) have been met effectively by mobilizing the resources of the Jewish community and by government support systems. Over time, the community has developed and institutionalized supports for immigrants. The Jewish Immigrant Aid Services takes direct responsibility for resettlement, and a number of other agencies have tailored their services to meet the needs of Soviet Jewish émigrés.

While resettlement has taken place relatively smoothly, the matter of integration, i.e., the whole range of activities that define ethnic affiliation, has remained a contentious and unresolved issue. The Jewish community of Toronto has had certain expectations regarding the ethnic self-identity of Soviet Jews immigrating to North America. The campaigns to 'Save Soviet Jewry' and the image of Soviet Jews as a group persecuted for their cultural and religious identity led the Toronto Jewish community, along with other Jewish communities in North America, to believe that an intense awareness of ethnic identity and a strong desire to enhance it through participation in Jewish institutions and activities were major factors in the choice to emigrate.

Furthermore, the Jewish community of Toronto expected that former

Soviet Jews would identify and affiliate with the existing Jewish community. The established Toronto Jewish community has developed a number of criteria for affiliation that reflect the unique combination of its own historical experience and the norms of the broader society in which it operates. Key indicators of ethnic identification for the established community that were applied in dealing with Soviet Jewish immigrants have included living in a Jewish area, being affiliated with a synagogue, providing children with a Jewish education, participating in Jewish communal organizations and activities, observing certain rituals, festivals, and life cycle events, supporting Israel, and giving financial support to the community through voluntary contributions.

In sum, the expectations of the established community were twofold. There would be a basis and motivation among the émigrés for Jewish self-identity. And the Jewish self-identity of former Soviet Jews would be actualized in activities and through institutions that had already been developed and legitimized by the established Jewish community.

Soviet Jewish émigrés in Toronto have not defined their needs for cultural development and their strategies for achieving cultural satisfaction in terms consistent with the values and behaviour patterns deemed appropriate by the established Jewish community. They have shown neither a strong interest in the Jewish traditions and practices valued by the existing community nor a willingness to express their ethnic identity through joining and participating in established Jewish communal organizations.

The large gap between the expectations of the established Toronto Jewish community and the self-identity of Soviet Jewish émigrés has created a number of tensions. Both communities have expressed resentments about their treatment and reception at the hands of the other. Within the established community there is debate over the responsibility of communal authorities for integration. Within the émigré community there are divisions over the appropriateness of established forms of ethnic identification.[1]

The slowness and reluctance of Soviet Jewish émigrés to identify with and take part in Jewish communal life are directly related to the 'cultural baggage' they have brought with them from the Soviet Union. What they have learned and come to believe in terms of their self-identity in the Soviet Union has shaped their perceptions of the ethnic community in Toronto and their desire and ability to relate to it.

What is the Jewish émigré's self-image, as a former Soviet citizen and as a Jew? And what implications does this self-image hold for ethnic integration in the multicultural pattern of North American society? We believe that the potential for successful integration into Jewish communities is related to an understanding of the Jewish émigré's association with both ethnic and secular values and institutions in the Soviet Union, motivations for leaving the Soviet Union, motivations for coming to Canada, and the types of gratifications and payoffs the immigrant expects to receive from his new community.

In this paper we will reconstruct some of the components of the ethnic self-identity of Soviet Jewish émigrés in Toronto. The basis for our work will be raw data obtained in a study conducted in Toronto in 1978 by Roberta Markus.[2] The study focused on the adaptation of Jewish children from the Soviet Union in the Toronto educational system, both public and private. It elicited a broad range of data that included information dealing directly with the Soviet and ethnic identities of children and parents. It involved interviews with 107 students and 53 parents who had arrived in Toronto from the Soviet Union between 1973 and 1978.

There is also sufficient information from other sources to help us construct a picture of the ethnic self-identity of Soviet Jewish émigrés to Toronto. Several scholarly studies have been completed and reported.[3] Many émigrés have told their stories.[4] This information has been enriched by reports presented by case workers, community representatives, and in the press.[5] These supplementary sources are used to broaden our understanding of ethnic self-identity and the issues of integration.

The Ethnic Self-Identity of the Soviet Jewish Émigré: The Soviet Experience

The experiences and changing status of Jews in the Soviet Union since 1917 have strongly shaped their attitudes toward their Jewishness and have implications for their pattern of adaptation in North America. Detailed accounts of the course of Soviet policy towards its Jewish population and specialized studies of the impact of major events on Soviet Jews are readily available in the Western literature.[6] What we propose to do in this section is simply to provide a brief overview, identifying some of the major events that have shaped Jewish self-identity in the Soviet Union. This background information may help to explain some of the difficulties Soviet Jewish émigrés have encountered in integrating into the Jewish community of Toronto.

In the Soviet Union, each individual, at the age of 16, assumes both the rights of a citizen and association with a nationality. This association, based on parental identification, is a legal status that is incorporated in a Soviet citizen's internal passport. In theory, national identity in the Soviet Union is fostered and encouraged through the embodiment of nationality rights in territorial entities (e.g., republics, autonomous republics, autonomous regions), in language rights, and in the maintenance of certain cultural traditions that may be national in form but socialist in content and which do not conflict with the overall goals that the regime has set for itself.

While the Jews constitute a legally recognized nationality group in the Soviet Union, they have undergone a number of experiences that have weakened their group identity and encased it with negative images. In the first decade after the Revolution, the regime's policies towards Jews were aimed at restructuring Jewish identification so as to strengthen support for the values of the new regime. This involved the creation of Jewish sections of the Communist Party that were empowered to undermine and destroy the traditional bases of Jewish identity, e.g., religion, Hebrew study, daily ritual, life cycle events, Zionism, and replace these with a secularly based Jewish culture in which Yiddish became the language through which socialist values and behaviour were communicated and internalized.[7] Secular Jewish cultural forms were to be a mechanism through which allegedly universalistic norms were to be communicated.

During Stalin's rule, the isolation of Soviet Jews from their cultural heritage and from international developments affecting Jews was reinforced in two ways. Official policy aimed to undermine group cohesion by depriving Jews of the means of religious and cultural expression. The regime set up a Jewish 'homeland' in Birobidzhan in the hope of isolating Soviet Jews physically. This experiment proved to be an unmitigated failure. At least three times during Stalin's rule, manifestations of official anti-Semitism undermined both the physical and moral strength of Soviet Jews. The purges of the 1930s included an anti-Semitic dimension through the identification of the Jewish origins of many of the accused and the implication that large numbers of Jews might be guilty of harbouring 'class enemy' elements through association. In the late 1940s Stalin undertook a campaign of Russian nationalism that included the persecution of so-called 'rootless cosmopolitans', leading to the liquidation of the leadership of the Jewish cultural élite. Finally, just before Stalin's death, the uncovering of the 'Doctor's Plot' led to the revelation of an alleged Jewish conspiracy aimed at the political leadership of the Soviet Union.

The fabric of the Jewish people in the Soviet Union was also destroyed by the Nazi invasion during World War II. Nazi-occupied territories included heavy concentrations of older Jews who had a strong sense of identification with traditional Jewish values. The systematic destruction of these people as part of the Holocaust deprived Soviet Jewry of an important link with its heritage. In addition, the official postwar Soviet treatment of the Holocaust, which did not give special significance to the tragedy of the Jews, made their experience seem like a Soviet historically isolated accident, rather than a major event in the history of World Jewry. Indeed, Soviet anti-Zionist propaganda has explicitly linked Hitler and Zionism, by claiming collaboration in the establishment of a Jewish state in Palestine.[8] Unlike Jews in the West, Soviet Jews were denied the full knowledge of the traumatic experience of the Holocaust and did not share in the meaning these events had in shaping present-day Jewish consciousness. In other words, these events were not part of the psychological and emotional environment which gives much meaning to Jewish life today.

Socio-economic trends in the Soviet Union under Stalin also served to undermine Jewish ethnic consciousness. After 1928, the Soviet Union underwent an intense process of industrial development that required an enormous expansion of the administrative, technical, and professional strata of the economy. For large numbers of Jews this was seen as an opportunity to escape the historical disabilities that had been imposed on Jews living in the Russian Empire. Furthermore, while the regime was pursuing policies aimed at destroying Jewish religion and traditional culture, Jews found that social and economic mobility were not hindered insofar as the regime was experiencing a shortage of skilled labour. In fact, the willingness of large numbers of Jews to assimilate into the dominant culture by adopting the Russian language, moving into large urban centres, and pursuing higher and specialized educational degrees meant that the aims of Jews and the regime coincided. Jews provided a disproportionate number of the newly emerging professional and skilled work force while at the same time demonstrating patterns of assimilation into the Russian-socialist culture that were highly favoured by the regime.[9]

Stalin's death may have relieved some of the pressures associated with being Jewish in the Soviet Union. However, the ambiguities and negative images associated with Jewish identity remained and new pressures emerged. Periodic official manifestations of anti-Semitism recurred under Khrushchev and Brezhnev. Jews were singled out in the campaign against economic crimes in the early 1960s. Anti-Zionist campaigns, triggered by the 1967 and 1973 wars in the Middle East, contained an unveiled element of anti-Semitism in which Jews as a group were held implicitly responsible for the 'imperialist aggression' of Israel. Throughout the post-Stalin period there have also been sporadic publications of books with anti-Semitic themes.[10]

The self-identification of Soviet Jews in the post-Stalin period became more complex and problematic for two reasons, First, the socio-economic mobility that had led to the rapid advancement of large numbers of Jews until the 1960s began to work against Jews. Other national groups had reached educational levels giving them access in ever greater numbers to higher and specialized education and intensifying their demands for positions in the educational system, the professions, and the economy in general proportionate to their numbers. Because of a complex system in the Soviet Union of allocating places in education and the economy on the basis of national representation through unpublished quotas, this change meant that access by Jews to higher education and career advancement was hindered by their national identity, regardless of their level of skill and degree of assimilation. Thus, reduced economic opportunity came to be linked closely with anti-Semitism.[11]

Second, the Six-Day War (1967) and the Yom Kippur War (1973) acted as catalysts in stimulating Jewish self-identification in the Soviet Union. For once, Soviet Jews, while they were being castigated for the actions of Israel, could also feel a sense of pride and positive identification with fellow Jews who had achieved major military victories in defending themselves. These events had a particularly strong impact on the middle and younger generations who had been born and raised under Soviet rule and had never experienced Jewish traditions in practice. Although still lacking what Alexander Orbach refers to as a 'Jewish historical consciousness',[12] they had for the first time in their lives a clearly defined, positive set of events associated with their historical traditions.[13]

In sum, the Soviet experience undermined and destroyed the traditional basis of Jewish identity and isolated the Soviet Jew from the outside Jewish community and international events. The persistence of informal and official expressions of anti-Semitism in the Soviet Union eroded ethnic self-esteem. A large proportion of Soviet Jews became urbanized and highly educated, and socio-economic mobility encouraged identification with the dominant secular culture.

For most Soviet Jews, especially those born under the Soviet regime, Jewish identity is an ascribed status and, according to the Soviet experience, a hindrance to educational and economic opportunities. Those émigrés who succeeded in retaining a strong and positive Jewish self-identity were attracted to Israel. Those who opted to emigrate to North America have tended, as a rule, to possess a weaker sense of Jewish identity. Large numbers have immigrated to North America from major cities that have been under Soviet rule since 1917. They are, mainly, second and third generation Soviet citizens who have grown up and been socialized in areas of the Soviet Union that are highly industrialized and have been saturated with a high level of the dominant Slavic culture. A large number are well educated and identify themselves as professionals and skilled tradesmen. They have been socially and occupationally mobile and had successfully adapted to the Soviet regime's dual requirements that self-identity be expressed in terms of a blend of Soviet socialist secular values and Slavic (predominantly Russian) cultural forms.[14]

Ethnic Identity and Reasons for Leaving the Soviet Union

The decision to emigrate from the Soviet Union is one that involves many uncertainties and risks in both the short and long term. Often the decision is made on the basis of very little information about the country of destination. The emigration process may be long, complex, traumatic, and potentially dangerous. There is no way of knowing what roadblocks may lengthen or even abort the process. A Soviet Jew who chooses to emigrate must receive an official invitation from a relative, preferably in Israel. The invitation must come through the open post. Once in possession of the invitation, one must apply for a visa through the Department of Visas and Registration (OVIR) division of the Ministry of Internal Affairs. Supporting documentation must be provided, including statements from employers and parents. A fee of 400 rubles for the visa and 500 rubles for renunciation of Soviet citizenship must be paid. The risks and uncertainties are great and numerous. The rules and criteria for decisions are not published. A refusal may be given without reason. Treatment by the bureaucrats may be capricious, arbitrary, and humiliating. Employment may be terminated, a disastrous situation for those whose visa application is delayed or refused. Various forms of harassment have been implemented, including denunciations by collectives of work colleagues, eviction from apartments, surveillance by the security police, the imposition of an 'education' tax, drafting of eligible males into the armed forces, and the laying of criminal charges. Family pressures against emigration are great since those who are left in the Soviet Union may be subject to additional forms of discrimination. There appears to be no systematic policy regarding regional or city quotas for visas or criteria for selecting families for refusal.[15]

The tensions involved in the decision to leave the Soviet Union are highlighted in the Toronto study. In response to a series of questions regarding the immigrants' perceptions of their life in the Soviet Union, 21 per cent of the adults replied that they had negative and 23 per cent mixed feelings about leaving the Soviet Union. The decision to leave was not always a clearcut and unambiguous one. The feelings of ambivalence surrounding departure from the Soviet Union are similar to those other immigrants experience when leaving their homeland. It is generally painful and frightening to pull up roots and leave the known, however difficult and unpleasant, for the uncertain. In addition, the Soviet Jew must face the severing of closely knit family relationships and separation from friends. These changes involve considerable emotional stress.

Over 60 per cent of the respondents claimed that they did not discuss feelings about leaving the Soviet Union with their children, suggesting that a good deal of tension was avoided by avoiding the issue. This conclusion is supported in responses elicited from the children. The majority (71 per cent) indicated that they had *positive* images about the Soviet Union and only 15 per cent replied that they were aware of negative aspects of life in the Soviet Union. The children's generally positive view of the Soviet Union and reluctance to leave the Soviet Union suggests that the Soviet socialization process is successful in building identification with, and loyalty to, the country. It is interesting to note that the positive image the children held of the Soviet Union was not necessarily based on ignorance of everyday Soviet life. Most children knew that in the Soviet Union people experienced shortages of food, housing, and clothing. These difficulties, however, were seen as part of normal life and were not generally blamed on the regime or its leaders. In fact, a number of children stated that the Soviet population was more fortunate than most people in the world because the government had eradicated poverty and provided for full employment.

The children's generally positive view of the Soviet Union may be a function of their socio-economic background. Most of their parents held responsible positions in Soviet society. Nearly 62 per cent of the fathers were within the professional and managerial stratum, 31.8 per cent were tradesmen, and 6.5 per cent were blue collar workers. The majority (85 per cent) of the mothers were also gainfully employed, many in professional or managerial positions. Despite the fact that the Soviet Union suffers from housing shortages, they had adequate or good accommodations and rarely lacked material necessities.

An awareness of the existence of officially sanctioned anti-Semitism in the

Soviet Union did not appear to undermine the children's feelings toward the country or to foster a negative image of themselves as Jews. Slightly fewer than half (43.9 per cent) of the children were aware of the negative portrayal of Jews by some Soviet writers and the Soviet media. The majority of the immigrant children interviewed (56.1 per cent) claimed never to have experienced anti-Semitism in the Soviet Union. Those who indicated that they had experienced anti-Semitism indicated that such behaviour had been expressed mainly through name calling. The children apparently lacked the long-range perspective of their parents; they were not aware of, or did not fully comprehend, the meaning of changes that have been taking place in Soviet educational policy and employment patterns that have set limits on career opportunities for Jews.

Given the circumstances surrounding departure, what are the motivations for declaring an intent to leave the Soviet Union? In the Toronto study, adult respondents indicated that their primary motivation for leaving the Soviet Union was a desire to improve what they perceived to be reasonably good economic circumstances and to ensure that their children had the opportunity to do the same (see Table 1). These strong feelings regarding economic opportunity, in combination with anti-Semitism, ranked highest both as a first reason for leaving and in terms of the total number of times mentioned. In addition, it appears that there is a strong relation between the Soviet émigrés' desire to improve career opportunities, for themselves and for their children, and ethnic identity.

The relationship between economic opportunity and ethnic identity as reasons for leaving the Soviet Union among Jews who come to North America has been substantiated in other studies. In examining émigré motives for leaving the Soviet Union, Jerome Gilison found that almost half of his sample (in Baltimore) gave 'discrimination against Jews' as the most important reason. However, when this was further explored, Gilison found evidence that the anti-Jewish discrimination to which respondents objected was prohibition against the practice of Judaism, the closing of synagogues and Jewish schools, or the strong pressure against the use of Yiddish. Rather, the evidence indicated that 'the primary source of disaffection occurred in the area of job discrimination, which makes their Jewish identity an extra burden in competing for the scarce resources of the Soviet economy, and makes them feel like second-class citizens.'[16] Stephen Feinstein's study of Soviet Jewish immigrants in Minneapolis and St Paul, and Ellen Frankel Paul and Dan Jacobs' study in Cincinnati also provides evidence that the high degree of political and religious-national alienation expressed by respondents was educationally and occupationally related.[17]

There are additional factors which may help to explain the Soviet Jewish émigrés' lack of identification with the North American Jewish community. In the Toronto study, a strong positive association of former Soviet Jews with the Soviet Union and with the dominant Russian culture appeared in responses about cultural heritage and language. In response to the question

Table 1 Reasons for Leaving the Soviet Union*

	FIRST REASON		SECOND REASON		THIRD REASON		FOURTH REASON		TOTAL	
	NO.	%	NO.	%	NO.	%	NO.	%	NO.	%
Economic opportunity	22	41.5	1	1.9	1	1.9	—	—	24	45.3
Political freedom	8	15.1	9	17.0	1	1.9	1	1.9	19	35.8
Anti-Semitism	10	18.9	14	26.4	7	13.2	—	—	31	58.5
Opportunity for young	6	11.3	11	20.8	8	15.1	1	1.9	26	49.1
Relatives leaving	5	9.4	2	3.8	2	3.8	1	1.9	10	18.9
Friends leaving	1	1.9	3	5.7	2	3.8	—	—	6	11.3
Shortages	—	—	2	3.8	2	3.8	4	7.5	8	15.1
No response	1	1.9	11	20.8	30	56.6	46	86.8	—	—

*As reported by parents

'Prior to contemplating departure from the USSR, were you interested in your Jewish heritage?' more than 60 per cent indicated that they were not interested and 36 per cent that they were interested only in Jewish history. The limited perspective on ways of identifying ethnically was demonstrated in response to the question, 'How did you satisfy your interest in Jewishness?' Over 60 per cent replied that, in the Soviet Union, they were not interested or had no opportunity to satisfy their Jewish interests, while 35 per cent said that they did this through listening to foreign radio broadcasting, i.e., BBC, Voice of America, and Kol Israel, celebrating holidays, information from relatives, or attending synagogue.

In contrast to the weak association with Jewish ethnicity, the respondents exhibited a strong, positive identity with certain Slavic and secular characteristics of Soviet society. All respondents indicated that Russian was the language spoken at home in the Soviet Union. All but one of the respondents indicated that Russian was also the language spoken with their parents, despite the fact that two-thirds claimed to understand Yiddish. When asked what they felt was most important to preserve from their heritage, the Russian language and Russian Soviet culture dominate.

In sum, the feelings of Soviet Jews who have left the Soviet Union and opted to emigrate to North America are mixed and their decision may be perceived in terms of a complex balance of costs and potential benefits. The overwhelming anticipated benefit is the possibility of pursuing a career that will not be limited by factors such as ethnic identity. The costs are associated with the risk and uncertainty of losing an acceptable and adequate standard of living and social status and losing the cultural infrastructure associated with Russian and the Soviet Union. For most, the potential for enrichment through enhancement of their Jewish ethnic identity was not a factor in their decision.

Table 2 What is Most Important to Preserve from Heritage

	FIRST CHOICE		SECOND CHOICE		TOTAL MENTIONED	
	NO.	%	NO.	%	NO.	%
Nothing	2	3.8	2	3.8	4	7.6
Yiddish/Hebrew	3	5.7	3	5.7	6	11.3
Russian language	48	90.6	3	5.7	51	98.2
Russian/Soviet culture	—	—	30	56.6	30	56.6
No second answer	—	—	15	28.3		

*As reported by parents.

Reasons for Coming to Canada

The evidence in the preceding section clearly indicates that being Jewish was an important factor in the decision to emigrate. This, however, did not necessarily signal a desire to rediscover Jewish roots and establish close ties with the Jewish community in the West, as interpreted by North American Jews. When asked for their reasons for immigrating to Canada, the respondents in the Toronto study indicated the following major factors: Canada's image as a peaceful country, Canada's geography, family reunification, information from previous immigrants, and economic opportunities for themselves and their children (see Table 3). Ethnic identity apparently played no important role in the decision. That is, the respondents indicated that a desire to pursue their Jewishness and to identify with a Jewish community and participate in it did not play an important role in their decision to migrate to Canada. There is no clear and compelling reason for choosing to migrate to Canada that would provide the basis for a strong identification with the Jewish community.

The single reason mentioned most often for coming to Canada is that Canada is a peaceful country. At least two meanings can be attributed to this response. If the reference point is the United States, then the choice of Canada may be seen as a means of avoiding the violence of some American cities (especially New York where the largest number of Soviet Jewish émigrés in America have settled). If the reference point is Israel (where the majority of Soviet Jewish émigrés have settled), then the choice not to go to Israel seems to be based, in part, on an unwillingness to resettle in a country under constant threat of war and the implications of this situation for the children. These fears may have dominated over the potential benefits of finding a homeland in Israel.

Ethnic Identity in North America: Institutional and Personal Dimensions

Soviet émigrés came to Toronto expecting to improve their career prospects

Table 3 *Reasons for Coming to Canada**

	FIRST REASON		SECOND REASON		THIRD REASON		TOTAL MENTIONED	
	NO.	%	NO.	%	NO.	%	NO.	%
Economic opportunity	6	11.3	2	3.8	1	1.9	9	17
Opportunity for young	2	3.8	4	7.5	—	—	6	11.3
Peaceful country	20	37.7	3	5.7	2	3.8	25	47.2
Multi-culturalism	1	1.9	2	3.8	3	5.7	6	11.3
Information from previous immigrants	8	15.1	6	11.3	3	5.7	19	35.8
Friends in Canada	1	1.9	6	11.3	1	1.9	8	15.1
Family reunification	10	18.9	4	7.5	2	3.8	16	30.2
Political freedom	1	1.9	—	—	1	1.9	2	3.8
Immigration policy	1	1.9	2	3.8	—	—	5	9.4
Geographical and climatic similarities	2	3.8	3	5.7	6	11.3	13	24.5
Social welfare system	—	—	—	—	1	2.9	1	1.9
No response	1	1.9	21	39.6	33	62.3	—	—

*As reported by parents.

and those of their children, attain economic wellbeing, and satisfy their cultural needs. They arrived with the expectation that Western Jews would be fully supportive of their personal plight, welcome them, and be willing to render assistance and well-deserved special treatment.

It soon became apparent that there was a clash between the two communities over values and services. The Jews from the Soviet Union showed a commitment to aspects of their Soviet Russian cultural heritage, whereas the established Jewish community rejected these and favoured adherence to the Jewish cultural heritage as it had evolved in Toronto. The Jewish Immigrant Aid Services and other agencies were prepared to provide traditional resettlement services. The Soviet Jewish émigrés asked for special consideration in view of their perceived unique circumstances and demanded additional services including: special efforts and programs in locating employment, retraining and licensing; financial support for dependent elderly relatives; and exemption from membership fees in organizations and programs such as the Jewish Community Centre, camps run by the Jewish Camp Council, and Jewish parochial schools.

The Jewish community was willing to satisfy certain demands, especially when these served to make immigrants economically self-sufficient and enhanced their identification with the Jewish community. Fees were waived for limited periods and scholarships were given to attract Soviet immigrant children to Jewish parochial schools and summer camps and adults to recreational programs. Special efforts were made on the employment issue, although these were limited by the prevailing economic constraints and agency budgets.

The speed and extent of changes rarely satisfy any client community and Soviet émigrés were no exception. They arrived in Toronto convinced that the established community should and could do considerably more, especially in the area of employment, which many considered a precondition for any further identification with the community. When the help they anticipated was not forthcoming, feelings of bitterness surfaced.

What aggravated the situation was the growing awareness among professional personnel and members of the Jewish community directly involved with the Soviet Jews that the demands made in the economic sphere were not matched by an interest in Judaism and/or Jewish cultural life. Soviet Jewish émigrés articulated demands that they be supported by the Jewish community in retaining certain aspects of their Russian/Soviet cultural heritage, and requested that Russian language instruction be provided for their children and that cultural programs of general interest (e.g., Russian films, concerts, poetry readings, ballet, folk dancing) be made available to the Soviet immigrant group.

The Soviet Jewish émigrés' strong identification with Russian culture and their ambivalence regarding their Jewish heritage weakened the possibility that, in the process of adaptation, they would voluntarily establish roots in the Jewish community. In the early stages of settlement and adaptation, immigrants generally experience socio-economic uncertainties and it is not uncommon for newcomers to cling to their cultural heritage in order to ease the pains of transition to a new life. The Soviet émigrés' reliance on Russian as their linguistic medium for cultural expression was, therefore, not surprising as it was in keeping with behavioural patterns common among other immigrant groups. The Soviet cultural experience provided the Jewish émigré from the Soviet Union with a sense of the familiar which he needed in order to cope with the insecurities surrounding him. Although the Jewish community recognized the émigré's need for his Russian cultural heritage, it was seen as decreasing the chances of bringing these Jews into the established Jewish community.

The danger of losing the émigrés to the non-Jewish, dominant Canadian culture was also made evident by an awareness that in the Soviet Union Jews gained social and occupational mobility by accepting the dominant linguistic and cultural patterns of Soviet society. It could be expected, therefore, that once in Canada they would repeat the adaptation pattern successfully applied in the Soviet Union and acculturate into the dominant secular cultural patterns. These predispositions are reinforced in the early stages of adaptation where, with very few exceptions, Soviet Jewish émigrés learn English in a secular environment and linguistics skills are acquired with an occupational and secular orientation that does not include the creation of positive Jewish identity. Acculturation to the broader, secular society takes precedence over the development of a sub-group cultural identity.[18]

The cultural background characteristics and adaptation tools that Soviet Jewish émigrés have brought with them have led to behaviour that clashes sharply with the expectations of the established Jewish community. Experience indicates that Soviet Jews are not likely to join and participate in Jewish institutions unless offered inducement in the form of exemptions from fees or dues, and there is no assurance that there will be a long-run commitment to such membership. As Zvi Gitelman warns, even where the experience with institutions has apparently been positive, we must assess the long-run impact with caution:

> We should not be misled into thinking that most of the immigrants had suppressed religious tendencies in the USSR and are now able to give them free expression. This is true of a few individuals, but the great majority have gone to synagogue in the US mainly out of curiosity, and because of pressure or invitation by local American Jews. Whereas in the USSR social stigma is attached to synagogue attendance, some American Jews seem to expect Soviet immigrants to rush to the synagogues, and the immigrants realize this. Moreover, many American families invite the immigrants to their synagogues and homes for the High Holidays and Passover ... The Soviet immigrants may fall into the typical American pattern of synagogue attendance three or four times a year.[19]

Stephen Feinstein adds to our understanding of the potential weakness of the synagogue (and other Jewish communal organizations) as the basis for institutional affiliation and Jewish identification for former Soviet Jews by suggesting that synagogue experience in the Soviet Union was a short-run phenomenon, specifically related to emigration, and cannot provide a firm basis for long-run affiliation:

> Furthermore, those sensitized to Jewish identity issues in the USSR appear to have drifted toward Jewish institutions or identity as a defensive gesture and as a means of finding out about the emigration movement itself. Those who had never been to a synagogue in Moscow or Leningrad before applying to emigrate often came to these institutions with enthusiasm after application for a visa. But once they arrived in America, as one immigrant put it, 'there is no need for the Jewish community to try to convert us', indicating that for many identification with Judaism would have to come gradually.[20]

What may be added to this profile is that, while North Americans have the cultural identity and learning experiences that will allow for their continued association with Jewish institutional life (and more intensive participation during certain life cycle events), there is a strong likelihood that Soviet Jews, who may show some initial, superficial interest in synagogue attendance for social or economic reasons or out of curiosity, do not have the religious-cultural basis that will ensure their long-run association with the Jewish community. What may be perceived as a temporary expedient to gain friendship, cultural gratification, and possible economic benefit in the short run may be discarded in the long run as new secular identities are established.

Evidence also suggests that initial association with Jewish communal institutions may be based on misperceptions of the payoffs. This was brought out in the Toronto study's focus on patterns and reasons for enrolment in Jewish parochial schools. Respondents indicated that the main factors affecting the choice of school were distance from home, peer pressure, family influence, and advice from community representatives. Desire for a Jewish education received low priority. In addition, those who chose to send their children to Jewish schools did so in the belief that discipline and curriculum were better than in the public schools. In Toronto there has been a heavy transfer of Soviet Jewish children out of the Jewish day school system. The two major reasons given by parents and children were the difficult curriculum and too much religious instruction. In fact, these may be the same reasons since they both may refer to the extra load of Jewish Hebrew studies. The responses to the questionnaires indicated that 'almost without exception, the Soviet parents did not comprehend the principles underlying Jewish education and that they selected the Jewish school system primarily because they thought it offered the child a better academic education and preparation for university'.[21] Once they understood that the Judaic component would not help, and might even hinder, students' chances of access to higher education (and, hence socio-economic mobility), the children were transferred to public schools.

In sum, once the immigrants have arrived in North America, there seems to be little indication of any basis for a strong and long-term commitment to the Jewish community. In the Toronto study it was evident that, despite initial material and social support from Jewish communal organizations, the respondents showed little interest in continuing the association. When asked about their interest in Jewish affairs, 83 per cent indicated no interest, while only 3.8 per cent showed an interest in the Jewish community, 11.3 per cent in Israel, and only 1.9 per cent in Jewish studies. The only two community organizations in which they participated were the Russian Association (34 per cent) and the YMHA (3.8 per cent).

Religious affiliation was even weaker. Almost all adult respondents indicated that they were secular. Nearly one fourth indicated that they would object to their children becoming more religious. Although a majority of parents did not object to or discourage their children learning about their Jewish heritage, there was little indication of positive support in this direction. When children were asked how their parents would feel about them becoming more religious, 42 per cent indicated that they thought their parents would be displeased, while only 11 per cent felt their parents would be pleased.

The Soviet Jewish émigrés' lack of interest in expressing Jewish ethnic identity through institutions and patterns of affiliation that are considered appropriate by the established community can be explained in terms of two sets of factors. First, most newly landed immigrants define their priorities differently from those of the established community in the short run because objectively their needs are different. New immigrants have to consider basic matters of subsistence before satisfying their cultural needs. Language, job training, licencing, suitable employment, appropriate housing, and the dozens of details of daily life that established members of the community do automatically have to be confronted in the process of developing a sense of self-confidence, dignity, and security that are preconditions for active involvement in the community.

For Soviet Jewish émigrés, however, a second set of factors must also be considered. There are major barriers that may inhibit their involvement in the ethnic community in the long run. Soviet Jews have come to North America with few resources that could form the basis for easy identification with established North American Jewish communities. Their identity as Jews was externally imposed by a society and regime that treated them as an alien element. They were denied access to experience that would provide them with a sound basis for relating to an organized Jewish community, e.g., knowledge of their history, familiarity with Jewish traditions, skills in relating to and working within an autonomous communal structure. Their success in Soviet society was directly related to their ability to deny and hide their Jewishness and assimilate into the dominant culture.

Conclusion: The Need for New Approaches

Despite the weak base for Jewish identity, former Soviet Jews now living in North America do bring with them a number of attitudes and behaviour patterns that may form the basis for successful integration on a personal level into a Jewish community. They bring with them a special pattern of friendship and a high value placed on association with Jewish friends. Soviet Jews provide little indication that they actively practised Jewish life styles in the Soviet Union that were congruent with North American patterns. However, they did indicate that they were very much aware of their Jewishness and that the majority of their friends in the Soviet Union were Jews. Gilison's study leads to the conclusion that:

> The fact of being a Jew, even when devoid of any substantial meaning, seems to have played a large role in their personal relations. While the anti-Semitism of non-Jews may have been a salient factor in the surprising 'clannishness' of Soviet Jews, it is hard to escape the conclusion that the *feeling* of being Jewish can be crucial in a Soviet Jew's life even without that person *knowing* anything about Jewish traditions.[22]

The former Soviet Jew brings with him to North America a diffuse sense of Jewishness in the sense of belonging to a Jewish ethnic group. This Jewishness has been expressed not through any institutional affiliation or the practice and transmission of Jewish traditions. Rather it has been expressed in the form of solidarity on a personal, friendship level with others of the same ethnic background.

The circumstances under which the Soviet émigrés meet members of the

host community in large urban settings are seldom conductive to the building of meaningful and lasting friendships based on equality and mutual
respect. Initial contacts is frequently generated by the desire of 'host families'
to volunteer help with settlement. The basis for the interaction is that of the
giver and receiver of help, and the nature of the relationship tends to produce
an unequal distribution of power. In a number of cases the 'host families'
have expressed resentment at the lack of appreciation and gratitude from
their 'wards', and the recipients of their help have voiced indignation at the
paternalistic and condescending behaviour of the 'host families'.

Even in cases where the contract comes through a social situation, the
basis for friendship is often lacking. The Soviet Jew is extremely proud of his
professional achievements and cultural perspective, and many North American Jews have difficulty relating to Soviet Jews on either level. The professional training the émigrés received in the Soviet Union is frequently not
recognized in North America, and licensing is denied until Western professional standards are met. While the émigrés struggle to achieve professional
status and live in a state of under-employment, it is difficult to build friendships based on equality and dignity with established colleagues.

On the cultural level, the value and importance the Soviet Jews place on
their Russian/Soviet heritage is not, as a rule, shared by most North American Jews. Many of their ancestors fled Russia to escape persecution and the
more recent revelations of Soviet abuse of basic human rights, anti-Israeli
propaganda, and acts of anti-Semitism do not encourage a positive view of
Soviet culture. Broadly speaking, North American Jews are not interested in
the Russian/Soviet cultural heritage, and the émigrés' identification with it
may, in fact, act as a deterrent to friendship with American Jews.

Soviet Jews appear to suffer from a sense of alienation in the Jewish community. Many say: 'In the Soviet Union we were considered Jews. Here we are
seen as Russians.' The implication is that they perceive themselves as outsiders
and feel unappreciated and unwanted. In part, the alienation Soviet Jewish
émigrés express is a reflection of a perceived cultural difference in the meaning
of friendship. For Soviet Jews, friendship has come to mean an intimate and
strong bond among the individuals involved. It is a relationship that requires a
great deal of commitment and mutual trust, and leads to a lifetime association.
For Soviet Jews, what most North Americans refer to as friends are merely
acquaintances. This cultural difference has led Soviet Jewish émigrés to voice
the opinion that North Americans are unfriendly, insincere, show lack of
interest, and are unsympathetic toward recent émigrés.[23]

The tensions between the émigrés and the established Jewish community
are deep-rooted. Some effort has been made to integrate Soviet émigrés into
Jewish communities.[24] However, the programs and services that have been
provided have met with only modest success. They have encountered resistance because they are not always viable options for large numbers of Soviet
Jewish émigrés. The ambivalent and diffuse sense of Jewish identity, coupled
with the strong sense of Russian/Soviet identity, that Soviet Jews have

brought to the West forms a tenuous base on which to build solid and lasting relations with established Jewish communities. It is likely that, unless more creative and intensive approaches to integration are developed and deployed quickly and on a broad scale, Jewish communities in North America may lose the opportunity of integrating Soviet émigrés. They will assimilate more easily into the broader secular community and lose whatever Jewish identity they brought with them to the West.

Notes

[1] For a discussion of the tensions in Toronto see, for example, the series of three articles in the *Canadian Jewish News*, 4, 11, 18 April 1975. For a discussion of the issues in American communities, see Dora Kass and Seymour Martin Lipset, 'America's New Wave of Jewish Immigrants', *New York Times*, 7 December 1980; Council of Jewish Federations, *Integrating Soviet Jewish Emigrés: The Continuing Agenda for the America Jewish Community* (New York, November 1980); Council of Jewish Federations, *Enhancing the Jewishness of Former Soviet Jews* (November 1979).

[2] Roberta Lander Markus, *Adaptation: A Case Study of Soviet Jewish Immigrant Children in Toronto, 1970-1978* (Toronto: Permanent Press, 1979). The information for the study was collected through interviews. Four separate questionnaires were designed for Soviet immigrant children, professional personnel, Canadian students, and parents of the immigrant children. Interviews were conducted with students and professionals in the North York and East York Boards of Education and in schools associated with the Board of Jewish Education. Interviews with parents were conducted at their place of residence. The questionnaires contained closed and open-ended questions and the format provided for a maximum richness in response. The length of the interviews varied. It took approximately 40-50 minutes to complete an interview with a student or parent, and 30-40 minutes to complete an interview with Canadian students or professional staff. The questionnaires designed for the Soviet students and parents were translated into Russian and the choice of language for the interview was left open to the respondent.

[3] For example, Dan N. Jacobs and Ellen Frankel Paul, eds, *Studies of the Third Wave: Recent Migration of Soviet Jews to the United States* (Boulder, Col.: Westview Press, 1981); various articles in *Soviet Jewish Affairs*; Rita J. Simon and Julian L. Simon, *The Soviet Jews' Adjustment to the United States* (New York: Council of Jewish Federations, 1982); Jerome M. Gilison, ed., *The Soviet Jewish Emigré* (Baltimore: Baltimore Hebrew College, 1977); R.L. Busch, 'Edmonton's Recent Soviet Immigrants,' in Martin L. Kovacs, ed., *Roots and Realities Among Eastern and Central Europeans* (CEESAC, Edmonton, 1983): 99-128.

[4] For example, Grigory Svirsky, *Hostages: The Personal Testimony of a Soviet Jew* (New York: Alfred A. Knopf, Inc., 1976); P. Panish, *Exit Visa: The Emigration of the Soviet Jews* (New York: Coward, McCann and Geoghegan, 1981); Bella Bytensky, *From Russia With Luggage* (Toronto: Annick Press, 1980).

[5] See various articles in the *Journal of Jewish Communal Service*, for example.

[6] See, for example, Lionel Kochan, ed., *The Jews in Soviet Russia Since 1917*, 3rd ed.

(Oxford: Oxford University Press, 1978); W. Korey, *The Soviet Cage: Anti-Semitism in Russia* (New York: Viking Press, 1973); Yehoshua Gilboa, *The Black Years of Soviet Jewry, 1939-1953* (Boston: Little, Brown, 1971).

[7]Zvi Gitelman, *Jewish Nationality and Soviet Politics* (Princeton, N.J.: Princeton University Press, 1972); Alexander Orbach, 'The Jewishness of Soviet-Jewish Culture: Historical Considerations', *Journal of Jewish Communal Service* 57, 3: 145-53.

[8]Howard Spier, 'Zionists "Unmasked",' *Soviet Jewish Affairs* 8, 1 (1978): 84.

[9]John A. Armstrong, 'The Ethnic Scene in the Soviet Union: The View of the Dictatorship' in Erich Goldhagen, ed., *Ethnic Minorities in the Soviet Union* (New York: Praeger, 1968): 8-11.

[10]For accounts of these, see the following articles in Lionel Kochan (ed.), *op. cit.*: B.D. Weinryb, 'Antisemitism in Soviet Russia'; Zeb Katz, 'After the Six-Day War'; Philippa Lewis, 'The "Jewish Question" in the Open: 1968-71'; and Lukasz Hirszowicz, 'The Soviet-Jewish Problem: Internal and International Developments 1972-1976'. Also see Leonard Schapiro, 'Antisemitism in the Communist World', *Soviet Jewish Affairs* 9, 1 (1979): 45-52; and Lukasz Hirszowicz, 'Soviet Perception of Zionism', *Soviet Jewish Affairs* 9, 2 (1979): 53-65.

[11]For an émigré view of the relation, see Igor Birman, 'Jewish Emigration from the USSR: Some Observations', *Soviet Jewish Affairs* 9, 2 (1979): 46-63.

[12]Orbach, *op. cit.*, p. 149.

[13]The Six-Day War acted as a catalyst for self-identification, which produced a large volume of printed material, mainly on Jewish history and culture. The literature included *samizdat* publications by Soviet Jews and *tamizdat* publications, mainly translated into Russian, of Western works. See Vladimir Lazaris, 'The Saga of Jewish *Samizdat*', *Soviet Jewish Affairs* 9, 1 (1979): 4-19.

[14]In contrast, a large proportion of the émigrés who have resettled in Israel come from areas that were incorporated into the Soviet Union only during World War II (the Western Ukraine, Latvia, Lithuania, Moldavia) or from areas that have not been as strongly affected by the combining of modernization and Slavic influence (Uzbekistan and Georgia). See Z. Alexander, 'Jewish Emigration from the USSR in 1980', *Soviet Jewish Affairs* 11, 2 (1981), 3-21, especially Table 12. Most of the émigrés who come from more recently incorporated areas or areas with less Slavic influence tend to have a stronger identification with Israel and Jewish traditions. In the former case, their experiences related more closely to times when they, or their families, lived outside the Soviet Union. In the latter case, local authorities have been more tolerant of their religious and cultural identity and traditional patterns of family and social relations.

[15]See Colin Shindler, *Exit Visa: Detente, Human Rights, and the Jewish Emigration Movement in the U.S.S.R.* (London: Bachman and Turner, 1978).

[16]Jerome M. Gilison, 'The Resettlement of Soviet Jewish Emigres: Results of a Survey in Baltimore' in Jacobs and Paul, eds, *op. cit.*, 38.

[17]Stephen C. Feinstein, 'Soviet-Jewish Immigrants in Minneapolis and St Paul:

Attitudes and Reactions to Life in America' in Jacobs and Paul, 57–75; Ellen Frankel Paul and Dan N. Jacobs, 'The New Soviet Migration in Cincinnati,' *ibid.*, 77–114.

[18]This argument is adapted from Alvin I. Schiff, 'Language, Culture and the Jewish Acculturation of Soviet Jewish Emigrés', *Journal of Jewish Communal Service* 57, 1: 44–9.

[19]Zvi Gitelman, 'Soviet Immigrants and American Absorption Efforts: A Case Study in Detroit' in Jacobs and Paul, 23–4.

[20]Feinstein, 64.

[21]Markus, 44.

[22]Gilison, 47.

[23]This theme is developed in each of the case studies in Jacobs and Paul. See pp. 26, 53, 69, 112–13.

[24]These issues will be dealt with in a forthcoming paper, 'Jewish Community Response to the Challenge of the Third Wave of Soviet Jewish Emigration: A Case Study of Toronto'.

This paper is a revised version of a paper presented to the Annual Meeting of the Canadian Association of Slavists, 4 June 1983, Vancouver, British Columbia.

Aliyah and Return Migration of Canadian Jews:

Personal Accounts of Incentives and

of Disappointed Hopes

Cyril Levitt

and William Shaffir

Countless generations of Diaspora Jews have traditionally prayed for a return to the Holy Land—'Next year in Jerusalem'. With the establishment of the State of Israel in 1948, a flood of Jews from 'free' countries, such as the United States and Canada, might have been expected to 'make *aliyah*', to emigrate to Israel. In fact, only limited numbers of North American Jews have settled in Israel in the course of the last four decades. One reliable estimate is that only about 7,000 Canadian Jews moved permanently to Israel since 1948.[1]

Research on this migration usually focuses on standard push and pull models.[2] Jewish commitments are the primary pull factors in such models, representing a basically ideological attraction to Israel, while the push derives from some form of dissatisfaction with one's community or lifestyle in North America. Studies by Antonovsky and Katz[3] and by Berman[4] have emphasized that these Jewish migrants were overwhelmingly influenced by the pull to Israel—they were not 'pushed' from their country of origin. Other studies, however, have maintained that there was in fact some general dissatisfaction with North American society arising chiefly from problems related to Jewish identity in a pluralistic context, and concerns about anti-Semitism.[5] Many authors have demonstrated that the migration experience involves a transformation of identity requiring an adjustment to a new culture and the modification of one's self-concept in relation to it.[6]

Studies of North American *yordim* (those who leave Israel) have related the reasons given for leaving Israel. Both Engel[7] and Jubas[8] have found that practical difficulties were the reasons most often offered. Engel stated: 'Job opportunities, housing, and cost of living were practical consideration for leaving'.[9] Antonovsky and Katz[10] and Jubas[11] have shown that encounters with Israeli bureaucracy were a source of anger and frustration for many immigrants in Israel (*olim*, those who make *aliyah*), while Gitelman has commented that American *olim* were especially disappointed by the inefficiency and waste, environmental pollution, crime, materialism, and lack of idealism that they encountered in Israel.[12] The research carried out by Dashefsky and Lazerwitz is the most comprehensive study to date of North American Jews who went to settle permanently in Israel but returned to the United States; these *yordim* were compared with other North Americans who had migrated to Israel and were still living there three years after their arrival. At first, it seemed that the religious factor was the major differentiating aspect; a closer examination of the data revealed that those who initially had a greater degree of self-confidence were more likely to be still in Israel three years after they had left their native land.[13] However, when Waxman analysed their data, he commented: 'Although the data suggest that those with higher education and those with weaker or less active Jewish commitment tend to return, no meaningful causal relationship could be established between the characteristics of the returnees and their decision to return.' According to his findings, the issue of separation from family was cited as among the main reasons for return migration, followed by problems with the Israeli bureaucracy.[14]

There is a sizeable literature on Diaspora Jews who migrated to Israel with the intention of settling there permanently[15] who then returned to their native countries, but few of the authors have attempted to examine the process by which *olim* arrived at their final decision to become *yordim*. This is surprising, for if international migration involves a series of adjustments, including changes in identity and commitment, then the decision to re-emigrate is just as likely to be fraught with such considerations.[16] This paper focuses on the decision-making processes of some Canadian Jews who have planned to emigrate to Israel in the near future and of another group of persons who did make *aliyah* but later returned to Canada. Our chief interest is to examine the kinds of inter-personal negotiations involved in the decision-making, although we also take into account the specific factors mentioned by our respondents.[17] We have found that people who are in the process of coming to the decision to make *aliyah*, or to return to Canada, develop an account of their decision-making process which rationalizes it for them and for significant others; essentially, there is in both cases the presentation and negotiation of an acceptable account.

This paper is based on two sets of informal interviews conducted with Canadian Jews in Montreal and Toronto. One set was completed in 1988 with 30 persons who had emigrated to Israel in the 1980s and then returned to Canada; we interviewed them within six months of their return. The other set consisted of 20 Canadians whom we interviewed at the end of 1989 and the first eight months of 1990. The list of all 50 respondents was developed by the technique known as 'snowballing'.

Those who had abandoned their plan to live permanently in Israel and had returned to Canada ranged in age from the early thirties to the mid-fifties and none was an observant Orthodox Jew. There were 18 men and 12 women; the men were mainly engaged in business activities or in professional occupations, while the women who did not stay at home to look after their young children had gone to work in Israel as English teachers or as English-language secretaries. None of the respondents claimed that emigration to Israel was the result of Zionist commitment or of having belonged to any Zionist movement or organization in Canada. During our conversations, we were mainly interested in their decision to return to Canada, but they themselves usually also referred spontaneously to their reasons for going on *aliyah*.

Aliyah: Expectations and Preparations

All the respondents who had emigrated to Israel had gone with the full intention of remaining there permanently, and had made thorough preparations to that effect. One married man described what the others had also told us: 'We moved lock, stock, and barrel. We had some misgivings about moving this way, but we realized that if we were serious about it, it was the only way to go.' Various reasons were given for the decision to go on *aliyah* but one which all the respondents mentioned was a desire to live in the Jewish State. They wanted to realize the long-standing dream of leading a Jewish life in a Jewish homeland. However, they did not say that they felt driven out of Canada because of rising levels of anti-Semitism or feelings of second-class citizenship. On the contrary, they spoke appreciatively about the range of freedoms and opportunities available in Canada; but they expressed a sense of unease about the Christian character of the country and especially the public celebration of Christian feast days.

By contrast, Israel was expected to offer a milieu where the celebration of Jewish festivals, even if undertaken in a secular mode, would no longer situate them in a minority position. They did not say that they had wanted to settle in Israel because they feared that their children might take Christian spouses in Canada; but perhaps this was because they either had very young children or adult married children. Our findings generally concur with those of Michael Brown, who concluded that Canadian Jews generally feel at home in Canada, where there are no strong push factors to stimulate large-scale *aliyah*.[18]

Apart from a single person who had been unable to secure an adequate income in Toronto, all those who had emigrated had lived in comfortable circumstances in Canada and had accumulated a respectable capital. They had visited Israel, had consulted not only friends or relatives living in Israel but also Israeli government officials, and were generally aware of the economic difficulties they were likely to encounter. However, they were prepared to lower their standard of living in exchange for the non-material benefits of living among fellow-Jews in a Jewish State. One man commented that he and his wife did not have unrealistic ideas:

> We knew that we wouldn't be able to live in Israel at the same standard we were living here. We certainly weren't extremely wealthy . . . but we were quite comfortable. We could always afford to buy those things we thought we needed or wanted. In fact, if we were really interested in making money, we knew that Israel wasn't the place to go. So, as far as economics were concerned, we were prepared to make sacrifices.

A common denominator for all respondents preparing for *aliyah* was their perception of approaching, or of having already reached, a 'turning point' in their lives. Strauss has noted that a turning-point may be conceptualized as a marker in development when an individual decides to take stock and evaluate the present position and then proceeds to embark upon a new course which will alter his or her identity in the eyes of others.[19] Turning-points may give rise to (or may be the result of) surprise, shock, anxiety, tension, self-questioning, or exhilaration. Examples were provided by one of our respondents who was retiring from full-time work, a young couple whose first child was about to begin to go to school, and a Quebec family worried about separatism: they all stated that a break in their pattern of living was imminent or was advisable. Another such case was a Toronto businessman who told us:

> I just seemed to be getting more and more bogged down in my work. I was in a real rut. When we decided to go for a brief vacation to Israel, I began to see a way out. Israel could be my place of renewal. The country was alive and I was dead. Here I could make a fresh start, do new things, and get moving again.

Some respondents told us that when they took stock of the particular circumstances in which they found themselves, including the long-term future of their young children, they were confident that they would be able to settle without great difficulties in Israel. The mother of three young children recalled: 'We moved in 1983. Our kids were at an age that unless we did it at that point, we would have to do it when we retired.' In another case, the impetus was provided by the changes which were reshaping the political landscape of the Province of Quebec:

> We had always considered *aliyah*, but we never had either the push or the pull. Lévesque [the then Premier of Quebec] gave us the push. We were getting the hell out of Montreal, not because we had to. There was nothing wrong with my practice and my French was fluent too. So we said, 'We're leaving'. We did toy with Toronto, and I had a business proposition in the States. . . . Then we said, 'Since we talked about *aliyah* potentially for many years already, so now that we're leaving there's only one place we can go. And that's Israel to see if we can live there permanently.'

In yet another case, a couple believed that they had sufficient capital to allow them to live in Israel without great hardship:

One of the reasons we decided to go, and decided to go when we went, was because we could do it then. We felt financially we could do it then. Because in any move, money is a big part of it. . . . I was coming off some very good years in business, the children's ages seemed just right, financially we could afford it.

Having reached the conclusion that *aliyah* was a realistic possibility, the prospective emigrant had to communicate this decision to relatives and friends — most of whom would probably react with surprise, disbelief, or even shock. Often, only one close relative or friend was approached in the first place and that person's reaction helped to plan how others would be informed. They might also be told in strict confidence and sworn to secrecy. One of our respondents, who was planning to go on *aliyah* with his wife, said:

Look, we're telling you, but nobody else knows. We've been thinking about this for the past six months and we finally decided this week. Don't tell anybody. If her mother hears about this, she'll lay a brick. Actually, we want to settle a few things before we drop the bomb.

Another one confided: 'We haven't decided to let anyone know just yet except our family and very close friends. Joe is still working and has a year to go until retirement. It's better that no one at work knows just yet.'

In other cases, there may not be a full disclosure because the decision to emigrate to Israel is not final:

Listen, it's too early, we feel, to let anyone know. . . . We're just about certain that we're going, but who knows, we can still change our plans. So I just don't want to get involved in having to explain to people why we changed our mind or whatever. Once we know for sure, then I can tell people.

Our respondents were aware that the announcement of their plans to settle in Israel would cause some surprise and they were particularly concerned about the effect which their decision might have one their close relatives, friends, and business associates. They had to present a well-argued account which would be convincing.[20] In other words, they had to persuade those with whom they had personal relationships that the decision to make *aliyah* had not been taken impulsively or lightly, but that both the advantages and the disadvantages had been carefully weighed. One of them said:

Most of our friends and relatives simply did not understand why we came to the decision we did. We told them first that we needed a change, that Israel was a good place to bring up kids. Then we told them that it would be great to live in a Jewish State with the holidays and everything. And we talked about the climate and the geography. And you know, we believed all these things, too.

The itemizing of reasons for settling in Israel also assumed a quality of self-justification,[21] as though the respondents were seeking to rationalize the decision to themselves. For example, a denturist who was about to retire listed a string of reasons which, taken together, provided a kind of fail-safe system for his *aliyah*:

> My children are grown and I am retiring from full-time work. I can sell my house and buy a nice apartment in Israel. I can live on my savings if I have to for a long time. But I have been promised work in Israel. And the climate is much better than in Canada. . . . Florida is not for me. We like the people in Israel and we made a lot of friends during our visits there.

However, the various arguments offered were not always convincing. One individual commented: 'You can't imagine how many people asked us why we're moving. What's interesting is that even after I tell them, you can tell they're searching for some deeper explanation.' Another said: 'The truth is that you have to come up with a story but, in a way, the story is as important for yourself as for others.' The following remarks reflect a respondent's awareness of the need to provide alternative explanations tailored to particular circumstances:

> It depends who I'm talking to. It depends who's asking. It depends on how well I know them and they know me. Is the person a friend or just an acquaintance who's asking to be polite? I have different answers. With some, I talk about Zionism, with others I know that they can more easily relate to the issue of Quebec nationalism. Once you know who you're talking to, you know what to say.

To use a stage metaphor, people developed a script, which was continually rehearsed, modified, and polished as the *aliyah* plans were crystallized. This process was described by one of our respondents:

> At first, when someone asked why we were leaving, I said that we weren't entirely sure, but we felt this was the right decision to make at this time. But as you keep on thinking about the decision, and as you become more confident that you're doing the right thing, you can explain it better. I've now reached the point where I can present my reasons for going very convincingly. It wasn't always like that.

Much like an actor who had memorized his lines and rehearsed his role, the prospective emigrant justified his decision with increasing authority and conviction as the departure date grew closer. Relatives, friends, acquaintances—and sometimes even strangers—who had already made *aliyah* were sought out and searching questions were put to them about their experiences in order to acquire a valuable pool of information.

The aim of both sets of respondents (those who were planning to make *aliyah* in 1989 and 1990 and those who had returned to Canada) was to settle permanently in Israel. There is, however, a possibility that those who have not yet emigrated may reconsider their decision. But why did the *olim* who had settled in Israel with the firm determination to remain there decide to return to Canada?

Re-evaluating the Dream: The Process of Return

It soon became evident to us that the decision to return to Canada had been taken very reluctantly and only after the conditions of living in Israel had progressively deteriorated to an extent which — in the end — the *olim* found almost intolerable. This was revealed by the phrase 'dropping the bottom line', which virtually every respondent used or implied. One of them, who had returned to Toronto after four and a half years in Israel, explained:

> The ground rules or the bottom line kept changing. You put your bottom line here [outlining the process with table cutlery], and then here, but then we kept dropping the bottom line. . . . And you can only drop the bottom line so far until things fall apart. . . . I don't know if it's a case of not wanting to admit defeat, but it's a case of not wanting the option of packing your bags and going back to Canada.

The final firm decision to return was apparently not precipitated by any one dramatic event but was the result of a series of setbacks over a period of time, in nearly every case. A married man told us that the decision to go back to Canada after two and a half years in Israel

> . . . was the culmination of seven or eight months of thinking and seeing what the alternatives might be to stay. Because there's no discussion that we would have preferred to stay. . . . On the day we made the decision, we had already explored all the other possibilities.

He and his wife had gone to meetings with officials of government agencies about their future financial prospects in Israel and they had also discussed their situation informally with relatives and friends.[22] In the end, the couple had to admit that financial constraints had become more severe than they had expected them to be[23] and that the situation had very adverse effects on marital and parental relationships.

In most cases, it was economic considerations which led the *olim* to reassess their position and prospects. One respondent told us:

> I was involved in work for which I was getting more than the national average but which was considerably below our lifestyle. We adjusted it considerably in Israel, but we had not adjusted enough to compensate. And basically, any kinds of savings we had, we went through it completely. And the saving grace was that when I left the business here [in Toronto], I received a sum of money and that helped tremendously. But we went through that very quickly. And the only asset that we had when we came back to Toronto was through the sale of our apartment in Israel.

(In this context, we were told wryly the following joke: Question: 'How do you get to have a million dollars in Israel?' Answer: 'Bring two million with you when you make *aliyah*.') That respondent said that he himself could have endured the financial constraints but he was greatly concerned that this wife and children were increasingly dissatisfied and unhappy:

> It bothered my wife when the kids wanted to go to Burger Ranch [a fast-food hamburger restaurant in Israel]. We said, 'No, you can't go to Burger Ranch. If you want a *falafel* [a vegetable savoury snack], we'll give you a *falafel*.' I'm just giving you one symptom. You see, we came from a lifestyle where we would go out to eat in a restaurant at least once a week, if not more often, and here we're talking about McDonald's or Harvey's [fast food chains].

According to him, the decision to return to Canada was taken in the interest of the family as a whole. Another respondent, the wife of a professional man, did not believe that she should have feelings of guilt because of a refusal to settle for a standard of living which was significantly lower than that which had been enjoyed in Canada:

> I said this in Israel and I say it here: you can't transfer that original kind of Zionist value to middle-class North Americans who, for whatever reason, want to go on *aliyah*. You have to appreciate what the North Americans bring with them in terms of their own personal values. They're not running away from something, they're hoping to aspire to something. But I used to think: 'Is it wrong to say that we've grown up with a value that living a lifestyle at base X is important? Why do we have to apologize for that?' That's not to say we aren't willing to take a cut in our standard of living. At what point do you have to say, 'I have to give up everything to live here?'

Another respondent, who had been a successful real estate agent in Toronto and had gone to settle in Israel in 1982, commented that he and his wife had been prepared to reduce their standard of living but had not expected the drastic reduction which became necessary:

> My wife saw the writing on the wall long before I did. And she's saying, 'This isn't going to work. We're losing money every month.' . . . But our ground rules or bottom line kept shifting. We figured out what it costs to live there and it came out, as I recall, about $2,500 a month, Canadian. Who makes $2,500 a month in Israel? So if you make $2,200 Canadian a month, you're losing $300 a month. So we see it's not working.

A couple who left Montreal to settle in Israel had invested their capital in a business enterprise which collapsed; they then seriously considered returning to Canada. But when they explained to their relatives and friends in Israel that the main reason for leaving was that their financial situation was rapidly and inevitably deteriorating, they were surprised by the reaction they encountered. Since most Israelis live under constant financial pressure, it was difficult for them to sympathize. The Montreal *oleh* said:

> And do you know what people said to us? 'So you're having a bad year. Sell your car, sell your washing machine, and you'll buy them back during a better year.' They really resented us when we said, 'Listen, we've come to the point where we still have enough money to move back. We haven't lost everything. You don't want us to get to the point where we have nothing left.' They resented that. They felt, if you really wanted to stay here, then you'll stay here.

It must be admitted that what the *olim* genuinely believed to be penurious circumstances (revealed by such statements as 'We suddenly felt poor' or 'We could not afford to buy things we considered important') might well have appeared to native Israelis as temporary or fairly minor financial difficulties which could be overcome in time with sufficient determination. On the other hand, there were cases when even if the Canadian immigrant was prepared to work tirelessly in order to make ends barely meet, other serious difficulties arose. One man said:

> Look, I was working the craziest hours because I had no choice. I had the store. I was basically alone and I was putting in 16-hour days. And there's no doubt the family as a whole suffered. I didn't have much of a chance to be with the kids, which I had always done. And although the kids didn't say anything, I sensed they felt cheated. And I think my wife felt the same.

Other respondents also told us of similar disruptive tensions in the home. One of them said:

> And my wife finally opened up by saying that the financial pressure which was her main concern at that point was just getting to her. . . . And then she put a bug in my ear: 'Just think what's the right decision for the family to make.' And then it sunk in what she was trying to say to me. . . . Our situation had begun to seriously affect our family life. I think there's a lot of friction involved, to be truthful.

Another related similar difficulties:

> I mean, the relationship becomes stressful. You have to look at yourself and ask, 'Is this what I want out of life? Is Israel worth a divorce? Is Israel worth that kind of stressful life?' Maybe some people would say, 'Yes', but we weren't going to say 'Yes'. My wife realized that it would difficult to make it financially. . . . And my wife was feeling the strain.

Some of the *olim* had friends and acquaintances who were also newcomers and who were also facing various hardships and uncertainties, but they hoped to overcome them in time. One respondent recalled: 'We probably should have left a year earlier than we did, but it was difficult leaving behind our close friends who were facing many of the same problems we were.'

It must be noted here that none of our respondents stated that the decision to return to Canada had been chiefly motivated by the unstable political situation or by the fear of physical danger from external or local Arab attacks — although they did refer in passing to these risks. When the *olim* did finally take the firm decision to leave Israel, they informed their relatives and friends in Canada — who had apparently not previously exerted any pressure to encourage them to return. They reported to us that these relatives and friends showed great support and understanding in their response to the news of the impending return.

Conclusion

When the *olim* returned to Canada, many of them said that they experienced 'culture shock', especially in cases when they had not visited Canada after they had settled in Israel. Many also found that the tensions and strains which had caused them to leave Israel were replaced by other stresses arising from the need to readapt to a Canadian lifestyle, the awkwardness of renewing some friendships, and especially from having to cope with feelings of failure, guilt, and regret about their unsuccessful *aliyah*. We hope to report in a later paper on the adjustments which the returned Canadian *olim* have to make.

Notes

[1] This figure is based on estimates provided by officials of the Association of Americans and Canadians in Israel (AACI).

[2] See, for example, C.M. Mills, C. Senior, and R.K. Goldstein, *The Puerto Rico Journey: New York's Newest Immigrants* (New York, 1959); R.C. Taylor, 'Migration and Motivation: A Study of Determinants and Types' in J.A. Jackson, ed., *Migration* (London, 1969); and N. Toren, 'Return to Zion' in *Social Forces* 54, 3 (1976): 546–58.

[3] See Aaron Antonovsky and David Katz, *From the Golden to the Promised Land* (Darby, Pa., 1979): 39–45, 52–3.

[4] See Gerald S. Berman, 'Why North Americans Migrate to Israel', *The Jewish Journal of Sociology* 21, 2 (December 1979): 135–44.

[5] See Ephraim Tabory and Bernard Lazerwitz, 'Motivation for Migration: A Comparative Study of American and Soviet Academic Immigrants to Israel', *Ethnicity* 4, 2 (June 1977): 91–102; Harry Jubas, *The Adjustment Process of Americans and Canadians in Israel and their Integration into Israeli Society*, PhD dissertation, Michigan State University, 1974; and Albert I. Goldberg, 'A New Look at Aliyah Influences Among North American Jews', *The Jewish Journal of Sociology* 27, 2 (December 1985): 81–102.

[6] In his study of Americans in Israel, for example. Avruch states that American *olim* are people who have invested heavily in their Jewishness: Kevin Avruch, *American Immigrants in Israel: Social Identities and Change* (Chicago, 1981): 117–22. Following Devereux, he argues that *olim* have a hypercathected ethnic identity so that it becomes the corner-stone of the self and the most salient element in the shaping of their identity. See George Devereux, 'Ethnic Identity: Its Logical Foundations and its Dysfunctions' in George de Vos and Lola Romanucci-Ross, eds, *Ethnic Identity* (Palo Alto, 1975).

[7] See Gerald Engel, 'North American Settlers in Israel', *American Jewish Year Book* 71 (1970): 161–87.

[8] See Jubas, *op. cit.*, n. 5 above: 191.

[9] Engel, *op. cit.* n. 7 above: 183.

[10]Antonovsky and Katz, *op. cit.* N. 3 above: 93-100.

[11]Jubas, *op. cit.* n. 5 above: 195-6.

[12]See Zvi Gitelman, *Becoming Israelis* (New York, 1982): 226.

[13]See Arnold Dashefsky and Bernard Lazerwitz, 'The Role of Religious Identification in North American Migration to Israel', *Journal for the Scientific Study of Religion* 22, 3 (1983): 263-75.

[14]Chaim Waxman, 'The Return Migration of American Olim', *Forum* 62 (Winter/Spring 1989): 103.

[15]See Dashefsky and Lazerwitz, *op. cit.* N. 13 above; Calvin Goldscheider, 'American Aliyah: Sociological and Demographic Perspectives' in Marshall Sklare, ed., *The Jew in American Society* (New York, 1974): 335-84; H.R. Isaacs, *American Jews in Israel* (New York, 1967); and Pearl Katz, *Acculturation and Social Networks of American Immigrants in Israel*, PhD dissertation, State University of New York at Buffalo, 1974.

[16]As in the case of the migration literature generally, the research on return migration mainly uses an economic model, arguing essentially that the probability of an individual's return varies with the calculated benefits and costs of the move. See, for example, R.I. Appleyard, 'Determinants of Return Migration: A Socio-economic Study of United Kingdom Migrants Who Returned from Australia', *The Economic Record* 38, 83 (1962): 352-68; Yochanan Comay, 'Determinants of Return Migration: Canadian Professionals in the U.S.', *Southern Economic Journal* 37, 3 (1971): 318-22; and Anthony Richmond, 'Return Migration from Canada to Britain', *Population Studies* 22, 2 (1968): 263-71.

[17]Thus, unlike Roskin and Edleson in their research on English-speaking immigrants in Israel, we are not concerned with the mental health of migrants but with the inter-personal dynamics involved in the process of migration and re-emigration. See Michael Roskin and Jeffrey L. Edleson, 'A Research Note on the Emotional Health of English-speaking Immigrants in Israel', *The Jewish Journal of Sociology* 26, 2 (December 1984): 139-44.

[18]See Michael Brown, 'The Push and Pull Factors of Aliyah and the Anomalous Case of Canada: 1967-1987', *Jewish Social Studies* 48, 2 (Spring 1986): 153.

[19]See Anselm Strauss, *Mirrors and Masks: The Search for Identity* (San Francisco, 1969): 153.

[20]See Marvin B. Scott and Stanford M. Lyman, 'Accounts', *American Sociological Review* 23 (December 1968): 46-62.

[21]We are particularly interested in those accounts known as justifications. Unlike excuses, which acknowledge that particular acts are undesirable, justifications are a form of account in which the person accepts responsibility for an act but denies that that act should be seen as untoward or wrong. Most significantly, justifications help to lubricate social interaction and attempt to project an identity. It follows that the outcome of a particular effort at organizing a justification for the act — whether it is successful or not — bears on the kind of identity an individual is able to claim.

[22]While about half of our respondents belonged to the Association of Americans

and Canadians in Israel (AACI), an association which provides a variety of absorption services for immigrants from North America, none indicated that they had consulted any AACI officials in the hope of alleviating what had become a very grave situation. It should be noted, however, that several of the respondents had availed themselves of AACI services during their stay in Israel, most notably by attending AACI-sponsored gatherings, where they had met other newcomers as well as long-established North American *olim*. However, by the time that our respondents had reached the firm decision to return to Canada, they did not believe that the AACI could be of any further help. For a brief consideration of the kinds of services offered by the AACI, see the 'Chronicle' in *The Jewish Journal of Sociology* 31, 2 (December 1989): 146-7.

[23]See Gitelman, *op. cit.*, n. 12 above: 133.

Index

List of Contributors

Jay Brodbar-Nemzer, Assistant Director, Community Planning and Allocations, Toronto Jewish Congress

Robert J. Brym, Professor of Sociology and Associate, Centre for Russian and East European Studies, University of Toronto

Steven M. Cohen, Professor of Sociology, Queens College, City University of New York

Leo Davids, Associate Professor of Sociology and Chair, Department of Sociology, Atkinson College, York University, Toronto

Michael Gillespie, Associate Professor of Sociology, University of Alberta, Edmonton

A.R. Gillis, Professor of Sociology, University of Toronto

Jean Laponce, Professor of Political Science, University of British Columbia, Vancouver

Jean-Claude Lasry, Research Associate, Department of Psychiatry, Sir Mortimer B. Davis Jewish General Hospital, Montreal, and Professor, Department of Psychology, University of Montreal

Rhonda Lenton, Assistant Professor of Sociology, McMaster University, Hamilton, Ontario

Cyril Levitt, Professor of Sociology, McMaster University, Hamilton, Ontario

Roberta L. Markus, Executive Director, Committee for Intercultural/Interracial Education in Professional Schools; Associate Professor of Nursing, University of Toronto

Sheva Medjuck, Associate Professor of Sociology, Mount St Vincent University, Halifax, Nova Scotia

Allan Reitzes, Director, Community Planning and Allocations, Toronto Jewish Congress

Carolyn Rosenthal, Professor of Sociology, Centre for Studies of Aging, University of Toronto

Donald V. Schwartz, Professor of Political Science and Associate, Centre for Russian and East European Studies, University of Toronto

William Shaffir, Professor of Sociology, McMaster University, Hamilton, Ontario

Charles Shahar, Research Coordinator, Department of Community Planning, Allied Jewish Community Services, Montreal

David Taras, Director, Canadian Studies Program, University of Calgary

Gary Tobin, Associate Professor of Jewish Community Research and Planning, and Director, Center for Modern Jewish Studies, Lown School of Near Eastern and Judaic Studies, Brandeis University, Waltham, Massachusetts

Jim Torczyner, Professor of Social Work, McGill University, Montreal

Harold Troper, Professor of History, Ontario Institute for Studies in Education, Toronto

Gerald Tulchinsky, Professor of History, Queen's University, Kingston, Ontario

Harold M. Waller, Associate Professor of Political Science and Associate Dean, Faculty of Arts, McGill University, Montreal

Gabriel Weimann, Senior Lecturer, Department of Sociology, Haifa University

Morton Weinfeld, Professor of Sociology, McGill University, Montreal

Conrad Winn, Professor of Political Science, Carleton University, Ottawa

Phyllis Zelkowitz, Research Associate, Department of Psychiatry, Sir Mortimer B. Davis Jewish General Hospital, Montreal